A SYSTEM

OF

BIBLICAL PSYCHOLOGY.

BY

FRANZ DELITZSCH, D.D.,

PROFESSOR OF THEOLOGY, LEIPSIC.

Translated from the German,

(SECOND EDITION, THOROUGHLY REVISED AND ENLARGED,)

BY THE REV. ROBERT ERNEST WALLIS, PHIL. DR.,

SENIOR PRIEST-VICAR OF WELLS CATHEDRAL, AND INCUMBENT
OF CHRIST CHURCH, COXLEY, SOMERSET.

Wipf and Stock Publishers
EUGENE, OREGON

Wipf and Stock Publishers
199 West 8th Avenue, Suite 3
Eugene, Oregon 97401

A System of Biblical Psychology
By Delitzsch, Franz
ISBN: 1-59244-223-4
Publication date: April, 2003
Previously published by T. and T. Clark, January, 1899.

TRANSLATOR'S PREFACE.

The translator is assured that nothing is needed on his part to commend this remarkable work to the philosophical student of theology in England, beyond an apology for the imperfections of the English garb in which it appears.

The great and growing interest of the subject, and the profound and exhaustive learning which the author[1] has brought to bear upon its treatment, had made the translation of this book a desideratum to many, who only knew it by casual reference and quotation, long before this attempt was contemplated. But the hope that such a work would fall into thoroughly competent hands was indulged in vain, when, by the enterprise of the publishers of the Foreign Theological Library, the present translator was encouraged to do what he could to supply the need. The result of his endeavour is here presented to the English biblical student as a mine of wonderful depth and fertility, which will well repay those who have the courage to pierce through a somewhat unattractive surface.

[1] The subjoined testimony of Dr Fuerst to the deserved reputation of Dr Delitzsch, may not be uninteresting to the English student:—

Extract from the Preface to Fuerst's Hebrew Concordance.

"Non possum quin publice gratum meum animum testificer Fr. Delitzschio Phil. Dr. adolescenti doctrina disciplinaque præstantissimo, cujus vivo literarum amore et adjutrice consuetudine non paucæ de disquisitionibus meis interioribus ac reconditis maturuerunt. Præclara ejus in literis biblicis ac judaicis eruditio—quam jam compluribus operibus satis luculente comprobravit, eum, quamquam in rebus theologicis prorsus a me dissentientem, socium atque adjutorem mihi adjunxit, quem in literis rabbinicis ac talmudicis antea auditorem et discipulum habuisse merito glorior. . . . . .

" JULIUS FUERSTIUS.

" LIPSIÆ, *Idibus Juniis* 1840."

The peculiar difficulties with which the translator has had to contend, were not unanticipated by the learned author himself, and may therefore be reasonably pleaded in bar of severe criticism on the way in which the task has been accomplished. Dr Delitzsch, in a courteous reply to a communication in which he had been informed of the intention to translate his book, says: "You are right: that book of mine greatly *resists* translation into English; it is full of newly-coined words and daring ideas; and both its form and substance are most elaborately involved." This witness is profoundly true; and should it approve itself so to the reader in the course of his perusal of the following pages, it is hoped that he will indulgently remember this testimony.

Any attempt to criticise the work itself, the translator conceives to be beyond his province. He contents himself, therefore, with briefly reminding the reader, that in giving all the author's views and statements without comment or qualification, he does not pledge himself to their indiscriminate adoption or approval. His desire has been, as far as he was able, to convey the writer's thoughts, in English which should as nearly as possible be equivalent to the original.

WELLS, *Dec.* 30, 1866.

PREFACE TO THE FIRST EDITION.

WHEN, in the summer session of 1854, I proposed a course of Biblical Psychology, I was compelled to discontinue it before beginning the middle division, because unforeseen circumstances had laid me under the necessity of limiting the number of hours appropriated to these lectures. Invited from many quarters to complete the fragment, I laboured ceaselessly onward; and thus appeared this book, wherein I discharge to my dear hearers of that time, a debt which, as I venture to hope, they had not forgotten.

My preparations for the subject are so old, that as early as the year 1846 I was endeavouring to arrange them. In a Latin dissertation upon the elements of man's nature—sketched out at that time, but suppressed—I proposed to myself an answer to the fundamental question: Whether the soul, so far as it is distinguished from the spirit, belongs by its nature to matter or to spirit? This question I proposed to consider apart from the ecclesiastical doctrine of dichotomy that had become prevalent, which, moreover, I defended in my *Theology of Biblical Prophecy* (1845), and in both editions of my *Commentary on Genesis* (1852 and 1853).[1] That dissertation, indeed, is absolutely right in maintaining the essential unity of soul and spirit; but it suffers from the great defect, that it does not do justice to the substantial difference between the two that is everywhere presupposed in the Holy Scripture. If this defect be not remedied, the psychologic mode of speech and matter generally in the Holy Scripture will be an obscure and formless chaos. The key of biblical psychology is found in the solution of the enigma: How is it to be conceived, that spirit and soul can be of one essence, and yet be distinct sub-

---

[1] The first edition of the *System of Biblical Psychology* (1855) comes between the second (1853) and third (1860) editions of the *Commentary on Genesis*.

stances? It was not until I was enlightened upon this question that my confused materials of biblical psychology formed themselves as if spontaneously into a systematic unity.

My problem was an historical one, standing indeed in a wholly different internal attitude to the psychologic views of the Holy Scripture, from that in which it stands—say to those of Plato or of the Indian Vedanta. In seeking exegetically to ascertain these views, and to combine them into a whole which should correspond to their own internal coherence, I proceeded from the auspicious assumption, that whatever of a psychologic kind Scripture presents will neither be self-contradictory, nor be so confused, childish, and unsatisfactory, as to have any need to be ashamed in view of the results of late anthropologic researches. This favourable assumption has, moreover, perfectly approved itself to me, without my having feared to consider the psychologic statements of Scripture in any other than their own light. For while the Scripture testifies to us of the fact of redemption, which is the revealed secret of human history and the universe, it gives us also at the same time disclosures about the nature of man, which, as well to speculative investigation into the final causes and connections of things, as to natural and spiritual self-contemplation, manifest themselves to be divine suggestions. So far, perhaps, the book before us may claim some consideration from inquirers into natural science and philosophy—from such, that is, as are not dissembling views of the same kind as were lately frankly avowed by Carl Vogt.

But especially would I commend my work to the examination of all those who are interested in the controversy on the fundamental question of psychology at issue between the Güntherish school and its opponents. For years the works of Anton Günther were my favourite study; and a book by a friend of his, J. H. Pabst, who preceded him into eternity on July 28, 1838, entitled *Der Mensch und seine Geschichte* (1830), which first called my attention to Günther, even attained the importance of a turning-point in my course of theological training. Nevertheless I could never make the view of Günther my own, on the essential distinction between the human soul and spirit, however I might have wished, and that for biblical and experimental reasons, which I have explained in this book in several places. The human soul gives life to the body by means of natural energies which appertain to matter, but the human soul itself is not the substance of these natural powers.

The now greatly extended literature of the psychologic controversy, which is raging in the Roman Catholic Church,—a controversy which has lately exploded in the face of all the world in the *Allgemeine Zeitung*,—has not been, I regret to say, very familiar to me. In general, in the immensely wide range of psychological literature, a great deal that is deserving of consideration, both old and recent, has undoubtedly escaped me. But I have read many writings also that were known to me which I have not spoken of, because they were of no use to me; for an exegetically careful, intelligent, and liberal probing into the depths of Scripture,—an investigation which in the church creed has its restraining barrier, but yet not its circumscribing measure,—this just mean between a false bondage and a false freedom craving after novelty, is a virtue not so frequently found in the literature of theology.

I have striven after this virtue; and as I seek at no point to overstep the limit of the church's judgment up to the present time, without at the same time assuring myself that I am abiding in harmony with the scripturally sound creed of my church, I shall not be blamed for some theosophic sympathies, especially as I have reduced what Jacob Böhme taught about God's sevenfold nature to the more biblical conception of the divine glory (*doxa*), and, moreover, have only so far appropriated it as it commended itself to me on biblical grounds. It was immediately in the light of this conception that the solution of the psychological problem occurred to me. In it (*scil.* this conception)—hitherto unduly neglected, and, as Weisse (*Philosophische Dogmatik*, i. 617) not at all too strongly expresses it, emptied of soul and life as it was under the hands of dogmatic philosophy—there are still to be found undiscovered treasures of knowledge.

I have still much to say to courteous readers. But I shrink from bringing myself any longer personally in the front of my book. In deeply conscious acknowledgment of its imperfection, but yet with a grateful retrospect to the enjoyment I have found in the inquiry, I resign it to the not less merciful than strict criticism of the divine Fire (1 Cor. iii. 11–15).

FR. DELITZSCH.

Erlangen, *September* 1855.

PREFACE TO THE SECOND EDITION.

THE reason why I so long resisted the general wish for a second edition of my *Biblical Psychology*, will be found in the book itself. I wanted first to ascertain whether the substantial view of the book approved itself to me anew. When this had been the case, however, I was bound to yield to that wish with the less hesitation, in consideration of the numerous studies of language and history that I have stored in this book independently of that fundamental view, to which I have now considerably added, studies in a more rigid historical apprehension of the nature of my undertaking.

I therefore beg all my readers carefully to distinguish the unassailable historical matter that is here placed before them, from that which is submitted to them for examination, and especially from those merely individual attempts to arrange it in general consistency with the scriptural view of God and the world; and to combine it systematically, agreeably with the suggestions of the Bible. He who in this behalf desires to form a competent estimate of my work, must first occupy a similar dogmatic, or, which is the same thing, ecclesiastical position to mine. That critics who are unprepared to answer the question, What is the Son of man? and who pare down the holy truths of faith in which they were baptized, and on account of which they are called Christians, nay, evangelical Christians, for the greater glorification of their scientific integrity, — that such critics should be able to find no enjoyment in my book, is wholly natural; and that the exact critics, who have no taste for a gnosis exercised in biblical paths, and the materialist critics, who know of no other induction than one which is calculated by atoms, should reject my book as a senseless production, is neither more nor less than might be expected.

PREFACE TO THE SECOND EDITION.

I rejoice in another estimate on the part of those who regard everything earnest and without duplicity—not merely the book of nature, but also the book of the Holy Scripture—as the attestation of a divine revelation, and who acknowledge the ground upon which I build (not without taking heed HOW I build) as the one that endures for ever. If my building on this ground should prove a failure, it is after all a first attempt, which still perhaps may supply many stones for a more solid and newer edifice. It is always something gained, that the doctrinal material of biblical psychology here at length more completely and successfully than formerly appears organically articulated, as is required by the idea of science. And if even many developments slip in, which appear to lose themselves in what is fanciful, and can pretend to no demonstrative force,—a reproach which no science will escape, if it be concerned with the invisible, the spiritual,—it is a fault that may be easily atoned for by the instructive communications of most manifold contents presented in connection therewith.

In such readers, thankful, and yet critically examining and sifting, the book has not hitherto been deficient. And if I thank those who, as Noack and Ströbel, have considered it intelligently, although unfavourably, and have not despatched it with an arrogantly brief notice, or still more arrogantly ignored it altogether, I am doubly and trebly indebted to those who, as v. Hofmann, J. P. Lange, Schubart, Werner, and v. Zezschwitz, have submitted it to a more or less severe but still friendly criticism. But I have been deeply ashamed of the very favourable consideration which President Dr. K. F. Göschel and General-Major v. Rudloff have devoted to my work. These two honourable veterans, grown grey in the noblest service, have prosecuted the examination of it step for step in special writings. The one is no more among those who live in this world, from whom he was removed on the 22d September in this year, in the seventy-seventh year of his age; but as the church above and the church below form an undivided living unity, my grateful greeting will find its way to him above. And how deeply I know how to esteem the loving service which the other has rendered to my work, this revision will, I hope, show him, for which the delightful study of his work has supplied me with an abundance of fertile suggestions.

But otherwise, moreover, dear friends, such as Besser, Biesenthal, v. Harless, Luthardt, J. Schubring, v. Strauss, by epistolary, others by oral communication of their critical observations, have rendered service to my work, especially " my Elberfeld Critic," whose critical annotations, communicated to me by the goodness of the mission-inspector, Dr Fabri, suggested to me rich material for the revision and elaboration of my views of biblical psychology. And although my book should even contain but little that is good originating from myself, yet care is taken that the reader should be made aware of the communications of such others as might partly dissent as to principles, partly might positively correct what has been written. Important inquirers, such as Molitor, Hamberger, R. v. Raumer, Fleischer, Tischendorf, have afforded such contributions. Moreover, there are not wanting extracts from rare books. There is found here the complete draught of the biblical psychology of C. Bartholinus, which I discovered at the library at Nordlingen in a compilation, where I had previously not looked for it; and passages important to the history of science from other writings: moreover, an extract from a mediæval manuscript, entitled *das leben der minnenden sele*, which is transferred from the library of Dr. Biesenthal into mine.

As only a few pages of the book have remained without improvement and enrichment, its extent, in spite of the unequally crowded print, has grown by four sheets. The relation of the soul to the spirit will be found even now also conceived as secondary, but everywhere more clearly and simply expressed. The relation of the *doxa* to the personal nature of God is represented, as I hope, more convincingly, as well exegetically as speculatively (I. Sec. 3., IV. Sec. 6). The distinction of nature and substance, which in the first edition was assumed, is now discussed (II. Sec. 4). The trichotomic fundamental text, 1 Thess. v. 23 (II. Sec. 4), and that of creationism, Heb. xii. 9 (II. Sec. 7), are searchingly considered. And equally so, the interpretation of the foundation texts of the conscience, Rom. ii. 15 (III. Sec. 4); of the relation of the soul to the blood, Lev. xvii. 14 (IV. Sec. 11); and of the antinomy of the spirit and the flesh unabolished in this world, Rom. vii. (v. Sec. 6), are investigated anew. The just claim of biblical psychology to be called a science (Proleg. Sec. 2); the ideal pre-existence of the historically actual (I. Sec. 2); the similitude of God, and not merely of the Logos in man (II. Sec. 2); the dualism of spirit and matter (II. Sec. 4); the distinction between a wider and a narrower conception of πνεῦμα (IV. 4, 5, V. 6); the fundamentality of the will (IV. 7); the priority of the spirit over the soul (IV. 8); the conception in the evangelical history of the Kenosis (V. 1); the importance to the history of redemption of the Descent into Hell (VI. 3); the actual reality, in the sense of Scripture, of the conjuration of the dead, 1 Sam. xxviii. (VI. Sec. 5)—are all established anew, with reference to the objections that have been advanced. Language, as a psychological manifestation, is better appreciated than before, as well in accordance with Scripture as experience (IV. 4, 10); the nature of the dream is more sharply defined, and its biblical name explained (IV. Sec. 14); and more attention is directed, in the region of extraordinary phenomena of the life of the soul, to the individual degrees and conditions of prophecy (IV. 14, V. 5). The earlier view of the psychologic matter of fact of possession (IV. 16), and the view of the relation of the resurrection-corporeity to the present one (VII. 1), are justified. Many psychologic definitions of relation, as soul, power, and matter (IV. 9), person (I) and nature (IV. 2), heart and brain (IV. 12), are newly examined, and the history of the views referring to them enlarged upon. In this manner the revision is extended to every paragraph. The substantial views, and the arrangement of the material, are nevertheless first and last the same.

To the doings of the later physiology, empirical psychology, and medical psychology, I have referred in this second edition, as compared with the former, not more frequently, but rather more seldom, because I have gained the experience, that the representatives of this school of inquiry do not quite approve of seeing themselves named by a theologian of my tendency. And such references might, besides, easily be misunderstood, as though biblical views ought to be modelled according to the results of natural science (precarious though they are), or the latter according to the former. Yet they were not always to be avoided. But my task is one wholly unconfused with that of these inquirers. The book whose answers to the questions respecting the source, the operations, the conditions, and destinies of the soul I have undertaken to discover, is not the book of nature, but the book of Scripture; and I have written for those to whom the answers of this book of books are not indifferent, and who know not merely a natural world of experience, but also one that does not give place to that, in reality of self-conviction.

Thanks be to God for the capacity bestowed once again to accomplish this work. May He bless it, to the stimulating of further labours in this field of biblical psychology. Should it, moreover, be impossible entirely to solve the problems which meet us here, still the Creator of all things is to be glorified, that He has granted to the human soul the capacity of raising itself above itself by self-investigation, and with the necessity for this investigation has imparted the blissful pleasure that proceeds therefrom.

FR. DELITZSCH.

ERLANGEN, *Mid-November* 1861.

CONTENTS.

PROLEGOMENA.

	PAGE
SEC. I. History of Biblical Psychology,	3
II. Idea of Biblical Psychology,	12
III. Method of Biblical Psychology,	19
APPENDIX. Caspar Bartholinus' First Sketch of a Biblical Psychology,	26

I. THE EVERLASTING POSTULATES.

SEC. I. The False Pre-existence,	41
II. The True Pre-existence,	46
III. The Divine Archetype,	55
APPENDIX. Letters of Molitor on Jacob Böhme's Doctrine of a Nature in God,	65

II. THE CREATION.

SEC. I. Man as the Object of the Six Days' Work,	71
II. The Divine Likeness in Man,	78
III. The Process of Creation,	81
IV. The False and the True Trichotomy,	103
V. The Origin of the Psyche in an Ethical Point of View,	119
VI. The Difference of Sex,	124
VII. Traducianism and Creationism,	128
APPENDIX. R. von Raumer on the Fundamental Import of the names "*Geist*" and "*Seele*,"	143

III. THE FALL.

SEC. I. The Sin of the Spirit and the Sin of the Flesh,	147
II. The Ethico-Physical Disturbance,	151
III. Shame and Fear,	154
IV. Conscience and Remoteness from God,	159
V. The Promise and Faith,	170
APPENDIX. From Pontoppidan's Mirror of Faith,	176

IV. THE NATURAL CONDITION.

SEC. I. Personality and the "I,"	179
II. Personal Life and Natural Life,	185
III. Freedom,	191

		PAGE
SEC. IV.	The Triplicity of the Spirit,	196
V.	Nous, Logos, Pneuma,	209
VI.	The Seven Powers of the Soul,	222
VII.	The Established View of the Capacities of the Soul,	241
VIII.	The Beginning and Development of the Threefold Life,	247
IX.	The Twofold Aspect of the Soul,	258
X.	The Body as the Sevenfold Means of Self-Representation to the Soul,	266
XI.	Soul and Blood,	281
XII.	Heart and Head,	292
XIII.	Within the Body—the Intestines and the Kidneys,	313
XIV.	Sleeping, Waking, Dreaming,	324
XV.	Health and Sickness,	337
XVI.	Natural and Demoniacal Sickness,	345
XVII.	Superstition and Magic,	360
APPENDIX I.	Passages from the Physics of Comenius,	373
II.	Theses on Fire and Light, Soul and Spirit. By Jul. Hamberger,	376

V. THE REGENERATION.

SEC. I.	The Divine-Human Archetype,	381
II.	The New Life of the Spirit,	393
III.	The Conscious and Unconscious Side of the Work of Grace,	401
IV.	The *Actus Directi* and *Reflexi* of the Life of Grace,	407
V.	The Three Forms of the divinely wrought Ecstasy, and the Theopneustia,	417
VI.	The Unabolished Antinomy,	433
APPENDIX I.	Luther's Trichotomy,	460
II.	Upon the "Spirit of the Mind." A. From H. W. Clemens' Work on the Powers of the Soul,	462
B.	From a Mediæval Tractate entitled *Das Leben der Minnende Seele*,	464

VI. DEATH.

SEC. I.	Soul and Spirit in the midst of Death,	467
II.	The True and the False Immortality,	473
III.	Future Life and Redemption,	479
IV.	The False Doctrine of the Sleep of the Soul,	490
V.	The Phenomenal Corporeity and Investiture,	499
VI.	The Relation of the Souls of the Righteous to the Corporeity of Christ,	513
VII.	The Relation of Souls to their Soulless Corporeity,	520
APPENDIX.	Johann Heinrich Ursinus on the Intermediate State of Souls,	526

VII. RESURRECTION AND CONSUMMATION.

SEC. I.	Spirit and Soul in the Act of Resurrection,	535
II.	The Metempsychosis,	545
III.	The Doctrine of Restoration,	547
IV.	Progress in Eternity,	555
APPENDIX.	From a Sermon of the Author's on Rom. viii. 18-23,	559

PROLEGOMENA.

"A Deo discas quod a Deo habeas, aut nec ab alio, si nec a Deo."
TERTULLIANUS (*De Anima*).

HISTORY OF BIBLICAL PSYCHOLOGY.

Sec. I.

BIBLICAL PSYCHOLOGY is no science of yesterday. It is one of the oldest sciences of the church. As early as the second century, we find, in the literature of the period, a book περὶ ψυχῆς καὶ σώματος ἢ (read καὶ) νοός, by Melito of Sardis,[1] of which Eusebius and Jerome make mention; and early in the beginning of the third century, the work composed by Tertullian in his Montanist days, *De Animâ*, as the first ecclesiastical attempts to supersede the *Phædo* of Plato, and Aristotle's three books, περὶ ψυχῆς. The work of Tertullian comprises all the leading dogmas on the subject of psychology, and pursues the history of the soul from its eternal source and temporal mode of origination, through its present duration and fundamental conditions, into the state beyond the grave. Tertullian's treatise, *De censu animæ adversus Hermogenem,* wherein he maintained against his opponent the divine and immaterial derivation (*census*) of the soul, is unfortunately lost to us. This loss is greatly to be deplored, because the writings of a teacher so able and so rarely endowed as Tertullian, are still an inexhaustible mine of profound knowledge. The tract περὶ ψυχῆς, addressed to Tatian by Gregory Thaumaturgus, the pupil and friend of Origen,[2] is a worthless and probably a spurious performance. Hence, therefore, Melito and Tertullian must be regarded as the only worthy inaugurators of the psychological literature of the church. In the fourth century its foundations were strengthened

---

[1] According to Rufinus, its title runs, *De anima et corpore et mente;* according to Jerome, as in the Syriac version of Eusebius' *Eccl. Hist.*, only *De anima et corpore.* See Cureton, *Spicilegium Syriacum,* p. 96, and the splendidly rhetorical passage there quoted from it, p. 53.

[2] See Möhler, *Patrologie,* i. 653.

by the abundant psychological elements contained in the works of the three great Cappadocians, especially in those of Gregory of Nyssa (and among them more particularly his dialogue, περὶ ψυχῆς καὶ ἀναστάσεως πρὸς τὴν ἀδελφὴν Μακρίναν, edited by Krabinger, 1837, and briefly known as τὰ Μακρίνια), which have been systematically elaborated by E. W. Möller in his treatise upon *Gregorii Nysseni doctrina de hominis natura* (1854), and thoroughly compared with the view of Origen; and the still more copious works of Augustine (among them *De anima et ejus origine*, and the anti-Manichæan treatise *De duabus animabus*), from which the Roman Catholic theologian Theodore Gangauf in Augsburg compiled his metaphysical psychology of St Augustine (1852). After this appeared, in the beginning of the fifth century, if not even earlier, the scientifically excellent work of Nemesius,[1] bishop of Emesa, περὶ φύσεως ἀνθρώπου, based on the Aristotelian plan, and the *Libri tres de statu animæ*, directed against Faustus Regiensis by Claudianus Mamercus (Mamertus), the special purpose of which is to prove that the soul is neither corporeal nor local; in the sixth century, the treatise of Cassiodorus, *De anima*, in twelve chapters, beginning from the meaning of the word, and the conception of the soul, and closing with its future condition; in the seventh century, the commentary of Johannes Philoponus on Aristotle's work on the soul, which appeared in Venice[2] in 1535, edited by Trincavelli. Moreover, to this catalogue belong the *Theophrastus* of the converted Platonist Aeneas of Gaza, finally edited by Boissonade 1836, being a dialogue on the immortality of the soul (about 490); and at the close of the patristic age, the fourth book of the dialogues of Gregory the Great, treating *de æternitate animarum* (593-4). In addition to these, when we name the numerous writings on the Hexaëmeron, and especially on the creation of man (*e.g.* those of Lactantius and Anastasius of Sinai), and the many writings upon the resur-

[1] Edited by Chr. F. Matthaei, Halle 1802-8. The treatise taken up into the editions of the works of Gregory of Nyssa, περὶ ψυχῆς καὶ ἀναστάσεως, is the second and third chapter of this work of Nemesius.

[2] The Δόξαι περὶ ψυχῆς published by Tarinus with Origen's *Philocalia* (Paris 1619), and by Caspar Barth. with Mamercus' three books, *De statu animæ* (Zwickau 1655), are *excerpta* from Philoponus. See Creuzer's Essay, *Schriften Christlicher Philosophen über die Seele*, in his German writings, sec. iii. vol. ii.

rection, beginning with Justin Martyr or (if his treatise preserved in fragments be considered spurious) with Athenagoras; finally, the multitude of Christologic and Soteriologic monographs, which entered upon psychologic problems,—it is plain that the ancient church had a psychological literature that claims respect no less for its extent than for its substance.

When, in the middle ages, Christian science became more systematic, and the most distinguished teachers confessed, after Augustine's example, that in the knowledge of one's self is the starting-point of all knowledge, the subject of psychology became a fundamental element of the *Summa*, or the complete doctrine. But psychology was treated of by scholars of all kinds in specific treatises also, not only by the specially scholastic, but by the natural philosophers and the mystics, partly in the form of commentaries on Aristotle's three books on the soul, as by Alexander of Hales, Peter de Alliaco, and others; partly in independent monographs, as by Erigena, William of Champeaux, Hugo of St Victor, Albertus Magnus, Thomas Aquinas, and others,—a long list which closed in the fifteenth century with the *Viola animæ seu de natura hominis* of Raymund Sabunde, an abridgment in the form of a dialogue of his great work on natural theology, which is in some sort the keystone of the whole scholastic literature. From these works there is still much to be learnt even in the present day; for with the dialectic mode of thought there was associated in those times a calm introverted contemplativeness, and a living experience almost elevated into ecstasy. But in general it is their reproach that their minds ran more in Aristotelian than in biblical modes of thought; in addition to which, it was an inconvenience, that as the readers of Aristotle did not understand his works in their original language, they were in a great measure dependent upon the Mohammedan translators and interpreters. Even in Dante's *Divina Commedia* the psychologic terminology is Aristotelian; for in Dante's estimation Aristotle is the master of those who know (*il maestro di color che sanno*). There runs, indeed, also through the literature of the middle ages, a strong tendency towards freedom from this dependent relation. Combining Plato with Aristotle, there is the attempt to read immediately in the Book of Nature, and to draw out of the depth of the soul's consciousness; but men did not see their way to a free and undivided reference to the teaching of Holy Scripture; and even had they wished to draw from that source immediately, their ignorance of its language would not allow them to appeal to it at first-hand.

It was only by means of the Reformation that a really free scriptural inquiry on all sides became possible. Psychology could then bring its traditional store of knowledge into the light of Scripture, and thus it advanced into a new phase. Contemporary with Budæus, Erasmus, and Vives, who were esteemed the triumvirate of science, the German Reformation had, moreover, as its representative a humanist of the highest rank; and the three books of Vives, *De anima et vita* (1538), which aim at simplifying the traditional Formulas,[1] appeared almost at the same time as Melancthon's *Commentarius de anima* (1540), the first compendium of psychology written in Germany. He frequently gave lectures upon it before immense audiences, and published it anew in 1552 under the title, *Liber de anima*. Even here also, Aristotle, whom Melancthon could read in the original as none of the scholastics could, is the highest authority next to Scripture, but its chains are nevertheless broken; and although many psychologic writings of the scholastics surpass that of Melancthon in fulness and depth of thought, it is superior to them all in a more elegant learning, and a sounder, a more liberal, and a more serene spiritual luminousness. As in Wittenberg, so also in other German universities during the sixteenth and seventeenth centuries, psychology was studied, and disputations were held on psychological questions with peculiar interest. The *Collegium psychologicum*, edited by John Conrad Dannhauer in his twenty-fourth year, at Altorf (1627), consists of seven such academical disputations. The internal progress of the science, however, was not so considerable as it might have been. The period in question was deeply conservative, and was satisfied with what was already known and dogmatically formulated. In matters on which the creed of the church had not yet decided, men clung too anxiously to views anciently established and maintained by the majority of orthodox teachers, and had no

---

[1] Vives is in favour of unity of the soul: *Anima humana inferiores omnes vita sua continet. Humana mens spiritus est, per quem corpus, cui est connexus, vivit, aptus cognitioni Dei.*

eyes to see clearly and without prejudice the rays of truth which shone outside the range of their own confessions of faith. Many a truth, sound, as rightly understood, was rejected on account of possible and actual heretical consequences: as, for instance, the trichotomy of human nature. Many a psychologically significant statement of Scripture—as, for instance, upon the intermediate state between death and the resurrection—was not done justice to. Mysticism, theosophy (with its master Jacob Böhme,[1] incomparably and divinely taught, notwithstanding all the errors into which he was hurried by his zeal against the dead orthodoxy and the miserable ignorance of natural science that then prevailed), the science of medicine, which acknowledged the authority of Scripture, and chemistry (represented especially by Paracelsus[2] and John Baptista von Helmont, investigators[3] who, in their daring originality, not unfrequently forestalled the lapse of centuries): these, in their more liberal movement, anticipated many a conclusion which has since been undeniably established by scriptural investigation and knowledge. At that time it was an additional misfortune for psychology as a science of the church, that the method of systematizing was so prevalent, and the habit of searching for the testimony of Scripture rather by reference to individual texts than to the general scope and harmony of Scripture,—a habit which, above all, changed the *analogia fidei* from a rule of scriptural interpretation into a measure of what Scripture contained. But Caspar Bartholinus (*ob.* 1629), the celebrated teacher of medicine and theology in the University of Copenhagen, drew out, in his *Manuductio ad veram Psychologiam e sacris literis*, a sketch of biblical psychology in which, although only slightly put together in an ungraceful style, and deficient in just exegetic basis, there may neverthe-

---

[1] To this place specially belongs his *Psychologia vera, or Forty Questions about the Soul,* and *Psychologiæ supplementum: Das umgewandte Auge* is on the same subject (vol. vi. of the collected works in the new edition of Schiebler).

[2] See Preu, *System of Medicine of Theophrastus Paracelsus*, 1838, in which also the psychology of the great reformer of medical science is exhibited in *excerpta* from his works.

[3] In his psychological writings, says Spiess (John Baptista van Helmont's *System of Medicine* (1840), sec. 53), Helmont exhibits himself in his greatest depth and peculiarity; and he not seldom succeeds in forcing his way into all the clearness of which so difficult a subject is capable.

less be discerned, in the courage which breaks through the customary formalities of scholasticism, some signs of promise in that province of thought.[1]

An entirely new era of scriptural investigation commenced with John Albert Bengel (*ob.* 1752). Hitherto scriptural inquiry had almost exclusively served for the apologetico-polemical proof of truth already acknowledged. Now men began, as well of free will as of divine necessity, to devote themselves to the Scriptures, that they might bring the knowledge already possessed into the light anew, and deepen and extend it. Oetinger's *Inquisitio in sensum communem* (1752), and the *Fundamenta Psychologiæ ex sacra Scriptura collecta* (1769) of Magnus Friedrich Roos, were fruits of this healthy revolution, as also were several psychological treatises of Chr. Aug. Crusius (who among the Saxons trod in the footsteps of the above scriptural inquirers of Wurtemburg), viz. upon superstition, upon magic, and generally upon man's relation to the spirit-world.[2] All these are only preludes to a biblical psychology; even the tract of Roos[3] itself, which has become very rare, brings together the texts of Scripture treating of $\psi v \chi \acute{\eta}$, $\pi \nu \varepsilon \hat{v} \mu a$, $\kappa a \rho \delta \acute{\iota} a$ without any principle, and in this lexicon-like and mechanical method neither formally nor actually satisfies the problem of biblical psychology. But the fundamental maxim, *ita accedere ad scripturam ut nullum præstruatur systema*, gives, notwithstanding, to this little volume an air of living freshness which enables it to contrast advantageously

---

[1] With respect to him, see Tholuck's *Martyrs of the Lutheran Church of all ranks before and during the time of the Thirty Years' War* (1859), p. 234. According to Michaud's *Bibliographie Universelle*, tom. iii. (Paris 1843), p. 193, the *Manuductio* appeared in Copenhagen in 1618–9; but I have failed to discover or to gain any intelligence of this edition: it is not even in the possession of the Library at Copenhagen. Subsequently, however, I found that the *Manuductio* is adopted into the *Systema Physicum*, which appeared at Hanover in 1628. It is from this compilation that I have given it in the appendix to these Prolegomena, only omitting some trifling and unessential matters.

[2] They are enumerated in my *Biblico-prophetical Theology* (1845), p. 140.

[3] It has now appeared in a German translation (by Cremer of Unna), under the title of *Grundzüge der Seelenlehre aus heiliger Schrift*, Stuttgart, at Steinkopf's, 1857. Compare the notice by Sprinkhardt in Reuter's *Repertorium*, 1858, pp. 41–45.

with writings of such low rationalistic views as the *Psychology of the Hebrews* of Friedr. Aug. Carus (published in 1809, after the author's death), and as Ge. Fr. Seiler's *Animadversiones ad Psychologiam Sacram* (1778-1787), which is not much higher in its view than the former.[1] And for this reason it has not been without influence. For, as the result of the *Fundamenta Psychologica* of Roos, appeared not only Stirm's extremely careful researches in anthropologic exegesis in the *Tübinger Zeitschrift für Theologie*, 1834, but also J. T. Beck's *Umriss der biblischen Seelenlehre*, 1843,—the first attempt to reduce biblical psychology into a scientific form, and to promote its claim to an articulated relation and an independent existence in the organism of entire theology. The author treats (1) of the soul-life of humanity as Nephesch (soul); (2) how it is distinguished from Ruach (spirit); (3) how it is comprehended in the Leb (heart). We do not misapprehend the propriety of this threefold division; nay, we thankfully acknowledge, that by its means Beck has succeeded in throwing light on many aspects of the subject of biblical psychology; but probably there would be few readers who would not gather from the compendiums of Roos and Beck the impression that this vast scaffolding is not sufficient to provide for all the varied abundance of the subject, and that there needs another less abstract principle of division to articulate it in a living manner, and to separate it intelligently. The historical method leads more surely to such a result. An excellent little compendium by J. G. F. Haussmann, *Die Biblische Lehre vom Menschen* (1848), adopts this course, adhering in other respects to Beck. It begins with the origin of man, and ends with the new humanity and its perfection,—a biblical anthropology, which in respect of psychology and somatology stands in the relation of the whole to its parts. Along with these two treatises of Beck and Hauss-

---

[1] The *Biblical Anthropology* of Franz Oberthür (Professor of Dogmatic in Würzburg), (vol. i. edit. 2, 1826; vols. ii.-iv. 1808-1810: according to the author's design, the second part of his dogmatics) misleads by its title, but deserves no sort of consideration at all. Equally misleading by its name is Grohmann's *Anthropologie des alten und neuen Testaments*, in Nasse's *Zeitschrift für die Anthropologie*, 1824, iii. It is a survey of the Old and New Testament history, "according to anthropologic points of view."

mann may be named the monographs of Gust. Friedr. Oehler, *Veteris testamenti sententia de rebus post mortem futuris* (1846); of Heinr. Aug. Hahn, *Veteris testamenti sententia de natura hominis* (1846); and, by way of a copious collection of the materials of biblical psychology, the work of Böttcher, *De inferis rebusque post mortem futuris* (1846). Moreover, also, those portions of the *Schriftbeweis* of J. Chr. K. von Hofmann which trench upon biblical psychology (especially in the doctrine of the creation and the last things), with which are to be compared the kindred sections on prophecy and its fulfilment (especially secs. iii. and iv.), as also with the *Christian Ethics* of G. Chr. Ad. von Harless,[1] and the full, carefully executed, but rather critically negative than positively constructive portion of Ge. Ludw. Hahn's *Theologie des Neuen Testaments*, which bears on the subject of anthropology (vol. i. pp. 385-475). Moreover, the compendiums of anthropology and psychology by G. H. von Schubert (1842, edit. 2), of Christian Heinr. Zeller (edit. 2, 1850), of Jos. Beck (edit. 4, 1852), and of Karl Phil. Fischer (1850), to which was added not long ago the *Seelenlehre* of G. Mehring (1857),—a work rich in substantial knowledge, but not yet noticed as it deserves;—all breathe a biblical spirit. These labours, and what the three veterans, Jos. Ennemoser (*ob.* 1854), Christoph. Ad. von Eschenmauer (*ob.* 1852), and G. H. von Schubert (*ob.* 1860), in the course of a long life of unceasing effort and rich in experience, have accomplished for experimental psychology and its history, supply such abounding materials for biblical psychology, that in the necessary process of rigid sifting, it has some difficulty to avoid being choked. The three last inquirers have in common the tendency to the profoundest depths of thought. The most spiritual and the finest of their works is von Schubert's *Geschichte der Seele*, in two vols. (4th edit. 1850), of which the compendium *Der Menschen und Seelen Kunde* is only an abridgment, and to which the book *Ueber die Krankheiten und Storüngen der Menschlichen Seele* (1845), together with the 3d vol. on the

---

[1] Both Harless and Hofmann dispute the possibility of a system of biblical psychology; but, nevertheless, the works of both the one and the other are substantially on subjects connected with biblical psychology, and are concerned in the reducing to system of views of the same science. More on this matter in the following section.

Geschichte der Natur (3d edit. 1855), and the *Symbolik des Traums* (edit. 3, 1840),[1] do in some measure belong as supplements. The above-named works of investigators, both theological and untheological, deserve our gratitude, as having rendered to biblical psychology a help not yet fully estimated. To this science also C. F. Göschel has afforded (apart from his speculative writings) welcome service, in his work on the profound fulness of meaning of the creative writings of Dante Alighieri.[2] Yet, nevertheless, when in the year 1855 this very work appeared,—the *System der biblischen Psychologie,*—theology was constrained to bear testimony to her own poverty, to the effect that, since the new era of scriptural interpretation that began with Bengel, the books of Roos and Beck had been the only attempts, with all the present exegetical resources, to establish anew a science whose necessity had been acknowledged as early as the first Christian centuries. At the present time, when after long delays I am for the second time putting forth my system of biblical psychology, the number of fellow-labourers in this field are seen to be most gratifyingly upon the increase. Besides the really valuable treatment of single portions and aspects of biblical psychology by v. Zezschwitz (*Profangräcität und biblischer Sprachgeist,* 1859), Schöberlein (*Ueber das Wesen der geistlichen Natur und Leiblichkeit,* in the *Annual Register of German Theology,* 1861), and others whom we shall have occasion to name further on, the entire scientific material of the subject is carefully elaborated anew, with critical reference to my treatment of it, in special writings of Göschel (*Der Mensch nach Leib, Seele, und Geist diesseits und jenseits,* 1856) and v. Rudloff (*Die Lehre vom Menschen nach Geist, Seele, und Leib,* 1858). Grateful for the positive instruction and critical suggestions received from these and many other sources, I am attempting the subject once more.

---

[1] Newly published by F. H. Rancke, 1862.

[2] Especially deserving of consideration are the following works: *Dante Alighieri's Unterweisung über Weltschöpfung und Weltordnung diesseits und jenseits,* 1842; *Dante Alighieri's Osterfeier in Zwillings-gestern des Himmlischen Paradieses,* 1849; and the Easter gift in a similar way, everywhere pointing to Dante, *Zur Lehre von den letzten Dingen,* 1850.

IDEA OF BIBLICAL PSYCHOLOGY.

Sec. II.

SOME well-known scriptural students of late have denied to biblical psychology the capability of verifying itself. Harless, in the preface to the fourth edition of his *Ethics*, avows, that while he has no fear at all of exact study of the so-called materialism in the field of psycho-physiology, yet, on the other hand, he greatly dreads the idealism and spiritualism, upon whose misty foundation such frequent and continued attempts have been made to rear a sound psychology; and in this behalf he refers to Carus' *Psyche*, and Ennemoser's *Geist des Menschen in der Natur*, as works in which he could place no real confidence. "I believe," he continues, "that our theologians would do well to concern themselves very little about this department of material investigation, which has only by a process of unauthorized abstraction come to be considered as if it were important of itself, and entirely distinct from the spirit. It is this circumstance which has prevented me from receiving the same pleasure that others have done from the late attempts to construct systems of biblical psychology.[1] For Scripture seems to me to occupy the same position in questions of psychology as in those of cosmogony. In each it is a finger-post directing attention to the position of the world, as to the position of the soul in questions of redemption; we must neither expect in connection with one nor the other natural description and natural knowledge, not because it could not have been given us in the Scripture, but because it was not intended to be given us. The meaning of its symbols is reserved for that scrutiny to explain, which, not in words and names, but in the facts of nature, toils after the understanding of the sacred hints in the sweat of its brow."

In accordance with this, Hofmann says in the second as well as in the first edition of his *Schriftbeweis*:[2] "A biblical

---

[1] The preface is of the year 1849. Probably he means Beck's *Umriss der biblischen Seelenlehre*. I am not aware of any *System der biblischen Psychologie* that had then appeared. Mine did not come out till 1855.

[2] I. p. 248, edit. 1 (1852); i. p. 284, edit. 2 (1857).

anthropology and psychology have been got together, but without finding any justification for it in Scripture, of which Harless rightly says that we must not expect from it natural description and natural knowledge, because it was not intended to be given there. That presumed science is based merely upon such Scripture texts as do not teach what the nature of man is, but on the hypothesis that it is understood what kind of creature is meant when man is spoken of, declare his relation or deportment towards God. "It has been replied," he adds in the second edition, with direct reference to me,[1] "that the Scripture does nevertheless give almost in its first sections disclosures which are deliberately anthropologic and psychologic, when it narrates the process of man's creation; and it cannot but be worth the trouble to bring together even its anthropological and psychological assumptions, since they could not be so trivial as to be understood of themselves, nor so inconsequent and unconnected as to be capable of no scientific organization. But in respect of these disclosures, they only serve the purpose of rightly defining in a general way the relation to God and to the world, without the knowledge of which there can undoubtedly be no anthropology and psychology corresponding to the reality; and as to the presumptions, no one doubts that they can be harmonized together, but without being justified in the expectation that they will form a scientific whole, since they only come to light in proportion as they are used for the expression of facts, which, while they touch on the anthropologic and psychologic region, themselves belong to another. A biblical psychology is just as little of a psychologic system as a biblical cosmology is a cosmologic system; and if it be found practicable also to call it theological instead of biblical, it will moreover be permitted to say that there is a theological

---

[1] Referring to p. 181 of the first edition of this book of mine. I have struck out in that place the words that I have here quoted from Hofmann, so as not to repeat myself. R. Wagner, in the *Evang. K. Z.* (1857), col. 189, and in his treatise *Der Kampf um die Seele vom Standpunkt der Wissenschaft* (1857), p. 119, approves of them. But when he says (p. 114), "Biblical anthropology and psychology is the section of theology which chiefly comes into consideration in the references to physiology," so, on the other side also, he agrees with me in acknowledging the scientific claim of biblical psychology, and rightly, as Fabri, in the *Evang. K. Z.* 1857, Nos. 96, 97, has proved in my defence.

psychology only in the same sense as a theological cosmology may be spoken of."

And thus the task which I propose to myself would be at the outset a failure, because it would be impracticable. This, however, is by no means the case. The problem, as I understand it, is not at all touched by those objections. For that all that Scripture tells us on the spiritual and psychical constitution of man is in harmony with the work and the revelation of redemption, which are the special burthen of Scripture, we deny so little, that we gather from it rather the idea of biblical psychology as distinguished from the empirical and the philosophical psychology of natural science. But what Scripture says to us in pursuance of that its great design for the salvation of man, is far more than is admitted by those two writers. For, from the announcement upon the substance of man's nature as it was created which we read in Gen. ii. 7, and which Harless places at the head of his Ethics, there runs throughout Scripture a many-linked chain of assertions upon the pneumato-psychical nature and life of man—of declarations which touch the most important fundamental questions of psychology, and throughout depend upon similar fundamental views, and are of such rich import that even Hofmann devotes to these announcements considerable portions of his *Schriftbeweis*. For all the great questions—How is man's soul related to his spirit? How is man's spirit related to God's Spirit? Is the substance of man's nature trichotomic or dichotomic? How is man distinguished as Nature and as Ego?—all these and many other psychologic questions are there attempted to be answered from Scripture; while, nevertheless, it is maintained that Scripture teaches nothing upon the whole subject. Now, therefore, whether it be called teaching or not, Scripture certainly gives us, on all these questions, the announcements which are necessary to a fundamental knowledge of salvation; and these announcements are to be exegetically investigated—are, because they are of a psychological nature, to be psychologically weighed—are to be rightly adjusted, so that they may cohere among themselves, and with the organism of the personal and historical facts of redemption. And here at once is a system; to wit, a system of biblical psychology as it lies at the foundation of the system of the facts and the revelation of salvation; and such a system of biblical psychology is so necessary a basis for every biblical summary of doctrine, that it may be rightly said of the doctrinal summary which Hofmann's *Schriftbeweis* seeks to verify by Scripture, that from the beginning to the end, from the doctrine of the creation to the doctrine of the Last things, a special psychologic system, or (if this expression be objected to) a special complex of psychological representations, absolutely supports it. What Scripture says to us of cosmology, may certainly appear insufficient to originate a system of biblical cosmology; but assuredly it says to us infinitely more about man's soul and spirit than about Orion and the Pleiades. And I would not assert that Scripture offers to us no natural knowledge of the soul; I believe it rather to the honour of God's word, to be compelled to maintain the contrary. For, for example, that the substance of man's nature is dualistic, *i.e.* that spirit and body are fundamentally of distinct origin and nature —that is surely a natural knowledge,—a dogma in the faith of which, in spite of all remonstrances of rigid natural investigation, we live and die. And although what Scripture gives us to ponder in such statements as Gen. ii. 7 and 1 Cor. xv. 45 may be called only suggestions, still a biblico-psychological investigation must be justified which takes the course indicated by these hints. Or are we to leave these hieroglyphs to the so-called *accurate* investigation? I hold this, no less than Harless does, in fitting honour; but the meaning of these hieroglyphs lies beyond the limit placed to experiment and calculation. It is possible to labour in the sweat of the brow even without the scalpel or the microscope. Even historical problems are not to be solved otherwise than in the sweat of the brow; and our problem is an historical one, only with the distinction arising from the fact that we stand in a different inward relation to the holy Scripture from that in which we do—say—to the Vedas or to the Avesta. We desire to bring out exegetically the views of Scripture, on the nature, the life, and the life-destinies of the soul as they are defined with a view to the history of salvation; and, in accordance with that inevitable requirement which we must impose upon our thinking when it is engaged on the subject of Scripture, to reduce it into systematic harmony. This harmony is only to be the scientifically intercepted reflection of the real harmony in which these representations subsist of themselves.

The risk which we run is not that of seeking to verify something which is impossible, but of substituting for that objective certainty of inward consistency, a feigned consistency, of the existence of which we have persuaded ourselves. For a systematizing of the material of biblical psychology is certainly not practicable, without the endeavour to unfold many a merely indirect scriptural saying, and to draw connecting lines here and there between individual points, according to the scriptural meaning. But as the Scripture is no scholastic book of science, this is more or less essential in every science that is based upon it as a foundation. Should we not always be successful in this task of construction in hitting the sense of Scripture, it will be just as little argument against the claims of the material of biblical psychology to scientific treatment, as it would be against the claims of Homeric psychology, that the inquirers in that region[1] contradict one another on some important points.

The task which I propose to myself is practicable; for under the name of biblical psychology I understand a scientific representation of the doctrine of Scripture on the psychical constitution of man as it was created, and the ways in which this constitution has been affected by sin and redemption. There is such a doctrine in Scripture. It is true that on psychological subjects, just as little as on dogmatical or ethical, does Scripture comprehend any system propounded in the language of the schools. If it taught in such a way, we should need as little to construct psychology from it as we should dogmatics and ethics. But still it does teach. If it proceeds upon fundamental views whose accuracy it absolutely takes for granted; if it narrates or predicts facts about which we should know nothing, or nothing certain, were they not testified to us by it; if the most manifold natural and supernatural conditions of the inner life of man find therein a self-evidence which admits no suspicion of self-deception or distortion; if it represents to us, in the way of consolation and warning,

---

[1] The Homeric psychology has found representatives in Wagner, in his *Psychologia Homerica* (Paris 1833); v. Nägelsbach, in his lately edited *Homeric Theology* (1840) by Autenrieth (1861); Grotemeyer, in his *Programm. Homers Grundansicht von der Seele* (Warendorf 1854); and others. The extent of this literature, which began with Halbkart's obsolete *Psychologia Homerica* (1796), is discreditable to biblical theologians.

the influence of superhuman powers, both good and evil, on the human life of the soul,—all this is so, and its purpose is, for our instruction, assuredly not to afford us an unfruitful learning, and to satisfy unspiritual curiosity (and neither indeed is this the purpose of theologically scientific doctrine), but to promote our salvation. But the science has the duty of bringing to light the materials of doctrine latent in the Scriptures,—of collecting that which is scattered there,—of explaining that which is hard to be understood,—of establishing that which is doubtful,—and of combining the knowledge thus acquired into a doctrinal whole, consistent and compact.

The formal possibility of the accomplishment of such a task is guaranteed by the undeniable unity of character prevailing in the doctrinal materials of psychology placed before us in Scripture. Or are the psychological assumptions and inferences of the biblical writers not in harmony with themselves? We maintain thorough fundamental agreement, without thereby excluding manifold individualities of representation and mode of speech; for in their essential spiritual unity the special writers have each their characteristic stamp. The passion for system exaggerates this. Its game is an easy one. How little is required to imitate it! Learned treatises would prove that the Elohist and Jehovist of the Pentateuch,—that the author of the book of Job and of the words of Elihu,— that David and Solomon,—psychologically differ from one another; even although the science for that purpose should be that of conceiving straw and bringing forth stubble. But let the first page of the Holy Scripture be only read, and the last compared with it; and not until the reader has felt himself transported with wonder at the majestic harmony of the word of God from Alpha to Omega, let him tell of the peculiarities of individual writers in the midst of this divine-human concert. That which is peculiar does not concern the fundamental views. There is a clearly defined psychology essentially proper to the Holy Scripture, which in like manner underlies all the biblical writers, and intrinsically differs from that many-formed psychology which lies outside the circle of revelation.[1] There-

---

[1] Thus we judge with Schöberlein, in his notice of v. Rudloff, *Studien u. Kritiken* (1860), p. 145, which in appropriate words comes to the defence of biblical psychology; and therefore we have, on scientific ground, the

fore the problem of biblical psychology may be solved as one problem. We do not need, first of all, to force the biblical teaching into unity; it is one in itself.

The biblical psychology thus built up is an independent science, which coincides with no other, and is made superfluous by no other in the organism of entire theology. It is most closely allied with so-called biblical theology, or (since what is accustomed to be most unaptly so called is rightly occupied, partly in the history of salvation, and partly in the history of revelation), with dogmatics. Biblical, or, as may be said, theological psychology (to distinguish it from the physical-empirical and philosophic-rational science), pervades the entire material of dogmatics, determining all the phases of man's psychical constitution, conditioned upon those facts and relations momentous to the history of salvation which form the substance of dogmatics. But it asserts in all these associations its own peculiarity, in that it considers all that is common to it with dogmatics only so far as it throws light or shadow into the human soul, draws it into co-operation or sympathy, and affords explanations upon its obscurities. Much which is only incidentally dealt with in dogmatics, is in psychology, which herein is subsidiary to it, a main feature: for example, the relation of the soul to the blood, as material to the doctrine of the atonement; and the question, as important to the doctrine of original sin, whether the soul is propagated *per traducem* or not: as, on the other hand, the scriptural doctrines of the tri-unity of God,—of the good and evil angels,—of the divine-human personality of Christ, which in dogmatics are principal matters, are only so far treated of in psychology as they are connected with the formation of the divine image in man, with the good and evil influences of the spiritual world upon him, and with the restoration of the true human nature. The new relation of God to humanity in Christ, which is the centre of entire theology, is also the centre of psychology as well as of dogmatics. Dogmatics have to do with analyzing and systematizing the believing consciousness of this new relation which rests on and in the Scripture. Psychology, on the contrary, has to do with the human soul, and forth from the soul,

right, which the critic in the *Literar. Centralblatt*, 1855, No. 45, refuses to us, to speak of the Scriptures almost entirely as of one subject.

with the constitution of human nature, which is the object and subject of this new relation.

From this conception of our science—which we are still as ever convinced, resists the fiery trial of criticism—we turn now to the method of realizing it.

METHOD OF BIBLICAL PSYCHOLOGY.

Sec. III.

SINCE the Holy Scripture regards man not from the physiologic point of view of nature's laws, but everywhere as in definite ethico-historical relations, we shall adopt the historical mode, and prosecute the history of the soul from its eternal antecedents to its everlasting ultimate destiny. Thus conceived of, the matter of psychology divides itself into the following seven heads:—1. Eternal Presuppositions. 2. Creation and Propagation. 3. Fall. 4. Present Constitution. 5. Regeneration. 6. Death and Intermediate State. 7. Resurrection and Perfection. Since psychology after this manner proceeds from eternity, and passing through time turns back again to eternity, there will not be wanting to it a completed unity; but the successful accomplishment of our task will depend on our not losing sight in any wise of the distinction between psychology and dogmatics. Our source is the Holy Scripture, in union with empirical facts which have a biblical relation, and require biblical examination. The Old and New Testament concern us equally; for the Old Testament, which is more directed to the creation and nature, *i.e.* to the origin of things and their external manifestation, gives us disclosures which the New Testament at once takes for granted; the New Testament, on the other hand, affords us, on the ground of the incarnation of the Son of God, far deeper and more accurate knowledge of the nature of God, and of the ethical relations of man to the invisible as to the visible world; and, moreover, it is there that we first learn to understand rightly the beginnings of man in the light of the clearly and specially revealed last things. We must carefully consider this difference of the two Testaments, and in general the gradation of the revelation; and we must take pains to distinguish between what Scripture designedly teaches, and what it adopts without close discussion,—as the psychologic view generally received in antiquity, or current among the Semitic tribes, or become stereotyped in language,— in order to attribute to it its peculiar doctrinal value in accordance with its character of revelation. Finally, it is not sufficient, by way of adducing proofs, to pick out individual texts from Scripture; but there is necessary, generally, inspection and inquiry into the entire scope of Scripture, that we may not fall back into the faults which made the ancient manner of referring to Scripture proofs, unhistorical, one-sided, and fragmentary. Moreover, we must guard ourselves against the self-deception of interpolating speculative thoughts suggested by Scripture, or physiologic notices foreign to it, in Scripture itself. To interpret into Scripture the circulation of the blood, or the importance of the cerebral system to the activity of the soul, would be just as foolish as to reject such new discoveries because no scriptural statements imply any reference to them. It is the peculiarity of revelation to accommodate itself to the degree of cultivation of every age, and to speak, not the language of the school, but the language of life. This observation is just, but it must not be pressed too far. It is incompatible with the purpose of revelation to make use of an absolutely inadequate means of representation, and incompatible with its truthfulness to base itself upon false presumptions. How, for example, could Gen. i. be a divine revelation, if the substance of what is revealed were limited to the fact that the world is a created work of divine power and wisdom, and if all the rest were mere pageantry, not to be received by physical science?—a low view, which has already been refuted in individual instances of importance by physical science itself! It is just the same with the psychological presuppositions of Scripture. From the standpoint of our present empirical knowledge they appear unsatisfactory, because, as in the case of what Scripture says on astronomical subjects, they are here or there only gathered from the external form of the phenomenon; but, nevertheless, they are not false: they only become so when the form of the revelation, borrowed from the modes of representation and expression of daily life, is regarded as belonging to its substance. Thus, for example, he who would reproach the Scripture, that it always places the soul in immediate relation with the blood, and not with the nerves, would be just as unjust as another would be foolish if he read in Scripture of electricity, magnetism, and such like things, or perhaps of the nervous fluid, abandoned as it is (I do not raise the question how rightly) by modern physiology. Of all these things Scripture can say nothing, since the Holy Ghost speaks there with a human tongue; and human representation and language had not in those times any ideas and words for those things. But we should deeply wrong the Scripture, if we thought that the glory of its psychologic representations must grow paler and paler in the daylight sunshine of the present day, and that biblical psychology is perhaps such as the psychology of Homer—nothing but a fragment of the history of the training of the human spirit, of only antiquarian value! Certainly, Scripture must forego the honour of having anticipated physical research in discoveries which have been made by sections and vivisections, and all kinds of experiments on animal bodies; but the honour of Scripture consists in the fact, that it offers us a knowledge just at that point where the knowledge of physical research (which, without it, is more physiologic than psychologic) hopelessly fails, unless man's impulse of knowing allows itself to be hushed up by idle promises of an undefined future. The path of knowledge of experimental physical investigation advances from without, inward, and has there before it a limit beyond which it cannot now or ever pass. The mode of evidence of the revelation, which gives itself to the internal experience, goes, on the other hand, from within, outward, and has no other bounds than those which it places to itself in accordance with man's attainment in culture and need of salvation.[1] Natural investigation, for example, can tell us most accurately how, by means of a purely optical process, the forms of the outer world

---

[1] "Where is the rule and the measure," cries to us, on the other hand, Noack, in his *Psyche*, vol. iii. 1860, p. 330, "whereby this way of evidence of the revelation which gives itself to the internal experience is to be judged?" We answer: In the trial of its genuineness, which only the real and genuine one can really undergo, and in the essential harmony of the internal experiences of faithful Christians of all times and of all places.

come in contact with the retina expanded on the background of the eye; but here it must stop: it can go no further; for how, by the further agency of the optic nerve and of the brain, the image becomes a perception—of this it can never tell us anything. It is absolutely impossible to show how, by means of the brain, irritation of the nerve of sensation is transformed into perception; how thence into the thought-product of perceptions; how thence into the self-consciousness that overrides and penetrates the entire physico-psychical mechanism. The final impulses of the process of life,—the Subject which, by means of the nervous system, stands in reciprocal relation with the outer world, and, as it were, superintends this telegraphic apparatus; the existence of the spiritual dignity and infinite perfectibility which distinguishes man from the brute;—these are things of too inward a character ever to be arrived at in the sensuous region of firmly grasped physical investigation. Its method proceeds from without inwards, and there strikes upon insurmountable limits, which it is compelled to acknowledge, if it would not fall into conceptions which by the laws and the necessity of thought would lead *ad absurdum*. Divine revelation, on the other hand, takes the reverse way: it begins at that which is innermost in man—the spirit; expands itself thence over the psychical life, and has no further interest in anatomizing the marvellous edifice of the bodily organs of that life (although the sacrificial worship promoted their study in brute bodies), since for it this present corporeity, degraded to sin and death, is a καταργούμενον. But as far as late experimental research has actually revealed to us the secrets of human bodily life, its results agree with the disclosures of Scripture about spirit and soul,—far removed from favouring a materialism which is opposed to Scripture; for, as a late opponent of the folly of the materialistic view of the world has with only too much truth observed, it is not the actual results of physical investigation, but the hypotheses grafted on to them, and arrived at from quite a different source, which imply the denial[1] of every

---

[1] F. Fabri, in his letters against materialism, 1856, and *Evang. K. Z.* 1857, col. 1069. "Where the question is about the fundamental views of a man, from which are built up his moral and spiritual views, there is primarily placed in the scale a factor which lies outside the domain of 'strict demonstration,' viz. the *will* of man."

nobler religious truth, and even of the substantiality and reality of the spiritual altogether.

Our task reminds us not to leave unconsidered many of those results attained by means of the dissecting knife and the microscope; for biblical psychology has not alone to bring out the psychologic aspects of Scripture, but also to show, in the face of later science, that, so far as they are well-founded and fairly-balanced presumptions of the revelation of salvation, there is due to them a continually better established claim to subsistence and authority on our consciousness. In these inevitable references to late physical science, and especially to physiology, we shall make it our duty to use the strictest care; and we believe, therefore, that we have no occasion to fear lest any one of the modern philosophers whom we shall name should be able to point out to us that we have not understood him, although he possibly might have to complain that we have not applied what he has said, as he himself intended it. But are we on that account to abstain from all references? Scientific theology has been lately admonished by a physical philosopher[1] for resting great hopes upon such rotten supports and in such troubled waters as the results of natural inquiry. And with reason. But neither has it any ground for entertaining great apprehensions. The book of nature and the book of Scripture are precisely two books which from the beginning were intended to be compared with one another. And if the student of nature asks the theologian or himself as a Christian, How readest thou? the theologian must also in return ask the student of nature, How readest thou? The reciprocity of this question has indeed almost ceased. It tends, however, to the honour of theology, that its interest in the book of Scripture is inseparable from its interest in the book of nature, just as it adds discredit to the later physical science, that for the most part it scarcely concerns itself about the book of Scripture, and establishes a yawning gulf between the two divine records. Theology cannot treat it in like manner, for the two books have as their author the one God, from whom the science itself is named. Therefore it cannot refrain from collating the two books, and, moreover, the exegesis of the two books. And it is this which is required in the nature of the problem itself,

[1] Rud. Wagner, in *Der Evang. K. Z.* 1857, col. 367.

in the field of biblical psychology. But if, in certain cases, a palpable contradiction appears between the interpretation of Scripture and that of nature, we shall be allowed to point out that, for the present at least, the biblical representations are not yet convicted of absurdity. With the materialism of our days, however, we shall concern ourselves little. Biblical psychology may remit the struggle against this barbarism to the empirical and philosophical science. There are still many other forms of vigorous opposition between the biblical manner of looking at things and the modern consciousness, and these must impartially be presented to us. On this account we shall certainly here and there be constrained to adopt an apologetic tone. And if we apply apologetically something of what has been said by natural philosophers in such a way that what they have not absolutely meant to say shall further the cause of Scripture, we are sorry to give them this cause of complaint, and we console them beforehand with the assurance that it shall not often happen.

For, for the most part, in our apologetic argument for the Scripture, which is associated with the exegetic-historic argument from Scripture, we shall rely partly upon undoubted facts of our own inward life, and partly upon well-attested facts of psychical occurrence without us. In respect of the former, we here upon the threshold make the avowal, that, in order to its right treatment and understanding, biblical psychology presumes above all, that the student has personal experience of that living energy of the word of God which is declared in Heb. iv. 12 to divide asunder the inward man with the sharpness of a two-edged sword. Even that natural philosopher[1] just referred to has not been ashamed to make the good confession: "Only he to whom it is given to apprehend the highest mysteries of revealed religion in full subjective faith, will be able with satisfaction to himself and to his age to philosophize upon the natural phenomena of the life of the soul." Such also is our conviction. That man only who in the way of repentance and of faith in God has returned to himself, is capable of any knowledge about himself which does not stop short at the threshold, and indeed, according to the unalterable law *ex fide intellectus,* is capable of a knowledge, genuine, resting on sufficient and reasonable grounds, and truly accurate.

[1] Rud. Wagner, *Der Kampf um die Seele,* p. 112.

Nevertheless, we are only here declaring the prerequisite of any intelligent penetration of the material of biblical psychology, and indeed we hereby desire to impress it chiefly upon ourselves as a matter of serious warning. In reference, however, to the well-attested facts of psychical occurrence external to us, there has never perhaps been a time more favourable to biblical psychology, as there has also never been a time that needed it more than the present, which, in features that are constantly becoming more manifest, earns the character of the last days. For the spirit-world, good as well as evil, which for all times has been the background of earthly events, is coming more and more to the front in our times; the end of the Christian era becoming, according to a divine law in the formation of history, increasingly like to its beginning. Powerful and awakening invasions of good spirits into the psychical life of men on the one hand, and on the other, all kinds of magic, even to the summoning up of the dead, are becoming more and more frequent. We would not be deaf to the preaching of repentance by the former phenomena, nor blind to the pernicious power of the latter, in which demoniacal influence and human quackery are adversely involved. By throwing light from the word of God upon these twofold phenomena, in order to draw from it the power of discerning of spirits as far as is attainable to every man, we are satisfying an increasingly urgent necessity of the present day. In the Holy Scripture we have the solution of these enigmas; but they are moreover a living commentary on the Scripture, which we must not ignore, if we would not, to our everlasting disgrace, neglect the consideration of the signs of the times.

Thus, then, for the second time, we tread anew the road of inquiry, whose plan we thus projected. May God bless our going out and our coming in! Thanks, moreover, to all those who have equipped us for this second pilgrimage by kindly critical consideration of our first attempt. We acknowledge good-will even in those who have not ignored our undertaking. They will all find their names inscribed here as in a genealogical table. They may all look on themselves as fellow-workers in this second edition; for it is only by mutual assistance that science makes progress. As it is said of the church, There are many members, but one body; so it may be said of science, There are many labourers, but one labour.

APPENDIX.

GUIDE TO A TRUE PSYCHOLOGY AND ANTHROPOLOGY,

TO BE GATHERED FROM THE SACRED WRITINGS.

ATTEMPTED BY CASP. BARTHOLINUS.

Prooemium.

PHILOSOPHERS have taken credit to themselves, and have almost triumphed in the course of many ages, in respect of human comments upon the nature of the soul, its diversities and faculties, and generally of dreams without sleep, and shadow without substance; closely written volumes having been published on this argument, to the great damage not only of paper, time, and labour, but also of truth.

As soon, however, as we consult the Spirit of God in His oracles and in His most sacred records, it is very manifest that the wisdom of the age has attained to little or nothing of the truth. And how could it be otherwise in so sublime an argument, when those who are wise after the manner of men are blind even to things which lie in their path and are obvious to their senses, and who, as Scaliger says, lick the glass vessel, but never touch the pottage? Wherefore, although in this imbecility of our nature we neither can nor will promise an exact and accurate ψυχολογίαν, yet we will contribute a compendious introduction, with the hope of making the whole matter more fruitful to others, and of affording both the occasion and the subject for its discussion and elaboration.

The first foundation, then, of the true doctrine of the human soul, appears as a sacred one in Gen. ii. 7, in these words: "Formavit Dominus Deus hominum pulverem de terra, et inspiravit in faciem ejus spiraculum vitarum, et fuit homo in animam viventem."

Formavit, i.e. He constructed like a potter. Whence Job (x. 9), "Remember that Thou hast made me as the clay;" and Jer. xviii. 2, God is compared to the potter, and man to the clay. The Hebrews will have the Hebrew word וַיִּיצֶר written with a double Jod, to signify the twofold formation, earthly and heavenly; for the reason that below, ver. 19 in the same chapter, וַיִּצֶר is found in reference to the construction of other animals with a single Jod, pointing to a single life, and that not immortal.

Dominus Deus hominem pulverem. Not only out of the dust of the earth, but man altogether was formed *dust* out of the earth. For which reason below. Dust thou art (not only "of dust"), and into dust shalt thou return.

De terrâ, or the mud of the earth.

Et inspiravit, i.e. He introduced breath with power. Where some persons are absurd who describe God anthropomorphically, as having blown into Adam's nostrils like one with distended cheeks, the breath or spirit, as if a particle of His own Spirit.

In faciem ejus. Thus the LXX. and Vulg. For in and by his countenance, man is chiefly seen, and his various affections, as anger, joy, sadness, etc. Therefore, although the inspiration was communicated to the whole body, yet that body is characterized from the most noble and conspicuous part—to wit, the countenance. In other respects, in the largest signification, *aph* and *anaph* mean that by which any kind of a thing is beheld, what and what like it is, except when $\tau\rho o\pi\hat{\eta}$, it is taken for other things. Hence it is taken also for anger or rage; because chiefly this affection is manifest, and especially in the face. Moreover, it is taken for the nostrils, by which the face is largely characterized; for an injury to the nose disfigures the entire face. Mercerus, therefore, takes needless trouble to induce us to understand nostrils as the actual meaning in this passage, since it cannot be denied that in many places of Scripture this word implies the countenance.

Spiraculum vitarum, doubtless of more than one, and certainly of a twofold life, Heb. נִשְׁמַת חַיִּים (for *neschama* is the same which in Greek is $\pi\nu o\acute{\eta}$, breath, blowing, breathing, respiration, and in construction *nischmat*), which two words placed conjointly Paul seems to repeat separately, Acts xvii. 25, where he says that God gives to all ζωὴν καὶ πνοήν, i.e. life and breath. Whence Forster, in his Lexicon, infers a distinction between the natural man who eats, drinks, begets, etc., and the spiritual and heavenly man regenerated by faith in Christ, who performs spiritual actions, such as are knowledge of God, love and praise and joy in God,—such an one as shall be in perfection in life eternal.

Et fuit homo in animam viventem. This is repeated in these words in 1 Cor. xv. 45: "The first man Adam was made a living soul."

And thus in that verse Moses impresses upon us all the causes of man. The efficient cause, the Lord God; the matter, earth; the form, the breath of lives; the object, that he might become a living soul.

Then, in the way of foundation, are to be adduced what things are said about the formation of man in God's image, in or according to His likeness (Gen. i. 26, 27). Finally, to this fundamental place is to be added what has been observed from the concordances of the Hebrew Bibles, that the words נְשָׁמָה, נֶפֶשׁ, and רוּחַ are so different, that *neschama* is the efficient soul, or the spirit with the idea of efficiency (although sometimes it is put for *nephesch*): *nephesch* is the spirit or soul, not simply, but efficient in dust, or the soul efficient in respect of the subject or the efficient subject (for which reason also it is sometimes taken for a corpse, or a lifeless body, as Lev. xix. 28): *ruach* is efficiency itself, or energy, or the force and efficacy of power. Wherefore, in the most sacred memorials, *neschama* and *ruach* are attributed to God, but not *nephesch*.

From these three words in the holy writings, as if *à priori*, the nature of the soul is aptly shown by the Spirit of God; that nature which the philosophers are compelled to investigate only *à posteriori;* and thus, the foregone foundations being given up to this point, we will approach the matter itself.

CHAP. I. *That Vegetables are not animated or living, notwithstanding the assertions of Philosophers.*

Those things which philosophers call living things—to wit, endowed with a vegetating soul as they call it, as roots, plants, trees, etc.—are not classed by God's Spirit among animate or living things; nay, they are absolutely distinguished and separated from these (Gen. i. 30); and therefore we most correctly say that herbs and trees are not animate or living. For the more abundant confirmation of which assertion, I adduce other passages of Genesis.

Gen. i. 24, the living soul is classified according to whatever species the earth produces; but herbs and trees are not enumerated, but cattle, reptiles, and beasts of the earth; and therefore in ver. 30 the herb is distinguished from the living soul by its being appointed for its food.

In Gen. vi.-ix. it is plain what things are said to have the spirit of life, or are said to be living things, or a living animal. For when God had determined to destroy every living soul that was on the dry land, He comprehended nothing under this designation except animals—winged, and living on the earth—beasts, and men; and these species He very often calls *omnem animam viventem, scil.* in the dry land (vi. 7, vii. 22). Wherefore the Hebrews never consider the vegetative life worthy of being called by philosophers by the name of soul or life.

Chap. II.—*Of the Senses.*

The instruments and servants for the bodily, and, in like manner, for the mental functions, are the senses. In brutes I say they are for the purposes of nutrition; in man correspondingly they subserve the intellect.

Chap. III.—*What Man is, and concerning his Origin.*

Although philosophers accustomed to human speculations do not speak with the Spirit of God, since they are left destitute of suitable words in so sublime a matter, yet we most rightly say, following the Spirit of God, that man is a soul, that man is a spirit in the dust, etc. Thus also cattle, reptiles, and beasts of the earth, are called living souls. But man is called a soul, not by synecdoche, but by a scriptural phrase in which *nephesch* is not a part of a man, but a spirit in the dust, or the spirit of dust, *i.e.* man.

Besides, man is often called the world in the sacred writings, because he is, as it were, the nucleus of creatures (that which, when it putrifies in the fruit, the rest also putrifies), and ἀπαρχὴ τῶν κτισμάτων, or chief of them all. Man especially is κτίσις and κόσμος, adorned and elaborated (and that not tropically or figuratively only) by God.

But every κτίσις has shone forth in God the Spirit, either that they may become only entities, or at the same time living entities, *i.e.* either entities potentially, or potentially living. For the efficacy of the Spirit of God is sometimes one thing, sometimes another, as some things may have received the spirit by which they are, others that they may live. All things, however, were made by the spirit of His mouth, *i.e.* by speaking. Hence being and living differ in the intensity of spirit, which indeed is plain from the intensity of the letters in the Hebrew words הָיָה and חָיָה, הָוָה and חָוָה (conf. Ps. civ. 29; Job xii. 10; Ezek. xviii. 4; Neh. ix. 6). Moreover, law and life have, according to Forster's *Annotations*, a great affinity between them.

Living things are divided, in respect of motion, into flying things, creeping things, and walking things (Gen. vi. 19).

But a certain κτίσις shone forth in the embrace of love in the moulded dust, to which, as there was its own face and form (*species*) (whereby it is looked at, so to speak, or known), the Lord, by the efficacy of His own Spirit, gave the spirit of lives, and then man was made a living soul; which peculiar efficacy is in this κτίσει beyond the rest, that to them it is not said that He breathed into them, although He made them by His own Spirit, and gave them the spirit of life.

And how intimately it shone forth in God, Moses declares (Gen. i. 26, 27), even into the very image of God with His likeness, to wit, the ἀπαυγάσμα and character of God giving itself as an image, in whose close embrace it might obtain the image of God Himself; that, as God Himself in His essence is an act of light knowingly true, of love mightily willing, and of the Holy living Spirit, so this κτίσις, in its essence mighty, might exist in light knowingly true, in love mightily willing, and in the Holy Spirit living.

Wherefore, as far as the spirit of lives is chiefly the spirit of this κτίσις, its proper potentiality is noted by the designation of God's image; but as far as it is of bodily dust, it is described in words of fructifying and subduing. For the life of the mental functions is to see God, ἐν οὐρανοῖς; that of the bodily functions is ἐξουσιάζεσθαι, etc., ἐν οἰκουμένῃ.

Finally, we must observe that soul and spirit are sometimes distinguished, as Heb. iv. 12 and elsewhere. For the soul is so called in its natural powers; but in so far as it is enlightened by the light of the Holy Spirit, it is called spirit.

Chap. iv.—*Of the Image of God in Man.*

Thus man shone forth even in the image of God, which before the fall was like, afterwards unlike. The likeness of the image was, that his spirit beamed with love, or that it was light, love, and spirit, as God is. After the fall the light indeed remained, but unlike; the love remained, but unlike, etc. Thus that likeness must be restored in holiness in regard of ourselves, and in justice in regard of λογισμοῦ τοῦ Θεοῦ. Before the fall God shone forth in a fitting image, that man might reflect God, which light was the life or the *to live* of man; and this life obtained from that light, that it might reflect God fittingly, by which very thing man was ἔνεικος, and moreover εὐδόκιμος (who in himself was ἔνθεος, and a partaker of the divine nature) and ἔννομος. For he was a law unto himself, his own essential conformity and perfection from within dictating to him what God in other cases from without dictates and prescribes; and that life was in very deed the vision of God, while God was shining forth in our spirit, and was thus being seen.

This light perished in the fall, and man died with death, and thus became ἄεικος and ἄνομος. The fallen Adam indeed retained his essence, and that a living one (Heb. ii. 14), but dead in respect of the perfection of its position. Hence Adam died. What life was left to him in life, was a dead life. And we all received from Adam such a flesh: dead we are, certainly, born of dead flesh. Wherefore it is necessary that we be transformed and daily assimilated to God, which assimilation, in proportion as we realize, in that proportion we see God; and because man has lost the likeness of the image of God, that is to be restored in Christ, in whom, as if in an image, we are built, and in whom intimately made to shine forth again, we have received εἰκόνα, from whom, I say, as if the head and beginning, the image of God Himself, the spirit living, although in moulded dust, has subsisted.

For God's counsel remains one and constant, and is not changed on account of the fall, *scil.* that we ought in λόγῳ to return εἰκόνα, and thus to be united to God in an eternal covenant. That real change was made in the fall and by the fall, that what we had before by nature is now conceded to us by grace.

CHAP. V.—*What στάσις and ὑπόστασις are in Man.*

Stasis is in its nature nothing else than that in which the internal perfection of everything consists, and, moreover, that by which the thing itself is made to stand perfect: it is the internal *status* of the thing itself which the apostolic language designates either by a simple expression στάσεως (Heb. ix. 8), or a compound one, whether συστάσεως (2 Pet. iii. 5) or ὑποστάσεως (Heb. i. 3, xi. 1).

Stasis and perfection, therefore, are one and the same thing, in such a way, however, that perfection may be said to belong to στάσεως, as that which is of stasis.

But στάσις and ὑπόστασις are different, although they sometimes concur in one. For mixed things, as this or that plant, this or that brute, have their στάσιν, but not ὑπόστασιν, because they have not yet attained to that στάσιν and τελείωσιν, beyond which it is not permitted them to ascend. For a living form, generally considered, is not restricted to the form of a plant, but may ascend to a nobler grade. In God τελείωσις or στάσις is called hypostasis, in whom all things are said to have σύστασιν and στάσιν, not ὑπόστασιν, man alone excepted, who is next under God, or His στάσει, and in whom the image is reflecting God; wherefore man is called both σύστατος and ὑπόστατος.

Σύστατος by reason of God, in whom all things have their σύστασιν, but ὑπόστατος in himself, and in respect of our inferior κτίσεως. Hence in this same ἀπαρχῇ τῶν κτισμάτων, ὕπαρξις and ὑπόστασις are different. For the rest of the κτίσις is ὕπαρκτος and σύστατος; man, over and above, is ὑπόστατος, on account of τελείωσιν, whereby he excels the inferior κτίσιν.

Hence Christ, in respect of His human nature, is called, not ὑπόστατος, but σύστατος, although He had an ulterior perfection differently from us men. For the natural στάσις of Christ, in which He was made like to us, is, that His human nature should be equally perfect as ours; whence it has the quality of being something, and not being reduced to nothing, otherwise He would not have assumed perfect human nature. But Christ in the divine στάσις is ὑπόστατος, which is a higher στάσις and τελείωσις, intimately in God, in whom it subsists in the most internal manner; whence His humanity obtains far greater things than the privilege of not being reduced into nothing. But because every essence consists of a threefold στάσις—as there will elsewhere be an opportunity of saying—completing its τελείωσιν, certainly also the human essence does so, essentially considered in its universal amplitude. And since, as regards the condition of matter when it is divisible, the individual is divided into various parts, even the units are called ὑπόστατα or ὑφιστάμενα.

CHAP. VI.—*Of the Human Reason and its Acts.*

Λόγος, or human reason, is that τελείωσις and στάσις of man, or of the human soul, by which, by its own internal essential light, he can both receive, consider, and acknowledge, and embrace, retain, and approve, whatever has any light to shine by.

Therefore λογικοὶ acts are *excipere* and *amplexari*. Some call them *intellectum* and *voluntatem*.

But that essential light of human reason, in which it was first established potentially efficacious by God, by that great judgment of God, has even perished and become deprived of its original perfection of brightly efficacious power, so that there has remained to it only a certain spark of light. Wherefore all men are exhibited by God's Spirit as τῇ διανοίᾳ ἐσκοτισμένοι (Eph. iv. 18), and in that respect are alienated from the life of God by the ignorance that is in them.

Hence it is not sufficient for vividly embracing things, and bringing them before one's self in the light,—the things, indeed, which refer to the life of God,—and it plainly has no light left by which they can shine forth to itself; but occult in perpetual mysteries, secret and profound, they will be able to be revealed by no spirit but that of God Himself, to be expounded or to be sought out by inquiry, concerning which thing we have spoken in our orations concerning the use of the human reason in divine mysteries.

Chap. vii.—*Of the Twofold Life in Man.*

Moreover, we have to determine how manifold that life is, in such a way that the number may not be needlessly great. Some people ridiculously understand by many lives the two openings of the nostrils. Others generally understand a threefold life—vegetable, sentient, and rational. But we have already shown above, that the vegetable is not anywhere called *a life* in the Holy Scriptures, but that rather the contrary is suggested. Wherefore, since there is said to be in man the breathing-place of many lives, it cannot be thought that they are either other or more than *corporis vita* and *mentis vita*, since nothing else in man can be said to live. That one spirit, breathed into the dust from the earth, lives and pervades each life for the safety of the body and the mind; or, which is the same thing, one living soul lives the life of either kind with one spirit. But that the spirit of lives is also given to brutes (Gen. vi. 17), is an objection which may be answered: (1) That they have not *neschama*, but *ruach chajim*; (2) That in the same expression men are comprehended; (3) That there is in brutes also a certain other life than the merely nutritive, yet not mental, but sensual, and in every one according to its kind (comp. Prov. xxx. 25, vi. 6-8). The spirit of man is so sublime, that in Prov. xx. 27, *nischmat Adam* is said to be the light or lamp of Jehovah.

Chap. viii.—*Of the Power of the Soul: in what way one, or manifold.*

Since, then, the essence of one soul is one, and if, where the essence is, the essence is potential, and that, moreover, in the one potentiality essential to itself its essentially potential essence is potential, and moreover one, its essentially one essential potentiality is living, or actually able to live, with a twofold life. But that the essence is created in which there is such a potential essence, is manifest because of existent creatures. It is one thing εἶναι, another thing στῆναι : the former is to be ; στάσις is to be able, or potentiality. Whence, moreover, on human ground, wise men concede that all created things, in respect to God, are a potentiality. But in God στάσις is an act, yea, it is to act itself; and when we speak of God, who gives στάσιν, then στῆναι also signifies to ordain, or to constitute. In order that this may be better understood, we must know that of every essence it is the essential condition to be prepared for action, or acting, which, if it is not prepared for not acting, then that essence is a mere act, or merely to act, because to act must always be thought of in an act, so that it may not be called potential in this sense that potentiality is opposed to act. But if, moreover, it is essentially prepared for not acting, and thus it is not a mere act, then it is understood and said to have a potentiality to act, so that it is not less essential to it not to act than to act, if the condition of the essence is turned to action ; which potentiality of every essence, and, moreover, even of human essence, is preserved and sustained by God in His στάσει.

But that one essence, with a certain universality and generic amplitude in proportion to the variety of objects around which either life is occupied, is potential to perform actions distinct in kind, although essentially participating in a generic community, as far as the actions are of an essence essentially potential, with its own only potentiality; which actions the one essence of the soul and of either life controls.

Wherefore, although in itself the essential potentiality is one in unity of essence, yet, in respect of its various effect in various objects, potential in various manners and in distinct actions, it is also invoked by distinct names; so that sometimes it is called the power of understanding, now of nourishing, of increasing, of changing, etc., that essential communion of the various actions in proportion to the variety of the objects mental and corporeal remaining meanwhile in the essential potentiality, as if with a general origin and general nomenclature, on account of the condition of the common essence.

As mind and body, as far as they are to be vivified by the power of the spirit of lives, are able to agree on many sides in this respect in a certain general community, but in respect of the special condition of every one, to differ also on many sides; thus also the destined objects of their life, and the actions of the same objects for either life and ample community, agree, and in special conditions differ. Whence, also, *actions* in either life, and in respect of the community indeed, are like to one another both in fact and in name, and for the special condition of every one are different.

As mental life alone is truly human life, so the potentiality which is called of the mental life in objects and actions is primarily potential; secondarily, it subserves the objects and actions of the bodily life. Hence, when in any action man or human soul is set forth as powerful, it will principally bear the appellation when around the mental life it is occupied in act; secondarily, when it serves the bodily life, unless in respect of either the one or the other, whether of mind or of body, from some special condition it is only peculiar to the other.

CHAP. IX.—*Of Death.*

Death is the destruction of actions, or the defluxion (not perishing and annihilation) of the perfection of every $\sigma\tau\acute{a}\sigma\epsilon\omega\varsigma$, as well of that which is common to man with the brutes, as of that in which he lives to God; and in respect of the latter, death is sin: for as far as it is $\check{a}\nu o\mu o\nu$ it is called sin, as far as it is $\check{a}\epsilon\iota\kappa o\nu$ it is called death. For all sin is death, but not the contrary. For death, as it is the privation of life by which we externally live, is not considered as sin. Before the fall, God communicated to man that he might be a $\nu\acute{o}\mu o\varsigma$ to himself; but afterwards, because he became $\check{a}\epsilon\iota\kappa o\varsigma$, he became also $\check{a}\nu o\mu o\varsigma$; and it is called sin as far as man is $\check{a}\nu o\mu o\varsigma$. This interchange of death and sin may be seen from Rom. v. 12, where it is said, "All have sinned," only it is not intended to refer to actual sin.

As soon as Adam fell, at that moment he began to die with death, or to sicken to death; for the potential essence was at once cast down from its status on account of the threatening uttered: In the day in which thou shalt eat of the forbidden tree, *morte morieris*. Therefore the human soul is not only mortal, but also most certainly dead, in a sense, not philosophical,—as if after death commonly so called it should survive,—but sacred. For any one is called dead by reason of the deficient image and δόξης τοῦ Θεοῦ, and of that vital image by which any one is called living.

For this reason, as soon as man is born, he is in the same position in which the fallen Adam was, as rightly said the poet, although ignorantly: *Nascentes morimur*, etc. Man dies, I say, daily; that is, he is subject to successive waste and abolition of his bodily actions, even to that sensible death, which death in this life is common as well to the pious as to the impious. But mental actions in the pious are renewed in this life gradually by regeneration, by which actions the pious are perfected in Christ and through Christ; and moreover the soul is spiritualized, until at length in the last day, joined with a spiritual body (which was sown an animal body), it becomes one spirit with God. In the wicked, neither is the soul spiritualized in this life, nor the body in the last day: it will not be subtle, agile, etc.; and although they rise again, yet they abide in that death in which they were before they were buried. Thus, in the Holy Scripture, resurrection *of* the dead is attributed to them, but not resurrection *from* the dead.

But if you should ask whether Adam, if he had not fallen, would not have been mortal also? I answer, To be mortal is said of the power of dying, or of the necessity. Any one may be in his essence prepared for the power of dying, and nevertheless of freeing himself from death. Because Adam was of the dust, he certainly had the capacity of dying; but if he had wished, he had at the same time before the fall the perfection of vindicating himself from death. But now, from the fall, necessity of dying has taken hold upon him.

CHAP. X.—*Of the State of the Human Soul after Death.*

When man dies by what is commonly called death, the soul of the pious is carried into Abraham's bosom; and where this is, since Scripture says nothing on it, it is fit that we also should be silent. It seems fitter to be said that the *soul is at rest*, than that it is locally moved by deserting the body (as the common people imagine), as a body from a body, since the soul is a spirit, not a body. Certainly, as in the good, everything which is corruptible perishes and becomes spiritual; in the wicked, that even *that* perishes and leaves the body which hitherto was as if good, in respect to future evil. In the resurrection the wicked will not indeed be so well off as they have been in the tomb; although, moreover, they may feel horrible sufferings immediately after death and burial, which before they were not able to feel on account of this carnal life, in which they were able in some measure to discharge bodily functions.

What things may be objected to the matters brought together in these few chapters, will be able to be solved from the foundations laid in the prooemium.

Moniti meliora sequemur.

I.
THE EVERLASTING POSTULATES.

Δι' ἐσόπτρου ἐν αἰνίγματι.—1 Cor. xiii. 12.

THE FALSE PRE-EXISTENCE.

Sec. I.

THE history of the soul, like all temporal history, has its beginning and its ending in eternity. Not as though eternity itself were like to time, and were related to temporal history in the way of before and after in time. Eternity, indeed, is essentially distinguished from time; it is something else than temporal endless duration: it cannot be conceived without getting rid of the idea of time, although eternity is derived from *ævum*, *æternitas* = *æviternitas*, and, as a word from the language of temporal existences, indicates by time that which is timeless, as a lapse of ages (αἰῶνες τῶν αἰώνων), veiled (עוֹלָם from עָלַם, to veil) both before and after, and thus illimitable.[1] Time is a mode of existence, unfolding itself according to regular measure and in regular progress, and arbitrarily limiting the existence that dwells within it. Eternity, on the other hand, is no continuous line, but a constant point without dimensions,—a centre always the same of absolute contents,—an absolutely present *now*, which suffers no abatement by past and future, but which, without being conditioned from without or limited in itself, is ever expanded or contracted according to the limitless will that rules therein (Ps. xc. 4; 2 Pet. iii. 8). Nevertheless it is possible to speak of an eternity *a parte ante*, and *a parte post*, in so far as eternity is that which was before time, and that which shall outlast time; yet not as though the time that lies between these extremes were a portion of eternity. Indivisibility is of the essence of eternity. It not only was before time was, and not only will be still when time is no more; but even in the midst of the current of time it is ever unchangeably existing.

[1] Otherwise חָלַד, which, reverting to the fundamental meaning, to slide noiselessly (Syr.), or probably to the root (Talm.), to conceal, imports the imperceptibly-wasting temporal life, as such.

Time proceeded forth from eternity, and goes back into eternity again, but it also exists in eternity. The time-world is a globe coming forth from eternity, and attracted by eternity, and pervaded by eternity, and is thus entirely suspended in eternity, and enclosed by it; and its destination is to be altogether received back into eternity, whether it be the positive eternity of heaven or the negative eternity of hell.[1] This is the view of Scripture from the first page to the last. For when it says that all things are from God ($\dot{\epsilon}\xi$ αὐτοῦ), that in God we live, and move, and have our being; that the things which are seen are temporal (πρόσκαιρα), but the things which are not seen are eternal (αἰώνια); that eternal life (ζωὴ αἰώνιος) is attainable even here, and that its manifestation only belongs to the future state,—it is therein asserting that eternity underlies the source and the Being, and the future and the ultimate end of time. It would be quite impossible for us to commence a study of psychology with the everlasting postulates, if there were not within time a self-evidence of eternity. But such a self-evidence there is, and indeed a twofold one: we have it in the Scripture, and in the inmost nature of our own soul. For the word of God, which as such comes forth from the region of the Everlasting, brings to us certain information upon what everlastingly was, and is, and is to come; and eternity is the innermost core of every human heart, as the ancients declared (Eccles. iii. 11): *æternitatem*[2] (אֶת־הָעֹלָם) *indidit cordibus eorum.* In the inmost being of every man is a sanctuary of everlasting being; wherein, in man's true craving for salvation, the everlasting Godhead enters to make it His dwelling-place, μονή (John xiv. 23).

It is, then, no over-bold beginning to take up the course of our psychological investigation from eternity. Still we must guard against too wide a grasp, such as Origen's, who regarded

[1] "Eternity," says my Elberfeld critic, "is a circle; the time-world a horizontal line, which, however, is to be formed into a circle. Heaven wills it, and so does hell." Another critic, on the other hand—Noack, in his *Psyche, l.c.* p. 336—finds "in the above apparent profundity nothing more than the simple fact, that every finite event is generally only a part of that which occurs and exists infinitely." But he who regards time as a segment of eternity, has no correct conception either of time or of eternity.

[2] LXX.: "Καί γε σύμπαντα τὸν αἰῶνα ἔδωκεν ἐν καρδίᾳ αὐτῶν." Eng. version: "He hath set the world in their heart."—Tr.

the earthly history of the human soul only as one epoch in an historical series of changeful decay and restoration, extending backwards and forwards into æons; and our temporal human body as the place of repentance and purification for our spirit exiled from a happier existence on account of committed sins. That is the false notion of pre-existence usually associated with the doctrine of the Metempsychosis, which, originating with Pythagoras and Plato, gained currency not only in the Jewish Alexandrianism and Essenism, but also in Pharisaism, in the Talmud and the Cabbala.[1] This doctrine has even lately been circulated as a most sublime revelation. Before man appears on earth, it is said, he lived an immaterial life in a spiritual world, where every one stays until his turn comes to appear upon earth, and here to enter upon a life of probation indispensable to him. Cahagnet relates of a person translated in vision, that she wished to embrace in her arms a child in the other world because it was so lovely, but she could not do so; and for this very reason, as it was told her, that this child had not yet appeared upon earth, and on that account no earthly spirit could come in contact with it.

Apart from the Metempsychosis, which is absurd, because it annuls the distinction between the spirit of man and the soul of the brute, in respect of which Augustine rightly says, "Anima humana facta est ad imaginem Dei, non dabit imaginem suam cani et porco," that doctrine of pre-existence which we call the false one is not in itself repugnant to reason, as is seen from the fact that Kant, Schelling, and among theologians Jul. Müller, have availed themselves of it, in order to transfer the ultimate ground of the moral constitution of individual men into a so-called *factum intelligibile* prior to time, (in contrast with *factum phænomenon*,) and thence to explain the beginning and root of sin in humanity. When Tertullian wittily observes against Plato's proposition (in the *Phædo*), that all $\mu\acute{\alpha}\theta\eta\sigma\iota\varsigma$

---

[1] The Talmud teaches that the Messiah will not come till the souls in the גוף, *i.e.* the super-terrestrial abode of souls, have all together entered upon earthly existence. Manasse ben Israel, in his work נשמת חיים (on the immortality of the soul), declares it to be perfectly orthodox Jewish faith that all souls were created within the limit of the six days' work. Upon the Cabbala in this behalf, see Joël, *Religions-philosophie der Sohar*, pp. 107-109.

is nothing else than ἀνάμνησις, " Plato scilicet solus in tanta gentium silva in tanto sapientium prato idearum et oblitus et recordatus est," his remark is more witty than true; for precisely the same thought is found outside the range of the Hellenic mind, in which, moreover, it is not limited to Plato; and when a von Schubert says, in his *Geschichte der Seele*, " In fact, I seem often to recall to light in my soul a presentiment which I have seen not with this my present, but with some other eye," it is an experience of which assuredly others than he can speak. But generally, the great principle frequently alleged against the pre-existence in question (lately, for example, by Staudenmaier in his *Dogmatics*), that man must needs have a distinct consciousness of that pre-temporal condition in which he sinned with freedom of will, is without any clear capability of proof. For it is matter of experience, that conditions of a higher kind through which the spirit of man consciously passes may be buried in total forgetfulness as far as he is concerned in his present normal state, without justifying the conclusion that they had not deeply impressed themselves on him; and in the presumed case, probably, many reasons may suggest themselves in the rectoral wisdom of God, why God should have sunk that existence, already lived through in a previous state, into such an unconsciousness for man.

Although, however, this doctrine of pre-existence is not in itself absolutely absurd, it is nevertheless—and this is sufficient reason for biblical psychology to reject it—absolutely contrary to canonical Scripture; only the platonically inspired apocryphal book of Wisdom refers to it in the words (viii. 19, 20), " For I was a witty child, and had a good spirit. Yea, rather, being good (just because I was good), I came into a body undefiled;" and Staudenmaier and others vainly seek to explain away,[1] in the interest of their several creeds, the intimation of pre-existence in this passage. For the rest, this doctrine is not exclusively Alexandrian and Essenian (Jos. *Bell.* ii. 8, 11): it is, moreover, talmudic and cabbalistic. The Cabbalists refer to Eccles. xii. 7, " The spirit returns to God who gave it." Origen infers a moral destination of the embryo originating in a pre-existent state (προΰπαρξις), from the fact that Jacob and Esau, while

[1] See, on the passage, Grimm in the *Handbook to the Apocrypha of the Old Testament*.

yet unborn, and prior to all earthly agency, are objects respectively of divine love and hate (Rom. ix. 11–13); as well as from the fact that John, while still in the womb of Elisabeth, leaped at the salutation of Mary (Luke i. 41). " John the Baptist," he says, enlarging on the interpretation of Mal. iii. 1, " was an angel sent from God into the flesh, to bear witness of the Light." In his unrestrained allegorizing exegesis, it is certainly easy to him to discover many other proofs of a dogma which he regards *à priori* as established. Even the men of the parable, who stand idle in the market-place, are in his view souls not yet sent down into this present state. Only one of his Scripture proofs is really striking, namely Jer. i. 5, where Jehovah says to the youthful Jeremiah, when He calls him to the prophetic office, " Before I formed thee in the belly I knew thee; and before thou camest forth out of the womb I sanctified thee, and I ordained thee a prophet unto the nations."

But our momentary surprise must at once yield to the recollection, that Scripture knows no creation of man other than that which comprises the body and the soul, which it records in Gen. i. and ii.; that it knows of no self-determination of a human soul, which could have preceded the self-determination of Adam, embracing as it did all human souls with it; that it traces back every moral destination under which man is found, no further than to Adam, and to the connection with our fathers and forefathers, by means of that procreation which entails it. These three fundamental principles, occupying the Scripture from beginning to end, substantially exclude the false doctrine of pre-existence. But with what propriety do we speak of the *false* doctrine? Is there, then, also a true one? Decidedly there is. How else could Jehovah say to Jeremiah, *Priusquam te formarem in utero, novi te?*

THE TRUE PRE-EXISTENCE.

Sec. II.

ACCORDING to Scripture, there is a pre-existence of man, although an ideal one; a pre-existence not only of man as such, but also of the individual and of all; a pre-existence not only of the human soul, but of the entire man, and not merely of the entire man in himself, but moreover of the individual, and of all, in the totality of their constitution and their history; a pre-existence in the divine knowledge, which precedes the existence in each individual consciousness; a pre-existence, moreover, in virtue of which man and humanity are not only a remotely future object of divine foresight, but a present object of divine contemplation in the mirror of wisdom. For let it be said at once, not only Philosophy and falsely boasted Gnosis, but Scripture also, knows and speaks of a divine ideal-world, to which the time-world is related as the historical realization of an eternal fundamental design. That all which is realized in temporal history exists from everlasting in God's sight as a spiritual pattern, and therefore as an idea in God, is not only taught in Plato, but also in the coherences of sacred history, of which Plato knew nothing: Isaiah, for instance (xxii. 11, xxv. 1, xxxvii. 26, and throughout in chaps. xl.–lxvi.); and the New Testament Scripture, which reveals the mystery in a way that was yet unattainable to the Old Testament. There are, moreover, two New Testament statements which even in form recall the speculative Hellenic mode of expression. For when Paul (in Rom. iv. 17) describes God as καλῶν τὰ μὴ ὄντα ὡς ὄντα, this is in terms Philo's formula of God the creator, τὰ μὴ ὄντα ἐκάλεσεν εἰς τὸ εἶναι; and although Paul, and Scripture in general, are as far removed as heaven itself from teaching an eternal ὕλη, a μὴ ὄν in the Platonic sense, yet still Paul, no less intentionally than Philo, says (where he expresses himself punctiliously) μὴ ὄντα, and not οὐκ ὄντα, on the ground that that which comes forward into historical existence is not previously an absolute Nothing. Abraham, as the father of the nations, becomes an everlasting subject of divine knowledge, and as such is a μὴ ὄν, waiting in readiness to come into existence forthwith, as soon as the creative καλεῖν is uttered. The other passage is Heb. xi. 3, where it is said that the world-system in all its parts, οἱ αἰῶνες, was created by God's word, εἰς τὸ μὴ ἐκ φαινομένων τὸ βλεπόμενον γεγονέναι. Here, also, the writer purposely avoids saying οὐκ ἐξ ὄντων, as 2 Macc. vii. 28 (although this expression might have been justified, as in the sense of *creatio ex nihilo*, by way of excluding the idea of eternity of matter), but μὴ ἐκ φαινομένων. All that was created by God's word was, prior to that creation, a μὴ φαινομένον; that is, something which was not yet brought forward into manifestation, into temporal historical actuality. It existed only as a divine idea. Even when μὴ is associated with γεγονέναι, the meaning is the same, for the contrast implied in addition is ἀλλ' ἐκ νοητῶν; and these νοητά are the very eternal invisible exemplars, whence proceeded, as from their ideal source, by means of the divine fiat, the visible reality. And faith is precisely that which pierces through the phenomenal externality of the world to this its supersensuous essential source, and to its production therefrom by means of the purely spiritual power of the divine creative word. Or could the author actually only mean to say, that no sensible material was at the source of the visible world? The mode of expressing an assertion in itself undoubtedly true, would be strangely chosen. The words themselves say, either that the visible did not proceed from that which was sensuous (but spiritual), or else that it proceeded from the supersensuous (spiritual). But what would be the contrary of this sensuous, or what would this supersensuous be, other than the thoughts of that world one day to come into existence,—thoughts formed and established by decree from eternity,—*scil.* the divine ideas? Thus, at least, that passage was understood by Albertus Magnus of old, and in later times by Staudenmaier, although the latter has made it the business of his life to combat that which is unscriptural in Philo's doctrine of Ideas, and generally in that of the philosophers. But we are not at all in need of these two texts. What they declare, as we understand it, is—as we shall now proceed to show, in order to draw therefrom psychological conclusions—the fundamental view of the entire Scripture.

We perceive and acknowledge on scriptural ground, (1)

that the idea of man as such is an eternal idea of God; for when Elohim says (Gen. i. 26), "Let us make man in our image, after our likeness," that is no decision come to in time, but only the revelation of an eternal purpose: for the whole six days' work was *à priori* intended to concentrate itself finally on the man, and the man as such was thus the substance of God's eternal plan even before the beginning of the temporal carrying into effect of this plan. What is true generally of the entire agency of God in time (Acts xv. 18), γνωστὸν ἀπ' αἰῶνος τῷ κυρίῳ τὸ ἔργον αὐτοῦ, is true especially in reference to man, the great object of the creative work. But (2) not only was man, as such, an integral element of the divine plan: moreover, every individual, in the totality of his nature and of his life's history, was a subject of eternal divine knowledge, and on that account also of eternal divine will, as says the Psalmist (cxxxix. 16), "Thine eyes did see me as embryo, yet being imperfect; and in Thy book were they all written, the days which were still to be fashioned,[1] when as yet there was none of them," for which the *Kerî* reads, "and His (God's) is every one of them," *i.e.* "He had eternally in His sight every one of these days before it came into being." What the Psalmist here acknowledges, Jehovah says Himself in another place to Jeremiah, "Before" (בְּטֶרֶם, properly, in the time when it was still to be expected that) "I formed thee in the womb, I knew thee;" whereby it is not only said that from the beginning Jehovah knew of the person of Jeremiah, but since, in accordance with the just observation of the ancients, the word יָדַע usually indicates a *nosse cum effectu et affectu*, that He chose this Jeremiah from everlasting for the prophetic office (comp. Gal. i. 15), into which He now calls the man who is manifested on the stage of temporal history. But still more than this, (3) the Scripture says to all who believe in Christ that God has pre-appointed and foreseen them πρὸ καταβολῆς κόσμου to the relation of children in which they stand (Eph. i. 4; 1 Pet. i. 2 et seq.); that the calling, justification, and glorification, by means of which He leads them from

---

[1] Or, moreover, "The days already formed, and while still there was none of them" (that is to say, actually manifested). At all events, יצר has the same meaning as in Isa. xxii. 11, xxxvii. 26, and elsewhere,— what is realized in time exists already long before as a spiritual type, *i.e.* an idea in God.

temporal foretaste to eternal enjoyment of blessedness, was preceded by an eternal προγνῶναι and προορίσαι (Rom. viii. 28–30); that all the grace which they experience is only the φανέρωσις of a grace bestowed upon them according to a divine purpose of love in Christ πρὸ χρόνων αἰωνίων (2 Tim. i. 9); that all who are faithful here below are ordained, τεταγμένοι, to eternal life (Acts xiii. 48, where the participle passive, according to the Hellenistic *usus loquendi, e.g.* Jer. xviii. 16, 2 Kings x. 27, LXX., can be understood in no other way), and assuredly from everlasting; for only those escape condemnation whose names have been written ἀπὸ καταβολῆς κόσμου in the Lamb's book of life (Apoc. xiii. 8, xvii. 8; comp. Isa. iv. 3). Thus what is there spoken of Jeremiah in reference to his office, is true of all believers in reference to their standing in grace. And it is true not only of the church of believers in Christ in its entirety, but of every one of its individual members. All these, with their future temporal relation, were everlastingly present to the knowledge of God, and were the object of His election, of His predestination, and briefly of His special loving purpose. We say of His *special* loving purpose, because there is also in Scripture a frequent and earnest testimony to a *general* purpose of love, in virtue of which He desires the happiness of all men, without exception; and this general purpose of love, not less eternal than the other, is the presupposition or postulate of that special one. But the particularizing of the general purpose of love has its reason in the fact that God does not merely contemplate men as such, but in their entire future moral destination, although this divine foreknowledge of their future actual use of freedom is to us absolutely inconceivable.[1] Scripture, however, expressly affirms this foreknowledge, as indeed the idea of God in itself requires it. For that very reason the election has a non-election as its reverse side. The godless and unbelieving are not only thus spoken of, whose names are not inscribed from the foundation of the world in the book of life of the Lamb slain (Apoc. xiii.

---

[1] When v. Hofmann, in the *Schriftbeweis,* i. 218, 257 (compare also *Mecklenburgisches Kirchenblatt*, 1845, iii. S. 209), says that the eternal will of God operates not on individual men, or of men as individuals, but on man and manhood, the distinction between a general and a particular will of God is thereby denied, but in my opinion wrongly.

8); Scripture does not hesitate also to say positively that they are appointed to condemnation, σκεύη ὀργῆς κατηρτισμένα εἰς ἀπώλειαν (Rom. ix. 22); still not in the sense of a purely arbitrary *prædestinatio duplex*, but in the sense that God has men everlastingly before Him, in the entire future actuality of their self-determination; and in conformity with it, yea, according as He finds them in Christ, or out of Christ, and adverse to Christ, He includes them in His love or in His wrath; and thus they minister to the future history of His glorification as vessels of mercy or of wrath in His household,—an everlasting προετοιμάζειν and καταρτίζειν, which is so far absolutely free, as it precedes all temporal self-determination of man, but still, moreover, not absolutely unconditioned, since it has as its object the foreseen man, not in the position of indifference, but in the condition arising out of his entire self-determination. For the everlasting general purpose of love in God embraces even the godless and unbelieving; nay, it embraces humanity foreseen to be sinful, as humanity. God the Father loves humanity from everlasting in His Son, or, as Scripture almost everywhere expresses it, in Christ. For (4) the eternal Son of God may rightly be called Jesus Christ in His relation to the future humanity, because the fact of the incarnation happening in time is for God an eternally present fact. In this sense Scripture speaks of a grace bestowed on us in Christ Jesus πρὸ χρόνων αἰωνίων (2 Tim. i. 9), and names the New Testament work of redemption the ἀποκάλυψις and φανέρωσις of a mystery existing from eternity, but hidden and kept secret (Rom. xvi. 25; Col. i. 26). It is thus an eternal event brought about by the reciprocally acting energy of the Father and of the Son, that the Son placed Himself to humanity while yet future, but eternally present to the Godhead, in a relation which was that of a covering (כִּפֶּר) for its sins; so that, instead of being an object of the wrath of the Father, it is the object of His love, in that He looks upon it no otherwise than in Him, the Beloved. There appertains as well to humanity and to men as to the man Jesus Christ, an absolute pre-existence, which, although an ideal one, is still so real and genuine, that Scripture refers all temporal events in the whole and in the individual to that everlasting root.

It has been objected to me, that, strictly speaking, pre-existence is not the true conception, since in the view of God the ideal-world is an eternal object of contemplation; consequently the existences that pass thence into history cannot by possibility leave this ideal-world or vanish therefrom. In such a case there is thus obtained a double-world, the drama of history is twice represented, and the fear occurs to one that the divine government may be only concerned with that upper world which is thus repeated and played over again here below; so that in our life we become detached from the heart of God, since He strictly is only interested in the ideal-world. These objections concern the Scripture itself, which neither regards the history of this world pantheistically as a constituent part of the divine proceeding itself, and as a segment of the infinity within which it is developed; nor—as here and there the modern Theism does—does it teach a self-limitation of the divine omniscience, lest the creative freedom should become a mere illusion. Scripture acknowledges a supra-mundane God exalted above the world which began in time, who from everlasting willed the world, and, in creative effectuation of this will, realized the world in time; a God whose eternal omniscience comprehends not alone that which is general, but also that which is most special of this world, thus eternally willed and temporally to be made actual; and not alone surveyed all the possibilities arising out of the use of freedom by the personal Beings to be created, but, moreover, looked through the future realization of this Free-being, even into its most individual and secret nature; a God who, in virtue of this all-comprehending and all-penetrating knowledge, exercising that formative power over the mundane relations which appertained to Him, without qualifying the freedom of the creature, moulded this eternally willed future world into a whole, issuing forth for the triumph of His love comprehended into a unity in Christ (Eph. i. 10)—the everlasting Son prepared for incarnation. It is just this *whole* that we call the ideal-world. Pre-existence is a conception rightly applied to it, because the decreed purpose is prior to its actualization; the salvation which comes into historical manifestation was already determined πρὸ καταβολῆς κόσμου (Eph. i. 4), and even in some measure promised πρὸ χρόνων αἰωνίων (Tit. i. 2) and granted (2 Tim. i. 9), to wit in Christ, the eternally beloved, who stands in the presence of the omniscience of everlasting love as the reconciler of the world (1 Pet. i. 20). Scripture is so little afraid of thus detaching us from the heart of God, that it rather reveals to us by this means how dear we are eternally to the heart of God. And assuredly we need not fear that our temporal history will thus become only a docetic reflection of that eternally ideal tissue of events. The realization of that which has been eternally known does not indeed happen below the sphere of God's care: it is a self-movement of God Himself, even to the depth of His heart. Every stage of history which absorbs into realization the ideality of that which has been decreed, is sympathetically experienced by God. And—say we with Dorner [1]—although God's agency is eternally decreed, as His knowledge of the present does not begin with to-day, yet the moment of that living effectual interference, which even for God is something more than the mere purpose, does not arise until the occurrence in every case of the actual present. Thus God Himself does not pass through the ideal that is everlastingly present to Him in His counsel historically, until the world does, and He interweaves into it His agency according to that purpose, and now also with corresponding meaning and motive, as on the other hand, in the divine counsel the moments of realization are inwoven into the world of His thoughts of love.

Thus we come back to the point whence we started, that there actually is, according to Scripture, an ideal-world, and indeed such an one as that of which the Son of God made Himself the centre by virtue of His incarnation—ideal in like manner. The mistake of all speculation, which, though pantheistic, has still claimed to be biblical, consists in having identified this eternal ideal-world with the eternal Son or Logos. But there is an infinite distinction between the two. The Son is God of God, the essential image of the Father veiling Him-

[1] See the beautiful argument in the *Jahrbb. für Deutsche Theologie*, 1858, pp. 592–605. Elsewhere, Stahl, *Die Luth. Kirche und die Union*, 1859, p. 226: "Our life is pre-existent in the sight of God, that is, it appears, according to His point of view of eternity, not as subsequent to His decrees, but as contemporaneously with them." According to this, the conception of an *æternitas a parte ante* would be unjustifiable. But it results necessarily from the creation beginning in time, as we said in sec. i. The life of God historically involved in the world, is to be distinguished from His eternal life.

self with His nature; but the Ideal-world is an epitome—existing indeed in eternity, but yet not by its nature infinite—of divine mental images of finite beings and their history: for since God knows Himself from eternity, He knows Himself moreover from eternity as the possible ground of a world which is not Himself; and the Ideal-world is just the thought apprehended and shaped forth of this possible Other-world, which is not God.[1] Therefore also Scripture calls this Ideal-world nowhere υἱός or λόγος, but חכמה, σοφία. For Scripture knows the Wisdom not only as an attribute of God the only and all-wise (Rom. xvi. 27); but, moreover, as the objective eternal reflection in God of the world-plan, distinguishing this wisdom in the fundamental design (*sapientia sciagraphica*) unmistakeably from that attributive wisdom. When it is said by Job, at the conclusion of the twenty-eighth chapter, that God, when He made a decree for the rain, and a way for the lightning of the thunder, beheld wisdom, and declared it; He prepared it, yea, and searched it out, and said unto man, "Behold, the fear of the Lord, that is wisdom," etc.; the meaning is, that God in the creation of the world took for an object the wisdom remote from man, by its pattern formed the world, and gave to man the fear of God for the law, by conforming to which he has his appointed portion in wisdom. The wisdom that is attainable to man is even here plainly distinguished from the wisdom which alone is known to God, and by which He brings the creatures into being, ordaining to every one a relative portion therein. Thus Prov. viii. 22–31, where the knowledge of this eternal wisdom is still further advanced. It is here personified, and declares of itself that God brought it forth before all creatures, as the first-fruits of His way of revelation, and in the beginning anointed it as a queen; that when He created the world, it was partaking in that work; and as from everlasting, so always, it is God's pleasure, and it rejoiced always before Him. That here the wisdom is not meant only as an attribute, but that an everlasting essentially divine fact is announced, the ancients probably perceived: their mistake was only in taking generally the birth of the Logos to be this fact. It is not the person of the Logos which

---

[1] See Dorner, in the *Jahrbb. für Deutsche Theologie*, 1856, pp. 369–372, whereby the above will be understood.

here proclaims its origin from God, but the Wisdom which is impersonal, and nevertheless existing still for itself, which is the eternal reflection of the world-plan of the Godhead; ἔσοπτρον ἀκηλίδωτον τῆς τοῦ Θεοῦ ἐνεργείας, as the book of Wisdom beautifully and pertinently says: for the Greek apocryphal writers, and generally the Alexandrian school, have prosecuted this knowledge offered to them by the Scripture more deeply, and yet not even they without confusing σοφία and λόγος; for it was not till the incarnation of the Logos in Jesus Christ that this mystery was cleared up, and the error of such avoided. On the ground of such disclosures, we say (5) that man and humanity are an everlastingly present object of divine contemplation in the mirror of Wisdom. The apostolic word assures us of this, in saying (Eph. iii. 10, 11), that for the angelic powers of heaven is made known in the earthly church ἡ πολυποίκιλος σοφία τοῦ Θεοῦ· κατὰ πρόθεσιν τῶν αἰώνιων, ἣν ἐποίησεν ἐν Χριστῷ Ἰησοῦ τῷ Κυρίῳ ἡμῶν. For that in this divine wisdom, which on account of the riches of its contents (comp. Rom. xi. 33) the apostle calls πολυποίκιλος, not only the creation in time, but also the redemption in time, has an eternal ideal objectivity before God, we need not, after what has been said above, be at any further pains to prove.

We have now pointed out in what scriptural sense a preexistence assuredly belongs to humanity, and to every individual of it. The whole history of time, with all the beings that enter upon it, and their development from the beginning to the end, in which divine providence and creative freedom so marvellously weave into one another, is present from eternity before God, and that in so concrete, although ideal, an objectivity, that even from eternity the Son of God has given Himself to be the centre of this history. As the Christ He is the centre of this objective eternal wisdom; and it is called with reason the mother of all things, for it bears them all before they exist, even every human soul, in its womb. It stands indeed below the Son, for without the Son the Father would not be Father; but it is an image of the Tri-personal purpose of love, and the Trinity would without it be what it essentially is. Nevertheless, although not the representation of the divine nature in such a way as to be of the same nature with it, it is still in its manner an image of God, and man is even called before other creatures the likeness of God. We must thus seek to have a clear understanding of how far the Trinity itself is the original type which comes to representative manifestation in that wisdom, and especially in man, in order that we may understand the nature of man.

THE DIVINE ARCHETYPE.

Sec. III.

In order to apprehend the nature of the ideal-world, the nature of the world of the actual, and especially the nature of the human soul, it is first of all essential to apprehend the nature of God, so far as it is γνωστόν, *i.e.* so far as it is permitted us to apprehend it, on the one hand in Scripture, on the other hand in the creatures themselves; for not Scripture alone, but, moreover, the works of God existing from the foundation of the world, reveal to us far more than the one simple truth that God is. In them is perceived by speculative thought (νοεῖν), as the apostle to the Romans says (i. 20), God's invisible nature, or, according to the still more significant Greek expression, τὰ ἀόρατα αὐτοῦ. Such a knowledge of God as presents itself to us in the mirror of God's word and in the mirror of the creatures is not the problem of psychology, but it is one of its most indispensable elements. Before advancing, therefore, from the eternal conditions which are assumed to precede the actuality of man, to the creative beginnings of that actuality, we must represent to ourselves the ἀόρατα of God, as they have been disclosed on scriptural ground to the general consciousness of the church, and thence, further, to sacred investigation of a profounder character. And here we say (1) to the catholic dogma of the Trinity, a sincere, unreserved, hearty yea and amen. The Godhead is one in three persons—a threefold self-consciousness in indissoluble and co-eternal unity of nature. God, moreover, is the Triune, irrespectively of the thought of creation, and irrespectively of the thought of redemption; for both the one and the other have their origin, not in the necessity of divine Being, but in the freedom of divine Life: even without them God would be what He is in the manner essential to His nature. Moreover, we do not conceive that, while there is in fact a Trinity immanent in the Divine Essence, Scripture nevertheless only speaks of it œconomically, *i.e.* in reference to its relation to creation and redemption, as Urlsperger[1] and, lately, Hofmann have taught. The Scripture passages concerning it have their purpose in the history of salvation; but this purpose is not the limit of what they contain: there are texts of a super-historical and metaphysical character, pointing to the final causes of the history of salvation—to the eternal design of God in the entrance of the Godhead into the field of history. Behind the loving counsel of God, which embraced the creation and redemption, Scripture leaves no unknown and unnamed x; but it is just the Trinity of God which is the background, the most remote of all and ever the same, of that counsel of love which it discloses to us. God is the Triune not only irrespectively of that counsel of love, which pertains to the substance of His free absolute life: He is so also irrespectively of His eternal essential manifestation, and irrespectively of His historical free revelation. What we mean by this, will soon be made plain: we have in the first place to show that the Trinity is the eternally disclosed divine nature itself, not merely a sundering of it adopted for the purpose of the revelation of redemption.

But, nevertheless, we reject all apprehensions of the essential nature of the eternal procession which are irreconcilable with the historical revelation of the Triune. Of this kind is the erroneous notion that God becomes conscious to Himself of Himself in the development of Himself in the triune relation. If the Son is ὁ λόγος, the Father is ὁ λέγων; and is λέγειν possible without conscious thought? And if the Logos is ὁ υἱός, the Father is ὁ γεννῶν; and is γεννᾶν possible without conscious will? Certainly God is πνεῦμα, and for that very reason He is the most absolute antithesis of every blind proceeding of natural necessity. If we get rid of the idea of the Trinity of

---

[1] See Thomasius, *Dogm.* i. 487–491. Ph. Matth. Hahn says on the subject in a letter (*Süddeutsche Originalien*, published by Barth, Pt. iv. p. 28), "I do not find Urlsperger's doctrine of the Trinity, as he describes it, in the Bible."

the divine nature, yet there is still infinitely conscious will, which clings to our conception. It is only an abstraction; but still it is justifiable, in order to enable us to perceive the fact that God is not infinitely conscious will for the first time at the conclusion of the procession of the Trinity, but that He already was so at the commencement and in the midst of that procession. But no otherwise than in this procession is He absolute Life living itself forth. The conscious will of the Father, itself stimulating itself, finds its satisfaction only in comprehending itself in the exactly counterpart conscious will of the Son; and while the latter lovingly turns back to the former as to the bosom of its origin, and the mutual operation of both is diffused as if by breathing itself forth, there arises a third conscious will, which concludes the unfolding of the nature of the Godhead—that of the Holy Spirit. Or, to speak in the words of the ancients: " Sicut dum Pater se ipsum in essentia sua contemplatur, verbum mentis exprimit et sic Filium generat: ita dum Pater et Filius se in unitate essentiæ diligunt, affectus voluntatis, qui est utriusque amor, simul ab utroque exprimitur sicque Spiritus Sanctus producitur."

In these three facts of inexpressibly rich significance, subsists God's eternally disclosed blessed life of love. And its relations are not such that the Father may beget the Son, and the Holy Ghost proceed from both, or not; but without Son and Spirit the Father would not be God, and without this threefold substance the Godhead would not be the Light, and the Love, and the Life.[1] Moreover, its relations are not such that the Father at any time might be without the Son, and both without the Spirit; and neither are they such, that the Son could at any time be so begotten of the Father, as that He should be begotten of Him no more; nor that the Spirit should at any time have proceeded from both, so as that it should proceed no more; but these are everlasting facts which, if eternity be conceived of as a duration without beginning or

---

[1] Thus also Philippi, *Glaubenslehre*, ii. 123. The Father requires—to his subsistence existing by itself as Father—the Son, not less in order to be a Father, than the Son in His subsistence conditioned through the Father, as a Son, needs the Father in order to be a Son: the nature of the Godhead itself consists from eternity only in these Three.

end, are apprehended as in ever-during *becoming,* and nevertheless are still absolutely completed in every moment of eternity. "Nec Deus pater ita generat," say our dogmatists in the words of Gregory of Nazianzen, "ut nondum perfecte generarit, neque ita generavit Filium ut generare desierit." And in a similar sense they call the *processio Spiritus Sancti, æterna et permanens.* It is a process of everlasting becoming without resting, and yet, moreover, of everlasting completion without deficiency; and although the Godhead is not the product of this procession, yet its Being subsists in the threefold producing of this procession. It is exactly this interaction of *being* and *becoming* which is the life of the Godhead.

But this Life of God, thus completed and hidden in itself, according to which He, the Triune, is πνεῦμα, has it not at all been manifested as in the presence of itself? Or, in other and plainer words, is there not in God, prior to all creation, an analogue of that which in the region of creation we call the appearance inseparable from all being,—the external corresponding to the internal of the nature,—its form, or even its earliest sphere of action? This question, as will soon appear, is of the greatest psychological importance; and although no sufficient answer is furnished us either in ecclesiastical dogma or in dogmatic philosophy hitherto,—although the subject itself has at least once been freely treated, namely in the controversy of the Hesychasts,[1]—yet we think, without opposing ourselves to the general consciousness of the church,[2] that we may say (2) that there is certainly an analogue of the relation of phenomenon to Being, or of the external to the internal in God; to wit, an everlasting glory, which from everlasting God has framed forth from the natural ground of His personality, for the heaven of His dwelling-place, and for the body of light of His spiritual nature, and for the sphere of His essential divine agency,—a glory which is not as yet a free self-revelation of God designed for the creature, but is first of all the everlasting radiation of His essential perfection, and which, without itself being personal, has its source of origination in the three persons of the Godhead, whose com-

---

[1] See the art. "Hesychasts," by Gass, in Herzog's *Real Encyclopædie.*
[2] Least of all to Luther himself, who in reference to this says, "The ore lies still half in the mine." See Thomasius, *Dogm.* i. 78.

bined reflection it is, eternally caused by the Father, eternally mediated by the Son, and eternally effectuated by the Holy Ghost. To the question, Where, then, was God before the creation of the world? our forefathers had the pertinent reply, God was in being. He was in His essence. And our dogmatists distinguish from the *gloria externa* of God, which has become manifest in time, an everlasting *gloria interna;* and from the created *cœlum angelorum* an uncreated *cœlum Dei;* whereof they say, " Cœlum Dei majestaticum nullis limitibus circumscribi potest, estque nihil aliud quam æterna et infinita Dei gloria et majestas, quam Deus in se habuit ab æterno et in æternum habiturus est."[1] With reference to passages where שְׁמַיָּא, οὐρανὸς, appears as God's name (Dan. iv. 23, Luke xv. 18, comp. Matt. xxi. 25, John iii. 13), they say, *hoc cœlum est ipse Deus.*[2] And this cannot be far from the true account of the matter, for the God of heaven swears (Deut. xxxii. 40) with hand uplifted to heaven: in which passage an old interpreter explains *ad cœlum* by *ad se ipsum.*[3] But we must go further, and say with more accuracy, this Heaven is the manifestation of the nature of God the Triune—a manifestation everlasting, infinite, immaterial; and God is called " the Heaven," as He also is named " the name, הַשֵּׁם" (Deut. xxviii. 58, comp. Isa. xxx. 27), for the name is the expression of the nature. The truth of the matter is this: As God, the absolute personality, is Himself absolutely revealed to Himself—Himself absolutely present to Himself (*sibi præsentissimus*)—personality, indeed, is presence to one's self;—so also, according to Scripture (without entering more closely into the metaphysical grounds of the question), there is an eternally glorious manifestation of the nature of the Godhead, which is and has itself absolutely present to itself. As in every nature there are distinguished an internal and an external, so also, apart from its relation to the world, are there in the *nature* of all *natures.* That which within the kingdom of creation we call appearance, externality, visibility, form, corporeity, is not without its archetype in the Divine Essence. We are not philosophizing *à priori*, but are forming a conception according to what is revealed in Scripture.

---

[1] Thus Quenstedt, in his *Systema Theologicum*, T. i. c. 624.
[2] The same, c. 626.
[3] Raschi, אֶל־שָׁמַיִם, *i.e* אֶל־עַצְמִי.

There is an eternal כָּבוֹד, in which the כָּל־טוּב of God, *i.e.* the entire fulness of His good and holy nature, becomes apparent in the way of manifestation.[1] The outward expression of the highest goodness can only be the highest beauty; but "beauty" is too trivial a form of speech for the Holy Scripture to use immediately of God:[2] it calls the manifestation of God's nature "Glory," and invokes every mode of expression to denote this inexpressibly great glory. The most usual appellations are כָּבוֹד and δόξα. The former indicates the glory, with reference to the impression produced by it, as weighty and majestic (comp. βάρος δόξης, 2 Cor. iv. 17): the latter, a conception akin to εἰκών (1 Cor. xi. 7); if it be derived from δοκεῖν, in the sense of φαίνεσθαι, suggests the appearance, especially that appearance[3] which is the expression of that which is preeminently excellent. Δόξα is the glorious appearance of the absolutely holy nature of God. More exactly defined, this glory is that which He had πρὸ παντὸς τοῦ αἰῶνος, prior to time, and therefore everlastingly (Jude ver. 25); the Light, נְהוֹרָא, which dwells with God (Dan. ii. 22), or God is called the blessed and only immortal King, who from everlasting dwelleth in this Light: φῶς οἰκῶν ἀπρόσιτον, ὃν εἶδεν οὐδεὶς ἀνθρώπων οὐδὲ ἰδεῖν δύναται (1 Tim. vi. 16). It is thus מָקוֹם, the place or sphere of the essentially divine self-life, whence proceeds God's mundane agency (Mic. i. 3; Isa. xxvi. 21), and His glorious self-demonstration in the face of heaven and earth (Ezek. iii. 12, comp. 1 Chron. xvi. 27), and whither He withdraws Himself from those who harden themselves in scornful thanklessness against His love (Hos. v. 15).

Scripture is not even afraid of prejudicing the exaltation of

[1] Kahnis, in his *Diatribe de Angelo Domini*, 1858, translates Ex. xxxiii. 19, *omnis pulcritudo mea*, and remarks thereupon with propriety, "Esse in Deo naturam quandam quæ ad revelationem in mundo vergit."

[2] That Ps. l. 2 calls the glory of God itself "the Perfection of Beauty" (*non plus ultra*) (LXX., Vulg., Luth.), is not so probable as that this is a surname of Zion (Syr., Aq., Hier.): for (1) according to the accents it must thus be construed; (2) Jeremiah (Lam. ii. 15) has thus employed this expression, and has probably thus understood it; (3) Beauty, יֳפִי, thus immediately predicated of God, is without precedent.

[3] See Schott on 1 Pet. i. 24. Δόξα is a relative idea; it is the external form, in any way perceivable, in which the life and nature of a personal or real subject comes to its actual manifestation, represents itself to itself.

SEC. III.]   THE DIVINE ARCHETYPE.   61

God above the creature when it calls this eternal light-dwelling of God, His body of light, His form of light: תְּמוּנָה, Num. xii. 8, Ps. xvii. 15; εἶδος, John v. 37; and μορφή, Phil. ii. 6. It still further discloses to us the mystery, in giving us to understand, that as, according to his self-revealing nature, God is threefold in persons, so this His essential revelation is sevenfold in powers. For the spectacle of the rainbow around Him who is beheld, is that in which the glory of Jehovah, כְּבוֹד יְהוָה, makes itself visible to the prophet Ezekiel (Ezek. i. 28); and also Apoc. iv. 3, an ἶρις of the colour of an emerald arches itself around the throne of the heavenly King. They are eternal *realissima* which are thus made manifest to the beholders. But Scripture says the same thing also without any figure. He who sits on the throne is there named (iv. 8), ὁ ἦν καὶ ὁ ὢν καὶ ὁ ἐρχόμενος. It is the same whose greeting occurs in i. 4; but here, in the place of the ἶρις κυκλόθεν τοῦ θρόνου, are named the ἑπτὰ πνεύματα who are before His throne—the same seven spirits which (iv. 5) appear as seven burning torches before the throne, and (v. 6) as the seven eyes of the Lamb. These seven spirits are not to be confounded with the seven angels; but neither are they, as is almost universally taught, identical with the Holy Spirit, even if they be regarded as closely related to Him, as may be gathered from Isa. xi. 2, and Zech. iv. 1–4, comp. 5, 6. That the seer should call the Holy Spirit in the immediateness of His nature " the seven spirits," is probably not in itself conceivable; and that he does not wish to be so understood, is clearly evident from iv. 5, where he sees the seven burning torches " before the throne," and from v. 6, where he calls the seven spirits those who are " sent forth into all the earth." They are the seven powers which, originating from the Father, the πατὴρ τῶν φώτων (Jas. i. 17), operating in the Son, the ἀπαύγασμα τῆς δόξης αὐτοῦ (Heb. i. 3), perfected through the Holy Spirit, and for that reason partaking His name and appropriated to Him in a special sense (Apoc. i. 4), form in their harmonious mutually interacting life and operation, the effected glory of the triune God, in unlimited possession of which, moreover, the Son of God now stands as the exalted Son of man.[1] Or is the *doxa* of God actually nothing else than His

[1] Philo is on the way to this acknowledgment when he interprets the burning torches (Gen. xv. 17) allegorically of the divine powers, αἱ θεῖαι

majesty in an attributive sense? It has been objected that our view confuses the personal conception of God by the adoption of an impersonal one.[1] But the *doxa*, far removed from being an impersonal accident[2] of the personal God, is certainly not nature in God, in the sense in which the assumption of a nature in God is rightly apprehended: it is not a nature which precedes the will of God; neither does it clothe itself generally with the conception of the nature, which (when this conception is otherwise applied) is its foundation and material, but not itself. The *doxa* is the nature carried out into form; the effective formulation of that foundation of nature which does not exist in God without His will, but, on the contrary, separates itself by His own will from the actuality of His *Ego*: it is in its everlasting perfection the eternal triumph of the personality of God, and in its light exalted above all mistiness, the absolute negation of unfreedom. Or is God's *doxa* perchance *à priori* absolutely light and absolutely harmony, without having become so by means of the balancing of contraries? It has been objected that the successive process of development from below to above is peculiar to the creature, and ought not to be transferred to God.[3] But, that development to a limited end—that separation of the original unity— that re-union into an adjusted unity—is not opposed to the

δυνάμεις (518, 16), and understands by the good treasure of God (Deut. xxviii. 12) the Logos teeming with divine lights, τὸν ἐγκύμονα θείων ζώτων λόγον (108, 20).

[1] Thus, for instance, J. P. Lange, in the *Deutschen Zeitschrift*, 1859, p. 22: "That God must have something impersonal in Himself, which should be distinguished from Himself as the absolute Spirit, we deny; and it is, in fact, contradicted when we call God the absolute Spirit." That God is Spirit (John iv. 24), proves certainly more than that He is incorporeal. He is absolutely free personality having power over itself, and the absolute opposite of blind necessity—Life entirely revolving on itself, indivisible, and having nothing external to itself. That all that God develops out of the ground of His nature must also itself be personal, does not follow therefrom, only that everything is overpowered and penetrated by His personality.

[2] Thus v. Rudloff, *Die Lehre vom Menschen*, p. 13, names it "an accident or attribute of the Divine Trinity, although it is one that belongs to the nature of it." But if it were an accident, it would not for that very reason belong to the nature; and if it were only an attribute, it would not be the unapproachable light in which God dwells, not the (uncreated) heaven after which God Himself is named "the Heaven."

[3] The letters of Molitor in the Appendix to this section.

nature of God, is shown already in the procession of the Trinity. And as to the *doxa*, the essential distinctive character of its nature, as different from that of all created aspiration, consists in this, that the basis of the development of the creature is one that subsists without its will—is given or communicated to it; and its development is one that is completed in temporal succession, whilst in God there is nothing which preceded His will, and nothing which at any time was not, and for the first time became. He is altogether *causa sui*, and His everlasting becoming is at the same time everlasting fulfilment; and the postulates of this eternal completion are only capable of being known from His creative and historical manifestation of Himself and of His nature.

We therefore introduce into the conception of God, who is utterly Spirit and absolute light, no limitation and no mistiness, when we say that God, considered in Himself apart from the creation, is threefold in persons, and sevenfold in revelation of Himself, the tri-personal One. But if we consider Him in relation to the creation, which according to Rom. i. 20 reflects τὰ ἀόρατα αὐτοῦ, we only need a glance to Gen. i. 2, 3, in the light of John i. 1-4, to apprehend that it is the Godhead in the totality of its nature which brings creation into temporal actuality; for the Father accomplishes it through the Logos with the perfecting co-operation of the Holy Spirit in seven days, of which the seventh is the blissful repose of perfection into which the six other days enter. But the creation realized in time is actually only the temporal realization of that which was everlastingly present to the triune self-consciousness of God; and of the latter as of the former, the same principle is true, that it is God in the totality of His nature from whom and in whom it has its ideal existence. The conceptions of the creation, future as to time, proceed from the Father through the Son, and proceed from both through the Holy Spirit, and form the ideal world of the triune Godhead which it fills with its sevenfold *doxa*; as it will be the final purpose of the world translated out of the idea into reality to be filled with the *doxa* of the Thrice-holy (Isa. vi. 3). It is one of the most genial flashes of Schleiermacher's spirit, when in his sketch of a system of moral philosophy he calls love "*the desire of reason to become soul.*" The *doxa* of God is the manifestation of His loving nature creating for itself out of itself a means and an instrument of revelation. In the *doxa*, God who is Spirit has not only what He inspires, but that wherewith He inspires it. He dwells in it, and unfolds through it, that it may be manifested in the world—the depth of that riches of wisdom and knowledge (Rom. xi. 33) which is personified in Scripture as the wisdom, חָכְמָה, σοφία, and has in the Logos its eternal Mediator, in the *doxa* its eternal medium.

Here we have attained the result which we proposed to ourselves at the close of the preceding section. God is All. All has its original in Him. He is I, and Thou, and He, and It. As I, the Father is the primal source of the Son. The Son, as Thou, is the object of the Father's love. The Spirit, as He, is the emanation of the love of the Father and the Son. The *Doxa*, as *It*, is the reflection of the Triune, and the origin of the Kosmos. We apprehend now the threefold personal and the sevenfold dynamical, the personally living, and the living archetype of the everlasting Ideal-Model,—in itself, indeed, impersonal, but effected by the personality of God, and wholly interpenetrated thereby,—including, moreover, the human soul and humanity in the image of God. We apprehend now, according to the measure of our knowledge, the everlasting postulates which precede psychological facts. And if anybody fables to us of an eternal matter in a falsely philosophical sense, we shall now have wherewith to answer him as Tertullian did Hermogenes (chap. xviii.) : " Habuit Deus materiam longe digniorem et idoniorem, non apud philosophos æstimandam sed apud prophetas intelligendam."

APPENDIX.

JOS. FR. MOLITOR ON J. BÖHME'S DOCTRINE OF THE NATURE IN GOD.

I.—*From a Letter of the 22d Sept.* 1858.[1]

I GREATLY regret that, through my ill health, we were prevented from going more deeply into the essence of God's nature. If the Böhme-Baaderish view of nature in God be well founded, it will follow that in God's essence there subsists, as the fundamental basis of existence, a dim natural impulse, or a dim natural instinct, which must, as in man, be overcome by the ideal or principle of freedom, and glorified from eternity to a higher spirituality. I think that this view could in no wise be adopted by a theologian; for it assumes too much of what is finite and naturally necessary in the nature of God, and degrades it therefore wholly into the range of finite existence. A God wholly distinct from nature—a spiritualistic Divinity—cannot be assumed: this view plainly contradicts the words of Holy Scripture. But still nature in God can just as little depend upon a blind, dark, instinctive impulse, which originally is antagonistic to the Spirit, and which, in the *eternal* process of the divine life, just as in the *temporal* process of the life of the creature, has to be overcome and elevated by the Spirit. But nature in God, which can

---

[1] The following was written with trembling hand by the grey-haired man, now at rest, when he was eighty years of age, and with a frame weakened by repeated attacks of apoplexy, but with a clear spirit, and a heart which desired for itself no higher good than "the grace of perfect submission and inward conformity to the most holy will of God." On the 23d March 1860 he fell asleep. "Jesus, my love," were his last words.— *Evang. K. Z.* 1860, No. 52.

be nothing else than the counterpart made objective of the eternally subjective divine Ideality, can only depend upon an *inner free absolute necessity*, of such a kind that, in the Godhead, we are not entitled to speak of an *overcoming* and *reconciling* of contraries, as we may in the creature, since the Godhead is originally, *in an absolute manner* that, after which the creature is bound to *aspire:* therefore in God the oppositions of life are all established in original harmony; whereas in the creature they require to be first of all combined into harmony. As this question of the nature in God is a matter of the deepest interest to theology and philosophy, I am very desirous of having your judgment on this view thus submitted to you.

II.—*From a Letter of the* 21st *Jan.* 1859.

It is undoubtedly certain that there can be nothing in created existence which has not in some manner, in the nature of the Godhead, its source of origination and of manifestation, inasmuch as the Godhead is the archetype of the creature. Only the question occurs, Does the creature form the *direct* or the *inverted* likeness of the Godhead? Since the Godhead has its source in itself, while the creature subsists by the Godhead, the creature and the Godhead appear to stand to one another in an inverted relation, of such a kind that what in the Godhead is the positive, and primitive without respect to time, in the creature is the secondary and subordinate. Thus, in the creature predominate ordination, externality, and conflict of contraries, or, generally, the natural aspect of things: it advances successively from a *minus* activity to a *plus* activity, from externality to internality, from the rough, rude, constrained rigour of nature, to the inward, gentle, free, higher ideality; whilst in the Godhead, which has its own origin freely from itself, the inverted current of life appears to find a place, in that here, receptivity, externality, natural ordination, are the *product* of the ideal constitutive actuality. Thus, moreover, there is not, in the nature of the Godhead, even conformably to the ideal, *a blind, impelled law of nature,* which cannot be overcome except in the divine process of life (certainly still only according to the idea), but in the peculiar nature of the Godhead intrinsically everything seems to me to be original harmony, which, merely operating externally, comes into relation with the opposing condition of sinners, as inharmonious action. According to the doctrine of Böhme, the process of life in the Godhead is conditioned in a precisely similar manner as that of the creature, and it depends only on a difference of degree—that the former is *infinite* and *not related to time*, while the latter is *finite* and *temporal*. As a result of this view, there appears, therefore, according to J. Böhme, in the procession of the Trinity, *the Father*, as the dark, rigorous principle of nature, which is propitiated by *the Son* as the gentle ideal principle. But this view, harmonizing as it does with the most inward fundamental nature of the doctrine of Böhme, is utterly false: —in the Father subsists *the same* principle of compassion as in the Son and in the Holy Spirit. The same is true also of the principle of strict righteousness. Yet, because the Divine Son, as the *outworking principle*, became man, in order to reconcile the fallen humanity, the notion has been indulged by many Christians, that the Son represents the *love*, and the Father the *severity*, of the Godhead.

II.
THE CREATION.

'Εξ αὐτοῦ, καὶ δι' αὐτοῦ, καὶ εἰς αὐτὸν τὰ πάντα.—Rom. xi. 36.

MAN AS THE OBJECT OF THE SIX DAYS' WORK.

Sec. I.

THAT God created the world in six days, and perfected it on the seventh, is not merely a humanitarian mould in which the scriptural history of creation has been cast; but, in the acceptation of the Thora,—which refers thereto not only the law of the Sabbath, but the week of seven days also,—it is an absolute fact.[1] We have observed how deeply this number seven of the days is founded in the nature of God; and if we consider attentively, we cannot help observing how remarkably this scheme of creation is reflected in the relations of the creature and its history. It is no mere chance, that in the so-called dual or binary system of notation, the number seven is denoted by three units placed in juxtaposition (III = 7), and that the seventh member of every geometrically progressing series is always a square, and a cube; for example, 1, 2, 4, 8, 16, 32, 64.[2] Seven is the number that represents the unfolding of the idea contained in the Trinity, the number that indicates the complete development of the possible, the number of the realization of the completion and repose of all progress and endeavour.

But there is importance also, not only in the number of the creative days, but in the consecutive order of the creative works. It is deeply significant, that on the fourth day, which forms the

[1] Thus also Hofmann, in his *Schriftbeweis*, i. 279. Yet this subject, in our view, has a far more comprehensive import when we derive the scriptural account of creation, not from the intuitive knowledge of the first created man, but from actual revelation, although not the revelation of vision, as Kurtz, Keerl, and others.

[2] Philo observed this (*Opp.* i. 26). Moreover, both he and the fathers of the church take great pains to bring forward this, that in the fundamental sequence of numbers (1-10) only the number seven has the two peculiarities, that it is neither produced by multiplication, nor ever produces by multiplication any other number occurring within the given limits. It is therefore called ἀειπάρθενος.—*Vid.* E. H. Lindo, *The Conciliator of B. Manasseh ben Israel*, London 1842, vol. ii. p. 262.

point of divergence of the two ternaries of days, the light of the sun, of the moon, and of the stars, shines forth, and that from that point, (assuredly not without harmony with its place and sequence, let the influence of the stars be ever so much or ever so little believed,) commence the creations of animated natures. But what chiefly concerns us here is this, that the creation of man closes the six days' work, and immediately precedes the beginning of the Sabbath. With respect to the six work-days, man stands at the end of all creatures as their close; and with respect to the Sabbath, man stands at the summit of all creatures as their leader on the way to God's rest, *i.e.* to their destination.

Palæontology, moreover, confirms the assertion that the creation of the terrene world attained its goal in man. A hundred years ago, who would have ventured to dream, that from the excavated bowels of the earth should emerge the most substantial proofs of the historical character of the story of creation which is the commencement of Holy Scripture? For the remains of plants in the primeval world are discovered as early as the transition and coal period, while the classes of vertebrate animals do not occur until later on, in an order corresponding to the degree of their perfection,—first fishes, then amphibious creatures, birds, and finally mammals; in respect of which classes, moreover, it is to be observed that the individual types, in proportion as they are more perfect in their organization, emerge so much the later, and under the more limitations. But human remains occur nowhere in a state of fossil petrifaction, but only calcined, and therefore pertaining to the historical period. Since the time that George Cuvier recognised in the fossil, which Scheuchzer called *homo diluvii testis*, a great salamander, the fact that human remains are not found among the fossil deposits has been established by continually increasing evidences. Thus, in those periods of creation in which the generations of plants and animals appeared and perished, from the primeval range of mountains down to the geologic deluge, to which still belong the mammoths, the cave-hyænas, and the cave-bears, man had not yet been created. This conclusion of palæontology, confirming as it does the statement of Scripture, is not a matter foreign to our scientific purpose; but, on the contrary, it is a psychologic result of the deepest importance. Man cannot be estimated psychologically, except as we know something of the position in the world assigned to him by God the Creator. He is the last link of the chain of degrees, which advances in systematic progression from the creation of the ruder and more incomplete, to the more noble and more perfect. Not as though man were the highest and noblest product of any unconscious natural development, left entirely to itself. It is in harmony with a view so pantheistic and substantially atheistic as this, that such absurdities are arrived at, as were lately promulgated by Bayrhoffer and others;—that the ape is the reflection of man as he was, while still undeveloped from the brute, and that there only needed one start of formative nature to reach from the ape to the man. In order to effect for superstition such a creative *natura naturans*, unnatural force must be put upon the understanding; and the man who, in the ape, greets his brother only a little left behind, must needs have first substantially brutalized himself, or he would rather shudder at this counterfeit of his own degradation. No! between the single steps of creation there are no primeval ova, or similar spawn of a *generatio æquivoca*, but the seeds of divine creative words, from which springs forth into temporal actuality that which had from all eternity in the divine wisdom its gradual progress accurately prefigured in the design of God. But this gradual progress forms no uninterrupted continuity; but as soon as, in the first half of the sixth day, the nature-life has been elevated to the summit of opulence and intensity, beyond which nothing further is possible, man, to whom the creation from the beginning aspires, appears on the stage of existence, in the realization of his heavenly pattern, which is no potentiality of the ape, but the image of the Godhead. In respect of the soul of man, there is between him and the chimpanzee or the orang-utang,—the most exalted among the ape tribe,—an infinite distance of origin and nature, absolutely immeasurable by any degrees. But, on the other hand, it is, moreover, true that man is a microcosm, not merely so far as he, being a mingled nature of spirit and body, presents, according to Gregory of Nyssa, ὥσπερ τινὰ μικτὸν κόσμον συγγενῆ τῶν δύο κόσμων; but also, because everything which distinguishes one above the other in the lower grades of nature is concentrated in man. For in man the vegetative life is subordinated to the animal, and the animal to the spiritual; and his body combines actually in itself all the primitive forms of the elements—fire, air, water, and earth (earths and metals), the body of the man of to-day indeed, as we shall find, combining them in a different manner from that of the body of the first created man.

We said (2) that man, as considered with reference to the divine Sabbath, is placed at the summit of all creation; as considered with reference to the divine six days' work—at its end. Regarding carefully this aspect of the position of man in the field of creation, we proceed from an empirical fact already mentioned, which we cannot forbear considering, and which, under the light of the Holy Scripture, leads us to important disclosures, or at least suggests weighty questions bearing on the subject. This is the fact—that before man came into being, entire races of plants and animals which we now find embedded in the mountain strata appeared, and again perished: perished in a great measure by earthquakes, which surprised them without warning; in a great measure by mutual destruction; and partly also by painful mortal disease. The adversaries of revelation do not fail to bring this fact triumphantly under our notice, by opposing to us—(to formulate their objection alike briefly and well)—that the δουλεία τῆς φθορᾶς, to which, in consequence of the fall of man, the creature was subjected (according to Rom. viii. 20 *et seq.*), was already in operation prior to the fall of man, and in general before man existed at all. What are we to reply to them? Must we deny the fact? It is undeniable. The fact is indeed as they state it; but it does not give them on their side any right to triumph. For what the Pauline testimony affirms by way of commentary on Gen. iii. 17-19, of the unwilling bondage of corruption of the creature, is true only of the present form of the world, and of its history as centralized in man. And, moreover, Scripture gives us many intimations which may save us from embarrassment, even although the fact of a bondage of corruption already existing, and indeed preceding the creation of man, obtrude itself upon us. When man was transplanted into Paradise, with the purpose of dressing it and keeping it (Gen. ii. 15); and when the secret meaning of these words—*ut custodiret*—soon became apparent from the fact that, by means of a magic spell, a brute becomes even in the midst of Paradise the instrument of speech for an evil spirit, who designed it for the ruin of the man who had been appointed to watch over Paradise,—these things, even apart from the tree of knowledge with its deadly fruits, are retrospective hints which give us to understand that there is a destructive power to which man was placed in opposition, that he might overcome it; and which, therefore, is older than the ruin which man's overthrow introduced into the last creation. This destructive power is not human, and yet it is self-conscious; and therefore it is an angelic power,—a conclusion which, in its progressive development, Scripture entirely confirms to us. It is true that the biblical story of creation tells us nothing of the creation of angels. But that which in itself is probable, we find taken for granted in Job xxxviii. 4–7, viz. that the angels were created before the creation of the corporeal world; for there it is asserted, that before Job, and absolutely before man existed at all, stars and angels—that is, the hosts of heaven—were there, and with songs of triumph and exultation beheld the earth come forth, as the residence of humanity, and the theatre of the great events which crowned the loving counsel of God. The creation of angels is thus included in the summary statement of Gen. i. 1 (comp. ii. 1, and in addition Neh. ix. 6); and the more particular narrative, i. 2, takes its point of departure at a time when the angels were already created.[1] In this we are saying nothing new. Among the fathers of the church, Gregory of Nyssa, Basilios, Gregory of Nazianzum, and others, have taught of old, and Jo. Philoponus (in his seven books of the creation of the world) has strenuously maintained against Theodore of Mopsuestia, that God created τὸν ὑλικὸν κόσμον after He had perfected τὸν ἁπλοῦν καὶ νοερώτατον τῶν ἀοράτων δυνάμεων κόσμον. If this be true, it is moreover obvious to place the fall of the angels— Lucifer at their head—(as we have no hesitation in adopting the church's view of the Satan as being the earlier prince of the angels of light, comparing Luke x. 18 with Isa. xiv. 12), prior to Gen. i. 2. The passage in 1 John iii. 8, ἀπ' ἀρχῆς ὁ διάβολος ἁμαρτάνει, suggests to us at least no limit in dating back this

---

[1] Hofmann rejects these consequences (*Schriftbeweis*, i. 400); similarly Philippi, *Dogm.* ii. 288. After repeated examination, we agree with Kurtz and Keerl, *Schöpfungsgeschichte*, 291. The book of Job is rich in angelological disclosures.

downfall; and our old dogmatists, in saying that the angels fell at all events *intra hexaëmeron*, are only careful to assert that their fall did not happen prior to the בראשית: for, without contradiction, ראשית here is absolutely the beginning inclusively of all creation. But the special narrative begins with the second verse, with an existing condition of the earth that was to be, which followed that primeval beginning. It is the condition of תהו ובהו. How we are to apprehend this condition, occurs to us when we reflect that *thohu* in every case, where it has not the general meaning of wasteness, of emptiness, of nothingness, betokens a condition of desolation by judgment of God (Isa. xxiv. 10), and especially fiery judgment (Isa. xxxiv. 9-11; Jer. iv. 23-26); that moreover here, in the narrative of creation, it is only said that in the beginning of the six days' work God *found* the earth in the state of *thohu wabohu*, but not that this was the original state in which He had created it; as also none of the extra-Israelitish cosmogonies regard God as Creator of chaos; that consequently this condition must have had a cause apart from God, which cause can be looked for in no other direction than in that of the world of those spirits whose creation preceded the six days' work, as is further shown by their unauthorized intrusion into human history, and as is expressly intimated in Job xxxviii. 4-7. Pondering this, and holding it in connection with the undeniable fact that, prior to the fall of man, painful death, mutual murder, and the like, phenomena not conceivable out of connection with sin, were present in the creation of the primeval world, we conclude that the creation described in Gen. i. 2 presupposes the fall of the angels; that the world which here is created out of the תהו ובהו stands in connection with that, which had been entrusted to those angels as a territory under their jurisdiction; that this world, when the prince of the angels, created for higher glory, instead of abiding in the truth (John viii. 44), as god of this world selfishly revolted against God, and fell into the fire of wrath; and that the תהו ובהו was the *rudis indigestaque moles* into which God gathered together the world, inflamed by the fire of the wicked one and of judicial wrath, when He quenched it down and materialized it, in order to make it the substratum for a new creation.[1] This coagulation did not abolish the prin-

[1] Lucifer, says the author of the *Quæstiones ex vetere et Novo Testamento*

ciple of wrath that had become operative therein, but placed to it a wall of separation and a limit; and thus, when the divine love, in the interpenetrating activity of its almighty Will and Word and Spirit, with the forming powers of the water and the light, began its work on this chaos, and raised it gradually to the condition of "*good*," טוב, there emerged—not without continual attempt of demonaic powers, but nevertheless with continual victory over them—a world mingled of wrath and love, but in such a way that the love had the dominion, and Satan was banished out of its territory, and was limited to the principle of wrath ($\sigma\kappa\acute{o}\tau o\varsigma$, Eph. vi. 12), narrowed by this dominion and supremacy. All, which in the primeval world resembles him, which in the mid-world, according to the testimony of Scripture, is the result of the sin that proceeds from satanic seduction, was the expression of the principle of wrath involved in the process of becoming conquered; above which the creative omnipotence in ever new deposits has reared higher and higher its structures, but which still, as at first, bear on themselves the traces of their chaotic origin. Then, when this conquest was so far advanced that the love and its blessing reigned supreme, it was required to place another, instead of the fallen and displaced and exiled Ruler, on the throne of the earth, that had been new created amid the songs of angels and of spheres; and with this purpose the Godhead proceeded, according to everlasting counsel in the depth of its being, to the creation of man; and the biblical story of creation soars aloft as it were in triumph, celebrating in three parallel members, as on a tripod, the crowning of the six days' work, in the words: "So God created man in His own image; in the image of God created He him; male and female created He them."[1]

(opp. Augustini, ed Bened. T. iii. Append. p. 35), beholding many spiritual powers beneath himself, which he in the Paradise of God had surpassed in knowledge of the heavenly mystery, puffed up with pride, wished to be called a god. Hence it was that God, in order to bring to nothing his arrogance, not by force, but by conviction, brought matter into being, this chaotic material of the world which was thence to be formed (*hinc est unde Deus, ut ejus præsumptionem non potestate, sed ratione destrueret, materiam condidit quæ esset rerum confusio, ex quâ faceret mundum*).

[1] I had just written thus far, when R. Rocholl, referring to my previous controversy on the hypothesis of Restitution, proposed to me the following questions for answer: 1. Whence are we to explain to ourselves the wild reck-

THE LIKENESS OF GOD IN MAN.

Sec. II.

SCRIPTURE nowhere says of any one of the visible creatures that surround us, that it is created after the image of God. They are works of divine wisdom, and therefore realized thoughts of God (Prov. iii. 19; Ps. xcii. 5). To intelligent and profound consideration they are emblems of divine ἀόρατα, and substantial proofs of the eternal power and Godhead of their Author (Rom. i. 20); and especially the nightly heaven of stars rays forth bright characters of the divine name (Ps. viii.); while, in face of the universe, the sun manifests and proclaims God's glory in more distinct, and generally more intelligible, announcement (Ps. xix.). But although, in Scripture, God is compared to the sun, and His spiritual operation to the light of the sun (Ps. lxxxiv. 11; Mic. iii. 6; Mal. iii. 10), yet we read nowhere that God created the sun after His image. Scripture says this only of man, and indirectly of the angels. For in Scripture the angels are called בְּנֵי הָאֱלֹהִים, sons of God (Gen. vi. 2; Ps. xxix. 1, lxxxix. 6; Job i. 2, xxxviii. 7); and it is characteristic of a son to be the likeness of him who begat him.[1]

lessness of the Evil One, whence, the animosity and *invidiam* of the Satanic Being, if not precisely by means of the lost *hierarchia?* 2. Whence is there a fully sufficient explanation of the ἄρχων τοῦ κόσμου κοσμοκράτορες, and of the appearance of Satan in the history of temptation, as generally in the New Testament, except by means of this hypothesis? The above reply will show, as far as it is here permitted, to what result further inquiry has led me since the second edition of my *Genesis*, and after manifold correspondence with Kurtz. On the other hand, Ströbel, in his criticism of this my psychology (*Luth. Zeitschrift*, 1857, p. 759), throws out, with reference to sec. ii., the question, "What think ye? Does the ancient Moses teach his modern interpreters, or do they teach him?" We answer: The Mosaic history of creation proceeded from revelation; and since knowledge of salvation, and generally knowledge of the truth, has endured subsequent to Moses for a period of thirty centuries, we are certainly in a position to read things which transcended the intelligence of Moses, between the lines of the Mosaic history of creation.

[1] The counter arguments of Keerl have not yet appeared, as vol. i. of his work upon man as the image of God (1861) only treats in a preparatory

THE LIKENESS OF GOD IN MAN.

But the angels were already created, as we saw in Sec. I., when God determined on the creation of man. It is thus possible, and—looking at other events recorded in Scripture, *e.g.* Isa. vi., as well as the extra-Israelitish traditions of creation—more than probable, that God, in saying נַעֲשֶׂה אָדָם בְּצַלְמֵנוּ כִּדְמוּתֵנוּ, uses the plural number to comprehend the angels with Himself; as, moreover, Philo explains it certainly according to the tradition, διαλέγεται ὁ τῶν ὅλων πατὴρ ταῖς ἑαυτοῦ δυνάμεσιν. Man therefore was to be created after the image of God, and of those who already by creation bore the image of God; for which reason, in Ps. viii. 5, these two things are both asserted, as well that man is a nearly godlike, as that (according to the LXX. and Targum translations) he is a nearly angel-like, being.[1] This is a matter of the deepest psychological importance. For (1) if man be created after the image of God and of the angels, it follows that the image of God in man refers primarily to his invisible nature.[2] And yet from that premiss an opposite conclusion has also been drawn. Because man in God's likeness has a bodily form, some have presumed to infer backwards therefrom that God also has a bodily form like to man, which is related by way of prototype to the human form. This confessedly in the fourth century was the doctrine of the sect of the Andæans or Anthropomorphites, and probably also pre-

---

way of the history of creation and of the doctrine of Paradise. The contradiction of Keil, *Genesis*, sec. xxvii., is merely a counter-assertion. We abide by the view that, in asserting that the angels are sons of God, Scripture declares at the same time that they are in the likeness of God, for that which is begotten always resembles him which begot (comp. *e.g.* John iii. 6).

[1] The words of the Psalm run: Thou hast made him fall a little short of the Elohim (מִן *partitivum*), *i.e.* of the nature of the Elohim (*derogasti ei paullum Deorum = numinis Deorum*), but the nature of Elohim is divine and angelic: God is Elohim, and the angels may equally be called so, for they are sons of Elohim, and form with God the heavenly, one heavenly family (πατρία).

[2] Man, says Philipp Nicolai, is *semi-angelus* and *semi-mundus*—of angelic nature in respect of the soul, and worldly in respect of the body. And: Because man was finally prepared for the possession of the world and for angelic fellowship, he has therefore a twofold nature also—he is half angelic and half of the world. For God has endowed him with body and soul; and as he subsists in these two natures, he is related by his soul to the angels, and by his body to the world wherein he dwells. *Vid.* R. Rocholl's communications from Ph. Nicolai, in the *Luth. Zeitschrift*, 1860, p. 193.

viously of Melito of Sardis, in his work, περὶ ἐνσωμάτου Θεοῦ. In the beginning of the fifth century, a portion of the Egyptian monks who dwelt in the desert of Scetys, maintained this doctrine against those of the Nitrian mountains who, with the so-called four Long Brethren at their head, subscribed to the doctrines of Origen. The church rejected this humanizing of God. We saw in the third section of the foregoing division, that what Scripture calls the form of God is something wholly different from a human form. Tertullian thinks substantially as we do, although he speaks of a corporeity of God; for when, for example, *Adv. Prax.* c. vii., he exclaims with a certainty of conviction, " quis negavit Deum corpus esse etsi Deus spiritus est," he adds, by way of absolute confirmation: " spiritus enim corpus sui generis in suâ effigie." We may, in a certain sense, speak of a corporeity of God; but as the idea of that which is material, elaborated, and articulated in the form of man, is so easily associated with this expression, this mode of naming the divine *doxa* is apt to mislead.[1] Certainly Scripture appropriates to God human members, but still without anywhere speaking of a body of God; and certainly such anthropomorphic expressions are more deeply founded, than when it speaks of the eyes and wings of the sun, of the womb and of the eyelids of the morning; for God, indeed, appears to the seers in human form: nevertheless, the thought of an everlasting self-investing of the divine nature with a corporeity of human form is absolutely foreign to it. The oft-repeated remark, that man thinks that God is anthropomorphic, because God created man theomorphic, retains its truth even although the human corporeity be not regarded as a copy of a divine one: it partakes only in its degree of the divine likeness of the entire man. But when God Himself represents Himself in visions anthropomorphically, it implies, according to John—for example, in his Gospel, xii. 41—an anticipation of the future incarnation of the Son. The anthropomorphic inference back from Gen. i. 26 is, however, proved to be false, from the consideration that its just consequence would be, that the angels also must have been

---

[1] For this reason I purposely avoid the expression, which has become a shibboleth in the use of J. Hamberger and others, just as, moreover, I do not name the *doxa* God's " nature," because the conception of the divine nature, 2 Pet. 1-4, is a different one.

formed like men. The biblical appearances of angels have in this respect misled many, although, *e.g.*, from Gen. xviii. we can as little conclude that the angels are formed in the likeness of men, as from Matt. xxviii. 3 we should be entitled to assert that they all wear raiment white as snow.[1] The angels have no bodies; but, by the miraculous power of their will, they can make themselves visible, and take what forms they please, according to the object of their mission, and the subjectivity of the beholder. In the view entertained by the ancient church, and now again very much ventilated,—that the angels are not absolutely incorporeal,—the truth intended is merely this, that their spiritual nature is not essentially hidden from sight, but, like the divine nature, it is capable of manifestation, and, moreover, is actually revealed by way of manifestation. They have a δόξα external to themselves, and essential, which, however, is not to be called σῶμα, for the σώματα ἐπουράνια (1 Cor. xv. 40) are not—as Meyer, De Wette, and others affirm they are—meant of angels' bodies in this sense.[2] Corporeity, whether it be material or spiritual, is, within the range of personal beings, absolutely only the specific peculiarity of twofold-natured man. The assertion of Kurtz,[3] that a creature without corporeity is altogether inconceivable, does not bear consideration. Certainly, being spirit-embodied men, we can form to ourselves no clear representation of pure spirits, but we are able to *conceive* of pure spirits without bodies; and if, in respect of the angels, we do not avail ourselves of this capability, we derange the limits of the creation, in that we confound one with another the several classes of being: for Scripture distinguishes the impersonal bodily world, and the personal bodiless spirits, and the spirit-embodied man, who stands between the two, and who, being at once exalted above the bodily world, and yet not purely spiritual, is the connecting link of all created things (Ps. viii. 5). His corporeity is, and

---

[1] Περίθες οὖν αὐτοῖς εἰ βούλει καὶ ἐσθῆτα λευκήν, says Jo. Philoponos (*de mundi creat.* i. 9), defending the view of Basilios, that the angels are absolutely incorporeal, and that while they have a περιγραφή (*circumscriptio*) κατὰ δύναμιν, they have none κατὰ τόπον or κατὰ μέγεθος, in opposition to Theodore of Mopsuestia.

[2] The heavenly bodies there referred to are the bodies of heaven,— moon, sun, and stars; *s.* von Hoffmann, *Schriftb.* i. 317, and Burger *in loc.*

[3] *Bibel und Astronomie*, iv. sec. xviii. p. 142 (ed. 4).

continues to be, a material one; and—because the monistic representation of the spirit itself forming to itself its own body is unknown to Scripture—it is an imparted one;—he remains even when risen from the dead a compositum, although thenceforth withdrawn from the region of birth and death (γένεσις καὶ φθορά), and therefore relatively of a nature like the angels (Matt. xxii. 30; Luke xx. 35).[1] If, then, the nature of God and of the angels be one, not indeed incapable of manifestation, but yet incorporeal and purely spiritual, the divine likeness in man is primarily, as we now repeat, referred to his spirit and his soul; and only so far to his body, as, in order that it may be the organ of the life of the spirit and soul in the image of God, it is formed suitably to this life, and is comprehended with it in unity.[2] We now conceive also (2) on what ground, and with what meaning, man is called אָדָם. Surprise has of late been expressed, that inasmuch as אָדָם imports one that is formed from the earth, the Hebrew language possesses no name of man which expresses the characteristic dignity of his nature. For the Indo-Germanic appellation *Mensch*, Sanscr. *manu, mânúsa*, from *man*, to think, denotes him according to his spiritual part; and the Greek ἄνθρωπος = ὁ ἄνω ἀθρῶν, the up-looking one, at least characterizes him by his external appearance, as exalted above the brutes; but אָדָם, whether it be represented by *homo*, from *humus*, or by χαμα in χαμαί, χαμᾶζε, χαμάθεν, only denominates him by the earthly side of his origin and condition. Even the Lapp language has two names for man, of which one (*olbmuk*) designates him by his spiritual, the other (*suddogas*) by his perishable nature. The Old Testament language has no word besides אָדָם and אֱנוֹשׁ to denominate man according

---

[1] From these very texts Kurtz infers the corporeity of the angels. The point of the proof, he says, is found (see on the place referred to, 137) in the fact that there are also creatures which are bodily, and still do not marry. But it is found rather in the fact that the Sadducæan question is, as such, absurd, because the risen natures, like the heavenly spiritual natures, neither marry nor die. We abide in this matter on the side of Philippi (*Dogm.* ii. 289-293), only there is wanted to him the truly reconciling conception of the *doxa* (Luke ii. 9; Matt. xxii. 30, comp. xiii. 43).

[2] Thus, for example, Sell also, *Die Gottbildlichkeit des Menschen*, 1856, p. 52. The likeness of God is concentrated in the spirit, as the deepest foundation of the human life, and is expanded in the soul and body into operations which exercise a power that transforms matter.

to his more exalted dignity. A Jewish scholar (Einhorn) and a Christian one (Richers) have therefore, independently of one another, both chanced on the conjecture that אָדָם might be derived from דָּם (Ezek. xix. 10) = דְּמוּת, and might thus indicate man as made in the likeness of God. But this is a notion just as verbally and practically untenable as when the first-named scholar derives the name of the earth, אֶרֶץ, in favour of Copernicus, from רוּץ, to run. Man has his name, אָדָם, from no other source than from the earth, אֲדָמָה, because it is not this which is his characteristic dignity, that God created him after His image; but this, that God created him the *earthly* one,—taken from the earth in respect of his natural constitution,—after His image. Man has the likeness of God in common with the angels; but that in his likeness of God he is אָדָם, is the peculiarity which constitutes him the point of union of two worlds,—the spiritual and the corporeal—the centre, the copula, or, as Ph. Nicolai happily expresses it, the heart (*focus vitæ*) of all created being—the final member of the work of creation, and the moving principle of the world's history. It is just in the fact proclaimed in Ps. viii., according to LXX. version (apart from the application to Jesus in the Epistle to the Hebrews), that man is made βραχύ τι παρ' ἀγγέλους, " a little lower than the angels," in that he bears his likeness of God in an earthen vessel; it is just in this fact that consists his exalted position in the universe above the angels. A third consequence which follows from the fact that man is made after the image of God and of His angels, respects the reciprocal relations of men and angels to one another in time and in eternity. For (3) in virtue of their common likeness to God, angels and men exercise upon one another an attractive power, in consequence whereof, from the beginning of human history, a close and active intercourse has subsisted between the two races, for the most part without the consciousness of men themselves, who have become, for supramundane things, dull and obtuse; and as fallen angels also make an evil use of this reciprocal relation established at creation, it has often resulted in the destruction of men. Further, because the likeness of God in man was in a mediate manner the likeness of angels, and his position antecedent to the fall was a position similar to that of angels,—as Ezek. xxviii. 13–15 does not teach, but presupposes,—the Holy Scripture indicates and describes the future condition of blessed men as a condition of likeness to the angels. They are ἰσάγγελοι, and, like the angels, υἱοὶ τοῦ Θεοῦ, and that, not because they are disembodied, but actually as υἱοὶ τῆς ἀναστάσεως (Luke xx. 36). For it is peculiar to man, as distinguished from the angels, that, as an earthly corporeal nature, אָדָם, he bears in himself and on himself the image of God; and therein will subsist the future restoration and completion of that which was originally begun in paradise, that even man's corporeity will then be the same thing perfected, for which God from the beginning had destined it, in associating it with the spirit. The body of man was appointed to be glorified into the image of God, and thus, to speak with Gregory of Nyssa, to become καθάπερ τινα εἰκόνα εἰκόνος. Originally it was not God's image, although it was God's likeness; but by means of the resurrection it attains also τὴν εἰκόνα τοῦ ἐπουρανίου (1 Cor. xv. 49), in that it is transfigured into the image of the God-man.

If, therefore, the likeness of God be something common to men and angels, it is natural enough, and, moreover, is generally not erroneous, with the teachers of the most ancient church, to regard the spiritual, and as such the self-conscious and free, nature of man (τὸ νοερὸν καὶ αὐτεξούσιον) as the image of God; not (as only a few among the fathers) the bodily formation, and not the dominion over earthly things, which is only an effluence of the divine likeness, and not the likeness itself. But this is far from being the true perception of that wherein the image of God subsists. The image of God in this sense is indeed incapable of being lost; but Scripture passages, such as Col. iii. 10, Eph. iv. 24,[1] take it for granted that we have lost the image of God. Our ecclesiastical creed, in what it asserts of the image of God, keeps to such clear apostolical words. And, moreover, our dogmatists for the most part know nothing of the image of God, save as of a likeness

---

[1] V. Hofmann, indeed, seeks to evade the force of proof contained in Col. iii. 10, by connecting "knowledge after the image of Him that created him" (*Schriftb.* i. 289); but it is contrary to the plain literal sense presented in Gen. i. 27. In the other quotation (Eph. iv. 24), κατὰ Θεόν might mean "in a divine manner;" but in the sketch of the contents of the Epistle to the Ephesians (*Zeitschrift für Protest.* 1860, p. 340), the author of the *Schriftbeweis* submits to what is doubtless the most natural meaning—"the new man, which is created in the likeness of God." These

THE LIKENESS OF GOD IN MAN.

absolutely lost through sin. Gerhard in the *locis*, and Calovius in the *Synopsis controv.*, actually deny that the image of God subsists *in iis quæ ad essentiam animæ pertinent et quæ etiam post lapsum naturaliter ei insunt*.[1] Yet the same Gerhard says in the *Confessio catholica*, that the likeness of God might be conceived as *generalis quædam congruentia, qua anima hominis τὰ θεῖα exprimit;* and thus conceived, it is incapable of being lost. Other dogmatists also express themselves thus, but almost only in the way of accommodation, saying that the divine likeness in its deeper meaning involves *ipsum esse spirituale animæ*.[2] It is this distinction of a divine likeness in a broader (physical) meaning which cannot be lost, and a divine likeness in a narrower (ethical) meaning which has been lost by the fall, which is subject to the charge of an unmodified dualism that has been felt even by our dogmatists themselves. Scripture only knows of one likeness of God in man, which is at once moral and physical, and which cannot be lost morally without being at the same time physically disordered. Scripture nowhere says that fallen man possesses the image of God still in living reality: it places the dignity of man as he is now, only in the fact that he is created after the image of God (Gen. ix. 6; Jas. iii. 9). If we adopt the view of the fathers, that the divine likeness subsists in the νοερὸν καὶ αὐτεξούσιον, or, as we say, in the personality, then the case is otherwise. The fallen man is a person also. But this definition of the divine likeness, with which the later theology rests satisfied, is insufficient. Personality is only the basis of the substance of the divine likeness, but it is not this likeness itself. Personality is only the unity of consciousness which comprehends the entire condition of the being in the likeness of God, and which is appropriate to it.

But this entire condition is a created representation of the entire absolute life of the triune God, and not merely of the Logos. For certainly it is true of man in particular, as of

Scripture testimonies claim for the divine likeness of the first created men, although only looking back indirectly to them, an ethical destination, with the loss of which the divine likeness itself, in the very essence of its nature, and the brightness of its manifestation, faded away. To this effect, Thomasius, *Dogm.* 24th sec. (p. 221), and Philippi, *Glaubensl.* ii. 365.

[1] *Vid.* Gottlieb Wernsdorf, *Disputationes*, vol. i. Disp. vii. (*de reliquiis imaginis divinæ*).

[2] Thomasius, *Dogmatik*, i. 174.

the whole universe, that he is created through Him and for Him who is the image of the invisible God, and has from God an origin which precedes that of all creatures (Col. i. 16); and if the Logos be the ultimate purpose of the world, it must also in some measure be its archetype. The world, and especially man, is actually created κατ' εἰκόνα τοῦ εἰκόνος, i.e. after the image of the Logos, who is the express image, as from the oldest[1] even to the latest[2] times has been unanimously taught. Scripture does not directly say so. It only says directly that God created all things by the Logos, not that He created them after the image of the Logos. It says in general only of man directly, that he was created after God's image, but not of the world. But from the biblical premises, and from the facts of the history of redemption, result both the propositions, that the world was created in the form of God, and that in a certain sense it was created in the form of the Logos. As the Son of God is the brightness of the Father's glory, so also within creature limits the world is a representation of the Father's glory; and the God-man laid in the grave is the grain of wheat, whence not alone proceeds a new humanity, but moreover a new heavens and a new earth. But if we should thence conclude that the world and man were created after the image of the Son, and not of the Father and of the Holy Spirit, it would be a mistake. We can only conclude thence, that God the triune created the world after the image of Himself in such a manner, that it, and especially man, stands to the Godhead in a similar relation of likeness, as that in which, within the Godhead itself, the Son of God stands to the Father. Upon the subject of this relation, no scripture leads us further. Everywhere Scripture says only that man was created after the image of the Elohim, or of the Godhead. And man, as distinguished from the woman who mediately comes into existence, is called (1 Cor. xi. 7) εἰκὼν καὶ δόξα Θεοῦ, not Χριστ-

[1] Not without the influence of Philo (and mediately also of Plato), but which does not in itself render the truth of the matter suspicious.

[2] So, for example, Staudenmaier (*Dogm.* iii. 474); Liebner; v. Hofmann, "Man, the image of God, the archetypal purpose of the world" (*Schriftbeweis*, i. 290); Thomasius (*Dogm.* sec. xx.); Philippi (*Glaubenslehre*, ii. 361); R. Löber (*Lehre vom Gebet*, p. 12); Schöberlein (art. "Ebenbild" in Herzog's *R.E.*; and appendix on the essence of the spiritual nature and corporeality, in the *Jahrbb. für deutsche Theologie*, 1861.

τοῦ. The idea of humanity stands certainly in closest relation to the Logos, which in all directions is the Mediator of its realization, but it is not exclusively reduced, as is manifestly seen from this constant mode of scriptural expression, (for example, in Jas. iii. 9, καθ' ὁμοίωσιν Θεοῦ), to the likeness of the Logos. It is the entire living fulness of the triune Godhead which is reflected[1] in man; and this reflection is at once[2] physical and moral, and by sin it is not only morally, but also physically corrupted.

We are here still speaking in enigmas. What we mean, and indeed, not as our meaning, but as the sense of Scripture, will become more clear as we now proceed to consider the story of creation.

THE PROCESS OF CREATION.

Sec. III.

If we compare the narrative of the creation of man in Gen. i. with the narrative in Gen. ii. 4 et seq., the latter seems to place man on a lower level than does the former. For the account of chap. i. raises man above all the other orders of being whose creation precedes his, by distinguishing him above them all, as made after the image of God; but the account of chap. ii. 4 has no other designation for what man became, as the result of the more closely detailed creative process, than that which in chap. ii. 19, i. 20, 24, is equally appropriated to the fishes, birds, and quadrupeds, נֶפֶשׁ חַיָּה. The Targums have sought to remedy this, by translating or paraphrasing נֶפֶשׁ חַיָּה by רוּחַ מְמַלְּלָא— "speaking, i.e. reasonable spirit"—λογικὸν πνεῦμα; but this paraphrase is an arbitrary substitution. Moreover, we do not need such a remedy. Between the two accounts there subsists, on closer consideration, no contradiction, but a hidden similarity. For the remark that we made on the appellation אָדָם, Sec. II., is equally true of the appellation נֶפֶשׁ חַיָּה. It is not characteristic of man, that he is in the form of God; but that, being in the form of God, he is also אָדָם, or, what is in a certain

---

[1] Thus v. Rudloff, *Lehre vom Menschen*, p. 95.
[2] So also Keil, *Genesis*, p. 28.

measure the same, נֶפֶשׁ חַיָּה. Since then the two names designate man from the side of that which is common to him with the lower living beings, the two accounts will be in perfect accordance, if the more closely detailed mode of man's creation in chap. ii. corresponds to the formation in the likeness of God, which according to chap. i. makes the earthly man אָדָם, the closing link of all creation. And it is so: the process of man's creation is essentially distinct from that of the brute creation. "Jehovah-Elohim," relates chap. ii. 7, "formed man dust of the ground, and breathed into his nostrils breath of life; and thus man became a living soul." If the conclusion were to be drawn—from the fact, that what was thus produced is called נֶפֶשׁ חַיָּה no otherwise than is the case in the creation of brutes —that therefore by the manner of human creation, thus expressed, nothing peculiar is intended to be affirmed,—it would be a conclusion just as false as to argue, from the fact that man is called אָדָם, that even his likeness to God established in him no essential distinction from the brutes. For the creation of man after God's image (chap. i.), and the manner of creation recorded (chap. ii.), stand, as we shall now show, in the closest parallelism—in a relation of reciprocal modification.

We must not represent to ourselves the process of creation in so anthropomorphic a manner as it is usually pictured. Scripture gives us no justification in assuming that God formed a clod of earth with His hands into a human form, and standing near it, breathed into it, from without, the breath of life. Though mythology may thus present to itself its Prometheus forming man in the likeness of gods, from water and earth (Ovid, *Metam.* i. 78–83: finxit in effigiem moderantum cuncta Deorum), with Jehovah-Elohim it is a different matter; and texts such as Job x. 8 and 2 Cor. v. 1 would only be foolishly quoted for the contrary: for, in the former passage, that external mechanical view is of itself excluded, since Job is speaking of his own coming into being in his mother's womb; and in the latter passage, the glorified body, as a "house not made with hands,"

---

[1] "Neque enim," we say with Augustine, *de civ.* xii. 23, "hæc carnali consuetudine cogitanda sunt, ut videre solemus opifices ex materia quacunque terrena corporalibus membris quod artis industria potuerint fabricantes. Manus Dei potentia Dei est, qui etiam visibilia invisibiliter operatur."

is contrasted not with the body of Adam, but with other habitations erected by the hands of man.[1] Man then came into existence, as did also the other creatures, as a work of divine omnipotence operating invisibly, and only appreciable in its results. And, moreover, man has it in common with the other creatures, that his endowment with spirit originates with the divine breath: for the creator of all beings is God; and the reason of the origination of everything that actually exists is His word, and the primal source of all life is His Spirit. But herein is distinguished the creation of man, that all other creatures of whom mention is made (chap. i.) were called into being by the divine command of power; whereas, in the creation of man, no such mighty command goes forth, but a solemn word of self-determination precedes. This distinction is important. The divine words of might go forth into the chaos, brooded over by the Spirit, but still at the time involved in an unreconciled struggle of powers.[2] In the Spirit the creative principle of effectual life is present, and in the chaos the general substratum of material capable of being formed; and the divine words of power are the forces which bring this material, and the life that proceeds from the creative Spirit, into order, and distributes them to their respectively appropriated natures. Thus, in the creation of the land animals that came into existence in the first half of the sixth day, the divine word goes forth to the earth. Spirit and matter are already present; and the manifold creatures which arise, are the diverse combinations of those two existing fundamental conditions of animal constitution, perfected by the significant divine summons. How totally different is the origination of man! The mode of his appearance on the stage of existence corresponds to the personality of his nature, as that of the brutes to the impersonality of theirs. For while, in respect of his corporeity, man comes into being, like the brutes, by means of a distribution of existing materials, still it is not on a command of God's power, but by an

---

[1] See v. Hofmann, *Schriftbeweis*, iii. 468, who thence draws the conclusion, that in general the human body is not to be understood of either the one or the other habitation.

[2] Comp. Keerl, *Schopfüngsgeschichte*, p. 324, where it is justly observed, the Spirit of God has to liberate and to appease the disturbed and agitated germs and powers of life from their state of conflict and tension.

act of God's immediate formation; and in respect of his internal nature, his origination is absolutely and wholly not by means of the distribution of the entire natural life already existing, but by a direct act of God's breathing. He comes forth in a twofold relation, since the divine fiat took the form of an utterance of God in the presence of Himself and His Spirits, in words of self-determination,[1] by means of a directly personal self-operation of God, by which, on both sides of his natural condition, man is constituted[2] *à priori* into a moral relation of personal kinship with God, and fellowship with God. For, assuredly, though heaven and earth, and all creatures, were made by the intervention of the divine Logos (Heb. i. 2; John i. 3), who is the mediator of the realization of the world-idea; and they did not come into being without the divine word ($ῥῆμα$, Ps. xxxiii. 6; Heb. xi. 3; 2 Pet. iii. 5), which is the seed of all things; yet, nevertheless, every created thing was not created, without exception, in one and the same manner. All created natures are God's thoughts become actual; constituted out of ideal being into actual existence, and therein maintained by the divine word of might, $ῥῆμα$, which is the application of the divine will as referred to the world, and the medium of the creating and maintaining operation of God through His Logos.[3] But none the less, on that account, there is a difference between the manner in which the chaotic original matter came into being, and that in which the world of bodies formed from it came forth; and man was created otherwise than the living beings inferior to him; and the super-terrene spiritual beings otherwise than the spirit-embodied man. And, generally, the idea of creation has no other essential characteristics than those of conditionality and temporal origination, as distinguished from the absolute and the eternal.

We cannot consider with sufficient care Gen. ii. 7; for this one verse is of such deep significance that interpretation can never exhaust it: it is the foundation of all true anthropology and psychology. If we first of all consider the origination of

---

[1] Rightly says my Elberfeld critic, the creation of living beings is not at all to be conceived of without a fiat.

[2] See the pertinent remarks in v. Zezschwitz, *Profangräcität und bibl. Sprachgeist*, p. 34.

[3] See my commentary on Heb. i., sec. iii. p. 12.

the human body, what follows is of the utmost importance. 1. The body of man came into existence prior to the soul. The view that the body is the soul's own formation, is thus contrary to Scripture: it is devised in the unscriptural endeavour to exalt the original dualism of the condition of man's nature into an original unity.[1] And although v. Rudloff[2] maintains that "the first man had a soul already before the divine inbreathing of the spirit," we maintain, in contradiction to this assertion, that Scripture says the contrary; and, moreover, we decline to enter any further upon the consequences flowing from premises that are opposed to Scripture. Still v. Rudloff himself confesses that he can only adduce in defence of his view one proof text, and that an apocryphal one, *scil.* Wisd. xv. 11; but this one proof text attests the direct contrary of what he has gathered from it. For it designates God as Him who inspired into man (not, as v. Rudloff interprets, *poured into* him) an active soul, and breathed into him a spirit of life ($\tau\grave{o}\nu$ $\dot{\epsilon}\mu\pi\nu\epsilon\acute{u}\sigma a\nu\tau a$ $a\dot{u}\tau\hat{\omega}$ $\psi u\chi\grave{\eta}\nu$ $\dot{\epsilon}\nu\epsilon\rho\gamma o\hat{u}\sigma a\nu$ $\kappa a\grave{\iota}$ $\dot{\epsilon}\mu\phi u\sigma\acute{\eta}\sigma a\nu\tau a$ $\pi\nu\epsilon\hat{u}\mu a$ $\zeta\omega\tau\iota\kappa\acute{o}\nu$). How is this passage to sustain the representation that the soul of man had been created before the inbreathing of the spirit? The denial of that unscriptural view cannot be more definitely formulated than in these very words of the book of Wisdom. But, moreover, to the reproach of J. P. Lange,[3] when he says that it is a trifling bondage to the letter, to regard the narrative of Gen. ii. 7 as implying successive acts, we reply with a downright "It is written!" For when he maintains that the soul was created at the same moment with the body, and even goes beyond v. Rudloff, in the fact that he regards the formation of the body, the origination of the soul, and the inspiration of the spirit, as actual contemporary impulses of one act of creation,

---

[1] God did not permit the soul to be present at the formation of the body, says Antiochos of Ptolemais (*Maji Collect. Vatic.* i. 3, p. 81), that it might not glory at having been a fellow-worker with God.

[2] *Die Lehre vom Menschen*, p. 14, against which Schöberlein (*Stud. u. Krit.* 1860, p. 153): "In Gen. ii. 7, the relation of causal conditionality of the soul upon the spirit is clearly declared."

[3] *Deutsch Zeitschrift*, 1859, p. 31. Moreover, Schöberlein, *l.c.*, declares himself against the "subsequent to one another in time;" and the like is true of Kurtz (*Bibel und Astronomie*, iv. sec. xi.), according to whom the two constituent elements of man are indeed *toto cœlo* diverse, but brought together *uno momento*.

—it may be philosophical, but it is not biblical. Not as though it only contradicted the fundamental passage (Gen. ii. 7): it contradicts the entire Scripture, it contradicts its representation of man's natural condition—of his life, his destiny, and his history; for everywhere the Scripture assumes that man is a nature originating first of all in respect of his earthly corporeity, composite, and on that account a limited and mortal nature.[1] As the six days' work is an ascending, gradual progression, so also is the coming into being of man: it begins with the earthly basis of his existence, in order that man may not forget that he is אֱנוֹשׁ מִן־הָאָרֶץ (Ps. x. 18), a mortal man who has the earth as his ancestor. But, moreover, for the reason that man, in order to become lord of the earth-world, must become, even in his coming into existence, closely associated with it, he is constituted with it, and it with him, in absolute connection: the being of man plants its foot on the earth, and the being of the earth culminates in man, for both are destined to the fellowship of one history. 2. The body of man, in order to unite all elements into itself, is formed from earth, the most composite of the elementary forms, and indeed, in accordance with the delicacy of its organization, out of עָפָר, therefore of the finest portions of the earthly material, and, what is not less worthy of note, out of moist red earth: moist, for a cloud had just ascended, and had watered it; red, for the earth is called אֲדָמָה, as πυρρά, according to the unexceptionable testimony of the fathers (Joseph. Theodoret, *quæst.* 60, etc.). The earth was watered, because man was to be a microcosm, an image and copy of the Kosmos baptized and drawn from the waters; as also actually the elementary ingredients of the human body are united with such a mass of water, that the quantity of water in the human body amounts to more than three-quarters of its entire weight. The earth was red, for red on white, צַח וְאָדוֹם, is the normal colour of man's skin, the fundamental colour of beauty (Cant. v. 10; Lam. iv. 7). And it was earth of Eden, the land of delight, and therefore of the same source and ground whence sprang the trees of paradise, and whence the beasts of paradise were

---

[1] Thus the interpretation of the mythos of Cupid and Psyche in Fulgentius' *Mythologicon*, lib. iii., is: Psyche of the three sisters, *Caro*, *Libertas* (*Mens*), and *Anima* the youngest; and, because it combines in itself *caro* and *libertas*, the fairest also.

formed. Eden was the central land whence the whole earth was to become Eden-like; and as the delight of Eden was concentrated in Paradise, so, on the other hand, the body of the first-created man was the highest of all concentrations of the possibilities of glorification contained in Eden. We say possibilities, for the beginning of the creature was the restraint of wrath by love—the possibility of glorification; and its end was to be a complete abolition of wrath in love—the realization of glorification. 3. The body of man was formed by God, not merely externally and mechanically, like a massive statue formed man-like in its outline, but in its inward parts unarticulated. There is, indeed, no trace of consciousness or presentiment in us, that the spirit in us had co-operated at any time or in any way in the organization of our body; but it knows and feels itself to have been associated, without its own participation, with the organized body. Consequently, in the formation of the human body, the same forces must already have been at work which complete the entire life of nature in their reciprocal action, but in such a way that these forces first of all had their unity only in the architect who made use of them. The general prior conditions of life were present, but were not yet combined into a living unity. The human body was material penetrated with power, articulated, organically combined, but as yet not an organic individuality, not an organism living of itself.[1]

This it did not become till Jehovah-Elohim breathed into it the breath of life. This breathing, says Hamann,[2] is the end

---

[1] It cannot be otherwise, for the thesis that pervades the whole of the later physics, and is developed in the clearest and most elementary manner by Dubois-Reymond, in the introduction to his remarks on animal electricity,—that matter is force, and force is matter, *i.e.* that there is no matter without force, and no force without matter,—maintains also, in the coherence of the biblical representation of the world, its irrefragable truth, without leading to the consequences deduced therefrom by Vogt, Moleschott, Büchner, and others. Physics and chemistry have to do with forces, whose operation they know and are able to turn aside, and teach how to turn to account; but will both ever be able to produce or to reproduce any living thing? The power of life, that inconvenient and yet indispensable conception of exact investigation, is something exalted above the physical forces of attraction and repulsion: how much rather, then, is the conscious soul, and still more the self-conscious spirit! Force, life, soul, spirit, form an ascending climax.

[2] *Works*, i. 65.

of the whole creation, which, in comparison with the creation of man, seems to be an *opus tumultuarium*. He is called נִשְׁמַת חַיִּים, a designation which later in Scripture occurs especially, perhaps exclusively, only of the breath of life. And the significant word for the creative act of inbreathing is וַיִּפַּח, LXX. ἐνεφύσησεν.[1] It is not said that God, externally to Himself, created a breath, and conveyed it into man, as our forefathers believe they are obliged to assume, in order to establish the created character of the human spirit. No: God breathes, He breathes forth into the bodily form; and he who breathes, breathes forth from himself.[2] Was it, then, an externally present πνεῦμα, when the risen Lord breathed upon the disciples, ἐνεφύσησεν, and said, λάβετε πνεῦμα ἅγιον? (John xx. 22.) He breathed out of the fulness of His nature, and thus also Jehovah-Elohim breathed out of the fulness of His nature. But there is a difference between the two actions: for the Redeemer gives to the disciples a communication of the absolute Spirit of His divine-human person as delivered from the restraints of the flesh; but God the Creator endows the human body with the relative spirit which henceforth is to belong to man's own nature. Nevertheless both acts are similar to one another in this respect, that they proceed from within outwards. God the Creator creates out of Himself that which man was to have of spirit in common with Himself; *de vitali fonte spiritus sui qui est perennis*, as Lactantius says; comprises it into an individual life, and thus creates the human spirit. This is as far from being God as a breath of man is from being man. "Nec tu enim," says Tertullian (*adv. Marc.* ii. 8), "si in tibiam flaveris hominem tibiam

---

[1] This verbal observation is old. Reuchlin, in his *Rudimenta*, p. 339 (the first edition, 1506), remarks: "Hoc vocabulum secundum rabi Abraham Aben-Ezra de solo homine dictum invenitur." There were some, as Aben-Ezra remarks, who derived נְשָׁמָה from שָׁמַיִם, and interpreted it "the heavenlies." Only Gen. vii. 22 is doubtful. But probably even here the words, "all in whose nostrils were the breath of life," are a periphrasis for the preceding "all men." When v. Hofmann (i. 286) pronounces this "impossible," this at least is an assertion which goes too far: for, 1*st*, the expression refers to chap. ii. 7; 2*d*, this would be the only place where נְשָׁמָה is attributed to the brute. At any rate, נשמה usually means (as even Keil, *Gen.* p. 39, admits) the human spirit, or the spiritual human soul.

[2] It is a talmudic maxim of incontestable truth, מִי שֶׁנָּפַח מֵעַצְמוֹ נָפַח.

feceris, quanquam de anima tua flaveris, sicut et Deus de spiritu suo." And the human spirit is similarly none the less a created thing: for it is a nature which came into being in time, and is conditioned by a temporal beginning; came into being by a free, but, in distinction from all other earthly natures, by an immediate personal, operation of God. The spirit of man is an inspiration[1] immediately passing over from God the personal into the bodily form, and by that very means constituting it a person. It did not emanate from God, if with emanation we associate those characteristics of natural necessity and passivity which conflict with the pure conception of creation; but if these characteristics be omitted, it may be said to have emanated.[2] Thus teaches Scripture. For the word of Aratos, τοῦ καὶ γένος ἐσμέν, which Paul appropriates, Acts xvii. 28, is true of man, not of the brutes. It is true of man precisely on account of that special act of divine ἔμπνευσις, of which Elihu speaks, Job xxxiii. 4. And the Gentile consciousness testifies to the same truth in myths. The Babylonish mythos makes man originate from drops of divine blood mingled with earth; and the Phœnician mythos makes him the son of Κολπία and *Báav*, i.e. of the divine breath infused into matter. *Báav* is בְּהוּ = בֹּהוּ (the solid mass without life or consciousness) of the biblical narra-

---

[1] Since the human soul, says Anastasios Sinaiticus (*in Origenis Philocalia*, ed. Tarinus, p. 606), did not originate from earth, nor from air, nor from water, nor from fire, nor from any other substance whatever, nor any created visible nor conceivable nature, but from the undimmed, and infinite, and incomprehensible, and unspeakable, and invisible, and illimitable, and immortal, and untransitory, and impalpable, and unwithering, and incorporeal being of God Himself; this our soul—the God-formed, the God-given, the God-related and God-created—is Being, and manifestation of being and source of life by the power of that divine inspiration. Thence it proceeded, as life and life-giving, as from a fountain of life, a little light from the treasury of light, a breath as from an abyss of infinite fragrance.

[2] Substantially thus, moreover, Oehler, *Veteris T. Sententia de rebus post mortem futuris,* p. 11; Auberlen, art. "Geist" in Herzog's *R.E.*; Fronmüller, art. "Mensch" in H. Zeller's *Biblischem Wörterbuch;* against which H. A. Hahn, *Veteris T. Sententia de natura hominis,* p. 10, revives the pre-existence view, that God in the beginning created a store of spirit, from which He infused spirit into individual beings. No. "Notre âme," we say with Avrillon in his *Sentimens sur la Dignité de l'Ame,* 1773, "sort du cœur, de l'esprit et de la bouche de Dieu; nous avons tous été formés dans ce cœur, exhalés de cet esprit, et nous sommes sortis de sa bouche adorable."

tive of creation, Gen. i. 2; and Κολπία is קוֹל פֵּיחַ (sound of breathing, i.e. inspiriting): the root-word is פּוּחַ, a similar root to נָפַח, whence וַיִּפַּח (he breathed), Gen. ii. 7.

As the breath of life proceeding from God, or the spirit of life, is now associated with the body, which is pervaded by living powers as yet without unity, man becomes נֶפֶשׁ חַיָּה, a living soul, i.e. a soul-enlivened nature. Let the suggestive distinction be here primarily considered between the modes of expression נִשְׁמַת חַיִּים and נֶפֶשׁ חַיָּה. In the designation of נְשָׁמָה, חַיִּים is a substantive, standing to the former in the relation of a dependent genitive; in the appellation of נֶפֶשׁ, on the other hand, חַיָּה is not a substantive (as which it is only used in poetical style), but an adjective, in opposition to which it can neither be urged that it sometimes has the article (i. 21, ix. 16, whereupon see Gesenius, sec. cxi. 2), nor that it sometimes is construed as a masculine (e.g. ii. 19, which never occurs except *ad sensum*). The *usus loquendi* in this matter is altogether distinct and consistent. On the one hand, נְשָׁמָה חַיָּה or רוּחַ חַיָּה is never and nowhere said (for in רוּחַ הַחַיָּה, Ezek. i. 20, x. 17, הַחַיָּה is a genitive substantive); on the other hand, nowhere and never נֶפֶשׁ חַיִּים. And even the LXX. in this matter is exact and strict: it always says πνοὴ or πνεῦμα ζωῆς, nowhere πνοὴ ζῶσα, πνεῦμα ζῶν; always ψυχὴ ζῶσα, nowhere ψυχὴ ζωῆς. Paul also says, with just consideration, 1 Cor. xv. 45, ψυχὴ ζῶσα; and John, in the Apoc. xvi. 3, hardly wrote πᾶσα ψυχὴ ζωῆς, as xi. 11, πνεῦμα ζωῆς. The oldest authorities here waver between πᾶσα ψυχὴ ζῶσα and πᾶσα ψυχὴ ζωῆς. The Cod. Alex. and Ephr. give ζωῆς; the Vat. and Sin.,[1] on the other hand, ζῶσα; and thus also read Andreas and Aretas, the two expositors of the Apocalypse.[2] In the German, moreover, *Geist* has the signification of a stronger, and *Seele* the signification of a weaker, moving principle;[3] and we speak perchance of the breath of life,

---

[1] The text of the Cod. Sinaiticus runs, as Tischendorf informs us, πασα ψυχη ζωσα απεθανεν επι της θαλασσης.

[2] The text of Andreas in Cod. Coisl. 224, collated by Tischendorf, has only πᾶσα ψυχή, and even Primasius drops *vivens* (*vitæ*). In favour of πᾶσα ψυχή, also, without addition, are many cursive MSS., and two MSS. of the Slavonic translation, of which one includes with it the commentary of Andreas. The Andreas collated by me, however, of the Cod. Mayhingensis reads: πᾶσα ψυχὴ ζῶσα ἀπέθανεν ἐν τῇ θαλάσσῃ.

[3] See the quotation of R. v. Raumer in the Appendix to this division.

the spirit of life, but never of the soul of life. It is the true reciprocal relation between spirit and soul which is reflected in this involuntary strictness of terminology apparent in the use of language. The spirit in man is the source of life. The commonly received passage, τὸ πνεῦμά ἐστι τὸ ζωοποιοῦν, John vi. 63, comp. 1 Cor. xv. 45, is anticipated in the collocation נִשְׁמַת חַיִּים. The soul, it is true, is also living in itself, but not by itself: it is that which lives in a derived and conditioned manner. How deeply language is conscious of this, is seen in the fact that, although רוּחַ (see the word, Gen. iii. 8) and נְשָׁמָה (from נָשַׁם, related to נָשַׁב, נָשַׁף), as well as נֶפֶשׁ (see Isa. iii. 20, and comp. *ni*, to breathe forth again, *respirare*), revert to the verbal fundamental meaning of breathing (πνέειν and ψύχειν), still nowhere is נֶפֶשׁ חַיִּים said. As נִשְׁמַת חַיִּים is referred to God the Inspirer, the God of the spirits of all flesh (Num. xvi. 22, xxvii. 16), so נֶפֶשׁ חַיָּה is referred to נִשְׁמַת חַיִּים.

Thus, when the narrative of creation says that God breathed into man's nostrils the breath of life, and that, in consequence thereof, man became נֶפֶשׁ חַיָּה, this certainly has in this place the metonymic meaning of a being נֶפֶשׁ חַיָּה אֲשֶׁר־בּוֹ (i. 30); as when men, because they have in them flesh and blood, are at once named σάρξ καὶ αἷμα (בָּשָׂר וָדָם). But without doubt it will therefore be said that man was endowed with soul by means of that inbreathing of the breath of life; that thus through that inspiration, not alone, as v. Rudloff teaches, was awakened the actuality of life, slumbering till then, of the soul that had been created in us with the body; but that thereby the living soul now for the first time came into existence, in virtue of which man is a being with a living soul. We have here two erroneous views to controvert. (1.) It is erroneous to regard the breath of life as being the creative spirit itself, entering into individually operative immanence in the man that is coming into being, so that thus the designation of the created immaterial inward nature rises into נֶפֶשׁ חַיָּה. According to this view, the soul is certainly related in a subordinate manner to the spirit, but it is to the Divine Spirit.[1] It has come into being

---

[1] Thus, for example, Engelhardt (*Zeitschrift für Protest.* 1856, p. 252), who concludes from Gen. ii. 7 as we do, but not in the same sense: The soul is thus not a presupposition of the spirit, but a consequence of the communication of the spirit. Just so Schöberlein (*Jahrbb.* 1861, p. 18):

through the Spirit of God, and subsists by the fact that that Spirit is immanent in it, and is spiritual because it is immanent in it, and so far as it is allowed to rule in it. Kindred to this also is the theosophic view, to which we shall return in Div. iv. Sec. viii., that the soul was contained as a potentiality in the bodily form; that through God's breath it became a living soul; and that this has first to realize the spirit forth from itself, by allowing the spirit-type (the Idea) manifest in it to attain to itself Form.[1] This is an ethical process, whose reality we do not here pause to question. But the denial associated with it, of the fact that the breath of God became the spirit of man, we pronounce arbitrary, even although it take the form, that through God's breath the human soul was first of all brought to life and set in movement only with the capacity to receive spirit, and the power to appropriate to itself spirit. That which is designated by a later representative of this view[2]—after the example of Beck—as the fundamental error of the modern so-called biblical psychology, to wit, " that man received a self-subsisting spirit," is, in truth, the fundamental assumption of the Holy Scripture. For, according to passages such as Isa. ii. 22, xlii. 5, Job xxvii. 3, נִשְׁמַת חַיִּים must be understood of the created breath of life of man. And of God it is not less said that He made the human נְשָׁמָה, than that He (עָשָׂה) made the human נֶפֶשׁ, Jer. xxxviii. 16, Isa. lvii. 16, and formed the spirit, רוּחַ, or the heart, לֵב, of man in his inward parts, Zech. xii. 1, Ps. xxxiii. 15. The נְשָׁמָה, spirit-soul, of man is called in Prov. xx. 27 a candle illumined by God; and Paul expressly distinguishes this self-conscious spirit of man (1 Cor. ii. 11) from the self-conscious Spirit of God. But the fact that נִשְׁמָה

God pours by inspiration His creative Spirit into the body of earth, and, as the result of this influence, goes forth the soul, the living!

[1] Thus my Elberfeld critic. The spiritual endowment is brought about first by the inward birth of the idea, not without man's own agency.

[2] Th. v. Thrämer, in his *Grundzügen einer Schriftgemässen Seelenlehre*, in the second part of the treatises of the Evangelical School Union, 1858, and equally Zöckler, *Naturtheologie*, i. (1860) 749. Man in himself, and as such, *is* soul, while he *has* a body and is to *become* spirit. The defenders of this view, indeed, say also that man has a spirit, but as a gift (Beck), or as a principle and completion of his being (Zöckler), or as an endowment *accessorium* (v. Rudloff), who, indeed, goes so far as to distinguish the spirit as an accident, from the soul as the subject.

and רוּחַ of man are directly called divine in other places, has, as we have pointed out, its reason in the special mode of the spirit's origination: it comes into being by means of divine inspiration; although in such a way, that as life of itself, it is none the less a made, a formed life immediately constituted by God, as the soul is constituted mediately: for the created breath of life is the power of man's life appointed by God; and the soul is the life which proceeds from this power of life, and is therefore life mediately constituted. But not in such a way that (2), as many of the ancients say, the creative breath of life conferred upon man should be a spiritual and physical principle of life in inseparable unity.[1] The endowment with soul, indeed, appears as a result of the endowment with spirit; and spirit and soul are therefore, in Scripture, actually distinguished. For that reason we cannot say that the created $\pi\nu\epsilon\hat{u}\mu\alpha$ entering into man was psychically individualized, or, to express it otherwise, that spiritual substance took to itself a soul-form, so that spirit and soul are distinguished as general basis and individual special manifestation. The $\psi v \chi \acute{\eta}$ must be more than the form of existence, the individuation of the spirit; for the Scripture certainly appropriates to the spirit and to the soul distinct functions, and often speaks of the two in juxtaposition. They must be distinguished yet otherwise than as general and special, for the general certainly only actually exists in form of the special, and man would then not be able to speak of his spirit specially, and of his soul specially. Rather might spirit and soul be apprehended as only two distinct sides of the one principle of life: so that it might be said that this נְשָׁמָה was named רוּחַ, $\pi\nu\epsilon\hat{u}\mu\alpha$, as immaterial in relation to the supersensual; נֶפֶשׁ, $\psi v \chi \acute{\eta}$, as organically associated with the material corporeity in relation to it, and determined by it. But even this distinction is far from being sufficient for the case in question. The spirit is certainly called נִשְׁמַת חַיִּים and חַיִּים: the latter, not from without, but from within, of the plural number, indicates the life as the summary of the reciprocally acting powers and phenomena of life: the spirit also bears the former name as a principle of life absolutely in

---

[1] So, for example, Calovius on Gen. ii. 7: "Spiraculum vitæ non est Spiritus S., sed ipsa anima rationalis, quæ in homine simul est vegetativa et sensitiva, ex qua oritur respiratio et exspiratio, unde $\psi v \chi \acute{\eta}$ et נֶפֶשׁ dicta."

all relations of life; and the soul cannot be the spirit itself in the latter or the former reference. No; it is the bearer and the mediator of the life that proceeds from the spirit. It proceeded from the spirit, in that the spirit unites the corporeity personally with itself, without the spirit being expended in it. The spirit is superior to the soul. The soul is its product,[1] or, what is most expressive, its manifestation.[2] Even the soul of the brutes, as all life, and every living soul, is a manifestation of the spirit; but only the soul of man is a manifestation of a *spiritus vitæ*, peculiar to him, and breathed into him immediately from God, the personal God.

But with what justice, then, do we avail ourselves of the inbreathing of the breath of life for the communication of the created spirit? It is indeed breathed into man's nostrils (בְּאַפָּיו, *in nares ejus*), and man has it in his nostrils, Gen. vii. 22, Job xxvii. 3, Isa. ii. 22 (בְּאַפּוֹ, *in naso suo*). Those parallel passages in which אַף is interchanged with אַפַּיִם, show that אַפַּיִם is not meant here in the more general signification of "the countenance" (LXX., Vulg.). It means the nostrils (Trgg. Lth.), as the avenue of the process of breathing, and as the organ of the sense of smell, closely associated therewith. All the less do we seem called upon to regard the breath of life as the thinking spirit

---

[1] "Of all the attempts," says v. Radowitz in the second vol. of his *Fragments*, "to approach more closely to the perception of the active impulses in man, the mode of explanation has always appeared to me the most suggestive, that, by the inbreathing of the Spirit of God into the matter of the body, the soul has been begotten in the body; the soul, which is appointed and equipped thence to become a product of the spirit in the body, and to bring about the efficiency of both in man." Exactly thus is the priority described, Gen. ii. 7.

[2] Thus, in a purely scientific interest, Damerow expresses himself, when he says, for example (*Allgem. Zeitschrift für Psychiatr.* 1860, p. 438): "We know that the spirit in man, although, in order to be able to be in reciprocal action with the material world, in order to appear as soul, it is united to the brain, operates through this organ, and acts as soul, yet still transcends the soul: we know this not only from our own inner experience, but also from our daily experience in errors, and in diseases of the soul." On the other hand, Schöberlein says (*Studien und Kritiken*, 1860, p. 159): "The soul is not independent existence, but only spirit appearing through the body." But is not, then, the effect the manifestation of the cause? Is not that which conditions revealed in that which is conditioned? And is not the soul also, in a certain measure, the embodiment of the spirit, in so far as it is the manifestation of the spirit conformed to the corporeity?

SEC. III.] THE PROCESS OF CREATION. 101

in man. But (1) it is still plainly intelligible, that what God breathes into man cannot be the air which man inspires and expires; for this is not itself that which breathes in man, but only that which is breathed. (2.) Thus נִשְׁמַת חַיִּים, referred to the breath, is the same thing in man which is the subject of the capability of breathing, and,—as with the inbreathing the life of man takes its first beginning,—the same thing in man which is the subject of life absolutely in every relation, $\pi\nu\epsilon\hat{\upsilon}\mu\alpha$ $\zeta\omega\tau\iota\kappa\acute{o}\nu$, as the book of Wisdom says (xv. 11), and therefore at the same time $\psi\upsilon\chi\grave{\eta}$ $\dot{\epsilon}\nu\epsilon\rho\gamma\upsilon\hat{\upsilon}\sigma\alpha$:[1] for the breath of the Almighty is not only the primal cause of human bodily life, but also of human spiritual life, נִשְׁמַת שַׁדַּי תְּבִינֵם (Job xxxii. 8). And as (3) man is not a living soul until the breath of life enters into him, the latter must needs stand to the former, if not in the relation of a temporal *prius* and *posterius*, yet in the relation of the *principium* to the *principiatum*; and we find ourselves thus thrown back upon the identity of the breath of life with the spirit, as distinguished from the soul (נְשָׁמָה or רוּחַ, as distinguished from נֶפֶשׁ). The inbreathing into the nostrils, therefore, can only be meant to affirm that God, by means of His breath, brought forth and united with the bodily form that same principle of life which became the source of all the life of man, and announced its existence thenceforth by the breath passing into and out of the nostrils. When Ezekiel in the vision (xxxvii. 1-14) is called upon to summon the wind (רוּחַ) from all the four quarters of the wind (רוּחוֹת), that it might breathe upon the bones of the dead (נָפַח בְּ) and make them live, the representation there is still more phenomenal. The wind is a figure of the Spirit; for in ver. 14 Jehovah says, in interpretation of the vision, "I will put my Spirit into you." It is the created spirit of God which is given back to the dead of Israel, so that they arise from their graves. The wind symbolizes it, because breath is the external naturally necessary manifestation of spiritually embodied life. Moreover, language could not indicate spirit and wind by one and the same word, and the wind (*e.g.* the thawing wind, Ps. cxlvii. 18), especially that which is raised up for the purpose of special demonstra-

---

[1] See Grimm, *in loco*. The book of Wisdom does not here agree with Philo, who distinguishes the *anima vitalis* ($\zeta\omega\tau\iota\kappa\acute{\eta}$) and *rationalis* ($\lambda o\gamma\iota\kappa\acute{\eta}$) as a lower (brutal) and higher (specifically human) principle of life.

tions of power (as Ex. xv. 8, 10; Num. xi. 31; 1 Kings xviii. 12; 2 Kings ii. 16), could not be called רוּחַ ה׳, if the wind were not the elementary phenomenon which most corresponds to the nature of the spirit, and if the breath were not a sensible analogue of the supersensuous spiritual life.

We may now at length form to ourselves an entire conception of the process of the creation of man. It begins with the constitution of the body, as the regeneration (Palingenesia) of man shall one day end with the reconstitution of the body. God first formed the human body, introducing the formative powers of entire nature into the moist earth taken from the soil of Eden, and placing them in co-operation; whereon He then breathed into this form the creature spirit, which, because it originated after the manner of breathing, may just as well be called His spirit as man's spirit, because it is His breath made into the spirit of man. This spirit, entering into the form of the body, did not remain hidden in itself, but revealed itself, by virtue of its likeness to God, as soul, which corresponds to the Doxa of the Godhead; and by means of the soul subjected to itself the corporeity, by combining within the unity of its own intrinsic vitality the energies of the bodily material, as they reciprocally act on one another in accordance with the life of nature. As Ezekiel beholds Jehovah, surrounded by His rainbow-like Doxa, enthroned upon the Mercaba (chariot); so the spirit, surrounded by the soul which originates from it, is enthroned within the body: for the soul, as Tertullian says, is the body of the spirit, and the flesh is the body of the soul.[1]

---

[1] Similarly the English physician, George Moore, *The Power of the Soul over the Body* (translated into German by Susemihl, 1850), S. xxv.: "As the dust was formed by immediate contact of Jehovah's finger, the human figure took the impression of the Godhead. But that this figure of earthly form and heavenly meaning might not remain like a temple without its indwelling glory, God breathed into the body of man the continuing spirit of separate life, and this enlightened it with the moral reflection of the divine character."

THE FALSE AND THE TRUE TRICHOTOMY.
SEC. IV.

IT is of no avail to say that either Dichotomy or Trichotomy exclusively is the scriptural representation of the constitution of human nature. There are such various kinds of views of dichotomy and trichotomy, that, in general, neither conformity with, nor opposition to, Scripture can be predicated of either. Scripture speaks at one time in a definitely dichotomic strain, as *e.g.* Matt. vi. 25, Jas. ii. 26, 1 Cor. vi. 20 (according to the reading of the *textus rec.*); at another in a strain as absolutely and undeniably trichotomic, as 1 Thess. v. 23, Heb. iv. 12. For there is a false trichotomy, and in opposition thereto a scriptural dichotomy; and there is a false dichotomy, and in opposition to it a scriptural trichotomy.

We proceed from the fact, that Scripture primarily requires of us to recognise the essential opposition, and thus the dualism, of spirit and matter. At the outset it is not to be denied that *matter* is not a word which occurs in Scripture. The word certainly does not occur, but probably the idea does. All life, according to Scripture, is activity and operation of the spirit, whether that that which is Living is spirit itself, as God, who as the absolute Living One is called πνεῦμα (John iv. 24, comp. Isa. xxxi. 3), and the super-terrene personal creatures which are called πνεύματα (Heb. i. 14); or that it is pervaded by the spirit, as is the whole of nature; or is endowed with soul by spirit, as are individual personalities. There is thus a distinction between the spirit as the living and the lifegiving on the one hand, and the corporeal as that which in itself is lifeless on the other; and this corporeal nature, lifeless in itself, is precisely that which we call matter. Scripture distinguishes so sharply and stringently, that, in its estimation, even flesh and spirit are considered as contraries, although in the flesh there is inseparable the conception of that which belongs to soul; for flesh is that which is bodily endowed with soul, or that has been endowed with soul. None the less בָּשָׂר[1] and רוּחַ are opposed

---

[1] The fundamental conception of this word may clearly be gathered from the Arabic, where *baschara* means to smooth over, to rub, to rasp, to

to one another, inasmuch as flesh is not itself spirit (Gen. vi. 3; Isa. xxxi. 3); and the Lord says (John vi. 63), "It is the Spirit which quickeneth; the flesh profiteth nothing." In the introduction to the history of creation, moreover, actually appears a *Hyle*, not eternal indeed, as that of the philosophers, but still a *Hyle* as yet absolutely formless and lifeless, the *thohu wa-bohu*, which,—as absolute negation, not so much of power, which indeed may also operate destructively, as rather of form and life,—may be called pure matter. The Spirit of God, which brooded over this Hyle constituted under the waters, for the purpose of creative formation—the aboriginal chaos—is the mediating cause of all endowment with form and life, co-operating through its whole course with the creative work now beginning. Thus, even on the first page of Scripture, matter and spirit are placed in essential opposition. And this opposition subsists not only between God's Spirit and chaos, but also between the Spirit that endues man with soul, and the body of man; between the Spirit that endues the brute with soul, and the body of the brute; between the Spirit that pervades entire nature, and the grossest as well as the most delicate material in which it comes to manifestation. The opposition, indeed, is no yawning gulf. The essentially different is united by unity of origin; for from God, as Scripture tells us, are all things (1 Cor. viii. 6), etc. "The unity of the source of all things," says a late natural philosopher[1] in harmony with this, "promises a homogeneity of the things among themselves."

But if, from this relation of the spiritual and corporeal realities to a final Cause, the conclusion be drawn that there subsists no essential distinction between soul and body, Scripture is diametrically opposed to it; for as it bids us from its first page to look upon the Kosmos, so also it bids us look on man dualistically. Another natural philosopher[2] acknowledges this; not, however, without observing by the way, that an abun-

scratch something on the surface; then generally to handle, to take hold of—*attrectare* and *tractare*. Flesh, *basar*, is thus *materies attrectabilis*, the opposite of the spiritual, impalpable, incomprehensible.

[1] E. Harless, in his *Rede über Grenzen und Grenzgebiete der physiologischen Forschung* (Munich, at the expense of the Academy, 1860), 27.

[2] R. Wagner, *Der Kampf um die Seele von Standpunkt der Wissenschaft* (1857), 47.

dance of reasons might be borrowed from the Bible in defence of a more spiritualistic, monistic, and even in a certain aspect, conditionally materialistic view. But the matter does not stand thus. Scripture teaches a final glorification of the material world, and still, for all that, does not conceive it spiritualistically. It comprehends the spiritually embodied man as a substantial unity, and yet does not on this account conceive it monistically. It subjects the entire man in the way of nature to death; and yet, for all that, it does not conceive of man in a materialistic way. But, that it calls spirit and soul by names which are borrowed from the most subtle forms of matter, arises from the fact that it speaks in human language, with which even the most abstract and the most exact philosophers must needs be satisfied. It is neither in favour of conditioned nor of unconditioned materialism; for the spirit, and indeed the derived spirit not less than the divine, is in its view something essentially different in its nature from matter. According to its representation, man is the synthesis of two absolutely distinct elements.[1]

The narrative of the creation of man in Gen. ii. is specially intended to give us the recognition of this composite nature of man, and thence, on the one hand, to tell us of the importance of his position in the world; and, on the other hand, of the possibility of his dissolution by death. It could not in any way more sharply indicate the essential reality of the opposition of spirit and matter, than by representing man as originating from the combination of an immediate breathing of God, with the body of earth. Beyond contradiction, therefore, it is against Scripture, to make man a Being, so to speak, out of one piece or at one casting. The body is neither the precipitate

---

[1] We cannot therefore adopt the opinion of Fabri, *Sensus Communis*, 1861, p. 62, in saying, "The dualistic division of spirit and matter, which, contradictory to Scripture as it is, has penetrated from philosophy even into theology, and even to this day is absolutely powerful therein, in numberless points stands in the way of a deeper acquaintance with biblical truths." For that "all matter is phenomenal, and only the revelation and embodiment of spiritual potencies," is absolutely a philosophic statement contrary to Scripture, according to which matter is certainly a sensible phenomenon, but, precisely as such, is the opposite of the purely spiritual. Moreover, Fabri appears not to reject dualism in itself, but only a dualistic division, which cuts asunder spirit and matter as opposites, without a higher unity and reciprocal relation capable of modification.

of the spirit, nor the spirit the sublimate of matter. Both views derange the limits of creation drawn by Scripture.

With the decision in favour of the dualism of spirit and nature, however, the question as to dichotomy or trichotomy is in nowise settled. Besides the apprehension that the essential distinction of spirit and nature might be obliterated, there are especially three errors, the fear of which has caused a prejudice against trichotomy: (1.) The pseudo-Gnostic view, that the spirit of man is a portion of Divinity incapable of sin, as Origen thought:[1] ἀνεπίδεκτον τῶν χειρόνων τὸ πνεῦμα τοῦ ἀνθρώπου τὸ ἐν αὐτῷ (tom. xxxii. *in Joannem*). (2.) The Apollinarian error, that Christ had body and soul in common with us, but that the eternal Logos had in Him usurped the place of the Spirit,—a narrowing of the true humanity of Christ, whereby the trichotomic view, after prevailing in the two first centuries of the church, came into discredit as a Platonic-Plotinian error among the orthodox teachers of the fourth and fifth centuries. (3.) The semi-Pelagian error, that the spirit is excepted from the original sin which affected the body and soul,—an extenuation of human corruption, which probably contributed most of all to make our old dogmatists averse from trichotomy. But, in the face of all these errors, its opponents must confess that man may be regarded trichotomically, without in the least degree implying the adoption of such erroneous views. And the reproach of Platonizing, which was cast upon trichotomy, contained nothing which could specially redound to its dishonour. Assuredly Plato teaches trichotomically concerning the soul, when he distinguishes from the undying part of the soul (τὸ λογιστικόν) two mortal parts (τὸ θυμοειδές and τὸ ἐπιθυμητικόν); and certainly the later academy taught in like manner a trichotomic view of man;[2] and it may be that Apollinaris, as Nemesios declares, constructed his peculiar dogma from the anthropologic trichotomy borrowed from Plotinus—σῶμα, ψυχή, and νοῦς. But is what Plato or what Plotinus teach to be absolutely

---

[1] But not without contradicting himself, in that he teaches of the soul, ἡ ψυχὴ ἦν ὅτε οὐκ ἦν ψυχή (*De Princ.*, ed. Redepenning, p. 10), it has fallen from the position of the νοῦς; it is chilled divine fire.

[2] Thus, for example also, the little book of Hermes Trismegistus, *An die menschliche Seele*, translated from the Arabic by Fleischer (*Zeitschr. für historische Theologie*, 1840-1). The active intellect which man, in himself

branded, because Plato and Plotinus teach it? Certainly the anthropologic fundamental conceptions which underlie the substantial fact of the history of redemption, will not be discovered in Plato and Plotinus. We must needs turn to the Holy Scripture, and accept without prejudice what it answers to us, whether it be Platonic or anti-Platonic.

But if we consider dichotomy first of all in its coarsest modifications, it is not difficult to point out its opposition to Scripture. When our dogmatists say that נֶפֶשׁ חַיָּה (Gen. ii. 7) does not denote a *tertium* proceeding from the combination of *corpus terrenum* and *spiraculum vitæ*, but the *compositum* proceeding therefrom which is named after the *pars potior;* it is sufficient, by way of reply, to recall the distinction, sharply stamped on the language, between נִשְׁמַת (רוּחַ) חַיִּים and נֶפֶשׁ חַיָּה, according to which the two are related to one another as cause and effect, and therefore cannot be absolutely identical; as well as that חַיִּים and נֶפֶשׁ are conceptions which in no way coincide (*vid.* 1 Sam. i. 26, Ps. lxvi. 9, Prov. iii. 22; comp. Job iii. 20, x. 1). Another dichotomic view according to which Scripture knows nothing of a created spirit, but only of a created soul (in opposition to which is a whole array of texts, as Rom. viii. 16, 1 Cor. ii. 11, and others), continues to have an interest for us, because it is an actual proof of the strong impression made by the assumption that governs the *usus loquendi* of Scripture, that the created spirit of man is a spirit that proceeds from God. It is the view propounded by Hofmann in *Prophecy and its Fulfilment.* Man—thus runs the teaching—subsists dichotomically of body and soul: the soul is that which constitutes personality in man, as the individual life willed into existence by the eternal Spirit and present in time; the spirit, distinguished from the man himself, is that in man which rules over him,—in respect of its actual occupation, the spirit of man,—but essentially, the Spirit of God. As this view—which stands in unmistakeable contradiction to unequivocal passages of Scripture, as Zech.

only potentially a reasonable nature, receives, is there considered as essentially distinct from the soul. To the original matter of the elements succeeds, in ascending gradation, the substance of the heaven of the spheres, and to this, the substance of the soul, and to this, the reason, which, of all created things, is necessarily the noblest, the subtlest, and possessing the highest rank.

xii. 1, 1 Cor. ii. 11, Rom. viii. 16, and Deut. ii. 30, 2 Cor. vii. 1
—has been given up by Hofmann himself, it is sufficient to refer
to my examination of it given elsewhere.¹ What this view has
to offer, in harmony with the dogmatic system of the Bible, the
shrewd systematizer has known how to preserve in another way,
by none the less maintaining an indwelling of God's Spirit in
man, established by the creation. For in the *Schriftbeweis*² it
is indeed admitted that Scripture knows just as much of a
created spirit as of a created soul : of both, not as two kinds of
substances, but in such a way as to name the breath of life as
the condition of the individual life, רוּחַ, and as the individual
life itself in its conditional state, נֶפֶשׁ : רוּחַ as power effecting
movement, נֶפֶשׁ as Being existing in movement. But there is
added the limitation, of immeasurably more consequence to the
system, that it is the everlasting Spirit of God dwelling in man,
by virtue of whom man has his breath of life, which is just as
much his spirit as his soul. The immanence of God's Spirit
in man, as the source and support of his life in him, is therefore also maintained in this form of doctrine.³ I find nothing
of it in Scripture. There is no indwelling of God's absolute
Spirit in man taught here, that is distinguished from that
general presence of the Godhead in the world which supports
every created thing in its own special character; and, indeed,
the scriptural proof adduced for it from some few passages, as

¹ In my *Theology of Biblical Prophecy* (1845), pp. 187–195, where,
however, as is remarked above, on account of the endeavour to maintain
the essential unity of the created spirit and the soul, the distinction between them is made of too little account.

² See the same, i. 292-300 ; comp. von. Zeschwitz, *Profangräcität
und bibl. Sprachgeist*, pp. 67-69, where the isolated texts brought forward
in von Hofmann's *Schriftbeweis* are rightly declared to be insufficient to
found on them a doctrine of a far-reaching character upon the facts of
creation.

³ Thus also teaches Schöberlein : Man consists of body, soul, and the
Spirit of God immanent in the soul ; for he remarks (*Jahrbb.* 1861, p. 24),
" The Spirit may be reckoned in man among the actual elements of his
being ; whereas of natural beings, because the Spirit forms a power which
only rules in them, but is incomprehensible to them themselves, it would be
said that they only consist of body and soul." Scripture does not say so,
and that the Spirit of God could be an element of human nature is a contradiction in itself ; for which Hofmann, in substantially a similar view,
consistently reproaches trichotomy.

Gen. vi. 3, Job xxxiii. 4, xxxii. 8, is manifestly feeble and inadequate. And as for the essential condition of man, I certainly agree entirely with the view that the spirit and soul of man are distinguished as primary and secondary, but not with the view that spirit and soul are substantially one and the same. In the abstract, it is difficult to conceive how, in such a case, they could be distinguished as conditioning and conditioned; but, moreover, there occur to us two New Testament passages (viz. 1 Thess. v. 23 and Heb. iv. 12) which here claim special consideration, because they denominate, not only casually but designedly, the condition of man's being; and their logically rigid trichotomic mode of expression cannot be summarily set aside with the assertion, that in them is meant the condition of man's life, and especially of the Christian's life, not in relation to its three distinct elements, but assuming the existence of only two elements, only in reference to its three distinct relations.

We direct our attention first of all to 1 Thess. v. 23.[1] In this passage of the earliest written of his epistles, Paul names at the outset of his prayer for God's blessing, "the God of peace," because sin has brought discord into man's natural condition and community, and peace, which takes away this discord, is God's will and gift. And the very God of peace, says the apostle, sanctify you ὁλοτελεῖς,—Lat. *vos totos*; German, as Luther pithily translates, "through and through," so that nothing in you remains uninfluenced by the sanctification; —and ὁλόκληρον ὑμῶν τὸ πνεῦμα καὶ ἡ ψυχὴ καὶ τὸ σῶμα, *i.e.* sound and entire (*integer*), may your spirit and your soul and your body be preserved blameless at the coming of our Lord Jesus Christ (or, "*to* this coming;" comp. Jas. v. 7)! The wish of the apostle, we gladly concede to Hofmann, is certainly not directed to their remaining entire men, but probably to their being so kept in the totality of their human condition of

---

[1] There was a time when this Pauline text could hardly be cited without incurring suspicion. Thus it happened to Freilinghausen, who referred to it in his admirable *Grundlegung der Theologie* (a popular dogmatic treatise), where he speaks of renewing and sanctification. The editor of J. J. Rombach's Lectures on the *Grundlegung* remarks, "The *auctores* of the *Unschuldigen Nachrichten* had created an offence out of the quotation of this passage, as if the author were appearing to *constitute* (*statuiren*) three essential parts of man"

being, that when the Lord shall appear in judicial glory, no blame may fall on them. And the apostle strikingly analyzes the human condition into πνεῦμα, ψυχή, and σῶμα; nay, he moreover regards every one of these three elements as being in itself again many-sided or many-parted, inasmuch as he refers the expression ὁλόκληρον[1] to every one of them. It is the view that forces itself upon every unprejudiced person. Should any one prefer to express it, that the apostle by πνεῦμα and ψυχή is distinguishing the internal condition of man's life, and especially of the Christian's life, in respect of two several relations, even this will not be false. For the three essential elements which he distinguishes are in nowise three essentially distinct elements. Either spirit and soul, or soul and body, belong to one another, as of a similar nature; and the apostle's view is thus in the final result certainly dichotomic. But supposing that he regards spirit and soul as the essentially similar inward nature of man, it seems to correspond very little with the regular ordination of the three anthropologic fundamental conceptions, if we attribute to the apostle the notion that πνεῦμα and ψυχή are only two several relations of that essentially similar inward nature, and not two distinct elements of it. It appears, therefore, that Paul distinguishes three essential elements of man, to every one of which the work of sanctifying grace extends in its manner.

How else, in the Epistle to the Hebrews, which, if not written by Paul himself, is still Pauline (iv. 12), could a dividing asunder of the soul and spirit, which God's word effects in us, be spoken of? This passage, which, together with 1 Thess. v. 23, is valuable as the special deposit of the Pauline view of the essential condition of man, is disregarded by Harless, when he confesses[2] that he can by no means find in 1 Thess. v. 23, a trichotomy, that cannot be proved from other passages of the apostle. Hofmann endeavours to avoid the concession, that in

---

[1] The fundamental idea of ὁλόκληρος, according to Schleussner, is *cui totum inest quod sorte obtigit.* Doubtless κλῆρος in this connection means "possession," "estate," "inheritance;" and ὁλόκληρον means what represents the whole undivided possession, what is not weakened by division, and thus subsists in perfect integrity. Hesychius explains it by σῶον, and ὁλοκληρία by ἕνωσις, "uniting," unity, in contrast with dissipation into parts.

[2] *Ethics* (1853-60), p. 30.

this case ψυχή and πνεῦμα are two separate elements of human nature, by saying that he regards the genitive ψυχῆς καὶ πνεύματος as depending upon ἁρμῶν τε καὶ μυελῶν; thus making the writer say that the word is so penetrating as to divide asunder and dissolve, as well the joints as the marrow of the inner life, *i.e.* the secret links of its coherence, and the innermost marrow of its substance. But we cannot consent to surrender the trichotomic view of the writer so plainly outspoken, at the price of this unnaturally-inverted expression, wherein, over and above the objection that the "inner life" is substituted for the twofold conception ψυχῆς καὶ πνεύματος, we can find, in the fact that in ἁρμῶν τε καὶ μυελῶν there is a figurative meaning associated with a literal meaning in ψυχῆς καὶ πνεύματος, no necessity for the adoption of a construction such as would require the writer to speak, in a daring figure indeed of the joints and masses of marrow (μυελῶν, not merely μυελοῦ), of the spirit and the soul. I maintain the view discussed in my Commentary, *in loc.*, that the writer attributes to the word of God a dividing efficacy of a moral nature, which extends to the entire pneumatico-psychical and corporeal condition of man; and that he regards as well the invisible supersensuous as the sensible sensuous condition of man as bipartite, dividing in the former the ψυχή and πνεῦμα, in the latter the ἁρμοί which serve for the life of motion, and the μυελοί which serve for the life of sensation. Riehm,[1] indeed, considers that, in applying the dividing power of the word of God, which analyzes and lays bare all things, to the human corporeity also, I am "confused and contradictory;" but if in our body and its members the law of sin and of death has become dominant, it is precisely the word of God which can take to pieces this structure penetrated with sin, just as it can divide in our immaterial internal nature, soul and spirit, not merely in conception, but actually; and can with exact subtlety analyze all that has therein been creatively constituted, or has been inherited by birth, or in any other way has from any source been superinduced, or has been spontaneously cultivated. Nevertheless, this is not the place to pursue this question further. As far as the matter concerns us here, Riehm agrees with us. It is pretty generally acknowledged, says

[1] *Lehrbegriff des Hebräerbriefs* (1858), p. 65.

he,[1] that the author of the Epistle to the Hebrews, in naming (ch. iv. 12) $\psi v \chi \dot{\eta}$ and $\pi v \epsilon \hat{v} \mu a$ in juxtaposition, as composing the immaterial substance of human nature, announces a trichotomic view of the nature of man.

But although, in accordance with such classical texts of Scripture as the above, to which v. Rudloff rightly adds 1 Cor. xv. 45, soul and spirit are separable elements of the internal structure of man, still we must guard against establishing a gulf between them. In the actual natural position of man, the Psyche has certainly attained a dominion and an independence, which, as it proves on the one hand that it cannot be identical with the Pneuma, so, on the other hand, must not be abused for the purpose of proving that, in relation to the Pneuma, it is the primary element, or that it is an element essentially distinct from it.[2] No! spirit and soul are not distinct natures. The Güntherish school makes them so, when it rightly conceives of man as the synthesis of spirit- and nature-life, but wrongly appropriates the Psyche to the latter as the highest internalization of the natural substance, as the capability of the formation of conception pertaining to the knowledge of itself, in contrast with the formation of ideas by the spirit. The trichotomy of Plato and Aristotle is in substance just this. For the soul of passion and the soul of desire ($\theta v \mu \iota \kappa \dot{\eta}$ and $\dot{\epsilon} \pi \iota \theta v \mu \eta \tau \iota \kappa \dot{\eta}$) are, according to Plato, mortal; and to the latter he adjudges sensibility ($a \ddot{\iota} \sigma \theta \eta \sigma \iota \varsigma$): so that it occurs at least as a consequence of his system, that to this mortal twofold portion of the soul are to be generally appropriated the forms of activity common to man with the brute.[3] And Aristotle, who, in like manner, declares that the sustaining and sensitive soul ($\theta \rho \epsilon \pi \tau \iota \kappa \dot{\eta}$ and $a \dot{\iota} \sigma \theta \eta \tau \iota \kappa \dot{\eta}$) is decaying, and only the reason ($v o \hat{v} \varsigma$, and indeed the $v o \hat{v} \varsigma$ $\pi o \iota \eta \tau \iota \kappa o \varsigma$) is immortal, attributes to this mortal soul expressly not merely appetite ($\ddot{o} \rho \epsilon \xi \iota \varsigma$), but, moreover, sensuous perception, imagination ($\phi a \nu \tau a \sigma \iota a$), memory ($\mu \nu \dot{\eta} \mu \eta$), recollection ($\dot{a} \nu \dot{a} \mu \nu \eta \sigma \iota \varsigma$), and thus every activity of the soul that belongs to the brute also.[4] That which is new in the fundamental view

---

[1] *Lehrbegriff des Hebräerbriefs*, p. 671.
[2] See the striking remarks in v. Zeschwitz, *Profangräcität und biblischer Sprachgeist*, pp. 48-50.
[3] See Zeller, *Die Philosophie der Griechen*, ii. (1846), 272-274.
[4] *Ibid.* ii. 486-489.

SEC. IV.] THE FALSE AND THE TRUE TRICHOTOMY. 113

of Günther, is only the distinction applied to the relation of spirit and soul of the formation of ideas and of conceptions, although, following the example of Paracelsus, J. B. van Helmont teaches, that to the soul, as distinguished from the intuitively and essentially perceiving spirit, belongs the *ratio, formatrix syllogismi, discurrendi sermocinalis facultas.* The distinction of the so-called higher and lower capacities of the soul has, as we shall be convinced further on, its substantial truth testified even by Scripture; but, for the rest, the false trichotomy consists actually in that distinction of spirit and soul which points to these two several spheres of being. There is no special need of a refutation of this trichotomy from the Scripture, since it is absolutely incapable of being established on scriptural authority. Since נֶפֶשׁ, ψυχή, according to the *usus loquendi* of all the books of the Bible,[1] frequently denotes the entire inward nature of man, and in more frequent metonymy denotes the person in reference to its whole internal and external life; and since the Holy Scripture still more frequently says that man consists of body and soul than that he consists of body and spirit, the soul, as essentially distinct from the spirit, cannot possibly, in the sense of Scripture, belong to the natural side of man; as also it is an unscriptural view, that the brute-soul is the "acme of the self-internalizing process of nature:" for all the life of the creature, even of the brutes, according to Scripture, is not a life which proceeds from the spontaneous activity of matter, but a life effected in matter by God (Ps. civ. 30; Job xxxiv. 14); and Josephus (*Ant.* i. 1, 2) rightly says, in reference to Gen. ii. 7, πνεῦμα ἐνῆκεν αὐτῷ καὶ ψυχήν, *i.e.* the divine inspiration was the endowing with spirit and with soul combined.

We maintain the dualism of nature and spirit as strenu-

---

[1] Even according to that of Paul, in whom, according to Krumm, *de notionibus psychologicis Paulinis* (1858), ψυχή is nothing more than *vis qua corpus viget et movetur* (similar to the αἰσθητική of Philo, and the ἐπιθυμητικόν of Plato). Then the idea of the Psyche in Paul would be different from the one in the Epistle to the Hebrews and in Luke; and the apostle, moreover, would not be consistent with himself in such passages as Eph. vi. 6, Col. iii. 23, Phil. i. 27. Krumm accordingly makes him speak in such passages in an inconsequent manner, according to the vulgar *usus loquendi.* In such *culs-de-sac,* the desire of system is checked without possibility of return.

ously as we maintain the dualism of God and the world, and in the same degree we regard the body and the spirit of man as being of a distinct nature. But the soul belongs to the side of the spirit. The essential difference between a human nature-psyche and the human thinking spirit is an invention contrary to Scripture and to experience. The dualism of Psyche and Pneuma, under which man, considered ethically, is groaning, is a consequence of sin, which has disunited in itself his life-principle which he had received immediately from God. For it is *one* principle from which are derived both his bodily and his spiritual life. The body without the spirit is dead (Jas. ii. 26). There is no natural-psyche between spirit and body, but only a life of the soul that proceeds from the spirit itself. We thoroughly agree in this respect with Thomas Aquinas, the ingenious elaborator of the fundamental thoughts of Aristotle. "Impossibile est," he says (Pt. i. 2, lxxvi. art. 3 of his *Summa*), "in uno homine esse plures animas per essentiam differentes, sed una tantum est anima intellectiva, quæ vegetativæ et sensitivæ, et intellectivæ officiis fungitur." Notice here the idea *essentia*. The understanding soul and the bodily soul are in their essence and nature one.

Moreover, the view of Göschel,[1] that the soul proceeds at once from body and spirit in order to unite the two, *i.e.* to elevate the body from the flesh to the spirit, and to appropriate the spirit to the body, and that, because otherwise there would be a dualism, it must be such a third nature as themselves, originating in like manner from the body as from the spirit,— this view, I say, is not to be received. For (1) it proceeds on the assumption that the body, prior to its endowment with spirit, was already a naturally living body of flesh, which not only contradicts the literal reading of Gen. ii. 7, but the scriptural view generally, according to which all fleshly life is the result of the spirit of life (נְשָׁמָה and רוּחַ) dwelling in the bodily creation; (2) although the soul is the medium of the dominion of the soul over the body, it is not the appointed mediator between

---

[1] In his work, *Der Mensch nach Leib, Seele, und Geist diesseits und jenseits*, 1856, p. 6, and throughout. On the other hand, according to Dante, by divine spiritual endowment the fruit of the body arises *un' alma sola che vive e sente e se in se rigira*,—an individual soul, which lives, and feels, and revolves within itself (*Purg.* 25, 70-75).

the two; and (3) a mixed nature originating at once from the body and the spirit, is absolutely inconceivable. On the other hand, it may be represented that the spirit, entering into the earthly body, combines the natural powers met with therein into the unity of soul; so that the soul should be indeed a nature-psyche, but originated through the union of the spirit with the body. But scriptural passages such as Matt. x. 28, and a hundred others, would then be inexplicable. The conclusion, then, is, that the soul is of one nature with the spirit.

But if, according to Scripture, the soul do not belong to the side of man's nature, but to the side of his spirit, it is either one and the same with his spirit, or it is a substance proceeding from it. When the above-named Thomas Aquinas, in his *Summa* (Pt. i. 2, lxxvii. art. 6), says, " Cum accidens proprium et per se causetur a subjecto secundum quod est in actu, et recipiatur in eo in quantum est in potentia, constat omnes potentias animæ ab ipsius animæ essentia emanare," the vegetative, sensitive, appetitive, motive, evidences of life which we attribute to the soul, like the intellectual, which we call spiritual, appear to him purely accidental emanations from the nature of the soul, which is potentially capacitated for them; or (to transpose his words into our manner of expression) the soul (Psyche) is to him only as an accident of the spirit (Pneuma), only as a sum-total of acts effected and determined by the body, that the spirit begets out of itself, and may take back into itself. If we, on the other hand, raise the question whether soul and spirit are not rather to be substantially distinguished, we are not apprehending *substantia* as one and the same with *essentia;* for that in this sense spirit and soul are of a like substance, we have already maintained against the Güntherish school;—moreover, we would not have understood by *substantia* that which has the foundation of its being in itself (*quod nulla alia re indiget ad existendum*);—for, apart from the fact that in this sense generally no creature is substance in any other than a very limited manner, we award to the soul *à priori* no other being than one derived from and dependent on the spirit, and therefore no subsistence in the sense of independence. But whilst we distinguish essence as existence thus or thus limited, and substance as real and permanent and existing by itself, we contrast substance with accident, and especially with the accidental *actus*, and ask whether then in truth what we call soul, as distinct from spirit, be nothing more than the actuality of the spirit referred to the corporeity; or, according to Tertullian, whether the spiritual-psychical inward nature of man is to be regarded as *uniformis duntaxat substantia*, and the soul as nothing more than *substantiæ officium*, *i.e.* the self-operation of the spiritual substance. This question we believe we must, in the sense of the Scripture, answer in the negative, and say, as does v. Rudloff, spirit and soul are of one nature, but of distinct substances.[1] If any one would rather say that the soul is a *Tertium*, or third existence, not substantially indeed, but potentially, independent, between spirit and body, but by its nature pertaining to the side of the spirit, we have no objection to it.[2] The principle in which it results is this, that the soul, whether it be called substance or potentiality, is not the spirit itself, but another nature conditioned by it, although standing incomparably nearer to it than the body. We do not purpose to prove it from individual texts where soul and spirit are named in juxtaposition, and are distinguished from one another, as Isa. xxvi. 9. The main proof is found, on the one hand, in Gen. ii. 7, according to which the human soul is related

[1] My reviewer in the *Catholic Literatur-Zeitung*, 1855, No. 48, characterizes my view as false, and contrary to reason,—that the soul emanates from the spirit, and is no distinct nature, but a distinct substance from the spirit. He remarks: " *Capiat qui capere potest.* For, apart from the fact that it is a question whether a created spirit can emanate from itself, still that which had emanated could not possibly be another new substance, in the same way as in the Trinity the three Persons are not distinct substances." This reproach I think I have now replied to in the above more accurate explanation. As far as concerns the emanation, it is conceded by my reviewer, (1) that in the Holy Scripture the spirit and soul of man are in nowise contrasted as essentially opposed; (2) that the human soul is nowhere placed in juxtaposition with the spirit as an independent monad. I add, moreover, (3) that they are none the less distinguished as conditioning and produced, and that precisely from these three points the conclusion results to me, that the soul stands to the spirit in the relation of emanation. For the rest, *emanare* is certainly an expression not exactly suited to the subject. The names רוּחַ (נְשָׁמָה) and נֶפֶשׁ rather suggest *spirare*. But both expressions are only natural figures of that which is supernatural.

[2] Thus v. Zeschwitz, *Profangräcität und Bibl. Sprachgeist*, p. 49, comp. 37, where $\pi\nu\epsilon\tilde{\upsilon}\mu\alpha$ is with perfect justice defined as the highest spiritual power, comprehending, ruling, penetrating all the powers of the soul and the body in the power of its own connection with God.

to the inbreathed creature-breath of life, just as the brute soul is related to the absolute Spirit which brooded over the waters of chaos; on the other, in the undeniably biblical representations, that in consequence of sin the human spirit is absorbed into soul and flesh, and man, who ought to pass over from the position of the ψυχὴ ζῶσα into the position of the πνεῦμα ζωοποιοῦν, has become, instead of πνευματικὸς, a being ψυχικὸς and σαρκικὸς; and further, that just for that reason, because the spirit stands in immediate causal relation to God, all the divine operations having redemption in view address themselves first of all to the רוּחַ, πνεῦμα, and only thence attain to נֶפֶשׁ, ψυχή: for when God manifests Himself, He appeals to the spirit of man; and if He deliver man from the old nature of sin, it is man's spirit which is renewed (*e.g.* Ps. li. 10; Tit. iii. 5). Not as though the soul were not a participant in such divine operations, but they determine themselves in the spirit, in order then to concentrate themselves in the soul; and we may thence conclude, that although it originates out of the essence of the spirit, it is not of absolutely identical condition with it, or, as we prefer saying, that it is not one and the same substance with the spirit, but a substance that stands in a secondary relation with it. It is of one nature with it, but not one distinct nature, as the Son and the Spirit are of one nature with the Father, but still not the same hypostases.

This internal divine relation, however, is not quite that which is prototypical herein. When Justin (*fragm. de resurrectione carnis*) says, οἶκος τὸ σῶμα ψυχῆς πνεύματος δὲ ψυχὴ οἶκος, and when Irenæus calls the soul *spiritus velut habitaculum*, they are referring to another prototypical relation; and when Philo (*de opificio mundi*) calls man, in relation to the powers of his soul, βραχὺς εἰ δεῖ τἀληθὲς εἰπεῖν οὐρανός; or when Peter, in the *Clementine Homilies* (xvi. 12), says of the eternal wisdom, ἥνωται ὡς ψυχὴ τῷ Θεῷ,[1] the true substance of the matter is still more plainly intimated: the human soul is related to the human spirit as the divine *doxa* is related to the triune divine nature. This is a similitude which is certainly not strictly completed in the Scripture,[2] but for which Scripture offers all

---

[1] See thereupon Möller, *Geschichte der Kosmologie in der Griech. Kirche bis auf Origenes* (1861), p. 471.

[2] It would be almost strictly completed if Ps. xxiv. 4 were translated,

necessary premises. For if the human נְשָׁמָה (= רוּחַ) is a candle of Jehovah (Prov. xx. 27), and if the Lord calls the spirit of man τὸ φῶς τὸ ἐν σοὶ (Matt. vi. 23, comp. 1 Cor. ii. 11), what can the soul be other than the ἀπαύγασμα of this light, since, according to the prevailing use of scriptural language, the soul is related to the spirit as life to the principle of life, and as the effect to that which produces it? And as the human spirit is the self-knowing nature, as is collected even from its origin, and as 1 Cor. ii. 11, comp. Prov. xx. 27, expressly says, how could נֶפֶשׁ, ψυχή, so very commonly denote the entire life—the whole internal nature—the person of man—if it were not the self-expression, and, so to speak, the reflection of the spirit—the sphere essentially like to it of its own self-knowledge? נֶפֶשׁ, in a general sense, is the name of the person, not because the soul is that which forms the personality of man, but because it is the mediating link of the spirit and the body, and the peculiar form of its personality. The spirit is the inbreathing of the Godhead, and the soul is the outbreathing of the spirit. The spirit is *spiritus spiratus,* and endows the body with soul, as *spiritus spirans*. The spirit is the life-centre provided for the body, as the Object of its endowment with soul, and the soul is the raying forth of this centre of life.[1] The spirit is (let it be well considered) the inward being of the soul, and the soul is the external

according to the original text, "who does not exhaust my soul for vanity:" for the soul of God would then be here His name, Ex. xx. 7, and then a revelation of the nature of God; as also Jer. li. 14, בְּנַפְשׁוֹ, *per animam suam,* is explained by בִּשְׁמוֹ, *per nomen suum*. The *Chethib,* "who does not lift his soul to vanity," certainly reads more naturally. But the *Keri* נַפְשִׁי is old, and recognised by the oldest testimonies (even LXX., Cod. Vat., τὴν ψυχήν μου); only Elias Levita rejects it, but on the ground of a misunderstood Masora (see Bär's *Psalterium Hebr.* p. 130). Norzi, whose critical judgment I followed earlier, and also Hupfeld *in loc.,* distort the fact.

[1] So far as spirit and soul stand related to one another as centre and circumference, we might express the relation also as Philo does in B. i. *de opificio mundi*. The spirit is, so to speak, the Psyche of the Psyche, as the apple of the eye in the eye (νοῦν ἐξαίρετον ἐδωρεῖτο ψυχῇ τινα ψυχὴν καθάπερ κόρην ἐν ὀφθαλμῷ); and so far as the soul serves to the spirit as the means of self-attestation and of operation on the cosmical side, we might say that the soul is as the chariot (the *mercaba*) of the spirit, and the spirit its charioteer (νοῦς ὁ τῆς ψυχῆς ἡνίοχος ταῖς αἰσθήσεσιν ἐπιστήσας).—*Const. Apost.* vii. 34, 3.

nature of the spirit; for there is nothing internal without a corresponding external, and nothing external without internal. From the side of the body it is the beaming forth *doxa* of the spirit—its immaterial bodily self—by means of which it governs the material corporeity, with the powers that are involved in it, as the Godhead, by means of its *doxa*, fills and pervades the world. Therefore in the Old Testament the soul also is absolutely called כָּבוֹד, Gen. xlix. 6 (where it is constructed as feminine because it is akin to נֶפֶשׁ), Ps. vii. 6, xvi. 9,[1] xxx. 13, lvii. 9, cviii. 2; for the spirit is the image of the triune Godhead, but the soul is the copy of this image, and is related to the spirit as the ἑπτὰ πνεύματα are related to the Spirit of God, or to God the Spirit.

How deeply penetrating the parallelism is, will appear as we now proceed to consider the psychical origin of man in an ethical point of view.

THE ORIGIN OF THE PSYCHE IN AN ETHICAL POINT OF VIEW.

SEC. V.

IF the soul be related to the spirit as the *doxa* to God, of whom the Scripture says πνεῦμα ὁ Θεός (John iv. 24), it might be supposed that Adam, even as he was created, was at once in the position of glorification. But we are forbidden to assume this, not merely by 1 Cor. xv. 45, but by the entire tenor of Scripture. Glorification is there never regarded as the beginning, but as the end and aim, of man. The apostle formulates it thus: οὐ πρῶτον τὸ πνευματικὸν, ἀλλὰ τὸ ψυχικόν, ἔπειτα

---

[1] Let these passages of the Psalms be compared with 1 Thess. v. 23, and לֵב will be found to correspond to πνεῦμα (νοῦς), and thus כָּבוֹד to the ψυχή, which, as Hupfeld observes, is so named either as the most precious possession of man, or as the brightness of the divine כבוד. We decide for the latter view. Just so does Böhner, *Naturforschung und Kulturleben* (1858), p. 21, who is with us in this matter.

τὸ πνευματικόν. What is affirmed in this thesis follows, moreover, of necessity from the nature of man as a creature spirit-embodied. For (1) the nature of man subsists not alone in the spirit formed in God's image, and reflected in the soul as the spirit's likeness: it comprehends besides the body of earth, which, as we have shown, Sec. II., was not itself immediately after God's image, but was created only for personal union with the spirit in God's likeness, and destined to become glorified into a similar likeness of God.[1] If this body were the effluent *doxa* of the soul, as the soul is the effluent *doxa* of the spirit, it might be thought that the existence of the first created man was immediately a glorified existence. But the body was created before the spirit, and thus the beginning of man's being was unconsciousness: the basis of his natural condition was an existence in itself blind and dark, preceding his knowledge and his will, to enlighten and to govern which, was the province of the spirit. This task, however, was no physical task, although it had reference to the innate physis, but primarily an ethical one. In the most peculiar sense it was a spiritual office: for (2) in order to discharge it, man had, on the one hand, to abide in the fellowship of God; on the other hand, opposed to the actual material corporeity imprinted on him, he had to maintain the dignity of his spiritual personal freedom. The attainment of the position of glorification was thus not possible without a twofold energy of man's own, which is to be conceived of not merely as a means to the end of glorification, but as an end of itself leading to the result of glorification. But as it conflicts with the conception of a free nature, that any kind of agency or action is innate therein, man is to be conceived of, as God his Creator completed him, only as provided with the means for that twofold activity. He found himself, indeed, not in the position of absolute moral indifference; but he was good, טוב, in every relation, although

---

[1] I cannot acknowledge the counter observation of my Elberfeld critic, that the body is also as certainly created in the form of God as pertains to the organic unity of the human nature, for "we did not become compounded in our mechanism till after the fall." Man is originally a *compositum*,— death, decomposition; resurrection, recomposition,— but in such a way that in the position of spiritual corporeity the composition is as good as abolished. The organic unity of man requires, in respect of the body, only a communication, not an immediate likeness of God.

the reality of this good was, in respect of ethical results, still only a potential, not yet an actual one : he was holy, but not yet *actu,* only *potentia.* His glorification depended upon the exchanging of this potential holiness into an actual one.

It would be a mistake to suppose that the coming forth of the soul from the spirit was the first step of this actuality. No! man bears here also the vivid impress of the opposition in which the creature, as such, stands to the divine. The question has been proposed, "How came the corporeity of man to stand in need of glorification through the spirit, before sin had penetrated it?" For this reason, that, even apart from the sin which intervened, man in the way of temporal development was to become relatively a partaker of that glory which God from eternity possesses, as always perfected. It has been further asked, "Why the light of consciousness which came into the corporeal being with the breath of the Spirit, did not enlighten and pervade this being with light at once, and entirely?"[1] For the reason that generally no creature is light in its own nature, in such a way as God is in His—not even the angels, much less spirit-embodied man. As the human existence manifests its conditionality by commencing with unconsciousness, so, moreover, with the human soul it is totally otherwise than with the divine *doxa.* This is the product of a known and willed process; but the human soul finds itself not only in a body which exists without its knowledge and will, but also in a body which is endued with soul without its knowledge and will. Not only the existence of man's body, but even of his soul, is prior to the beginning of his actual consciousness. For as man received the breath of life by the creative act, he became a living soul precisely in consequence of this creative act. When he for the first time conceived the thought of I, it was the totality of his nature that had originated without his concurrence, and consisting of spirit, soul, and body, which in this thought of I he comprehended. But the glorification of man was not to, and could not, ensue without the knowledge and will of his spirit. God had left nothing wanting to man which could make him capable of glorification; but, in order to become glorified, it was essential that man should not be wanting to himself.

[1] A. Schubart proposes these questions in the *Pädagogische Revue,* 1857, p. 223.

The apostle designates this advance from the possibility of glorification to the actuality of glorification, as an advance from ψυχὴ ζῶσα to πνεῦμα ζωοποιοῦν. Man was created psychical, but with the destination and the means to become spiritual. The important point of his beginning lay in the soul, which unites his spirit-life and his corporeal life, by means of which, spirit and body stood in a reciprocal relation, whose aim was the glorification of the body. The life of the spirit, attaining to constantly increasing intensity, was to make the soul, and by its means the body, the reflections of itself; so that the twofold life of man, as it has, in a natural and naturally necessary manner, the soul for its connecting link, so in an ethical and spontaneous way might receive the spirit as its all-determining and all-pervading principle.

In order to estimate rightly the position of the ψυχὴ ζῶσα into which, and the position of the πνεῦμα ζωοποιοῦν for which, man was created, we must consider that the process of the soul from the spirit is just as little a fact completed at once, once for all, as is the procession of the *doxa* from God. The soul, as little as the *doxa* of God, has an existence severed from its origin, and stiffened into passive deliberate neutrality; the egress of the soul from the spirit is a continual process engaged in constant accomplishment, whose progress is only distinguished from the creative commencement, by the fact that, after man is once created, both, without any temporal before and after, have an existence absolutely contemporary, and placed under a similar law of development. Moreover, that we are to conceive of the being of the spirit, and its manifestation as soul, not as an inflexible neutrality, but as a living process, necessarily follows from the indissoluble coherence in which spirit and soul stand related, and from the characteristic of ever-during actuality subsisting in the appellations רוּחַ (נְשָׁמָה) and נֶפֶשׁ. If it be really so, it follows thence that the God-established formation of the mutual relation of spirit and soul in which man found himself at the first moment of his consciousness of himself, was thenceforward transferred to the power of his freedom. The soul, as God created it mediately with the spirit, was the reflection, harmonious in the manifoldness of its powers, of the spirit in the form of, and united with, God, proceeding from it, and unselfishly reverting to it: it

SEC. V.] THE ORIGIN OF THE PSYCHE. 123

was, if I may avail myself of a natural analogue, the pure and beautiful sevenfold refraction of its light. The essential condition of man bore the stamp of holiness. The soul was the likeness of God's image, and the body was to become so by the expansion of the God-established relation of the spirit to the soul, strengthening to ever-deepening intensity, over the corporeity. The decision, however, of the problem, whether this was to be the case or not, lay hidden in the mystery of human freedom.

Up to this point we have considered man in the condition in which he was placed prior to his becoming subject to the distinction of sex. For as the human history would be without unity of beginning, and thus without unity of coherence, if God (although His eternal foresight was directed to one humanity, consisting of many individuals) had created many men at once, He did not create man at the very first in pairs, because not until man was created as *one*, did the unification of the male and female principle in the one become manifest as לֹא־טוֹב. But how? Unification of the male and female principle! We leave, in this matter, out of consideration, that still even now the sexual determination of man is only gradually formed out of a state of uncertainty and slumber into a state of contrasted semiety or halfness, to which the poet refers, when he says—

> Lo! in the tender child two lovely flowers united
> Maiden and youth; the bud still veils them both.

We refer only to the important fact of the primeval beginning, that the woman was created out of Adam; and it was only as a consequence thereof that Adam became the husband of the woman. What thus became independently existent in the woman, had existed previously in Adam. We say it was in him, not it was his; for a glance at scriptural passages such as Luke xx. 35, 1 Cor. vi. 13,[1] which point to the abolition of the

[1] Keil (*Genesis*, p. 49) will not allow this passage to avail for the conclusion which, with Hofmann, we draw from it; but the apostle says (certainly with reference to nourishment and digestion) that the belly is appointed for duties with which it itself shall cease to be; and as he, in 1 Cor. xii. 23, acknowledges among the members the existence of $\dot{\alpha}\sigma\chi\dot{\eta}\mu o\nu\alpha$, and therein is thinking, doubtless, of the organs of excretion and of sex (v. Burger, *Corintherbrief*, i. p. 174), he denies the perpetuation of the belly in respect to both kinds of uncomeliness.

bodily distinction of sex in the future life, instructs us that, as the end is but the fulfilment of the beginning, Adam was externally sexless.[1] But being externally sexless, the distinguishing of the sexes was effected by a separation of opposites, which up to that time had been united, not outwardly, as pertaining to Adam, but inwardly in him; and the bodily distinctions of sex are only the external manifestation of the bodily organism transformed in conformity with that inward separation. The psychological importance of the distinguishing of the sexes is self-evident, after these preliminary observations.

THE DISTINCTION OF SEX.

Sec. VI.

IF the contrarieties of male and female, or rather the contrarieties which lay at the foundation of the separation of male and female, prior to their independence of one another, were united in the man, we ask, Wherein did they consist? And the answer is at hand. The male principle in man was the spirit, and the female was the soul. There would indeed be little ground for this assertion, if it were based simply in the grammatical distinction of genders of the two German appellations, although it is always worthy of remark, that this distinction of genders is impressed also on the Latin (*animus* and *anima*),

---

[1] We cannot form to ourselves any representation of the body of Adam before the creation of the woman, without falling into a monstrosity (as *e.g.* is shown by the eccentricities of the Bourignon). " Man is, by virtue of the power of thought given to him, only made capable of repeating in himself, of imitating, and of acknowledging the thoughts, expressed and visible, in the universe: he can create nothing originally—no atom, no reflection, no thought."—P. Jessen, *Psychologie* (1855), p. 70. When, therefore, Noack refers scornfully to the form of the embryo prior to the fourth month of pregnancy (*Psyche*, 1860, p. 330), this scorn affects us not; and when he asks whether the brutes of that obscure primeval period are in like manner to be represented as sexless, we are ready with an answer, that, for the above reasons, it is evidently only man who, according to the biblical history of creation, was not at once created in pairs.

and in some measure on the Greek ($\pi\nu\epsilon\hat{v}\mu a$, $\lambda \acute{o} \gamma o s$, $\nu o \hat{v} s$, and $\psi v \chi \acute{\eta}$); and that also in Hebrew, נֶפֶשׁ only once occurs in the masculine gender by means of a *constructio ad sensum*, while, on the contrary, רוּחַ is not less usual as a masculine than as a feminine word (*e.g.* 1 Kings xix. 11, Ps. li. 12, and especially Gen. vi. 3, "My Spirit shall not always strive," *i.e.* the spirit granted to him, in man; for that he, man, is flesh). The substantial proof of our assertion consists herein, that the distinction of the woman from the man in all its characteristics coincides with the distinction of the soul from the spirit. If we compare the external form of the man and of the woman, the appearance of the man is beautiful in proportion as it bears the stamp of a noble spirit; and the appearance of the woman, in proportion as a beautiful soul becomes visible therein. Genuine masculine beauty is like the nature of the spirit itself become transparent, and genuine feminine beauty like the nature of the soul itself become transparent; wherefore the significant Greek myth personified the soul in conformity with its profoundest and most delicate features in the female form of Psyche. The relation of the woman to the man is the impression of the secondary receptive relation of the soul to the spirit. Man and woman are distinguished, as are spirit and soul, by self-conscious energy on the one hand, and resigned passiveness on the other. Those faculties of the soul which correspond to the will, and thought, and experience of the spirit, *scil.* the desire and longing, the fancy and imagination, the feeling and foreboding, and those properties which correspond to the relation of external and internal in which the soul stands to the spirit, *scil.* of sensitive excitability, of variable vivacity, of delicate power of observation, and of direction to the individual and the special;[1] these are predominant in the woman. And as the spirit is connected with nature only through the soul, while the soul is interwoven with the harmony of nature with all its powers, the life of the woman is more manifoldly and more closely linked with the whole life of the creature, and, moreover, more instinctively and more necessarily dependent upon the natural basis of its own kind, than that of the man.

[1] See v. Thrämer, *Grundzüge*, p. 57. Beside the distinctions here given of the nature of the man and woman, we find in this arrogant production nothing worthy of reference.

THE CREATION. [SEC. VI.

We say this without in any way being led to these thoughts by the Jewish Cabbala. But that this latter has glanced with extraordinary profundity into the relation of the woman to the man, has been proved by Molitor. According to it (the Cabbala), man forms the principle which is positive, independent, operating productively, and expanding from within outwards, corresponding to the נְשָׁמָה, *i.e.* to the spirit. The woman, on the other hand, is the man inverted: in her preponderates the principle negatively active from without inwards, turned from the circumference to the centre, living itself forth in adopting and receiving, which corresponds to the נֶפֶשׁ, *i.e.* to the soul. Man, more independent of nature, represents the spiritual, ideal, sunlike aspect; and woman the psychic, real, moonlike aspect: in the former lies hid the mystery of the spirit; in the latter, the mystery of nature. These are only the most external outlines of the observation on the distinction of the two sexes [1] recorded in the Cabbala, and admirably reproduced by Molitor. One confirmation of this distribution of the spiritual and the psychical principle respectively to man and woman is moreover found, among others, in the fact, that when, in the Holy Scripture, soliloquies occur, the spirit is nowhere addressed. Everywhere the spirit speaks as the stronger manly part of the man, to the soul as the σκεῦος ἀσθενέστερον (Ps. xliii., xliv., ciii., civ., cxvi. 7; Jer. iv. 19; Luke xii. 19; comp. Ps. xi. 1, xvi. 2, cxxxi. 2). Even when David, in Ps. lvii. 8, says, "Awake up, my glory," it is his soul that he thus names כְּבוֹדִי.[2]

In consideration of this, we say, without any need of appealing to the Cabbala, with Tertullian (*de anima*, ch. xli.), that the relation of spirit and soul resembles a *connubium*, in that

---

[1] See the epitomized communications from the 3d vol. (1839) of Molitor's *Philosophy of History*, in v. Rudloff, *Lehre vom Menschen*, pp. 122-126.

[2] As כָּבוֹד, so also יְחִידָה, Ps. xxii. 20, xxxv. 17, is a name of נֶפֶשׁ. It signifies not merely the soul of the rejected or tempted one as abandoned of God, but, as the parallel word נַפְשִׁי and the analogy of כָּבוֹד show, the soul in general, as the only one, *i.e.* not twofold, present, and therefore invaluable because incapable of being replaced. The denomination is not to be explained according to Ps. xxv. 16, but according to Gen. xxii. 2, Judg. xi. 34. Thus LXX. τὴν μονογενῆ μου, and Vulg. *unicam meam*. Isychius on Lev. xix. 29 says: Anima nostra nobis filia unigenita est. The translation μονογενῆ is significant. Μονογενής, according to Wisd. vii. 22, is a surname of the Sophia. As it is related to God, so is the soul to the spirit.

the spirit of man (to speak with Augustine, lxxxiii. *quæst. qu.* 64) is *quodammodo animæ quasi maritus*,[1] and conclude further, that the internal reciprocal relation of the spirit and the soul, this mother of life, received a representation external to man by the creation of woman. Whether this externalization was necessary in order that man might be propagated, is a dogmatic question with which here we have nothing to do. This only is psychologically important to us, that the bodily distinction of sex is the sensible representation of an inward one, which subsists in the fact that man as such has his definite character from the prevalence of the spirit, and woman as such has her definite character from the prevalence of the soul.[2] Observation and Scripture confirm this. Observation confirms it; for, apart from what has been already remarked, the creatively established dependence of the woman on the man, as probably nobody denies, is founded on the fact that the man is constituted pre-eminently spiritual. Scripture confirms it still more directly than in the hints that we have mentioned, by the history of the origination of the woman, for the woman was formed from the lowest rib of Adam; thus from the bone and flesh of that region of the body where, as we shall see further on, the most important organs of the life of the soul are situated. And the tempter approaches her, for the reason that he hopes to arouse in her, rather than in the man, on account of the predominant life of the soul, a selfishly inflamed craving for sensual gratification, whereby the divine prohibition should be superseded. She, moreover, is not without the spirit in the divine image; but she has it not immediately from God, but mediately from God through man.[3] Her flame of life is kindled at that of man, אִישׁ, whose name is allied to אֵשׁ. She is absolutely and wholly ἐξ ἀνδρός, as she is διὰ τὸν ἄνδρα. The man is, as Paul says

---

[1] The principle often asserted by the fathers, *anima sexum non habet*, remains true none the less in the sense in which they mean it.

[2] This is what Joannes Scotus means when he says, *de divisione naturæ*, iv. 18: *Naturæ humanæ vir est intellectus, qui a Græcis vocatur νοῦς, mulier sensus, qui feminino genere αἴσθησις exprimitur;* for, according to his doctrine, man consists *ex corpore h. e. formata materia visibili, et anima h. e. sensu et ratione, et intellectu, et vitali motu* (*ibid.* sec. ii.). And all this is found literally in Philo.

[3] V. Dietrich., *Abhandlungen für Semitische Wortforschung* (1844), p. 248.

(1 Cor. xi. 7), immediately εἰκὼν καὶ δόξα Θεοῦ, but the woman is δόξα ἀνδρός; whereupon Grotius admirably observes, *minus aliquid viro, ut luna lumen minus sole.* As the soul is originated from the spirit (*anima ex animo*), so the woman is originated from the man; and as the soul is the image of the image of God, so the woman is the *doxa* of the *doxa* of the man. And as, according to 1 Cor. xi. 3, Eph. v. 23, God is the head of Christ, and Christ is the head of the man, so is the man the head of the woman; and the true relation of the woman to the man is, as is the true relation of the soul to the spirit, ὑποταγή. Man, says Saint Martin, is the spirit of the woman, the woman is the soul of the man, and the two are one under the common Lord.

In these statements we have everywhere assumed that the woman, not only in respect of her bodily external nature, but also in respect of her pneumatico-psychical, internal nature, is from the man. We have now to justify this assumption. This justification is inseparable from the question which from the primitive times has been discussed in the church: Whether the pneumatico-psychical nature of man is propagated, as we are accustomed to express it, *per traducem?* or, Whether in every act of begetting there is the product of a superadded divine act of creation?

TRADUCIANISM AND CREATIONISM.

Sec. VII.

SETTING aside the details of the answers that may be or have been given, the question runs, Is the pneumatico-psychical nature of the descendants of the first created man the immediate, or only the mediate constitution of God? Psychology cannot evade this question, even if its conclusions in reply should be the confession of Lucretius (i. 113):

"For it cannot be said what are the conditions of the soul,
 Whether it is itself begotten, or produced in those who are begotten."

And biblical psychology must especially investigate this question, since Scripture meets it, not only with numerous statements, but also with the facts of the history of redemption, which are closely associated with this question. Its importance in respect of the doctrines of the incarnation and of original sin is manifest. Hence in the church, from ancient times till now, it has ever been a point of controversy, debated with great earnestness and zeal. Within the range of heathenism, contrary to what one might have expected, creationism was the old Italian view. The ancient Latin Church abandoned it. In its fold, Tertullian was the most decided and the boldest defender of traducianism: " Duas species confitabimur seminis, corporalem et animalem, indiscretas tamen vindicamus et hoc modo contemporales ejusdemque momenti." It was thus he spoke, and with him, according to the testimony of Jerome, *maxima pars occidentalium.* Jerome himself was a decided advocate of creationism. In the East, Apollinaris was a declared traducianist; but when he maintained that souls are derived from souls, as bodies are from bodies,[1] it must not be forgotten that he regarded man as consisting, in the sense of Plotinus, of three elements, σῶμα, ψυχή, and νοῦς; and therefore he doubtless excepted the νοῦς from this mode of origination. The Apostolic Constitutions, however, teach concerning the soul indiscriminately, that, as in the primal beginning, so also after conception, God creates it into that which is becoming man, ἐκ τοῦ μὴ ὄντος; and most of the Orientals were of this opinion, so far as they were not pledged, as probably even Clement of Alexandria was, to the theory of pre-existence. Nevertheless this latter theory is not less strongly opposed to traducianism than is the creationism which identifies, as to time, the origination of the body with begetting, and that of the spirit with creation. Augustine, of whom it would be thought that he must have been the most exclusive traducianist, was wrestling with this question all his life; and it does great honour to his scientific accuracy and candour, that he openly acknowledges his dissatisfied wavering between for and against, although Pelagius availed himself of creationism to oppose the dogma of inherited sin. From this

[1] See his foundation for this assertion, in Nemesius, c. ii. (ed. Matthæi), p. 108.

hesitancy of the great church teacher,—in which, in excessive dread of notions accordant with materialism and emanation, he still substantially inclined rather to creationism,—and from the semi-Pelagian tendency of the ecclesiastical anthropology, which was ever growing stronger and stronger, it is plain that the dominant church doctrine tended to become more decidedly in favour of creationism. The saying of Peter Lombardus, *Creando infundit animas Deus et infundendo creat*, became an authentic formula; and in the Roman Catholic Church, this view, inherited from the Scholastics, of creationism, or, as it was also called, infusionism or inducianism, was maintained the more strongly in proportion to the facility with which it accorded with the semi-Pelagian view, that had become prevalent, about the corruption of man. Anton. Günther defended it with great ingenuity, on the ground of the essential dualism of spirit and nature, referring emanation and procreation to the life of nature as exclusive attributes, and making the soul only to be propagated with the body, but the spirit to come into existence by an immediate act of God's creation. Just so also Baltzer, in his *diss. de modo propagationis animarum* (1833); Staudenmaier, in his *Dogmatics;* Gangauf, in his *Metaphysical Psychology of St Augustine*, and many other adherents of the system of Günther; whereas traducianism in the Romish Church has only a few isolated defenders, as Klee, Oischinger, Mayrhofer, and Frohschammer. In the Lutheran Church, the opposition to the Romish semi-Pelagianism so strongly suggested the traducian view, that creationism was almost rejected as heresy. In the meanwhile, the German reformers themselves were still undecided on this matter. In a sermon preached on the day of the conception of Mary, Luther expresses himself still remarkably in favour of creationism.[1] Melancthon, in his *Psychology*, declines any decision of the question. Brentius declares himself absolutely and decidedly on the side of creationism, yet, as Quenstedt observes, *solus fere ex γνησίως Lutheranis;* for Martin Chemnitz, in the *Locis*, designated the

---

[1] *Works* (Erlangen edition), xv. 54, where he distinguishes the infusion of the soul as the second conception, from the first bodily conception. Yet, in the year 1545, Luther declared himself only inclined to maintain *traducem;* but he went no further, although especially Bugenhagen very much urged him to do so.

principle *animas creando infundi et infundendo creari* as a *temeraria assertio,* which was responsible, or partly responsible, for the disfigurement of the pure doctrine of inherited sin. Calovius went so far as to adopt the maxim, *Hominem generare hominem idque non tantum quoad corpus sed etiam animam,* among the articles of a creed in his *consensus repetitus,* not only in opposition to the Romish, but also to the Calvinistic theology, which, as it sharply distinguishes dualistically divine and human nature in the person of the God-man, so also distinguishes spirit and body in the person of man, and besides also, in its predestinarian view, would rather acquiesce in creationism.[1] In the seventeenth century there was hardly left one Lutheran teacher who interested himself in creationism, but many who opposed it by all the means in their power.[2]

And we are of their opinion. Although later Protestant thinkers—*e.g.* Göschel (in his doctrine of the last things)—rend asunder spirit and Psyche, and assume that the latter is propagated by way of procreation, the former by way of creation, it is, according to Sec. IV., a view which to us is wholly untenable. Nor is the view any more acceptable to us, that the human soul comes into existence through the operation in every case of the creative spirit upon the material element which is propagated, and does not become spiritual until the creative spirit is implanted into it, making it its own, and making it one, as is taught by Schöberlein (in his *Abh. über das Wesen der geistlichen Natur und Leiblichkeit*).[3] For as it is true that spirit, and idea,

---

[1] Compare Schneckenburger, *zur Kirchlichen Christologie* (1848), pp. 82-84. Calvin himself says: Animas creatas esse non minus quam angelos certo statuendum est.

[2] So, for example, Balth. Meisner, in his *Philosophia sobria;* Theodore Thummius, in his treatise *de Traduce,* against which the Jesuit Wangner-Eck wrote his tractate, *de creatione animæ rationalis;* Vake, in his work on the origin of human souls (1692).

[3] *Jahrbücher*, 1861, p. 28: "The creation of souls occurs on the basis of the material element, therefore not in such a way as that the soul would be independently formed and then placed into matter, but so that it is called forth as the higher potentiality of the general nature of the power which reigns in the matter through the operation of the spirit in the matter;" and p. 31: "The soul of man is essentially a natural soul; but a distinction between man and the mere natural being is established, in the fact that the created spirit is absorbed into the soul of man, into a true internal union with it, and the soul thereby is participant and possessor of

and word, are from the era of creation continually operative powers in that which is created, and as it is true that man only attains by the operation of God's Spirit to that spirituality, or rather holiness, which is his ideal destination, so the trichotomy which is assumed in this modification of creationism is destitute of sufficient Scripture foundation, and is contradictory in itself, —a trichotomy according to which the Spirit of God Himself is an element of human nature; and a spirit distinguishable from his soul, created and personal, is *à priori* denied to man. No; the man of creation is not unity of bodily-psychical life in the power of the Divine Spirit, but unity of bodily-spiritual life by means of the connecting link of the created soul. And his pneumatico-psychical nature is either, according to the Romish doctrine, God's immediate constitution in every case, or, according to the old Lutheran doctrine, it is God's immediate constitution in every case through the mediation of the act of begetting. We purpose inquiring for which of these two special possibilities Scripture decides.

As Scripture nowhere declares in a doctrinal manner anything on the origination of the pneumatico-psychical nature of man as distinct from the origination of his bodily nature, so no result is to be attained in the ordinary way of proof from Scripture; and it is not to be wondered at, if Augustine says, "De re obscurissima disputatur, non adjuvantibus divinarum scripturarum certis clarisque documentis." The proof is not to be gathered from individual passages of Scripture (as, perhaps, Gen. xlvi. 26, Acts xvii. 26), but from facts which are equally certified throughout the whole of Scripture. There are such facts as, in our conviction, are inconsistent with creationism. Among these occurs to us—1*st*, THE CREATION OF WOMAN. The act of divine ἐμπνευσις by which the pneumatico-psychical nature of Adam came into being is not repeated in the origination of the woman (Gen. ii. 21); on which account St Paul (1 Cor. xi. 8) says, without any limitation, γυνὴ ἐξ ἀνδρός; and Epiphanius, by way of developing this passage, says, "The woman was formed for him (Adam), out of him, resembling him, out of the very same body, and by the very same inspira-

the spirit itself, so that it can be comprehended and defined with a conscious free meaning in reference to the divine idea of its being regnant in the spirit."

tion (καὶ τοῦ αὐτοῦ ἐμφυσήματος)." That Adam calls the woman only flesh of his flesh, and bone of his bones, is no argument against this, for he designates marriage only as the union of man and woman לְבָשָׂר אֶחָד, without thereby excluding the idea that it is a fellowship of two souls, mutually complementary of one another. The narrative, indeed, throughout adheres to the externality of the manifestation, without on that account disowning the supersensuous background that exists therein. Still with the relation of the woman to the man, let the antitypical relation of the church to Christ, according to Eph. v. 22, be compared. This also is ἐκ τῆς σαρκὸς αὐτοῦ, but it is moreover ἓν πνεῦμα with Him (1 Cor. vi. 16): it has its being and life not only from Christ's glorified corporeity, but primarily from Christ's Spirit. It has been objected,[1] "The inspiration (endowing with spirit) was given to Adam and the woman, both in one, in the still undivided, complete man. Eva is certainly not Adam's child, but Adam himself in a different sex." This is true; but does not this very duplication of the one principle of life speak very strongly in favour of traducianism? Another fact which militates against creationism is, 2d, THE SABBATH OF CREATION. This is a limit sharply drawn by God Himself between His direct creative foundation, and His continuous mediate creative control (John v. 17). Scripture does not make any distinction in expression between the immediate and mediate production of God; but between the two kinds of operations of God's power, closely connected as they are, but yet absolutely distinct, there stands as an actual wall of separation, the Sabbath of creation, with which it is impossible to reconcile the principle that God is still every day immediately creating millions of souls. Of a *creatio continua*, in the special sense of the idea of creation, Scripture knows nothing, although it frequently speaks of the creation as of a continuous agency of God (especially in such characteristic descriptions as Isa. xl. 28, xlii. 5);[2] and certainly it looks upon the divine maintenance of the world as a *creatio continua*, but only for the reason that all duration of things subsists in continuous pulses of the primeval creative impulse, and it is absolutely by

---

[1] Göschel, in his publication, *Der Mensch diesseits und jenseits*, p. 14.

[2] The disconnection of such participles in historical relative passages is at least not always allowable (see *e.g.* Ps. xxxiii. 7).

the same omnipotence which first created and now sustains the things, that they endure, in that the endless chain of causes and effects in every one of their members remains conditioned by the overruling and all-penetrating will of the Author. When, then, it is said that God makes our souls (נְפָשׁוֹת) and נִשָׁמוֹת, Jer. xxxviii. 16; Isa. lvii. 16), that God's Spirit makes us, and the breath of the Almighty gives us life (Job xxxiii. 4), that God forms the spirit within us (Zech. xii. 1, comp. Isa. li. 13), it proves absolutely nothing for creationism: for in these cases, without raising the distinction between immediate and mediate production, the origination of our pneumatico-psychical nature is referred back to God's absolute original causation and power as its final source[1] (comp. Ezek. xviii. 4); and elsewhere, from the supposition that every mediate calling into being is only the repetition of the primal immediate one (Ps. cxxxix. 15; Job xxxiii. 6), is ascribed to God just in the same way even the formation and development of the fœtus (Ps. xxii. 10, cxix. 73, cxxxix. 13–16; Job x. 8–12, xxxi. 15; Isa. xliv. 2), as the Lord likewise in Matt. vi. 30 speaks of the lilies of the field, and the apostle in 1 Cor. xv. 36–38 of the grain of seed of the plant, equally in the tone of creationism. Another fact which compels us to the adoption of traducianism[2] is, 3d, INHERITED SIN. There subsists between all men, and the first created pair who became sinful, according to the teaching of Scripture, confirmed by well-founded experimental self-knowledge, a close connection, in virtue of which every individual regards the beginning of the human race as his own beginning; so that not only the sin of the race is his sin, but also the transgression of Adam is his transgression, and thus also his guilt.[3] Thus it cannot be otherwise than that the spiritual-bodily origin of humanity is one which, by virtue of the creative foundation, and of the maintaining providential co-operation of God, continues itself from itself; and thus the spirit of the individual comes into existence by an immediate appointment of God on each occasion, just as little as does his body. It has been, indeed, remarked in the Roman Catholic

---

[1] As when Eusebius, on Ps. c. (xcix.), says, εἰ καὶ δοκοῦσιν οἱ πατέρες ποιεῖν τὰ τέκνα, ἀλλ' οὖν ὁ Θεὸς ταῦτα ποιεῖ, καὶ ὁ μὲν αἴτιος, οἱ δὲ συναίτιοι, ὡς τῷ ἐξ ἀρχῆς αὐτοῦ διακονοῦντες προστάγματι.

[2] Frank., *Theologie der Concordien-formel*, i. 53.

[3] Hofmann, *Schriftbeweis*, i. 540

interest, sophistically enough, that the transmission by inheritance of Adam's sin can only be spoken of on the hypothesis of creationism, since the divinely created spirit which enters into the sensitive nature derived from Adam, inherits at the same time with it the sin inherent in it.[1] But the meaning and substance of inherited sin is rather this—that man, as soon as he attains to the thought of I, and to self-knowledge, finds everything that he, the I, the person, has in himself, *i.e.* the entire circumference of his spiritual-bodily natural condition, permeated with sin. It is not only the corporeity of man, but the totality of his entire nature absorbed in the σὰρξ, in and with which sin is transmitted, so that the sinful disposition of the entire being of the individual anticipates his actual self-conscious and self-determining life; or, in other words, is prior to the commencement of his personal life. But if it be supposed that the spirit of the individual is at every time immediately created by God,[2] there result therefrom the consequences, contrary to Scripture and experience, that the human spirit stands independently, without any actual relation to original sin; that it is God Himself who concludes the human spirit under the consequences of it; that there is only a sinful determination of the bodily nature including the so-called natural-psyche, but not an inherited sin comprehending man's whole personality, and certainly not an inherited guilt; that substantially every begetting is a new commencement of human history: for, since freedom belongs to the essence of the spirit, and God cannot imprint upon it the impotency of unfreedom, without becoming Himself the originator of evil, it cannot continue to be an absolute necessity for it to subject itself slavishly to the sinful σὰρξ of Adam; and there could at least be no question of an imputability of inherited sinfulness, so long as the spirit had not yet actually consented to this condition, and extinguished in itself the image of God. Such

[1] *e.g.* Staudenmaier, *Dogmatik*, iii. 447–449.

[2] Thus *e.g.* also Fronmüller (art. "Geist und Seele," in the *Zeller. Bibl. Wörterb.*), who says that, "to the soul at its origination is added immediately the spirit, as a spark of the Divine Spirit, and that this does not prejudice the fact of inherited sin, but rather places the expressions of Jesus about the childlike mind in their true light." Opposed to this, we hold to the above consequences, and refer to their further development in Frohschammer, *Ueber den Ursprung der Menschlichen Seelen*, 1854.

results, and others, contrary to Scripture and experience, flow, in respect of inherited sin, from creationism. Augustine plainly perceived this. When, therefore, the young Vincentius Victor, disapproving Augustine's wavering, very decidedly embraced the side of creationism, Augustine in the most earnest way reproached him with his youthful inconsideration; and although he was the older teacher, he even conjured the younger Jerome and others to help him over those difficulties of creationism of which Pelagius knew so well how to avail himself.[1] But, moreover, 4*th*, THE INCARNATION bears an actual testimony against creationism. Wherever Scripture speaks of Christ in conformity with the human aspect of His personality, it places it under the point of view of begetting, conception, and birth; nowhere of immediate divine creation. Since the temporal beginning of his existence corresponds to the everlasting beginning, Christ is, even in His human nature, υἱὸς τοῦ Θεοῦ, but so that at the same time He is, in full absolute truth, υἱὸς τοῦ ἀνθρώπου. He has all that belongs to the human natural condition on the one side ἐκ πνεύματος ἁγίου, on the other side ἐκ γυναικός. He has it by the reception of the Holy Ghost, and overshadowing of the power of the Most High (Luke i. 35), from Mary—not only the body, but also spirit and soul. Only on this supposition is He in truth (not merely according to the natural basis of human nature) our ἀδελφός; and only upon the supposition that on all sides of human natural condition He is rooted in the compact consistency of humanity, was its universal redemption possible through Him: for, proceeding from the maxim of Gregory of Nazianzum, τὸ ἀπρόσλεπτον ἀθεράπευτον, our dogmatists rightly say—*Si Christus non assumsisset animam ab anima Mariæ, animam humanam non redemisset.*[2]

The last and principal support of creationism is the principle, that the assumption of the spirit's ability to propagate

---

[1] See Gangauf, *l.c.* pp. 250–266, where the position of Augustine to the question in debate is set forth with praiseworthy impartiality. That Augustine convinced himself of the truth of creationism after many inward struggles, as Staudenmaier says in his *Dogmatik*, is untrue. Even in the retractations he still confesses that upon this question he is still, as ever, unable to give an answer (*nec tunc sciebam, nec adhuc scio*).

[2] These counter evidences against creationism are very well collected in the sketch of physiology by E. A. Mirus, in his *Kurtzen Fragen aus der*

itself is contrary to the dualism of nature and spirit, and transfers the nature of the latter to the former, thus confounding two departments that are sharply distinct. This reproach, however, touches Scripture itself, and proves itself unjustifiable there. For although the Scripture, as well of the Old as the New Testament, teaches that God is a Spirit, yet it reveals to us an eternal act of begetting and of birth in the Godhead itself (ὁ πατήρ and ὁ υἱός), and an eternal emanation of God the Holy Spirit from God the begetting, and God who is born. Moreover, Wisdom says, "When there were no depths, I was brought forth," חוֹלָלְתִּי (Prov. viii. 24); and Scripture does not shrink from calling God's creative production הוֹלִיד (Job xxxviii. 28) and חוֹלֵל (Ps. xc. 2; Deut. xxxii. 18), compare יָלַד, Ps. xc. 2; and His new creative production ἀναγεννᾶν (1 Pet. i. 3) and ἀποκυεῖν (Jas. i. 18): nay, it speaks directly of a divine σπέρμα (1 John iii. 9; compare 1 Pet. i. 23). The Scripture could not teach and speak in this manner, if begetting and participation, indivisibility and propagation, were coincident ideas; and if there were not a manner of begetting which corresponds to the nature of spirit, in which the essential distinction of the spirit from the nature remains unabolished.

After these counter evidences against creationism, the one passage of Scripture which for the most part favours it (Heb. xii. 9), will not be able to suggest to us another to succeed it. Our fathers are there, as τῆς σαρκὸς ἡμῶν πατέρες, contrasted with God as πατὴρ τῶν πνευμάτων, and certainly in a physical, not in an ethical sense. God is not called our spiritual Father, in opposition to the merely natural paternity of our parents; but the divine co-operation in the origination of our spiritual-bodily existence is raised so much the higher, as the spirit is exalted above the flesh; the latter we have from our ancestors, the former from the Father of spirits, *scil.* the spirits of all flesh (Num. xvi. 22, xxvii. 16).[1] There can hardly be a more classical

Pneumatica Sacra (1710), pp. 206-209. Gen. v. 3 is here rightly referred to. The likeness of God did not propagate itself in the immediateness of its origin, but in the mediateness given by Adam's self-determination, which ensued in the meanwhile, whereby human instrumentality is required for the origination of the entire man, even of his spirit.

[1] See my Commentary *in loco*, and Riehm's confirmation of the argu-

proof text for creationism. But if it be considered in connection with other statements of Scripture, and especially of the Epistle to the Hebrews itself, the matter appears somewhat differently. For when (vii. 5) the writer says that the Israelites came out of the loins of Abraham, and (vii. 10, comp. Gen. xlvi. 26) that when Abraham met Melchizedec, Levi was still in the loins of the former, his ancestor, he means thereby, that the subsequent family,—on the one hand indeed, not by the necessity of nature, but according to promise, but, on the other hand, not only partially according to the flesh, but generally according to its entire substance,—was determined in Abraham; for only on this supposition is the meaning conveyed, that in and with Abraham, Levi also had mediately paid tithes. The passage xii. 9 cannot thus be quoted in favour of creationism, in such a sense as that the writer's traducian view, so strongly expressed above, should be afterwards negatived by it; rather it will appropriately supplement this latter view, by taking up into it that which is true in creationism.[1] In other words, the writer does not mean to say that the new beginning of a human life is effected bodily indeed by procreation, while spiritually it is constituted by a divine new creation; but rather that the body as well as spirit of the child comes into being at the moment of procreation: the former, however, in virtue of an act of human will, by means of material impregnation; the latter in virtue of a divine impulse of creative power, by means of an inspiration performed through the medium of the spirit of the person that begets,—an inspiration in which the original method of endowing with spirit is continued. For this reason God is called (Zech. xii. 1) the Former of the spirit of man within him, and (Ps. xxxiii. 15) the Fashioner of the hearts of all men. Our corporeity is referred to a process of nature, our spirit to the creative concurrence of the Father of spirits.[2]

ment there for the (briefly) creationish sense of the passage in his *Lehrbegriff des Hebräerbriefs*, pp. 678-681.

[1] In the same way, Göschel, *Der Mensch diesseits und jenseits*, p. 13; comp. Philippi, *Glaubenslehre*, iii. 102, "It is possible that the *concursus generalis* of the sustaining activity of God in procreation is changed into a *concursus specialis* (*miraculosus*) of a more creative character."

[2] Luther also aimed at this when he thus expressed himself: Animam Deus ex semine patris creat. He means to say that the creative operation does not resemble the *creatio prima ex nihilo*, but is *creatio secunda*

SEC. VII.] TRADUCIANISM AND CREATIONISM. 139

The origination of man is, indeed, on all sides a mystery (Prov. xxx. 19; Eccles. xi. 5). That which in these passages was said by the ancient Israelitish Chokma, must also still be said by the latest physiology. But, without seeking to unveil this mystery, we may, on the ground of Scripture, and of our previous scriptural inquiry, state the following principles: (1.) In the pneumatico-psychical nature of Adam, was at the same time potentially constituted that of all men who were to come into existence; for according to Scripture, without any limitation, the woman is ἐξ ἀνδρὸς, and the whole human race is ἐξ ἑνὸς αἵματος (Acts xvii. 26). (2.) After the distinction was established between the sexes, this potentiality was a divided one; for the bringing into existence of man is thenceforward conditioned by the fact that the man *knows* the woman, and the woman the man (Gen. iv. 1; comp. Num. xxxi. 17, Judg. xi. 39); a biblical mode of expression, which, as also בוא אל, is everywhere used only of human, and never of brute coition; because the former, as distinct from the latter, is a free moral act, not merely performed by the flesh, but moreover by the spiritual-soul. It is a figure in harmony with Scripture, when the ancients say that the tree of humanity, in its entire ramification, as it stood before God in the mirror of wisdom, was originally enclosed in the soul of Adam as a grain of seed, which after the creation of the woman is distributed to man and woman. (3.) Not only in the man, but in the woman also, is the potentiality of the whole man that was to come into existence according to his spiritual-bodily nature.[1] It is in both, according to distinct aspects, for in both is spirit and soul, but in man prevails the spirit effecting life, in the woman the soul

---

ex præjacente termino. Leibnitz says, with reference to the divine concurrence: Ordinaria an extraordinaria operatione Dei non definio. See Göschel, *l.c.* p. 26. Together with other places referring to procreation in v. Lasaulx's *Philosophie der Geschichte* (1857), the expression communicated from the Indian book of law of *Jágnavalkja* is very remarkable: "In the union of man and wife, if blood and seed be pure, the Lord takes the five elements (ether, fire, air, water, earth), and is Himself the sixth."

[1] Among our old theologians, Sal. Gesner says, that the soul of the child is lighted at that of the father, as a light at a light. In the same way, Balth. Meisner excludes the mother, but remembers at last the truer representation, that the souls of the parents, in the act of procreation, act reciprocally, and that the soul of the child is derived from the souls of

representing and developing life.[1] From the fact that the Logos receives from Mary the entire natural condition of a man, proceeds the result that even in the woman, although partially, is the potentiality of the entire man. And from the fact that this potentiality is made actual in Mary by the operation of the Holy Spirit, we appear to be compelled to the conclusion that, in virtue of the divine creative power mediately operating in the act of procreation, the establishment of a new human beginning of life is effected by the man's prevailing spiritual nature, to which corresponds the fructifying male sperma, exerting an influence upon the woman's prevailing psychic nature, to which corresponds the female ovum waiting for fructification; as we in comparing מְרַחֶפֶת, Gen. i. 2, with Luke i. 35,[2] are the better able to assert, because Scripture does not attribute to the woman a sperma of her own; and yet not merely the capacity of conception, but also of the perfecting of the male sperma (Lev. xii. 2), and therefore an accessory participation in the production of the man. We might refer also, for the distribution of the spiritual and psychical portion of the power of procreation, to Gen. vi. 1-4, comp. Jude 6, where the sons of God, who are still רוּחוֹת, engender with the daughters of men; yet we fear that we may be accused of confounding that which is divine, natural, and demoniacal, both, as when a torch is illumined at two others, where it cannot be said that its light comes exclusively from this or from that.

[1] When the Jerusalem Targum, on Gen. ii. 7, says that God created man סומק שחים וחיור (red, black, and white), and a Midrasch (see a collection of small Midraschim brought out by Ad. Jellinek, Pt. i. p. 155), האיש מזריע לבן והאשה מזרעת אדום (the man impregnates white, and the woman red), it coincides with what is said above. For white (the colour of light) is the symbol of the spirit, red (the colour of fire) the symbol of the soul, and black (the colour of earth) the symbol of the body. According to another view, resting on Lev. xii. 2, which must be taken into consideration in Heb. xi. 11, a male fruit is produced when the female seed anticipates the male, and a female when the male seed anticipates the female. This also agrees with the above. The spirit has the impulse to become soul, and the soul has the impulse to become the medium and the representative of the spirit.

[2] This reciprocal relation is doubtless aimed at; and as Basilios (after the example of his friend Ephrem) remarks, in reference to the מרחפת of the genesis of the Kosmos, κατὰ τὴν εἰκόνα τῆς ἐπωαζούσης ὄρνιθος, so not less strikingly (after the example of Theophylact) Maldonatus, on the ἐπισκιάσει of the genesis of the God-man: Sicut solet avis ova sua tegere, ut ejus calore pulli gignantur excludanturque.

especially as of late an emphatic protest has been made again by Keil, Philippi, and Keerl, against the angelological apprehension of what is there narrated (which we, with v. Hofmann, Kurtz, and v. Zezschwitz, maintain). But, on the other hand, it is still an undeniable truth, that divine and spiritual are in many ways the transcendental archetype of created and natural, and that the latter is an anagogic type of the former; as well as that in the demoniacal kingdom (as will be confirmed further on by the examination of many experimental facts of psychology) is manifoldly represented that caricatured counterfeit (which is characteristic of the darker magic) of the divine. (4.) From the fact that conception frequently ensues when the passions of the man and woman are worn out, and does not ensue in spite of all the fervour of love where any bodily hindrance of any kind, often pathologically incapable of recognition, is opposed to it, manifestly results the principle that the event is completed by means of a creatively established and providentially conditioned natural necessity within the department of nature withdrawn from the self-consciousness and freedom, as moreover the act of begetting is truly an absorption of the person into the natural ground of the species, and is always associated with a veiling of the self-consciousness, and a surrender of the freedom to the force of nature. Thus it will probably remain an enigma, how, through the mutual agency of the man and woman, the man in his spiritual aspect comes into being; and the formula borrowed from the propagation of cuttings *per traducem* is not a solution, but only an imperfect resemblance.[1] Better in proportion is what the ancients say: Cum flamma accendit flammam neque tota flamma accendens transit in accensam neque pars ejus in eam descendit: ita anima parentum generat animam filii ut ei nihil decedat. But even this is only a similitude borrowed from the region of that which is natural.

[1] Therefore Quenstedt says: Distinguendum est inter traductionem vel propagationem animæ ipsam et traductionis vel propagationis modum. Propagationem animæ fieri manifestum est, modus vero definitus non est adeoque ab ejus determinatione et definitione abstinemus. Klee, a Catholic adversary of creationism, has coined the name Generationism instead of Traducianism (see v. Berlepsch, *Anthropologiæ Christianæ Dogmata*, 1842, p. 61,—a youthful work of Romish zeal),—a name to which even Frohschammer gives the preference: "*Generare* is not a *traducere*, but a secondary, a created *creare*"

We know inferentially only thus much, that while in the world of angels no spirit can produce another out of itself, the human pneumatico-psychical nature, because it is associated with matter, is planned for the purpose of propagating itself out of itself at the same time with the bodily procreation. But how this happens is a still greater mystery than the bodily process of procreation, which is only as the dim shadow of the more exalted spiritual process; and since the *magnificat* of the first mother, "I have brought forth a man with Jehovah!" every birth is and remains a marvel, only to be explained by the co-operation of God's creative power. Aristotle says man begets man with the co-operation of the sun ($ἄνθρωπος$ $ἄνθρωπον$ $γεννᾷ$ $καὶ$ $ἥλιος$), we say with the co-operation of the Father of spirits.

APPENDIX.

SPIRIT AND SOUL ("GEIST" AND "SEELE")

REFERRED TO THE FUNDAMENTAL IDEA OF THEIR GERMANIC APPELLATIONS.

BY R. VON RAUMER.

THE words "*geist*" and "*seele*" (spirit and soul) are of those whose derivation is not yet satisfactorily ascertained.

In the word *geist*, it does not assist us much to refer to the oldest forms accessible to us. The Gothic does not possess the word, at least so far as our sources reach; rather the Gothic translates the Greek πνεῦμα by *ahma*. The Anglo-Saxon has the word in the form *gâst*; in the old Saxon it appears as *gêst*; and even in the old High German it reaches far back in the forms *geist* and *keist*. On the other hand, again, it is wanting in the old northern, which reproduces the idea of πνεῦμα, *spiritus*, in the word *andi* (masc.). But even this *andi* does not occur in the rhythmical Edda, and seems generally only to be used in prose, and in such poems as bear a distinctly Christian character. All the forms in which the older Germanic languages present the word *geist*, testify (1) that the initial sound is a mute in the Gothic degree of sound *g*; (2) that the vowel of the word (High German *ei*, Anglo-Saxon *â*, old Saxon *ê*) corresponds to the Gothic *ai*. Hence it follows that the derivation of the word *geist* from the old High German *jesan* (*fermentescere*, to ferment) is untenable. Grimm (*Gramm.* ii. 46) traces *geist* back to the root *geisan*, *gais*, *gisun* (*ferire*); but this root itself is only assumed to exist. There remains, therefore, nothing **to** do but to bring together the words of the Germanic languages whose sound accords with *geist*, and whose import points to a connection with this word. In a peculiar manner the two old Germanic languages from which the word *geist* proceeds, actually present some words which probably lead us to the fundamental idea of the word. The old-northern has a trace of a word *geisa*—*cum impetu ferri, cito cursu ferri, ruere*. But the Gothic renders ἐξιστάναι, Mark iii. 21, by *usgaisjan*; Luke ii. 47, and elsewhere, ἐξίστασθαι by *usgeisnan*. We should thus be led to suppose that the idea lying at the root of the word *geist* is that of quick, hasty movement. The old northern substantive *ôðr* (*Völuspâ* 18), spirit, offers an analogy with this ideal affinity in its reference to the adjective *ôðr*, rash, impetuous, fierce, and to its root, *vaða præt.: ôð*, to go along eagerly, with force.

The word *seele* (soul), Gothic *saivala*, seems to be connected with the Gothic *saivs* (late High German, *See*); and the connecting idea appears, in like manner, to be that of movement, although of a gentler kind. The word *seele* occurs in the Gothic (*saivala*), old High German (*sêla*), Anglo-Saxon (*sâvul, sâvl, sâul*), old Saxon (*sêola, siola*). On the other hand, the word does not seem to have appeared in the old-northern until the period of Christianity. In the whole rhythmic Edda, only the distinctly Christian *Sôlarliod* contain it. We have the original psychological mode of expression of the north German in *Völuspâ* 18, where *ôdr* is interchangeable with *geist*, and *önd* with *seele*, without, however, implying thereby that these ideas are hidden there in all their meaning and extent. At all events, it looks as if Christianity had been the first means of representing the *ôðr* of the Edda as *andi*, the *önd* of the Edda as *sâl*. The Icelandic translation of the New Testament (Kaupmannahaufn, 1807) renders πνεῦμα by *ande*, ψυχή by *sâl*. There needs still further investigation to tell us how far, in the other Germanic languages also, the promulgation of the words *geist* and *sêle* might be associated with the introduction of Christianity.

III.
THE FALL.

Τέκνα φύσει ὀργῆς.—EPH. ii. 3.

THE SIN OF THE SPIRIT AND THE SIN OF THE FLESH.

SEC. I.

WE have already seen, in the sixth section of the previous division, what was the reason that the tempter did not appeal to the man, but to the woman. The woman was, briefly to repeat it, only mediately in the form of God; she was comparatively less spiritual than psychical; and just for that reason she was more susceptible of the influences of the *natural* upon her and around her. For this reason the tempter approaches her, not as a pure spiritual nature, but in the form of the crafty serpent, which speaks by the power of demoniacal delusion. By this means the woman allows herself to be enticed into a dialogue. The disguised tempter renders the divine command suspicious to her, as being unlovingly strict, and falsely tells her that want of love was its motive and origin. Thus inwardly led into error respecting God, the woman surrenders herself, with her sight and imagination, to the forbidden tree; and this appears to her so delicious to the taste, so attractive to the sight, so enticing to a closer contemplation, that she takes of the fruit of it, and eats. In thus surrendering herself up to the tree, her soul is already stained, and sin is received into it. The eating is only the external performance of the deed which had already been internally committed. As soon as the woman had succumbed to the serpent, she became the serpent to her husband. The tempted one became, in her turn, a tempter; and Adam abides not in himself and in God; but in sight of the enticing fruit in the hand of the beloved one, every thought of God's love, and of the death which He had threatened, vanishes from his mind. And thus he incurs an equal sin.

The essential condition of man subsisted in three concentric circles. The innermost was his spirit; the inner, his soul; and the external, his body. With his spirit, man lived and moved in the love of God. The body stood, by means of the soul, under the potential influence of this light of love, and was thence expecting its glorification. By sin all this has now become reversed. It began by the spirit becoming dislocated from the divine love, its true life-centre. For the temptation proceeded from the suspicion of God's love, and thence advanced to the absolute denial of that love. Let this be well considered. Sin did not begin by the discovery of the woman that the forbidden tree was so irresistibly enticing; but by the infused suspicion of the loving reason of the prohibition, and generally of God's love. The sin was not the result of the darkening of the consciousness of God's prohibition to the woman, by means of the sensual charm of the tree; but it was the result of her giving admission to the serpent's insinuations that envy and jealousy were the grounds of the prohibition. The point of departure of the original sin was therefore in the spirit.

Nevertheless, there is a vast difference between this and the sin by which Satan became Satan. Scripture, indeed, tells us nothing directly of what the fall of this lofty spirit consisted in; but when it speaks of him, we always see in him (although he is compelled to serve God) the enemy of God as such, and of godly-minded people as such. He behaves as if he were God (Matt. iv. 8); and in some measure, moreover, he is a god, ὁ θεὸς τοῦ αἰῶνος τούτου (2 Cor. iv. 4). His sin was, therefore, what it still is—revolt against God: striving to surpass the glory which was conferred on him by creation, he wished to rule in divine pre-eminence. We have to conceive of his sin and his overthrow, with the Fathers, according to scriptural statements, such as Isa. xiv. 12-15. Arrogantly reflecting himself in his glory, he did not continue in submission to God's light and love; but, desirous of exalting himself above measure, he incurred the divinely ordained punishment of such frantic selfishness.

The primal sin of man had this in common with the primal sin of Satan, that, like it, it was a forsaking of God's love, wherein every creature has its good original position, a continual advancement in which is its true development. For God is ἀγάπη, and because ἀγάπη, He is φῶς (1 John i. 5); and loving God, and loving what God loves, the creature, self-conscious and free, abides and moves ἐν τῷ φωτί (1 John i. 7, ii. 10), and its life is a progressive μεταμορφοῦσθαι ἀπὸ δόξης εἰς δόξαν (2 Cor. iii. 18). All sin is transgression of the limits imposed by this love (παράβασις), and attendant degradation and decline from the sphere of this love (παράπτωμα): it is ἀνομία, for every law of God is an appointment of His love, as even the Thora was a gift of love to Israel (Deut. xxxiii. 3), and לְאַהֲבָה אֶת־ה׳ is its first and last claim. Departure from God's love is the common nature of all sin; and when the departure from this love was associated with a desire to progress in the direction of a selfishly appointed end, rather than of the end divinely appointed, this was the common nature of the primal sin of the spirit-world and of humanity.

But the distinction is, that (1) Satan was the originator (πατήρ) of sin, while men succumbed to the power of sin already intruded into the good creation of God; that (2) Satan revolted against God of himself alone, but men were withdrawn from the love of God by being ensnared from without; and (3) that, in the immediateness in which Satan, as purely a spirit, stood opposed to God, his sin was a direct, perfectly conscious rebellion; whereas the sin of men, as spiritual-embodied beings, was accomplished in that being misled in respect of God's love, without absolutely conscious denial of it, they received the decisive impulse of the forbidden object through the power of sensual attraction. By the first distinctive characteristic, the sin of the first-created man is distinguished from the sin of Satan, but not from that of the angels who fell with and after Satan. By the second and third, however, man's sin is also distinguished from that of these latter. For the angels that fell with Satan decided also absolutely of themselves—they fell by imitation, not by seduction; and the sons of God of which Gen. vi. speaks, did not fall as men did, in consequence of a possibility of becoming fleshly, established in the reciprocal relation of their nature to that which was natural outside them, but by an unnatural violation of the divinely appointed limit below, as Satan and his angels fell by an unnatural violation of the divinely established limit above.

To shorten the matter: the distinction is this, that the primal sin of Satan was a direct, purely spiritual revolt against

God; the primal sin of man was indirect revolt corporeally effected against God—brought about by means of a masked power of deceit coming from without (Gen. iii. 13, הִשִּׁיאַנִי, comp. ἐξηπάτησεν, 2 Cor. xi. 3, 1 Tim. ii. 14), and by the superadded material and sensual attraction of the forbidden tree.[1] Not as though there were an evil principle in matter in itself: the material world of the six days' work is good; but considered apart from God, it becomes actually, by means of its goodness, an evil enticement.

The world was good, and man was good; the world crowned by the creation of man was very good. But it was brought forth from chaos to this very good position; and even the very good position of man rested upon the chaotic foundation which was made the substratum of his life. The potentialities of this foundation, which of themselves alone were possibilities of wrath and of death, were made serviceable to life by the spirit of life; and this life was linked in the personal man, on behalf of the whole earthly world, to God the living one; and in fellowship with Him, it was to be maintained and to be progressively established. But as man fell away from his life which had its being in God's love, the natural ground of his life became the abyss of death.

After having psychologically discussed the nature of the primal sin of man, in distinction from that of demoniacal beings, we proceed, in a similar psychological point of view, to consider its consequences.

[1] Satan, says my Elberfeld critic, wished in his arrogance to surpass God; man failed in love to God by means of love to the vain world, and therefore by endeavours after that which was sordid.

THE ETHICO-PHYSICAL DISTURBANCE.

SEC. II.

CERTAIN and inevitable death (Gen. ii. 17, iii. 3) was the penalty threatened upon transgression; death, in the sense of a return to dust. If men do not become dust immediately after indulgence, it is to be gathered therefrom that the threatening of punishment did not imply this. Meanwhile, as by the creation of the woman the possibility of a ground of mitigation of the guilt had been created, so also had been the possibility of a fulfilment of the threatening, without breaking off the course of human history. But that man, as an individual, from the same day incurred the punitive decree of death, is shown (iii. 19); and that by the sin of one, as the sin of all, death became an inevitable power for all men, is proved by Rom. v. 12.

Death as a return to dust, and therefore a dissolution of the body, is only the sensuous external side of the penalty of sin established in the natural constitution of evil. Evil is a product of the will, that wills itself out of God and against God. The body that belongs to the nature of man, and to the unity of his personality, would not be liable to death if there had not preceded it, in the spirit and in the soul of man, a change which tended to the death of the body.[1]

The spirit which was breathed into man was, indeed, the condition of life to his body. But life, light, and love, are throughout the whole Scripture, ideas that are interwoven one in the other. Departed from the love of God, the spirit had thus become incapable of being the principle of life and of glorification for the body. Instead of the life that aspired to glorification, had appeared a life that was sinking back downwards to corruption.

---

[1] Pruys van der Hoeven (Prof. der Medicin zu Leiden) says, in accordance with this, in his *Studie der Christelijke Anthropologie* (ed. 3, 1856): "That man, conscious to himself of his own independence as a person, who can rule over himself in his life, should die, is an enigma that can only be solved by the fact of the degeneration of his nature" (*door de ontaarding zijner natuur*).

But the spirit itself cannot possibly die in the manner in which perishes the bodily form of dust. Such a death is contrary to its nature, and contrary to its origin. It cannot be dissolved into its elements, for it is not composed of elements. Moreover, it cannot be annihilated, for it is of immediate divine origin. It might indeed be conceived, that, without substantially annihilating it, God should place it back into the condition of non-self-subsistence and of unconsciousness; but that God does not do this, is seen in the condition of the evil angels, whom He did not annihilate, although they are incapable of redemption. Thus, when Scripture appears to declare a resorption of the spirit into God's nature (as Ps. civ. 29, Job xxxiv. 14), nothing else is meant than that the impersonal spirit of the brute, whose individuality is constituted by the spirit (Eccles. iii. 21), is taken back into the general spirit of nature; but the personal spirit of man returns to God who gave it (Eccles. xii. 7), and, indeed, to God the Judge (ver. 14); and therefore probably still without any loss of consciousness. And that Scripture, in saying even of the soul מוּת, and even calling the dead body נֶפֶשׁ, is not proceeding on the notion of the dissolubility and corruptibility of the soul, we shall see subsequently: for the present it is sufficient to refer to the Old Testament representation of Hades, which quite plainly supposes a perpetuation of souls. According to Scripture, the soul is as little mortal, in the way of dissolution or annihilation, as the spirit whence it proceeded.

But Scripture knows of a spiritual death (1 John iii. 14; Matt. viii. 22; Luke xv. 24; Eph. ii. 1, 5, v. 14; Apoc. iii. 1), and of a second death (Apoc. ii. 11, xx. 6, 14, xxi. 8); thus, of a kind of death which, without being annihilation, may yet concern both spirit and soul. The second death is the condition of punishment in hell, that lies on the further side of the first death; but spiritual death is the natural condition of punishment in this life, wherein every man apart from grace finds himself, and it is thus a consequence of the primal sin. If it be said that this spiritual death is the alienation of the inner man from God the living, this declares less wherein it consists, than whence it proceeds. It must consist in a dissolution similar to bodily death, and in a disappearance of the previous life similar to bodily death. And this is just the case. In con-

THE ETHICO-PHYSICAL DISTURBANCE.

sequence of the first sin, the internal nature of man became possessed by death, by the dissolution of the previous unity of the manifold powers reciprocally acting in the life of the spirit and of the soul; and by the disappearance of the spiritual life in God's image, and its reflection in the soul. Hitherto God's love filled the spirit's will, thought, and feeling: this threefold divinely filled life of the Spirit was the holy image of the Godhead in man. But when satanic thoughts of a loveless God found entrance into man's mind, then entered enmity ($\xi\chi\theta\rho\alpha$, Rom. viii. 7) into the place of love, and Turba[1] into the place of peace: the powers of the soul, at peace in God, fell into confusion, and kindled in passionate eagerness opposed to God. The spirit had fallen away from the love of God, and the soul from the dominion of the spirit. This is the background of *morte morieris*, and since its fulfilment we must all chime in, in the song of lamentation: *Quaternis elementis componimur et quaternis corrumpimur.* Our life is since only a shadow of life, and from the ground of nature whence it has risen extend many arms,[2] which finally draw down the fleeting shadow into the darkness of death.

As, however, there is a great distinction between the primal sin of Satan and that of man, so also is there between the

---

[1] As science is entitled to bring biblical representations to terminologic expression, we shall further on sometimes call this disharmony of the powers previously united in God, by an expression borrowed from theosophy—the "*Turba*," a word of the same meaning as ἀκαταστασία, or, as Luther and Melancthon say, ἀταξία, *confusio partium*. It is the opposite of εἰρήνη (1 Cor. xiv. 33) and δικαιοσύνη (which, moreover, in Plato, especially in the *Republic*, indicates the perfect relation of the fundamental elements of the natural condition of man, which corresponds to his idea), of ἑνότης, as unity of the differing, and ἁρμονία (by which Pythagoras characterized the essence of health, and every good, and God Himself), as the Hebrew שָׁאוֹן (שְׁאִיָּה) means a confused savage noise, and in opposition to harmony, euphony, and a condition of union,—devastation, and destruction. The "*Turba*," as the abolition of that which the *Apology for the Augsburg Confession* calls *æquale temperamentum qualitatum corporis*, is the antecedent of φθορά; and the position was maintained by Flacius, that, since the fall, the Turba, or *animæ partium horrenda perturbatio*, is the *forma substantialis* of man (v. Preger Flacius, ii. 409).

[2] Comp. Keerl, *Schöpfungsgeschichte*, p. 420. The human organism could never more be subject to death, if the latent causes of this corruption were not hidden in it.

results of both. In men, by the first sin, was laid the foundation of all sins; in Satan, however, and his angels, the first sin was, as it were, the summit of all sins. The opposition to God into which Satan emerged was an absolute opposition. After he had inflamed his being in sin, and had fallen like lightning from heaven (Luke x. 18), he hardened himself in the darkness of his extinguished glory; and ἐξουσία τοῦ Σατανά and ὁ Θεὸς are now the contrasts symbolized by τὸ σκότος and τὸ φῶς (Acts xxvi. 15). The primal sin of man, however, had not that insuperable intensity of self-induration. Through their fall, men had fallen into the power of Satan, without being able by their own help to deliver themselves thence; but they were not froward in their position, changed as it was by sin; but they were ashamed of it, and afraid.

SHAME AND FEAR.

Sec. III.

THAT men, after they had fallen, were ashamed of their nakedness, and on account of their nakedness were afraid in the presence of God,—these are certainly indications that they had not become absolutely satanic; but Scripture relates them to us as the evil consequences of their fall.

In the position of innocence they were not ashamed of their nakedness. They were naked, but yet they were not so. Their bodies were the clothing of their internal glory, and their internal glory was the clothing of their nakedness.[1] Their bodies were not yet spiritual, but they were of the Spirit; not yet pervaded, but illumined by its light; not yet glorified, but

---

[1] It is this which Ph. Nicolai (see *die Mittheilungen Rocholls*, in *Luth. Zeitschrift*, 1860, p. 201) simply describes when he says: Men before the fall were invested and clothed, and as it were shadowed, with an external glitter and shining, as is the moon, instead of clothes. Comp. my *Commentary on Genesis*, ed. 3, p. 163.

surrounded by the power of glorification.[1] The earthly, animal element of their bodies retreated, as if vanishing away, towards the super-terrene, God-resembling element of the spirit, which by means of the soul controlled them.

But when the divine efficiency of the central spirit upon the soul, and outwardly from this upon the body, yielded to the satanic influence proceeding from the surrounding body upon the soul, and from this upon the spirit, and the spirit had fallen away from the love of God, and thus from the truth of its nature, the likeness of God in the spirit, and in consequence thereof the likeness of the spirit in the soul, and in consequence thereof the corporeity conformed to both for glorification, became a distortion. The bodies of men had now forfeited the glory which proceeded from the spirit and the soul upon them, which had hitherto clothed them. Thus the Scripture says, that after the transgression the eyes of both were opened, and they knew that they were naked. The longer these words are pondered, the harder, but also the more weighty and important, they will be found. It cannot be said from these words that they now for the first time became aware of their nakedness; such blindness contradicts the assumed self-knowledge of the first created men. The meaning of the words is, that as well in respect of their nakedness in itself, as of their subjective relation to it, a great change occurred in the instant of their fall. In respect of their nakedness in itself: for the nakedness, although it was not of another nature, was still an essentially different thing. Hitherto subjected to the influence of the spirit in God's image, it was now displaced and distorted: it had become a nakedness itself, and thus, because deprived of spirit, it had become, from a material thing, a coarse materialistic thing; from a σαρκίνη, it had become a σαρκική. In respect of men's subjective relation to their nakedness: for the sight of sense had till now been in the service of the spirit,

---

[1] Jo. Scotus Erigena, when he says, *de div. nat.* iv. 12, "Illud corpus, quod in constitutione hominis primitus est factum, spirituale et immortale crediderim esse ac tale aut ipsum, quale post resurrectionem habituri sumus," goes, like the later theosophy, too far. The resurrection body is the perfect completion of the beginning constituted in the original body, and our present fleshly body is the reversed operation of the advancement for which the beginning was designed.

which in God ruled over itself and the outer world; but now, when the spirit had become the slave of sense, and that which was natural had escaped from its authority, the sight of sense for the first time began its special existence, insomuch as it had now become its own, and the spirit was slavishly surrendered to the impressions which it transmitted. In other words, sensible sight had until then been a sight effected by sense ἐν πνεύματι; now it had become a sight absolutely sensual—immersed in itself, hurrying away the spirit with itself, and reflecting upon it its own ruin. And now, when, with the eyes of their sense opened, men perceived their degraded corporeity, and in this as in a mirror the degradation of their spirit and their soul, they felt for the first time the experience hitherto unknown to them of הִתְבּשֵׁשׁ. When anything that degrades us in the judgment of others, not without our own guilt, becomes public, or when we are apprehensive that it may become public, we are ashamed.[1] The first result is, that we recoil before that which brings or may bring us shame (Ps. xxxv. 4, cxxix. 5, etc.); the second, that the retreating blood accumulates upon the heart, and causes it to fall into violent and stormy contractions, the result of which is, that the blood streams forth to all those parts which by their demeanour can betray our sense of guilt, especially to the countenance and its immediate vicinity (comp. *e.g.* Ps. xliv. 16). Thence arises the blush of shame, חָפֵר (from the root פר, doubled in πορφύρεος, *purpureus*); and if the blood, when terror rises high on account of the impossibility of concealment, recedes, the paleness of shame, בּוֹשׁ (akin to בּוּץ, comp. Aram. בְּעַץ, עֲבַץ, אֲבַץ, tin, and עֲבַץ as a verb, Ps. xxxiv. 5, Targ. to be ashamed). That חָפֵר and בּוֹשׁ originally indicate these several colours of shame, is plainly seen from Isa. xxiv. 23, comp. xxix. 22. Moreover, these hues are only the most external manifestation of the events that transpire within the pneumatico-psychical-somatic nature. Scripture does not analyze for us the shame of fallen men; but when it tells us that they sewed fig-leaves together, and made themselves aprons, it gives us in a few words the profoundest disclosure on the way in which shame came into existence. It is the region below the hip that is veiled by men: complete nudity, without covering this region of the body, is confessedly regarded even among

[1] F. W. Hagen, *Psychologische Untersuchungen*, p. 41, etc.

savage nations as disgrace. And this has as its reason—that there are situated the outlets of excretion for the food that has been used, but especially that there are placed the organs of propagation, which in biblical language, and generally in the common speech of men, are called shameful parts (*pudenda*). These are directly called עֶרְוָה (*e.g.* Gen. ix. 22) and בָּשָׂר (*e.g.* Lev. xv. 2, comp. Ex. xxviii. 42), because nakedness and flesh, which men are required by shame to hide, culminate in them. Even without supposing that a physical change passed upon these parts by reason of the fall, yet it is plain wherefore the bodily results of the fall must just in this place be most evident. After man had been distinguished into man and woman, he resembled (in respect of propagation, and looking to the physiologic-anatomical externality of its apparatus and accomplishment) the brutes. But in reference to its pneumatico-psychical background, and to the ethical character stamped upon it beforehand by the spontaneous power and sanctity of the spirit, he was in this respect also elevated above the brute. But when men succumbed to a temptation of Satan effected by means of a brute, and the power of glorification had been changed into the efficiency of a materiality become absolutely selfish, the contrast between the former time and now, forced itself nowhere so sadly upon the perception as in the members of propagation, where converged all the rays of the naked naturalness, now divested of the glory of the spirit, as in their source. The opposition, now without unity, of the spiritual and natural, was here at the coarsest, and the likeness to the brutes of the human corporeity appeared here as the most brutal: therefore men were ashamed, and covered themselves, in order to hide from themselves, and from every beholding eye, the sight of their honour converted into shame.

A second feeling which seized the fallen ones was fear. That they were ashamed, was an advantage which they possessed over Satan; but that they were afraid, was common to them with him. We mean the conscious fear before God with which they were possessed, when they were aware of the sound of Jehovah-Elohim, as He walked in the garden in the cool of the evening, and they hid themselves in the midst of the trees of the garden (iii. 8-10). Fear in the presence of God, as distinct from the fear of God—and comprehending in itself the manifold gradations of apprehension and anxiety, terror and anguish, fright and dismay—is the consequence of the sense of the wrath of God, which is inseparable from the feeling of guilt and shame. But the wrath of God, as Scripture teaches us to recognise it, is (1) self-excitement of His holy personality in the presence of sin; (2) excitement of the lower strict potentialities of His glorious splendour, or, as we may also say, of His nature, in itself wrought out into cloudless light; (3) sending forth powers of destruction operative in the world from the judicially aroused *doxa;* (4) kindling of the lower natural potencies of the created personality itself, that has become opposed to God. In other words: The wrath of God has a personal aspect, and a natural aspect: it is a purpose of wrath, the correlative of *Echthra* on the side of the creature; and fire of wrath, the correlative of the *Turba* on the side of the creature (Div. IV. Sec. VI.). God is angry, in that His personal holiness repels sin, and in that He stirs up the flaming aspect of His glory. Wrath, as such a stirring up, is called אַף, זַעַם, זַעַף, רֹגֶז, ὀργή (θυμὸς, Apoc. xix. 15, from θύειν, synon. of ζέειν, to seethe); and as such a setting on fire, it is called חָרוֹן or חֵמָה. And man is afraid, in that feeling, consciousness, experience, of this divine excitement places him in fear and quaking; for the characteristic behaviour of this fear, to the fundamental idea of which almost all appellations revert (עָרַץ, פָּחַד, יָרֵא=יָרֵע, פְּלָצוּת, etc.), is trembling. This trembling, in its highest degree, resembles the convulsion that follows electrical shocks, to wit, as the Scripture says, the lightning of God's wrath (Ps. xviii. 15, cxliv. 6). Fear in this sense, and love, exclude one another. Φόβος οὐκ ἔστιν ἐν τῇ ἀγάπῃ, 1 John iv. 18.

That men were ashamed, was the essential consequence of the fact that their glory, that clothing of honour of their body, had been perverted into the shame of nakedness (Apoc. iii. 18); and that they were afraid, was the essential consequence of the fact that they had retrograded from God's love, and had therefore incurred God's wrath. Doubtless it was better that they should have been so ashamed and afraid, than that they should not have been ashamed and afraid. It is true this shame and fear were not anything positively good—they were only the arbitrary reflection of lost good; but in this, that men allowed themselves to be mastered by these feelings, without crushing them by forcible resistance, is shown that their fall, deep though it was, yet did not approach in depth to that of Satan. They had sinned against their conscience; but after they had sinned, they did not put to death their conscience, which testified against them. For as well shame as fear operated by means of the conscience; by men now perceiving themselves out of God, not without a knowledge of what they ought to be, and what they had been, in God.

CONSCIENCE, AND REMOTENESS FROM GOD.

Sec. IV.

The systematic treatment of a scientific matter has the great advantage, that isolated thoughts, which had previously been entertained upon questions associated therewith, as they must be brought within a closer and more many-sided connection, have to undergo an examination which, for the most part, leads to their adjustment, their definition, or their completion; and the historical method which we have chosen benefits us besides, by relieving us of the associated prejudices derived from deceptive self-observation, and teaching us to recognise their true nature in the first beginnings of psychologic facts, with at least far less risk of delusion. Thus it is with the questions, What is the conscience? and of what kind was the intercourse of God with the first man, before and after the fall? On both questions not a few fallacious views are prevalent, which, because they are not absolutely without truth, are liable to corrupt the truth, and to be transmitted in almost traditional formulas. It will be manifest how false they are, when we compare them with the judgments that we have previously come to, and with the inexhaustibly instructive records of primitive history contained in the first pages of the Bible.

Nothing is more commonly read, than that conscience is a voice of God within us. Surely, literally and logically regarded, this is wrong. For conscience (*conscience*, from *con* = *cum*, συν) is closely related to the Greek συνείδησις (*conscientia*), and is thus a subjective idea, and indeed a purely subjective and not a correlative idea, as v. Schubert defines it in his *History of the Soul*, after v. Baader's example: " Privity of the soul with the omnipresent, omniscient God." The συν is not that of fellowship or intercommunion, but συνείδησις imports (keeping in view the distinction between the *I* as knowing and the knowledge, *vid.* 1 Cor. iv. 4) the knowledge dwelling in the person of man; and indeed, as an ethical conception, the knowledge proceeding from man's consciousness of God, *i.e.* from his inalienable knowledge about his conditional nature arising through God, as it were inalienable knowledge about his moral reciprocal relation to God—briefly, his moral-religious consciousness. It must therefore be said, conscience is the moral-religious consciousness, adapted to man by virtue of an inner self-attestation of God. But, moreover, this is not true, if it is meant thereby that there are continually repeated self-evidences of God, of which conscience is the echo, and of which man stands in need in order to have a conscience at all. Scripture nowhere speaks thus of the conscience. It speaks of it everywhere as of something belonging to the most special nature of man. The Old Testament, in which this conception is not yet distinctly defined—since מַדָּע, Eccles. x. 20 (LXX. ἐν συνειδήσει σου), indicates only the quiet inward consciousness—expresses it as לב (לבב).[1] Conscience appears there as a knowledge of the heart (1 Kings ii. 44); the rebuke and punishment of conscience, which man experiences as חָרַף and הִכָּה of his heart (Job xxvii. 6, comp. LXX.; 1 Sam. xxiv. 6; 2 Sam. xxiv. 10); reproaches of conscience, or shocks of conscience (προσκόμματα, comp. Acts xxiv. 16), as מִכְשׁוֹל לֵב, 1 Sam. xxv. 31. The New Testament Scripture also ascribes to the heart the functions of conscience (Rom. ii. 15; Heb. x. 22; 1 John iii. 19); but it has at the same time attained in συνείδησις a clear conception and expression for the fact of the testimony of conscience; and has assigned to it, under this name, its distinctive place henceforth in the spiritual nature of man.[2] If we ask about the nature of the conscience, it is

---

[1] Luther translates, accordingly, Josh. xiv. 7, Job xxvii. 6, *conscience*, but elsewhere *heart*.

[2] See von Zezschwitz, *Profangräcität und biblischer Sprachgeist*, pp. 52-57. The whole of Grecian antiquity knows the fact of the testimony of

everywhere found that it is not God who gives witness to the conscience, but the conscience that gives witness to man (2 Cor. i. 12): συμμαρτυρεῖν is not said of the conscience, in the sense that it bears witness with God who witnesseth, but in the sense that it testifies with, or in man, Rom. ii. 15, ix. 1 (comp. συμμαρτυρεῖν in a similar sense, of an inwardly given and indwelling attestation, Rom. viii. 16). Accordingly, also in 1 Pet. ii. 19 (comp. Rom. xiii. 5), συνείδησις Θεοῦ is not the consciousness having the conscience as God dwelling in it, and testifying, but as consciousness of God, to wit, of His will and pleasure. The view is not well established in Scripture, that the conscience is the reflex of an immediate self-evidencing of God in man, still less that it is this self-evidencing itself. Moreover, supposing that man had dwelling in him, from creation downwards, God's Spirit as the foundation and support of his life,—a view to which we must on the surface deny the conformity to Scripture that it claims on the strength of a few texts that may easily be differently understood,—conscience would still not require to be defined as the self-attestation of this spirit.[1]

If we look into primitive history, the erroneousness of this view is confirmed. When, in the presence of the serpent, the woman shows herself aware of the rigid divine prohibition, and expresses herself accordingly, that which she so utters is the testimony of her conscience. And when she and Adam, never-

conscience, says the author, but its wavering expression betrayed the deficient apprehension of its nature. And " even the Old Testament was no favourable ground on which to build up this conception. The positive law took its significance from the natural moral consciousness." We observe thereupon, that the Grecian antiquity nevertheless very much anticipated the Israelitish, in the impression of the idea of conscience. For Periander is said to have replied to the question, τί ἐστιν ἐλευθηρία, by the words ἀγαθὴ συνείδησις. It is plain here, moreover, that Christianity has melted together the Old Testament truth with the elements of Hellenic truth; and it is consistent with this, that (except in the section of the woman taken in adultery, John viii. 9) συνείδησις does not occur in the Gospels.

[1] It must at least be said, as Thomasius, i. 167: There occurs a constant inner living intercourse of God with man, and the RESULT of this communion is that which we call conscience. For assuredly the conscience is an impulse of the human spirit, but this impulse is ESTABLISHED by the Divine Spirit testifying itself in it.

theless, transgress the divine prohibition, it is the result of their having declined from God's love to sensual lust, and having crushed the warning witness of their conscience. But when the sin is committed, and is manifest to them in its consequences, the restrained conscience breaks forth again. Looking upon their nakedness, they are seized with shame; and perceiving God's nearness, they are seized with fear. The two things would not have been possible, if their conscience had not reminded them of the divine prohibition, and represented to them the guilt of its transgression. Let it now be considered that an immediate self-attestation of God to Adam preceded the transaction between the serpent and the woman, *scil.* the prohibition of the tree of knowledge; and an immediate self-attestation of God follows it, *scil.* the conviction and the sentence; and the narrative could not give us more plainly to understand that the conscience is not itself even the reflex of an inward immediate self-evidencing of God, to say nothing of its being itself such a self-evidence.[1]

The apostle tells us, however, in Rom. ii. 15, precisely that the conscience, in regard of the objective factor of its nature, is not the echo of an immediate divine self-evidence at every moment, but

---

[1] Nevertheless v. Hofmann says (*Schriftbeweis*, i. 572): "Both shame and fear were announcements of the conscience. But the conscience is, according to its nature, not a something in man, nor an effect produced in him, that he could ascribe it to himself, but an immediate self-evidencing of God in him, to perceive which, is neither a sign of a right relation to God, nor serves to restore such a relation." Then further on it is said, p. 573: "Men, become sinful, in those experiences of shame and fear neither recognised announcements of conscience, nor consequences of their sin; but there was needed an expressive word of God before they acknowledged in themselves and confessed to themselves that they, only in consequence of their sin, were ashamed before one another, and afraid before God." Marvellous! The conscience is no knowledge, but only an *actus directus* of divine self-attestation to men which causes shame and fear, but—no knowledge. For this definition of conscience there is no reference to a scriptural word, as it upsets the subjective idea; but to v. Harless' *Ethik*, p. 59, where we read, "Conscience to me is generally so far identical with the human spirit, as it is not spirit in the spirit, not the divine in the created, and generally not anything." What then? "It is actual reciprocal relation of God with the human spirit, and the reverse. It is, according to its nature, an ever operative assurance of God to our spirit, and the like." We cannot appreciate all this, and we must hold every definition of the idea *à priori* as a failure, which does not start from the fact that conscience—συνείδησις, as the *rationale* of the word implies—is a species of knowledge.

the knowledge of a divine law which every man—even he who does not know the positive revelation of the law—bears in his heart. The final destiny of a man (this is the connection of the thoughts) is decided not according to the possession of the law as such, but according to his moral conduct (ver. 12); "for not the hearers of the law are just before God, but the doers of the law shall be justified" (ver. 13). The heathen furnish the proof for this, for they indeed have no law that they could hear (therefore no law historically revealed); but if the heathen, who are still without law, do by nature works that the law prescribes to them, they are, in spite of their being without law, a law unto themselves, and prove thereby that a godly conversation is possible even without the possession of a law, to wit, of a positive law. They are, moreover, not absolutely without law; but, doing by nature ($\phi\acute{v}\sigma\epsilon\iota$) what the revealed law claims, they bear actual witness to the fact that a knowledge of what is right before God is established in the $\phi\acute{v}\sigma\iota\varsigma$, *i.e.* in the creatively ordained constitution of man: they have, as they prove by such conduct according to law as is possible to them, $\tau\grave{o}$ $\H{\epsilon}\rho\gamma o\nu$ $\tau o\hat{v}$ $\nu\acute{o}\mu ov$ $\gamma\rho\alpha\pi\tau\grave{o}\nu$ $\acute{\epsilon}\nu$ $\tau\alpha\hat{\iota}\varsigma$ $\kappa\alpha\rho\delta\acute{\iota}\alpha\iota\varsigma$ $\alpha\grave{v}\tau\hat{\omega}\nu$; *i.e.* the conduct by which God's law is performed, of whatever kind this conduct is, stands as an objective pattern, written with ineradicable traces in their heart, as it stands for Israel on the stone tables and the document of the Thora; wherefore in Isa. xxiv. 5 it may justly be said of all the dwellers in the earth, in relation to the final judgment, " They have transgressed (God's) laws, changed the ordinance" (LXX. $\pi\alpha\rho\acute{\eta}\lambda\theta o\sigma\alpha\nu$ $\tau\grave{o}\nu$ $\nu\acute{o}\mu o\nu$ $\kappa\alpha\grave{\iota}$ $\H{\eta}\lambda\lambda\alpha\xi\alpha\nu$ $\tau\grave{a}$ $\pi\rho o\sigma$-$\tau\acute{a}\gamma\mu\alpha\tau\alpha$). When the apostle adds, $\sigma v\mu\mu\alpha\rho\tau v\rho o\acute{v}\sigma\eta\varsigma$ $\alpha\grave{v}\tau\hat{\omega}\nu$ $\tau\hat{\eta}\varsigma$ $\sigma vv\epsilon\iota\delta\acute{\eta}\sigma\epsilon\omega\varsigma$, he places conscience in a relation to that inner law, which resembles that of prophecy to the Thora. As prophecy (which has been strikingly called the conscience of the Israelitish state) testifies to the Thora, and places the circumstances and conduct of Israel from time to time in the light of the Thora,—thus conscience gives witness to that inner law in man in his own sight ($\sigma v\mu\mu\alpha\rho\tau v\rho\epsilon\hat{\iota}$), impels and directs man to act according to that law (the so-called precedent conscience), judges his doings according to this law, and reflects his actions and his circumstances in the light of this law (the subsequent conscience): not as though the conscience were a special spiritual activity associated with the will, the thought (judgment), and feeling; but it is the effectual power in the spiritual forms of activity concerned in those internal experiences.[1] From the side of this critically judging or condemning activity, the conscience is conceived of in reference to one's own doing (Heb. x. 2), and in reference to the doings of others (1 Cor. x. 29; 2 Cor. iv. 2, v. 11). The conscience, therefore, is the natural consciousness to man, as such, of the law in his heart; the religious-moral determination of his self-consciousness dwelling in the human spirit, and effectuating itself even against the will in all the forms of life of man; the ethical side of the general sense of truth (*sensus communis*), which remained in man even after his fall; the knowledge concerning what God will and will not have,[2] manifesting itself progressively in the form of impulse, and judgment, and feeling. Inasmuch, then, as the conscience gives witness to the inward law, there appear in some degree before a man, and there arise in him—whether it be that he reflects on his own individual conduct, or upon his entire condition—thoughts called forth by the testimony of conscience, on the one side accusing, on the other side excusing, which

---

[1] In substance thus Güder, *Die Lehre vom Gewissen*, in *Stud. u. Kritiken*, 1857, pp. 265–270; and Schenkel, art. "Gewissen," in Herzog's *Real-Encyklopädie*, v. 138. But while the former teaches that conscience is an activity which is effected by a co-operation of the various capacities of the spirit, *scil.* the form of manifestation of the consciousness of God immanent in the consciousness of self, practically certifying itself to the self-activity; the latter teaches that in its nature it is no activity, but a determination of the self-consciousness, which, however, as such, regulates the activities of the spirit in which the self-consciousness expresses itself, *scil.* the thinking, feeling, and willing. The two views, as is frequently the case, contradict one another only logically, not substantially. Conscience, according to its nature, is no activity, but a determination, although an effective one; and according to its expression it is an activity, but no contingent one: for, as Güder says, to the consciousness of God is appropriated the practical tendency to bring on the conditionality of the free personality corresponding to him; and what is conscience other than, in all forms of spiritual life, this self-effectuating knowledge of man about God, as the morally determining absolute will?

[2] The scholastics distinguish *synteresis* or *synderesis* (συντήρησις) as the habitual knowledge of the divine will in general, which is considered as the *scintilla spiritus* remaining in man, and *conscientia* as the actual synderesis, *i.e.* as the operation of conscience administering that general knowledge normally or judicially. The *synteresis* seems to them in the *syllogismus conscientiæ*, as *propositio major*; comp. Schenkel, *l.c.* p. 135.

occur as in a law-suit, in controversy with one another (μεταξὺ ἀλλήλων). With this law written on his heart, with this continuous attestation of it by conscience, with these thoughts of self-accusation, or moreover of self-justification, called forth by the testimony of conscience,—the heathen, as says the apostle to the heathens, comes to stand eventually before the judgment of God, which He executes by Jesus Christ, the Saviour not only of man, but of humanity.[1]

Conscience, therefore, is not an echo or abode of an immediate divine self-attestation, but an active consciousness of a divine law established in man's heart; for all self-consciousness of created natures capable of self-consciousness, is naturally at once a consciousness of their dependence on God, and a consciousness of their duty to allow themselves to be determined by the will of God, and consciousness of the general purport of that will. That which is said by ancients and moderns of the conscience as God's voice in us, has in it this truth, that the testimony of conscience certainly rests on a divine foundation woven in our natural condition, *scil.* on a divine law in man, ordained with his created constitution, the existence of which, its claims and judgments, are removed from his subjective control. If a man know his doing to be in harmony with this law, his conscience is ἀγαθή (Acts xxiii. 1; 1 Pet. iii. 16, 21; 1 Tim. i. 5, 19), καλή (Heb. xiii. 18), καθαρά (1 Tim. iii. 9; 2 Tim. i. 3), ἀπρόσκοπος (Acts xxiv. 16). If his doing be evil, so also is his conscience, inasmuch as it is consciousness

---

[1] "If a heathen,"—thus v. Hofmann fills up the meaning of v. 14 in the *Zeitschr. f. Protest.* 1860, p. 69,—" if a heathen do what is claimed by the revealed law, he is in nowise ashamed before God that he has not the law: he is to himself what the Jew has in his law, in that he, by his doing, proves that its contents is the desire of his heart testified by conscience, and accompanied by the interchange of thoughts accusing, or—in the day when God through Jesus Christ judges the hidden heart's-ground of men, in the spirit of the gospel message appointed even for the heathen world— moreover excusing him." This linking of the ἐν ἡμέρᾳ with the clause ἢ καὶ ἀπολογουμένων I do not approve, as appears from what has been said above; but the thought that, in that day in which God exercises His judgment through Jesus Christ the Mediator of grace, even heathens may be accepted to grace, is without doubt in the meaning of the apostle. We remember the expression of Jesus on the men of Nineveh and the queen of the south (Matt. xii. 41) Compare also Hebart, *Die Natürliche Theologie des Ap. Paulus,* 1861.

of such evil ($\pi o \nu \eta \rho \acute{a}$, Heb. x. 22): it is $\mu \epsilon \mu \iota a \sigma \mu \acute{\epsilon} \nu \eta$ (Tit. i. 15; 1 Cor. viii. 7), so far as the evil deeds shadow themselves in it like blots; or $\kappa \epsilon \kappa a \upsilon \tau \eta \rho \iota a \sigma \mu \acute{\epsilon} \nu \eta$ (1 Tim. iv. 2), so far as it bears them in itself ineradicably and indelibly like brands. All these characteristics prevail in the so-called subsequent conscience. In respect of the so-called precedent conscience, prevails in Scripture generally the fundamental position that man is to act in proportion to himself, *i.e.* according to the measure of his conviction and his faith (Rom. xiv. 23; comp. Ecclus. xxxvii. 13, xxxv. 13), without thereby exalting the conscience to an infallible oracle. The precedent conscience may be right or wrong, weak or strong ($\dot{a} \sigma \theta \epsilon \nu \acute{\eta} s$, $\dot{a} \sigma \theta \epsilon \nu o \hat{\upsilon} \sigma a$, 1 Cor. viii. 7, 12); it may err and waver in that which is right before God; but in all cases it remains the norm, or law, for the occurrent doings of man. For action without conscience is, as such, absolutely blameable, although action according to conscience is not absolutely on that account right before God. For man, even on account of the confusions and perversions of his conscience, is responsible to God; and the weakness of conscience, which depends on deficiency of right knowledge (1 Cor. viii. 7), and is to be spared (1 Cor. viii. 9), may, in its exercise of judgment upon the freedom of conscience of another (1 Cor. x. 29), result in a self-induration and vain-gloriousness most perilous to the soul.

If man, indeed, were not fallen, the conscience would be in us the always truthful and assured witness to itself of the will of God, and the blessed consciousness of the unity of our will with the divine; or was there really before the fall of man no need to appeal to conscience? "So long," say many,[1] "as man lived in immediate fellowship with God not yet interrupted by sin, he had no conscience, *i.e.* his self-consciousness harmonized immediately with his divine consciousness: there could as yet arise no distinction of the two, as of two natures essentially diverse from one another, or forms of consciousness contradicting one another." But self-consciousness, world-consciousness, consciousness of God, are still absolutely three several sides and tendencies of the personal life of the spirit; and

[1] Thus, for example, Schenkel, art. "Conscience" in Herzog's *Real-Encyklop.* v. 132; comp. K. v. Raumer, *Geschichte der Pädagogik*, ii. 212, where conscience is called the correlative of original sin.

man's will and God's will are always two, if not different, still several, wills; and God's will was, and is, and remains our law, as surely as the sense of absolute dependence on God—to which even the seraphim give utterance—will not leave us even in the blessed eternity.[1] Why, then, ought not man's knowledge about his relation to God from the first beginning to be called conscience, especially as, even to those who were first created, the will of God, having in view the confirmation of their freedom, was made known in the form of a positive law? Conscience in its primitive form was precisely knowledge knowing itself in God, and knowing itself not otherwise than conformed to God's will. But, in consequence of the fall, it not only became a painful consciousness of disunion of the two, and therefore a consciousness of guilt, of which man, although for a time he may hush it up, can never wholly get rid;[2] but, moreover, in its claims, which it urges upon human conduct, it has incurred the corruptions of eclipse and stupefaction. It is no longer the perfectly true mirror of God's law in us. This law itself, however, subsists in man as the ineradicable dowry of his divinely constituted nature. Even in man fallen is written, that abiding in the divine love is the truth and the peace of his nature; that his conduct must be so ordered as to be conformed to the divine love; and that, if it be otherwise ordered, it incurs the divine anger. The powers of the spirit and of the soul themselves are as the decalogue of this creative Thora established in us. Only the prophecy of conscience, although inextricably related to this objective law of God, is subjected to the consequences of the fall; and after man had fallen from God's love, there needed a re-establishment into this holy sphere (comp. Rom. ix. 1), that the conscience should testify to him just as faithfully and surely of the will of the divine love as of the incurred divine wrath.

[1] We cannot therefore agree with Harless (*Ethik*, p. 34), who refuses to conscience, considered according to its nature, the form of the law; because he regards consciousness of the divine will as law, and dissent of the human will from the divine, as inseparable.

[2] Objectively represented by heathenism in the Furies, the personified *terrores conscientiæ*, as is acknowledged by heathendom itself, as soon as the spell of the mythology is broken. See the expressions of Cicero, Juvenal, and others, in Thomasius, *Grundlinien z. Religions-Unterricht*, sec. xi. (ed. 3, 1858), and Harless, *Ethik*, p. 26.

And as it is wrong to name conscience the voice of God, so it is also wrong to name conscience, as such, the voice of God the Redeemer. It is the one generally received view, since Günther and Pabst, that conscience is not a psychologic fact appertaining to the creation, but to redemption. No; conscience is inseparable from the personal nature of man, and comes into being contemporaneously therewith. For the self-conscious man is, as such, conscious to himself also of his conditionality in respect of God and his duty, to allow himself continually to be conditioned in his self-determination by the will of God. The existence of conscience, therefore, reaches beyond the fall, and has, in its manifestation of itself, run through a changeful history: it was one thing in its original position; it is another in its position under sin; it becomes another in its position under grace, through which it becomes renewed, together with our likeness to God. While it testifies to man of his separation from God, and excites the longing after harmony and peace with God, it assuredly helps to prepare the way for redemption; but it is so little a gift of redeeming grace, that rather it needs itself not only purification through grace (Heb. ix. 14, comp. ix. 9, x. 2), but correction, establishment, sharpening (comp. 1 Cor. iv. 4) through grace. Thus, moreover, what has often been maintained, after Günther's example, is unsound, that the call of God, אַיֶּכָּה, is the origin and essence of conscience, and that this latter is therefore the beginning of the grace that seeks the sinner.[1] When Eve, in the presence of the serpent, shows herself conscious of the divine prohibition and of its rigid obligation; when shame and fear seize upon the fallen ones, it is God's law (established in the first, as in all men,) of the obedience of thankful love due to God, which then made itself manifest. The call of Jehovah-Elohim, Where art thou? is not therefore the first beginning of conscience, and conscience is not the continued echo of that call. Men had a conscience which testified to them of God's loving will, even in the relation of nearness to God in which they stood before the fall: they had a conscience which placed them in shame and remorse, in the relation of remoteness from God in which they stood after the fall; and it is nothing else than the struggle of

---

[1] See the chief passage from the school of speculative theology that preceded Günther, in Thomasius, *Dogm.* i. 854.

thoughts of self-accusation and of self-exculpation in the court of conscience, to which Jehovah-Elohim puts an end by bringing the testimony of conscience concerning their guilt to a certainty.[1]

But when God approaches them as a Judge, he at the same time approaches them as a Redeemer. This advance of Jehovah-Elohim in the garden is the first historical movement of God to the work of redemption—the first historical step to the incarnation. For that this mode of intercourse of God with men was the primitive mode, is a prejudice that rests upon no demonstration. The intercourse that till then had subsisted, took another form in consequence of the fall. The life of men, while still unfallen, was a life in God, and in His love. If they addressed themselves to themselves, they communed with God in the spirit; and if they turned to the outer world, they communed with God in His works. But when they swerved from God's love, they became strange to God, and God became remote from them. But, according to His eternal counsel of love, He would not remain remote from them. He approached them again, but now in a manner that corresponded to their materialization and alienation. He gives to Himself a manifestation limited by the sensuous perceptions of men, and probably human. This is no childish representation or mythologic investment of the narrative. Certainly the being of man, even

---

[1] We refer here to (F. Weber) *Die Lehre vom Gewissen mit bes. Absehen auf ihre Bed. für die Kirchliche Praxis*, in the *Zeitschr. f. Protest.* 1860, pp. 65–89. This appendix is a well-considered commentary supplementary in many ways to this paragraph of my Biblical Psychology. Compare also the opinions of Güder, acquiescing in previous opposition to the false making-objective of the idea of conscience, in his *Lehre vom Gewissen, l.c.*: "The conscience is in nowise a transcendent operation of God in the subject." Göschel, *Der Mensch diesseits und jenseits*, p. 56; Philippi, *Glaubenslehre*, iii. 13, "Knowledge of the human spirit about the divine law implanted in it;" Fronmüller, art. "Gewissen" in the *Zellersd. Bibl. Wörterbuch;* v. Zezschwitz, *l.c.*; v. Rudloff, p. 142; Riehm, *Lehrbegriff des Hebräerbr.*, p. 675, where is well and briefly given, by way of definition, "Συνείδησις is the knowledge of man about himself concerning his relation to God." Schenkel, art. "Gewissen" in Herzog's *R.E.*: "It is not accurate to define conscience as an existence, or a voice of God in man. In the conscience God is not the subject, but man is the subject; while, on the other hand, God is the object. Man has God objectively in the conscience; God is objectively to man in the conscience." My Elberfeld critic, following Baader, defines· "Conscience is the knowledge of our *being known.*"

after the fall, is a being in God (Acts xvii. 28); or, what is the same thing, God the omnipresent is in man also after his fall.[1] But because man is no longer in God's love, it is true equally that he is out of God, and God out of man. The relation of love is severed. It is this which now becomes historically manifest. How distant God has become from men, is plain from the fact that He now advances to them from without; and how strange men have become to God, is plain from the fact that they hide themselves from His presence. The breach of the relation of love, however, becomes manifest in so historical a manner, because a new restoration of men in the course of the history is the loving purpose of God. The preparatory form of this restoration is this, that on the part of God, the promise, and on the part of man, the faith, penetrates the separating wall of partition,—a psychological event of the profoundest significance to the history of redemption.

THE PROMISE AND THE FAITH.

Sec. V.

ALTHOUGH shame and fear, the effects and expressions of conscience, do not constitute any real atonement, yet it is not to be denied that fallen men, by the immediate self-evidence of God the Judge and the Redeemer, very soon enter upon a position truly prepared for atonement. How comes it now, that God's grace did not make that which had happened, in

[1] According to Scripture, no more can be said; for that God's Spirit is inborn into man as the ideal principle of divine fellowship, without nevertheless being able to manifest it of itself, and that the Holy Spirit—the Spirit of the incarnate Son of God, as the real principle of the divine fellowship—was the first that brought the actual personal unity of man with God into operation (Schöberl. *Jahrbücher*, 1861, p. 59), is a view irreconcilable with the unity of God's Spirit. Scripture knows nothing of an immanence of God's Spirit in man, as such, even fallen. The Spirit of God, in passages of Scripture such as Gen. vi. 3 (see my Comm.), is the Spirit in virtue of which humanity has its origin from God, in a manner exalted over all earthly creatures, and can say, We are His offspring (Acts, *l.c.*).

such a way not to have happened, that the history of mankind, placed back at its commencement, established by creation good, might have begun anew? Why was there needed, in order that the loving relation of God and men should be restored, such a fact influencing the Godhead in its own proper nature, and effected from eternity into time, as the incarnation of the Son? Wherefore did God permit, that, from the fall of the first man downwards, sin and grace, without extirpation of the former by means of the latter, should propagate themselves in an historical course of thousands of years? and wherefore did He ordain, that not till the middle—as the fulness—of these long periods, should the Restorer appear, who would perfectly retrieve the good beginning that had been lost? To these questions the general answer is, that the work of restoration was a work of free divine love, but that, if it were to be effected, it could only be effected thus, and no otherwise. The reasons of the kind and manner of its accomplishment lay in God's nature, and in the divinely constituted nature of man. On the one hand, it was in the nature of freedom that the sin of men, as their free action, could not become annihilated, without at the same time annihilating men themselves together with this beginning of free self-demonstration; and it was in the nature of spiritual-corporeity, in virtue of which men are not only independent persons, but also a self-propagating species organically linked together, that the determination against God of the first created ones must become of decisive consequences for the whole of humanity constituted in them, and developing itself forth from them. On the other side, it was in the nature of the divine holiness, that God cannot abrogate the self-punishment which sin bears in itself, and produces from itself, without atonement offered; and that He cannot love the sinners, without the sin—which rejects Him, and which He rejects—being completely made amends for. These answers to the above questions are right in outline, but they do not become convincing, until we apprehend that the ethical consequences of sin are at the same time physical. No atoning pains of men were sufficient to restore to them again an internal and external form conformed to the holiness of God; for sin had disordered their likeness to God, and there needed a new creative restoration of this, that God might again recognise Himself in men, and love them. Further, wrath and love are not merely two different modes of feeling in God; but two principles, distinct as fire and light, of the everlasting revelation of the glory of His nature. God is love, but He is so in everlasting, absolutely cloudless, bright, triumph over the ground of fire which, in historical revelation of God, is called $\mathit{\mathring{o}\rho\gamma\acute{\eta}}$, and according to which God Himself is called $\pi\hat{\upsilon}\rho\ \kappa\alpha\tau\alpha\nu\alpha\lambda\acute{\iota}\sigma\kappa o\nu$. The spirit of man dwelt in God's love, and his soul was the copy of that triumph of light. But when man swerved from God's love, he sank down into the fire-ground of his nature, which originated in the fire-ground of the divine. Man was now a $\phi\acute{\upsilon}\sigma\epsilon\iota\ \tau\acute{\epsilon}\kappa\nu o\nu\ \mathit{\mathring{o}\rho\gamma\hat{\eta}\varsigma}$ (Eph. ii. 3)—one that had incurred wrath. He was no more $\kappa o\iota\nu\omega\nu\grave{o}\varsigma\ \theta\epsilon\acute{\iota}\alpha\varsigma\ \phi\acute{\upsilon}\sigma\epsilon\omega\varsigma$ (2 Pet. i. 4); and if he were to become so again, not only was a change of disposition in God necessary, but an act of divine love, to lift him up out of the depth of wrath again to the altitude of the light. This act of divine love is the everlastingly decreed and temporally fulfilled redemption of men from wrath through the Son to love, who betook Himself down into the depth of the Godhead's wrath, clothed the humanity, which had forfeited the divine likeness, with His own absolute divine likeness, took the wrath upon Himself, and in Himself annihilated it,—and thus brought back the creature that had fallen from love, again to the principle into which it had been created. It will be objected that these are words of the fancy, and not of the understanding—pictures, and not ideas. But of such mysteries we can only effectually stammer in figures; and your abstract conceptions,—we appeal to the objectors,—are nothing but a perforated sieve for these most intensely real of all realities. Scripture says, moreover (Gal. iii. 13), that Christ must first become $\kappa\alpha\tau\acute{\alpha}\rho\alpha$, that the promised $\epsilon\mathring{\upsilon}\lambda o\gamma\acute{\iota}\alpha$ might be brought forth: $\kappa\alpha\tau\acute{\alpha}\rho\alpha$ is the manifestation of the anger, and $\epsilon\mathring{\upsilon}\lambda o\gamma\acute{\iota}\alpha$ the manifestation of the love. The $\kappa\alpha\tau\acute{\alpha}\rho\alpha$ of the Sinaitic law which He, as the crucified, תָּלוּי, set forth in Himself, is only an historical expression of the $\mathit{\mathring{o}\rho\gamma\acute{\eta}}$, which abideth on all those who despise the act of reconciliation (John iii. 36), which humanity had thus incurred (Eph. ii. 3), and subject to the penalty of which, without Christ, it would have remained.

This change of the divine wrath into love through the self-surrender of the Son of God to and for fallen humanity, is an eternal fact; for God's will of love and counsel of love, in respect of humanity, in eternal prevision of its fall, are everlasting. When, therefore, the fall of man had been realized historically, then also began at once, rooted in the eternal fact of reconciliation before God, the historical self-manifestation of the divine loving will, and the historical self-fulfilment of the divine counsel of love. The judicial sentences upon the serpent, the woman, the man, are expressions of the divine wrath; but the wrathful will becomes at once manifest as a wrathful will of love, *i.e.* not absolute, but a will of wrath subdued and enclosed by love; for the extreme of the curse upon the serpent, the bruising of its head by the seed of the woman, is blessing for humanity. At first it is only a ray of light, which breaks through the gloom of the alienation of men from God,—only a gleam of light, which shines out in the midst of the fire of wrath. It is a word which speaks of a future One; for, because God has become remote from men, their salvation also now comes from afar. And because men have externalized themselves by sin, this word of promise points thus externally to victory over the serpent. What the divine love means, remains concealed, as behind an emblematical form of enigma. And yet the whole gospel is contained in this Protevangelium. The זֶרַע אִשָּׁה, the הוּא, thoroughly understood, is no other than Jesus, the Son of God, and the son of Mary. Yea, this is He who, in and with this word, establishes the foundation of His coming in humanity; for from this word inwardly, and from this word outwardly, He advances through the Old Testament to the purpose of His incarnation, and through the New Testament to the purpose of His mission. But that the self-demonstration of the divine love, that the self-proclamation of His coming, should subsist in such dim, and more or less external words, concerning a future person, is the result of the remoteness of humanity from God.

Salvation moves towards humanity from the distance; and by what means does it become near to it? By faith. Scripture appropriates the activities of faith and conditions of faith, as well to the spirit (*e.g.* Ps. cxliii. 7, lxxviii. 8, li. 12) as to the soul (*e.g.* hoping, waiting, trusting on God, depending on God, resting in God, Ps. cxvi. 7, cxxxi. 2). But Scripture nowhere says, the spirit believes, or the soul believes; because faith ($\pi\iota\sigma\tau\epsilon\acute{\nu}\epsilon\iota\nu$,

הֶאֱמִין) is an operation of the human Ego, which is distinguished from spirit, soul, and body. It says, indeed, that with the heart it is believed, καρδίᾳ πιστεύεται (Rom. x. 10), because faith is a central, yea, the most central human operation;[1] but, moreover, it distinguishes from the heart itself that which is itself believing in us: for the peculiar nature of faith scarcely anywhere expresses itself more plainly than Ps. lxxiii. 26, where Asaph says, "My flesh and my heart faileth; but Elohim is the rock of my heart, and my portion is Elohim for ever." His Ego remains trusting in God, even although the body, and even the heart—therefore the spirit- and soul-life, or his external and internal man[2]—decayed: even then he held fast to God, as to the rock which abides when everything is wavering, and to the possession which must remain to him when all else is lost; he held fast to him for ever, himself imperishable, because associated with the imperishable. This recourse, breaking through all inward and outward contradictions—through sin, sorrows, death, and hell—to God the Redeemer; this longing after God's free, merciful love, as His own word declares it,—a longing, reaching forth, and grasping it; this naked, unselfish craving, feeling itself satisfied with nothing else than God's promised grace; this eagerness, absorbing every ray of light that proceeds from God's reconciled love; this convinced and safety-craving appropriation and clinging to the word of grace;—this is faith. In its nature, it is the pure receptive correlative of the word of promise; a means of approaching again to God, which, as the word itself, is appointed through the distance of God in consequence of sin: for faith has to confide in the word, in spite of all want of comprehension, want of sight, want of experience. No experimental *actus reflexi* belong to the nature of faith. It is, according to its nature, *actio directa*, to wit, *fiducia supplex*.[3]

[1] Thomasius, *Dogm.* iv. 158.

[2] Thus is removed the doubt of Oehler in Herzog's *R.E.* vi. 20, that "heart" in connection with "flesh" seems to indicate the bodily heart: it indicates that which is within the body, and generally that which is *within*. Comp. also my *Commentary on the Psalms, in loco.*

[3] Nowhere is this discussed more instructively, or with more profound experience, than in Ehrich Pontoppidan's (author of the *Menoza*) *Clear Mirror of Faith*, Copenhagen and Leipz. 1726, 1768; *vid.* the Appendix to this division.

While now from the God of love—the remote God—the word of promise comes to meet man; and man as Ego, with all the powers of his spirit and his soul, reaches forward to meet it faithfully, the primitive relation of love renews itself once more as in its budding commencement. This incipient form is retained, moreover, through the entire history of salvation here below, although the revelation of salvation progresses, and the difference of the two testaments is considerable. For even after Jesus had historically appeared, and had completed the redemption, it is the word which with all its clearness is still ἔσοπτρον ἐν αἰνίγματι (1 Cor. xiii. 12), and the faith, which no otherwise apprehends Him than in the word, which encloses all other means of grace. Our natural life remains subjected to wrath, and finally succumbs to the attack of death; but in the midst of this wrath we live, who believe, with our Ego, with our innermost man delivered from wrath, in the principle of divine love; and all the wrath which we experience is of no effect any more upon us according to our true nature, but for the disintegrating of the Natural, from which we ourselves are ever longing to become delivered. Our likeness to God, our *doxa*, is lost; but in Christ, whom we have apprehended in faith on His word, we have it again. He is our divine image, and our *doxa*, till the time when all wrath, not merely in the way of imputation, but also actually, shall be extinguished for us, and our whole natural condition shall be transformed into the image and the glory of Christ.

We return to the psychological elucidation of these facts of the redemption in the concluding divisions. The strictness of the systematic method would have properly bidden us to be silent on the subject for the present. But we could not deny ourselves this precursory glance, since the ground of our natural condition established by the creation, which the section that now follows will determine, is already, from the first historical moving of the solution of the enigma of redemption, pervaded by grace, and only remains in existence because it has this for a background.

APPENDIX.

From Pontoppidan's " Mirror of Faith."

PETRUS MOLINÆUS (Du Moulin) has briefly and clearly shown,[1] that the special nature of faith consists merely in the repentant soul's recourse to Christ; and that the consolatory experience, with the strong assurance that arises therefrom, belongs not so much to the nature as to the perfectness of the faith: for the nature, or *forma essentialis*, of faith may be found in him who, like the father of the boy with a dumb spirit, is compelled to acknowledge with weeping eyes, " Lord, I believe; help Thou mine unbelief." Du Moulin distinguishes in that respect a twofold assurance,—an assurance of refuge (*confiance de recours*), and an assurance of experience (*confiance de sentiment*), or, what is the same thing, *fiducia supplex* and *fiducia triumphans*. The recourse of faith to Jesus, and the laying hold of His merits, is *actio fidei directa*; and the powerful experience that follows thereupon of the attestation and the firmness of faith, is *actio fidei reflexa*. The believer attains to reflex faith, *i.e.* to faith which recognises and experiences itself in the divine light with joy, partly by proving himself according to God's word (2 Cor. xiii. 5), and finding himself standing in the faith (*reflexio activa, rationalis vel syllogistica*); partly by receiving without his own agency impressions of the Holy Spirit, which in the ground of his heart give to him the sweet and comforting assurance of his standing in grace, and assure him that he is a child of God (*reflexio mere passiva et supernaturalis*). The reflex faith in this latter sense is separated from the direct faith, just as the repeating echo is distinguished from the voice that calls it forth.

[1] In his excellent *Traité de la Forme essentielle ou nature de la Foi justifiante*, an appendix of his *Traité de la Paix de l'Ame*.

IV.

THE NATURAL CONDITION.

———•———

"Nil dignius est anima, nil excellentius hac unica cognitione, quam qui perfectam haberet Deo similis esset, imo Deus ipse."—FRANCISCUS SANCHEZ.

PERSONALITY AND THE "EGO."

Sec. I.

HAVING now considered the fall of man psychologically, and having, moreover, taken a psychological anticipatory glance at his restoration, we proceed to consider, apart from this work of grace, his present condition. The method which we adopt for this purpose is from within outwards. That which is most external of man is his corporeity. Powers which are common to this with the whole of nature are active herein—the presuppositions or postulates of bodily life. In these powers, rules the soul, combining them into the unity of individual life. The soul, on the one hand, is turned towards these powers, and towards corporeity; on the other hand, it is turned inwardly towards the spirit, whence it has its origin. The soul is the external aspect of the spirit, and the spirit the internal aspect of the soul; and the most internal nature of man is his Ego, which is distinct from spirit, soul, and body. From this we begin. It is the same course which is adopted by the work of restoration. This also addresses itself first of all to the human Ego, and thence extends to the threefold condition of man's being. For the faith with which it commences is, as we saw at the close of the previous paragraph, the union of the Ego with the word of grace.

It is then no philosophic abstraction with which we begin, but a natural psychologic fact of the greatest soteriologic importance; for which reason we may expect that the self-distinguishing of man as Ego, from all which belongs to his nature, will be very sharply impressed on Scripture. And it is so. How clearly is man as Ego distinguished, Isa. xxvi. 9, from his spirit and his soul! how clearly (Prov. xxiii. 15, לִבִּי נַם־אָנִי, and Eccles. vii. 25, אֲנִי וְלִבִּי) from his heart! And how ingeniously is the twofold relation of the Ego to the human natural condition indicated, by the fact that the Israelite — speaking of the spirit, soul, heart—says not less frequently עָלַי than בִּי or בְּקִרְבִּי! In the former case, the Ego appears as the centre, which has the natural condition above itself, or around itself; in the latter case, as the circumference, which encloses the natural condition, and contains within itself all that belongs to it. (See רוּחִי עָלַי, Ps. cxlii. 4, cxliii. 4; נַפְשִׁי עָלַי, Ps. xlii. 5, 6, 7, 12, xliii. 5, Job xxx. 16, Lam. iii. 20; לִבִּי עָלַי, Jer. viii. 18, Neh. v. 7; and compare with these, passages such as Ps. cvii. 5, Lam. i. 20, where we read instead, בִּי or בְּקִרְבִּי.)

So far as man is able in the innermost depth of his innate being to apprehend himself as Ego, and to comprehend the entirety of this being in the thought of Ego, we call him a person. Scripture indeed makes use of πρόσωπον (LXX., 2 Cor. i. 11), פָּנִים, not in this sense, but of man, or even of God in His self-representation in the externality of His manifestation. Ὑπόστασις also (Heb. i. 3, comp. xi. 1) indicates in itself not that which knows itself, but the substance that underlies the appearance. But "person" has now come into use, to express a nature self-conscious, capable of introspection, even to the thought of the Ego, and self-consciously determining itself. The classical use of the word has most undoubtedly the tendency to give it this later meaning, which is brought about by the Romish law and the ecclesiastical dogmatics. It were only to be wished that "personality" should not be confounded with "individuality," as still so frequently occurs. Personality is that which is common to all men as such, whereby they are elevated above plants and beasts (for even between the idea, feeling, and instinct of the brute, and the subjectivity of man, which knows itself, and determines itself from itself, is an impassable gulf). Individuality, on the other hand, is the peculiarity of the individual man, whereby he is distinguished from the other beings of his kind.[1] In Scripture we cannot naturally expect these conceptions of scholastic language. But even in the narrative of creation, where מִין is only used of plants and beasts, and not of men, it suggests that man is more than an individual of a מִין—he is a person. And Paul says, in connection with a word of Aratos, that humanity is γένος

---

[1] Let it be observed how Cicero, de offic. i. 30, expresses himself hereupon: Intelligendum est, duabus quasi a natura nos indutos esse personis, etc. The one is "personality," the other "individuality."

τοῦ Θεοῦ (Acts xvii. 28): it is an entirety of individuals, which at the same time are persons, as God is a person.

Everything which pertains to man's essential condition and his inborn individuality, he possesses without his own agency. But in apprehending himself as Ego, he constitutes himself as the centre of this inherited being, and makes it the circle of his knowledge and his power. It is to this being that belongs, as was said above, even the נֶפֶשׁ. Nowhere does נֶפֶשׁ indicate the Ego of man as distinguished from his substantial nature. For although נַפְשִׁי, ψυχή μου, is in many cases interchanged with אֲנִי, ἐγώ, and may be substituted for אֲנִי, ἐγώ, yet it does not signify "my Ego;" but in saying נַפְשִׁי, I distinguish myself as Ego from the soul which appertains to me. But that נֶפֶשׁ may indicate not only the entire inner nature of man, but also his entire personality, i.e. all that pertains to the person of man (the personality, conceived, as our dogmatists say, not *formaliter et præcise*, but *materialiter et concretive*), has its reason in the fact that the soul, and indeed (let it be well considered) the soul capable of spirit and spirit-like, is the mediator in man, having two aspects, bearing upon the spirit and the body respectively. רוּחַ would only very unintelligibly indicate man, since he is not pure spirit; and בָּשָׂר, σάρξ (Ps. lvi. 5; frequently in כָּל־בָּשָׂר, πᾶσα σάρξ, and in the New Testament σάρξ καὶ αἷμα = בָּשָׂר וָדָם), indicates him only in reference to the sensuous, perishable side of his nature. As little as נֶפֶשׁ is the Ego of man, so little could it be concluded, from this mode of using it, that it is this which constitutes the person of man. It is not, as we have already said in Div. II. Sec. IV., that which constitutes the person, but it is the bond of the personality, i.e. of the spirit-embodied nature of man. Precisely on this account נֶפֶשׁ is used in the sense of Person. נֶפֶשׁ is used in the sense of somebody; כָּל־נֶפֶשׁ, πᾶσα ψυχή, in the sense of everybody (for which, after the example of Deut. xx. 16, also is used כָּל־נְשָׁמָה, Josh. x. 40, xi. 11, 14, 1 Kings xv. 29, as in the Arabic *nesemeh*, but nowhere כָּל־רוּחַ); and numbers are reckoned, as well in the New Testament as in the Old, by souls (e.g. 1 Pet. iii. 20, ὀκτὼ ψυχαί, and often in the Acts of the Apostles). It would thence be wrongly concluded that the soul is what constitutes the person of man; for the brute is also called נֶפֶשׁ. In נֶפֶשׁ in itself is not involved the conception of the personal living, but only of the self-living (the individual). In such cases נֶפֶשׁ indicates the person of the man, but not the man as a person. That we are able to translate it "person," is accounted for not in the idea of the word, but in the nature of what is denoted by it (comp. Rom. xiii. 1 with ii. 9); for man and beast are נֶפֶשׁ in essential diversity. The beast is נֶפֶשׁ, as a self-living nature by the power of the spirit that proceeds from God and pervades entire nature, the individual constitution of which spirit is the soul of the brute; but man is נֶפֶשׁ, as a self-living nature by the power of the spirit that proceeds from God, and is in the form of God, and is therefore personal, the operation of which spirit is his endowment with soul. That which constitutes the person of man, *i.e.* that, by virtue of which he is a being knowing himself, and determining himself out of himself, is his spirit; for the God-breathed נְשָׁמָה is the light of God which searches through all the chambers of his internal nature, Prov. xx. 27; on which passage Elster rightly observes: "It is the mystery of self-consciousness which is here represented in a sensible form. The human spirit, when it is trained to the height of the capacity of development quiescent therein, is able to make objective to itself, its own life, its own nature; it can set opposite to itself its own feeling by its reflection, and thus can reflect itself in itself. This capability of self-consciousness, however, is the most essential part of the divine likeness, and it is therefore called a Light of God, because herein especially the human spirit announces itself as a ray of the divine."[1] The New Testament Scripture says just the same of the created

[1] In this passage Hitzig understands by נשמה not the spirit, but the soul, appealing to a word of Kafswini (*Cosmogr.* i. 355). The soul (*en-nefs*) is like the lamp which shines around (with which all around is enlightened) in the corners of the house. But in this expression *en-nefs* means the spirit-soul; for النفس, according to a *usus loquendi* that has become prevalent, is the spirit-soul, originating out of the spirit-world, and الروح the soul of nature turned towards the sense-world—the bearer (حامل) of the natural powers of life. Therefore *ruhi* (روحی) in Arabic is used quite in the same sense as in Hebrew, *nafshi* = myself (*ipse*). Moreover, according to a prevailing rabbinical terminology, נפש is the intelligent, immortal; נשמה, on the other hand, the animal soul, which passes away with the body (see Scheyer, *Das psychologische System des Maimonides*, 1845). According to a better distinction, נֶפֶשׁ is the lower soul, רוּחַ the spirit of life ordained

human spirit. It is there called the internal eye, the internal light (Matt. vi. 23).¹ Τίς γὰρ οἶδεν ἀνθρώπων τὰ τοῦ ἀνθρώπου, εἰ μὴ τὸ πνεῦμα τοῦ ἀνθρώπου τὸ ἐν αὐτῷ (1 Cor. ii. 11). Therefore in the New Testament, where those testimonies and operations of God which are addressed to our self-consciousness are spoken of, we nowhere find the ψυχή named. God manifests Himself τῷ πνεύματι ἡμῶν (Rom. viii. 16), and we become renewed τῷ πνεύματι τοῦ νοὸς ἡμῶν (Eph. iv. 23). The spirit is that which constitutes man's person, and there accordingly begins the work of grace, which restores the intercourse of the personal man with God the absolutely personal, and has in view the entire condition of man's nature, held together by the Psyche, and encircled by the self-consciousness of the Pneuma. The object of the saving facts of redemption is called ψυχή, for ψυχή indicates the individual entire life of man; but the object of the internal operations of grace, completing themselves in the light of the self-consciousness and of the self-determination, is called πνεῦμα (καρδία, νοῦς): for this is the abode of all self-conscious will, thought, and perception, where the personal relation of man to the proffered salvation is determined and formed.²

above it, and conditioning its standing, and נְשָׁמָה the intelligent soul. Thus distinguish Saadia, Abenezra, Schemtob.; *vid.* Egger's *Psychologia Rabbinica* (an excellent Basel dissertation), 1719. Here at least נְשָׁמָה occupies the highest place; but, according to a representation absolutely opposed to the Bible, רוּחַ appears as *spiritus vitalis* between the inferior and the rational soul. This confusion of the use of language is widely spread. According to Hermes, in *Stobæos*, i. 1, 40, the νοῦς is the most internal, and the πνεῦμα (the life-spirit traversing throughout by veins, and arteries, and blood) the most external of the inner man: ὁ νοῦς ἐν τῷ λόγῳ, ὁ λόγος ἐν τῇ ψυχῇ, ἡ δὲ ψυχὴ ἐν τῷ πνεύματι. Similarly Robert Flud (died 1637), "Spiritus interpositus est inter animam et corpus haud aliter ac aër inter solum et terram;" and Campanella (died 1639), "Triplici vivimus substantia, corpore scilicet, spiritu, et mente. Spiritus vehiculum mentis, mens vero apex animæ in horizonte habitans, quæ spiritum et corpus item informat." This also is the terminology of Comenius: *anima* or *mens*, the spirit; *spiritus*, the animal soul (see the first Appendix to this Division). Similarly Lord Bacon of Verulam.

¹ In like manner, Aristotle says of Nûs, that it is the divine eye of the soul (ψυχῆς θεῖον ὄμμα), that it is in the soul what the power of vision is in the eye (ὄψις ἐν ὀφθαλμῷ).

² See v. Zezschwitz, *Profangräcität u. bibl. Sprachgeist*, p. 45.

But has the soul, then, no self-consciousness of its own? We answer provisionally: the self-consciousness of the soul is just the self-consciousness of the spirit. The spirit is substance knowing itself; the soul is substance, but knowing itself only in virtue of the immanence of the spirit;[1] and the Ego is not substance, but the thought of the spirit combining in thought the entire essential condition into this one luminous point.[2] Since J. G. Fichte, it has of late been often and urgently said, that the self-consciousness of the spirit is its existence itself.[3] This assertion is not without meaning, if by spirit be understood the realization of the soul's foundation of self-consciousness. But for us, who hold the self-consciousness to be the realization of the foundation of the spirit itself, it is without meaning and intelligence. The spirit is potentially and actually self-conscious, *i.e.* Being reflected in itself,—not the self-consciousness itself. The spirit is essence; the self-consciousness, in its actuality, is the confirmation of this spirit-essence; and the self-thought is the result of the consummation of self-consciousness—is the general self-thought, which underlies all special thoughts, of the spirit which apprehends itself and its sphere of operation as its object. How rightly and in what meaning we assert this, will appear more clearly when we examine the distinction which has grown usual and important in the later biblical theology, of the personal life and the natural life, according to Scripture and experience.

[1] In a similar but not an absolutely identical sense, Schöberlein, *Jahrb.* 1861, p. 49: "The soul is the subjective principle in man. The spirit, indeed, causes the soul to soar up into the Ego: the spirit is that which constitutes the person, but the seat of the Ego-personality itself is the soul; in the soul man leads his own, his self-life." This representation, that the spirit is that which constitutes the person—the soul is itself the human-personal—can only be carried out, if, with Schöberlein, we understand by the spirit the Divine Spirit, but not if we distinguish spirit and soul as separate created substances (see below, Sec. VI.).

[2] It is only a confirmation of the above, when my Elberfeld critic says: Ego is not a fourth nature by the side of the Trine—Soul, Spirit, Body—as the one God is not a fourth nature.

[3] V. Preger; Flacius, ii. 401.

PERSONAL LIFE AND NATURAL LIFE.

SEC. II.

NATURAL life is neither an idea nor an expression absolutely foreign to Scripture. It is true that the Old Testament has no word for nature. Even the LXX. nowhere uses the term φύσις. But in the New Testament, φύσις occurs frequently. In its largest sense, it signifies the kind and manner of being, proper to an existence in consequence of an internal tendency to become, which precedes its actual manifestation; or the constitution inherent in it of itself, apart from any other kind of determination, or even of self-determination superadded, than the nature itself thus constituted.[1] Thus ἡ θεία φύσις (2 Pet. i. 4) is applied to God, who is what He is and appears, by virtue of a spontaneously powerful conscious becoming so; but usually the term is used of brutes and men, who have become what they are and appear in the manner of creation and procreation, (Jas. iii. 7,) where ἡ φύσις ἡ ἀνθρωπίνη indicates the class of being to which men belong, with reference to their innate eminence above all kinds of brutes. With this use of φύσις, in contrast with that which is imparted from without, is associated the adjective φυσικός (Rom. i. 26), *i.e.* what is according to the implanted inborn constitution. The contrast is applied somewhat differently, 2 Pet. ii. 12, comp. Jude 10. In this case the brutes are called φυσικά, as natures whose life is passed in necessary expenditure of the being implanted in them. In the former case, φύσις, comprehending in itself, according to the nature about which it is used, that which is corporeal, psychical, and spiritual, was the opposite of art,—of grace,—of what was abnormal; here it is the opposite of the λογικὸν, of action with intelligence and freedom. The two opposite relations meet, if by nature we understand that which anticipates man's will, and thus interpret it—that which is already in existence in him when he first comes to self-consciousness.

[1] V. Hofmann, *Schriftb.* i. 564.

In this sense Hofmann distinguishes between natural life and personal life. Man is both: he is the conscious Ego, and the occupant of a nature thus or thus qualified, in which he already finds himself before he becomes personally conscious of any self-determination. In his personal life he is free: the spirit of God which dwells in man from the creation, is to him an actively present ground of self-consciousness and capacity of self-determination; and according to the reality of his personal conduct, is determined his relation to God, and his eternal destiny. In his natural life, on the other hand, man is not free: he stands here under the determining operation of the divine spirit dwelling in him; and according to this is moulded the form of his personal conduct, and his historical position, serving to the self-fulfilment of the will that rules the world. That which is natural in man, that which is inborn in him, together with all the conditions appertaining to it, is ordained of God: man is free as Ego, but necessary, as his own nature using himself as a means.

Apart from the divine spirit implanted in man by way of creation, which I do not find taught in Scripture (but with which the view presented in Ps. cxxxix. 5, Acts xvii. 28, and other places, may easily be confounded), all this is scriptural undeniably, and consistent with experience. That man, in entering into the position of conscious self-determination (Isa. vii. 15, comp. Deut. i. 39, 2 Sam. xix. 35), finds himself constituted as Ego into an individual condition of life, and established into relations of life individually and generally historical, which are conditioned thus and not otherwise, without his knowledge and will, is manifest. This sphere of life, which is inborn in man, and into which he is born, began without man's co-operation, and even in respect of its being or not being, is withdrawn from the freedom of man. It is a sphere of unfreedom, in which the Ego finds itself as a centre, and related and referring itself to which, it determines itself in accordance with, or in opposition to, that which is godly. In this self-determination man is free; but in the determination of that which he has in himself, and around himself, he is not free. It is not his agency, although he not merely experiences influences therefrom, but also exercises influences thereupon. For "man's personal relation to God, to which he determines himself, stands in a constant reciprocal relation with the operation of God which determines him in his nature, by virtue of which the moral self-determination of man even reaches into that region in which, as nature, he is determined, and on the other side has the prior determining operations of God of the latter kind, as their precedent ground."[1]

It is not to be denied, that this distinction of person (Ego) and nature, with a view to indicate the idea, has something of inconvenience about it. "Nature" thus becomes a homonym, inasmuch as one and the same word serves to denote two ideas that are not congruous. For when we elsewhere say, that the soul, according to its essence, belongs to the side of the spirit, and not to that of nature, then spirit and nature are apprehended as contraries: spirit as that which constitutes the person personally living, and producing all life, even the psychical; nature as that which is corporeal, and unconsciously, or even consciously, *i.e.* psychically, but not personally, living. And the meaning of our dictum is this, that the human soul, as distinguished from the brute soul, is not merely that it is the individuation of the entire life of nature, but that it is the principle of the bodily life, personal, and proceeding from the personifying spirit. Here, on the other hand, where we contrast man's person (Ego) and his nature, we comprehend by nature, not merely the corporeity, but also soul and spirit, inasmuch as the Ego of man makes even these objective to itself, and is distinguished from them.[2] And not only so: soul and spirit, as well as corporeity, have their determined natural constitution even before the personal conduct of man begins: there is, indeed, the whole threefold natural condition of man, which is developed out of the basis of unconsciousness, and subsequently becomes the substratum and means of free conscious self-demonstration. We thus comprehend the idea of nature at one time in a narrower sense, at another time in a wider sense. But, moreover, the language of Holy Scripture itself does not escape this homonymy: for as, on the one hand, it names the brutes φυσικά, as belonging to the impersonal world (2 Pet. ii. 12), so, on the other hand, it names man, in the epitome of his entire creatively constituted being, ἡ φύσις ἡ ἀνθρωπίνη (Jas. iii. 7);

[1] Thus v. Hofmann, *l.c.* i. 312.
[2] Thus also v. Hofmann, *Schriftb.* i. 296, comp. 313.

and from the idea of φύσις it so little excludes the spiritual side of his being, that it speaks, moreover, of a θεία φύσις (2 Pet. i. 4), and thereby understands not the divine *doxa*, but the entire essence of the personal God (θειότης). We are not therefore departing from the biblical *usus loquendi*, when we understand by nature, all in us which is prior to the beginning of our personal life, including soul and spirit in their condition as transmitted to them in the way of birth, precisely as Scripture names the entire nature of man in its condition transmitted by inheritance and implanted in us, in some measure *per synecdochen*, σάρξ.[1]

And thus, therefore, we call natural life, the man's individual mode of existence, involved in continual ordination of itself, which, without his own knowledge and will, he has from nature, *i.e.* has by God's appointment from his birth,—and which is peculiar to him; even although he does not raise himself above it as Ego, and place himself into this or that freely chosen and conscious relation thereto. By this natural life the personal life is most closely fenced in,—that is to say, the assertion of the man as Ego in the midst of that existence which is transmitted to him without his knowledge and will, and which, moreover, manifests itself without his conscious influence thereupon, and his conscious acquiescence in its influence upon himself. The person is the man in every stage of his growth, and in all conditions; even in the embryonic state, and in the state of morbid unconsciousness; but personal life is first present, and only present, when the capacity of the man to apprehend himself as Ego—as contrasted with that which he has in himself, and experiences—comes forth into activity out of the bondage of the germ and of potentiality. In the man of mature age, with whom we are here concerned, is no longer found the natural life in such nearly pure abstractness of its conception as in the child; and yet it is easy to him, although natural life and personal life are artificially involved, to distinguish the manifold appearances of the former from the manifold relation which the Ego assumes to them.

[1] *Schriftb.* i. 559; comp. Philippi, *Glaubenslehre*, iii. 218, where likewise is conceded that Hofmann does not merely understand by σάρξ (as *e.g.* Meyer) the materially psychical, and thus the lower, but the whole sensuous spiritual nature as it is inborn in man burdened with sin and death.

Man has not only a corporeal, but, moreover, a pneumatico-psychical nature. The spirit is indeed also included in the individuality transmitted to us by birth ($\phi\acute{\upsilon}\epsilon\sigma\theta\alpha\iota$, *nasci*); and, besides, in the general human corruption transmitted to us from Adam. Now it is assuredly the spirit itself, by virtue of which man is a person, and can apprehend himself as Ego. The thought of Ego is of the spirit; but in man's apprehension of this thought, everything which he has in himself, even his spirit, is objective. And this is possible in a twofold manner: either in such a way that man apprehends himself as Ego within the natural life itself; or that he elevates himself above it, and releases himself from it. Philosophy, as is well known, distinguishes between the empirical and the higher Ego. Scripture distinguishes between them both in the profoundest ethical relations. When the apostle (Eph. ii. 3) says that we formerly had our conversation in the lusts of our flesh, $\pi o\iota o\hat{\upsilon}\nu\tau\epsilon\varsigma$ $\tau\grave{\alpha}$ $\theta\epsilon\lambda\acute{\eta}\mu\alpha\tau\alpha$ $\tau\hat{\eta}\varsigma$ $\sigma\alpha\rho\kappa\grave{o}\varsigma$ $\kappa\alpha\grave{\iota}$ $\tau\hat{\omega}\nu$ $\delta\iota\alpha\nuo\iota\hat{\omega}\nu$, he means that our personal life was wholly absorbed into the natural life, which, even on its spiritual side, was determined by the impulse or the direction of the inherited sinful nature.[1] On the other hand, in Gal. v. 17, when he says to the Galatians that spirit and flesh are contrary the one to the other, $\tilde{\iota}\nu\alpha$ $\mu\grave{\eta}$ $\hat{\alpha}$ $\mathring{\alpha}\nu$ $\theta\acute{\epsilon}\lambda\eta\tau\epsilon$, $\tau\alpha\hat{\upsilon}\tau\alpha$ $\pi o\iota\hat{\eta}\tau\epsilon$, he supposes an Ego which is withdrawn from the nature-life, and has as its basis a spirit with a renewed constitution of nature.

For the nature-life of man, as it is by birth, is in the position of ill-regulated harmony, and therefore of commotion opposed to the likeness of God. In the language of theosophy, as has already been observed (Div. III. Sec. II.), there is found for it the appropriate and scripturally consistent expression *turba*, the opposite of שָׁלוֹם, as if of a wildly excited sea (Isa. lvii. 20), or of a constantly flowing poisonous spring (Jer. vi. 7). Even in the etymon of רָשָׁע the condition of the sinner is conceived as disharmony; for this word has, as the Arabic shows, the primitive idea of a loosening and dissolution: thus he is called loose, and indeed loosed from God, Godless,—who, because he has lost his hold upon God, is in the condition of a characterless freedom from restraint, and of fierce convulsion;

---

[1] This impulse is called by v. Hofmann nature-will, in distinction from personal-will, *Schriftb.* i. 517.

according to Isa. lvii. 20, like a sea opened up by the storm.[1] And even the most general name for the wicked, רָע, points to this *turba*; for רָעַע signifies as well to rage as to become evil (Isa. viii. 9). The spirit, too, is swallowed up into this nature-life, penetrated throughout by the principle of ὀργή. Because it is withdrawn from God's love, it has therefore lost God's image, and therewith the truth of its nature. Therefore man abides as he is by nature, when he apprehends himself as Ego, imprisoned within the nature-life. He abides so, because even his spirit has fallen into the power of the *turba*. There proceed, *e.g.* from the flesh, enticements to sensuality: the spirit, no longer having control over itself, yields to these without effort and power of resistance; and the man is placed in the midst of the sensually stimulated flesh as a centre,—that is, θέλημα τῆς σαρκός. Or the man is in the condition either to sin or to die; but his ψυχή, which has become superior to the spirit, clings to the body, and trembles at the sight of death; and the man is placed in the midst of this death-shunning ψυχή, craving in an unspiritual manner after self-preservation as a centre,—that is, θέλημα τῆς ψυχῆς in the sense of Matt. x. 39. Or there arise in the spirit suspicious, loveless thoughts: the spirit is continually torn asunder by them, and the man is placed in the midst of this rush of ungodly thoughts as a centre,—that is, θέλημα τῶν διανοιῶν. The θέλειν in all three cases is of the spirit, but of the spirit absorbed into the σάρξ, —into the ψυχή,—into its own corrupted φύσις; and of its Ego establishing itself here or there in the midst of this nature-life as a centre. But if, for example, he who is attracted to sensuality by his flesh, confesses that he who yields to these allurements disorders his body, and ever incurs tormenting stings of conscience,—these are thoughts of the spirit, on the foundation of which the Ego seeks to resist, although it may be without result, or even without the right motive. But already there is a disunion between that which wishes to establish itself as a centre in the sinful nature-life, and the Ego that wishes to oppose itself thereto. There is a disunion in the Ego itself, which on the one side is imprisoned, on the

---

[1] Accordingly, רָשָׁע appears to be akin to רָעַע, רָגַשׁ; but the Arabic refers for this word to another fundamental meaning,—to wit, to be slack, loose, in opposition to צָדַק, which originally means to be hard, firm, close.

other side wishes to set itself at liberty. In what way this disunion expresses itself if grace has effected it, is shown by the cry of the father of the child possessed with a dumb spirit (Mark ix. 24), πιστεύω, βοήθει μου τῇ ἀπιστίᾳ; and Joseph flying from the wife of Potiphar with the loss of his garment is a type of this better Ego, which withdraws itself from the seductive power of the nature-life, and leaves behind all that it has attached to itself. But we must here break off, that we may not stray over into the subject of the fifth division, where, considering the pneumatico-psychical life of the regenerate person, we shall return to this dualism, even then still unabolished, although overcome.

These are facts of experience of which we speak, although they are the more mysterious the longer we reflect on them. This mystery of the Ego, which is distinguished from the spirit, and disunites itself in itself, is the mystery of human freedom.

FREEDOM.

SEC. III.

MAN as such is free: this is a thought which, thus expressed, nowhere occurs in Scripture; for חָפְשִׁי is everywhere in the Old Testament (apart from Ps. lxxxviii. 5, where it implies relaxed, stretched forth, languishing; comp. 2 Kings xv. 5) the free man, and indeed the freed man (as distinguished from נָדִיב, חֹר, and other words, which usually denote the free-born man). נָקִי points to this or that obligation (*e.g.* the duty of defence, Deut. xxiv. 5) being released and made void. דְּרוֹר is the freedom from imprisonment, debt, and slavery, which the year of jubilee brought; and even in the New Testament, the external political legal meaning of ἐλεύθερος is prominent (see, among other places, ὁ αὑτοῦ ὤν, οὐκ ἄλλου; comp. לְנַפְשָׁהּ for חָפְשִׁית, Deut. xxi. 14). As, in the classical ἐλεύθερος, the word proceeding from this sense takes the moral signification *liberalis*; so also, in the passages of the New Testament, where they are used in a meaning of spiritual internal enlightenment, ἐλεύθερος, ἐλευθερία, ἐλευθεροῦν, return everywhere to that primitive politico-legal sense: freedom as the peculiarity of man, as man, is everywhere taken for granted in the Scripture, without anywhere being so named.

Instead of saying man is free, Scripture says man can choose (בָּחַר, LXX. αἱρεῖσθαι, αἱρετίζειν, ἐκλέγεσθαι); he can act בִּרְצוֹנוֹ; he can do הַטּוֹב בְּעֵינָיו. Life and death, blessing and cursing, were put before the first men, the people of Israel, as the result of the giving of the law on Mount Sinai: they could choose; and Joshua gives to his assembled kindreds of the people the choice between Jehovah and idols. Man can choose what God wills, and can choose what he himself, and not God, wills: he is free in his conduct towards God, as moreover God the righteous is in His conduct towards man (Isa. lxv. 12, lxvi. 3). The New Testament, moreover, everywhere takes this for granted: man has the choice to occupy a given position, or otherwise, with respect to Christ. Christ came not into the world ἵνα κρίνῃ (John iii. 17, xii. 47), but yet He came into the world εἰς κρίμα (John ix. 39), in that man in His presence must determine himself, and thus decide upon his own eternal destiny. Οὐκ ἠθελήσατε is one of the last parting words of Jesus to Jerusalem (Matt. xxiii. 37).

That this freedom of self-determination is a common possession of humanity, Scripture indirectly says when it indicates the entrance into maturer age as an entrance into the position of דַּעַת מָאוֹס בָּרָע וּבָחוֹר בַּטּוֹב (Isa. vii. 15, comp. Deut. i. 39). Decision supposes distinction, and free self-determination supposes conscious discrimination (διάκρισις, Heb. v. 14) of that which is diverse, and conscious reference of the same to the discriminating subject. Freedom of self-determination is thus something that is developed contemporaneously with the self-consciousness; and personality and freedom in this sense are inseparable correlatives. It is no contradiction of this, that הַדַּעַת טוֹב וָרָע was attached to the forbidden tree of Paradise, as the result of man's self-determination; for knowledge of good and evil is in some sense the consequence, and in some sense the postulate, of self-determination. Men already knew good and evil prior to their determination: the divine prohibition distinguished the two for them. But this theoretical knowledge did not become practical until their self-determination. They first knew what good and evil were, then they knew from their own experience what were the relations of good and evil; in such a manner, nevertheless, that they recognised the contrasted good from the position of evil, instead of recognising the contrasted evil from the position of good.

We call this freedom of self-determination the freedom of choice. "Man is free to choose" would, according to the Old Testament mode of speech, be, "he is בַּעַל הַבְּחִירָה." God thus originally created man, and put into his hands the free decision for good or for evil—ἀφῆκεν αὐτὸν ἐν χειρὶ διαβουλίου αὐτοῦ (Ecclus. xv. 14); and thus it is still. An external constraint may be used upon man's freedom of choice, which makes impossible its being carried into effect outwardly, or, as Paul expresses it (1 Cor. vii. 37), takes away from him the ἐξουσία περὶ τοῦ ἰδίου θελήματος; but only God could exercise an inward constraint which would compel man to do that which, in the moment of doing it, is not his own will; and God does not use this power: it would be a neutralizing intrusion into the nature of man; for, to be compelled to will what a man does not will, is a contradiction which annuls will itself in his nature. The strongest impulses might bias and urge the will of man in one or other direction; but for it to come to determination and action without man's self-determination and consent, is impossible. The ancients name this freedom *libertas naturæ;* in Bardesanes and other Syrian writers, it is called *chirutho* (Heb. חֵרוּת). That it is just as incapable of being lost as the will itself, to whose nature it belongs, is among our dogmatists not at all questioned. They for that reason do not regard it as the image of God, as do Raymond of Sabunde, Bernhard, and others; even these, however, not without distinguishing between *imago* and *similitudo*.

Since the fall also, man is free to choose, and for that reason is accountable; but equally certain it is, from Scripture and from experience, that by his own guilt he is not free. He is free to choose, in so far as no foreign will can irresistibly constrain his to will against his own will. He is not free, in so far as within his own personality the sin is dominant which has been allowed by himself which enslaves his will (Rom. vii. 14); and even when his Ego wills what is good, makes it impossible to him to execute that which corresponds to the will of the Ego (ποιεῖν, πράττειν, ἐνεργεῖν, κατεργάζεσθαι), Rom. vii.

19. In the former case the will itself is absolutely enslaved, in so far as, having forfeited its holy original position in which it was the free power over the opposites of good and evil, it fell under the power of evil, and thus became not independent in the presence of good. In the latter case also the Ego of man is enslaved, which on the one side has become free from the sinfully-excited nature-life, and the spirit-will absorbed into the flesh (θέλημα τῆς σαρκός); on the other side is impotent, by the entire downward tendency of sin, to bring the desired good to the only actuality. But in both cases it is man who does not succumb to sin without willing it, and is thus free to choose.[1] In the former case he wills the sin with his whole will; in the latter case, according to the better part of his Ego, which in itself is twofold, he wills not sin; but the part of the Ego absorbed into nature-life—the ἁμαρτία—with which it has become one, gains the upper hand (Rom. vii. 20). Man in both cases acts with formal freedom, but without substantial freedom;[2] or, as we prefer to say, he acts in both instances with freedom of choice, but not with freedom of power.

Man never has been and never is in a position of absolute indifference with respect to the contrasts of good and evil. God made man יָשָׁר (*rectus*), Eccles. vii. 29. The will of the first created men had its position in good. But instead of becoming permanently independent in good by willing obedience to God, they became permanently independent in evil (Gen. iii. 22). The entire natural condition of man fell thereby into the principle of wrath, and even the will of man became choked by the Turba. This situation, not to be rectified by any determination of human will, is what is natural to all men.[3] By nature we are δοῦλοι τῆς ἁμαρτίας, and hence

---

[1] Very justly says Harless, *Ethik*, p. 42: "Precisely in the obligation to one's own inclination the will is free. The will is not free only when, instead of one's own inclination, any kind of outward or internal pressure conditions the volition; whereas, by virtue of his own inclination, man has the ground of determination of his will absolutely in himself, *i.e.* is free. Thus obligation by an evil inclination, considered in the abstract, is certainly not unfreedom. Man, in this obligation to his inclination, is perfectly free, as certainly as inclination is perfectly different from constraint."

[2] Ed. Nägelsbach, *Der Gottmensch.* i. 58-66.

[3] The church dogma expresses itself thus: the *liberum arbitrium* is lost. In opposition to the Pelagian melting away of freedom into mere freedom

ἐλεύθεροι τῇ δικαιοσύνῃ (Rom. vi. 20). For either man resigns himself to righteousness, to love, or he resigns himself to sin, to wrath: a third alternative is not possible; the freedom is thus, withal, always a voluntary bondage (δουλεία), in that man either allows himself to be conditioned and determined by God, or by that which is foreign to God (1 Pet. ii. 16). If man succumbs to sin, to wrath, his freedom is degraded to a shadow; for although sin is manifest to him in its results, as bringing ruin, he yet has no more power over them and over himself: it is a power opposed to his Ego, which he increases by every sinful motion of his will, and every sinful action. If he, on the other hand, surrenders himself to righteousness, to love, he remains in his true nature,—wills and does what is good, as that which is according to his nature, for his own satisfaction, without needing an external law, and has power over evil, in that he keeps it off from himself, as that which is destructive of his peace and his happiness. Of such an one, Old Testament language says (Ex. xxxv. 21, 26, xxxvi. 2), נְשָׂאוֹ לִבּוֹ ,נְדָבַתְהוּ רוּחוֹ, *i.e.* he rises from within outward to the good deed: he is spurred to it not from without, but from within. The spirit of such an one is רוּחַ נְדִיבָה (Ps. li. 14); for without inward constraint, such as sin exercises over him, out of the innermost, freest excitement of its nature in the likeness of God, it impels him to good. Such a man is נְדָבוֹת, *i.e.* absolute voluntariness (Ps. cx. 3). He cannot will, and do otherwise: he wills and acts joyfully, according to his nature, and according to his inmost need, not κατὰ ἀνάγκην —that is, an externally compelling necessity; possibly, however, according to an inwardly impelling necessity, or, which is the same thing, κατὰ ἑκούσιον (Philem. 14), בְּנֶפֶשׁ חֲפֵצָה (1 Chron. xxviii. 9.

Only such a man is truly free, for he is free as God is, because he is free in God. God, indeed, is never called in Scripture, the Free; but in calling Himself אֶהְיֶה אֲשֶׁר אֶהְיֶה (Ex.

of choice, *liberum arbitrium* (*libertas arbitrii*) has become almost exclusively used in the sense of freedom of power; but it is necessary, especially in the face of the Romish dogmatics, always to remember that even the Lutheran doctrine attributes to man in all cases of responsibility the *libertas a coactione:* for will without freedom, as Joh. Gerhard says, is a self-contradiction, like something warm without warmth. "Voluntas quæ potest cogi et cogitur," says Luther himself, "non est voluntas sed noluntas."

iii. 14, comp. with the expression, Ex. xxxiii. 19, 2 Kings viii. 1), and thus unfolding His name of Jehovah, He designates Himself, the Controller in history, as the absolutely Free. As He is so in history, He is so in Himself. The Divine Existence, as such, is an existence engaged in constant self-fulfilment, *i.e.* living; and in this His manifest life is directed and determined by nothing else than His own nature. Similarly the will and deed of the man surrendered to God are conditioned by nothing else than by his own nature in the divine image, existing in God; he is thus free, like to God. But our natural position out of God is unfree: for allowing sin to rule in us, we feel— as is no otherwise possible—ourselves in contradiction to our true nature, and are nevertheless imprisoned in this contradiction, yielding ourselves up therein to freedom of choice, but without being able to struggle forth therefrom into freedom of power.

This is the case with man. Apart from grace, his freedom is nothing but the shadow of that freedom in the image of God, which he lost. The same is moreover true of his spirit, the living source of the thought of Ego, and of freedom. The spirit of man was the image and mirror of God, as the Triune. Out of this, his past, which also is his future, Scripture teaches us to understand his present. But, moreover, this divine mirror reflects it to our gaze only in enigmas: therefore the consciousness ought never to forsake us during the progress of the following investigation, that they are only fragments which our present knowledge grasps,—fragments, however, which serve to enhance our eager longing to attain thither where we shall know God even as we are known of God.

THE TRIPLICITY OF THE SPIRIT.

Sec. IV.

MAN is in the likeness of God, but God is spirit (John iv. 24): the first and most special subject of the divine resemblance, therefore, is the spirit of man. From what has been thus

asserted, it follows that, in the human spirit, the triplicity of
the spiritual nature of God is referred to as a type. What we
thus conclude, is everywhere the scriptural assumption. It takes
it for granted, when it attributes to God even the same modes
of activity that are proper to the human spirit. It takes it for
granted when it calls the mediating divine Hypostasis by the
name of ὁ λόγος; for λόγος, however it may be conceived, is a
spiritual mode of activity, or the product of such an activity:
hence the divine λόγος is the divine archetype of exactly that
which is so called in the region of man's spirit-life. And
how closely Paul suggests to us the resemblance of God's
spiritual nature and man's spirit, when he compares (1 Cor.
ii. 11) the knowledge about the depths of the Godhead which
belongs to the Spirit of God—not as distinguished from the
Father and the Son, but as a Spirit of revelation, as distinguished from all other beings—with the knowledge of
man's spirit about what is in man! Hence the old church
literature is full of the thought that man's spirit is εἰκὼν or
μίμημα of God's spirit-nature. As a piece of glass, says
Gregory of Nyssa, reflects the entire form of the sun, although
in very diminished proportion, thus out of the limited nature
of our spirit shine forth the copies of the inexpressible attributes of the Godhead. In the same sense he calls our spirit,
an eye, created of a kindred nature with the sun, in order to
look upon the sun.[1] If this be scriptural, the triplicity of the
human spirit will not be too bold an expression for us to use.
Moreover, Jo. Scotus Erigena is not the first to speak of a
trinitas nostræ naturæ in the form of God (*de div. nat.* ii. 23),
but Augustine, before him, teaches a *trinitas mentis* like to
God's (*de trin.* xiv. 12); and, that this is an expression corresponding to a matter of fact, which obtrudes itself not only on
the path of scriptural inquiry, but also on that of self-observation, how many testimonies—intentional, and by no means
arbitrary—may be accumulated to prove! "Les perfections
de Dieu," says E. G. Leibnitz, in the preface to his *Theodicee*,
" sont celles de nos âmes, mais il les possede sans bornes : il est
un océan, dont nous n'avous reçu que des gouttes. Il y a en
nous quelque *puissance*, quelque *connoissance*, quelque *bonté*,

---

[1] *Vid.* E. W. Möller, *Gregorii Nysseni doctrina de hominis natura*, secs. 9, 10.

mais elles sont toutes entières en Dieu." Among the moderns, Carus confesses in his *Psyche*—although as little allied to Scripture as dependent on Augustine—a " triplicity of the higher psychical life;" and both he, in his *Grundzügen einer neuen und Wissenschaftlichen Cranioscopie,* and E. Huschke, in his work, *Schädel, Hirn, und Seele,* place this trinity of our fundamental spiritual powers in connection[1] with the trinity of the convolutions of the skull and of the brain,—an association which had obtruded itself on the ancients, and not on the ground of arbitrary fancy, but of pathological consideration, as the later physiologists of the brain, certainly not without surprise, may perceive from Nemesios.[2]

The triplicity of the human spirit is a fact which is established, even although we should not succeed in attaining the exact truth in its development. But, in attempting this, we have to adopt a different method from that of the empirical or rational psychology. For the treatment of this latter is regressive: it analyzes the human spirit, and thus attains to its triplicity, perhaps as a result; whereas, for the biblical psychology, on the other hand, this triplicity is a postulate. For its method proceeds according to scriptural direction, which leads from knowledge of God to knowledge of ourselves—not backwards from the spirit to God, but from the archetype forwards to the antitype. We are primarily concerned about nothing less than about the right knowledge of the internal divine process of the Trinity, so far as the Holy Scripture and living experience render this knowledge *à posteriori* possible to us.

We have already referred (Div. I. Sect. III.) to a modern conception of this process wholly foreign to Scripture. It is considered as the growth of the divine self-consciousness. If it be thus supposed, that it is in the Spirit generally that God first attains to self-consciousness, so that thus commences the growth from unconsciousness, or even from a mere potentiality

[1] Similarly *e.g.* Hanne, in his *Confessions* (1861), p. 64.

[2] He teaches that the fore-brain is the organ of the $\varphi \alpha \nu \tau \alpha \sigma \tau \iota \varkappa \acute{o} \nu$ (the power of representation), because from it proceed the nerves of sense—$\nu \epsilon \tilde{\upsilon} \rho \alpha$; the mid-cavity of the brain the organ of the $\delta \iota \alpha \nu o \eta \tau \iota \varkappa \acute{o} \nu$ (the intelligence); and the hinder, the organ of the $\mu \nu \eta \mu o \nu \epsilon \upsilon \tau \iota \varkappa \acute{o} \nu$ (the capacity of memory). Certainly this rests upon a false view of the division of the brain, and of the nerves of sense, among which only the nerve of smell is associated with the fore-brain.

of consciousness, the process is a blind and naturally necessary process, whereby the nature of God is annulled, except for those who identify it pantheistically with the world. Or the self-consciousness, which is engaged in the *becoming*, is conceived as growing higher by the use of means, so that the *becoming* thus proceeds from immediate self-consciousness. In this case, the process comes under the partial point of view of the thought, and there results the supposition, unworthy of God, that in advancing from a lower degree He attained to a higher; in that He proceeds, although not from unconsciousness or mere potentiality of consciousness, still from consciousness undeveloped, and not yet become capable of itself. 1 Cor. ii. 11 is only seemingly in favour of this. Certainly God's Spirit in a peculiar manner is that in God which knows, but not as distinguished from Father and Son, but as distinguished from all creatures by virtue of its proceeding from the Father and the Son: it alone knows both, because its nature primitively exists in both, and is immanent in both; and as the historical process of salvation corresponds to that which is within God, so there is no knowledge of the nature and will of the Father and the Son possible, which does not proceed from Him who proceeds from Father and Son. Where could there be found even one scriptural passage, whence could be gathered that the Father is not already, at the commencement of the process, perfectly conscious of Himself? God becomes objective in an exact resemblance of Himself, but not in order to become perfectly conscious of Himself to Himself. This likeness is, indeed, called λόγος, in so far as it is the perfect knowledge of the Father about Himself, which comprehends and imprints itself therein; and υἱὸς, inasmuch as the bringing forth of this exact likeness is not merely an act of thought, but at the same time, and primarily, an act of will.[1]

But if the proceeding of the Trinity is no process of growing self-consciousness, the antitypical triplicity of the human spirit does not subsist in the triplicity of the momenta wherein the

---

[1] Against the view which prevailed in the middle ages, that the begetting of the Son was effected *per intellectum divinum*, and the emanation of the Spirit *per voluntatem divinam*, Duns Scotus observed with much justice, that the *intelligere* did not become *gignere* until the interference of the *velle*.

higher self-consciousness is accomplished. When the spirit, for instance, itself takes its place as *existing*, it first of all represents itself to itself as something else which it has in front of itself, and further attains to higher self-consciousness by the recognition of itself in this other nature, knows it to be one with itself, and thus returns into itself as a self-conscious spirit from this externalization, in other words, in the act of this higher self-consciousness, the Ego is a nature presenting itself to itself, a nature presented, and a nature recognising itself in this presentation, and thus a threefold nature in uncancelled numerical unity.[1] We do not deny that even in this the process of the Trinity is reflected by way of likeness, but very far from exhaustively. There is generally no act of the human spirit, in which the process of the Trinity is not in some way shadowed forth. Even that completion of the higher self-consciousness is such an act. It is the beginning of all thought—that which underlies all thought, and the general basis which accompanies it. But, assuredly, thought is a reality which partially and in some degree resembles the divine life of the Trinity. The name λόγος proves this, for *word* is surely nothing else than composed and formed thought. But does God attain for the first time to the thought of Ego in the Logos? So little, that He rather comprehends His entire perfectly conscious nature in the Logos as His exact image. The process of the Trinity is made finite, by conceiving of it as the accomplishment of self-consciousness; and, at the same time, it is made one-sided when it is conceived of only as a process of thought.

The process of the Trinity, as the Scripture instructs us about it, comes chiefly (1) under the point of view of the will; for the Father, in begetting the Son, desires an object of His love, who, in order to satisfy His loving will, must be of like nature with Himself : (2) under the point of view of thought and knowledge; for, in begetting the Son, He thinks Himself, and combines the whole fulness of this self-thought in Him, the Logos, *i.e.* the Word;—He knows Himself in begetting the Son; and after He has begotten Him, He knows Himself in Him: (3) under the point of view of experience; for, after that God

[1] Read the instructive article "Trinität," by Hagemann, in the *Wetzer-Welteschen Catholic Church Lexicon.*

had attained an object of His love, the love of the loving one, and the responding love of the loved one, as the one finds Himself in the other, become a reciprocal experience of love, which is hypostatized in the Holy Ghost, who proceeds from both.[1] The process, in all the momenta of this its self-completion, is undergone by the divine self-consciousness, which does not come into being first of all in the middle of the process, but precedes it, and throughout accompanies it; for neither will, nor thought and knowledge, nor experience, are possible without self-consciousness: they are all personal acts. It is a trine of acts, which, however, form an indissoluble unity. For as little as it can be said that God first attained to self-consciousness in the third hypostasis, as little also can it be said that He then first attained to experience. For (1) the will which becomes the fact of the begetting of the Son, has as its precedent ground the perception of the want of the *Ego* in respect of a *Tu*, and the experience of the longing of love for such a *Tu*. This perception and this experience are the impelling forces of the will. (2) The thought and knowledge which become the objectiveness of God in His own likeness in the Word—the Logos—have, as their precedent ground, the experience of want of satisfaction, and the will to make to themselves an object, in order to find satisfaction therein. (3) The experience has, as its precedent ground, the knowledge of the one by the other, and the will passing over into one another, reciprocally immanent in one another. There are three acts, but in such a way that every single act involves both the others in itself; and it is thus a tri-unity of acts. These three acts are not the three persons of the Godhead themselves, but the foundation of their *actus personales*.

"In the divine love-nature," says an old theological scholar,[2] "which is merely unending life, there is a *central*, or most inward of all, infinite, and experiencing will, or willing experience, which power of experience may be called the disposition; and in it the feelings may be distinguished from the understanding (the *subjective* primitive wisdom of God). The infinite will of God must have an infinite desire, longing,

---

[1] On the internal necessity of this hypostatizing, compare the discussions of Richard of St. Victor, brought to remembrance by Liebner and Sartorius.
[2] The anonymous German editor of John Pordage's works.

and aspiration after an *adequate*—that is, infinite—object, that it may unite itself therewith; and because there is no other infinite nature than the spirit of eternity itself, it has an infinite hunger after itself, as the only object which can suffice all its craving and appease all its hunger. Therefore it excites its whole nature, and turns and impels it upon itself into its *central* or innermost disposition. And thus the eternal will begets or generates, by such inward turning of its whole nature upon its own foundation upon its everlasting heart, an eternal infinite essential living, all-filling, all-satisfying, and sufficing *experimental notion* and knowledge of itself, which is the essential image of itself, and the sufficing immediate object of its desire.

" In this birth we have to observe the coincidence of two things, attributes, or perfections,—one active, the other passive,—to wit, (1) the strong, eager desire of the divine will, which stirs the whole nature of the Godhead, forces together and throws all its rays as a divine seed into its own innermost being; and (2) the passive disposition, (which, although in itself it is absolutely life, power, and influence, is nevertheless passive in respect of the will, and of this impregnation,) that receives into itself all these irradiating powers, grasps them, holds or *fixes* them,—gives to them, as it were, an abiding nature, and *moulds* them into an eternal birth of a blessed essential knowledge,—perhaps the deep source of the two *infusions*[1] in nature, male and female, which concur in the bringing forth of all things.

" From these two (the infinite desiring *subjecto* or base, and the all-filling infinite *objecto* or object) originates and proceeds infallibly a third,—to wit, an infinite essential triumphant joy,—which flows through the whole being, and *tinges* it, as it were, with an infinite, all-surpassing, inconceivable restorative flavour of its own, and thereby concludes and perfects its own infinite blessedness. For by virtue of the divine unity of nature, every *reality* or perfection in God communicates itself to all the rest, which can occur no otherwise than by one influencing the other, and therefore by one beaming into the other its essential effluences. And thus all the powers of the contented and satisfied *subject* or ground, in most intimate union with the all-satisfying object, must communicate to one another a taste and comfort of their

[1] *Tincturen*, orig.

joy, by essential irradiations of every one of them into all the rest; which most holy *mutual* irradiations of every one into all the others together, constitute, as it were, a divine air, respiration, breath, or spirit, which penetrates the entire divine nature."

Let not offence be taken at the quaint grossness of these words ; the process of the Trinity can hardly be better exhibited *à posteriori* than is here accomplished. Chiefly it is rightly concluded from them, as elsewhere from theosophy, that the primitive ground of the Godhead is a will originating by nothing, infinite, and conceiving itself: not as though this will in God could in any way have temporally preceded being and self-consciousness,—a representation militating against the eternal absoluteness of God, against which we have already sufficiently declared ourselves;—but the true conception of God requires that, even in relation to being and self-consciousness, the will should be apprehended as the primitively causal first in God.[1] Later theology will be compelled to acknowledge this more and more ; for the great problem of Christology—the Kenôsis—is absolutely insoluble without this prior assumption. In carefully weighed consideration of the incarnation, Thomasius therefore conceives of the will as the absolutely primitive in God: " The nature of God is not inflexible dead substance, but throughout is will, life, *actus*,—is itself ordaining itself, itself willing itself, itself absolutely powerful over itself."[2] And he remarks thereupon, that this definition of all effort must be placed at the summit of theology. When God Himself declares His own most mysterious name (Ex. iii. 14) by אֶהְיֶה אֲשֶׁר אֶהְיֶה, He gives to its meaning the will which wills itself and determines itself out of itself as the root.[3] And when the apostle (1 John iv. 8)

[1] Thus, what J. P. Lange remarks against this (*Deutsche Zeitschr.* 1859, p. 23), does not touch us: "The will, without which the thought and experience are not yet consecutive, cannot be conceived of as spirit; as a dim impulse of becoming, it comes under the category of natural development." We are far from attributing to God self-unconscious will, which indeed would be a blind natural impulse; but none the less His self-willing will passes with us as the ground of His being, and his one self-comprehending will as the ground of His self-consciousness.

[2] *Dogm.* § 8, comp. 41 (ii. 203).

[3] See the remarks of Drechsler in my *Commentary on Genesis*, p. 67, ed. 3. In the personal creature, being precedes will: in God, indeed, the will does not precede existence; but, as distinct from the creature, God

says of God, not that He is *the* love, but that He is love (ἀγάπη),—*i.e.* that He is love in the deepest ground and entire circuit of His nature living itself forth,—we obtain the disclosure—which follows, besides, from the fact, that He is light, absolutely free from darkness (1 John i. 5),—that the will which is the root of His being has love as its impulse, and is thus the will of love. Therefore Scripture places the process of the Trinity under the point of view of love. It is mediated in the Son of Love. The loving will of the Father begets, when entering into the ground of His self-conscious and self-experiencing nature, engenders the thought and longing there after an object of love that is present, forms it into the Word, and satisfies it in the Son; and the Son is the brightness of the Father's glory, and the very image of His hidden nature, in whom the Father knows Himself, and which acknowledges the Father in itself and of itself,—the substance of His self-acknowledgment brought forth and realized by the Father's loving will; and the Holy Ghost is the breathing forth of the mutual love of both—the breath of love of the loving one and the beloved one—the emanation of the experience of love, in which the loving one discovers the beloved one, and the beloved one discovers the loving one. If I were to picture to the senses in a figure the process of the Trinity, I would paint a fiery circle as the symbol of the fiery loving will of the Father; and in this circle a sunlight centre as the symbol of the Son,—the object of love, which lights the whole infinite depth of the divine nature of love; and proceeding from this sunlight centre to the circumference of the fiery circle, an abundance of rays, as the symbol of the triumph of love going forth from the Father through the Son, and entirely filling Father and Son.[1]

is Lord of His own existence, absolutely *causa sui* (opposed to Philippi, *Glaubenslehre*, ii. 63–65). The name of Jehovah designates Him, be the etymological origination of the idea what it will, as the absolute Ego—as the absolute personality, ruling with unconditioned freedom (Keil, *Genesis*, p. 37).

[1] In the Lutheran monthly publication *Lehre und Wehre* (St Louis 1858, iv. 63), a word of Gregory of Nazianzum is recalled to me, in reference to the above passage: "On the subject of God's birth we ought with reverence to be silent." But Gregory, with the other fathers who were faithful to the Nicene faith, has himself pointed out that it is not unbecoming to speak of this mystery with adoring veneration, and to reflect

THE TRIPLICITY OF THE SPIRIT.

If we now consider the human spirit, there are three fundamental forms in which its life manifests itself: a striving forwards, a going forwards, a going into itself and being still. It strives and longs after the attainment of its destination in God: it attains in the way of thought to its object; and then reposes in His nature, as in a continual current and constant circular motion.[1] Briefly, the life of the spirit is a threefold unity of will, thought, and experience. We say—of experience;[2] for as there is a psychical experience, which consists in direct perception of the irradiated sensuous charms of experience, and a psychical feeling of pleasure or displeasure, which proceeds from furthering or restraining impressions which intrude into our psychical life, so there is also a higher spiritual experience, which receives its excitements even from the thinking and willing life of the spirit itself: as, for example, the peace and the joy which are the reflex of the idea of God taken up by the spirit into its thought and will, which idea nevertheless, in fact, has nothing to do with our nerves of perception. Without thus interchanging experience and feeling, in the sense of these conceptions that is now customary, we analyze the life of the spirit into will, thought, and experience. There are three well distinguishable realities, of which, however, none comes into operation, none is present in actuality, without the other two being somewhere therein—like to the περιχώρησις of the three divine acts and the three divine persons, which, by virtue of their likeness of nature, invariably penetrate and live through one another: so that every person, by its relation, shares in the possession of the nature of the two others; and their knowledge and will, reflecting itself in reciprocal love, is an absolutely united nature.[3]

on the hints of the Holy Scripture with trembling joy: for to be able to think is the dignity of man; and even to be allowed to think upon the holiest of all subjects is one of his most blessed prerogatives, which indeed must be exercised in the consciousness of our infancy in this state (1 Cor. xiii. 11): for "woe to the wise in their own eyes,"—we are nothing but stammering children.

[1] According to Göschel, *Der Mensch diesseits und jenseits*, p. 35.

[2] Not,—"of feeling," as *e.g.* Kahnis, in the *psychologic section*, ix. 2 (p. 135), of his Dogmatics, according to which the feeling, thought, will, of the spirit, correspond to the experience, perception, desire of the soul.

[3] Zöckler, *Naturtheol.* i. 758, says, with reference to the above, that I compare thought to the Son; and that this comparison of the will, thought,

The threefold life of the willing, thinking (word-forming), and experiencing spirit which points back to this archetype, is man's own, even still in his present natural condition, without its being possible to call it a remainder of the primitive divine likeness; for it is only the framework that is left to man of that which has faded away. Willing, thinking, experiencing, are indeed, in themselves, mere forms of life. In the original condition this threefold life of the spirit was a life of love in the likeness of God, filled up by the power of a glad conscience, which knew itself one with God,—an image of the eternally resting flow, and the eternally flowing rest, of the blessed life of the Godhead. As God has satisfaction in Himself, so the human spirit sought and found satisfaction in God. God was the object of his will, the contents of his thought, the fountain of his experience. Not as though he had not also made created being the object and contents of his will, thought, and experience, but everything in God, and with a view to God. For the necessity is based in the nature of the spirit to possess an object corresponding to the nobility of its original source, with which it might make itself one, and in the union with which with itself it might feel itself blessed. God is indeed love, and the spirit of man is the inspiration of this God; therefore the life of the spirit is love, and nothing truly satisfies it but the love whence it originated. After he has fallen from this love, still his life does not renounce this character of love implanted in it. For what he continues to make the substance of his will, thought, and experience, has the purpose of satisfying this necessity of love, or of removing what is adverse to this satisfaction. What a French philosopher lately maintained—*Aimer c'est vouloir, et vouloir c'est aimer*—is, in substance, true also of thought and experience. Each of the three has for a final purpose the apprehension, acknowledgment, and experience of an object of

and experience, with Father, Son, and Spirit, almost corresponds to the Taulerish triad *concupiscentia, ratio, ira*. But this triad is the wholly useless dregs of a Platonic representation; and the case does not stand thus, that I compare the thought to the Son; but the act by which the Father—the will, having its original foundation in Himself—brings forth the Son I compare to the thought: for the Son is λόγος, Word, *i.e.* embodiment of the thought which the Father conceives in thinking of an object of His loving will, that may be like to Him with exact likeness.

love which satisfies the spirit's need of love. In the present natural condition of man, none of the three indeed have the right direction and the right contents; but the triad of spiritual activities, and their working one into the other, is nevertheless a shadow of the three acts of the divine life, and their Perichorêsis.

This consideration of the spirit in the light of its archetype, affords us the great advantage of making known to us those capacities and activities which belong to it, even apart from the Psyche. As in this division we wish to advance gradually from the most internal to the most external nature of man, this is to us doubly important. We do not even become till now capable of finding our way in the biblical nomenclature of spiritual powers and efficiencies. Proceeding from the psychological mode of speech in Scripture, we should have been entangled in a labyrinth, as the psychological researches of Roos and Beck show. For the use of language in Scripture is absolutely swayed by the fundamental view, that the spiritual life in itself, that the spiritual and psychical life, that the threefold life of man—the spiritual, psychical, and corporeal life—is a unity. The same Perichorêsis which unites the three spiritual activities compactly into efficiency, shows itself also in their verbal denominations. Willing, thinking, experiencing, are never distinguished in Scripture with terminologic sharpness. The word יָדַע indicates not merely knowledge, but also experience; the word טָעַם, not merely taste, but also understanding; the word דָּמָה, not only thinking or representation, but also remembering or purpose to do anything. In יָצַר, thought and will are combined as one forming activity of the heart. And rich as the Old Testament language is in words which signify to will, and to desire, yet there is never once imprinted on it the distinction between inclination of the will, and determination of the will, which in the Greek is represented by βούλεσθαι (wherewith וַיֹּאֶל, Hiph. הוֹאִיל of a like root) and θέλειν. The efficiencies of the spirit are neither distinguished in themselves, nor are the activities of the spirit, as such, sharply distinguished from those that are psychico-somatically effected. Will, thought, and experience, and all the higher and lower activities into which these spiritual fundamental activities ramify, are predicated of רוּחַ, לֵב, and נֶפֶשׁ indiscriminately,—in so far as רוּחַ is the supreme principle, נֶפֶשׁ the secondary principle, emanating herefrom towards the side of the corporeity, and לֵב is the internal focus of the threefold life of man. Thus all three, in their manner, partake in the highest and lowest activities and affections of that life. It may, at any rate, be said that the spirit of man, in the immediateness of its origin, is called נְשָׁמָה; in the concentration of its activities, especially of its thought and will, לֵב; in the circumstantial and sensitive unity of its thought and will pervading from נְשָׁמָה throughout the לֵב,—רוּחַ. But even this distinction is not clearly marked; although certainly רוּחַ by far the most frequently designates the spirit, not as thinking and willing, but as experiencing,—or the general circumstantial character and disposition which includes thought and will in itself. A reflex of the relation of the trinity is not easy to be mistaken in the mode of speech; but it is not to be gathered from it by itself, without close examination through the typical relation that has just been considered by us.

In the New Testament, especially in the Pauline writings, the psychologic mode of expression is much sharper and profounder. The mystery of the Trinity, that has become historically revealed in the work of redemption, throws here its noonday light into the depth of human nature; and it is, indeed, the conceptive, highly-cultivated Greek tongue, in which the primitive condition, the actual condition, and the destination of man are treated upon,—not without the interposition of the endeavour already made in Alexandrianism, to introduce into the religion of revelation at the same time with the elements of truth contained in the Greek philosophy, the forms of speech that it had coined. There are especially three ideas, to which the New Testament disclosures upon the likeness of God in the spirit-life of man are bound. The psychologic main and universal idea which the New Testament, as distinct from Hellenism, primarily establishes, is Pneuma, spirit; the three ideas which we have now to consider strictly, according to the New Testament meaning and use, are the threefold development of this one main and universal idea.

NOUS, LOGOS, PNEUMA.[1]

SEC. V.

WHEN the eternal person who was manifested in Jesus Christ is called by John ὁ λόγος, we are plainly pointed back thereby to an intrinsically divine archetype of the created human λόγος. Humanity is Θεοῦ γένος precisely for that reason, that it is essentially distinguished by means of the λόγος from the ἄλογα ζῶα, which know that which they know—φυσικῶς, not λογικῶς (Jude 10). Nevertheless ὁ λόγος, as the name of the eternal person manifested in Jesus Christ, signifies not *ratio*, but *oratio* or *verbum*. In the New Testament Scripture

[1] V. Zezschwitz, *Profangräcität und bibl. Sprachgeist*, p. 33, objects to this triad, because the bringing forward of λόγος as an independent capacity of the spirit contradicts the biblical *usus loquendi*, which constantly rejects λόγος in the sense of reason, and because πνεῦμα occupies a position which contradicts its meaning. But (1) they are not three independent capacities of spirit which I put forth in the above triad, but the three factors in which, as in the theogonic procession of the Trinity, the human spirit-life is brought to complete development. (2) I do not understand (as the reader will find) λόγος in the sense of reason, but in the sense of word; and find the circumstance not a little favourable to my parallel of the divine type, that the Scripture so constantly rejects the former meaning, guarding thereby against the arriving at a false representation of the divine Logos, by starting from the constituent factors of the human spirit-life. (3) It need not appear strange, that within the pneumatic nature of man is assumed the existence of a Pneuma in a narrower sense, since even within the pneumatic nature of the Godhead we distinguish a Pneuma in a special sense. This, moreover, answers the objections of the eminent Swedish physician, O. M. Witt, in his work on empirical and biblical psychology, *Själen, i normalt och sjukligt tillstånd* (the soul, its normal and morbid condition), Pt. i. (1858), p. 84, that *Logos* nowhere occurs in Scripture as a part of man, and *Pneuma* does not occur in a double signification. Krumm also, in his treatise *de notionibus psychologicis Paulinis* (1858), finds in the above triad a strange *divisio spiritus in tres partes*, and remarks against it, (1) that λόγος is not at all a conception of biblical psychology; (2) that he does not perceive how πνεῦμα in the narrow sense is distinguished from καρδία. But it is only in the immediate meaning of *ratio* that it is not a conception of biblical psychology, but probably in the meaning *oratio* (word and faculty, or gift of the word) it is a most weighty and important one; and if human πνεῦμα is distinguished from human νοῦς, πνεῦμα can certainly not coincide with καρδία, because, even according to the repre-

generally, λόγος nowhere occurs in the meaning *ratio*, not even in John among his many other significations,—a fact which, as observed by an ancient investigator of biblical psychology, has its reason in a divine decorum.[1] In the Johannean writings it means throughout the Word, sometimes the individual word, as an expression of Jesus, John ii. 22; of God, x. 35; of the prophet, xii. 38; of the Scripture, xv. 25; of the people generally (proverb), iv. 37; sometimes the entire word of Jesus, as *e.g.* viii. 31, if ye remain ἐν τῷ λόγῳ τῷ ἐμῷ; or of God, *e.g.* xvii. 17, ὁ λόγος ὁ σὸς ἀλήθεια ἐστίν, both of which are essentially one and the same word (xiv. 23). Thus also ὁ λόγος, John i. 1; ὁ λόγος τῆς ζωῆς, 1 John i. 1; ὁ λόγος τοῦ Θεοῦ, Apoc. xix. 13, will signify respectively the Word, the word of life, the word of God. Elsewhere it is the word of the proclamation, the tenor of the ῥήματα τοῦ Θεοῦ, which is so called

sentation and *usus loquendi* of Paul, discursive reflective knowledge is a function of the καρδία itself: for man knows the mystery of his salvation by the enlightened eyes of his heart (Eph. i. 18), in which the light of spiritual knowledge shines forth out of darkness (2 Cor. iv. 6). In his passion for system, Krumm attributes to the apostle a different mode of conception from all the rest of the biblical writers, even from Luke (*vid.* Luke i. 51, xxiv. 25), in that he (and this is the fundamental thought of his whole treatise) makes him the author of the division of the πνεῦμα into νοῦς as *intelligendi organum*, and καρδία as *sentiendi organum*, and limits the reference of the passages, in which the heart appears as the organ of knowledge, to immediate experimental knowledge as perception. But, in truth, it is the case in Paul's writings, as everywhere in the Holy Scripture, that καρδία is the internal spiritual-psychical hearth of man's life, and, moreover, the workshop of the νοήματα (Phil. iv. 7). On the other hand, Paul gives us in the Hellenic νοῦς, less frequently used than καρδία, the first member of a distinguishing of the spiritual process of life in itself, to which καρδία is in no way the second member; but πνεῦμα τοῦ νοός (Eph. iv. 23) is at any rate the closing link. For the rest, Krumm more nearly agrees with the above triad than he thinks; and though this Sec. V. looks to him strangely theosophic, we will still not be angry with the young philosopher, since even he acknowledges the important premiss, *Spiritus humanus et substantiâ et efficientiâ simillimus est divino* (p. 20), which we have ventured to consider somewhat more deeply, and will confidently await the result which Göschel, agreeing with us, states, confessing out of his riper and richer experience (in p. 37 of his work, *über den Menschen diesseits und jenseits*), "He who observes himself in his thinking, will learn from his own experience to distinguish νοῦς, λόγος, and πνεῦμα τοῦ νοός."

[1] H. W. Clemm, *Schriftgemässe Gedanken von der Kräften der menschlichen Seele* (1760), p. 90.

(comp. John vi. 68; Apoc. i. 2, 9, etc.). The word of the proclamation, and the word that appeared in Jesus, are distinguished in such a way, that the latter is the personal Word, which preceded the former; in which God has from everlasting given to His counsel of love an objective existence in His own sight. Moreover, that He, in this everlasting Word, has not only expressed His will, but also His nature, in His own presence, John affirms in the brief Θεὸς ἦν ὁ λόγος. The Pauline testimonies which lead up to John i. 1—*e.g.* Col. i. 15–17; Heb. i. 3 —say it still more circumstantially. And if further proof were needed for this metaphysical apprehension of the Logos, it would be found in Philo: for it is an undeniable fact, that the Johannean doctrine of the Logos is not without relation to the doctrine of Philo. The apostolic proclamation did not scorn the forms of ideas already coined by the Alexandrian philosophy, but it filled them with the contents presented by the history of their New Testament realization. As Christianity withdrew the limits from the spirit of the Old Testament revelation, and separated the imperishable gold of its substance from the dross of the cosmical elements, so it became a refining fire for Hellenistic and Hellenic philosophy, the transfiguration and consecration of what was true, and of the forms in use in both for the presentation of the truth.

The admitted propriety is sufficient for us here, of the assumption, that ὁ λόγος, in the trinitarian sense, is the God-spoken eternally personal Word, which comprehends in itself God's nature and will. From this assumption we can much more clearly apprehend the antitypical threefold spirit-life of man. That in man which wills, thinks, and experiences, is called in general πνεῦμα, as God is the Tri-personal πνεῦμα. But in this self-conscious πνεῦμα are distinguished νοῦς, λόγος, and πνεῦμα,—a representation of the Father, Son, and Spirit.

That which, or by means of which the self-conscious spirit, thinks and wills, is called νοῦς (*mens, animus,* as distinct from *anima*), or also διάνοια (*ratio*). According to its etymon, νοῦς, from the Sanscrit root *gnâ,* signifies spiritual perception and comprehension (for γνοῦς, as *nomen, narus, navus,* for *gnomen, gnarus, gnavus*), certainly only the thinking nature;[1] as also

[1] *Vid.* Autenrieth on v. Nägelsbach's *Homerischer Theologie* (1861), p. 393.

mens (μένος, v. Passow), Sanscr. *manas*, is named from *man—mnâ*, to think; but the will (θέλησις) allows itself to be taken up into the thought (νοεῖν, διανοεῖσθαι), inasmuch as all will is an endeavour of the spirit, from a ground that has become conscious, towards an object that has become conscious, and thus is enclosed on both sides by thought: as again the thought is a seeking—and, as such, a will—of that which is to be found.[1] This is the universal scriptural view, on which account, *e.g.* רָעָה (רְעָא)—whence רַע, רְעוּת, רַעְיוֹן—unites in itself the ideas of will or endeavour, and of thought (comp. especially Ps. cxxxix. 1, 17). That νοῦς is both, as well the willing as the thinking faculty in man, is seen from Rom. vii.: in man, when by the divine law he has attained to consciousness about what is good and evil, commences a conscious will for the good that is known and approved of God. The subject of this will is his νοῦς. The moving causes of conduct lie herein, effectuated by the thought (Rom. xiv. 5). That, therefore, by virtue of which man thinks and determines himself, the thinking and willing faculty in him, is his νοῦς. As the will of the νοῦς is to be distinguished from longing, so is its thought to be distinguished from conception, and its knowledge from perception. The ἀόρατα of God are called (Rom. i. 20) νοούμενα: the created world is sensuously perceived καθορᾶται by man when his eye falls upon it; and in penetrating through the multiplicity of that which appears in this or that manner, to the root of its source in this or that way constituted, he attains by means of his νοῦς the idea of the Godhead. In a similar sense, the Epistle to the Hebrews (xi. 3) pronounces the fact of the origination of the world by the word of God to be a νοούμενον of faith, *scil.* of the believing νοῦς. To recognise the not phenomenal eternal source of origination of the visible universe beginning in time, is a concern of the νοῦς. And in Apoc. xiii. 18, comp. xvii. 9, it is the νοῦς which unriddles the cipher of the future. Thus νοεῖν is the radical, ideal, penetrating thought and knowledge, directed to the essence of things, and which, in a word, are spiritual or rational, and the will determining itself in conformity thereto, distinct from the kindred psychical facts of presentation, perception, and desire.

The product of the νοῦς is the λόγος; for the human spirit, as

[1] Similarly Gregory of Nyssa, in Möller, *l.c.* p. 27.

not merely endowed with consciousness, but with self-consciousness, for that very reason is also, as the Targums (Gen. ii. 7) interpret, רוּחַ מְמַלְלָא, *i.e.* speaking spirit—spirit capable of speech.[1] The νοῦς is related to the λόγος, as the speaking λόγος (*ratio*) to the spoken λόγος (*oratio, verbum*). In the New Testament Scripture, as already observed, λόγος in this signification does not occur; but its use of λογικός, ἄλογος, λογίζεσθαι, ἀναλογίζεσθαι, συλλογίζεσθαι, λογισμός, διαλογισμός, refers to this aspect of the idea: λόγος is distinguished from φωνή and ἦχος, as the speech or word of a personal nature endowed with λόγος (capacity of thought). This twofold λόγος, the thinking and the spoken, is related, according to Philo's expression, as πηγή and ἀπορροή; and as λόγος in the former sense is a capacity or an efficiency of the νοῦς, so in the latter sense the λόγος is the organ of the νοῦς: they are related, once more to quote from Philo, as Moses and Aaron (Ex. iv. 15)—ὑποβολεὺς λόγου νοῦς.[2] What we are here asserting, is nothing foreign to the Scripture. The Old Testament use of the word אָמַר proceeds from the essential identity of thought and speech, for אָמַר signifies both,—the thought as inward speaking (with or without בְּלִבּוֹ), and the speech as audible thinking; just as also הָגָה and שִׂיחַ (LXX. μελετᾶν, ἀδολεσχεῖν) denote meditation, as wholly internal, or as faint, solemnly audible, speaking. Thinking and speaking, spirit and speech, are necessarily associated. Human speech, indeed, is effected psychically and corporeally, and is indissolubly bound to this agency; but speech in itself, even in the pure spirit, even in the Godhead itself, is inseparable from thought, for the word is the comprehension of the thought. And that word which, according to Rousseau, it is necessary to presuppose in order to supply the foundation for[3] the human use of the word, is finally no other than the word of all words—the archetypal Logos.[4] Νοῦς and λόγος, in the way of likeness, stand

---

[1] In the later Hebrew scholastic language, הַמְדַבֵּר is the speaker, Arab. *en-nâtik*, and thus, as related to it, man, and הַנֶּפֶשׁ־הַמְדַבֶּרֶת, the speaking soul, Arab. *en-nefs en-nâtikeh*, and so, as akin to it, *anima rationalis*.

[2] *Vid.* thereupon Grossmann, *Quæstionum Philonearum*, p. 11 (1829), 4.

[3] See Bautain, *Experimental-psychologie*, transl. by Dalhoff, ii. 145-156.

[4] See my *Jesurun*, pp. 43-45; and besides, the opinion of Hamann in reference to the origin of language (*Works*, iv. 33; comp. Gildemeister, *Leben*

in such essentially necessary relation as God the Father and God the Son;[1] for if we wish to name Him in a way corresponding to ὁ λόγος, the Son's name, the Father is ὁ νοῦς, *scil.* ὁ τῶν ὅλων νοῦς (Philo), ὁ ἀΐδιος νοῦς (Athenagoras), ὁ τέλειος νοῦς (Justin), *i.e.* the absolute *nûs*, whereof it is said, τίς ἔγνω νοῦν Κυρίου (Isa. xl. 13, LXX.; Rom. xi. 34; 1 Cor. ii. 16). His *nûs*, which designed the plan of the universe, is unsearchable. And there are infinitely many of the divine words proceeding from this *nûs*: for of His thoughts (רֵעָיו, Ps. cxxxix. 17), how immeasurably great is the sum! But the Son as Logos (מֵימְרָא; and Jerus. Targum, Gen. xxviii. 10, דִּבְּרָא or דִּבּוּרָא) is the one eternal self-thought of God—ἐννόημα τοῦ Θεοῦ (in Clemens Alex.)—the thought of His whole proper nature, made objective, independent, personal in the Word—the Word absolutely —the Word of words. As the Logos is the basis of all other thoughts and words of God, so It is the archetype of the human Logos, primarily of the thought of Ego, wherein man becomes objective to himself as a person,—and of the word for it;—then of every thought or inward speech that is effected on this ground of the self-consciousness involved in thought and word. For the νοεῖν does not begin until man becomes objective to himself as Ego; and this νοεῖν is no otherwise possible than by the originating thought, completing itself by taking upon it the form of the word. Intelligible speech is only the sensibly perceptible announcement of this inward speech, this λόγος ἐνδιάθετος.[2] Thoughts, according to a biblical figure, are branches (שְׂעִפִּים or שַׂרְעַפִּים, Job iv. 13, xx. 2; Ps. xciv. 19, cxxxix. 23), and words are flowers and fruits, which, rooted in the spirit, and springing from it, blossom and ripen forth through the mouth and lips (Isa. lvii. 19 comp. Prov. x. 31, Prov. xviii. 20 comp. xii. 14, xiii. 2). Man thinks by speaking inwardly: this speech often occurs so rapidly as not to be *Hamanns*, ii. 63). All that man heard in the beginning, saw with his eyes, and his hands handled, was a living word, for God was the Word.

[1] As in man is *Logos creatus*, says Ph. Nicolai, quoted by Rodwell, *l.c.* p. 199, thus God the Father has *Logon æternum increatum*.

[2] Precisely thus Eusebius says on Ps. lvii. (lvi.) 5: Our Logos, which has its substance in syllables and words and names, and is spoken out by means of tongue and voice, is not properly and truthfully to be called Logos: for it has another as a producer—the inward Logos; and this only is specially and properly to be called the true Logos.

observed; but there are always words by which the thought is thought, as all reckoning, even the most rapid, is by means of figures. To think apart from language, is to think apart from thought itself. Unreflected consciousness without language is possible, as manifestly in the case of brutes; and as there is a condition of being Ego, as foundation and ground, whence the realized self-consciousness and the realized conscious self-determination are developed, so consciousness reflected in itself is also possible without language, as was manifest in the first created man. For there was implanted in him, indeed, the capacity of speech, but not the speech itself. His first condition was an intercommunion of speechless love for the God of his origin. His will, produced by his condition of Ego, but not yet enlightened by actual self-consciousness, inclined thankfully to the will to which he was indebted for his being; and from this relation of self to God, proceeded a feeling of delight, which still lay at the threshold of self-consciousness, and was no precipitate of darkened conceptions, but, so to speak, a chaos of ideas that were not yet lifted up into light. The external world copied itself in his senses, and presented itself in psychical forms of perception before his soul: his spirit was only first turned to this world of forms *actu directo*; the apperception, the transformation of these forms of intuitive perception into ideas, was first impending; but as soon as this spiritual efficiency began, language also began with it: for the moulding of the contents of the supersensuous, or of the sensuous, consciousness, is thinking; and this thinking is, as such, speaking also, primarily internal,—and inasmuch as man is a spirit-embodied being not purely spiritual, but pneumatico-psychical, wherein the word is as absolutely pre-formed, as it is subsequently uttered by means of the bodily organs of speech. What is related to us in Gen. ii. 19 is not the first genesis of language. By way of illustration, however, it is there set forth to us how language came into existence. Previously the individual kinds of beasts were objects presented by means of the five senses for the primal man's contemplation; but now those considerations which sensible perception supplies to him, become to him an object of inward contemplation, his spirit forms from them ideas: he grasps them as compact, strongly outlined thoughts; or, which is the same thing, he gives to the beasts names, which are the apprehended expression of the impression that proceeds from the individuals, and is now spiritually apperceived or comprehended.[1] We may here forego the question as to the original formation of language, whether Adam's language came to perfection by the spiritual ground of things itself being that which entered into the region of his spiritual being, and then assuming for his Ego the form of the inward word.[2] It is only necessary here for us to observe, that, beyond all doubt, language was the creation of the spirit as distinguished from the soul; and, moreover, the creation, sensibly and psychically accomplished, of the spirit capable of speech, and in itself created (even apart from the fact of association) in need of language. Certainly the primal man was the only one whose existence preceded language: subsequently, language has a concrete subsistence independent of man, by which his special capacity of speech is determined *ab extra*, and his spirit is replenished with material already formed and regulated. And assuredly there subsists for us a knowledge only imperfect, and still to be acquired in any scientific method, about the value of the meaning of words in their relation to things; language, as a transmitted possession, is for us only a system of conventional signs of ideas, which we have instinctively appropriated to ourselves. And this language which we speak is one of many: it bears absolutely the stamp of the individual character of the people to which we belong: it is no longer the one speech of the beginning, the pure language of the divinely formed spirit: it remains, inasmuch as it was transmitted, always something more or less external to the thinker, however natural it may have become to him, and however masterfully he may handle it: deeply as he penetrates it, it is still to him always a substance more or less opaque; and thus it limits and obscures his thought, just as much as it is its inalienable means. None the less, in itself, language is, and remains—apart from its materializing produced by the fall of man, and its nationalizing produced by the confusion of tongues—a shadow of the divine Logos; and, in its

---

[1] Comp. Steinthal, *Charakteristik der hauptsächtlichen Typen des Sprachbau's*, 1860, p. 76.

[2] See thereupon the anonymous (theological) work on *Language and its relation to Psychology*, Freiburg, vol. i. 1860.

indissoluble connection with the thinking spirit, a shadow of the unity of nature and life between the Father and the Son.

In this analysis of the life of the spirit, as it lives itself forth, we are upon a biblical and experimental track, which must lead us, from this beginning, and by this means, to a right result. The human understanding, thinking in all directions, comes to the word, and by the word it advances further. It meditates, and breaks forth, as it were, out of the chrysalis, and wheels round, and, as in birth-pangs of reflection, attains to form and shape—to the sharply outlined thought-investiture of the word. The word is the means, the organ, the conditioning of the thought; the word is the expression of all will and thought, whereby it first of all comes to itself by defining itself. But the third and final stage is that in which words are at an end, where the understanding is at a pause,—where the spirit, although in a more realized sense, is again in thought, as in the beginning before the birth of the word. For the thought and will, which serve to develop the spirit, and find their expression in the word, cease without a word: the crown of the word is the spirit without the word—the innermost sanctuary of the heart.[1] This is what the apostle means in Eph. iv. 23 (comp. Rom. xii. 2) by πνεῦμα τοῦ νοός. There is thus not only a νοῦς, which according to its nature belongs to the πνεῦμα, and in the natural man is νοῦς τῆς σαρκός (Col. ii. 18), instead of νοῦς τοῦ πνεύματος; but, moreover, a πνεῦμα which, according to its nature, belongs to the νοῦς, and is therefore inversely called πνεῦμα τοῦ νοός.[2] What kind of a πνεῦμα this is, is to be gathered—although it has escaped the commentators[3]—from 1 Cor. xiv. For here—vers. 14, 15, 19—the apostle, speaking of the speech with tongues, distinguishes between a human πνεῦμα and the human νοῦς. Five words spoken διὰ τοῦ νοός μου, he says, are more profitable for the church, than ten thousand ἐν γλώσσῃ; and wherefore? Because the five words serve for the instruction of others, and the ten thousand do not, unless that a διερμηνευτής translate them into the lan-

---

[1] According to Göschel, *Der Mensch. diesseits und jenseits*, p. 36.

[2] The Latin *mens animi*, by which Krumm, *de notionibus Paulinis Psychol.* p. 23, renders it, does not correspond. Πνεῦμα τοῦ νοός is, on the other hand, *animus (spiritus) mentis*.

[3] See, on the other hand, Hilgenfeld, *Glossolalie*, p. 56.

guage commonly understood. Inasmuch as the five words proceed from the νοῦς thinking with reflected consciousness in the mother tongue, they are all ideally intelligible, and capable of being expressed in language. But he who prays or sings γλώσσῃ, prays or sings not τῷ νοΐ, but τῷ πνεύματι; and therein his νοῦς is ἄκαρπος. The actuality of the self-consciousness is repressed by the divine influence, which absolutely takes possession of him who is speaking with the tongue: the activity of thought of the νοῦς, bringing forth fruit in thoughts and words, benefiting itself and others without any further agency, ceases. The divine influence occurs in the human region of immediate experience and intuition, and expresses itself in a language corresponding to this immediateness, not passing through the νοῦς of the actual utterer, and thus therefore unintelligible to the νοῦς of the hearers. The apostle calls this region of immediate experience and intuition, the πνεῦμα, as distinct from the νοῦς, of man. It is the spirit in the narrower sense (distinguished from πνεῦμα in a wider sense, as 1 Cor. v. 3, vii. 34, 2 Cor. vii. 1), as experiencing, and especially as seeing with immediate intuition—the image of the divine πνεῦμα ἅγιον. For as the activity of the loving will and the loving thought of the Father and the Son in the Holy Ghost goes forth into the actual condition of loving experience, in which loving will and loving thought are reciprocally satisfied, and as it were combined; so the human πνεῦμα in this narrower sense is the seat of the experience of the divine love, and of the immediate intuition of its mysteries (טָעַם and רָאָה, Ps. xxxiv. 9);—a Tertium in which will and thought, passively surrendering themselves to a new form of love, blend and dissolve.[1]

[1] Even Krumm understands πνεῦμα (1 Cor. xiv.) of the capacity of mystical intuitive absorption into the divine depths; and gives, to my apprehension of it, involuntary testimony, when he says, p. 18, "Cogitatio in spiritu nondum sejuncta est a sensu et voluntate, sed hæ tres actiones una quasi comprehenduntur;" and when, p. 67, he observes upon the boasting spirit-seer puffed up, ὑπὸ τοῦ νοὸς τῆς σαρκός (Col. ii. 18), "ἔκστασις Christiana atque veræ revelationes in spiritu gignuntur" (IN THE HEART, NOT IN THE FANCY). For if νοῦς as the capacity of reflective thought, and καρδία as the capacity or organ of immediate experience and perception, be distinguished from the πνεῦμα, as from the undivided unity of both, then becomes absolutely necessary also the distinction of a πνεῦμα in the

But as man is by nature, it is not the divine love which man experiences in this his πνεῦμα. The νοῦς has become νοῦς τῆς σαρκὸς, given up to the flesh (comp. Prov. xxxi. 3; LXX. διδόναι τὸν νοῦν γυναιξί); the διάνοιαι, like the θελήματα, are determined by the flesh (Eph. ii. 3); and the πνεῦμα, in its God-resembling nature, glowing and panting with love (1 Thess. v. 19; Rom. xii. 11; Acts xviii. 25), is, as it were, extinct and dead. The true nature of the πνεῦμα is not indeed destroyed, but it is buried beneath a tendency which contradicts it. Therefore man needs to be renewed (τῷ πνεύματι τοῦ νοός, Eph. iv. 23). "But ye," says the apostle (Eph. iv. 20-24) to his christianized heathen readers, contrasting them with the actual heathens,—" but ye have not so learned Christ; if so be that ye have heard Him, and have been taught in Him, since truth is in Jesus: that ye should put off,[1] concerning the former conversation, the old man, which is corrupt in consequence of the lust of delusion; and be renewed in the spirit of your mind; and that ye put on the new man, which after God is created in righteousness and true holiness." The renewal seeks to make the νοῦς spiritual again, this fundamental power of the human spirit, which has become fleshly, and therefore lays hold of πνεῦμα τοῦ νοός, which, instead of being penetrated by the Holy Spirit, whose image it is, is possessed by the spirit of this world. It is the life of the heart that is meant, which on the one hand is the summative unity into which the willing and thought-forming activity of the νοῦς is dissolved; and, on the other, the secret spring whence the νοῦς receives its impulses, which it adopts into consciousness, and translates into acts of will.[2] Here divine love gives to man to taste its hidden manna. Here God and the soul, which are not according to substance

narrower and wider sense,—namely, a πνεῦμα proving itself in thinking and experience, and one that proves itself in both at once.

[1] The additional ὑμᾶς is in itself not opposed to this association of the infinitive with ἐδιδάχθητε; and, moreover, the repetition of the subject here is explained as occasioned by the parenthesis. Vid. Alex. Buttmann, *Gramm. of the New Testament Language*, p. 235.

[2] Πνεῦμα τοῦ νοός resembles very closely the Homeric θυμός, e.g. in the combination, κατὰ φρένα καὶ κατὰ θυμόν (in mind and heart). I do not find that this important psychological idea is illustrated by anybody satisfactorily, or at least searchingly, (*Schriftb.* iii. 292, " renovation to a newly inspired personal life;" v. Zezschwitz, " the spirit which reigns in the νοῦς.

and nature one, become one through love.[1] Here is the standing-place of the peace of God, which surpasses πάντα νοῦν (Phil. iv. 7); here is the bottom of all ethically profound experience (*vid.* Luke i. 47; Mark viii. 12; John xi. 33, xiii. 21, and elsewhere); here, the sanctuary of all immediate communion between God and man.[2]

In Scripture, this innermost threefold personal life is called ὁ ἔσω ἄνθρωπος (Rom. vii. 22; 2 Cor. iv. 16; Eph. iii. 16); and in reference to the unity of its origin, its seat and home, ὁ κρυπτὸς τῆς καρδίας ἄνθρωπος, the hidden man within the heart (1 Pet. iii. 4). These ideas do not belong exclusively, as does ὁ καινὸς (νέος) ἄνθρωπος, to the life of regeneration. Every man is, as such, an external nature subject to the perceptions of sense, and an inward nature not sensibly perceptible; although, in the position of nature the inward man

the spiritual power of the sense;" Krumm, *interna spiritus restoratio*), except only perhaps H. W. Clemm, in his *Scriptural Thoughts of the Powers of the Soul* (see the epitome in the Appendix of Div. V.). Luther, in his translation, "in the spirit of your heart," points in the right direction; for *heart* is " the deepest inwardness of the free personality, in which thought and will rest, together with the testimony of the conscience, in immediate unity" (Schöberlein, *Jahrbuch*, 1861, p. 53). Only the genitive ought not to be taken appositionally, as Master Eckhart (p. 317 of the *Pfeiferschen Ausg.*): *in the inner spirit, which is called mind,—that is, in the heart.*

[1] See G. Charles Schmidt, *Etude sur Jean Rusbroek* (1859). It is, as Luther says on one occasion (*Opp. Lat.* xviii. 252, ed. Erlang.), *thalamus conscientiæ ubi sponsus et sponsa soli cubant.*

[2] Anastasius of Sinai, in his beautiful and thoughtful work on man's creation after God's image and likeness, which at first was edited by Jo. Tarinus, together with *Origenis Philocalia* (Paris 1618, 4), recognised the importance of 1 Cor. xiv. for the assertion that the Spirit is a μονὰς ἐν τριάδι καὶ τριὰς ἐν μονάδι: ὅτι γὰρ καὶ μία ἐστὶ τῇ οὐσίᾳ (ἡ ψυχή) καὶ οὐ μία τῇ θεωρίᾳ τῆς ἑαυτῆς μερῶν, ἐδήλωσε σαφῶς ὁ εἰπών· ψαλῶ τῷ πνεύματι, ψαλῶ καὶ τῷ νοΐ· προσεύξομαι τῷ πνεύματι, προσεύξομαι δὲ καὶ τῷ νοΐ (1 Cor. xiv. 15). According to Anastasius, the ψυχή corresponds to God the Father; the νοῦς or λόγος to God the Son; the πνεῦμα (πνεῦμα τοῦ νοῦ) to the Holy Ghost; which (*scil.* πνεῦμα) he designates as τὸ ζωτικὸν καὶ συστατικὸν καὶ συμπληρωτικόν, so far as the intelligent soul has in the spirit the condition and the completion of its life. It is plain that this is not the right conception of the πνεῦμα attributed to the ψυχὴ νοερὰ (λογική) in 1 Cor. xiv.), but Anastasius is on the right track; and so much the richer in grand and true thoughts is his comparison of the Son to the word born from the soul (*oratio*), whose internal silent origination he regards as the copy of the internal divine birth of the Son, and whose external origina-

has lost its independence of the outer, and is estranged from its true being. But, moreover, distorted as the life of the inward man is, still the features of the archetype are recognisable therein. " Ego et Pater," says the Lord to the soul, " et caritas nostra unus Deus sumus, tu mens rationalis et verbum et dilectio tua unus es homo, ad similitudinem auctoris tui factus, non ad æqualitatem; creatus nempe, non genitus. Recede ab his quæ infra te sunt, minus formosa quam tu es. Accede formatrici formæ, quo possis esse formosior, eidemque semper adjungere, quia tanto ab illa speciei amplius capies, quanto te illi caritatis pondere magis impresseris."[1]

But—a consideration which inevitably obtrudes itself—is then experience the unity into which will and thought coincide, and not rather the unity out of which both proceed ? To this we answer, for the present, that as, in the triune life of the

tion, effected by the instrument of language, he regards as the copy of the temporal birth of the Son: "For the word is first born in the heart, in incomprehensible and incorporeal manner of birth, and remains unrecognised in the internal nature of man; then it is born in a second and corporeal mode of birth by means of the lips, and this without destroying its connection with the soul which bare it: this is a general, manifest, and instructive resemblance of the two births of God the Logos." Augustine formulates his trinitarian conception of the human spirit variously,—now as *memoria, intelligentia, voluntas,* or *mens, intellectus, voluntas* (as, after him, Thomas Aquinas, Dante in *Purg.* 25, 83, Eckhart, Rusbroek, and others);— now as *esse, velle, scire,* or also *esse, novisse, diligere ;* and in conformity therewith, *mens, notitia sui, amor.* Jo. Scotus Erigena, on the other hand, distinguishing after Dionysius Areopagita the three divine hypostases as οὐσία, δύναμις, ἐνέργεια (a distinction which is partially founded upon misunderstood passages of Scripture), divides also the spiritual nature of man into *essentia, virtus,* and *operatio.* None of these triple divisions is capable either of biblical, or logical and empirical examination. On the other hand, Erigena approaches the true state of the case when (as he thinks without self-contradiction) he distinguishes in yet another manner. " Quid tibi videtur," he asks, *de div. nat.* ii. 23, " de famosissima nostræ naturæ trinitate, quæ intellectu et ratione et sensu intelligitur? Sensum autem dico non exteriorem sed interiorem;" in Greek, as he himself states them further on, νοῦς, λόγος, διάνοια, the *tres motus animæ* according to Dionysius, and mediately according to Proclus. Verbally, Gregory of Nyssa entirely agrees with us, in his work on the likeness of God, separating πνεῦμα, λόγος, νοῦς, as factors of the human trinity; but he adopts these words more in a philosophical than a biblical sense.

[1] Claudianus Mamercus, *de statu animæ,* i. 26 (partially according to Philo); p. 96, the edition of Casp. Barth.

Godhead, all three acts of life are together immanent in everlasting presentness, without temporal sequence; so also in the threefold life of the human spirit, all its impulses so work one into the other, that every individual one, although prevailing at the same time, bears the others in itself. A more satisfactory answer will occur when we analyse—as we are now about to do—the nature of the human soul.

THE SEVEN POWERS OF THE SOUL

Sec. VI.

WE have shown from Holy Scripture in Div. I. Sec. III., that there is an eternal sevenfold *doxa* of God; and, as was indicated in Div. II. Sec. IV., the relation of the human soul to the human spirit corresponds to the relation of this eternal sevenfold *doxa* to God the Triune. We here assume both of these positions to be scripturally affirmed. But from the fact that Scripture designates ἑπτὰ πνεύματα as the constituent powers of the divine *doxa* carried into operation by God's Spirit,[1] there occurs to us the problem in conformity with the parallel once drawn between *doxa* and *psyche*—to show the nature of the human soul to be a sevenfold nature. And here first of all arises the question, what those ἑπτὰ πνεύματα are, whose possessor, according to Apoc. iii. 1, is the God-man, and in what order they stand to one another. And our first glance falls on Isa. xi. 2. Here they are named, and named so as to be enumerated from above downward, or from right to left; for the spirit of the fear of Jehovah is the basis of all, as חָכְמָה is the object which, from יִרְאַת ה׳, is arrived at (Ps. cxi. 10;

---

[1] J. P. Lange (*Deutsch. Zeitsch.* 1859, p. 23), with reference to Apoc. i. 4, questions the impersonality of the seven spirits; but however it may be interpreted, they are certainly not seven persons, but seven powers or operations of the personal God, and of His Spirit, whereof J. Böhme (*Dreif. Leben*, iv. 82) strikingly says, "It is the Holy Spirit who reveals God in nature. He spreads forth the glory of the Majesty, that He may be beheld in the wonders of nature."

Prov. i. 7; Job xxviii. 28); and the Spirit of Jehovah absolutely is the heart of all, corresponding to the midmost flame on the shaft of the seven-flamed lamp (Zech. iv.)—the fourth therefore, as four is the middle of seven.[1] If we arrange them in a row, in which, from left to right, they correspond to the seven flames of the typical lamp, their order is as follows: (1) רוּחַ יִרְאַת ה׳; (2) רוּחַ דַּעַת ה׳; (3) רוּחַ ה׳ (4); גְּבוּרָה; (5) רוּחַ עֵצָה; (6) רוּחַ בִּינָה; (7) רוּחַ חָכְמָה. But the seven spirits are here named, not so much according to what they are in themselves, as according to what they effect. In such sevenfold efficiency, the sevenfold *doxa*, which proceeds from the Father and the Son by means of the Spirit, is to descend upon the second David. It may be expected that the ethical efficiency of the seven spirits will correspond to their metaphysical nature. Our inquiry, therefore, must proceed from another quarter.

And from what other quarter than from those portions of Holy Scripture which narrate to us how the divine *doxa* has allowed itself to be beheld? To Abraham it appears as a smoking furnace, out of which a burning torch appears (Gen. xv. 17); thus flaming and enlightening from a dark ground. On Sinai, its manifestation begins just in the same way with gloom of smoke and cloud, from which breaks forth מַרְאֵה כְּבוֹד ה׳ as consuming fire (Ex. xix. 16, xxiv. 15); wherefore it is said indiscriminately, that Jehovah spoke to Israel מִתּוֹךְ הֶעָנָן, or that He spoke מִתּוֹךְ הָאֵשׁ (comp. *e.g.* Deut. iv. 12 with Ex. xxiv. 16); and here therefore, also, the manifestation was that of flaming and enlightening from a dark ground. In the leading of Israel through the wilderness, the self-manifestation of the divine glory by the cloud or by the light of fire was assigned to day and night (Ex. xiii. 21, xl. 38; Deut. i. 33; Ps. lxxviii. 14), but in such a way that אֵשׁ וְעָנָן are in one another; and even in the day-time, if Jehovah will, fire breaks forth from the cloud (Ex. xiv. 24). In Ezekiel, this involution of fire, light, and

---

[1] The accentuation which gives *Athnach* to רוּחַ ה׳ is thus therefore justified. For the most part, it is held that "Spirit of Jehovah" is the general idea, which is separated into three pairs. But thus we have not an actual seven according to the apocalyptic requirement. Seven is the divine in the multiplicity of its development (*vid. Genesis*, p. 640). Even the unfolding of the principle opposed to God, appears in the Apocalypse sevenfold.

gloom, is circumstantially described. He sees a great cloud, and אֵשׁ מִתְלַקַּחַת reciprocally enfolding itself, *i.e.* fire whirling, circling, and נֹגַהּ, the brightness which beams from the fire, round about the cloud (i. 4). This brightness into which the appearance is projected, is expressly designated as like a rainbow, and as the exact מַרְאֵה כְּבוֹד ה' (i. 28). The fire thus goes forth out of the gloom, and the light out of the fire. This relation, moreover, is manifested even in Him who sits upon the throne. From His loins upwards He appeared to the Seer as brightness, זֹהַר, and from His loins downwards as fire, אֵשׁ (Ezek. viii. 2, comp. i. 27, LXX.).[1] The Johannean description of Him that sits on the throne (Apoc. iv. 3) agrees with this: "And He that sat was to look upon like a jasper and a sardine stone; and there was a rainbow round about the throne, in sight like unto an emerald." The jasper, which in ch. xxi. 11 is called as clear as crystal, and stands in ch. xxi. 19 as the first foundation, corresponds to the bright side of the divine *doxa;* and the sardine, which has the appearance of fire and of blood ($\pi\nu\rho\omega\pi\grave{o}s$ $\tau\hat{\omega}$ $\epsilon\emph{i}\delta\epsilon\iota$ $\kappa\alpha\grave{\iota}$ $\alpha\emph{i}\mu\alpha\tau\sigma\epsilon\iota\delta\acute{\eta}s$, as Epiphanius says), corresponds to the fiery side of the divine *doxa*.[2] Fire and light, moreover, are the elements and modes of appearance of the stream or sea before the throne of God, which comes into the visual horizon of the seer. John beholds just the same river proceeding from God, which becomes visible to Daniel as a fiery stream (vii. 10), as a pure river of water of life, clear as crystal (Apoc. xxii. 1), and another time as a sea of glass mingled with fire (Apoc. xv. 2). The fire (נוּר) points to the wrath, and the crystal clearness to the love; and the mingling of the fire with the glassy clearness, to love that does not come to breaking forth without manifestation of wrath. And as John beholds the seven spirits as seven burning torches before the throne of God (iv. 5), so God as Father of glory is called by James (i. 17) Father of lights—$\tau\hat{\omega}\nu$ $\phi\acute{\omega}\tau\omega\nu$. Thus everywhere in the divine *doxa,* appear united the potencies of the fiery gloom and of the

---

[1] Züllig, in Hengstenberg, *Comm. über die Offenb.* i. 263, observes, in addition: Below, opposite the earth, appeared to me, He who sits on the throne in the angry glow of His function of judge and avenger, above in the pure brightness of His calm, undisturbed heavenly majesty.

[2] Hengstenberg, *l.c.* p. 261. The sardine stands here for an indication of the primitive righteousness of God—of His wrath.

brightness. Let it not be said that these are only types. Types they certainly are, but types of heavenly realities, which thus portray themselves. How otherwise could the Scripture say of God, He is light, φῶς, and on the other hand, He is fire, πῦρ? (Deut. iv. 24, ix. 3; Isa. xxxiii. 14; Heb. xii. 29.) Certainly He is neither of the two in the sense of earthly elements; for the bush in which the fire of the *doxa* appears to Moses is not destroyed (Ex. iii. 2), and the light which shone around Saul and his companions was far "above the brightness of the sun" (Acts xxvi. 13). God is fire and light, in a sense the most actual of all, but in a way that is absolutely supersensual, and above that which is created. He is light, and in Him is no darkness at all (1 John i. 5). According to Jas. i. 17, He is the Father of lights, in whom is found no change from the light to the darkness (παραλλαγή), or falling of a shadow, such as sun and moon suffer in consequence of a changing (τροπῆς ἀποσκίασμα). On the other hand, however, Scripture also says that God is a consuming fire; that there is in Him a power of wrath, which He being angry arouses (Ps. lxxviii. 38); that His purpose of wrath has flaming fire as its result, which is His judicial manifestation (2 Thess. i. 8), by which His anger effectually proves itself (Heb. x. 27), which proceeds from Him (Lev. x. 2, comp. Num. xvii. 11). It considers the wrath absolutely, not merely as an affection of God's will, and an action of God's will; but, at the same time, as something belonging to God's nature, which is in God, and is through sin (Jer. xvii. 4) judicially aroused against sinners, and is sent forth (*e.g.* Ex. xv. 7) or poured out from God (*e.g.* Ezek. xxii. 20-22). And as for the darkness, Scripture does not hesitate to name God not only the former of light, but the creator of darkness (בּוֹרֵא חֹשֶׁךְ, Isa. xlv. 7); and, where it describes the manifestation of the divine glory, to distinguish in it darkness, fire, and light. How otherwise is all this to be reconciled, than by assuming that God, in respect of His personal nature, is indeed love, but love which has as its reverse side the might of wrath; and that God, in respect of the *doxa* of His nature, is indeed absolutely light without disturbance, but light which, in the face of the world opposed to God, can let loose powers of gloomy fire eternally excited in Him? In His *doxa*, the darkness is eternally swallowed up by means of the fire in light. In the fire, darkness and light are distinguished; wherefore Scripture comprehends fire and light sometimes as primarily contrasted, sometimes as synonymous ideas: for the fire, as the fire of love (Lev. ix. 24), is light; contrary to which, as fire of wrath (Lev. x. 2), it is the synonyme of darkness. Dwelling in this His *doxa,* God the triune dwells omnipresent in every created thing. In itself it is the absolute triumph of light. But in the presence of the creature, it externalizes itself as fire or light, even as the creature takes its position in the dark-fiery or in the fiery-light principle of the same. In the godly, God reveals Himself as light,—namely, as חַנּוּן וְרַחוּם וְצַדִּיק (Ps. cxii. 4); but to the view of sinners, the light of Israel becomes fire, and the Holy One of Israel—*i.e.* that which in itself is absolute light and purity—becomes flame (Isa. x. 17), to wit, by means of a backward grasp at the potentialities which form the substratum of His glorious light. The fire and darkness of hell proceed from God's *doxa,* not less than the light of glorification (Isa. xxxiii. 14; Ps. cxxxix. 8). So far as by the power of His wrathful will, fire and darkness prevail in the creature, He rules over both in the might of His light (Ps. cxxxix. 12). In Him Himself is neither darkness nor fire which are not merged in absolute light. Without such views as these, Scripture—unless its statements are emptied of all meaning—is in a great measure absolutely unintelligible. We know probably the ingenious representations into which the presumed fantastic symbolism of Scripture allows itself to be interpreted; but they are only the *caput mortuum* of its infinitely more ingenious figurative expression. We believe that we rightly interpret this, in saying that God's *doxa* has a dark-fiery and a fiery-light side,—that in the fire both principles are distinct,—and that the former principle is absolutely overpowered and pervaded by the latter.

We go further: if the *doxa*—which is by the Father and the Son effectuated by the Holy Ghost—be a reflection of the Godhead, then as well the loving will, and the loving thought of the Father, as the loving satisfaction which the Father finds in the Son, and the Son in the Father, as also the loving experience of the Holy Spirit, will be reflected therein. The light that shines forth in the midst of the process of the *doxa* is the reflection of the birth of the Son of God; for He is, as we so frequently read in the Gospel of St. John, the self-living absolute light that goeth forth from the Father (i. 4, viii. 12)—the ἀπαύ-γασμα of the paternal *doxa* (Heb. i. 3; comp. Wisd. vii. 26, ἀπαύγασμα φωτὸς ἀϊδίου of the σοφία).¹ It follows thence that the three first πνεύματα describe the offspring of the Father's love. But how otherwise than by prototypically representing the three-fold law of every φύσις: (1) the contraction into itself, (2) the outward pressing beyond itself, (3) the unrest of becoming; to which there follows, (4) the breaking through of that which has been aimed at, as it were, *à priori*? This agony of becoming, which at the same time is a pleasure of becoming, is the characteristic of all self-life. It is a constant circle—a wheel revolving around itself—τροχὸς γενέσεως, according to Jas. iii. 6.² Of late, the power of attraction, the power of expansion, and the polarity which results from the operation of these two polar forces, has been named the "trinity of power."³ Jacob Böhme calls it the fiery triangle in every living thing. These three forces or forms in themselves are the principle of life (חַיִּים), whose emblem is scarlet (*coccus*), as the colour of fire and of blood,⁴ but not yet the principle of the life of light or of love. They do not become this until a further advance of the process. In themselves they are infinite agitation and excitement—θυμός or ὀργή in the first primitive meaning. Therefore they are expressed, when God's love is repelled, as instruments of divine

---

¹ Athanasius, *C. Arian.* iv. 2: ὡς γὰρ ἀπὸ πυρὸς φῶς, οὕτως ἐκ Θεοῦ λόγος. Augustine, *de Symb.* ch. iii.: Occurrat vobis (he is addressing the catechumens) ignis pater, splendor filius, ecce invenimus coævos.

² According to Böttcher, *Schriftproben*, p. 83, there exists even in the root of חָיָה—to wit, חִי—the fundamental idea of the circling line returning into itself. According to the Arabic, on the other hand, the root-meaning is rather *comprehendere* or *contrahere*. For the word حَوَى indicates, according to the Kamûs, to bring together and to secure: conjug. viii., to lay one's self around something; conjug. vi., to wind into one another, to curl one's self (of the serpent), to wrinkle, to crisp one's self. According to this, life may be called *el-hajât*, as close-binding (contrast of death, *maut*, מוֹת, as stretching out, *i.e.* loosing of that which has been hitherto bound and contracted); as Shame, *ḥajâ*, Beidâwi on the Koran, Sur. ii. 24, is defined "as a retraction of the soul to itself (*contractio sui*), apart from that which is shameful from fear of blame." The serpent, however, is called *el-ḥajja*, as curling itself, or as the living one κατ' ἐξοχήν.

³ Prof. Owen, in a work so entitled (Nürenberg 1856).

⁴ Bähr, *Symbolik des Mosaischen Cultus*, i. 333.

wrathfulness; and so far—not as though there were everlasting wrath in God—they are called also the principle of wrath.

The impelling power of the process is indeed the God of love, in whom the urgency of love, the satisfaction of love, and the triumph of love, eternally coincide. Therefore the three first forces—those of contraction, expansion, and rotation—are only the basis of the fourth, the force of decussation[1] or intersection, in virtue of which, out of the released fire the light of love shines forth, as, in Ezekiel, from the midst of the fire shone a flashing brightness, כְּעֵין הַחַשְׁמַל (i. 4). The emblem of this fourth power is the fourfold figure of the cross, significant to all the orders of heavenly and earthly existence.[2] The other powers or forms correspond to the Holy Spirit, which, on the one hand, is receptively related to the loving relation of the Father and the Son, by adopting into itself its impression; on the other hand, is productively related thereto, by becoming the expression for the promulgation of this impression (comp. John xvi. 13–15). Corresponding to that is the fifth power—that of the passive resignation to the light of love; and the sixth —that of the distinct and manifest production of the nature imprinted by God on the *doxa* as it comes into being. The fifth is the prototype of the fruitful and moulding water, which receives into itself, and reflects, the forms of things: for in Scripture water and light are things very closely bordering upon one another (Ps. xxxvi. 9); and there is an everlasting spring of living water, of which it may equally be said that God Himself is it (Jer. ii. 13, xvii. 13), just as He is light—as that it is in God (Ps. xxxv. 9; Apoc. xxi. 6, etc.), just as the light is in God (Dan. ii. 22). The sixth is the prototype of the sound or of the voice (קוֹל, Ezek. xliii. 2), which, considered in respect of itself alone, is the *doxa* or glory of the word. The Holy Ghost reveals Himself in the fifth power rather as the Spirit of the Father, and in the sixth, rather as the Spirit of the Son (Logos). In the sixth grade the *doxa* is the intelligent and intelligible revelation of the nature of God, and its substance. But there is still wanting one power, which unites all the powers together with their contents into a substantial and compact whole. It is the efficiency of the seventh. As the

---

[1] See the article "Geist" in Oetinger's *Biblischem Wörterbuch*.
[2] See the article "Cross" (*Kreuz*) in Oetinger's *Wörterbuch*.

sixth power corresponds to the day of the creation of man, so this seventh power answers to the Sabbath of creation. Seven is everywhere the number of peace. Thus the seventh beatitude of the Preacher on the Mount concerns the peacemakers (Matt. v. 9); thus the seventh of the attributes which, according to *Aboth de-Rabbi Nathan*, ch. xxxvi., attend before the throne, is Peace. The seventh power unites all the powers of the divine *doxa* into peace. Its emblem is (Apoc. iv. 3) the emerald, for green is the most comforting and the mellowest of all combinations of colours. The seven spirits are an organization of sabbatic harmony, and they are this, without beginning and without end; for the formation of the *doxa* is an everlasting, but never incomplete, *becoming*. All the seven spirits exist from eternity in majestic light and peaceful activity of love.[1] "I was by Him," says Wisdom (Prov. viii. 30), "as His workmistress;[2] and I was daily His delight, rejoicing alway before Him." The *chokma* which is here personified is not distinct from the *doxa*. The *doxa* is called *chokma* (חָכְמָה or חָכְמוֹת) so far as it involves in itself the divine ideas in pre-existent elementary actuality. Both are sevenfold. The wisdom that is from above has, in James' epistle (iii. 17), seven characteristics, as the house of wisdom, according to Prov. ix. 1, has seven pillars. For the divine wisdom, as the divine *doxa*, is πολυποίκιλος (Eph. iii. 10). In both is reflected the divine nature and its rich substance. This reflection, as a reflection of the divine nature, is called *doxa*; and as a reflection of the contents of the divine nature, *i.e.* of the ideas, it is called *sophia*, or wisdom. But both are one. For if the *sophia* says (Prov. viii. 23), "I was anointed a king[3] from everlasting," in what respect does that differ from the everlasting δόξα of the βασιλεὺς τῶν αἰώνων (1 Tim. i. 17)?

These are the seven spirits—or, as we may venture to say, the seven powers or forms—of the divine *doxa*: spirits, in consideration of their vitality, spiritually effected, excluding

---

[1] See the beautiful statement of this movement, reciprocal Source and harmonic Unity, in Rocholl, *Beiträge zu einer Gesch. der deutschen Theosophie* (1856), pp. 57-59.

[2] (German, *Werkmeisterin*. Auth. vers.: "one brought up with Him."—Tr.)

[3] (Auth. vers.: "*I was set up* from everlasting."—Tr.)

everything material and accidental, pure and simple; powers, in consideration of their peculiar manifestation, and the cosmic operations of which they are the sources of efficiency; forms, in consideration of the divine *doxa*, which they all together in indissoluble unity, but every one in special manner, show forth. We have here attempted to solve the problem which Scripture, without offering its direct solution, proposes to the gnosis that proceeds from faith. The knowledge of the problem is primitive, for long ago Philo and the Cabbala have striven to solve it, by placing at the head of the ten δυνάμεις or סְפִירוֹת, a triad; and thence deducing a heptad—the seven brooks into which the ocean of the divine nature is divided.[1] But in these attempts there is missed not only the inward necessity, but also all scriptural foundation that is in any measure satisfactory. Moreover, the seven names are only names of divine attributes (as 1 Chron. xxix. 11), from which attributes the reference of the typical relation of the human soul to the divine *doxa* is wholly incapable of being drawn out; and apart from all, the gloom in which these attempts grope after the mystery, is set aside by the New Testament unveiling of the trinity of the divine nature. Whether our endeavour, which for the most part is due to Jac. Böhme,[2] approaches to the truth, will now be proved, as we come to confront the archetype with the copy.

[1] v. Grossmann, *Quæstionum Philonearum*, Pt. i. p. 241, and the late works of Franck and Joel on the Cabbala, but especially that of Molitor (*Philosophie der Geschichte oder über die Tradition*, 4 vols.), besides its replies by Hamberger (*Die hohe Bed. der altjüd. Tradition*, 1844) and Rocholl (*Beiträge*, 1856). The three last named Christian scholars assume, after the example of Mirandola and Knorr von Rosenroth, a too respectful attitude to the Cabbala. This latter is not without lights (see *e.g.* above, Div. II. Sec. VI.), but it is full of false lights. Above all, there requires historical criticism to distinguish the actually old tradition from the mediæval and new.

[2] Naming him, I cannot forbear recalling the words of Lavater in his review of his physiognomical predecessors: "And then I name one more, *absit blasphemia dicto*, Jacob Böhme! Whether we laugh now or weep, probably nobody had more natural perception, feeling of nature, or sense of the language of nature, than this unintelligible theosophist. Doubtless our dictatorial journalistic age will finely impale this thought, and cry, Crucify him! I know that I have friends, who, from love to my theological and philosophical reputation, would be sufficiently weak-hearted and good-hearted to buy out of this page these four or five lines with as many

As the divine *doxa* is related to the tri-personal spiritual nature of the Godhead, so the human soul is related to the personifying human spirit. But the same process, which in respect of God falls into the domain of self-consciousness, and of that freedom which is one with internal necessity, on the side of man falls into the domain of entire unconsciousness and entire unfreedom, because man is a creature, and the beginning of his existence, by which he is a witness to himself of his own character of a creature, precedes in every relation his own knowledge and will. As the spirit of man is the product of the divine inbreathing, so the soul, by virtue of the continuously operative impulse of this divine inbreathing, is the product of the human spirit: its origination is a וַיְהִי (Gen. ii. 7), and thus full of mystery as all God's creations. The necessity is implanted into the nature of the created spirit, to bring itself to essential manifestation, and, so to speak, spiritually to embody itself. So it is even with the heavenly spirits, as we see in their self-manifestations in visions; for although they make themselves visible in such cases in a manner accommodated to human perception, still the diversity of their forms (*e.g.* cherub, seraph) points back to an actual supersensuous externality of their nature. Not as though the angels also had souls: we could only speak of the souls of angels, as of a נֶפֶשׁ of God (*e.g.* Amos vi. 8; Isa. i. 14), by means of an anthropomorphism.[1] Soul, נֶפֶשׁ, is the

louis d'ors, if it were possible; but if they were willing, and, if at the same time a poor man stood by me who might want these louis d'ors, I would not take them." The rest may be referred to in Lavater's *Ausgen. Schriften*, edited by Orelli, iv. 64.

[1] The question whether, without contradicting Scripture, we may speak of the souls of angels, is discussed by Origen, *de princ.* ii. 8. He considers that, if by soul is understood a *substantia rationabiliter sensibilis et mobilis*, it is allowable to speak of the souls of angels. This is certainly true. In this sense, Philo calls the mid-natures between God and man (the angels or demons, *i.e. Logoi* and spirits of the air) everywhere in his works bodiless souls; *e.g.* i. 431: ἔστι καὶ κατὰ τὸν ἀέρα ψυχῶν ἀσωμάτων ἱερώτατος χορός, ὀπαδὸς τῶν οὐρανίων· ἀγγέλους γὰρ τὰς ψυχὰς ταύτας εἴωθε καλεῖν ὁ θεσπιῳδὸς λόγος. The mode in which Plutarch speaks of demons (spirits of the air) is entirely the same. But the New Testament Scripture, even where the same might be expected, as in Eph. ii. 2, vi. 12, expresses itself otherwise. Hahn, *Theologie des N. T.* i. 404, very justly observes: "The angels are named πνεύματα, but never ψυχαί; living men are called ψυχαί, but never πνεύματα."

peculiar *doxa* in which the spirit of corporeal natures is reflected. Therefore Scripture only speaks of souls of men and of brutes. Even of brutes, for they have souls which are the individual particularizations of the spirit of life inwrought into universal nature by the creative spirit of God, which the ancients call—by a name certainly not to be justified from 1 Cor. ii. 12[1]—*spiritus mundi*. The Scripture acknowledges in plants life indeed, but no soul. Even although חי (Ps. lviii. 9) is not to be referred to the thorn-bush, yet the notion of the life of plants is evident from Job xiv. 8, Ps. lxxviii. 47, Jer. xiv. 30, Jude 12; for only what is living can die. But they do not belong to the κτίσματα ἔχοντα ψυχὰς (Apoc. viii. 9). The prevalent idea of an *anima vegetativa*, which scholasticism adopted from Aristotle, is foreign to Scripture. They are endowed with life, but not self-living. The general spirit of life lives in them, contracting its essence in the grain of seed, and unfolding it in the shoot, according to the idea of the plant already pre-formed in the seed. Its wheel of life does not oscillate itself, but it is oscillated; as also is that of the lowest of the brutes when just engaged in the transition to psychical life, and partaking thereof.

We turn back to the soul of man, to the effluence of his spirit, which is essentially distinguished from the spirit of the brute by the fact that it is no individualization of the general spirit of life, but the immediate constitution of the spirit itself by God. Before we set out the seven powers of the soul, let the position be very clearly established, that the soul, made personal indeed by the spirit, is yet in and for itself impersonal, as its archetype, the divine *doxa* or *chokma*, of which therefore we just now said that it is personified in Prov. viii. That the divine *doxa* or *chokma* is impersonal, although brought forth from God's will, and pervaded by God's self-consciousness, and enclosed by God's personality, needs no proof; thence it follows of necessity that God, as He has revealed Himself and declared

---

[1] For in this place πνεῦμα τοῦ κόσμου does not mean the Spirit of God, as it dwells as a created spirit of life, as a physical-psychical power of life in the world, and even in Christians as men (thus Theod. Schott in the *Luth. Zeitschr.* 1861, p. 232); but, as the contrast shows, the spirit which is not from God—therefore the principle opposed to God, and operative in the worldly life, which is breathed into the world by the prince of the world.

Himself to us, is a tri- and not a quadri-personal nature. That the soul is impersonal, strange as it may sound, is at least no new view. It is, moreover, the view of all those who attribute the soul to the corporeity of man, and essentially distinguish it from his spirit,—the dualism of the Güntherish school, defended of late by Zukrigl, Gangauf, Esser, and others. But still, if we only read Gen. ii. 7, we see that man is not already endowed with soul before the spirit is breathed into him, but that it is even by that inspiration that he is endowed with soul. And how could Scripture say that the body without the spirit is dead (Jas. ii. 26), if the soul belonged to the body? The whole Scripture, from beginning to end, contradicts this view of a dualistic distinction of the soul and the spirit. Spirit and soul are not essentially distinct. Even in Homer, $\theta\upsilon\mu\acute{o}\varsigma$ and $\psi\upsilon\chi\acute{\eta}$ do not stand in this relation. The view of Nägelsbach, that $\theta\upsilon\mu\acute{o}\varsigma$ in Homer is the spiritual, and $\psi\upsilon\chi\acute{\eta}$ the animal principle of human life, essentially distinct from the former, has been already shown to be untenable. That which continues to flourish of man after death is called $\psi\upsilon\chi\acute{\eta}$, but sometimes also $\theta\upsilon\mu\acute{o}\varsigma$ (*Il.* η. 131); because both are of one nature, and for the rest are only separated just as spirit (mind) and soul are. Yet that trichotomic view which places the soul on the side of corporeity is not absolutely destitute of truth. That which is true therein is, (1) that spirit and soul are substantially distinct; and (2) that the spirit, and not the soul, is the personifying power in man. We have already often seen for what reason Scripture is accustomed to call the *self* or Ego of man by the name of נֶפֶשׁ: it is because the soul is the medium and link, and the proper and essential form, of the human personality.[1] But itself is only personal so far as the spirit is immanent in it; it is impersonal when we consider it in itself, abstracting it from the concrete matter of fact. The self-consciousness—*i.e.* that consciousness in virtue of which man apprehends himself as Ego—and all the functions conditioned by it, belong originally to the spirit, and come to the soul only in a derived manner, by means of the immanence of the spirit.[2] The spirit is the *power*

---

[1] The spirit is the essential foundation of man; the soul his peculiar essential form; the body his essential manifestation. Thus J. P. Lange, *Dogm.* p. 298. The expressions are excellently chosen.

[2] Comp. Oehler in Herzog's *R.E.* vi. 16: "The soul is the supporter

of self-consciousness, and the soul, its *place;* and the spiritual soul, its *subject,* and the whole man, its *object.* It has its root in the spirit. Therefore, when the Scripture speaks of spiritual functions as such, it never says נֶפֶשׁ, ψυχή, but always רוּחַ, πνεῦμα. Thus, for instance, in 1 Cor. ii. 11, where the writer is speaking of the self-consciousness of man, probably ψυχή could as little be substituted for πνεῦμα, as in Ps. lxxvii. 7 נַפְשִׁי for רוּחִי, or the לֵב which is commonly used in the Old Testament instead of νοῦς. Even in 1 Chron. xxviii. 12, where it is said of David, that he had before him in the spirit the design of the future temple, בְּנַפְשׁוֹ would not be allowable in place of בְּרוּחַ. And although, moreover, יָדַע is rarely and exceptionally said of the soul in the sense of higher perception, as Ps. cxxxix. 14,

of the Ego-life, the peculiar *self* of man, certainly by the power of the immanence of the spirit; but so that this latter is only the personifying principle, not the human person himself." Fault is found by Oehler, that I characterize the soul as impersonal in itself; but if, according to his own words, it is indebted for its personality to the immanence of the spirit, it follows that in itself it is not personal, but is related to the spirit, as, perhaps, the moon to the sun. Moreover, v. Rudloff, p. 34, says: "Without the spirit, the soul would be no reasonable soul, no human soul, would have no self-consciousness—would be no Ego." In other words, man is a personal *anima viva,* by virtue of the spirit immediately inbreathed into him by God (comp. Gen. ii. 7, Prov. xx. 27, 1 Cor. ii. 11): the spiritual soul is its proper essential form (*forma informans,* according to the Aristotelian expression), but the personifying spirit is the principle and ground of that essential form which distinguishes him from the brute. V. Rudloff's formula —the soul is the *principale,* the spirit the *accessorium*—according to this, is inconsistent with itself. It must be said the spirit is the *principale,* the soul the *secundarium.* When finally, moreover, Zöckler (*Naturtheologie,* i. 734) puts it down as a complete reversal of the true state of the case, that I should regard the spirit as the peculiar personifier in man, I hold, in opposition to him, that he himself looks on the spirit as the energetic principle which completes the personality of man. But if it be that which completes the person, it is also self-consciousness; and if it be self-consciousness, it is also the personifying power, or with the distinction of a self-conscious spirit and a soul self-conscious, not through the spirit, but in itself, the unity of man's natural condition is altogether lost; since that cannot otherwise be maintained than, as says Schöberlein (*Studien u. Krit.* 1860, pp. 153–155), by regarding the spirit from which the soul has existence and personality, as the absolute divine spirit entered into man, or by looking on spirit and soul as only two aspects of one substance, or the self-consciousness of the soul as the self-consciousness of the spirit immanent in the soul.

Prov. xix. 2, still in passages such as Ezek. xi. 5, xx. 32, נַפְשְׁכֶם could hardly be said; as Scripture speaks indeed of an erring spirit (Isa. xxix. 24) or heart (Ps. xcv. 10), but never of an erring soul (against which, for two obvious reasons, is not to be alleged Num. xv. 28); because perception of the truth in the deeper sense is a function of the spirit, and not of the soul. Just so, in texts such as Judg. viii. 3, Job xv. 13, Isa. xxxiii. 11, xxv. 4, Ps. lxxvi. 13,—where רוּחַ, as often elsewhere, denotes the spirit of wrath vehemently declaring itself in pantings,—נֶפֶשׁ could not be used: passionate excitements overcome man, from his spirit (Eccles. vii. 4), and take possession of him from thence outwards. And why does Scripture speak of the truly humbled one—נִשְׁבַּר־לֵב (broken heart) and דַּכָּא־רוּחַ (contrite spirit)— everywhere naming heart and spirit (Ps. xxxiv. 19, li. 19; Isa. lvii. 15, lxvi. 2, etc.), and not soul? For the reason that the selfish Ego-life which penitence breaks down has its root in the heart, and the self-consciousness, from whose fallacious elevation penitence brings down, has its seat in the spirit. Similarly, according to the New Testament mode of expression, which in this respect is still more stringent, the renovation of man's person-life has its seat in the πνεῦμα or νοῦς (Rom. xii. 2; Eph. iv. 23): it is there that man receives the testimony of his adoption (Rom. viii. 16). For that man is ψυχικὸς, *i.e.* that the ψυχή has become that which designates his person-life, is the result of sin. But, moreover, this psychical self-consciousness is the self-consciousness of the spirit only psychically determined. For the soul is, indeed, the very counterpart of the spirit; but not as the Logos is of the Father, but rather as the *doxa* is of the Trinity. It is of similar nature with the spirit, but not similar to it. The psychical functions which are the types of the spiritual, correspond to the spiritual functions, but are not like to them: they are rather the broken rays of their colours. The soul is no Ego, distinguishing itself from the spirit. The self-consciousness which forms the background of its spirit-copied functions, is that of the spirit from which it has its origin, and of which it is the organ made essential by the spirit-corporeity of man, and the first sphere of its operation.

The existence of the soul has its origin in the spirit, and, indeed, in its struggles to reveal itself. It reveals itself first of all to itself, and this its revelation of itself to itself is the soul. In order to have any deep understanding of the sevenfold character of this, we must enter in thought into the process, by means of which, when God breathed into man the spirit in God's likeness, immediately therefrom proceeded the soul. In doing this, we are conceiving as separate and consequent, what in reality was associated without place, and contemporaneous without time. Still we are at liberty to do this, because that which we are conceiving as distinct is absolutely separable; and that which we are conceiving as consequent actually forms a chain of cause and effect; and that in such a manner, as that every effect is always again the cause of a subsequent effect.

The beginning and basis of the soul's existence are the three constituent fundamental powers of all life—חיים—that of contraction, of expansion, and of rotation. At the first stage, it is substance contracted into itself; at the second, striving away from itself, and out beyond itself; at the third, fallen into the restlessness of becoming; the effect of the first power, and the counter effect of the second, begets, for instance, an excitement or commotion, which becomes a revolution ($\tau\rho o\chi\grave{o}\varsigma\ \gamma\epsilon\nu\acute{\epsilon}\sigma\epsilon\omega\varsigma$), as the soul, coming into existence, has in itself no satisfaction, and still is not willing to lose itself: for in every moment of self-comprehension, it urges itself away from itself, and in every moment of this avoidance of itself, it comprehends itself. The impelling power of the process is the spirit, which is engaged in producing a living likeness of itself—a likeness of its own light, threefold, nature. The constituting of the soul, as of a living thing, is the founding of this likeness. The purpose of the process is light, in the divine spiritual sense. Embracing itself, the soul is dark; fleeing itself, it presses outwards to the light; oscillating on itself, it is, as it were, in birth-pains (comp. חיל, to revolve, *circumagi*, to bring forth). The form in which it proceeds out of this agony of becoming, is, however, not at first light, but fiery. In the fourth power, that of breaking forth, fire and light are distinguished.

Fire and light! If to any person this sounds too purely physical, let him consider that the life of fire is a scriptural designation of the selfish life of self; and the life of light a scriptural designation of the self-life, after the likeness of God or the spirit. These two several kinds of the self-life are distinguished in the fourth power. The form of the spirit, which is the central agent of the process, here comes to light: the self-life of the soul in itself, transforms itself here to self-life in the spirit. It becomes the life of love, which is turned in love towards the spirit. Therefore the next power is that of perception ($αἴσθησις$), of reflection, or of spirit-like receptivity: the soul surrenders itself passively and receptively to the spirit, and becomes, as it were, impregnated with its thoughts: the substance of the spirit becomes, as in a copy, that of the soul. And by means of the sixth power—that of manifestation, of revelation, or of spirit-like productivity—it reveals this conceived substance, serving to the spirit as a means to imprint the spiritually formed material of its consciousness on words which, before they pass over by means of the organs of speech into sensible externality, already bear on themselves the pre-formed complete determination of the word which is to be outwardly dispersed in sound: for as the soul, on the one hand, is the mirror in which the outer world is reflected to the spirit; so, on the other hand, it is the workshop or laboratory in which the spirit forms its thoughts into words, and, as it were, embodies them. For the $λόγος$ $ἐνδιάθετος$ of the spirit becomes $λόγος$ $προφορικός$ in the soul; and it is there that the word, with its sound and its form of speech, is made ready, before it comes forth as $φωνὴ$ $ῥημάτων$ (Heb. xii. 19) into sensible perceptibility. The seventh power embraces all the former in one harmonious organic unity: it is the power of substantiality; for the powers of the soul that have been referred to, are not its inherent attributes distinct from the soul; all these powers together are the substance of the soul itself; and therefore the seventh is that in which the spirit-resembling essence of the soul is sabbatically completed.

But in all this we have only considered the nature of the soul in its intercourse with the spirit; but not yet, as we shall do later, in its aspect towards corporeity and the outer world; for primarily, as has been said, it is the externalization of the spirit itself. And in representing its origination, we went back to the primeval process; because, after the loss of the spirit's likeness to God, the soul's presence still only makes itself perceived by its primeval going forth from the divinely-imaged spirit. For the soul has lost by the fall nothing of its sevenfold substance—only its spirit-resembling determination. The fifth and sixth powers, which brought the spirit-resembling nature of the soul to its completion, are still only the remaining outlines of a failing type—the forms that are left of a lost substance, but still only truly intelligible from this their original constitution and destination.

The soul thus consists, in conformity with its archetype—the divine *doxa*—of seven powers.[1] As are the seven spirits to the Spirit of God, unfolded in a sevenfold aspect towards the world, so is the soul to the human spirit unfolded in sevenfold-wise towards the body. It resembles—as we say with Luther in his exposition of the *Magnificat*—the candlestick in the sanctuary, with its seven branches and lights; for this, as it were, is an embodied doxology of the church[2] giving back sevenfold to God in the echo of praises, the sevenfold glory in which He has revealed Himself (comp. the psalm of the seven thunders, Ps. xxix. 1). The holy candlestick, rightly understood, is thus, in reality, a fitting type of the human soul, which indeed is for that reason called כָּבוֹד.[3] Its constitution, as we have shown, is sevenfold. There are seven circles: the first (contraction) is the narrowest; the centre, which here still is concealed in its

---

[1] How—even apart from Jac. Böhme (v. Hamberger, *Lehre Jac. Böhme's*, p. 129), and Pordage—psychology strives after such a sevenfold expression of powers, is shown by the *Religions-lehre* of C. A. H. Clodius (1808), pp. 122–125, the author of *Eros and Psyche*, an ingenious poem of a psychologic and religious character, that appeared after the poet's death, in twelve cantos (1838). And Flacius' representation of the genesis of the faith in Thomasius, *Dogm.* iii. 2, 185, offers an analogue of our psychical sevenfold nature. But the knowledge of the gospel beginning to soften the sting of conscience is the fourth degree, not the third.

[2] Hofmann, *Weiss. und Erfüllung*, i. 143, has shown that the sacred candlestick does not signify so much the light proceeding from God, as rather the light by which Israel makes visible the dwelling of its God, just as he also has rightly interpreted the visionary candlestick in Zechariah (*ibid.* p. 343). The remark of Zöckler, *Naturtheol.* i. 787, against me, goes on the mistaken supposition that the candlestick is a symbol of the Spirit of God in its operation on the spirit of man. The lights burn, indeed, by being fed with the divine oil of the Spirit. It thus signifies, in any case, the human endowed with divinely produced light—which even Köhler misses in his interpretation.

[3] The most learned Jewish epigraphist of late times says of the symbol frequent in Rome on the Jewish cemeteries, *e.g.* of the *Via Portuensis*—the *Menôrah* (*Epigraphische Beiträge zur Geschichte der Juden*, in the *Jahrb.*

impulse, but typically disclosing itself, is the spirit. In the fourth power shines forth, for the first time, the spirit-resemblance of the soul, while the spirit's will immanent in the process maintains the supremacy. In the ternary beyond, is repeated the first ternary in inverted order; so that the fifth power is the correlative of the third, the sixth of the second, and the first of the seventh. To the expansion according to its nature (2), corresponds the expansion of the spirit-resembling nature (6); to the excited restless circling round itself (3), corresponds the gentle, submissive surrender to the spirit (5); and to the unity of the germinating origin (1), corresponds the perfected unity in multiplicity (7). The three first powers correspond to the procreative urgency of the Father's love reflecting itself in the *doxa;* the fourth to the birth of the Son exhibited in the *doxa;* the fifth and sixth to the inhalation of love and the exhalation of love of the Holy Spirit, manifesting itself in the *doxa;* and the seventh completes the nature of the spiritual soul as the image of the threefold spirit, as in the archetype the nature of the divine *doxa* was completed as the image of the threefold Godhead.

The biblical use of נֶפֶשׁ, ψυχή, is conformed to the powers that we have inferred, on the supposition that the human soul is the type of the divine *doxa.* For in respect of the first power, נֶפֶשׁ imports the self of man, *e.g.* Deut. xiii. 7, 1 Sam. xviii. 1; in regard of the second power, נֶפֶשׁ imports in the most manifold reference, desire, longing, *e.g.* Prov. xxiii. 2, Ps. xxvii. 12, xxxv. 25, and the internal impulse (Eph. vi. 6; Col. iii. 23); in respect of the third power, נֶפֶשׁ implies life, *e.g.* Job ii. 6, John x. 11; in respect of the fourth power, נֶפֶשׁ signifies, in virtue of the immanence of the personifying spirit, the Ego, *e.g.* Isa. xxvi. 9; in respect of the fifth power, נֶפֶשׁ implies the disposition of mind, as it may be inclined and determined by natural (Ex. xxiii. 9) or by spiritual (1 Pet. ii. 11) events; in respect of the sixth power, נֶפֶשׁ implies the expressed will, Ps. cv. 22 (synon. with פֶּה, Gen. xli. 40, as also in the second meaning (Isa. v. 14) it is synonymous with פֶּה); in respect of the seventh power, נֶפֶשׁ imports the soul in the totality

für d. Gesch. d. Jud. ii. 282): "The candlestick with the seven branches is a type of that which is placed in the sanctuary, and, according to Prov. xx. 27, it passes for the symbol of the human soul."

of all its powers, *e.g.* Jer. xxxviii. 16, and as the spiritual medium of the spirit and body, the entire person of man, *e.g.* Gen. xlvi. 26. Thus, moreover, the biblical mode of expression teaches us to recognise the soul, (1) as comprehending itself; (2) as stretching itself beyond itself after another; (3) as self-living; (4) as penetrated by the spirit, which knows itself; (5) as thus or thus affected; (6) as speaking, *i.e.* forming the thoughts of the spirit into audible words; (7) as united in one in a multiplicity of powers. And even in the seven spirits which are named by Isa. xi. 2, our result is confirmed so far as they without constraint correspond to the seven powers or forms of life of the soul. For if we consider man in the position of the restored likeness of God, even as God by His Spirit dwells in the spirit of man, so God's Spirit proves itself to the spirit of man, by means of the first power of the soul, as רוּחַ יִרְאַת ה׳ (comp. Ps. lxxxvi. 11), in opposition to sinful selfishness; by means of the second power of the soul, as רוּחַ דַּעַת ה׳, in opposition to sinful craving; by means of the third power of the soul, as רוּחַ גְּבוּרָה, in opposition to sinful passionateness; by means of the fourth power of the soul, as רוּחַ ה׳, in opposition to secularity; by means of the fifth power of the soul, as רוּחַ עֵצָה, in opposition to worldly bondage; by means of the sixth, as רוּחַ בִּינָה, in opposition to worldly thoughts and customs; and by means of the seventh, as רוּחַ חָכְמָה, *i.e.* in opposition to the *Turba* of all the powers, as the spirit of the wisdom which holds them all together, and regulates them harmoniously, or still more biblically expressed (comp. Rom. xi. 33 with Eph. iii. 9), œconomically.[1]

We do not suppose that we have proved our view of the sevenfold unity of the soul from the Scripture by these means. But it is sufficient that it is the not unscriptural result of an inquiry, towards which we found ourselves led by Scripture hints worthy of consideration. The capacities of the soul which psychology is accustomed to enumerate, and copiously to treat of, are different. We desire to show how our analysis maintains its claims in the face of that psychological analysis which diverges from it.

[1] See the admirable recapitulation of this paragraph in Göschel, *Der Mensch, diesseits und jenseits*, p. 37.

THE ESTABLISHED VIEW OF THE CAPACITIES OF THE SOUL.

Sec. VII.

Where, then, it will be asked, are the capacities of perception and representation, with memory, fancy, and understanding? where the capacity of feeling, where the faculty of desire, with inclination and choice? We formulate the question even as it is required, when we leave out such faculties as have been already shown to belong to the spirit, as such (reason, disposition, free-will). All the capacities named are actually proper to the spirit-resembling soul, as such. The soul is the perceiver in us. "Thou hearest, O my soul," says Jeremiah (iv. 19), "the voice of the trumpet, the sound of war." As it is here said that the soul hears, so elsewhere, that it thinks, and speaks, and knows (1 Sam. xx. 4; Lam. iii. 24; Ps. cxxxix. 14): it must therefore so far partake in the spirit's capacity of thought and knowledge, that the faculty of representation is proper to it: to make to itself anxious representations is called, in Ps. xiii. 2, שִׁית עֵצוֹת בְּנַפְשׁוֹ. Imagination is called, in Eccles. vi. 9, הֲלָךְ־נֶפֶשׁ, to conceive, to think with one's self; Esther iv. 13, דִּמָּה בְנַפְשׁוֹ. That memory and forgetting are affairs of the soul, is shown by Deut. iv. 9. Thus, that passions and affections of all kinds are declared of the soul, as subject and object, there need absolutely no special texts to prove: נֶפֶשׁ indicates in that behalf absolutely the general disposition of a man's mind, proceeding from events or circumstances (Ex. xxiii. 9, comp. שָׁפַךְ נַפְשׁוֹ, 1 Sam. i. 15). That there is a capacity of desire belonging to the soul, is shown by the customary phrase אִוַּת נֶפֶשׁ, e.g. Deut. xii. 15, comp. Apoc. xviii. 14. Nay, נֶפֶשׁ, ψυχή, signifies in that respect absolutely the longing, e.g. Prov. xxiii. 2, and the thing longed for (Ps. xxxv. 25). It implies, in contrast to the external urgency, the impulse (Col. iii. 23); and in opposition to the self-dominion of the spirit, the internal arbitrary choice.

We have therefore formulated the question which we proposed at the beginning, as it requires. The faculties of the soul, which are wanting in our representation, certainly belong to the soul—to wit, in virtue of the fact that it is the copy of the spirit, and that the spirit is immanent in this its likeness. But in the arrangement of the deficient faculties of the soul we have followed the established method, by which it is usual to place the capacity of perception and of representation first, and the capacity of desire at the end.[1] This arrangement is nevertheless neither consistent with the fact, nor with Scripture. It is not according to Scripture; for in the idea of נֶפֶשׁ, ψυχή, as Scripture uses it, is altogether manifest the characteristic of desire, predominant over everything, and pervading everything; so much that נֶפֶשׁ even signifies by metonymy the most external bodily organs of desire, the mouth and throat (Isa. v. 14), and the stomach (Isa. xxix. 8, xxxii. 6; Prov. vi. 30); and similarly the counterpart of appetite—food (Isa. lviii. 10), and the means of providing the daily bread (mill and mill-stone) (Deut. xxiv. 6); and רְחַב נֶפֶשׁ (Prov. xxviii. 25) is broad-souled, as opposed to greedy, covetous (narrow-souled).[2] Generally, Scripture considers will, knowledge, and experience absolutely as one unity. We showed this when we treated on the triplicity of the spirit. We shall prove it further, when we discuss the biblical use of the word לֵב, καρδία. For that in man which thinks and perceives could not be called in Scripture לֵב, καρδία, unless the will were the peculiar central feature in man, which precedes perception, and comprehends it in itself; while through the perception superadded, the will becomes self-determination and self-decision.

Arthur Schopenhauer[3] has built his philosophical system on

[1] Thus, for example also, in the able psychological compendiums of Jos. Beck and Christ. Heinr. Zeller, founded as they are on biblical principles.

[2] Distinct from רְחַב לֵב (Ps. ci. 5), broad-hearted, which is contrasted with puffed up, arrogant.

[3] In his work, *Die Welt als Wille und als Vorstellung;* comp. his work on the will in nature (2d ed. 1854). We might, moreover, have proceeded above from Schelling; for that there is no other means of being able to know the being and life of the Godhead, as of the soul and of the spirit, than by the will (that which first of all wills itself, and is not objective)— this is also the fundamental thought of the (later) system of Schelling. We have, however, avoided it, in order to avoid the false appearance of being dependent on this system whilst we have the Holy Scripture before us, and independently follow the guidance of the profound German thinker, through the study of whom Schelling's thoughtful labours since the inquiries on the nature of human freedom, 1809, have appeared newly fertilized and made young.

the fundamental position, that the thing in the abstract, or the final *substratum* of every phenomenon, is the will; for that it has been a mistake hitherto to regard will and knowledge as absolutely inseparable—nay, to regard the will as a mere operation of knowledge, which is the supposed basis of every spiritual fact. Will and choice were confounded, which latter is only a mode of appearance of the will. For the will is the agent, moreover, of all occurrences without cognizance; but choice is will where knowledge enlightens it; and thence arise motives, that is to say, representations which are moving causes to it. The difference between movements which are arbitrary and not arbitrary does not concern the essential and primary element, which in both cases is the will, but merely the secondary—the calling forth of the externality of the will, whether this occurs, for instance, in the guiding clue of special causes (as in inorganic bodies), or by attraction (as in vegetable-animal life), or by motives, *i.e.* through the knowledge of pervading causes (as in psychico-spiritual life).

These principles are not without truth, if only this were not abused, in connection with this system, into a foundation of the most peculiar idealism and wretched atheism, so as to be disfigured thereby. Even K. Fortlage indicates the "will or impulse" as the fundamental relation of the psychical nature— as the empiric Ego: "the impulse," says he,[1] "is built under all being as its deepest foundation." And Hinrichs, although distinguishing will and impulse, in opposition to Schopenhauer, still defines all life as the appearance of impulse, inasmuch as in his work,[2] which exhibits very ably the essential likeness and essential difference between brute and man, he proceeds from the position, "that the feeling of self is the foundation of the possibility of life, inclination or impulse the internal condition of its coming into existence: the possible life in the feeling of self, which as such is an inseparable unity, is rendered effectual by inclination." On our side, we maintain that experience attributes to inclination, not to the perception of self, the priority. For the sense of self of the living nature awakens in the degree that the inclinations natural to it —*i.e.* innate, stimulated by sensational allurements, and ideas associated therewith—begin to express themselves,—a process

[1] *System der Psychologie*, i. 464.   [2] *Ueber das Leben in der Natur*, 1854.

of development which reaches back even into the still restrained life of the fœtus swimming in the amniotic fluid of the womb.[1] The inclination aroused by sensations and ideas, and thus found in existence by them, is, however, the lowest ground-form of the will, willing in the light of self-consciousness; yet,—as appears from the fact that the willing power can transplant itself, by virtue of its will, into the position of unconsciousness,—not first begotten by self-consciousness. At least the Godhead would not be *causa sui*, if its being, and even its self-consciousness (as we have seen in Div. IV. Sec. IV.), had not will, and indeed, will purely self-determining from itself (without stimulus from without) as its primitive ground, or,—as we might even say, as here is the limit of all thought losing itself in the infinite— its *no*-ground. God is prior to all will, for He is love; and to love, אָהַב, is before all, to will, אָבָה (אָוָה), *avere* (corresponding to the Vedic root *av*, to desire, to love) : true love is good-will itself. But even elsewhere, Scripture does not make the will subsequent to perception. "Scriptura de cogitationibus," says M. F. Roos, with careful consideration,[2] "non ita loquitur ut voluntatem vel volitiones sejungat, quemadmodum id in scholis philosophorum fit, qui discrimen inter intellectum ac voluntatem ingens constituerunt et intellectui regimen, voluntati obsequium attribuerunt." "What is will?" asks Oetinger;[3] and answers, "My soul is pure will, *nisus indifferens*, which is first determined by certain *objectis* and becomes *sui conscius*; so that, as it were, the will gives birth to the understanding by the *objecta*." This answer is scriptural. All existence, הָיָה, is in its deepest source will, אָוָה (comp. הַוַּת נֶפֶשׁ, Mic. vii. 3, for אַוַּת[4]); for which reason also an immediate θέλειν (John iii. 8), *i.e.* a θέλειν not produced by the way of knowledge, is attributed to the entire life of nature unconscious of itself. But in the latter instance the question of the priority in the Godhead itself is decided in favour of the will. Therefore, when we considered the triplicity of God as the archetype of the triplicity of the spirit, we everywhere gave will the precedence before thought and knowledge. According

---

[1] See Kussmaul, *Untersuchungen über das Seelenleben des neugeborenen Menschen*, 1859.

[2] *Fundamenta Psychologiæ ex S.S. Collecta*, p. 182.

[3] In his work on the Psalms, p. 627.

[4] See, on הָוָה (whence הַוָּה), *hiare* and *inhiare*, Hupf. on Ps. v. 10.

to Scripture, the will is the root of the Godhead and of the spirit, having its primary existence in God, and consequently also the root of the soul, having its primary source in the spirit.

Although, therefore, in our view of the soul, the faculty of desire seems to be omitted, yet, in case the seven powers comprehend it in themselves, it will probably be contained in the first of them. And thus it actually is. For what is the first power wherewith the being of the soul commences, other than a will as yet immediate, having no object but itself, embracing itself, and therefore dark? In the second power the immediate will is already become an effectuated will with a motive. There is associated with it the idea of a purpose placed outside of itself; and this idea becomes a motive which forces it out of its immediate existence within itself: desire has here stepped forth from its mere reference to itself, and has become impulse. In the third stage we find passion and conception striving with one another; passion seeking to possess itself of the thing conceived, in opposition to other possible conceptions: desire here appears as arbitrary will, or faculty of choice. Thus, in respect of its three first powers, the soul is a copy of the spirit's loving will and loving thought, just as this latter is the copy of the Father's loving will and loving thought directed towards the Son. The destination towards which the soul struggles in the third stage, is that it may press through to a conformity with the spirit. This pressing through is carried into effect in the fourth stage, where the spirit has before itself the soul, as the image of itself, and the soul has before itself, itself as the image of the spirit. Here is the place of the plastic power of the imagination or fancy ($\dot{\epsilon}\nu\theta\dot{\upsilon}\mu\eta\sigma\iota\varsigma$, Acts xvii. 29), which, if it dissolve the harmony with the spirit, becomes a scene of confusion, of entangled and ignoble phantasms, and not less also of the faculty of foreboding, since it is here where the soul is penetrated with misgivings from the veiled depth of the future, and generally of that which is mysterious, *i.e.* immediate perceptions, like lightning, or like glimpses of light. In the fifth stage, the soul, pervaded with likeness to the spirit, is receptive of the substance of the spirit so formed into it, and is passively turned towards it. It perceives it, it sensitively reflects it, it preserves that which is perceived and felt,—in all, a true mirror of the spirit, which unfolds itself to it as a pattern. Perception, feeling, memory, have here their place; for perception and feeling (*sentire*) are inseparable, and memory is nothing else than the retaining of that which is received by way of perception and feeling. In the sixth stage, the soul is confirmed in possession of this important deposit, in that by the power of the *nous* (manifesting itself here as understanding) of the spirit immanent in it, it divides it, and arranges, or comprehensively systematizes it, and translates it into the sound-forms of audible speech. In the seventh stage, the spirit-resembling nature of the soul is then completed by the organizing power of wisdom.

Thus, in our view of the soul, none of the faculties are omitted which are usually enumerated as psychical. Their sequence, indeed, is different from that which is commonly received, but it is more accordant with their genesis: we see one unfolded out of the other in gradual progression. In all, however, it must not be forgotten that the soul has no self-conscious existence for itself; its capacities are the refractions of rays of the spirit's light; it is what it is, and as what it proves itself, by the power of personal association with the personifying spirit. The seven powers of the soul are not the soul's own powers, but the psychical powers of the spirit itself; as the "seven spirits" of the Apocalypse are, so to speak, the powers of God the Spirit, and especially of His Spirit, brought into operation as the *doxa*, or in the way of the development of His glory. The understanding (בִּינָה, מַעַם, φρένες, σύνεσις) is a mode of operation of the reason psychically effected (שֵׂכֶל, דַּעַת, νοῦς, γνῶσις[1]), Job xxxii. 8, 1 Chron. xxii. 12, 2 Chron. ii. 11; and wisdom (חָכְמָה, σοφία) is in the highest sense a mode of operation of the knowledge of the spirit (דַּעַת, γνῶσις) psychically carried into effect: for as God has γνῶσις, so far as He knows Himself the Triune, but σοφία in relation to His *doxa* and to the world; as γνῶσις and σοφία (Rom. xi. 33) are so distinguished, as that the former is the *knowledge* of God, by means of which the world's history with all its intricacies and abysses is eternally known to Him, but the latter is the *wisdom* of God, by means of which

---

[1] It is a very just tact by which Luther (although not consistently, still very generally) translates בִּינָה, תְּבוּנָה, φρένες, σύνεσις, by "understanding," and דַּעַת, שֵׂכֶל, γνῶσις, λόγος, νοῦς (νόημα), by "reason;" comp. especially Prov. xviii. 15, xix. 25, xxi. 11.

He has established for the world's history its destination, and selects the right means to lead it towards this destination—the design and substance of the οἰκονομία τοῦ μυστηρίου (Eph. iii. 9);—even so σοφία, as the completion of the nature of the human soul, is the typically reflected knowledge of the spirit itself, in the harmonious disposition and regulation of all its powers. All wisdom, which pertains to the spiritual soul by virtue of the immanence of a spirit detached from God, is ψυχικὴ in an evil sense (Jas. iii. 15; comp. on the other hand, Col. i. 9).

The soul has, however, not merely a side turned towards the spirit, but a side turned towards corporeity and the world. But before applying ourselves to the consideration of this aspect of the soul's life, we have to deal with a weighty objection. According to the usual view, the spirit's life is related to the soul's life, as its blossom and flower; according to our view, it is its root. The human process of development appears to contradict this view, to which we attach ourselves on the ground of Scripture. It is this which we are now engaged to investigate.

THE COMMENCEMENT AND DEVELOPMENT OF THE THREEFOLD LIFE.

Sec. VIII.

WHEREVER the Holy Scripture speaks of the act of begetting and conception, *e.g.* Ps. li. 5, it speaks of it as of a fact to which is referred the beginning of the being and the threefold life of the whole man—of man absolutely and without exception entire. Even the male or female sexuality is already distinguished according to Scripture in this moment of commencement (Job iii. 3; Luke i. 36).

The embryo is called in Hebrew גֹּלֶם (Ps. cxxxix. 16). As is known, the embryo does not lie straight, but so that the front of the head is inclined forwards to the front of the belly; the extremities are folded, and all is as much as possible thrown into the form of an egg. The Israelite had skill in this knowledge, in consequence of the practice then frequent in war times of laying open the womb of the mother (בֹּקֵעַ הָרוֹת, 2 Kings viii. 12, xv. 16; Amos i. 13; Hos. xiv. 1). A more significant word for the embryo could hardly be found than that גֹּלֶם, derived from גָּלַם, to roll together.[1]

The development of the embryo, to the wisdom of the Israelite, stands for one of the profoundest mysteries. "As thou knowest not what is the way of the wind," says the Preacher (xi. 5), "nor how the bones do grow in the womb of her that is with child" (as thou knowest not the growing of this into a man); even so thou canst not know the works of God, who maketh all." "I know not," says the mother of the seven in the time of the Maccabees to these her children (2 Macc. vii. 22), "I know not how ye came to being in my womb; neither gave I you spirit and life, nor did I arrange the members of you (στοιχείωσιν διερύθμησα)." Two poetic passages of the canonical Scripture speak at large of this mysterious development. We translate them: first of all, vers. 13–16 of the 139th Psalm of David:

> " For Thou hast brought forth my reins.
> Thou inweavedst me in the womb of my mother.
> It was a fearful wonder, therefore I thank Thee.
> Marvellous are Thy works!
> And my soul knoweth it right well.
>
> My bones were not hidden from Thee
> When I was made in secret,
> Variously wrought in the lower parts of the earth.
>
> Thine eyes did see me as an embryo,
> And on Thy book were they all written;
> The days of the future, of which none existed then."

Then verses 8–12 (one strophe) from ch. x. of the book of Job:

> " Thine hands have formed me and fashioned me
> Altogether round about; and now Thou hast destroyed me.
> Remember still, that as clay Thou hast fashioned me;
> And wilt Thou change me into dust again?

---

[1] The LXX. translates ἀκατέργαστόν μου, Symmachus, ἀμόρφωτόν με. In the Talmudic, גֹּלֶם implies the unformed man, especially the still unformed vessel.

> Hast Thou not poured me out in form as milk,
> And allowed me to curdle like cheese?
> Thou clothedst me with skin and flesh,
> And interweavedst me with bones and sinews.
> Thou hast shown to me life and grace,
> And Thy protection defended my breath."

The most important matter to us in these two passages is this, that the female uterus is called אֶרֶץ תַּחְתִּיוֹת.[1] It is called thus, as the secret workshop of the earthly principle, with the same reference back to the first origination of man's body from dust of the earth, as when Job (i. 21) says, "Naked came I out of my mother's womb, and naked shall I return thither again." This back reference is expressed according to both aspects, when, on the one hand, it is said of Elihu (Job xxxiii. 6), "Behold, I am, even as thou thyself art, of God: I also am moulded out of the clay;" on the other hand, ver. 4: "God's Spirit hath made me, and the breath of the Almighty hath given me life." In the origination of every man is thus repeated, according to the view of Scripture, the mode of Adam's creation.

But if it be the case that the primeval coming into being is the type of every following instance, we are not, with Fr. Nasse,[2] at all to assume in respect of Gen. ii. 7, that the child has no soul of its own until its birth; but, on the contrary, the substance of the germ from which man is developed must be taken for an interaction of body and spirit effectuated by the soul, which proceeds from the spirit; and this view is to be held although it cannot be proved by inquiry, and has the apparent evidence against it. Thus (1) the view is objectionable, that the body is even from its first beginning the image of the soul embodying itself.[3] "When we suppose," says K. Heyder,[4] "that

---

[1] Reuchlin had previously interpreted briefly and well in his *Rudimenta* (1506): Contextus sum in inferioribus terræ id est in matrice.

[2] In the Appendix, "of the Animation of the Child," *Zeitschr. für die Anthropologie*, 1824, i., and 1825, iii. In both, the author depends on Gen. ii. 7.

[3] So, for instance, the author of the *Seelenfreundlichen Briefe* (1853), p. 57, and especially J. H. Fichte.

[4] In his notice of the Wagnerian work on the struggle about the soul, *Zeitschr. für Protest.* 1857, p. 345. Just thus decides A. Zeller, art. "Irre" in Ersch and Gruber's *A.E.*

God has endowed the soul with anything of creative power, by which itself produces its own bodily appearance,—and, indeed, in such a manner that, by divine contrivance, its previously existing material offers itself as the conditioning of its operation,—we think that we are not therein coming into contradiction with the Holy Scripture." As a recommendation of this opinion, the observation is premised, that in general " it is not the purpose of Scripture to give us scientific disclosures on the problem of the union of body and soul." But, however that may be, the Scripture certainly has a fundamental view on the relation of the soul to the body, which it holds unchanged from its first page even to its last; and this fundamental view, it must be conceded, is decidedly dualistic. This decisiveness is not diminished by the fact, that it none the less comprehends the union of body and soul as an internal and essential fact. The narrative of creation (Gen. ii. 7)—which certainly has another purpose than that of making scientific disclosures—is actually, with respect to this its other purpose,[1] the most express protest against monism. And as in this foundation text, so throughout, Scripture considers body and soul as distinct creations of God, and the latter, not as that which produces the body, but only as that which enlivens it; as also the brute soul has not formed to itself its own body,[2] but it is the constitution of the creative Spirit, which came forth at the divine call to being, at the same moment with the body. Nevertheless the origination of the child differs from that of the first man in this respect, that certainly the beginning of the individualized corporeity absolutely coincides with the beginning of the individual soul that vitalizes it; so that, from the first moment of its beginning to be, the embryo is a germinating concrete unity of body and soul. And, moreover, it is true, that from this first moment the soul is a coefficient factor of the bodily development; but it is false to say (2) that it is a plastic or organizing principle of this development,[3] and the body only the external formation of the soul's inner natural life, effected by attraction from the natural world

---

[1] See thereupon Drechsler, in my *Commentary on Genesis* (1860), p. 138.

[2] Thus Keerl, *Schöpfungsgeschichte*, pp. 576-578.

[3] Thus *e.g.* K. Ph. Fischer, in his *Anthropologie* (1853), see especially sec. 82.

of the corresponding material.¹ This view is only another variation of that which has just been rejected, which makes the soul a productive principle. For if the soul, according to an idea dwelling in it, forms the material beginning of the body into a skilfully articulated organ of itself, it is the creator of the body, although it does not bring it forth out of nothing, but out of a plastic chaos. And this is contrary to Scripture, and contradicts itself. It is contrary to Scripture; for, looking to the history of creation in Gen. ii. 7, the skilful structure of the body is prior to its endowment with soul; and in the origination of the child, the body, according to Scripture, equally as then, is God's structure, and the soul, equally as then, God's inspiration,—equally, although effectuated by those who beget it, inasmuch as the creative impresses of the primitive beginning are continuing to operate in the act of procreation. But, moreover, it confutes itself; for if the origination of the body and the origination of the soul absolutely coincide, so that neither of the two precedes the other, then the body is, even in the first moment of its individualization, a germ, preformatively bearing in itself the idea of its development,²—a גֹּלֶם, *i.e.* an undeveloped thing, but a thing capable of development out of itself; in conformity with that capability, it is already all that it subsequently becomes; and the final impelling cause of its development, according to Scripture, is God, not the soul. To understand this, it must be remembered that the elementary germinating substance of the body, even apart from the soul, is not an absolutely dead mass. It has already a part in organic nature-life, although as yet it is not individually living. It is indeed fructified from the father's life; it is rooted in the mother's life; it is pervaded by powers from which its vegetative development may be comprehended even without the addition of a soul. But there is implied in the preformative idea of this development, that the corporeity has to be moulded

¹ Thus literally Schöberlein, *Jahrbb.* 1861, p. 47.

² We know well what modern psychology is pleased to say against this: "It is nothing but a phrase—which pretends to satisfy, but dissolves in the hand that would grasp it—to say that it is the idea of the creature involved in the egg, which is confirmed by the development, and that the idea is awakened by fructification."—Bergmann-Leuckart, *Vergleichende Anatomie und Physiologie,* 1855, p. 572. Assuredly ideas cannot be grasped with hands.

into a suitable organ of the soul. The soul is thus the purpose, and link, and support of this growth into being: it is the self-living centre, round which all the atoms of the body are grouped and arranged. Certainly also it influences this growth into being, in that it not merely lets it happen that a body forms itself, but it operates for this purpose, that a body corresponding to this soul, in such or such a way determined, should form itself to it—thus conceiving for the growth into being of the body the stamp of its individuality. So far it is, as the unity of the end of this growth into being, so also the unity of its foundation, but not absolute, only in a certain measure.

A third view is confuted by that resemblance which Scripture assumes between the act of procreation and the primeval act of creation. For instance, (3) it has been often and much taught, under manifold modifications, that the spiritual soul, free in itself as it forms its real external organization (the body), so further, by spontaneous relation to this organization, develops also its ideal spiritual nature, or internal organization, which is the medium of its self-realization into the concrete spirit, or to the spiritual personality.[1] The human soul (in this respect distinguished from the brute soul) is thus, as it were, *à priori* spiritual, but only potentially so: the spirit does not become actual until the soul realizes this potency, and thus completes itself. This is not only the prevailing philosophical view, but also the theosophic view, although the latter considers the process of development not as physical, but ethical. It pertains to the fundamental views of J. Böhme, and his great interpreter Fr. Baader, that the soul has its primitive standing in the fire-life of the Father, which is as well a longing after light and existence, as the power towards both; that in it is implanted by the Son, as the bearer of the world of ideas, the idea or the divine image of human destination; and that it has in the body the essentiality, which must come to a spiritual conformation through the Holy Spirit by His actualizing that idea, and so making the soul itself spiritual.[2] We will not dissemble it, but, on the contrary, in love for the truth, we will most urgently declare it, that this is the point at which our conception of the relation of soul and spirit has to undergo

[1] See K. Ph. Fischer, *Anthropologie*, sec. 84.
[2] See J. Hamberger, in the second Appendix of this division.

the hardest and most decisive trial. Here is the motive which first decided me, after long delay, to allow this my system of biblical psychology to issue to the world a second time. For whether the development of man is to be placed under a natural or a spiritual point of view, most weighty considerations occur to us here. But they still cannot determine me to subvert my fundamental view. In writing biblical psychology, we are concerned to know whether the fundamental view in question is biblical; and of this foundation we are now as ever assured.

The act of divine inbreathing (Gen. ii. 7) is not apprehended by theosophy as endowing with spirit, but as the enkindling of the essentials of the soul present in the bodily form, and the awakening of the idea, or of the spirit-form of the soul, by the Holy Spirit. It is this which calls the soul into life, and makes manifest the idea in it, which primarily is a gift, but at the same time a charge, so far as the soul is to allow it now to attain form in itself, and, as Baader expresses it, to become spirit through the inbirth of the idea as seed of the spirit. But these are thoughts which cannot be read from the biblical text. For the breath of life (*nischmath chajim*) is a breath of God which not only effects this and that in the construction of the body, but, as is shown by Gen. vii. 22, Isa. ii. 22, and other passages, enters into man as a continual element of his nature. Man is henceforth living soul by the power of the spirit of life, wherewith God has endowed him in a manner elevated above the origin of the brutes. He is an individual endowed with soul, and, at the same time, a spiritual personality. The endowing with soul is the consequence of the endowing with spirit, and the endowing with spirit is not previously the object into which the endowment with soul was developed. The God-willed object of development is penetration by the spirit, *i.e.* spiritual permeation of the whole condition of being, but not the outworking of the spirit itself. The realization of the idea is not the becoming of the spirit itself, but the problem proposed to the threefold spirit with the co-operation of the seven powers of the soul. In the spirit shines forth the light which corresponds to the birth of the Son. The entire threefold life of man has as its destination to develop itself forth from its ground of fire to the life of light. The entire man is to become a child of light by becoming a light in the Lord, the everlasting Light which became the Light of the world. This is the biblical truth of the theosophic view.

The philosophic view of the priority of the soul, and of its first gradually ensuing self-development into spirit,—not merely dynamically present, but actual,—has, at all events, experience in its favour, so far as man does not enter except with advancing growth into the position of intellectual self-determination; as, moreover, Scripture assumes (Isa. vii. 16). This gradual progress is altogether undeniable; and, moreover, we are far from opposing to the proposition that the soul develops itself into spirit, the reverse proposition, that the spirit develops itself into soul. No; we concede that we should thereby be flying in the face of experience. But this consequence is not at all involved in our premiss, that the priority in relation to the soul belongs to the spirit. For we maintain this priority with reference to the created origination of the two, and their position in respect of creation to one another, but not with regard to the development of the man, which in general, following the procedure of creation, begins from below upwards, in order then to complete itself from above downwards. What results from that premiss, with reference to the development of man, is only this: that in the first germinating beginning of man, spirit and soul also are placed together in the way of germ; that they both together emerge by degrees into actuality; and that the life of the soul does not unfold itself, without, at the same time, the self-consciousness of the spirit glimmering near it in the background, and so glimmering on throughout the development. The Scripture at least knows absolutely nothing of a נֶפֶשׁ developing itself into רוּחַ, of a ψυχή becoming πνεῦμα; rather it supposes, that with the embryonic beginning of bodily life is produced, at the same time, the beginning of the spirit's and soul's life. The human life, says a philosopher —who in this matter agrees with us[1]—comprises three periods of development and training,—the bodily, psychical, and spiritual, the characteristic features of which are predominantly denoted by the age of life—of childhood, youth, and manhood. None of these elements is wholly absent in any one epoch of life; but the rest are subordinated to the spiritual, not only manifestly in

[1] Windischmann, in Fr. Nasse's *Zeitschr. für d. Anthropologie*, 1823-4, p. 382.

the time of greater maturity, but also from the beginning, only in a more hidden manner: in the psychic element they have their natural effectuation and reciprocal action.

For when, according to Luke i. 25, John even in his mother's womb was said to be full of the Holy Ghost, it is plainly assumed that the fruit of the body has not only soul, but also spirit; for it is precisely the human spirit which is the organ for the reception of the divine. Besides, moreover, Scripture relegates secret events, which primarily concern the spirit, back into the life of the embryo, especially the separating and sanctifying to a lofty call (Isa. xlix. 1, 5; Jer. i. 5; Gal. i. 15). And as well believing love of God (Ps. xxii. 10 *et seq.*, lxxi. 6), as self-turning departure from God (Ps. lviii. 4; Isa. xlviii. 8), are dated back at least without any limits into the period of infancy, to say nothing of Gen. xxv. 22, Hos. xii. 4, Luke i. 41. It is therefore impossible that the Scripture should so separate spirit and soul in the child, as that the former should be only potentially included in the latter. Spirit and soul are factors, present from the beginning in proportional correlation in the process of man's development. If the Scripture apparently contradicts this, by saying that the beginning of man is psychical, and the aim of his development is pneumatical, it is meant of the ethical development that is to be completed on the ground of the physical condition. The first position of man is the implanted or inborn one of psychical immediateness determined in this or that way; and from this position he is to pass over into the self-effectuated spiritual one of all, even to the outermost end of the self-determination that rules over the corporeity.

We stand here before a riddle, which, however, is equally enigmatical, whether we suppose that the soul is the self-copy of the spirit, or that the spirit is the culminating point of the soul. In both cases it is mysterious, that the existence of the spirit— to which it is essential to be conscious of itself—begins with a condition of unconsciousness. For the actual and reflex knowledge, especially the knowledge of itself, begins, like the perception of the sunlight, not until after birth (Eccles. vi. 3–5). How is it possible, it is asked, that man, beginning to be, should have spirit without yet having self-consciousness? Personality, as Philippi teaches in reference to the question, is that which lies at the foundation of self-consciousness and free self-determination·

something deeper—that peculiar internal nature which is reflected in these two forms of appearance—that spiritual *Ego-ness* of which man becomes conscious in his self-consciousness, and which, in his self-determination towards the external, he disregards, as is shown in the child in which the *Ego-ness* is already present as a germ, and still does not develop itself in consciousness and freedom.[1] The fact is true, although its mode of indication may be questioned. This *Ego-ness* is the personally implied, but not yet personally efficient, individuality of man, which is not so much the essence, as it is rather the ground of possibility of self-consciousness and of freedom; or still more plainly and definitely, this *Ego-ness* is the spirit of man itself, to which self-consciousness and freedom already potentially belong before they become energetic. The human spirit is thus a self-conscious spirit before man becomes conscious of himself. That is just the enigma. But this enigma is a fact which could not be otherwise. If spirit and body were to enter into a *unio personalis*, it was indispensable that the spirit should be subjected to a similar law of development with that of the body. How this was possible may be guessed, if we remember that (as has been shown) the basis of the life of the spirit and of the soul is not knowledge, but will; but it can just as little be apprehended as the *unio personalis*—infinitely more mysterious—of the divine and human nature in Christ. We experience the actuality of this incomprehensible thing in ourselves daily. For there are many normal and abnormal conditions, in which the human spirit is put back into that state of unconsciousness or restrained consciousness with which its existence began. And as it has forced itself upwards from darkness to light, it has (itself herein being a witness of its conditionality) even now still a gloomy depth, in which everything great that it brings forth is wont embryonically to ripen [2] before it is born into the light.

[1] *Glaubenslehre*, ii. 144.

[2] C. Gust. Carus, in his book entitled *Psyche*, has exquisitely represented the region of unconsciousness still ever subsisting in the neighbourhood of the conscious life of the soul. Also in the work, *Schädel, Hirn, und Seele* (1854), of E. Huschke, there occur some profound considerations having reference to this subject. "In our spirit," we read, p. 186, "there is constantly active gloom, half gloom, and clearness; and while the clear sinks back into gloom, a gloom is labouring upwards to the daylight of

But if spirit and soul stand in inseparable causal connection, and if the spiritual functions of the soul are the beamings forth of the spirit itself, the development of the spirit in its normal consummation must of necessity keep equal pace with that of the soul, and the advance of the spirit must at the same time be the advance of the soul. And thus it actually is. Of the child normally developing itself, Scripture says, κραταιοῦσθαι πνεύματι (Luke i. 80, comp. ii. 40, 52). It is readily felt how almost impossible to be said is κραταιοῦσθαι ψυχῇ,—for this reason, namely, because the latter is comprised in the former, and would have specially suggested the idea of speaking of a strengthening of the soul in distinction from the spirit—therefore of a defective development. That for the rest even in children, and plainly in them, a determinate development of the three activities of the spirit is possible, no one will doubt, who remembers that the mysteries of the kingdom are revealed to infants—νηπίοις (Matt. xi. 25); and that God has chosen τὰ μωρὰ τοῦ κόσμου to bring to shame the wise (1 Cor. i. 27, comp. Ps. viii. 2). Precisely in the child—that is to say, in the rightly trained child—the spirit comes to the first development, which corresponds to its nature of love originating from God; and the soul of the child—which is not yet clouded by the gloomy shadows of sensuality, and is not yet thoroughly disordered by the magic power of the passions—is the still clear lovely mirror of that firstling life of the spirit.

In the commencement and advance of the threefold life of man, closely considered, there thus appears no counter-proof against our view, founded on Gen. ii. 7, of the priority of the spirit in relation to the soul. Undisturbed in our view, we may advance to the consideration of the aspect of the soul which is turned towards the body and to the world, just as we have already more closely considered the aspect turned towards the spirit.

consciousness." Similarly, J. H. Fichte, and especially Fechner in his *Psychophysik* (2 vols. 1860), in which he, with a Herbartish application of mathematics to psychology, seeks to establish the wave-like vicissitude of consciousness and unconsciousness according to law.

THE TWOFOLD ASPECT OF THE SOUL.

Sec. IX.

EVERY spirit has its *doxa*, even as God has; but not every *doxa* is called נֶפֶשׁ. Scripture nowhere speaks of souls of the angels, and only anthropomorphically of a soul of God.[1] For נֶפֶשׁ is, in any case, only the *doxa* of the spirit united with a material body. Man has a soul, and the brute has a soul. The soul of the brute is the individualized breathing forth of the spirit of entire nature; the soul of man is the self-out-breathing of his personal spirit. There are always in bodies living natures, to which Scripture adjudges נְפָשׁוֹת. With respect to such, God is called אֱלֹהֵי הָרוּחֹת לְכָל־בָּשָׂר (Num. xvi. 22, xxvii. 16); and with respect to such, He says, Ezek. xviii. 4 (comp. Job xii. 10), הֵן כָּל־הַנְּפָשׁוֹת לִי הֵנָּה. In the idea of נֶפֶשׁ there is thus involved the fact that it is the incarnate *doxa* of the

---

[1] Ex ea istud (scil. esse Dei animam) significatione commemorari solitum est, qua et manus et oculi et digiti et brachium et cor incorporali Deo connumerantur. Thus with great propriety Hilary *de trinitate*, x. 58. Beidâwi, on the Koran, observes, that God has *ruach*, but not *nefs;* and thus if it be said to God, "in my soul is not what is in Thy soul"—that the المشاكلة (a rhetorical figure similar to the Zeugma) is as if, *e.g.*, the one who possesses a hut were to say to the other who has a castle, I find myself just as well in my hut as thou in thine. When Scripture speaks anthropomorphically of a soul of God, there is brought into consideration, man's soul transferred to God, as the means and link of the spirit-embodied condition of nature. God swears "by His soul," *i.e.* by His very own self. God's soul hates this and that (Ps. xi. 5; Isa. i. 14); or abhors it as repulsive (Lev. xxvi. 11, 30; Jer. xiv. 19); or satisfies itself by punishment (Jer. v. 9); *i.e.* He Himself, in the innermost depth, and in the entire circumference of His nature. It is only once said that God's "soul" delights—namely, in His servant (Isa. xlii. 1; Matt. xii. 18, εἰς ὃν εὐδόκησεν ἡ ψυχή μου). Even here, soul seems to mean the very deepest inward self, comprehending the entire condition of nature. Origen (*de princ.* ii. 5) conjectures that the Son of God, who is God's word and wisdom, is named *anima Dei*. But this is untenable; and altogether, there is only one single text in which God's soul implies a name of God; and this is allied in meaning to *doxa* of God, *scil.* Ps. xxiv. 4, whereupon we have spoken above, Div. II. Sec. IV., towards the end.

spirit—that it is the principle of bodily life in the form of the spirit. In conformity to its nature, it is double-sided:[1] for, on the one side, the spirit is manifested in it in its own sight; on the other side, the unity is effected by the spirit through it, for which the spirit is allied with corporeity.

It is a question of very ancient times, and of history that reaches into the latest periods, how any reciprocal action is possible between spirit and body. We refer to the much discussed suppositions of a physical influx (originated by Thomas Aquinas); of a divine assistance (to the so-called Occasionalism of Cartesius: "Deum occasione animæ in corpus agere et vice versa); of an action upon one another only occasioning, and furnishing opportunities (the occasionalism as *systema causarum occasionalium* of Malebranche and De la Forge); and of a *parallelismus inter corpus et animam*, by virtue of a harmony preestablished by God (Leibnitz),—as well as to the later strained attempt to supply the void, either by an idealizing of matter, or by a materializing of the spirit. Even scriptural-minded inquirers have not known how to help themselves otherwise than either by regarding the spirit as the final link in the advancing process of the centralization of matter, and as such for its arbitrary counterpart;[2] or than by explaining spirit and body as two several modes of manifestation of one power, or one life, as space and time, form and law, perceptibility and perception;[3] or than by seeking to grasp in any other way the last existing element (τὸ ὑποκείμενον) in spirit and matter, as being essentially one and the same.[4]

The answer of Scripture is none of all these. If God, who is spirit, created matter,—and if God's Spirit, as we read in the first page of Scripture, gave life to matter, and formed it,—it follows of necessity that the created spirit which is originated from God will be able to exercise a powerful agency upon matter, resembling the creative power of God and of His Spirit.

---

[1] The soul—Haussmann, in his *Biblical Doctrine of Man*, 1848, briefly and well says—is a twofold and mediate nature, fleshly and spiritual soul in one.

[2] Rothe, *Ethik*, i. 170.

[3] Heinroth, *Psychologie*, p. 264.

[4] Thus v. Schaden, in his work, *über die Hauptfrage der Psychologie für die Gegenwart* (1849), according to which the power of extension is that common substratum.

It is implied in its nature that it is super-ordinated to matter, and in its appointment to act through and to pervade matter. And there is no insurmountable barrier between them, for although they are opposites, yet, on account of the unity of their final source, they are no absolute opposites;[1] so little, that the son of Sirach, in an absolutely scriptural sense, is able to express the proposition, that sounds so entirely pantheistic, τὸ πᾶν ἐστὶν αὐτός (Ecclus. xliii. 27). The powers of the spirit, as of the matter, have, in a like manner, the actual presence of God in every created thing as the background that supports them (Jer. xxiii. 24). All life, individual as well as universal, has, as its ground of origination and subsistence, as its root and its link, God's λόγος (Ecclus. xliii. 26), and God's πνεῦμα (Wisd. i. 7, xii. 1). There is therefore no need of a pre-established harmony. Everything lives, and moves, and subsists, closely united, and reciprocally attracted to itself in one element, ἐν αὐτῷ (Acts xvii. 28). "As an army is organized by its general, and is arranged according to his plan of battle,"—thus speaks a theological scholar, who stands at the summit of the present scientific knowledge of nature,—" even so are banded together the starry hosts and the groups of atoms according to the will of the one eternal Spirit. This creating and ordaining Spirit pervades every cell, generates and regulates the flight of every working bee, according to the eternal purpose of the whole. Everywhere in nature, the relative contrasts stand in the closest reciprocity, by means of their higher united nature. That which generates the galvanic current in the most opposed elements of the voltaic pile—that which gives the living weapon of defence to the electric eel, by the contact of moist heterogeneous parts—that which inclines the magnetic needle to the north,—precisely the same creative principle orders and controls the whole fabric of the world—creates and vitalizes the organic cell—arranges the intercourse between spirit and matter, the association between soul and body. Everywhere the inner living unity of the larger system rules over all the parts that

---

[1] It is true (as in Div. II. we have already ascertained), as E. Harless said in his *Grenzen u. Grenzgebiete der physiol. Forschung*, p. 27, "the unity of the foundation of all things suggests a homogeneity of the things with one another, and thus is assured the possibility of their substantive reciprocal action."

belong to the whole."[1] Above the material stands the power as the material of materials, and above the power stands life as the power of powers, and above life stands the spirit as the life of life, and above all spirits stands God as the Spirit of spirits; and there is no solution for the enigma of the reciprocal action of all things, but this all-effecting and pervading chief monad, which unites all contraries in itself and through itself, and has united them in man as in a microcosm, as even in itself it is no monad in the sense of the doctrine of monads, but the absolute unity of diverse and infinitely manifold life.

The reciprocal action of spirit and matter is thus explained on the one hand by reference to the origin and the destination of the spirit, on the other by reference to the common ground of existence in God, which systematically includes together all things (Col. i. 17). The influence of matter upon spirit is, however, essentially of a different kind from the influence of spirit upon matter. Spirit acts upon matter by the power of a conscious will, but matter acts upon spirit when spirit makes matter the object of its cognizance, which it is able to do by virtue of its eminence above it (Ps. xciv. 9), and allows it to act upon itself. There is in matter no will which overpowers the will of the spirit, but matter becomes manifest to the spirit in its own light, as when, *e.g.*, the narrative of creation says of God, וַיַּרְא ; and the impressions which are made upon it by that which was manifest to it are feelings, thoughts, determinations, to which it is decided by reason of that manifestation, as when, *e.g.*, Ps. civ. 31 says that God rejoices in His works, or when, according to Gen. vi. 2, the daughters of men became an object of attraction to sin for the sons of God. Matter with its powers is incapable of carrying its action over into the region of the spirit. But in that the spirit takes up this or that material fact into its consciousness, or enters into it with its consciousness, it may allow that of which it is conscious to become a moving impulse to one of its three fundamental powers. Briefly, matter has no power over the spirit, except so far as the spirit itself makes it to have, for it is the power over matter.

But hitherto we have only had in view the relation of

[1] Böhner (pastor in Dietikon at Zurich) in his work, *Naturforschung und Kulturleben* (1858), p. 216.

matter to the spirit as such. In man it is otherwise. In him, spirit and matter are combined into a personal unity, by means of which the spirit not only, as we saw Sec. VIII., is brought under the law of natural development, but also is in many ways conditioned by matter in a fashion withdrawn from its own spontaneity. Here, for the first time, the relation of spirit and matter becomes really for us a closely veiled mystery; and Augustine is quite right in saying that this mystery is in no respect less deep—nay, if possible, is still deeper—than that of the personal union of God and man in Christ.[1] We must not indeed forget that the present condition of man represents to us a conditioning of the spirit by matter, which is a deplorable caricature of the original relation. But even apart from this, spirit and matter in man are in such wise fenced in, that the spirit is limited by matter; for development and limitation, which the former is gradually overcoming, are altogether inseparable. How are we to explain to ourselves this conditioning of the spirit by matter in man? Holy Scripture gives us the disclosure on the subject with which we may be satisfied. It does not explain to us that which is inconceivable physically, but as it were from God's level.[2] It teaches us that the body is an image of God, and that God has established the spirit under conditions of this body, wherewith it may prove itself in progressive strengthening as a power over matter. That is the distinctive task allotted to it, the importance of which, in connection with the world's entireness and the world's history, we know. This present crass materiality is no original creation of God. It came into existence by the perversion of this (*vid.* Div. II. Sec. I.). Man is destined to overcome this perversion. For this purpose the spirit of man is absorbed into this crass matter, that it may raise it up again to the lost standing, and to its completion,—a result, however, although the spirit was added to the matter, which could accrue in no other way than by the Logos Himself becoming flesh.

---

[1] Gangauf, *Psychologie des h. Augustinus*, p. 308; v. Thomasius, *Dogmatik*, ii. 63. On the other hand, it has lately been maintained by Lotze with much truth, that "in the reciprocal action between body and soul there subsists absolutely no greater enigma than in any other instance of causality, and that only the idea of knowing more in that other matter has begotten the astonishment that here nothing is known."

[2] Thus, for example, also Gregory of Nyssa, in Möller, *l.c.* p. 33.

Scripture, therefore, opens up to us the mystery, at least so far as that it gives us to apprehend the reason in the history of redemption for that which is physically inconceivable. For that destined vocation man is created, and indeed εἰς ψυχὴν ζῶσαν. The soul is the link between spirit and matter in man, as he himself, as the unity of both, is the link of all created things. Only, in man, spirit and matter are united in one individual life, standing in mutual reciprocity of action; and that which effectuates this reciprocal action is the soul, which only in man is an individual manifestation of an individual spirit; but in the brute world, on the other hand, is the individual manifestation of the general spirit that pervades it. The soul, indeed, is not less immaterial than the spirit; but yet, by the object of its existence, it is more nearly and more immediately related to matter than it.[1] It is, so to speak, the outside of the spirit, whereby the spirit is personally united to the externality of the body. It is the *speculum* conveying to it, the *speculator*, the *spectra* of the outer world; or, moreover, as Augustine permits himself to say, *specula mentis*, the watch-tower whence the spirit looks forth, and receives objects of sight. It is the mirror of the spirit in twofold relation, as well in respect of the spirit reflecting itself in it again, as in respect of the outer world reflecting itself in it to the spirit. Besides this one soul, man has no other. It is this by which the powers of nature, operative in the body,

---

[1] E. Harless, *l.c.* p. 26, denounces those who, proceeding from the erroneous supposition of a specific opposition between spirit and matter, wish to arrange this opposition by means of an interpolated phantom which is neither fish nor flesh. This does not concern our biblical-psychologic view, for (1) we indeed separate spirit and matter specifically, but still recognise a profound homogeneity of both in the unity of their original ground; (2) we do not interpolate the Psyche between spirit and body as a third element, but it stands to us as a phenomenon of the spirit itself; and (3) to the question whether it belongs to the side of the spirit or of matter, we give the decided answer that it is not a mongrel thing, but of a spiritual nature. The appendix of E. Harless, on the Apparatus of the Will, *Zeitschr. für Philosophie*, 1861, i., is in favour of this our subdivision. For the nervous system, which is stimulated from without, still has the Psyche, in which the stimulus becomes a reflex of sensation, as its background; and the Psyche, on the other hand, has as its background the self-conscious spirit, to which it conveys the sensations, and which governs the physically caused ideas (perception, form, and inducement of motion) with the light of thought and the freedom of the will.

are comprehended into a united life. There is no especial fleshly soul, and the hypothetic nervous æther, if there be such a thing, is no soul.[1] Man consists only of three essential elements, which the Latin language appropriately designates by the masculine *animus*, the feminine *anima*, and the neuter *corpus*. The spirit vivifies the body by endowing it with soul. As God, the eternally Triune, reveals Himself in eternal *doxa*, in order to fill eternity, and to fashion it into his heaven; and as, within the range of history, He lowers His *doxa* to fill the temple of Israel; and as at last the whole earth is to become the vessel and reflex of His *doxa* (Isa. vi. 3, comp. Ezek. xliii. 2),—so the human soul is the *doxa* proceeding by the power of the creative impulse from the human spirit, for the purpose of filling the body as its house, and of absorbing[2] it into the region of spiritual life. The trine of the fundamental powers of the spirit is here developed by the power of creative arrangement into a septet of powers, by means of which the spirit takes possession of the body, and propagates even upon it its psychical image. As the seven spirits of God on the one side are turned to God as the sevenfold glorious mirror of His threefold nature, on the other side, to the world as the powers that carry out the process of the glorious realization of the world-idea; so the seven spirits of the soul, or powers of the soul, are on the one hand turned to the spirit as the sevenfold glorious mirror of its godlike threefold nature, on the other hand, to the body as the powers that effectuate the process of its becoming united into the life of the spirit, or more briefly, of its spiritualization: for the body may become pneumatical, because matter and spirit are only opposites relatively, not absolutely. The soul is the double-sided mid-nature which unites the two; as the seven-coloured rainbow, originating from the effect of the sun on the dark cloud, symbolizes the willingness of the heavenly to per-

---

[1] V. Rudloff (*Lehre vom Menschen*, p. 90) regards the nervous spirit as the *anima*, the principle of animal life.

[2] Göschel (*Letzte Dinge*, p. 181) strikingly calls it Personation: "The personality which has its root in the self-consciousness of the spirit, is in man the principle of development; for the process of development subsists essentially in progressive penetration and personation of the entire organism." Augustine has previously used *personare* in a similar way, when, for example, he says, *Deus est qui nos personat*.

meate the earthly, and, according to the tradition, is the bridge (ἴρις from εἴρειν) between heaven and earth.

I think that thus we gain a profounder glimpse into the essential condition of man, than when Philo regards the soul, considered in Plato's sense, as tripartite (λόγος, θυμός, ἐπιθυμία),—as "the reflected brightness of the blessed, thrice blessed nature of the Godhead" (ii. 356); or when Augustine (*de symbolo*) says, "Homo habet tres partes, spiritum, animam, et corpus, itaque homo est imago S. S. Trinitatis" (although he elsewhere limits the resemblance to the three fundamental powers of the spirit-soul), and when later writers suppose, in conformity with this fallacy, that the body corresponds either to the Holy Spirit[1] or to the Son.[2] Both views are prodigies. That the human body should correspond typically to one of the three persons of the Trinity, is in itself a notion unworthy of God. If we say, on the other hand, spirit, soul, and body are related as are God, *doxa*, and the world, we therein maintain as well God's supramundane spirituality as man's likeness to God, and microcosmic world-position closely connected therewith. For man's resemblance to God does not merely subsist in the fact that God's nature is imaged forth in him, but, moreover, that God's relation to the world is so typified. As it is the object of the world's development that the thrice-Holy should, so far as it is permitted by creature limits, assimilate it to Himself by filling it with His *doxa;* so it is the purpose of

[1] J. F. Von Meyer, *Glaubenslehre*, p. 71, and previously Göschel, in a wholly peculiar manner. V. Rudloff (*Lehre vom Menschen*, p. 102) also places spirit, soul, and *nefesch* (= nerve-spirit) in typical relation to the Father, Son, and Holy Spirit. Even Witt draws the nerve-spirit herein into the parallel, remarking, p. 138, that if anything in man corresponds to the divine *doxa*, it is not the soul, but rather the nerve-spirit (*sa vore det väl snarare nervanden*).

[2] Thus the author of the work, *Der Mensch nach Geist, Seele, und Leib dargestellt*, Düsselthal 1844. And equally (*Seele Abbild des Vaters, Leib Abbild des Sohnes, und Geist Abbild des h. Geistes*) Zöckler, *Naturtheologie*, i. (1860), 727, where (p. 739) more ancient defenders of this conception of the relation are named, among whom, however, J. Böhme is reckoned, only according to expressions entirely misunderstood. According to Böhme, the body is an image of the essentiality effected by the spirit, which forms the dwelling, the enclosure, and, as it were, the body of the Ternary. The emblem thereof is

the development of corporeity, that the spirit, which bears in it the form and the idea of the thrice-Holy, should, so far as is permitted by the boundary drawn between matter and spirit, assimilate it to itself, by taking it up by means of the soul into its own region, and imprinting upon it the full effect of its own likeness to God. This is the scriptural parallel. Between its two members there subsists, according to Scripture, even the closest causal relation. For, in proportion as the body of man is the reflection of the spirit-resembling soul, the world also is the reflection of the God-resembling *doxa*. The glorification of the world has its point of issue in the glorification of the human body. This latter is a microcosm, not alone in respect of its construction :[1] it is so, moreover, as the first object of man's worldly calling, and as the historical centre to which the circle of the microcosm is contracted; for, according to the fundamental view of Scripture, the history of man is the heart of the history of the world. In it is decided the future of heaven and of earth.

But if the body is destined as the microcosm, and in it the world as the macrocosm, to become spiritual, it must now of necessity be shown how the soul—which in the septenary of its powers reflects the nature of the spirit—possesses in the body an organ conformed to this septenary, by means of which it can bring itself, and mediately the spirit, to living manifestation.

THE BODY AS THE SEVENFOLD MEANS OF SELF-REPRESENTATION TO THE SOUL.

Sec. X.

THE saying of Thomasius[2] is true, in addition to that of Harless and Hofmann, that Scripture has no intention of giving a physiology of man. For this reason biblical psychology is not a

---

[1] According as κόσμος is conceived of as the entirety of all creation, or (as Gal. iv. 3, Col. ii. 8, 20, Heb. ix. 1) as the entirety of all material existence, man, or even only man's body, may be named microcosm. Both are really as well as literally scriptural.

[2] *Dogm.* i. 166 (2d ed.).

natural philosophy of the soul of man. But as Scripture considers man not merely under the point of view of redemption, but also under that of creation, and inextricably interweaves its doctrines of salvation with some constant and fundamental considerations of the natural condition of human existence,[1] so it contains, moreover, abundant material in reference to the natural knowledge of the human soul; although this natural knowledge is not its object, but only a means to its purpose of salvation. And even this material having reference to the nature and the natural life of the soul, falls into the region of the psychological problem. Certainly Scripture is a book just as much human as divine. It speaks of man, when it is not giving announcements that bear the specific character of revelation, in the language of antiquity, and especially of the Hebrew people. But it will be a justifiable endeavour, to compare these its appropriate popular representations with its revealed fundamental doctrines, and to see whether there is manifest an internal consistency between them, and whether the truthfulness required of them is inherent in these representations. How copious is the material of biblical psychology, is shown as a matter of fact, by our not finding ourselves more than midway advanced, after the long course that we have already traversed. And nobody can reproach us with having hitherto anywhere displaced the boundaries between Scripture and natural science. The risk of doing this does not begin until now, when we are undertaking to bring into juxtaposition the declarations of Scripture on the relation of the soul to corporeity. We trust that we may escape this risk. Or have we already incurred it, in proceeding upon the useful prejudice, that Scripture declares nothing about the relation between soul and body, whereof it needs to be ashamed in the presence of the present physiological knowledge of man?

The most popular biblical figure of the relation of the soul or of the spirit to the body, is the figure of the body as of the

[1] " It is a weak objection," says Ebrard, *Dogm.* i. 206, "that it is no purpose of Holy Scripture to give instructions in natural history. It is very true. But it supplies first principles in the consideration of nature, which have a significance of an immediately religious character." And Fabri, in the *Evang. K.Z.* 1857, col. 1072 : " The result consequent on the canon, that we must not expect from Scripture any natural knowledge, will not only be to mislead dogmatic philosophy from the perfect sense of Scripture, but continually to entangle it in unscriptural spiritual views."

house of the inward man. This house is called, with reference to its origin (Gen. ii. 7, comp. Job xxxiii. 6), a house of clay, בֵּית־חֹמֶר (Job iv. 19): the body, as φθαρτὸν σῶμα, is called γεῶδες σκῆνος (Wisd. ix. 15). In this σκῆνος (or, as Doric poets and the Pythagoreans call the body, σκᾶνος) there is an allusion to the fragility and the final breaking up of the habitation of gross elements. The body, as St Paul more accurately expresses it, is a tent-house, οἰκία τοῦ σκήνους (2 Cor. v. 1), in which we are not at home (ἐνδημοῦμεν) without at the same time being in a foreign country (ἐκδημεῖν): we depart from it at length (ἐκδημοῦμεν), and as a shepherd's tent, אֹהֶל רֹעִי (Isa. xxxviii. 12), it passes away from us: death is ἀπόθεσις τοῦ σκηνώματος (2 Pet. i. 13). According to another representation—which likewise refers to the dissolubility of the double condition of the human nature—the body is called the sheath, נִדְנֶה (נִדָן), of the spirit (Dan. vii. 15),—a figure which, even apart from the Holy Scripture, was propagated from further Asia as far as Rome.[1] Death is as the drawing forth of a sword from its sheath, שָׁלַה (Job xxvii. 8). According to a third figure, the body is the vesture, ἔνδυμα, of the soul (2 Cor. v. 1), as flesh and skin are the vesture, לְבוּשׁ, of the body (Job xxx. 18, comp. x. 11). In all three figures [2] there is only expressed the relation of the temporal association of the soul and the body, and that indeed (which is important) as a relation that is capable of dissolution without the destruction of the soul; but there is not expressed in any way the cause of this mutual relation. Such an expression is given in some degree, when, in carrying out further the figure of the tent, the soul is called the tent-cord, יֶתֶר (Job iv. 21), which holds the tent upright and expanded; or when the life is compared to a web (*scil.* the life of the soul, since this is the

---

[1] See Gesenius, *Thesaurus*, p. 854. The Talmud, *b. Sanhedrim*, 108, interprets accordingly לֹא־יָדוּן (Gen. vi. 3). Moreover, the Indian Vedanta says that the soul is in the body as in a sheath (*Kosha*), or a succession of sheaths, proceeding from within outward (Colebrooke, *Misc. Essays*, i. 372; and Graul, *Bibliotheca Tamulica*, i. 139).

[2] See thereupon Tobler's essay, *Haus, Kleid, Leib*, in Pfeifer's *Germania Vierteljahrsschrift für Deutsche Alterthumskunde, Jahrg.* iv. Pt. ii. (1854, pp. 160–184). That the body is called (Gen. xlix. 6) כָּבוֹד and (Ps. ciii. 5) עֶדְיִי, and therefore the *doxa* of the soul, as Juda ben-Bileam supposes (see Aben-ezra on Gen. *l.c.*), is not confirmed.

cause of the bodily life), the cutting loose of which from the thrum is death (Job vi. 9, xxvii. 8; Isa. xxxviii. 12). But nowhere is the original connection of the soul and the body more designedly symbolized, although in enigmatic and allegorical form, than in one of the latest canonical books, which is called Ecclesiastes, because Solomon, to wit (*Solomon redivivus*), is there introduced speaking as the incarnate preaching Wisdom. There (xii. 6) the young man is warned, mindful of his Creator, to rejoice in his youth, " or ever the silver cord be loosed, or the golden lamp be shattered, or the pitcher be broken at the fountain, or the wheel be broken at the cistern." The first image places before our eyes a lamp hanging down from the tent-covering (Job xxix. 3) by means of a silver cord. The silver cord is without doubt the thread of life, or more accurately the soul, which holds and supports the body in life. By the silver cord being suspended from above, may probably be intimated that the soul, to which the life of the body is attached, itself depends again upon a higher cause—to wit, on God. It is further plain that the hanging down, dependent גֻּלָּה, is the body. But that this is called a golden vessel, because it is royally and wonderfully made,[1] seems to me very improbable; for a golden vessel is certainly not shattered when it falls down: moreover, the body would not consistently be said to be of gold, while the soul is represented as of silver.[2] The body is indeed σκεῦος ὀστράκινον (2 Cor. iv. 7). Thus also it is here meant; for the writer has in view Zech. iv., where, in the description of the seven-branched candlestick of the vision, גֻּלָּה is the oil reservoir, which is in the midst of the lamps, and above them; and of the two ejects of this oil reservoir, it is said that they empty out of themselves the oil necessary for the burning of the lamps. But the oil is here called הַזָּהָב. It is the golden oil which flows from the two olive branches, which are close to the two ejects, into the גֻּלָּה, wherewith then from the גֻּלָּה, by means of the seven pipes, the seven lamps are supplied.[3] Thus

---

[1] Mich. Baumgarten, in *Schleswig-Holstein Gnomon*, 3d ed. p. 170.

[2] Thus justly observes Hitzig in his explanation of Ecclesiastes, p. 214.

[3] Hofmann, *Weiss. u. Erf.* i. 344, understands the gold of the lamp itself taken up in the flow of constant becoming; but the gold in the representation of the prophet comes from the olive trees. It is thus golden oil. Thus also Köhler, *Zachariah*, i. 142.

by גֻּלַּת הַזָּהָב is to be understood the designation of the body. But if the gold is not the material, but the contents of the vessel, then that the soul is represented by silver can only imply the spirit, of which ch. v. 7 says that it returns to God who gave it. When the silver cord of the lamp gives way (יֵרָחֵק, according to the Keri יֵרָתֵק, is unchained, or—as certainly *Ni.* in privative meaning is without example—when it collapses), the lamp full of gold is shattered, the body becomes πτῶμα (Matt. xiv. 12, comp. Num. xiv. 32), and the golden oil and light of the spiritual life, whose reservoir it was, is all lost.[1] Up to this point the interpretation is tolerably certain, but the two other types can only be conjecturally explained. That they are only general personifications of death,[2] in connection with the preceding very special symbolism, is to me not probable. Perhaps כַּד (the bucket or pitcher) is a symbol of the heart, and גַּלְגַּל (the wheel of the draw-well) is a symbol of the respiratory apparatus.[3] For נִשְׁבַּר, which is here said of כַּד, is a usual scriptural word applied to the heart when it has come into the

---

[1] The spirit—the one spirit—says an Indian didactic poem in Grant. *Bibl. Tamulica*, p. 185—enlightens the senses at whose summit is the understanding, as the lamp does a vessel.

[2] So Jerome, "Contritio hydriæ super fontem et confractio rotæ super lacum per metaphoram mortis ænigmata sunt;" and just so Winzer, who, with many others, in all the three figures only finds the thought, *antequam machina corporis destruatur* (in *Commentationes theol.* 1825, i. 1, p. 104).

[3] Rich. Mead takes a different view in his *Medica Sacra* (in the sixth chapter of which this allegorical description is explained of old age): he understands the golden lamp, of the head (*distillationes humoris ex capite in nares, fauces et pulmonem*), the urn, of the bladder (*fœdum stillicidium urinæ*), and the wheel, of the circulation of the blood (*cor vi sua defectum concidit*). Similarly the interpretation given by Witt in his Swedish work on the soul (*Själen*), from Westerdahl (in his *Helsans bevarande*, Maintenance of Health, 1768). The latest interpreters of the book of Ecclesiastes have different explanations—Hengstenberg (1859) and H. A. Hahn (1860). According to the former, the pitcher = individual life, the fountain = general life, the wheel = life by reason of the swift movement, the well = the world; according to the latter, the pitcher = the body, the fountain = the spirit, the wheel "to the cistern" = the life turned to the spirit supplying to the body the powers peculiar to it. A plain and sensible interpretation of this allegorical passage is contained in Göschel's work, *über das Alter.*, 1832. He finds in ver. 6 the gradually ceasing aspiration, expiration, and inspiration represented (ἀναπνοή, ἐκπνοή, εἰσπνοή), while he regards the "silver cord of the gold fountain" as the draw-rope.

condition of death, or of nearness to death (Jer. xxiii. 9; Ps. lxix. 21); and Scripture says as well שָׁפַךְ לֵב (Lam. ii. 19) as שָׁפַךְ נֶפֶשׁ: moreover, the heart can actually be compared to a bucket, in relation to the blood that courses through the body. And if we reflect that the words which come out of the mouth are compared to deep waters (Prov. xviii. 4), and the mouth of the righteous to a well of life (Prov. x. 11),—that to draw air (comp. שָׁאַף רוּחַ, Jer. ii. 24, xiv. 6) is spoken of as well as σπᾶν ἀέρα (Wisd. vii. 3), and that the throat (with the larynx) is called נַּרְגְּרוֹת, from נָּרַר, to draw, as also נָּרוֹן (Isa. lviii. 1; Ps. cxv. 7, cxlix. 6), in probably similar meaning, from נָּרָה;—it is not so very unreasonable to find the thought in the third image—before the breath is stifled, or stopped, and in the second—before the heart is broken or paralyzed. Still these are only conjectures. For us at present the important point is only this, that the soul, or the life of the soul, is represented as the link which is the condition of the continued union of the body and the spirit.

Proceeding now from the incontestable position which Nemesios[1] very rightly formulates, τὸ σῶμα τῆς ψυχῆς ὄργανον ὑπάρχον ταῖς ψυχικαῖς δυνάμεσι συνδιαιρεῖται, we have indeed no direct scriptural statement in our favour, when we further assert that the soul, as in its inclination towards the spirit it reflects the nature of the spirit in seven forms of life, so in its inclination towards the body, and by its means, it sets forth its own nature in seven forms of life. We do not wish to appeal to the fact that the number seven has already been found to be significant in the origination and development of life, by the natural philosophers of antiquity,[2] among whom, as the Canticles belong to the range of the literature of the Chokma, their author might be referred to, as speaking of a sevenfold corporeal beauty, which is praised (Cant. iv. 1–5) in Shulamith.[3] We would rather rely upon the fact that the number seven is absolutely, plainly, and confessedly a fundamental number in

---

[1] *De Natura hominis*, ch. v.

[2] According to the view of the Græco-Roman philosophers and physicians, the capacity of life of the fœtus does not begin till the seventh month, and the whole life of man runs in a gradual progression of weeks of years (Hebdomads); v. Sprengel-Rosenbaum, *Gesch. der Arzneikunde*, i. 427, 465, 488.

[3] This observation of Hengstenberg and Hahn is just.

the human body; for the head of the full-grown man, or the region of the head that reaches to the middle of the neck, exactly measures the seventh part of the entire length of the body; and as in the neck of man (also of almost all mammals) there are found seven vertebræ, so seven ribs form the enclosure of his breast.[1] But the point on which we depend is another— to wit, that guidance of Scripture which bids us to understand spirit and soul by the relation of God to His *doxa*. We proceed from the fact that the soul is the image of the spirit, and makes the body the image of itself. It will be manifest that, from this scriptural assumption, all things which appear in the Scripture as a pervading prevailing representation of the bodily life, articulately work into the whole texture, and mutually explain one another.

The first of the seven forms of life is that of the גֹּלֶם, or embryo. The soul—which, upon the lowest basis of its spirit-resembling nature, is direct will—appears here, at the lowest grade of its nature, manifested as corporeal—as a blind, even still undeveloped agent of the idea that forms the body: spirit, soul, and body are in process of becoming, but בַּפֵּתֶר (Ps. cxxxix. 15), *i.e.* in the dark laboratory of the womb, and, as the spirit is still as undeveloped as the soul, in the dark region of absolute unconsciousness. This original unconsciousness remains even subsequently as the gloomy foundation of man's life; it is the root of life, all the processes of life which are performed in unconsciousness are based in this lowest psychico-corporeal form of life, which enters into the subsequent forms without becoming destroyed by them. The second form of life is that of the נְשָׁמָה, or of the breathing;[2] for immediately after separation from the circulation of the placenta, the child

---

[1] M. Fränkel, *Trifolium*, p. 48, where occurs, moreover, the striking remark, that "in the physical nature of man the number *seven* predominates; in the spiritual, on the other hand, *three*." The anatomical consideration of man in Zeller's *Seelenlehre*, secs. 13-22, has the same suggestive view.

[2] J. P. Lange (*Deutsche Zeitschr.* 1859, p. 30) finds that here there is a jump into another category; since after the embryo should follow the suckling, the child, etc. But we wish to show how the embryonic beginning itself advances even to the perfect working out of the body as the organ of the soul. The subsequent form of life is developed always on the basis of the preceding, which is modified by it, but carried on with it.

SEC. X.] THE BODY SELF-REPRESENTATIVE OF THE SOUL. 273

breathes and cries: hitherto the mother has breathed for the child, now it breathes itself. We ought here to be reminded of the now generally known fact, that breathing in its fundamental nature is one and the same chemical process as the heating of an oven—that chemical process, to wit, whose manifestation is fire, and whose result is the warmth of the body and the blood.[1] Thus the second form of life is fiery, as the first is dark. Without wishing to substitute for Scripture a knowledge of that bio-chemical process, we still think that we may observe that breathing and burning are regarded in Scripture, especially where it speaks of God's wrath, as very neighbouring ideas, *e.g.* Job xli. 13, Isa. xxx. 33. We lay a greater stress on the fact that נֶפֶשׁ actually signifies the breathing (Job xli. 13), and that the same words by which the spirit is named, denote also the breath exspired and inspired through nose and mouth: to wit, נְשָׁמָה, Isa. ii. 22, comp. Gen. ii. 7, vii. 22; רוּחַ, Job xxvii. 3, Lam. iv. 20, etc., comp. Isa. xi. 4, Ps. xxxiii. 6, cxxxv. 17; נִשְׁמַת רוּחַ, 2 Sam. xxii. 16; so that spirit and air (Job iv. 15), life and wind (Ezek. xxxvii. 5), are nearly related ideas, and breathing out of the soul is associated with dying (Job xi. 20, xxxi. 39; Jer. xv. 9). Whence arises this prevailing mode of representation and expression in Scripture, except from the fact, that really the breathing or the self-sustenance by the element of life which is found in the air, is that form of life wherewith the life begins to become self-life, and in a continual succession of ejection and intraction (הֵשִׁיב רוּחַ, Job ix. 18) to evidence itself outwardly? With the commencement of breathing, the current of the blood of the child, which hitherto has been dependent on that of the mother, becomes independent. We purposely avoid saying the circulation of the blood, for antiquity was aware that the blood flowed through the body, but did not know that it circulated. With the first drawing breath of the child, the soul is manifested in its third form of life—the form of life of the דָּם, or the blood: this also is fiery, for the blood is red, אָדֹם; and τὸ πυρρὸν is at once the colour of fire and of blood;[2] the bright red of the blood

---

[1] The breathing, on the one hand, regulates the animal heat as a process of cooling, perfecting itself in interchange and exchange; on the other hand, it effects the same as a process of fire.

[2] V. Hofmann (*Weiss. u. Erf.* ii. 329) on Apoc. vi. 4: "The horse of

S

actually passed with the ancients, and not without reason, as the effect of a process of fire.[1] Moreover that the soul, immediately after operating in the breathing, whence it has its name, reveals itself in the blood, is declared by the direct testimonies of the Noachian (Gen. ix. 4) and of the Mosaic Thora (Lev. xvii. 11–14, etc.): to pour out the soul is equivalent to die (Isa. liii. 12; Ps. cxli. 8). This moving of the soul in blood which is independently the infant's own, begins with the first breathing (not first with the dividing and binding up of the umbilical cord, Ezek. xvi. 4), so closely is linked the third form of life to the second. And not less closely is the fourth form of life to the third—that of the לֵב, or heart. In the heart, whose movement presupposes the breathing, and is suspended at once by its cessation, the soul attains for the blood in which it rules, a reservoir (comp. יָבֵשׁ, to wither from the heart, Ps. cii. 5): it is the pitcher at the fountain of blood which draws and pours forth: it is the principal vessel of the blood-life become independent, whereinto it discharges and whence it proceeds, for מִמֶּנּוּ תּוֹצְאוֹת חַיִּים (Prov. iv. 23).[2] The heart is the centre of the wheel of life (Jas. iii. 6),—a representation which is so prevalent in Scripture, that it speaks even of a לֵב, i.e. of a middle of heaven (Deut. iv. 11), of the earth (Matt. xii. 40), of the sea (Ex. xv. 8; Jonah ii. 4), etc., yea, even of an oak-tree (2 Sam. xviii. 14). But if the heart be the centre of the life revolving round itself, as the individuation of this life is fundamentally completed in it, we may scripturally say that the natural light of life, אוֹר הַחַיִּים (Job xxxiii. 30, Ps. lvi. 14, comp. Job iii. 20), proceeds in it on the ground of the preceding forms of life; and we are justified in the conclusion that the form of life of the לֵב will be just as much followed by three, as it has been preceded by three. And this expectation is actually and without any constraint realized. The next which follows on the concentration of the three first forms of life in the heart is this, that now nourished by the blood which moistens all the organs, even

the second rider is fiery red, and points, in contrast to the former, to bloodshed and burning."

[1] See Schubert, *Gesch. der Seele*, i. 142; comp. Fr. v. Baader, *Werke*, xv. 566: "The water of life—the blood—is at once fluid and heat; and it perishes when both of these elements are separated from their concrete condition."

[2] See Hitzig, *in loco* (p. 37 of his commentary of the year 1858).

SEC. X.] THE BODY SELF-REPRESENTATIVE OF THE SOUL. 275

the nerves, the life of experience and of sensation, carried on by means of the sensitive and sensuous nerves, begins, by means of which the soul comes into relation with its own corporeity, and with the outer world. It is the form of life of the מֹחַ, or of the nerves. But as, in the idea of מֹחַ (Job xxi. 24), there is no distinction between the marrow of the bones and of the nerves,—and as generally the nerves, as organs of feeling and of sensation, were unknown to antiquity,[1]—this name might appear ill chosen. It is not, however, so ill chosen as it appears, for מֹחַ is also a name of the brain and of the spinal marrow, which, as is known, are the central portion of the nervous system, although in the sense of antiquity they are not named as such. The brain (Syr. *mûcho*) was probably called in ancient Hebrew מֹחַ;[2] and of this (as is primarily implied in the plural form μυελοί, Heb. iv. 12: v. Passow) it was the cerebral medulla, with the spinal medulla, whence the ancients attained a glimpse of the nature of the nerves, and of their causal relation to feeling and perception. This being considered, מֹחַ, if we open up the idea still undeveloped in the Old Testament, is no unsuitable and unauthorized denomination of this fifth form of life.[3] Primarily there are, on this fifth stage, the organs of the five special senses (רָאָה, ὁρᾶν; שָׁמַע ἀκούειν; הֵרִיחַ, ὀσφραίνεσθαι: from which in the New Testament only ὀσμή = ὀσφρασία; טָעַם, γεύεσθαι; מִשֵּׁשׁ נָּשֵׁשׁ, ψηλαφᾶν, ἅπτεσθαι), which are the means of the receptive relation of the soul corporeally

---

[1] Herophilos in Alexandria (about 300 years before Christ) is the first in whom there is a dawning perception of the functions of the nerves; vid. Sprenger, *l.c.* p. 511.

[2] It is said in *b. Menachoth*, 80, *b*, of a man without judgment: I fancy that he has no brain in his skull (שאון לו מֹח בקדקדו).

[3] More suitable than גִּידִים (Gen. xxxii. 33; Job x. 11; Ezek. xxxvii. 6, 8), which, without distinction (as νεῦρα, τένοντες, τόνοι, σύνδεσμοι, in the older medical language of the Greeks; *vid.* Harless, *Gesch. der Hirn und Nervenlehre in Alterthum.* i. 23–30), denotes muscular fibres, ligaments of the joints, and generally every elastic and tense fibre in union with the body (from גִּיד = אָגַד, עָקַד), and thus excludes that which we now call nerves. Hupfeld, *Psalms*, i. 99, and Rödiger in the *Thes.*, translate Prov. iii. 8, "It shall be healing to thy nerves" (*nervis tuis*); but this would not be understood in the present current meaning. שֹׁר (from שָׁרַר, strong) means the sinews, and especially the umbilical cord, and then generally the navel.

manifested to the outer world; the organs of the αἴσθησις, or the αἰσθητήρια (Heb. v. 14; comp. Jer. iv. 19, LXX.), for which, biblical Hebrew has not as yet any generic name,[1] among them chiefly sight, which in the Holy Scripture is the most general and comprehensive characterization of psychico-corporeal feeling and perception: so that, *e.g.*, it says, I have *seen* the heat, instead of feeling it (Isa. xliv. 16); and speaks of seeing that which was spoken, or generally audible, instead of hearing it (Jer. xxxiii. 24; Mark v. 38); of seeing life instead of enjoying it (רָאָה חַיִּים, Eccles. ix. 9; comp. ὄπτεσθαι ζωήν, John iii. 36); and seeing death or corruption, instead of suffering them (רָאָה מָוֶת, Ps. lxxxix. 49; ἰδεῖν θάνατον or διαφθοράν, Luke ii. 26, Acts ii. 27, and elsewhere; θεωρεῖν θάνατον, John viii. 51; comp. γεύεσθαι θανάτου, Matt. xvi. 28, and elsewhere, = rabb. טְעַם מוֹתָה). Every perception, whether it be effected by means of the organs of sense or not (as the prophetic perception and seeing), from the most spiritual apprehension to the mere passivity that loses itself in unconsciousness, is comprehended in and named by Scripture, as *seeing*. We are certainly not wrong, if we gather in this *usus loquendi* an assistance towards the naming of that common perception, which is wanting in the biblical as generally in human language, which perception lies at the base of all feeling and of every experience, which immediately affects the organs of sensation. The Scripture calls this common perception (*sensus communis* or *sensorium*),[2] in default of another word, a *seeing;* and as it endeavours to reduce the multiplicity of the sensual perceptions and sensual organs to a unity, in which all their radii combine, and whence

[1] The post-biblical Hebrew names it חוּשִׁים, according to the Aramaic חֲשַׁשׁ (comp. Isa. xxxiii. 11, LXX. and Grdt.), to perceive.

[2] "Est addita sensibus exterioribus," says Melancthon in his *Liber de Anima*, "alia superior facultas magis miranda, quam simplex adprehensio sensuum exteriorum." This *superior facultas* is just the *sensus communis*, which the ancients comprehended with the *compositio objectorum*, scil. *ratiocinatio* and the *memoria*, under the name of the three *sensus interiores*, manifestly confounding heterogeneous things. Comp. K. Fortlage, *System der Psychologie*, i. 18, where it is rightly observed, that Locke indeed established the analysis of the inner sense, but did not first introduce the expression into science; which expression was already known to Albertus Magnus and his predecessors. The Arabians compare this common perception to a membrane stretched like a sounding-board under the five external senses.

SEC. X.]   THE BODY SELF-REPRESENTATIVE OF THE SOUL.   277

they proceed, it is manifest that, in speaking of the ears of man as of an ear,[1] and still more frequently of the eyes of man as of an eye (*e.g.* Ps. xxxi. 9; Lam. iii. 48–51, etc.), it does so in order to indicate the sense of all the senses. And this is just the fifth form of life of the soul manifesting itself corporeally, that it sets at work this common perception, whose organ, as we know, is the nervous system, in the multiplicity of external perceptions, and thus first of all comes into a receptive relation to the outer world. To this stage of the sensual and nervous life the outer world, and primarily its own corporeity, becomes for the soul luminous; for רָאָה and אוֹר (comp. Matt. vi. 23) are correlatives. To this receptive fifth form of life is allied the productive sixth. In proportion as the soul thus shows itself capable of receiving and of acting upon the influences of the external world made clear,—which occurs at the latest in the domain of the sense of hearing,[2]—there is developed also, under the co-agency of the blood, the action upon the external world effected by the influence of the nerves upon the muscles, and especially speech effected by the muscles of inspiration and of the larynx, and the cavity of the mouth, including the tongue, the work of the understanding, the externalization of the Nous or Logos. This form of life might be called that of the קָו, if it were proved that קָו as τόνος (τοναία) unites in itself the meanings of sinew or muscle, and sound or voice.[3] It corresponds to the second form of life, as the fifth to the third. The fifth corresponds to the third, for the blood is concerned in the formative process of the nervous germs of the embryo: it nourishes the nerves, and maintains and stimulates their activity. Moreover, there are generally in man no two factors

[1] Thus always in the expressions הֵעִיר, פָּתַח, גִּלָּה אֹזֶן, in which אָזְנַיִם is never used.

[2] Kussmaul, *Unters. über das Seelenlehre des neugebornen Menschen* (1859), p. 27: "There may not be an absolute defect of the sense of hearing in the newly born child; but of all the senses, hearing slumbers the most deeply."

[3] In Ps. xix. 5, the LXX. translates קַוָּם by φθόγγος, Symm. by ἦχος, Jerome by *sonus;* but perhaps it is to be explained by Jer. xxxi. 39, and other passages. Moreover, whether קַו־קָו (Isa. xviii.) means muscular, strong, is uncertain; but it is acknowledged that the Semitic designations of strength recur most to the fundamental meaning of tension and elasticity of the muscles.

of his bodily life which stand in such close reciprocity as do blood and nerves. The sixth form of life, moreover, corresponds to the second: for, on the one hand, the breathing—standing in the closest causal connection with the blood, in so far as it is instrumentally effected—is the first setting at work of the muscles of the child, proceeding in contraction and expansion; on the other hand, the in- and ex-spiratory stream of air—without which no vibration of the ligaments of the glottis and no breathing murmurs are possible—is the inevitably necessary means to the origination of all sound of speech. The progressive character of this sixth form of life, compared with the others, is plain. In the fifth, the soul attains for the corporeity an external mirror, receiving the impressions of the outer world, just as itself is the internal mirror of these impressions to the spirit; but in this sixth form it makes the corporeity a means of influencing the outer world in word and deed. In speech, the nature of man, united in multiplicity, comes to the most spiritualized material manifestation. The air (רוּחַ, πνεῦμα), by which man is placed in the closest reciprocity to the whole life of nature (it is indeed his *pabulum vitæ*), becomes in speech the material (comp. Ps. xxxiii. 6 with cxxxv. 17) in which the reasonable spirit (רוּחַ) portrays the substance of its thought (therefore in Aramaic called רוּחַ מְמַלְּלָא, speech-spirit, *i.e.* thought-spirit); but this occurs through the mediation of the soul, which, in conformity with its twofold aspect, on the one side receives and prismatically refracts the thoughts of the spirit; on the other side, blends the sounds that have become distinguishable in it, with the distinguishableness of the sounds formed out of the air (קוֹל), and thus begets language (קוֹל מְדַבֵּר, Deut. iv. 33, etc.; קוֹל דְּבָרִים, Deut. i. 34, v. 25, etc.; קוֹל מִלִּין, Job xxxiii. 8; φωνὴ ῥημάτων, Heb. xii. 19).[1] For thus the individual impulses of the origination of speech may be thought of as distinct from one another. The things of the outer world are first formed in the perceptions of man, *e.g.*, upon the retina of the eye, and thence become representative pictures which the soul offers to the spirit: the spirit receives them into its self-consciousness, makes them, as thoughts, its own property,

---

[1] Otherwise language is called by metonymy לָשׁוֹן or שָׂפָה, γλῶσσα, the mouth, as the organ of speech is called, Cant. iv. 3, מִדְבָּר.

and gives to these thoughts in the soul the sounding elementary form of speech of the inner word, and then, by means of the power that it exercises by means of the soul over the organs of speech, establishes this inner word in a condition of sensible perceptible external realization. Human speech, therefore, is the creation of the spirit by the mediation of the soul.[1] We find ourselves here on the outermost light side of the corporeal self-manifestation of the soul; for all that becomes manifest, says the apostle, Eph. v. 13, is light; but in speech the spirit becomes manifest: it comes by way of the soul to light-like manifestation; as, moreover, φάναι with φάος (φως) goes back to the like-sounding root ΦΑ (Sanskr. *bhâ bhâsh*),[2] and generally between seeing and hearing, light and sound, colour-scale and tone-scale, there subsist noticeable connections which are referred to in the Old Testament language.[3] This corporeal self-manifestation of the soul pressing out from darkness to light is completed in the seventh form of life. We call it the form of life of the תֹּאַר (Judg. viii. 18; 1 Sam. xxviii. 14), or of the πρόσωπον τῆς γενέσεως (Jas. i. 23), as the third is

---

[1] When H. Steinthal (*Grammatik, Logik, und Psychologie*, 1855) says that the formation of language is the effort of the soul to transform itself into spirit, this is, if rightly understood, not untrue, for the soul in the formation of speech serves the advancing ideal self-realization of the spirit, which is the alpha and omega of human development.

[2] I say intentionally like-sounding, not "like;" for although the view that in the root *bhâ* the ideas of lighting and speaking lie side by side, has authorities such as Wilson and A. W. v. Schlegel on its side, I still always entertain the scruples expressed in my *Jesurun*, p. 142. But the word אָמַר has in no case anything to do with the light (see Gesenius, *Thes.* p. 119): it has the fundamental meaning of bringing aloft, sounding aloft. What a pity it did not please Bähr, in his *Symbolik*, i. 445, to prove the position that he there expresses, that " nearly in all the ancient languages light and word, to lighten and to speak, are kindred ideas."

[3] See thereupon, *Neue Beiträge zu dem Geist in der Natur* of Oersted (Leipz. 1851), p. 87. In הָלַל, the meanings, to be clear, and to sound, coincide; in צָהַל, the meanings to glitter, and to cry out; in חָצַר, the meanings to be bright green, and to crash; in הוּד, the meanings to shout, (הֵידָד, הֵד) and to glisten (הוֹד). In the Greek there belong to this category, λιγύς (*e.g.* in σελεναίη λιγυφεγγέτις), and the expressions ὕμνοι φλέγονται (Bacchyl. xiii. 12, Bergk), παιὰν λάμπει (Soph. *Œd. Tyr.* 182), ἔλαμψε φάμα (*ibid.* 468), τηλωπὸν ἰωάν (Philoct. 216), and more of a similar kind.

that of the τροχὸς τῆς γενέσεως. In this seventh, the preceding forms of life come to a united blending; and the psychical-corporeal individuality, which in the first form of life was only constituted as a germ, becomes here a completed stamped psychico-corporeal or natural determination (natural temper or disposition). Temperament and character, physiognomy,[1] and the entire bodily *habitus*,—inclusive of the formation of the cranium, as the psychically effected expression of the spirit,—are here realized in manifestation. As in the seventh form the *doxa* becomes God's perfected μορφή, and the soul becomes the spirit's perfected μορφή, so in this seventh form the body becomes the perfected μορφή (ἰδέα, Matt. xxviii. 3) of the soul; and as the spirit attains from the revolving thought to the word, and from the word to the profound internal voiceless memory which fulfils itself on the basis of the spirit (πνεῦμα τοῦ νοός), and to contemplation that cannot be expressed, so the bodily life culminates in the physiognomy,—that pervading combination of all the impulses of the nature of man, that speaks without words. And, which is not less deserving of consideration, in all three regions, that of the spirit, of the soul, and of the body, the end (Pneuma, the concentration of all the powers of the soul, physiognomy) is associated with the beginning (will as impulse, intention, embryo).[2]

These are the seven forms or stages of the corporeal self-representation of the soul. They do not follow one another in sections of time, and the growth of one is generally not sharply cut off from that of another. It is a sevenfold process, in which the coming into being of the first is at the same time the coming into being of the last, and all mutually acting, are comprehended in one another; but still so that every individual of the seven in every involution maintains its own peculiar nature.[3]

[1] The most admirable thing that has lately been written on this subject occurs in Mehring's *Seelenlehre*, of which the third part treats of the forming soul, or of the self-expression. In Scripture, physiognomy is characterized as the expression of the countenance, giving the heart to be known, Isa. iii. 9, הַכָּרַת פָּנִים, especially *agnitio vultus h.e. id quo se agnoscendum dat* (comp. τὸ εἶδος τοῦ προσώπου, Luke ix. 29).

[2] Thus Göschel, *Der Mensch diesseits und jenseits*, p. 41.

[3] Ἐμοὶ δοκέει, says Hippocrates, *de locis in homine*, ii. p. 101, ἀρχὴ μὲν οὖν οὐδὲ μία εἶναι τοῦ σώματος, ἀλλὰ πάντα ὁμοίως ἀρχὴ καὶ πάντα τελευτή· κύκλου γὰρ γραφέντος ἀρχὴ οὐχ εὑρέθη.

Moreover, let us guard ourselves against misunderstanding, as though we had fallen into the self-deception of supposing that such a septenary of psychico-corporeal forms of life is directly taught in Scripture.[1] We say only that Scripture offers us fundamental views of the relation of the soul to the spirit, and of the body to the soul, from which its scattered declarations on the psychico-corporeal life arrange themselves into such a combined form as corresponds to the physiological result,—a form which, in order to be recognised in its internal necessity, is to be considered in its all-sided associations.

Having now seen how the soul presents its sevenfold nature corporeally, the relation of the soul to the blood, upon which direct and richly suggestive statements of Scripture occur, still attracts to itself our special attention.

SOUL AND BLOOD.

Sec. XI.

Upon the relation of the soul to the blood, Scripture contains statements not merely casual, but deliberate, to which it attaches itself the greatest fundamental importance. We assure ourselves at once, without further reflection, that there is a meaning and coherency in these statements. Such are the following: (1.)

[1] The reproach of R. Wagner, *Der Kampf um die Seele*, p. 120, that "in this paragraph such a breadth is given to the arbitrariness of scriptural interpretation, that no criticism can be brought to bear against it," is none the less unjust. I have the assurance, that what I have said upon the individual forms of life, not only permits, but also bears criticism: the association of each individual will of necessity only be regarded as arbitrary, when the postulates of this association are regarded as untenable. This is true also against Noack, who, in respect of Sec. VI., at least concedes: "It certainly cannot be said that the play of these powers was carried into the psychical life of man absolutely, and that in reality nothing at all may be referred to that of the analogue" (*Psyche*, 1860, p. 346); and in respect of Sec. XI., declares, "Something true there always is in the propositions of the biblical-theological writers; but as soon as they are laid hold of decidedly and in earnest, they appear equally ill-founded and arbitrary. They are a play on words, figures, and relations" (*ibid*. p. 347).

Gen. ix. 4–6. The word אַךְ introduces a limitation of the permission to eat flesh, freely given in ver. 3 : " But flesh with its soul, which is its blood, ye shall not eat." דָּמוֹ is an apposition to נַפְשׁוֹ ; and in this closer determination of the נַפְשׁוֹ by דָּמוֹ subsists, briefly intimated, the foundation of the prohibition. The blood of beasts is for this reason excepted from the permission to eat, because it is the soul of beasts. But, according to ver. 5, man's blood and man's soul are even more closely associated. Man is to eat of the flesh of beasts, *but* not the blood of beasts. To this restricting "*but*" is added, in the "*nevertheless*" (Eng. ver. "and surely") of ver. 5, a restriction referring to man's own blood: the former is not to be eaten, and is therefore to be poured out; but the latter is strictly forbidden to be shed. "Nevertheless, your blood of your souls," *i.e.* whosesoever soul it may be to whom it belongs, " will I avenge:" thus the life of man contained in the blood of man is not to be touched by beasts or men, under the penalty of death. (2.) Lev. xvii. 10–14. That he who eateth any manner of blood (no matter whether it be the blood of sacrifice or not), whether he be Israelite or stranger, is to be destroyed, is here established in the following manner : Ver. 11. "For the soul of the flesh," *i.e.* of the nature living in the flesh, " is in the blood; and I have given it to you upon the altar, to make an atonement for your souls: for the blood by means of the soul (בַּנֶּפֶשׁ) is an atonement." To translate this בַּנֶּפֶשׁ, with Luther, according to the LXX. (ἀντὶ ψυχῆς, Cod. Alex. ἀντὶ τῆς ψυχῆς) and Jerome (*pro animæ piaculo*), the blood is the atonement " for the life " (as even Ewald, sec. 282*a* : the blood atones for the soul), we are compelled to regard with Kurtz as inadmissible, since כִּפֶּר may perhaps be constructed with בְּעַד (*e.g.* Lev. ix. 7), but otherwise never with בְּ, of that which is to be atoned for. Rather it might be explained with Hofmann, the blood atones as the soul in this character; for the noun with which *Beth essentiæ* is associated, may just as well be grammatically defined (as " the soul") as undefined (as " soul") : it occurs with proper names, which (without adopting the article) are determined by themselves, and with appellatives which are more closely defined by suffixes annexed to them.[1] But why should the בְּ be otherwise

[1] *Vid.* Hofmann's *Schriftbeweis*, ii. 1, 239, and my *Commentary on the Psalter*, vol. i. p. 272.

understood here than as it is to be taken elsewhere in connection with כַּפֶּר? In the action of the atonement, it is the *Beth instrumenti* which indicates the means of the atonement (as *e.g.* Gen. xxxii. 21; Lev. vii. 7; Num. v. 8; 2 Sam. xxi. 3). The blood atones by the means or by the power of the soul which is in it. The life of the sinner, says Knobel *in loco*, has specially incurred the punitive wrath of Jehovah; but He accepts for it the substituted life of the sacrificial beast, the blood of which is shed and brought before Him, whereupon He pardons the sinner.[1] The prohibition of eating the blood is thus doubly established: the blood has the soul in itself; and it is, in consequence of a gracious arrangement of God, the means of atonement for the souls of men, in virtue of the soul contained in it. The one reason lies in the nature of the blood, and the other, in its destination to a holy purpose, which, even apart from that other reason, withdraws it from a common use: it is that which contains the soul, and God suffers it to be brought to His altar as an atonement for human souls; it atones not by indwelling power, which the blood of beasts has not, except perchance as given by God for this purpose,—given, namely, with a view to the fulness of the times foreseen from eternity, when *that* blood is to flow for humanity which atones, because a soul united to the eternal spirit (see on Heb. ix. 14) has place therein, and because it is actually of such absolute value, that it is able to screen the whole of humanity. When hereupon it is said that the blood of slaughtered beasts is to be poured forth, and the blood of game slain in the open field is, besides, to be covered over with earth, the above reason follows once more, somewhat otherwise applied and solemnly sanctioned (ver. 14): "For the soul of all flesh הוּא בְנַפְשׁוֹ דָּמוֹ—whereof I said to the children of Israel,—blood of all flesh (whether it be of beasts sacrificed, or slaughtered for the common use) ye are not to

---

[1] Thus also Bähr, *Symbolik*, ii. 207, and most of the Jewish interpreters, according to the traditional maxim תבא נפש ותכפר על נפש, one soul covers or atones for the other, *i.e.* the offering atones so far as it is a substitutionary surrender of the life of the beast that flows in the blood, instead of the life of man: *e.g.* David b. Abraham in his *Lexicon*, written in Arabic, אגדון (see in Pinsker. *Zur Gesch. des Karaismus*, p. קכד). The blood atones through the soul: this is its fundamental ground, and for this reason it atones for souls (*'an en-nufûs*), and takes their place (*janûbu*, from which *nâïb*, the representative).

eat, for its blood is the soul of all flesh: whosoever eats of it shall be destroyed." The passage here (which the LXX. has simplified by omission of the בְּנַפְשׁוֹ) is difficult. Wessely and other Jewish commentators explain, as concerning the soul of all flesh (whether it be of tame cattle, wild beasts, or feathered fowl), its blood is most closely associated with its soul: it cannot be said of the blood of the slain beast, that the soul is as little therein any more, as a man is in the house from which he has gone forth; for there remain in the blood, the elements which served the soul as *media* of its efficiency, and thus are themselves of a psychical kind. This explanation is not inconsistent with the meaning of the Thora; for the prohibition of eating blood has actually its reason in the continuous psychical arrangement of the blood. Otherwise Knobel, who, however, takes the preposition בְּ similarly in the sense of the prohibition: "The life of all flesh—it is its blood with its life, *i.e.* it subsists in its blood, nevertheless, only so far and so long as this latter is united with its נפש, and includes and contains it: it is not the material of the blood in itself that is the life, *e.g.* not therefore coagulated and dried blood, from which the נפש has vanished, but blood associated with the נפש. But this distinction between blood that still contains soul, and blood deprived of soul, lies altogether outside the range of the prohibition of blood: it comes into consideration only in a certain measure within the law of sacrifice, in that there the atoning power cleaves pre-eminently to the blood of the soul flowing forth of itself—the so-called life's blood (דַּם הַחַיִּים)." Against both explanations, as well that of Wessely as that of Knobel, it is, however, to be observed, that a passage which regards blood and soul as united, and therefore holds them as distinct from one another, does not truly agree with those that identify them (11*a*, 14*b*) by which it is surrounded, according to which it is more probable that בְּ is to be apprehended in the sense of immanence, rather than in the sense of concomitance, which, besides, in such a simple declaratory text, is more according to the *usus loquendi*. Moreover, neither does Baumgarten's explanation commend itself: "As regards the soul of all flesh—its blood is in its soul (הוּא referred back to דָּמוֹ), *i.e.* it has therein its being—it is its manifestation;" nor the explanation proposed in the first edition: " This is (הוּא referred back *per attractionem* to נֶפֶשׁ) its blood in its soul, *i.e.* its blood existing in its soul—having this for its existence, and bringing it to manifestation."[1] Both explanations are hair-splitting, not sufficiently simple and natural. Equally conformed to the connection and to the *usus loquendi*, on the other hand, is Hofmann's explanation, according to which בְּנַפְשׁוֹ is a predicative idea, introduced by *Beth essentiale:* " Of all flesh, soul avails thus much, that to it its blood is that which constitutes its soul."[2] The blood has the peculiarity of being the soul of the nature living in the flesh; therefore it is even to be allowed to flow from the body of the beast not offered in sacrifice, and to be covered with earth. It is to flow forth because it is not to be eaten, and, as it were, to be buried,—out of respectful awe, to wit,—for the blood is נפֶשׁ as the corpse is נֶפֶשׁ,—the former as that which has been the vehicle, the latter as that which has been the shrine, of the soul. (3.) Deut. xii. 23. Beasts of sacrifice, it is said here, may be slaughtered and eaten for common use, generally like the roebuck and the hart, *i.e.* beasts not of sacrifice: " Only be sure that thou eat not the blood; for the blood is the soul, and thou mayest not eat the soul with the flesh. Thou shalt not eat of it; thou shalt pour it upon the earth like water." How much the Thora relies upon this prohibition of the eating of blood, is seen from the fact that, without closer reasons, it is often repeated (Lev. iii. 17, vii. 26); so that in the Mosaic legislation itself, it occurs in all seven times (Lev. iii. 17, vii. 25–27, xvii. 10–14; Deut. xii. 16, 23, 24, xv. 23).[3] The later literature, moreover, shows us that eating of blood was acknowledged in Israel as sin (1 Sam. xiv. 32). Even in the prophets, who otherwise meddle little with the prescriptions of the law in detail, the transgression of this special one is not left unpunished (Ezek. xxxiii. 25, comp. Isa. lxvi. 3). And even in the New Testament, where the seasonable occasion of the prohibition in the sacrificial use of the blood ceases, abstinence from blood outside or inside the body of the beast (αἷμα-

---

[1] Thus also David b. Abraham, from Fes. *l.c.*: " The blood is in the soul, *i.e.* the one is in the body, in and with the other, so that with the condition of the one, that also of the other stands or falls."

[2] *Schriftbeweis*, ii. 1, 238, with which I have declared myself agreed in the *Commentary on Genesis*, p. 272 (3d ed.).

[3] The pre-Mosaic texts (Gen. ix. 6), and that which does not specially belong to the subject (Lev. xix. 26), are left in this out of the question.

τος καὶ πνικτοῦ) is maintained (Acts xv. 20, 29, xxi. 25) as binding upon the Gentile Christians. The ancient church adheres strongly to it, as numerous witnesses testify: Erubescat error vester Christianis—Tertullian is able to oppose to the suspicions of the heathens—qui ne animalium quidem sanguinem in epulis esculentis habemus, qui propterea suffocatis quoque et morticinis abstinemus.[1]

The idea of the unity of the soul and the blood, on which the prohibition of blood is based, comes to light also, everywhere where the Scripture speaks of violent death, in its mode of expression. In the blood of one mortally wounded, his soul flows forth (Lam. ii. 12), and He who voluntarily sacrifices Himself pours out His soul unto death (Isa. liii. 12). The blood of man shed, which as plural is named דָּמִים,[2] cries to heaven for vengeance (Gen. iv. 10; Heb. xii. 24), for which, in Job xxiv. 12, comp. Apoc. vi. 10, it is said that the soul of those that were slain cries out. Of the murderer of the innocent, Scripture says that he slays the soul of the blood of the innocent (ψυχὴν αἵματος ἀθώου, Deut. xxvii. 25), and that the blood of the souls of the innocent (αἵματα ψυχῶν ἀθώων) cleaves to his skirts (Jer. ii. 34, comp. Prov. xxviii. 17, blood of a soul). And because the blood is the soul, that which is true of the person is said of the blood: דָּם נָקִי (Ps. xciv. 21), αἷμα δίκαιον (Matt. xxiii. 35).[3] This idea of the unity of the blood and the soul is not exclusively peculiar to the Holy Scripture. How harmoniously antiquity thus expressed itself, has been set forth by Bähr in his *Symbolism of Mosaic Worship*. That in the ancient Egyptian hieroglyphics, the hawk, which according to old tradition feeds on blood, implies the soul, proceeds, according to Horapollo (i. 7), on just the same idea. Virgil, in his *Æneid*, gives to it the boldest expression, when in ix. 349 he says of a dying person, *purpuream vomit ille animam*. Many Greek and Roman philosophers and physicians sought to establish it scientifically as the true view among the many various notions of the situation of the soul.[4] Critias taught absolutely: the blood

[1] *Opp.* ed. Oehler, i. 149.
[2] *Vid.* on this plural of the product, my *Commentary on Genesis*, p. 204.
[3] Beck, *Biblische Seelenlehre*, p. 5.
[4] *Vid.* Aristotle, περὶ ψυχῆς, B. i. ch. 2, and Tertullian, *de anima*, ch. xv.

is the soul.¹ Pythagoras and others: the soul is nourished by the blood. Empedocles: the heart's blood (αἷμα περικάρδιον) is the seat of the soul.² The Stoics: the soul is the exhalation (ἀναθυμίασις) of the blood. In the supposition of these last that the soul is developed from the blood as gas from the fire, they derived ψυχή from ψύχειν in the sense of cooling.³ The better knowledge is found in Homer. The Psyches in Hades, when it is granted to them to take up blood into themselves, attain again the power of thought, language, and experience. The blood is thus not absolutely one with the soul. It is only—as, moreover, Scripture supposes it—the means of its self-attestation.

Turning back again to the Scripture, it is first of all

---

¹ Matthæi observes, *in loco*, when Nemesius mentions this, that this Critias at any rate, if anybody had, had a soul of blood:—he was one of the thirty tyrants.

² He says it in the verse often cited in the church fathers, αἷμα γὰρ ἀνθρώποις περικάρδιόν ἐστι νόημα; comp. Cicero, *Tusc.* i. 9: *Empedocles animum esse censet cordi suffusum sanguinem.*

³ The Stoic derivation of the name ψυχή appears, moreover, differently used, *e.g.* by Chrysippus, in Plutarch, *de Stoicorum repugnantiis*, ch. xli.: "The child is naturally nourished in the womb like a plant; but when it is born it is cooled by the air (ψυχόμενον), fills the mouth with breath, and thus passes into a living life; wherefore the soul is fittingly so named from the cooling breathing (παρὰ τὴν ψῦξιν)." Just so the physician Hicesius, in Tertullian, *de anima*, ch. xxv. (where he contends against the view that the child is not endowed with soul till birth): Hicesius jam natis animam superducens ex aëris frigidi pulsu, quia et ipsum vocabulum animæ penes Græcos de refrigeratione respondens. Plato succeeds better in etymology, in the *Cratylus*, p. 399: "The soul is the cause of life, which procures to the body the capacity of breathing, and refreshes it (ἀναψῦχον);" for ψύχειν signifies to breathe, to blow, and also to cool, inasmuch as a man breathing cools himself, and blowing cools anything else. The simplest is Dio Chrysostomus, *Or.* xii. p. 387 (in union with the view of the endowing with soul at its birth): "When the child has left the womb, the air awakens it to life by means of breathing and inbreathing (εἰσπνεύσας καὶ εἰσψύξας)." Moreover, Origen assumes that the soul has its name from ψυχρόν, but *a refrigescendo de statu diviniore ac meliore*, as it were cooled by its journey down into the world of darkness (ἀποψυγεῖσα). See Lobeck's *Aglaophamus*, i. 759. One remembers in this, Plato and Heraclitus; for the latter (see Gessner, *de animis Heracliti*) distinguished damp or moist (sinking down) and dry (ascending) souls: the latter are those akin to the primitive fire, and drawn from Him whose ἀποσπάσματα or σπέρματα the souls are.

deserving of consideration, that it always combines soul and blood only—nowhere spirit (רוּחַ) and blood, as a unity. Philo has noticed this. It is only the sensuous soul—he says quite correctly—not the intelligent and thinking soul, whose οὐσία is called the blood: the blood is the οὐσία of the soul; but the οὐσία of its nobler part, which is related to it as the apple of an eye, to the eye—as it were the ψυχὴ ψυχῆς—is the spirit which originates from God.[1] The spirit, say we—on the foundation of such christologic passages psychologically applicable, as Heb. ix. 14,[2] Acts xx. 28—is only mediately immanent in the blood, in that it is immanent in the soul. The spirit reveals itself in the soul, and the soul lives and moves in the blood. How sharply the Scripture here separates and defines, is seen from the fact that internal bodily organs such as the heart, the kidneys, etc., are frequently named as the localities of spiritual occurrences, but never the blood. It is thus only the soul on its physical side which is so pre-eminently in the blood, that it can be said to be one with the blood: not in the sense of identity, for the expression "the soul is the blood" alternates with "the soul is in the blood;" and not in the sense of local enclosure, for the soul, although an unextended nature, is certainly capable of being localized in an organic body, but not in such a way as that one part of the organism should exclusively include it in itself. The scriptural view, at least, is entirely opposed to such a localizing of the soul in one part of the human corporeity. According to Scripture, the soul is not in the blood in such a way that it could not also be outside the blood.[3] For it is also in the organs of respiration and of nutrition: the breath is actually called נֶפֶשׁ (Job xli. 13), and even the yawning mouth is called נֶפֶשׁ (Isa. v. 14). It is everywhere where

---

[1] See *Philonis Op.* ed. Mangey, i. 206, 480, ii. 356, and *Opp.* ed. Tauchnitz, l. vi. pp. 258, 390.

[2] The πνεῦμα αἰώνιον of Christ stands here in contrast with the perishable soul of the beast; according to the difference of their πνεύματα, is measured the respective value of the bloody self-sacrifice of Christ and of the sacrifice of beasts. The bold assertion of the contrary, by Lünemann, *On the Hebrews*, p. 289 (ed. 2, 1861), that the Scripture throughout knows nothing of a πνεῦμα of beasts, is contradicted by Ps. civ. 30, Eccles. iii. 21, Gen. vii. 15, comp. 22, and other places.

[3] Cassiodorus thinks, in naïve ignorance of language, that *anima* is perhaps therefore related to ἄναιμα.

bodily life is; and where it is, there it is always entire, although here and there in different manifestation.[1] The question only occurs: With what justice is the soul, that manifests itself in all corporeal forms of life, brought into so pre-eminently close a union with the blood?

The identification of the blood with the soul which prevailed in antiquity, appears at first to have no further foundation, than that a sudden diminution of the quantity of blood in the body causes death. But this phenomenon itself has the deeper reason, that all activity of the body—namely, that of the nervous and muscular systems—depends on the quantity of the blood; for if a part of the body be deprived of the flow of blood, all activity therein ceases—a sensible part in a few minutes loses all sensibility—a muscle no longer either serves the volition, nor is it susceptible of reflex irritability. The consequence which antiquity gathered from the phenomenon that blood-shedding and death coincide, is thus perfectly justified on physiological grounds. Irritability, sensibility, capacity of movement,—all activity of the body,—are lost with the loss of blood. The blood is actually the basis of the physical life; and so far, the soul, as the principle of bodily life, is pre-eminently in the blood. Therefore in the

[1] Our old dogmatists express both the above propositions in the following manner: "Anima in ubi est corporeo, sed non corporaliter neque localiter;" and, "Anima in toto corpore tota et in singulis simul corporis partibus tota." Even the Calvinistic dogmatists maintain the former position, but not the latter. It is true also of the brute soul. Claudius Mamertus (i. 21) says even of the plants, not without truth: Aut cuncta quæ de seminibus prodeunt intra eadem semina corporaliter ostende, aut herbarum quoque vitam incorpoream confitere. In extreme opposition thereto, it is said now, pointing to the fact, that from the lower beasts, *e.g.* polypi and worms, from the one hydra or naid, by mechanical division, two, three, or several hydræ or naids may be formed by divisibility of the soul—yea, indeed, "of the consciousness." The expression is old (*e.g.* in Albertus M., *de anima*, i. 15, with reference to the same experimental fact: Anima quæ uno numero fuit in toto efficitur duæ numero per divisionem), but inappropriate; for, as it has been rightly said in opposition, "that which is divisible must, moreover, be extended; and what is extended is a body." That which is multiplied as the result of the cutting up of the bodies of lower creatures (comparable to the setting of a plant), is only the body, to which neither individualized life, as in the higher kind of beasts, nor, what is the same thing, psychical life, cleaves. As concerns the multiplication of souls, however, in the process of generation, this is no division, and ought not therefore to be called so.

sacrifice, the blood of the sacrificial beast represents the soul of the offerer, and, indeed, as we have elsewhere shown, not in symbolical, but in intercessory and substitutional worth.[1]

There is still, besides the principle that the blood is the basis of the psychical life, a second, without the addition of which the biblical prohibition of the eating of blood, although it doubtless seeks to prevent a brutal degradation of man, cannot at all be comprehended. The blood is not only the all-conditioning basis, but also the all-embracing source, of the physical life. Scripture expresses itself on this point as decidedly as possible (certainly without purposing to give us physiological information), when, in Acts xvii. 26, it says that God hath made ἐξ ἑνὸς αἵματος all nations of men on all the face of the earth; and in John i. 13,[2] that man by nature is born ἐξ αἱμάτων. The blood is there plainly considered as the original material, and, as it were, the chaos, from which the whole human organism proceeds. This view, moreover, is scientifically confirmed: for it is generally acknowledged, that from the point at which in the embryo the nervous marrow and blood have come into existence, all further secretion and formation arises from the blood; and that even after birth, in every body endowed with soul, all the material for growth, *i.e.* for all sorts of nourishment, as well as of secretion, proceeds from the blood. Only it is still scientifically in debate, whether the various kinds of material are contained in the blood in a state of actual diversity, and thence,

[1] See the second final consideration of my *Commentary on the Epistle to the Hebrews*, 1857: "When the priest," says Nachmani on Lev. i. 5 (to appeal to a Jewish witness), "sprinkles the blood on the altar, this represents the position of the blood and of the soul of the offerer,—that he may consider, when this occurs, that he has sinned in his body and his soul; and that properly his blood ought to be shed and his body burnt, if God had not graciously ordained this substitution (תמורה)."

[2] In this passage, οὐκ ἐξ αἱμάτων denies the material basis; οὐδὲ ἐκ θελήματος σαρκός the causality of the fleshly, therefore unspiritual, unsanctified will; οὐδὲ ἐκ θελήματος ἀνδρός the causality of man's, and therefore of created will. An Old Testament parallel does not occur to the above two New Testament passages. For the "blood-relationship" is in Hebrew שְׁאֵרָה (fellowship of the flesh), Lev. xviii. 17. My blood relation is שְׁאֵרִי, בְּשָׂרִי, or עַצְמִי וּבְשָׂרִי. In both those New Testament passages, Hellenic and Israelitish views appear to prevail. Comp. Euripides' *Ion*, ἄλλων τραφεὶς ἀφ' αἱμάτων. But it is only the Hellenic *usus loquendi* which here defines the biblical: the view is old-Israelitish.

by virtue of the relations of affinity which the several organs have thereto, are transferred to these as actual products;[1] or whether they are first changed by the organs themselves, by virtue of the functional powers of these organs, in such a way as to furnish them with certain characters and qualities. If the former view be true of some materials, and the latter of others, it is the fact that the restlessly prosecuted investigation of the blood, in respect of the manifold material of healthy and unhealthy life, supplies to the view of its pre-existence in the blood, a continually extending support.[2] The same acknowledgment, although not as yet scientifically stated, lies at the base of the biblical prohibition of the eating of blood. The blood is thus stringently forbidden, because it is the substantial centre whence the animal life in all its forms is radiated into development. Everything fluid and firm, which, in the body endowed with soul, separates itself, by way of assimilation or secretion, exists already either as a product, or else potentially, in the blood. The immanence of the soul in the body is thus, physically regarded, nowhere so intensive as in the blood. The blood is the soul, not only as the principle of bodily life, but also as the principle of bodily formation in its sensible manifestation.

But only the blood of beasts is forbidden, in order to prevent the contact of the human soul with the brute soul. That the traditional practice allows the blood of fishes, arises from the fallacious idea that the blood of fishes has not the same relation to their life as the blood of other creatures. Meanwhile the Thora certainly does not expressly forbid the blood of fishes; and, moreover, it does not forbid human blood. Human blood, says Wessely, is legally permitted, for no reason exists to forbid it.[3] Wherefore not? Because it is homogeneous to man. He, therefore, who thus sucks the blood perchance from one who has cut himself, does nothing unlawful. And when

[1] See *e.g.* Rösch, *Bedeutung des Blutes*, p. 8: "The blood as the primitive fluid is a homogeneous liquid, which, notwithstanding, contains all differences, whereby it is possible that even the most different things can be formed from it, and be nourished from it,—depositing this in one place, that in another, and thus it is dispersed as the light is broken up into colours." It is the so-called humoral-pathologic view.

[2] See, for example, Budge, *Memoranda*, ii. sec. 268.

[3] דם אדם מותר מן התורה שאין טעם זה לאסרו.

the Lord, in the last supper, ordains His blood for drink, that is not, on the legal standing, so startling as when Peter receives the command to eat of the living things in the descending vessel. In the former case, the purpose is to transplant the life of the God-man into us; and this life is so far homogeneous to us, that it is the life of man, in which the idea of humanity has attained to its highest conceivable perfection.

Thus much upon blood and soul. That spiritual functions are nowhere attributed to the blood, we have already observed above. So much the more multifarious are the functions which Scripture attributes to the heart, which is the reservoir of the blood. And in conjunction with the heart, there scarcely occurs any mention of the head, which is the reservoir of the brain. Here, if anywhere, biblical psychology encounters difficult problems, which, however, when they shall be solved, are equally evidences for the just claims of the science, with the building up of which we are concerned.

HEART AND HEAD.

Sec. XII.

"Quid sine capite est homo," cries Ambrose, "cum totus in capite sit!" According to thorough investigation and evidence of Scripture in all its parts, however, the heart is the innermost centre of the natural condition of man, in which the threefold life of man blends together; wherefore קֶרֶב, inwardness, internality (although properly of a broader meaning than לֵב, Ps. xxxix. 4, lxiv. 7), is used in a sense almost the same as לֵב (Arab. *qalb*) (*e.g.* Ps. v. 10, xlix. 12); and לֵב, καρδία, denotes also the middle or centre of other natural things (see Sec. X. of this division). The heart is (A) the centre of the bodily life, it is the reservoir of the entire life-power (Ps. xl. 13, comp. xxxviii. 11), and indeed in the lowest physical sense; for eating and drinking, as strengthening of the heart (Gen. xviii. 5; Judg. xix. 5; 1 Kings xxi. 7; Acts xiv. 17; Jas. v. 5, comp. Luke xxi. 34), becomes the strengthening of the whole man. It is (B) the centre of the pneumatico-psychical life, and (a) of the life of will and desire. When the man determines of himself upon anything, it is called מְלָאוֹ לִבּוֹ (Esther vii. 5, comp. Eccles. viii. 11, ix. 3), or נָדַב לִבּוֹ אֹתוֹ (Ex. xxxv. 29), or נְשָׂאוֹ לִבּוֹ (Ex. xxxv. 21), or נָתַן לִבּוֹ (Eccles. i. 13), or שָׂם עַל־לִבּוֹ (Dan. i. 8); in the New Testament, προαιρεῖται τῇ καρδίᾳ (2 Cor. ix. 7). When the man designs anything with a consciousness of the motive and object, it is called הָיָה בִלְבָבוֹ (Isa. x. 7) or עִם־לְבָבוֹ (1 Kings viii. 17, x. 2): it is תַּאֲוַת (Ps. xxi. 3), εὐδοκία (Rom. x. 1), πρόθεσις (Acts xi. 23), of his heart; and when he is strongly determined, he is ἑδραῖος ἐν τῇ καρδίᾳ (1 Cor. vii. 37). What is done gladly, willingly, and of set purpose, is done מִלֵּב, ἐκ καρδίας (Lam. iii. 33; Rom. vi. 17; comp. Prov. xxiii. 7). The heart is the seat of love (1 Tim. i. 5) and of hatred (Lev. xix. 17). Whom a man loves, to him he gives his heart (Prov. xxiii. 26; Judg. v 9), and him he has in his heart (Phil. i. 7; 2 Cor. vii. 3). The heart is (b) the centre of the pneumatico-psychical life, as the life of thought and conception. The heart knows or perceives, Deut. xxix. 3, Prov. xiv. 10; it understands, Isa. xxxii. 4, Prov. viii. 5, Acts xvi. 14; it deliberates, Neh. v. 7; it reflects, συμβάλλει, Luke ii. 19; and estimates, Prov. xvi. 9. The heart is set or directed (שִׂים, שִׁית) when one gives heed (Deut. xxxii. 46; Ps. xlviii. 14): it is turned away from, or inclined towards, according as one's sympathies are turned away or turned towards an object (Deut. xxx. 17; Josh. xxiv. 23). That which one impresses on one's self, and makes one's own, is said to be settled, bound, written on or in the heart (Deut. xi. 18; Cant. viii. 6; Prov. vi. 21, iii. 3); one knows in his heart if he is conscious to himself (Deut. viii. 5), and with his whole heart if he is absolutely conscious (Josh. xxiii. 14; comp. לֵב, knowledge about anything, in the phrases, 2 Kings v. 26, Gen. xxxi. 20); and everything which comes into our mind or memory rises in the heart (עָלָה עַל־לֵב or אֶל־לֵב, Isa. lxv. 17, Jer. iii. 16, or בָּא עַל־לֵב, 2 Chron. vii. 11; ἀναβαίνει ἐπὶ καρδίᾳ, Acts vii. 23, 1 Cor. ii. 9); the heart is the storehouse of all that is heard and experienced (Luke i. 66, ii. 51, xxi. 14). Thinking is called אָמַר בְּלֵב, Gen. xvii. 17, or אֶל־לֵב, Gen. viii. 21, xxiv. 45; דִּבֶּר עִם־לֵב, Eccles. i. 16, or עַל־לֵב, 1 Sam. i. 13; λέγειν or εἰπεῖν ἐν τῇ καρδίᾳ, Matt. xxiv. 48, Apoc. xviii. 7. The heart itself discourses inwardly, and then speaks, by expressing itself outwardly (אָמַר, Ps. xxvii. 8; דִּבֶּר, Ps. xli. 7, Prov. xxiii. 33; הָגָה, Prov. xv. 28, xxiv. 2, Isa. xxxiii. 18). The heart is the birth-place of the thoughts: thought is called הָגוּת, Ps. xlix. 3, הָגָיוֹן, Ps. xix. 14, or רַעְיוֹן, Dan. ii. 30, of the heart;—its thoughts, מַחְשָׁבוֹת, Gen. vi. 5; חִקְקֵי or חִקְרֵי, Judg. v. 15; מְזִמּוֹת, Jer. xxiii. 20; מַעַרְבֵי, Prov. xvi. 1; מַשְׂכִּיּוֹת, Ps. lxxiii. 7; מוֹרָשֵׁי, Job xvii. 11; βουλαὶ, 1 Cor. iv. 5; διαλογισμοὶ, Matt. xv. 19, Luke v. 22, ix. 47, xxiv. 38; ἐνθυμήσεις, Matt. ix. 4; ἔννοιαι, Heb. iv. 12. Wise thoughts, as well as inventions (1 Kings xii. 33; Neh. vi. 8; Isa. lix. 13) and deceits (Jer. xiv. 14, xxiii. 16), originate from the heart: it is the heart which forms them (יָצַר, Gen. viii. 21), and devises them (חָרַשׁ, Prov. vi. 18). Because it is the birth-place of the thoughts, the heart is, moreover, the birth-place of words. Words are brought forth from the heart (Job viii. 10), are spoken with the heart (Ps. xv. 2); the mouth speaks ἐκ τοῦ περισσεύματος τῆς καρδίας (Matt. xii. 34). The heart thus comprehends both νοῦς and λόγος; therefore the wise man is called חֲכַם־לֵב (Ex. xxviii. 3), and לֵב is pregnantly used as equivalent to understanding (Job xii. 3; Prov. xv. 32; Hos. iv. 11): thence אִישׁ־לֵבָב, the man of understanding (Job xxxiv. 10, 34), and חֲסַר־לֵב (Prov. x. 13) or אֵין־לֵב (Hos. vii. 11; Jer. v. 21), the man void of understanding; for heart without שֵׂכֶל (Job xvii. 4) or חָכְמָה (Prov. xiv. 33) is no better than none. The heart is (c) the centre of the pneumatico-psychical life, as emotional, *i.e.* the life of the feelings and the affections (affections of the mind). To the heart are attributed all degrees of joy, from pleasure (Isa. lxv. 14) to transport and exultation (Acts ii. 46; Ps. lxxxiv. 3); all degrees of pain, from discontent (Prov. xxv. 20) and sorrow (John xvi. 6) up to piercing and crushing woe (Ps. cix. 22; Acts xxi. 13; Isa. lxv. 14); all degrees of ill-will, from provocation and anger (Prov. xxiii. 17; Jas. iii. 14) to raging madness (Acts vii. 54) and glowing desire of vengeance (Deut. xix. 6); all degrees of dissatisfaction, from anxiety (Prov. xii. 25) to despair (Eccles. ii. 20); all degrees of fear, from reverential trembling (Jer. xxxii. 40) to blank terror (Deut. xxviii. 28; Ps. cxliii. 4). The heart melts and writhes for anguish (Josh. v. 1; Jer. iv. 19), becomes weak by despondency (Lev. xxvi. 36; Deut. xx. 8), glows and ferments for sadness (Ps. xxxix. 3, lxxiii. 21), dries up and withers under the weight of sorrow (Ps. cii. 4;

Ezek. xvi. 30), is broken and crushed by the anguish of adversity, wrath, and punishment (Ps. cxlvii. 3; Jer. xxiii. 9; Ps. li. 19), is turned for sympathy (Hos. xi. 8); is set into a sacred burning by God's word (Jer. xx. 9; Luke xxiv. 32). Briefly, לֵב, καρδία, is the conscious unity of the pneumatico-psychical life in all its directions; and therefore לֵב אֶחָד, καρδία μία, is the conscious perfect unity of will, thought, and feeling (Jer. xxxii. 39; Ezek. xi. 19; 1 Chron. xii. 38; Acts iv. 32). But as will, thought, and feeling are always conceived by Scripture from an ethical point of view, it is thence understood of itself, that the heart, moreover, is (C) the centre of the moral life; so that all moral conditions, from the highest mystical love of God (Ps. lxxiii. 26), even down to the self-deifying pride (Exek. xxviii. 2, 5), and the darkening (Rom. i. 21) and hardening (Isa. vi. 10, lxiii. 17; Jer. xvi. 12; Lam. iii. 65; 2 Cor. iii. 14), are concentrated in the heart as the innermost life-circle of humanity (1 Pet. iii. 4); and the moral character is called precisely לֵב (comp. לֵב וָלֵב, an ambiguous character, Ps. xii. 3, 1 Chron. xii. 33), or with reference to the heart, יֵצֶר (Deut. xxxi. 21; New Testament, διάνοια, Luke i. 51, ἐπίνοια, Acts viii. 22). Therefore בַּר, clear; טָהוֹר, pure;[1] יָשָׁר, upright; שָׁלֵם, whole; תָּם, perfect; נָכוֹן, strong; נֶאֱמָן, faithful; and so further, with their opposites, are appellations of the heart,—the discussion of which, however, is not a problem of psychology, but of ethics. The heart is the laboratory and place of issue of all that is good and evil in thoughts, words, and deeds (Mark vii. 21; Matt. xii. 34); the rendezvous of evil lusts (ἐπιθυμίαι) and passions (πάθη ἐπιθυμίας, Rom. i. 24; Mark iv. 19, comp. 15); a good or an evil treasure (Luke vi. 45). It is the place where God's natural law is written in us, and effectually proves itself (Rom. ii. 15); as also the place of the positive law put within by grace (Isa. li. 7; Jer. xxxi. 33). It is the seat of conscience (Heb. x. 22); and all the testimonies of the conscience, *e.g.* 1 John iii. 19–21, are ascribed to it. With the heart it is believed, καρδίᾳ πιστεύεται (Rom. x. 10); and also disbelief places there the dregs of all wickedness (Heb. iii. 12). It is the field for the seed of the divine word (Matt. xiii. 19; Luke

---

[1] It is characteristic of the rather Hellenic than Hebraic language in which the idea is expressed, that the book of Wisdom (vii. 27) says ὁσίαι ψυχαί, where the Old Testament (Prov. xxii. 11, LXX.) says ὁσίαι καρδίαι.

viii. 15). According as it makes its decision, it stands under the inspirations of God (*e.g.* 2 Cor. viii. 16) or of Satan (John xiii. 2 ; Acts v. 3). It is the dwelling-place of Christ in us (Eph. iii. 17), of the Holy Ghost (2 Cor. i. 22), of the peace of God (Col. iii. 15); the receptacle of the love of God shed abroad (Rom. v. 5), the place of rising of the heavenly light (2 Cor. iv. 6; 2 Pet. i. 19), the closet of secret communion with God (Eph. v. 19 ; comp. Lam. ii. 18, iii. 41, Hos. vii. 14); a great mysterious depth, which only God fathoms (Prov. xv. 11 ; Jer. xvii. 9 ; Ps. xliv. 22 ; Rom. viii. 27).[1] To speak with Beck, it is the centre of the entire man—the very hearth of life's impulse—the supporter of the personal consciousness, combined with self-determination and the activity of the reason—the training-place of all independent actions and conditions; it is the agent of all relations and conducts, as well on the spiritual as on the bodily side, so far as they ensue with self-consciousness and free agency. It is by the heart that is characterized the moral condition of the man : in the heart are found the postulates of speech ; in the heart is affirmed the natural law, and, by means of regeneration, the new law of God as a living power. The question of v. Rudloff,[2] whether the heart belongs to the domain of the spirit or of the soul, needs not at all to be proposed in this mode of comprehension. It is the pneumatico-psychical inward nature of the man in its concrete central unity, and on all sides of its dynamic efficiency and its ethical determination. All that Hellenically and Hellenistically is called $νοῦς, λόγος, συνείδησις, θυμός$, is involved in $καρδία$; and all by which בשר and נפש is affected, comes in לב into the light of consciousness. The heart, says Solomon (Prov. xiv. 10), knoweth the bitterness of his soul. It is obvious, from this mode of conception, that the heart is the place where, as Oehler expresses it,[3] the soul is at home, and becomes conscious of all its doing and suffering, as its own. All the rays of the life of soul and body converge thither, and again develop themselves thence (comp. *e.g.* Prov. xiv. 30, xvii. 22). Heart,

---

[1] Where hitherto, in the individual cases, only one illustrative text or a few or many of them are cited, it has always occurred with design, and after a previous review of the collected texts pertaining to the point.

[2] *Die Lehre vom Menschen*, p. 42.

[3] Art. "Herz" in Herzog's *R.E.*

soul, and flesh, is the Old Testament trichotomy (Ps. lxxxiv. 3, xvi. 9); heart and soul, the Old Testament designation of the pneumatico-psychical inner life (Deut. iv. 29, vi. 5; Josh. xxii. 5, xxiii. 14; 1 Kings ii. 4; 2 Kings xxiii. 3; 1 Chron. xxviii. 9; 2 Chron. vi. 38; Prov. ii. 10).

We have purposely spared neither ourselves nor the reader the trouble of a tabular survey thus dry and wearisome, that the importance of the questions might be duly estimated which are associated with the view which is expressed in so continuous and various a manner in Scripture, from beginning to end. Maimonides disregards all difficulties, when, in view of this biblical mode of speaking, he says that לב is a homonymous word, which primarily denotes the principal organ of life, and then, moreover, thought, sentiment, will, and intellect.[1] Between heart in the lower bodily-vital sense and heart in the higher pneumatico-psychical sense, there must subsist a deeper and more real consistency than that of a mere figure of speech. From the fact that Scripture speaks nowhere of a heart of the brutes in a higher sense (a fact to which Roos first of all calls attention),[2] as moreover the Arabic *Hamasa*, p. 513, says directly, the brute is without heart (بغير لب), it cannot be proved that the higher conception of the human heart is a purely spiritual one: for the difference of the human and the brute heart has its foundation in the distinction of the human and the brute soul; the organ of which in both cases is the heart of flesh: the fleshly heart of man is divested of humanity, when his soul is brutalized (Dan. iv. 16). That, moreover, when Scripture speaks of the heart in the higher sense, its reference is not to be so entirely withdrawn from the fleshly heart, is proved by almost all the passages where the heart appears as the object and subject of affections, *e.g.* Job xxxvii. 1: " At this also my heart trembleth, and is moved out of his place." These are for the most part symptoms of the fleshly heart, as Ps. xxxviii. 10; the impetuous quickly recurring contraction and expansion,[3] by which

---

[1] *Moreh Nebuchim*, i. 39.

[2] See also Beck, *Seelenlehre*, p. 70.

[3] Not to say movement of rotation, for which סחרחר is the strict expression, the heart revolves in every condition of its efficiency a little round its axis—*leviter sese quasi contorquet*, as Harvey expresses it; and with

the sentiments are indicated. But, moreover, Scripture conceives of higher spiritual occurrences in association with the fleshly heart. "I will give them," says Jehovah, in Ezek. xi. 19, of the Israel of the future, "one heart, and I will put a new spirit within you; and I will take the stony heart out of their flesh, and will give them an heart of flesh" (לֵב בָּשָׂר). And Paul says to the Corinthians (2 Cor. iii. 2): "Ye are our epistle written in our hearts, known and read of all men: inasmuch as it is manifest of you that ye are the epistle of Christ ministered by us, written not with ink, but with the Spirit of the living God; not on tables of stone, but on fleshly tables of the heart." Irenæus not unjustly avails himself of this passage as a prooftext for the resurrection of the flesh: Si ergo nunc corda carnalia capacia spiritus fiunt: quid mirum si in resurrectione eam quæ a spiritu datur capiunt vitam![1]

Will it perchance be opposed to us, that this concentration of all pneumatico-psychical life in its sensuous agency upon the heart is not at all peculiar to the Holy Scripture? Even according to the Indian view, the sun of knowledge rises in the æther of the heart: there dwells the part "which stands at the crest" (*Kûtasṭa*) of the universal Brahma, who, by his reflection, bestows the needful light on the spiritual capacities.[2] Of the Persians, Firmicus Maternus tells us that they regard the heart as the source and ground whence the thoughts branch forth like a wood[3] (*in modum silvarum*). In Homer, κραδίη (ἦτορ) likewise serves as the central living hearth of man, and stands to φρένες directly in the relation of an internal nature. It is only because of the distinct and more elevated position which philosophy and physiology award to the νοῦς, that the brain gradually attained a higher significance. Pythagoras was the first who isolated the νοῦς in the brain. Alcmæon, his pupil, considered the brain as the organ, as well of perception (αἴσθησις) as of thought. Even Plato located the νοῦς in the head, wearing the form of a terrestrial globe. In like manner,

---

convulsive states of the heart is associated at times a feeling as if the heart were in a rolling motion.

[1] *Opp.* ed. Stieren, i. 753.

[2] Grant, *Bibliotheca Tamulica*.

[3] In a passage given in full in the following section, in Gersdorf, *Bibliotheca Patrum*, vol. xiii. p. 67.

the younger Hippocratic school,[1] and most of the Alexandrian physicians. Nevertheless Erasistratos taught (under Seleucus Nicator), according to Galen's testimony, that not alone the spirit of life, but also the spirit of the soul, had its seat κατὰ τὴν καρδίαν. This view, moreover, found scholastic support elsewhere. Empedocles gave the heart's blood to the soul, Diogenes of Apollonia the cavity of the chest to the νόησις; the author of the Hippocratic work, περὶ καρδίας, gave the left ventricle to the γνώμη (intelligent soul), as its place. But the chief assertor of the heart as the central organ of the soul is Aristotle, with the school of physicians that adopt his philosophy. The heart, from which the formation of the embryo takes its beginning, is, in his estimation, the centre whence proceed all the organs of sense, and whence, therefore, the soul, as the *entelecheia* of the body, develops its activity.[2] Moreover, among the Stoics, Chrysippus taught that the heart is the abode of the reason and the affections; and Posidonius, that the one soul, with its three fundamental powers (λογίζεσθαι, θυμοῦσθαι, ἐπιθυμεῖν), has its one proper dwelling-place in the heart.[3] And generally, the heart appears to the entire Greek science something more than a mere mechanical forcing-pump of the blood; for even Plato (followed by Philo), although he regards the head with the senses as the seat of the λόγος, places the θυμὸς in the chest or the heart, as the ἐπιθυμία in the liver, or the umbilical region. In Homer, the slain man, as wanting the light of consciousness, is called ἀκήρεος, without heart; and also in the Latin, *cor*, although here superseded by *animus*, is used in a pneumatico-psychical sense, as is shown by the adjectives *excors, socors, vecors*, and the forms of speech, *cordi esse, cordi facere*, and the like. Of a clever, cunning girl, it is

---

[1] Hippocrates himself, in his genuine writings, nowhere attributes to the brain the functions of the soul. This Galenistic view did not occur till the later apocryphal Hippocratic works: see Herm. Nasse, *Commentatio de insania secundum libros Hippocraticos*, 1829, iv. p. 4. The work, περὶ ἱερῆς νούσου, would therefore not be genuine; for there (*Opp.* ed. Littré, vol. vi. p. 392) it is expressly said that the brain, and not the heart, is the seat of the intelligence.

[2] See Brandis, *Aristoteles und seine akademischen Zeitgenossen*, second part (1857), p. 1144. Zeller, *Philosophie der Griechen*, ii. 487; comp. v. Zezschwitz, *Profangräcität und bibl. Sprachgeist*, pp. 24-31.

[3] See Max. Heinze, *Stoicorum de affectibus doctrina* (1860), p. 50.

said in Plautus : Ut habet sapiens cor, quam dicit quod opust.[1]

It is thus a fact, that this mode of regarding the heart is common to Scripture with classical and oriental antiquity, and that, in classical antiquity, even great scientific authorities look on the heart as the central organ of the soul. But is the marvel of the matter thereby explained? Is it, on that account, the less an enigma that needs explanation? In the extra-biblical sphere one might pass on, and be satisfied with the fact that this idea of the heart—as, perhaps, that of the revolution of the sun round the earth—is one of the many puerile ideas which belong to the early times of humanity; ideas, of which science has not even yet been able altogether to divest herself. But in Scripture it is so involved with the idea of the blood, and this so much implicated with the ritual of sacrifice[2] and the doctrine of atonement; and even were this not the case, it has there so pervading an influence upon the mode of thought and expression, and such an all-pervading control, that it is impossible to be satisfied with that cheap and superficial mode of explanation. For only the book of Daniel sometimes names the head, where, according to the prevalent mode of speech in Scripture, the heart might have been expected: it considers the head as the *locale* of visions (ii. 28, iv. 2, 7, 10, vii. 1, 15 ; comp. on the other hand, ii. 30). This חֶזְוֵי רֵאשֵׁהּ by the side of רַעְיוֹנֵי לִבְבָךְ in the book of Daniel, is a hint of the greatest value; but it is also the only trace of the reference of pneumatico-psychical events to the head: for, in respect of such passages as Eccles. ii. 14, it would only be a misapprehension of the true matter of fact to assume any.

Certainly moreover the head is, according to Scripture, evidently the noblest part of man; standing in the closest relation as well to soul and spirit in the man, as to all psychic-spiritual influences which arise to the man. Because in the head, the human organism culminates, Christ is called the κεφαλή[3] of

---

[1] Persæ, iv. 4, p. 84, ed. Ritschl.

[2] In the whole-offering the head and heart of the beast were burnt upon the altar (Lev. i. 3, viii. 20); otherwise, only the fat, kidneys, and the liver : Philo (*Opp.* ii. 190) neglects the former, while he finds the reason of the latter in the fact that head and heart are the seat of the ἡγεμονικόν, *i.e.* of the νοῦς.

[3] See my *Four Books of the Church*, p. 14.

the church His body, (see especially Eph. v. 23; Col. ii. 19; comp. 1 Cor. xi. 3); and for the same reason, ראֹשׁ is the general metaphorical appellation of him who is most exalted, the most excellent, the chief. He who blesses lays his hand upon the head of the person to be blessed (Gen. xlviii. 14, comp. xlix. 26; Prov. x. 6), and he who consecrates, on the head of the person to be consecrated (Jer. viii. 10); so that from thence, blessing and consecration, like the anointing oil (Ps. cxxxiii. 2, comp. Lev. viii. 12), should flow down upon the whole natural condition, and pervade it. Precisely for the same reason, tongues of fire are distributed on the heads of the apostles, and they become thus full of the Holy Ghost (Acts ii. 3): it was their heavenly laying on of hands (סְמִיכָה). There is a similar reason for the healer laying his hand upon the person to be healed (Matt. ix. 18): the power of healing (Luke vi. 19) goes forth upon the head, in order to go forth from thence upon the whole man. And it scarcely needs a proof, that the countenance or front of the head is, moreover, regarded in Scripture as the mirror of divine influences upon the man—of all affections, and of the entire life of soul and spirit. When Moses beheld the glory of God upon Sinai (Ex. xxxiv. 29, comp. Matt. xvii. 2, 2 Cor. iii. 13), it was his countenance which shone long afterwards. The wisdom of a man, says the Preacher (viii. 1), brightens his face, and, through boldness, his countenance is defaced or changed. In the physiognomy is reflected the moral condition of the man (Isa. iii. 9: see above, Sec. X. towards the end). Therefore God's פָּנִים is Himself, in His essential revelation (Ex. xxxiii. 14; Deut. iv. 37); as the Angel of Jehovah, as the medium of this revelation, is called מַלְאַךְ פָּנָיו (Isa. lxiii. 9). As the person, in respect of its internal nature, is called נֶפֶשׁ, ψυχή; so, in respect of its external nature, it is called פָּנִים, πρόσωπον, or רֹאשׁ (Judg. v. 30; 1 Chron. xii. 23), and even גֻּלְגֹּלֶת (Ex. xvi. 16, xxxviii. 26). The visible personal presence of any one is called his countenance, *e.g.* 2 Sam. xvii. 11. In all these relations the head is very highly exalted, but without, as v. Schubert[1] thinks, attributing to it any spiritual or higher

---

[1] *Geschichte der Seele*, i. 270; against which Einhorn, *Princip. des Mosaismus*, i. 174, observes: "The head is to the external appearance what the heart is to the internal agency of the soul; and only on this view is a prominent position attributed to it in the biblical point of view."

psychical functions. And even where Scripture speaks of the functions of the organs of sense, especially of seeing and hearing, as of conscious functions, and transfers the appellations to purely intellectual and spiritual transactions, it nowhere justifies us in supposing that there the head—which, even as the chief organ, unites in itself the organs of sense—is represented as the seat of the soul and the spirit, which are the background of every sensuous perception or perception similar to it.

The result of our investigation is pretty much this: that the Scripture, without excluding head and brain (as we may see on a glance at Dan. ii. 28, etc.) from the psychico-spiritual activities and affections, attributes the central agency of these to the heart. We have set forth the state of the case wholly without prejudice, considering the Scripture in its own light, and not in that of the later physiology and psychology. So much the more uncompromisingly is manifested the contradiction in which the scriptural view stands not only with the scientific idea that has been customary since the middle ages,[1] but also with our own natural self-observation. For as it is indubitable that, by the blood in its normal design, the integrity of the psychical functions is conditioned; and that privation of blood by disease, or violence, or superfluity of blood, has, as its consequence, a scale of symptoms, from their most extreme agitation even to their absolute suppression; and as it is experimentally certain, that with anger, love, and every eager psychical excitement, is associated palpitation of the heart—that the blush of shame has its cause in the heart-beats which drive the arterial blood towards the countenance—that generally, in a mysterious manner, mental affections change the pulsations of the heart; —so it is to us also indubitable, and experimentally certain, that anything which mentally affects us from without, does not become a conscious affection, without the brain being interested, as well in its origination as in its consequences. That the brain

[1] Thus teaches, for instance, the Jewish physician and astronomer, Schabtai Donolo, that the נשמה—which withal he takes strictly in a dichotomic sense, as spirit of thought and life—has its seat in the membrane of the brain, which is expanded over the brain and the fluid, as the divine Schekinah in the highest heaven arched over the waters. Below the membrane there is, without anatomical division, the *dura mater*, together with the *arachnoidea*.

is the organ of all conscious vital activity, and therefore the peculiar organ of the soul,—*i.e.*, as Damerow strikingly expresses it, the central organ of the spirit which appears in man as soul,—is not only the testimony of science, but is assured to us by every headache that results from over-strained thinking, and every congestion of blood towards the head that checks our thinking, by every self-reproach to which we give expression by striking our forehead, by every sense of stupefaction arising from forcible depression of the skull.[1] It is further a fact, that after destruction of the brain and spinal marrow, the animal muscles, *i.e.* the muscles that obey the volition, sink into absolute quietude, from which they can only be aroused by external stimulus,—a proof that brain and spinal marrow are the chief organs whence proceed all those stimuli which from within put the animal muscles[2] in motion. Thus, for the present, there prevails no doubt at all that the higher self-conscious activity of the soul, in all its tendencies, has its laboratory in the brain,[3] although, even to the present day, we have not succeeded in discovering

---

[1] "The problem of the biblical significance of the heart is solved very simply by the absolute ignorance of the brain and nervous life." Thus Noack dismisses me (*Psyche*, 1860, p. 348). But is it necessary to know the life of brain and nerves, to feel that we think with the head? Such a solution is none at all.

[2] In contrast to the organic muscles, which are the agents of the vegetative life, and withdrawn from the volition,—a usual distinction since the time of Bichat.

[3] "By heart ($\kappa\alpha\rho\delta\iota\alpha$)," says Harless, *Ethik*, p. 15, "we understand nothing else than the naturally offered designation of the living spiritual-bodily personality, so far as it is capable of inclination or disinclination,—of love or of hatred. Of a seat of this capability in the heart, we need speak just as little, as of a seat of the intelligence in the brain, or of other similar seats of the spiritual life." Where, then, is left the respect for the "so-called materialism of exact criticism," expressed in the preface to the *Ethik*? Nothing is more certain to him, than that the brain is the special seat of the soul; and how does it agree with this, that, according to a thorough biblical inspection, the heart is not only the seat of the impulse and of the inclination, but also of the intelligence and the will? It is just the question put to the science of biblical psychology, which is surely not satisfactorily solved by the fact that the heart is the natural centre of man. For the rest, the "spiritual-corporeal personality of man" is nowhere in Scripture called לֵב, but always נֶפֶשׁ. The heart nowhere appears as personal power (רוּחַ), nowhere as personal link (נֶפֶשׁ), but always only as a personal organ.

that unique constituent of the brain which is the indispensable condition of psychical phenomena, and therefore the peculiar ultimate—as it were, definite—seat of the soul. Nevertheless, all disturbance of the soul is esteemed pre-eminently a morbid state of the organ of the brain; and it has not sufficed to regard the thoughts as coinciding with the nervo-electric oscillations of the brain fibres, or as being at least accompanied by them,—even a plastic corporeal existence has been attributed to them in the brain.[1]

The treatise of Fr. Nasse which appeared in the year 1818, on the psychical reference of the heart, is of still undiminished value for the question with which we are here concerned.[2] This eminent investigator, whose glance was not limited to his own department, and who embraced all regions of science and of the spirit with observant and living sympathy, declares himself here decidedly against the hypothesis of a single organ of the soul—for the soul united in itself. Thence he ventures the conjecture, that a psychological significance belongs not merely to the brain, but, moreover, to other organs of the internal corporeity,—a significance which antiquity anticipated and stamped upon their language, but which later science has not yet dispassionately examined, and therefore, moreover, has not duly estimated. Above all, it is the heart, to which, in opposition to the exclusive reference of the psychical life to the brain, he seeks to win back the hitherto mistaken close relation to the soul, especially to its capacities of feeling. But he goes too far when he attributes to the heart an immediate psychical agency, *i.e.* a proper production of psychical functions taking place without concurrence of the brain. For although the heart in itself is only a great muscle, and is thus a mechanism without sensation, which drives round the blood in the body, by means of the pressure which it brings to bear upon it, it yet includes ganglia (nervous centres) and nerves, which belong to its nature not less than the muscular mass. These

---

[1] Thus *e.g.* Buchez, s. Edel. *Untersuchungen über das Intellectuelle Leben*, 1855.

[2] In the first quarterly part of the *Zeitschr. für psychische Aerzte*, but to whom also the treatise on the relation of the chief tendencies of the soul to those of the body is to be attributed, in addition, in the *Zeitschr. für die Anthropologie*, 1823, 1.

nerves are partly of cerebro-spinal, partly of sympathetic nature, as generally between the two systems of nerves there subsists a close reciprocity. This is not the place to allege the results of an anatomical investigation of the nerves of the so-called organic region, and to adduce the facts of experimental observation which place that relation of reciprocity, probable as it is, *à priori* beyond a doubt. When for a long time the cerebral system had been regarded as too dominant, the reaction prepared by Fr. Nasse, experimentally established by Volkmann and Bidder in favour of the sympathetic system, laid claim to an independence for it, which, if not absolute, was yet a relative one; and the result of it was the acknowledgment of the nearest material relationship and causal reciprocity of the two systems. And if I be not deceived in my judgment of the present position of the inquiry, the heart, in the measure that this compact dualism of the nervous system has become recognised, has again attained significance; and although, at the present time, not much will be thought of the experimental facts asserted by Fr. Nasse,—that sometimes melancholy and mania are associated with defects of the heart in the most manifold forms, without, at the same time, any noticeable affection of the brain, and without any disease of the brain appearing in the corpse; and that the *post-mortem* investigation of men, brutal and degenerated into the inhuman, has shown all kinds of deformities of the heart,[1]—still, it might become conclusively manifest, that brain and heart both together are the nearest and most influential bodily organs of the human soul. If the notion of finding the point of the brain wherein is the abode of the psychic-monad be only first substantially given up, then, instead of the view of the single seat of the soul, the ancient Stoic supposition of an extended seat of the soul, lately experimentally demonstrated by

[1] See on both, moreover, Steuder's *Diss. de Cordis Morborum vi ad Animum*, Kiel 1855. Against the former, it may be said that the proof *per enumerationem simplicem* (from individual cases) is too weak to build thereon the assumption of a deeper causal-connection; the latter has not yet been confirmed, at least for the present, by later observations. Charles II., the last of the House of Hapsburgh on the Spanish throne, the favourite of the Inquisition, and the amateur of the *auto-da-fé* (died 1700), presents an example not mentioned in Fr. Nasse: "The heart of the king was not larger than a pigeon's egg, and soft as moistened chalk" (see Kayserling, *Ein Feiertag in Madrid*, p. 9).

Fechner,[1] will be more and more confirmed; and then, moreover, the acknowledgment of the fact, that the ganglionic system serves for the perception of the general conditions of life which proceeds from external impressions and single sensations, will further tend to this result, that the expansion of the seat of the soul extends not only to the heart, but that this latter, moreover, is a principal hearth of the soul's activity.[2]

Thus, while considering the contradiction which the biblical assertions on head and heart meet, we have attained a point from which may be anticipated a possibility of arrangement. It is certainly too little, when Beck, in order to apprehend the spiritual significance which Scripture attributes to the heart, makes the following observation, which, in itself, is entirely true:[3] "Centrality, with independently acting combined power, as well as with power of circulation stimulating and nourishing in all directions—this forms the essential characteristic of the heart's life; and as the soul, with its peculiar character, is organically involved in the blood, so the central chamber of the blood-life, the heart in its declared peculiarity, forms the organic basis of the entire soul-life." It is too little; for although Scripture makes blood and lower soul-life to coincide with its spirit-resembling functions, it nowhere makes blood and higher soul-life: there subsists a mediate connection between these two, but no immediate; the spiritual significance of the heart must yet be found elsewhere than in its being the central organ of the blood. But if it can be proved that the heart, considered in respect of its nervous character and not of its muscular mass, is the central point, in which, because it is the fountain of the blood, the two nervous systems coincide in a more significant manner than anywhere else, as it has already been shown

---

[1] In his *Elements of Psycho-physics*, ii. 382-428 (against Lotze, who, with Herbart, postulates for the simple soul-nature also a single place of retreat, and is inclined to consider the annular protuberance in the brain as this seat of the soul).

[2] Comp. Mehring, *Seelenlehre*, 1857 (sec. 46, on the seat of the soul).

[3] *Seelenlehre*, p. 65; compare, however, also p. 13. Granfelt expresses himself less definitely in his *Observationes circa Notionem cordis humani biblico-psychologicam* (Helsingfors 1847), that, from the biblical presumption that the heart is the centre and laboratory of the blood, we are led *ad simile quoddam centrum adytumque intimum, cui basin visibilem et naturalem cor carnale præbeat.*

that brain fibres go to the heart, and not merely sympathetic nerve-fibres are inwoven therein, then the spiritual importance which, according to the view of Scripture and antiquity, attaches to the heart, might be explained from the fact, that everything which mentally affects man comes to his consciousness indeed in the brain, but from thence it stimulates the heart, and from the heart reacts upon the brain, as sentiment, *i.e.* affection taken up into consciousness; in other words, from the fact, that the capacity of being subject to emotions of external or internal impressions, *i.e.* impressions originating either in the way of perception or idea, begins and ends in the brain, while it has its intermediate place in the heart. Nevertheless, this explanation is only partially satisfactory still; for, according to Scripture, the heart is not merely the seat of emotion, but also of the will and the thought. All the three spiritual activities, so far as they are reflected in the soul, and accomplished in the body, converge in the heart.

We shall approach the true solution, if we do not refuse[1] to give an unprejudiced and inquiring consideration to a phenomenon, to which—in spite of a scepticism only seemingly scientific, that closes its eyes to it, and in spite of the abuse and fraud whereby it has been degraded—must be attributed, on the ground of the most harmonious and credible testimony, the most indubitable authenticity. It is the phenomenon of somnambulism. It only so far comes within the range of our investigation here, as the declarations of somnambulists remarkably and unintentionally accord with the statements of Scripture on the spiritual significance of the heart. A perfectly trustworthy reporter, who had opportunity of observing two somnambulists,—a little girl of ten years old, and a young man who for twenty years, in the condition of so-called magnetic sleep, preached Christian devotedness in a manner that marvellously transcended his own educational position and human capacity—both somnambulists, not by human agency, but by divine dispensation,—says on this matter: "From the presumable hypothesis, that the two natural forces of positive and negative electricity correspond to the two spiritual forces of knowledge and will, whose result is perception, and that positive currents are conveyed by the several

[1] We are glad herein to have the agreement of Oehler in Herzog's *R.E.* vi. 21.

nerves of sense to the knowing power of the spirit, while the willing power conveys negative currents to the muscles, and thus through them reacts upon the external world, I conceived of the place where occurs the flowing into one another of the two electricities, as being in the two hemispheres of the brain; because all our physiologists acknowledge the brain as the chief seat of the spiritual activity. It was not until after the somnambulist said to me that the light-beam of knowledge not only penetrates to his heart, but that it also streams forth from our heart to him, that I was able to renounce this general assumption; and I am now conjecturally of the opinion, that the region of the heart and of the stomach (namely, the so-called ganglionic system, which directs all the involuntary movements of the internal organs, as the chief conductor of the negative element) is the abode of the spiritual perception; and that here is formed, by the overflow of the two electricities, the spiritual light of conscious actions stimulated from without, or of purely subjective acts." We are far from wishing to appropriate to ourselves this combination, not only of nervous power, but also of psychico-spiritual capacity, with electricity: it lies altogether beyond the horizon of our capability of judgment; but the facts from which the originator of that conjecture proceeds, are, in our estimation, uncommonly weighty, and it will not be found without result if we record at least two of them.

When the somnambulist K. (the second of those above designated) observed that one of the auditors wished to question him, but hesitated, he said, "I see through your thoughts even without question; but in order that I may glance through them with facility, would you be good enough to place your hand at the pit of my heart, and with vivacity think of a question which you wish to have answered, without asking it aloud? I will then at once answer." At this moment, his wife, who was separated from his sleeping couch by other auditors, and stood at the door of the room, thought very vividly how she would like to press forward and submit to him in thought the question long ago contemplated, whether he could long bear the bodily exertions which somnambulism caused him, in addition to his heavy smith's work, or whether her melancholy prognostic would be fulfilled, that he could not live long?

Immediately the character of his speech sympathized with the mournful tone of feeling and the anxious cares of his wife. What he replied, notwithstanding the heavenly consolation mingled therewith, made upon her so deep an impression, that she was carried out fainting, and all further question ceased.

The above-mentioned narrator relates the second fact supplied by way of illustration in the following manner. When I asked the somnambulist H., of ten years old, whether she could even see my thoughts in undulations of light which penetrated from my heart to her, she answered me, "No, I cannot see them; I am as yet still too weak for that; but I feel them dimly in my heart." As she answered me to no thought questions, but to questions expressed aloud in words, I asked her whether then she could hear my words, and she replied, "No, I hear them not with my ear; but I perceive them in my heart and in my breast, as they press into my spirit."[1]

Another somnambulist, when questioned on the nature of thoughts, gave the remarkable answer: "I apprehend the thought in the nervous system, and neglect it in memory. It seems to me at first like an electric spark which circulates in the nervous canals; hereupon it passes into the blood in the form of a crystalline atom, and comes forth thence to the daylight after it has burst the husk of its birth, and begins its operation." The conversation then continued in the following manner: *Q.* Where does it come to light? *A.* In the heart and in the brain. *Q.* In which of these two organs does it show itself first? *A.* I say to thee, in the heart and in the brain. *Q.* Which agency does it express in the heart? *A.* That of the feeling: it there makes itself visible to the spiritual eye. *Q.* I thought, on the contrary, that the brain sees it, and the heart

---

[1] Thus far from the writings of the head-master, M. Beesel, in Schöneck at Danzig, upon somnambulists and somnambulism there. There are the following works: (1) *Communications of the Somnambulist C. W. Köhn to Suckczyn at Danzig*, 1851; (2) *Last Sayings of the Somnambulist Köhn*, 1851; (3) *Literal Statements of several still living Somnambulists in the neighbourhood of Danzig*, 1853; (4) *Vital-Magnetism, or Association of the oscillating-formative Spirit- and Life-Powers with the Vibrations and Currents of the Æther*, 1858 (in commission at Homann in Danzig). These four works may serve rather than others to enable us to form a well-founded judgment on somnambulism. We commend them to such as may be capable of testing it.

merely feels it? *A.* No, the heart sees it first; but the sympathy between the two organs is so great, that it is seen almost at the same time by brain and heart.[1]

We see from these facts and statements, which might easily be multiplied by hundreds, that the head as the apex of the cerebro-spinal system, and the heart as the centre of the so-called vegetative nervous system, are two corresponding poles of the bodily agency of the psychico-spiritual life,[2] and that the heart is related to the head, as the hidden root to the manifest and outwardly-turned top of the tree. The root contains in itself all that is developed out of it. In those conditions in which the external senses are closed, the sensitiveness of the outer corporeity is as it were dead; the blood from the external parts is withdrawn, and the breathing is almost imperceptible: then the powers that are concentrated in the root break forth in fullest intensity. Although now somnambulism is a phenomenon which always falls under a pathological point of view (by which, moreover, the interference of divine or demoniacal powers is not excluded),[3] yet still it is precisely that which is morbidly abnormal, that is recognised as a principal means of ascertaining that which is normal and primitive. And we do not at all want somnambulism to prove that the internal nature of man, with its centre the heart, is the place of the deepest internalization of all psychico-spiritual activity. As well the most intensive degrees of mystical self-internalization, as the divinely effected prophecy in many of its modes of manifestation, are an evidence of it. "Like the tortoise," says an Indian religious treatise,[4] "man must draw all senses into himself. Then Brahma appears in him as fire, as lightning. In the great fire, in the aperture of the heart, a little flame will blaze upwards, and in its midst will be *âtma* (the spirit); and he who makes

---

[1] From a work of L. A. Cahagnet, which, for the rest, I put aside, as in a great measure trenching on the department of the magic forbidden in the Holy Scripture.

[2] See Solger, *Nachgel. Schriften*, i. 230, which, together with many erroneous consequences, draws moreover this right one, and places it at the head.

[3] "It is not known," says Purkinje somewhere, "whether the magnetic conditions are to be classed among the pathologic or the hyper-physical." I conceive it is not a dilemma that concerns us.

[4] See in Steinbeck, *Der Dichter ein Seher*, p. 125.

all longing after external knowledge to be silent in him—he breaks like a hawk through the meshes of the net, and has become one with nature." And in respect of prophecy, it is indeed the characteristic of false prophecy, that it originates out of the prophet's own heart, and follows the tendency of his own spirit (Ezek. xiii. 2); but, moreover, the true prophet receives the perception of the impulse of the Divine Spirit in his heart (Jer. xx. 9); and with what else does he see, except with the internal eye, which is not opened unless the activity of the outward man be withdrawn to the position of the inward man? Therefore Balaam calls himself the man of the closed eye (Num. xxiv. 3, 15). Therefore he whose inner eye is opened sees, while others see nothing, and only perhaps receive a vague impression of an extraordinary occurrence (Dan. x. 7; Acts ix. 7). It is "the concealed paradisiacal glory (restrained in materially forming activity) of central doing and seeing"[1] which is there released. For "faith, power of faith, divination, the degrees of religious ecstasy and convulsion, the steps of the wonder-working operation of faith,—these are all manifestations of the inner man, set free from bondage in the night-side, in the vital vegetative region, and established into the eternal centre."[2]

But still the question always remains unanswered, how Scripture and antiquity came to the determination of regarding that spiritual importance which the heart attains in the various kinds of manifest and obscure forms of ecstasy, as the usual normal fact; and of giving it an expression in language, which—from its first unanticipatory coinage, even to the latest time, which still always distinguishes psychically between head and heart—has maintained an almost undiminished dominion.[3] I know not how to answer it otherwise, than that the view which forces itself upon us, that all psychico-spiritual life has its seat in the head, is the result of a psychico-spiritual one-sidedness, which was

---

[1] Thus J. P. Lange, in the *Zeitschrift für Christl. Wissenschaft*, 1852.

[2] Rocholl, *Beiträge zu einer Gesch. der deutschen Theosophie* (1856), p. 109.

[3] We say "almost," for we should hardly now continue to express ourselves as *e.g.* Luther on the Holy Communion (*Works*, 30, 87): "The heart eats that spiritually, which the mouth eats bodily; but because the mouth is a fellow-member with the heart, it must finally live in eternity also for the sake of the heart."

foreign to the ancient world. "The humanity of those times," says, moreover, a later Homeric commentator,[1] "knew no one-sided activity of the understanding—no abstract thought : its perceptions were directed to practical life ; and were therefore accompanied by greater or less excitement of feeling, which manifests itself in the breast by deeper and quicker, fainter and more slow breathing, as well as by a more or less lively pulsation of the heart. Therefore it conceived of the breast as the chief place of the life of the soul. It was not until an abstract mode of thought was developed, certainly with the sacrifice of unprejudiced simplicity of mind, that the significance of the head in respect of the spiritual life was apprehended." This is precisely our judgment, but without foregoing the hope, that the simple self-consciousness of the yet unbiassed man of antiquity will one day still vindicate itself to modern science, as it did in Aristotle to ancient, in the way of physiological knowledge.[2] In any case, the present excentric preponderance of the brain-life is, on the one hand, the result of a one-sided intellectual advance, wherein we have far surpassed antiquity; but, on the other hand, it is the result of a one-sidedness of the psychico-spiritual life, wherein we are far inferior to antiquity. For this life has its root in the heart, and its crest in the head; and is therefore only then perfect, when between these two poles there subsists, without any confusion of them, but also without absolutism of the one or the other, the destined reciprocal relation.[3]

We have hitherto everywhere considered the heart not as isolated, but inclusive of what surrounds it,—namely, of the nervous tissues woven through the cavity of the breast, and

[1] Grotemeyer, *Homer's Grundansicht von der Seele* (1854), p. 5.

[2] As v. Zezschwitz, *l.c.* p. 30 : "This is the way of all spiritual development of man, that what was once consciousness of living possession of nature, is found again on the path of science." Fr. Nasse says, in his treatise on the psychical relation of the heart (1818), p. 88 : "We find confirmed, at least in the main features, what Plato, what Pythagoras, taught of the immediate relation of the heart to the soul : we must also here confess that in earlier times very many a thing was better known than in later."

[3] Grace re-establishes this life, and then, moreover, there corresponds to it, the condition of truly spiritual self-knowledge, as *e.g.* is proved by J. Böhme's answer to the question, How and in what place is the seat of the soul in man? (Q. 11 of the 40 questions on the soul.)

the abdomen, and the viscera in its neighbourhood. The following section will show with what well-founded scriptural justice we have done so.

WITHIN THE BODY—THE INTESTINES AND THE KIDNEYS.

SEC. XIII.

THE most usual Old Testament denominations of the parts inside the body, situated below the head and neck, bounded towards the back by the true and lumbar vertebræ, and held together below by the pelvis, are קֶרֶב and בֶּטֶן, of which the former especially designates the cavity of the chest with heart (1 Sam. xxv. 37, and frequently), and lungs (1 Kings xvii. 21, although their Hebrew name, רֵיאָה, does not occur in the Old Testament): the latter especially designates the cavity of the abdomen with the stomach (Prov. xiii. 25, xviii. 20, etc.), and the cavity of the pelvis with the organs of generation (Job xix. 17; Prov. xxxi. 2, etc.). That קֶרֶב appears not only as the *locale* of feeling (Isa. xvi. 11), but also of the spirit (Zech. xii. 1), of spiritual life (Ps. li. 12; Isa. xxvi. 9), and of divine wisdom (1 Kings iii. 28), cannot appear strange, since the heart is the centre of the קֶרֶב. Even the psychico-spiritual entire condition of man, and the effort and endeavour that realize it, are called his קֶרֶב (Ps. v. 9, xlix. 11).[1] But in the Old Testament also, בֶּטֶן is not only the name of that within the man which feels (Hab. iii. 16; Job xx. 23); but, moreover, of that which thinks and wills (Job xv. 35), the recipient of that which is spiritual (Prov. xxii. 18), and its moulder (Job xxxii. 19); and it signifies חַדְרֵי־בָטֶן (chambers of the body), with its many secret corners and recesses, which the spirit penetrates with its light of self-examination and self-knowledge (Prov. xx. 27, comp. 30). Used in just this way, we read κοιλία (Ecclus. li. 21, xix. 12), and in that utter-

---

[1] The LXX. frequently translates קרב, καρδία, *e.g.* Ps. v. 9 : once, when it would not be expected (Ps. li. 12), very materialistically—τὰ ἔγκατα; once very spiritually—διάνοια (Jer. xxxi. 33): neither of the two without reason.

ance of the Lord so abundantly stimulating to reflection, John vii. 38: "He that believeth on me, from his belly (ἐκ τῆς κοιλίας αὐτοῦ), as the Scripture saith, shall flow streams of living water." Here every spiritual possession is placed in the κοιλία; for the spring of living water which flows over upon others in streams, *i.e.* in abundant and efficacious manifestations, is the gift of the Holy Spirit. Thus, not only the head with its instruments of sense, but moreover, and even especially, the interior of the body, is regarded in Scripture as the place of psychico-spiritual experiences and activities; as in Ps. xxxi. 9, נַפְשִׁי, my soul, stands significantly in the midst, between עֵינִי, mine eye, and בִּטְנִי, my belly.

The bodily contents of the interior of the body are the intestines or viscera. These, as well those which are situated in the cavity of the chest, as those which are below it (see *e.g.* Gen. xv. 4, xxv. 23), are called (קְרָבִים only in Ps. ciii. 1) usually מֵעִים.[1] When David (Ps. xl. 8) says, "Thy law is within mine inward parts" (marg. my bowels), they are here named (as elsewhere—לֵב, Ps. xxxvii. 31, Isa. li. 7; קֶרֶב, Jer. xxxi. 33; καρδία and κοιλία) as the place of the most profound spiritual occupation. But far more frequently the Scriptures of the Old and New Testament, including the apocryphal Ecclesiasticus (xxxiii. 5, etc.), place the viscera in passive relation to the vehement affections. The intestines are in pain on account of sorrow (Jer. iv. 19), boil and ferment for pain (Job xxx. 27; Lam. i. 20, ii. 11), groan for sympathy (Cant. v. 4; Isa. xvi. 11; Jer. xxxi. 20). They are especially the seat of lively sympathy; wherefore רַחֲמִים,—proceeding from רֶחֶם, the womb,[2] properly signifies the viscera of the abdominal and pelvic cavity,—but directly signifies compassion (see the parallelism, Isa. lxiii. 15). The LXX. usually translates it by οἰκτιρμοί, and in a few places, where the transition from the bodily meaning into the psychical is very evident, by μήτρα (1 Kings iii. 26), ἔντερα or ἔγκατα (Gen.

---

[1] This is the traditional expression, not מֵעִים; the sing. is מֵעִי (as מֵי to מַיִם), *e.g.* in Schabtai Donolo (in the tenth century): see his treatise, *über den Menschen als Gottes Ebenbild*, edited by A. Jellinek, 1854.

[2] The connection is an actually established one; for stronger sympathy is readily reflected, and especially in the sexual organs. The word רָחַם, to love tenderly, is denominative: no deeply experienced compassion without the shadowing of the feeling of love.

xliii. 30), and σπλάγχνα (Prov. xii. 10): in this latter passage especially, another translation was hardly possible. In the New Testament (comp. also even Wisd. x. 5), σπλάγχνα and σπλαγχνίζεσθαι are altogether usual words to express tender, sympathizing, and especially compassionate love. Paul names Onesimus τὰ ἐμὰ σπλάγχνα (Philem. ver. 12); as also in Latin, *viscera mea,—in medullis ac visceribus hærere*, and similar expressions are used of every one who is deeply beloved.[1]

In that passive relation in which Scripture places the affections in respect of the viscera, there is as little remarkable, as in the passive relation in which the bones (עֲצָמִים or עֲצָמוֹת)—those bodily frameworks which contain the marrow of life—stand to deep internal good or ill health, or to powerful spiritual-psychical excitements and commotions;[2] for experience and self-observation in this matter confirm the statements of Scripture. That deep passionate excitements of mind stimulate the intestines into sympathy, we have the opportunity of feeling frequently enough. But while active expression (not merely passive emotion) of exulting joy is attributed to the bones only in two passages (Ps. xxxv. 10, li. 8),—and that with a poetic boldness whose justification is to be sought for in the idea, not in the reality,—Scripture (without, in this case, the poetic language sufficing as a ground of explanation) places even special intestines in causal relation to definite affections, and even to higher spiritual events. It is here first of all noticeable, that the cross-membrane which parts off the cavity of the chest below, from the abdominal cavity—this dividing wall (*diaphragma*) of the upper and under *præcordia*, which, moreover, itself is called *præcordia*, Gr. φρένες,[3] and is, according to the ancient Greek idea, the seat of the θυμὸς and νοῦς—nowhere occurs in Scripture (although the "walls of the heart," Jer. iv. 19, appear to comprehend in them the diaphragm on which the heart obliquely rests): only once (1 Cor. xiv. 20) φρένες occurs in the usual metonymic meaning, as understanding. Even the liver, placed on the right hand at the top in the

---

[1] E. F. Nägelsbach, *Lateinische Stilistik* (1858), p. 361.

[2] See the passages in Hupfeld, *Psalmen*, i. 99.

[3] Sometimes as the integument of the heart—κραδίη, or ἦτορ ἐνὶ φρέσ.—so that the name thus comprehends in it the membranes covering the cavity of the chest.

abdominal cavity under the ribs (כָּבֵד), and the gall (מְרֵרָה, מָרָה, χολή) fixed on to the under surface of the liver, are never named, or certainly only rarely, in a psychical connection. Bitterness, venom, gall, are in the Scripture kindred ideas. "The gall of bitterness," therefore (Acts viii. 23), is a metaphorical designation of malicious envy and ill-feeling: the reciprocal relation of the organ, and of the affection that is expressed thereby, is nowhere more closely intimated. But the liver—which, according to a widely diffused idea of antiquity, is considered as the seat of sensual desire and pleasure[1]—seems actually to be named not without this reference, when (Prov. vii. 23) it is said that the young man suffers himself to be enticed by the prostitute, till the "dart (of sensual love) strikes through his liver;" which reminds us of *jecur ulcerosum* (the love-wounded liver) in Horace (Od. i. 25, 15), and the designation of love in Plautus, as *morbus hepatarius;* against which, in Lam. ii. 11, "My liver is poured upon the earth" is only meant of the extremest bodily experience of pain; and Gen. xlix. 6, τὰ ἥπατά μου, is a false translation of the LXX. The spleen is wholly unmentioned in Scripture: its old name, which the Talmud has preserved to us, was מְחוֹל.[2] Before all the other intestines there are the kidneys

---

[1] The firm elastic mobile heart is, according to Nemesios, ch. xvi. (p. 215, ed. Matthæi), the organ of the θυμικόν, and the soft liver the organ of the ἐπιθυμητικόν τοῦ δι' αἰσθήσεως, i.e. of the longing effected by sensual feeling. Mamertus (iii. 9) therefore names insensible, dull men, *tepidi jecoris homunculi.* Firmicus Maternus says of the Persians: Unam partem capiti assignant, ut hominis iram quodammodo denotare videatur; aliam in corde statuunt, ut diversarum cogitationum varietatem, quas multiplici intentione concipimus, in modum silvarum tenere videatur; tertia pars constituitur in jecore, unde libido nascitur et voluptas. Among the Arabs, on the other hand, the liver (*kibd*) is regarded as the seat of courage (Daumas, *Pferde der Sahara,* p. 185), and the Talmud Berachoth, 60a (comp. Midrasch, Ps. ciii.), where the functions of the individual bodily organs are enumerated, says of the liver, כבד כועס, thus attributing to it anger and passion. Among the Malay peoples, the liver (*afi*) is the seat of all moral impressions and feelings. One names another caressingly, "My liver." "My liver is sick" is, in other words, "I am angry." "My liver is anxious," "My liver wishes," is absolutely equivalent, in other words, to "My heart," "My soul" (*Ausland,* 1860, p. 90).

[2] The Talmud says, *l.c.,* טחול שוחק; and this gives to the spleen a share in laughter. We recall, in connection with this, the distich: Cor sapit, pulmo loquitur, fel concitat iram; Splen ridere facit, cogit amare jecur.

SEC. XIII.] WITHIN THE BODY—INTESTINES AND KIDNEYS. 317

(כְּלָיוֹת, νεφροί), placed on both sides of the lumbar vertebræ on the hinder wall of the abdomen, of which the Scripture makes such frequent mention, and in the most psychically significant manner. It brings the tenderest and the most inward experience of a manifold kind into association with them. When man is suffering most deeply within, he is pricked in his kidneys (reins, Ps. lxxiii. 21). When fretting affliction overcomes him, his kidneys are cloven asunder (Job xvi. 13, comp. Lam. iii. 13); when he rejoices profoundly, they exult (Prov. xxiii. 16); when he feels himself very penetratingly warned, they chasten him (Ps. xvi. 7); when he very earnestly longs, they are consumed away within his body (Job xix. 27); when he rages inwardly, they shake (1 Macc. ii. 24). As the omniscient and all-penetrating knower of the most secret hidden things of man, God is frequently called (from Ps. vii. 10 to the Apocalypse) the Trier of the hearts and reins;[1] and of the ungodly it is said, that God is far from their reins (Jer. xii. 2), that is, that He, being withdrawn back into Himself, allows not Himself to be perceived by them. Moreover, טֻחוֹת (Ps. li. 8; Job xxxviii. 36) is, without doubt, a name of the kidneys, very significant (from טוּחַ, to cover with fat), as the kidneys are embedded in a cushion of fat. In the latter passage, which I translate, "Who hath placed in the reins wisdom, and given to the cock insight?" the kidneys are regarded as the organ of the faculty of foreboding,[2] as the cock is considered as a weather-prognosticator. According to the former passage, it is the kidneys into which a spiritually upright nature (אֱמֶת, as ἀλήθεια, Eph. iv. 21) is implanted.

We have thus made good what we wished to substantiate, that the Scripture subjects, not only the heart, but also the organs surrounding it,—or, as without speaking against the sense of Scripture, we may say from the standing of later physiological

[1] In Wisd. i. 6, kidneys, heart, and tongue are placed in association, as feelings, thoughts, and words.

[2] In Plato, it is the liver (not the kidneys) which, so far as the craving portion of the soul experiences influences of the reason, is the organ of foreboding (μαντεία) and of enthusiasm (Zeller, *Philosophie d. Griechen*, ii. 275). Therefore the prophetic inspection of entrails among the Greeks, Etruscans, and Romans, was especially inspection of the liver (ἡπατοσκοπία): the liver and gall are called absolutely τὰ σπλάγχνα (*exta*), and the liver τὸ σπλάγχνον.

knowledge, the entire ganglionic nervous system (the sympathetic, or, as it is also called, the *vaso-motor* nervous system), —to the influences of the soul and of the spirit; nor yet so as to place the head and the intestines in opposition to one another, as the life of thought and of feeling; but so as to suggest to us to apprehend the two in both relations, as poles corresponding to one another. The heart is the centre, whence, according to the Scripture, the soul pervades the body,—everywhere present in a manner which manifests itself locally, but yet is not local. That this pervading presence is effected by a bipartite compact nervous system, is not asserted in Scripture; but it is only by assuming the fact, that what Scripture says becomes intelligible. The nervous system, which extends through the entire corporeity, even to its most delicate and extreme subdivision of tissue, is the inner body of the soul, ever anew restoring itself from the blood. It is, as Reil[1] ingeniously expresses himself, "the peculiar body of our Ego (rather of our soul): the other parts are the body of this body, the nourishing and protecting bark of this its tender pith." Whether, besides this anatomically attested nervous system—which of itself has a wondrous arrangement that is lost in mystery[2]—there is also a so-called nerve-spirit, is questionable. The Holy Scripture knows nothing of it; the name of the soul, נֶפֶשׁ, has nothing to do with it. We cannot be satisfied when v. Rudloff[3] defines *nephesch* as the immaterial spiritual inner body of man formed from the nerve-spirit, and, in exposition of Gen. ii. 7, makes of a being with a living soul, a being endowed with a nerve-spirit.

[1] Huschke, *Schädel, Hirn, und Seele*, p. 165.

[2] "In order to give only a weak conception of the character of this marvellous mechanism," says Spiess, in a discourse of the bodily conditioning of the activities of the soul (1854), "I will mention that here generally microscopic relations are treated of, and that the thickness of single nerve-fibres themselves being taken at 1-200th part of a line (and the central fibres of the brain are incomparably finer still), in a single square inch nearly six millions of such fibres are packed, and that the mass of a civilised man's brain may, perhaps, contain upwards of 60 cubic inches. Astonishment seizes us when we think upon the marvellous riches of such an organization; and, perhaps, we may doubt whether we shall ever attain to penetrate into its mysteries, and ever to learn to know only the coarser relations of this disposition of filaments, and only the general relations of their activities entwining with one another."

[3] *Lehre vom Menschen*, p. 54.

Even the Cabbala understands by *nephesch,*—conformably to its ascending triple division, *nephesch, ruach, neschama,*—not nerve-spirit, but the animal soul. And this nerve-spirit can in no case be taken to be spiritual, in the special sense: rather it forms (if we assume its existence) the imponderable inner corporeity, adjacent to the soul, and effecting its connection with the material body—in certain circumstances probably also operating outwardly; for anything else than an excessively subtle fluid, withdrawing itself from sensible perception, as the agent of nervous activity, has never been understood thereby. The case is different, however, with this nervous æther, from what it is with the light-æther. The latter is a postulate of physics, which is on all sides experimentally confirmed; but the former is an auxiliary hypothesis of the ancient physiology, which the present science avows that it needs no longer, in that the doctrine of innervation finds, in the laws of electricity, that illustration in defect of which the nerve-spirit was discovered. Nevertheless, even now some scientific suffrages are still found to befriend it; and in the manifold departments of magnetic clairvoyance, it is a thing harmoniously and unanimously maintained and proved by numberless facts for which credibility is claimed. We do not venture to declare it a phantom; so much the less, as there are only the ordinary natural phenomena of life, for whose explanation science does not need it. But since no difficulty has been made in asserting, as an hypothesis, by way of explaining this, the existence of a periphery outside of the nervous system withdrawn from perception,—*i.e.* of a nervous atmosphere,[1]—it might perhaps be possible that this hypothesis should establish itself scientifically, if science be no longer too proud to examine inquisitively the extraordinary phenomena of the life of the soul, and no longer so frivolous as to be deservedly mocked by them. We conceive that it is modest, and yet not superstitious, when we will not deny the existence of a medium like to æther, by means of which the nervous system—this skeleton of the inner body of the soul—forms a compact whole; and that the soul under certain circumstances, by means of this medium, can produce extraordinary effects upon bodies, both endowed and unendowed with soul, and can come into relation with a world closed to its ordinary intercourse. But, as already

[1] See Hoppe, *Medicinische Briefe,* p. 288.

observed, this medium is in no case purely spiritual. It is a physical power, falling, under a physical point of view, into union with the most subtle material as its vehicle.[1] And as the anatomically recognisable nervous body, so this also—the nerve or soul æther, which from the scientific stand-point is still hypothetical for the present—is by no means the substance of the soul itself, but only the most delicate material manifestation of the soul, which in itself is immaterial.

But in order rightly to understand the relation of the soul to that many-branched light-tree of the nervous system, and generally to the corporeity, it is necessary to renounce the monistic view as contrary to Scripture as it is to experience—that the body is the self-formation of the soul. We have already referred to this error in Sec. VIII., and shown that the body, if we regard its original, does not at all proceed from the soul in the way in which the soul proceeds from the spirit. Thence it happens that the natural laws of the body bind the soul, and mediately the spirit also, against their will: thence also that the soul, in spite of its ubiquity in the body, can still only receive impressions and exercise influences in the measure of the existence of conditions which are present without its co-operation: thence that the organic processes of healthy life, and, moreover, those which accompany the functions of the soul, take place without our knowledge and will, and, in a great measure, are withdrawn from our consciousness and our control. It must not here be forgotten, that dependence and powerlessness of the soul in relation to the body actually subsist in a measure which entirely contradicts (as we have shown in Div. II. and III.) the original position, and (as we shall show further on) the destination, of man; neither, on the other hand, must it be forgotten, that even in the present position we can still always bring into experience the eminence of the soul over the corporeity, by being able to draw the unconscious into our consciousness, and to affect that which is independent by intention and direction of will. The soul knows that all the life of the body, even to its extremest end, and most delicate atom, goes forth from it; but it must also know, that the conformity to its purpose of the so wonderfully complicated nervous and muscular processes, to

[1] Rightly therefore rejected by Kurtz, *Bibel und Astronomie*, 1858, p. 580, on behalf of the angelic corporeity maintained by him.

which it is related passively,—or, whether in an instinctive or conscious and voluntary manner, actively,—is neither its own work nor its own operation. It is the impelling power of the body; but the mechanism, however conformably to the soul it is constructed, is still not constructed by it. The body, with the regularity of its organic processes, is related to the soul as a Pandean pipe, which is so arranged, that, however unskilfully the player applies himself to it, a certain harmony of tone is inevitable. If the melody which the instrument gives forth originate from the soul, the soul must know the height and depth of the individual pipes, as also their arrangement with one another. But if it know nothing of all this, the melodious association of tones is only conditioned by the organization of the pipes: and the soul effects nothing but the impulse of breath, which awakens that, which, in a designed form, is already, although only passively, present. In this similitude of a distinguished philosopher,[1] we are at once reminded of Isa. xvi. 11, where the excitement of the intestines in the deepest compassion is likened to the sounding of a harp; and of Jer. xlviii. 36, where the excitement of the heart in a similar affection is likened to the sounding of pipes. It is the breath of the soul which vibrates the strings of this harp, and blows this pipe; but neither the stringing of the harp, nor the pipe's capacity and fulness of sound, are the soul's own work.

If we now glance once more back to the relation in which the Scripture places the intestines to the affections, it cannot be denied that it makes definite organs to be made use of by this or that affection, and refers it to them. It would, indeed, be involved in an untenable popular view, if Johannes Müller were right in saying, "I know no single proof, but mere traditions, that in the healthy man a passion acts more upon one organ than upon another. No special passion acts regularly upon the stomach or the heart: in the sound man, their effects extend *radiatim* from the brain over the spinal marrow, over the animal and organic nervous system. Every special effect is also individual."[2] But this assertion, directed against Bichat

[1] A. W. Volkmann, in R. Wagner's *H.W.* ii. 542, 546.
[2] *Physiologie*, i. 815 (1834); and not otherwise Henle, Volkmann, and moreover A. Zeller, art. " Irre" in *Ersch und Gruber's A.E.* : " In the affections is shown that the entire body is a psychical organism; and only a

and Fr. Nasse,—who consider the organs of the abdomen and of the chest as the seat of the passions,—although it has otherwise become popular, does not bear the test of close examination, and analysis of the appropriate phenomena. The following is the remark of a philosopher who has entered into the most special investigation of this matter: "The assertion that the several movements of feeling do not affect the special organs of the body in a different manner, both quantitative and qualitative, is one-sided, and in contradiction to the experiences of life: it is not true that sorrow and joy stir the heart in the same measure; it is an error to say that every passion may be intensified into weeping; it is false to say, that only in the case of those who already have diseased liver, or an innate excessive tendency to disease of the liver, does anger disturb this organ. Who by unprejudiced examination would ever come to the conclusion, that the bodily phenomena of amazement and of cheerfulness, of persistent heart-breaking sorrow, and of unrestrained joyousness, are the same? The more the affections are considered without prejudice, and the more closely they are psychically analyzed, the more firm is the conviction, that as well the kind of excitement, as the most special nervous lines in which that stimulus proceeds, are peculiar to individual emotions. Why this is so—why sorrow acts upon the lachrymal duct, and confidence and hope upon the tone of the muscles, is certainly not to be understood. We may, indeed, call in the help of teleology and symbolism; but the wisdom as well as the poetry of these arrangements is not unfrequently exposed to serious risk."[1] Damerow also acknowledges the undeniable fact of experience, and commends it to general and casuistic investigation. "Altogether special consideration," says he,[2] "is required in connection with the bodily effects of the affections and passions, for the altogether individual, special, constant, or varying effects upon this or that organ." The hypothesis of Scripture, that peculiar false tradition makes the special passions act exclusively upon special organs. Only in the affections, which require a distinct member for the realization of an urgent idea and craving, does a special current towards that organ occur."

[1] Domrich, *Die psychischen Zustände ihre organische Vermittelung und ihre Wirkung, in Erzeugung Körperlicher Krankheiten* (1849), p. 207.

[2] Damerow, *Ueber die Grundlage der Mimik u. Physiognomik*, in the *Allgem. Zeitschr. für Psychiatrie*, 1860, p. 429.

effects upon single organs are proper to different affections, is thus something more than a traditional popular superstition: it is actually a scientific problem.[1] Besides, also, Scripture, in this matter, does not draw too sharply defined limitations. Among what manifold affections does it distribute the reins! It is marvellous that it thus appropriates the reins—the kidneys. The kidneys confessedly suggest the urinary apparatus;[2] and even a mutual relation of the function of the kidneys and the sexual function has been observed, which must depend upon the co-operation of the renal and spermatic nerves. Our self-observation, however, allows us only to detect mediately an influence of terror on the kidneys, by a resulting secretion of a watery urine. With what justice Scripture associates the kidneys, *e.g.* with aspiration, we cannot conceive. Does Scripture perchance name them only by way of illustration, instead of the innermost inward parts of the body? Or did antiquity feel, in this respect, otherwise than we do—namely, more profoundly and more plainly?——

The solution of our psychological problem has here reached its result. The natural state of man, as Scripture conceives and represents it, is now plain to us. We have sought to make it plain to ourselves, by pursuing it from within outwardly, according to our design expressed in the opening of Sec. I., and considering first the spirit; then its self-manifestation, the soul; thirdly, its means of representation to itself, the body. From the natural condition, we turn now to the two-fold pair of contrasted fundamental circumstances which interchangeably prevail over it. These are the contrasted conditions of waking and sleeping, of health and disease. Our position here also is the biblical one, and our point of view the psycho-

---

[1] What occurred in the investigation of the psychical significance (*psychica dignitas*) of special inner organs, may be found in Friedrich's *New Magazine of Psychology*, 1832, i. pp. 101-104, to which we direct succeeding labourers in the field of biblical psychology.

[2] The method and manner in which Haussmann, *Die biblische Lehre vom Menschen*, p. 33, after Beck, squares together the action of the kidneys in secreting urine, with the psychical importance attributed to them in Scripture, is altogether too vague. The thought of Hegel (*Encycl.*), that even the intestines are a "system of the corporealization of the spiritual," easily leads to results without foundation. For the body is *for* the soul (in its attraction to the material), but not *through* the soul.

logic one. The material on which we work consists in the direct statements of Scripture on these circumstances, and the indirect means of knowledge which it presents to us for forming a right judgment of them. Our next subject is waking and sleeping, with the intermediate condition—much referred to in Scripture—of dreaming.

SLEEPING, WAKING, DREAMING.

Sec. XIV.

THE soul, as we have concluded on biblical grounds, as well in respect of the spirit whose self-manifestation it is, as in respect of the body, by means of which it brings itself to manifestation in the midst of its sensible surroundings, is sevenfold (*septiformis*). In virtue of its seven spirit-like forms of life, it is the *doxa* of the spirit; and as it fills the seven soul-like forms of life of the body with its life, it must make this body its own *doxa*, and mediately that of the spirit also. When these twice seven forms of life are engaged, in full activity of their interacting, ascending, and descending functions,—so that even the bodily life is disclosed outwardly, and, so far as this is possible, serviceably accompanies conscious and voluntary emotions of the soul,—this is the condition of waking, the condition of עוּר (Hellenistic γρηγορεῖν, formed from ἐγρηγορέναι), or, so far as it is purposely maintained, of שָׁקַד (ἀγρυπνεῖν).

But sleep is the periodical sinking of the seventh, sixth, fifth form of life, back into the fourth, even to the first. To this nature of sleep corresponds in the most marked manner the Greek καταφορά, from καταφέρεσθαι (Acts xx. 9). The Old Testament appellations of sleep form a climax of three degrees: 1. תְּנוּמָה (נוּמָה), from נוּם, LXX. νυσταγμός, from νυστάζειν (Matt. xxv. 5); 2. שֵׁנָה, from יָשֵׁן, LXX. ὕπνος (ὑπνοῦν), the intensive of the previous word (Isa. v. 27; Ps. cxxi. 4); 3. תַּרְדֵּמָה, from נִרְדָּם, LXX. ἔκστασις, for which other translations have καταφορά or κάρος or κῶμα, i.e. deeper (Acts xx. 9) or heavier sleep (Luke ix. 32). The highest degree of profound

SLEEPING, WAKING, DREAMING.

sleep, effected or ordained by God for a special end, is designated by תַּרְדֵּמַת ה׳ (1 Sam. xxvi. 12; comp. Gen. ii. 21, xv. 12).

When man falls asleep, the first thing is, that the activity which unites everything that characterizes waking, and which is the essence of the seventh form of life, withdraws. The activity, moreover, of the sixth form of life ceases, in that the speech, which proceeds from the understanding that prepares the ideas and words, as far as it is outwardly spoken, with the organic functions that co-operate to produce it, and generally every action that is related to the outer world, and accomplished by the muscles, are suspended. Thirdly, the outer senses are closed; the origination of perceptions and ideas caused by sensation, and thus also the subjective impression of them on the mind, ceases; the receptivity of sensible perception, wherein subsists the essence of the fifth form of life, is checked. It is no extinction of these manifestations of life, only a binding; still more correctly expressed, an involution. A further retrogression is not possible. The activity of the fourth form of life continues, in the pulsation of the heart; that of the third, in the flow of the blood; that of the second, in the breathing in and out; that of the first, in the incessant renovation of the organism from the fountains of its origin. A sick man's sleep affords hope of his recovery (John xi. 12; Ecclus. xxxiv. (xxxi.) 2),[1] because that renovation is more intensive in sleep than in waking. It resembles the embryonic plastic power, as sleep, when it is profound, recalls in other ways also the embryonic condition. "Every night we sink back into that state whence we came; and the spiritual, as the bodily, life of every day contracts itself to its first roots, in order to spring up again on the following morning with new living vigour. In sweet distraction of thought, our spirit retires at first out of the hemispheres of the brain, into the chain of the large cerebral ganglions. They also become paralyzed, however: the *corpus striatum*, the *thalamus opticus*, and *corpora quadrigemina* are

---

[1] It may be translated: Sleep recovers heavy sickness, *i.e.* (with special reference to feverish disease) heals it; or, since ἐκνήφειν is elsewhere only used intransitively—according to the reading, ἐκνίψει—sleep washes away (*eluit*) severe sickness. But this occurs, moreover, in the reading ὕπνον, which gives a more fitting meaning to the first half verse; as this, that heavy sickness does not suffer sleep to come on.

able no longer either to enliven the glance or to support the limbs; the eyelid droops, forsaken by the paralyzed nerve of the muscles of the eyes; the balance is lost. Only the ever-wakeful source of our life—the *medulla oblongata*—remains unaffected by this retirement. Like the heart—*primum movens* and *ultimo moriens*—it still maintains the play of the vital muscles of the body, and the vital processes themselves. If these limits are passed, there ensues powerlessness and death."[1]

To the four bodily forms of life, to which in sleep life retreats, correspond also the spirit-like psychical: for the dream is a characteristic psychic phenomenon, in which the spirit, with the activities proper to it, transferred, as it were, into a position of repose, represents the spectator, and which it annuls as soon as its will, appearing out of inactivity, or out of a reaction as yet only feeble, begins to interfere either by way of restraint or stimulus.[2] If the sleep be profound, the sleeper does not dream at all: the soul has retreated absolutely into the unconsciousness of the first form of life, which consists in direct yet dim self-apprehension; it lives, and is moreover active, but without being manifest to itself in the lowest hidden ground of its nature. If the retreat of the forms of life pause at the fourth, or if it raise itself from the deeper submergence back again to this, the dream begins, חֲלוֹם, ἐνύπνιον (ὄνειρος only in the book of Wisdom; ὄναρ only in Matt.).[3] The unconscious will proceeds out of itself as an impulse, which, according to the man's disposition, expresses itself in this or that way, but always with less restraint and more strongly than in waking life. And the impulse seeks for itself within the world of forms, that has been stored up during the waking

---

[1] E. Huschke, *l.c.* p. 161; compare the able treatise on sleeping, waking, and kindred states, by Purkinje in R. Wagner's *H.W.* iii. 2, 431. Also Erdmann, *Psychol.* p. 19, apprehends sleep as "a return into the embryonic life."

[2] Hence we perceive a meaning, when Erdmann (*Das Träumen, ein Vortrag*, 1861, 12) calls sleep the feminine, and waking the masculine, side of human life.

[3] Göschel, *Der Mensch diesseits und jenseits*, p. 43: "As sleep may be represented as sinking (καταφορά), the dream may be represented as the rising (ἀναφορά)." Comp. the luminous representation of the course of events in Köhler, *Zachariah* (1861), p. 42.

SEC. XIV.] SLEEPING, WAKING, DREAMING.

life, an object corresponding to its own determination, in the representation of which, or its fantastic new formation, idea and volition are concerned,—a kind of birth-labour, which comes to breaking forth in the fourth form of life; ὡς ὠδινούσης φαντάζεται καρδία, i.e. as the heart deviseth to itself forms in travail[1] (Ecclus. xxxi. (xxxiv.) 5). For the proper laboratory of the dream, according to Scripture, is the heart. Thus the Scripture names the seat of the imagination (Sec. VII.), where that, which in the first forms germinates, and expands, and struggles forth, comes into daylight prepared,—and the seat of the capacity of presentiment, which does not bring forth images, but receives images into itself—that is, receives immediate impressions of the future, and generally impressions full of mystery. The head indeed is so little unconcerned in dreaming, that in the book of Daniel dreams are even called "visions of the head," and forms of the brain therefore; but depending on the day's activity of the brain, this relation is rather secondary and passive. The activity of the region of the heart, on the other hand, is increased; and thence—where, moreover, lie the roots of thought—spring forth (without piercing to the clearness of the spiritual, daylight consciousness of the free, fully conscious thought) dreams formed and coloured by sense, and, as it were, painted on the cloud-gloom of the vegetative life. "I slept," says the Shulamite, beginning to relate a dream (Cant. v. 2), "and my heart was waking."[2] Dream-forms which obtrude themselves falsely upon man as divine revelation, are called deceit of the heart (תַּרְמִית לֵב, Jer. xxiii. 26).[3]

There is none of the manifestations of life belonging to the three highest forms of life which is not carried on in the dreamer; but although not in unconsciousness, still only in phantasy, not in outer reality. For the genuine activity—which is

---

[1] Grimm remarks that the mention of women with child was rather to be expected. Not only, however, in the case of pregnant women, but also in those who are actually bearing (and even those who are shortly about to bear), various nervous disturbances may be considered as degrees between the morbid impulses and high degrees of psychical alienation (*e.g.* mania)—degrees which not seldom express themselves in hallucination.

[2] See my *Canticles*, p. 123.

[3] Corresponding to this biblical representation, the spirit of Clytemnestra, in Æschylus' *Eumen.*, says, v. 104, to the sleeping chorus of furies, ὁρᾷ δὲ πληγὰς τάσδε καρδία σέθεν.

instrumentally carried on by the body—of those powers that act externally, has ceased; they have, as being reduced to potentialities, entered into the fourth form of life, and there—often in such a lively manner, that the dreamer, without knowing it, becomes the speaking echo of the impressions inwardly received[1]—carry on their play in the picture-world of the heart. The dream is only a phantom of the waking life, a shadow which fleeth when one awaketh (Job xx. 8). Therefore the melting of the dream at awakening is in Scripture a favourite image for destruction without trace left (Ps. lxxiii. 20; Isa. xxix. 7). And emphatic warning is given against trusting in dreams. "Where many dreams are," saith the Preacher (Eccles. v. 7), "there are many vanities and words." The son of Sirach carries on this, when in ch. xxxi. 1 he says: "The hopes of a man void of understanding are vain and false, and dreams lift up fools. As he that catcheth at a shadow, and followeth after the wind, so is he that regardeth dreams. The vision of dreams is a resemblance ($\tau o \hat{v} \tau o$ $\kappa a \tau \grave{a}$ $\tau o \acute{v} \tau o v$), even as the likeness of a face to face ($\pi \rho o \sigma \acute{\omega} \pi o v$ $\acute{o} \mu o \iota \omega \mu a$)."

But this prevailing illusory character of dreams has, moreover, its reverse side. The dream is a domain of experience, to which is appropriated an intellectual, ethical, and spiritual significance far transcending the unimportance of appearance or seeming. As spirit and soul are associated as essence and manifestation, and as the peculiarity of man as such subsists in the reciprocal modification of his spirit-life and bodily life by the soul, which is the link that associates the two, it is certainly impossible, that when the soul and its corporeal self-manifestation retire to the sources whence they originated, there should not at the same time follow a withdrawal of the spirit. It may be said without hesitation, that when the man sleeps, his spirit also sleeps, so far as it does not make itself manifest outwardly as in waking life; just as the Scripture says of God, that He, as it were, sleeps (Ps. xliv. 24, lxxviii. 65), when He does not interfere in what is happening externally, as might be expected from His righteousness and truth. But, on the other hand, what the Scripture says of God, Ps. cxxi. 4, is also true of the

---

[1] This sleep-talking is called in Scripture חִזָה, Isa. lvi. 10; comp. Cant. vii. 10.

spirit, that He neither slumbers nor sleeps. As the activity of
the soul and of the body only changes its character, and does not
cease, still less does that of the spirit. " Quiescit a munere suo
externo," says Hamann in his Latin *Exercitium*,[1] " uti conditor
ab opificio suo quievit; attamen pergit operari, æque ac vivere in
somno haud cessamus, quamvis per quietem vitam non sentia-
mus." The distinction is only, that in God there is no distinction
of the consciousness of day and night; but to the self-conscious
creature its own nature is never so transparent as that of God
is to Him. And especially we, the men who live in an earthly
body, have, as the background of our being, a dim region, out
of which our thinking labours forth to the daylight, and in
which much goes forward, especially in the condition of sleep,
of which we can only come to a knowledge by looking back
afterwards. Experience confirms to us the assertion of Scripture (Ps. cxxvii. 2), that God giveth to His beloved in sleep.
Not only many poetical and musical inventions, but, moreover,
many scientific solutions and spiritual perceptions, have been
conceived and born from the life of genius awakened in sleep;
and as Lavater confesses in his *Pontius Pilatus*:[2] "If we take
together all the dream-visions in the Bible, and consider them
with a calculating glance; if, of the innumerable histories of
ancient and modern days, of all which Plutarch, Valerius
Maximus, Pliny, Suetonius, Velleius Paterculus, and so many
wise and honourable men of antiquity relate, we grant nothing,
and are willing to explain all, without exception, as deliberate
falsehoods or childish superstitions,—a course which seems to
me to involve no praise of our reasonableness and wisdom, of
our love of truth and perception of truth; if we, moreover,
bound by the spirit of our free-thinking age,—declare the whole
to be falsehood and folly, and merely hesitate at the review of
all the biblical dreams,—can we, as reverencing the Bible—we
who pardonably believe in the Bible histories—can we help

---

[1] Comp. Kahnis, *Dogmatik*, i. 186: " At the source of the actual consciousness, *i.e.* that which is definitely imprinted on the individual powers,
directed to a definite purpose, and associated with the nervous functions,
lies the potential self-consciousness, the innermost core of the spirit, which
is affected by no change of the nervous functions,—an image of God, who
neither slumbers nor sleeps."

[2] Lavater's *Ausgewählte Schriften*, von J. K. Orelli (1841), Part i. p. 155.

confessing that there is in human nature a sensorium for invisible, absent, remote, future, contingent things, for real images and sensuous symbols of such things; which sensorium, under certain contacts of higher natures, under certain influences, which in natural ways are hidden from us, may be set in motion and disposed for the perception of such things as can be perceived by no other sensorium?"

Certainly the deep of man's internal nature, into which in sleep he sinks back, conceals far more than is manifest to himself. It has been a fundamental error of most psychologists hitherto, to make the soul only extend so far as its consciousness extends: it embraces, as is now always acknowledged, a far greater abundance of powers and relations than can commonly appear in its consciousness. To this abundance pertains, moreover, the faculty of foreboding, that leads and warns a man without conscious motive, and anticipates the future,—a faculty which, in the state of sleep, wherein the outer senses are fettered, is frequently unbound, and looms in the remoteness of the future; as, among the ancients, especially Æschylus beautifully and appropriately says:[1]

> Εὕδουσα γὰρ φρὴν ὄμμασιν λαμπρύνεται,
> ἐν ἡμέρᾳ δὲ μοῖρ' ἀπρόσκοπος φρενῶν.
>
> For in sleep the spirit is clear-sighted;
> By day the spirit's vision of the future is limited.

With respect to this natural gift of divination, the Talmud names the dream the sixtieth part of prophecy;[2] and Tertullian, with respect to it, suggests, in his psychological section *de somno*, the question, *Quis tam extraneus humanitatis, ut non aliquam aliquando visionem fidelem senserit?* The dreams of Joseph in his father's house (Gen. xxxvii. 5-11), which, as became plain

---

[1] *Eumen.* v. 106.

[2] The ingenious talmudic passage *Berachoth*, 57b, runs: "Five are a sixtieth. Fire, honey, and Sabbath, sleep and dreaming. Fire is a sixtieth of hell; honey is a sixtieth of manna; Sabbath is a sixtieth of the future world; sleep is a sixtieth of death; dreaming is a sixtieth of prophecy." Similar to this is another passage, *Genesis Rabba*, c. xvii.: "Three things are fallings off (as foliage from the tree): sleep is a falling off from death; dreaming is a falling off from prophecy; the Sabbath is a falling off from the future world." R. Abin adds to these two more: "The sun is a falling off from the light of heaven; the Thora is a falling off from the wisdom of heaven."

to him subsequently (xlii. 9), figuratively predicted to him his future eminence over the house of Jacob; the dreams of the chief butler and the chief baker of Pharaoh (Gen. xl.), which, as Joseph interprets them, signify beforehand the forthcoming several issue of their destiny; the dream of the warrior in the Midianitish camp in the time of Gideon (Judg. vii. 13),—are illustrations of such dreams of presentiment (φαντασίαι ὀνείρου προμηνύουσαι, Wisd. xviii. 17-19). In all these cases the dreams are not designated as divinely produced; and there is no need of any other source of origination than that natural gift of insight[1] innate in the soul, and variously allotted to individuals and peoples, which slumbers when the man wakes, and often wakes up when he slumbers. Its representation of the future is often concealed behind enigmatical symbols; and with reference to this, Scripture recognises a science of dream-interpretation (פִּתְרוֹן or שֵׁבֶר), but as a capacity bestowed from above (Dan. i. 17; comp. Gen. xl. 8, xli. 16).

Another significant aspect of dreaming is the ethical. It is not alone the external world, with its operations echoing and growing dim in the distance, which is represented in the dream (wherefore the Preacher says, v. 3: "The dream cometh from the multitude of trouble"); but, moreover, our entire innate and acquired subjectivity is manifested there in a natural truthfulness, that breaks through the pressure of external relations and the simulation of the waking life. In the dream the man has himself before himself as in a mirror (κατέναντι προσώπου ὁμοίωμα προσώπου, Ecclus. xxxi. 3). And not merely the constitution and contents of the soul, including the state of the body, but mediately also the constitution and contents of the spirit, come to manifestation in the dream as in a hieroglyph. Is the man of a carnal tendency? It may be said of him, in some measure, when he is unconsciously sleeping, what is said of a dead man in Rom. vi. 7 (ὁ ἀποθανὼν δεδικαίωται ἀπὸ τῆς ἁμαρτίας), so far as the actual sinning ceases, although in sub-

---

[1] *Vid.* J. P. Lange, art. "Ahnung" in Herzog's *R.E.*, and E. von Lasaulx, *Die prophetische Kraft der Menschlichen Seele in Dichtern und Denkern*, 1858, 4. "As," says the Spanish physician Huarte, "there are men who excel others in remembering past events, or in the perception of the present, so there are also men who have, more than others, the natural capacity of representing to themselves the future."

stance it is only dammed up at its fountain. But as soon as ever dreaming is combined with the sleep, the spirit suffers, from the side of the dark and fiery life of the soul withdrawn from its light—driven about by the flesh and self—a degradation towards the soul; and from the selfishness of the soul, its selfish impulses, its restlessness stimulated by selfishness, are formed in the heart all kinds of sinful images, of which the man is ashamed when he awakens, and on account of which remorse sometimes disturbs even the dreamer, especially those dreaming forms that proceed from the sexual impulse and its allurements, which will be all the more dominant and unchaste the less the man in his waking state strives, and is accustomed, to keep himself in strict discipline on this side of his natural disposition. The modern doctrine of the soul, indeed, regards these dreams as free from guilt;[1] but Scripture decides otherwise, and even looks upon the involuntary emission of seed, as a loathsome contamination, which makes him who suffers it unclean for the current day (Lev. xv. 16), and even banishes the warrior from the camp (Deut. xxiii. 10); for it is a disgrace of the spirit that it has lost its royalty, and must allow itself to be involuntarily driven about by the wheel of nature. Our own conscience confirms the judgment from which the institutions of the Thora proceed; and the whole of antiquity, from India to Egypt, is unanimous on this μιαίνειν τὴν σάρκα of the dreamer (Jude ver. 5). These licentious dreams show just this, that the spirit has let go the reins; it attains to the perception of it in the veiling of the spirit that follows them. For so far as man in God has once more attained power over himself, the spirit of the sleeper sinks not into the flesh,[2] but into God, from whom it originated: it communes with God, and finds

[1] Thus, for example, Scherner, *Das Leben des Traums* (1861), p. 192: "Collectively, the sexual impulses, and their dream-images that occur in sleep, are morally wholly indifferent."

[2] The Semitic חֲלוֹם (Syr. *chelmo*, Arab. *ḥulm*) specially designate such sexual, lustful dreams; see the true development of the meaning of the verbal stem in Ges. *Thes.* But the word has become then the conception of a species of the dream: "so nevertheless, that, at least in Arabic, this denomination of the dream, on account of the sexual-sensual meaning attached to it, is avoided when prophetic, spiritual, pure, and true dream-visions are spoken of, and *manâm* or *ruja* is used. It would be a kind of *contradictio in adjecto* to say *ḥulm fsâdik*, a true dream; all the world says *manâm*

itself with its senses in God, as in falling asleep, so also still in awakening (Isa. xxvi. 9; Ps. cxxxix. 18, comp. iii. 5, iv. 8).

A third significant aspect of dreams is the spiritual: they may become the department and means of a direct and special intercourse of God with man, for specific purposes, individual, or general. We divide dreams, in this view, into dreams of conscience and dreams of revelation.[1] The witness of conscience—which, besides, in man's conscience, instinctively and judicially attends all his doings—may make itself objective, and expand within the dream-life, and the night-life generally, into inwardly perceptible transactions between God and the man. Thus God appeared threatening and warning Abimelech (Gen. xx.) and Laban (Gen. xxxi. 24) by night, in a dream; and the wife of Pilate warned her husband against being concerned in the death of the Just One, in consequence of the terror that she had experienced in a dream (Matt. xxvii. 19). Such a phenomenon, with the purpose of establishing the conviction of the sinfulness and nothingness of man, is the vision of the night with the spirit's voice, which Eliphaz relates in Job iv. 12-21. And Elihu describes (with reference to Job's utterance, vii. 13) such experiences of the sleeping man as may kindle repentance (xxxiii. 15): "In a dream, in a vision of the night, when deep sleep falleth upon men, in slumberings upon the bed; then He uncovereth the ear of men, and sealeth warnings to them, to release man from crime, and to withdraw arrogance from man. He keepeth back his soul from the pit, and his life from falling on to the sword." Dreams, or even dream-like visions, that overtake man within his nightly perception, bring him to self-acquaintance, self-consideration, and draw him back from the brink of the abyss

fsâdik or *ruja fsâdekeh*. On the other hand, *ḥulm*, plur. *aḥlâm*, is entirely in its place, when disordered, nonsensical, confused, and phantastical, vain, and lying dreams are spoken of; as the Koran (xii. 44, xxi. 5) says confusion of dreams, *ahlâmin* = confused chimeras" (Fleischer).

[1] According to Synesius (*de insomniis*), these correspond to those respectively which we call dreams of foreboding, of conscience, and of revelation —the Greek expressions ὄνειρος, χρηματισμός, ὅραμα, contrasted with which the dream as a reflex of experience is called ἐνύπνιον, and as the picture of the creating imagination, φάντασμα. Compare, for the rest, also Philo's two books on dreams. Of the original five books, only the second and third remain to us.

They print the call to repentance deeply and past forgetting, on his heart, and seal the work of grace that brings him round by chastisement from destruction. These are the dreams which we call dreams of conscience.

There are, moreover, dreams, by means of which God's special will is made known to man by the voice of God, or of an angel, in a way that it could not be known to him only from God's written word, and the points of view and motives presented by conscience; and dreams, by means of which future occurrences are made present to man,—events, the foresight of which, on account of their speciality, and their relation to God's counsel, and its fulfilment in redemption, lies far beyond the limits of the faculty of presentiment, and is essentially distinct from the mode of expression of presentiment. The prevailing psychological tendency does not acknowledge the truth of such occurrences thus apprehended: it says that in them the man becomes his own genius, and the substance of his own religious inward nature is there portraying itself. But the Holy Scripture, which has for the beginning, middle, and end of its contents and purpose, a personal intercourse of man with the personal God, although, on the other hand, warning expressly enough against dreams on account of their predominantly illusory subjective nature, yet claims a recognition of such dreams of revelation as those in which God and man stand in presence of one another as I and thou, and divinely produced forms enter into the dream-life of the sleeper, in that the Spirit of God applies ideas and conceptions which man has attained in a natural way during waking life, to give him by their means an expressive experience of the future and of eternity. The means of representation here also are human; but that which is represented itself, and its efficient cause, are divine. Such dreams as, like everything divine, bear in themselves the evidence of their divine original, are an essential link in the chain of the temporal working out of redemption. Scripture relates a great multitude of them. Illustrations of such, by which God's mind and will are revealed to the individual, are found in the dreams of Jacob in Bethel (Gen. xxviii. 12) and in Haran (Gen. xxxi. 10–13); the dream of Solomon in Gibeon (1 Kings iii. 5); the dreams of Joseph the husband of Mary (Matt. i. 2); the nightly visions of Paul (Acts xvi. 9, xviii. 9, xxiii. 11, xxvii. 23), if (which is not expressly said) they were experienced by the apostle in a sleeping condition. In such dreams as relate to the way of life of the individual, God perhaps even at times answers to sincere inquirers (1 Sam. xxviii. 6). And the dreams of Nebuchadnezzar and Daniel are examples of dreams concerning the history of the future having a more general horizon; perhaps also, considering their introduction into the history of God's people, the dreams of Pharaoh (Gen. xli.), although these moreover—not excepting xli. 25—may be regarded as God-ordained dreams of presentiment. If he who has such dreams of revelation be an appointed agent of divine revelation, they are prophetic dreams in the special sense. Waking visions probably are to be distinguished from these prophetic dream-visions, which the seer—whether by day (Ezek. viii. 1; Dan. x. 7; Acts vii. 55, x. 9-16), or, as for example Zechariah (comp. Acts xvi. 9, xviii. 9), by night—receives in a waking state. In both cases the external senses are in repose; and in both cases the freedom of action is limited to the range of that which is beheld, and otherwise is in bondage. But in the former the restraint is the natural manifestation of sleep, in the latter, the extraordinary result of an operation of God. Every deep sleep, indeed, so far as the soul is withdrawn from its relation to the outer world into its relation to itself and the spirit, and through the spirit to God, is an ἔκστασις (LXX. for תרדמה);[1] but there is also in the waking state an internal withdrawing like to sleeping and dreaming, which may arise to such a point, that the man is taken out beyond the limits of the region of his temporal life, and comes into contact with a remote world withdrawn from his usual perception (comp. נִרְדָּם, Dan. viii. 18, x. 9). This is ecstasy (from ἐκστῆναι, opposed to σωφρονεῖν, i.e. daylight, calm, discursive thinking, 2 Cor. v. 13, and to γενέσθαι ἐν ἑαυτῷ, i.e. being in one's self, Acts xii. 11), the condition of prophetic visionary intuition (Acts x. 10, xi. 5, xxii. 17), or of special *charisma* (1 Cor. xiv. 2), or, moreover, of individual extraordinary events (Acts

---

[1] Just so Philo, *in Genesin*, p. 17, ed. Aucher: Somnus in se proprie ecstasis est, non ea quae propior est amentiae (μανία) sed secundum sensuum solutionem absentiamque consilii (λογισμοῦ). Tunc etiam sensus recedunt a sensibilibus, et intellectus abest a sensibus, non roborans nervos eorum neque praestans motum illis.

ix. 3, comp. ix. 7 with xxii. 9; 2 Cor. xii. 2–4),—in the Old Testament חָזוֹן, as distinguished from חֲלוֹם (Joel iii. 1; Dan. i. 17),—a divinely wrought concentration of the entire human life upon the spiritual (Apoc. i. 10),—an internalization which is effected to the limit of the bodily life and of death, *i.e.* of the separation of the soul from the body (2 Cor. xii. 2–4). This ecstasy in waking stands above the dream of revelation, wherefore the revelations which Daniel receives begin with dreams or visions of the night (Dan. ii. 19, vii. 1); as, on the other hand, that immediate constant vision of God of which Moses was declared worthy (Num. xii. 6–8),[1] is above them both: for neither in the dream nor in the ecstasy is the object seen altogether without the veil of symbol and enigma, which are occasioned by the remoteness of God and of the spirit-world from man. That, for the rest, even in dream and ecstasy, phantoms of the heart may assume the appearance of divine revelations, Scripture is fully conscious. It warns of them, specifies the criteria to distinguish them (Deut. xiii. 2; Gal. i. 8), and is rich in warning examples. For that is the very blinding and deception of the false prophets, in whose dreams the fleshly wishes and hopes of the people that they are beguiling are embodied (Jer. xxix. 8, comp. xxiii. 32, etc.).

This classification of dreams has already led us some steps beyond the limit of this division, in which we have to consider the natural psychological condition. The dreams of the second and third kind (those of conscience and of revelation) pertain to the sphere of grace and of miracle, which break through nature. If the spirit of man, according to its original intention and destiny, rested in God, all the sleep of man, without needing supernatural operations of God's grace and power, would be a union into God; and the fulness of the spirit like to God, and united with God, would be reflected in the soul all the more intensively, that it would be the less developed by being retracted from the last forms of life to the first. Of such a kind was the sleep of Jesus. For of Him—the sinless Son of man—we read indeed that He slept, but not that He dreamt. Our sleep, on the other hand, is associated either with total obstruction of our consciousness, or with confused dreams. For after the soul has come into the service of the body,

[1] Tholuck, *Die Propheten u. ihre Weissagungen* (1860), pp. 50–52.

and the divine image of the Spirit is faded and darkened, the sleeping life of man bears the character of the Turba that the harmony of man's powers has become; and that which is in man is there manifested in confused and sinful images. Even when the innermost nature of man—the will of his spirit—is directed to the God who is his original, it has the enticements, pollutions, and disturbances that proceed from the Turba incessantly to drive away and to retreat from; and, that it may express itself more freely and purely, and become a more fitting organ of divine revelation, there is necessary a restraining and putting to death of the self-life of man's psychical body, which has incurred sin and materiality—a restraining of a more pervading and overmastering kind than that which is usual in healthy and normal sleeping and dreaming.

It will become still clearer to us how distorted and disturbed is the relation of the bodily life to the life of the soul and spirit in the present natural condition of man, when we proceed to consider psychologically, according to the hints given by the Holy Scripture, the alternate states of health and sickness between which the life of man vibrates backwards and forwards.

HEALTH AND SICKNESS.

Sec. XV.

In what, then, according to Scripture, consists the essence of sickness? Many will think that an answer to this question is neither to be sought nor found in Scripture; yet Scripture does, in truth, give us the profoundest disclosures on the essence of sickness. It tells us what is the essential origin of sickness,—namely, wrath. It tells us what is the essential condition of sickness,—namely, Turba. It tells us what is the essential process of sickness,—namely, dying, or a tendency to death.

The essential reason of sickness is wrath. "We are consumed," says the Israel of the wilderness (Ps. xc. 7), "by Thine anger, and by Thy wrath we are troubled. Thou hast set our misdeeds before Thee, and our secret sins in the light of Thy countenance." Death is declared (Gen. iii. 19) to be a wrathful decree of God; so therefore is sickness, that "lightning of death." A man's falling sick indeed, as the book of Job shows, may also be a dispensation of divine love, which desires to chastise and prove him; but sickness on that account just as little fails to be an effect of anger as death does, the sting of which is sin (see Num. xxvii. 3, where the daughters of Zelophehad say of their father, who was not implicated in the sin of the company of Korah, בְּחֶטְאוֹ מֵת, he died through his own sin). Sickness is an effect of the wrath that prevails in the world, and especially in humanity, in consequence of sin; and its relief—the relief of sickness in its entire extent—is for that very reason declared in Matt. viii. 17 to be the office of the Redeemer. By Him, love has made wrath subject to itself, in order to bring itself in humanity through sin and death to the sole dominion. But although the will of wrath has become a pure will of love towards all who lay hold of the finished redemption, yet the natural consequences of wrath still continue; and our sinful body must first yield to the fire of wrath, before the love set free by the Redeemer can begin its work of glorification in it.

The fundamental peculiarities of wrath, moreover, are also really the fundamental peculiarities of sickness: it drives man into a dull, obtuse, gloomy condition of inward being, breaks forth in violent pains, transposes the action of the wheel of life into a feverish, fiery oscillation, for which reason so many names of sickness express the ideas of burning and glowing heat.[1] Sickness thus manifests itself as an abnormal enhancement of the three first forms of life, and as a hostile exaggeration of them above the others.

For its essential condition is Turba. Sickness is always a fiery excitement, alternating with dark depression, which disturbs the equilibrium of the powers, and puts them in opposition to one another. It is always רִיב (Job xxxiii. 19), the opposite of שָׁלוֹם. How profound a fact it is, that the Old Testament language has the same word for health or soundness (*valetudo*), and peace, שָׁלוֹם (*e.g.* Gen. xxix. 6)! When in the relations and mutual relations of the bodily, and psychical, and spiritual powers, peace prevails, the man is sound,—a condition

---

[1] To these belong דַּלֶּקֶת, חַרְחֻר, קַדַּחַת, שְׁחִין, πυρετός.

which, since sin has gained possession of humanity, is never predicable in an absolute, but merely in a relative manner. Sickness is dissolution of this relative harmony. It is no parasitic form of life, which intrudes by the side of those which constitute the life of man:[1] it is a partial or total, a greater or less, setting of these themselves at enmity one with another.

Moreover, its essential process is dying, or tending towards death. Scripture gives to this fundamental feature of sickness a very definite expression in naming recovery חָיָה (מֶחֱלְיוֹ), (*e.g.* Josh. v. 8; 2 Kings i. 2, xx. 7). Sickness is therefore always a disposition towards death, a slow decease, as convalescence is always a reviving.[2] It is in this sense that the threat, "In the day that thou eatest thereof, dying thou shalt die," is actually fulfilled on the day of the transgression. Men are from that time not merely mortal, but dying. Their healthy life, for the nourishment and strengthening of which the tree of life was appointed, is from that time forward subject to the wrathful decree of death, and does not incur it immediately, only for the reason that grace maintains the decaying organism. It is still always thus. That living we die, is the result of God's wrath; that although dying we nevertheless live, is the result of God's grace.

Since sickness has God's wrath as its essential reason, and man's sin as its cause, the root of sickness lies in the spirit. Sickness in humanity began in the fact that the spirit of man became sick; both soul and body became sick only after the spirit had become so. This indeed ill accords with the view of the later psychiatry. "That, in the true sense of the word, the spirit or the soul can be sick," says an acute French maddoctor,[3] "no one can possibly grant. It is logically impossible that a spiritual potentiality—a power of pure unity and pure activity—can be affected by anything at all, that would be analogous to our idea of sickness. Sickness is a peculiarity, or

---

[1] Thus v. Ringseis in his so-called "*Ontologic*" *Medicine;* and thus also, among the older physicians, Leonh. Fuchs, in the time of Flacius (v. Preger, *Matth. Flacius*, ii. 235), calls sickness a substance by the side of, and in the substance of man.

[2] [The point of the original antithesis of expression is lost in the translation: *ableben* and *aufleben=living-down* and *living-up*, have no exact English equivalent.—TR.]

[3] Buchez, *bei Edel. Untersuchungen über das Intellectuelle Leben*, p. 9.

rather a destiny of things in the corporeal world, *i.e.* of things that are composed of parts, of things which are not unconditionally one like the soul, but, on the contrary, are formed by an aggregation of manifold molecules, which are mutable, and subjected to a constant change." On this view, according to which soul-sicknesses or soul-disturbances are properly only bodily-, and indeed brain-sicknesses, it is maintained that the spirit of a crazy man is perhaps related to the outer world, somewhat as the performer on an instrument spoiled and out of tune, to his auditors; and that sickness of soul or of spirit can only be spoken of *per synecdochen*, just as, when a man has ragged clothes, he himself is called a ragged man. But that axiom of the modern psychiatry is false. For the soul, although not composite, is still not simple; and although not simple, it is nevertheless a unity. The same is true of the spirit. Scripture teaches us, in the archetype of the Spirit, which is the essence of God the Triune, that unity and simplicity are not at all coincident ideas. Assuredly spirit and soul fall sick in their manner, as does the body in its manner. The bodily sickening affects the material means of self-representation of the soul's seven forms of life; the psychic-spiritual sickening affects these seven forms of life themselves, and the three fundamental powers of the spirit.

As Scripture names the result of departure from God spiritual death, so must it also be said, since this death does not consist in annihilation of the spirit and the soul, that the life of both is sick in the ethical sense, when it either is tending to spiritual recovery or ends in spiritual decease. In this sense we read in 1 Tim. vi. 4, νοσεῖν, of a morbid desire of the spirit (νοῦς) after a knowledge indifferent to the blessedness of God, and estranged from it; and in similar reference, in 1 Tim. vi. 5, 2 Tim. iii. 8, of men with corrupted spirit (διεφθαρμένοι τὸν νοῦν). And Jeremiah says (xvii. 9) of the heart of man as it is by nature, that it is uneven or rugged (comp. Isa. xl. 4; Ps. cxxxi. 2), and deadly sick (אָנֻשׁ), in a manner that is only altogether manifest to God. The relation of the spirit and the soul to God, to themselves, to their own corporeity, and to the world, has sustained a perversion militating against the will of God and the destination of man, which is of necessity at the same time a morbid affection of the constituent powers of the

nature of the soul and spirit (Div. III. Sec. II.). But if soul
and spirit be morally perverted, the body also is not in a normal
condition. The primal sin of the first created men had decease
of their bodies as its consequence; and the inherited sin, in
which it is propagated, has a manifoldly diversified, but still
never absolutely failing, bodily inherited sickness as its accom-
paniment. And as inherited sin breaks forth into actual sins, so
does the inherited sickness, in consequence of those actual sins,
break forth into all kinds of actual sickness. Spirit and soul,
when they in a conscious manner pervert themselves, make the
body sick, either by making use of it directly as an instrument
of their sinful impulses and lusts, or by consuming it by their
passions (*e.g.* sensual love, 2 Sam. xiii. 2), or by not knowing
how to regulate it, by reason of the discord prevailing in themselves and thus disproportionately cultivating it, wantonly
exposing it to danger, and generally disturbing and distorting
the compact co-operation of its elements. The prevailing sin
in the human race, into which the individual is entangled by
his birth and relation, is the cause of all sickness; and the
actual sins of the individual are the cause of many sicknesses.
Very few physicians have a perception of these sources of
sickness. One who really cares for the soul is here the best
physician, but power and blessing come from God the Saviour.

We class the sicknesses caused by excessive affections with
those that are caused by actual sins. "Hope deferred," says
Solomon (Prov. xiii. 12), "maketh the heart sick." Deep inward sympathy, anxious care, is called directly, in 1 Sam. xxii.
8, חָלָה (*vid.* Ges. *Thes.*); and the highest degree of heart-
sorrow bears the name of אֲנוּשׁ (Isa. xvii. 11; Jer. xxx. 15).
Experience corresponds to this manner of speaking. If the
affections, by which passing or abiding feelings are accompanied, become so strong and deep, that they make the life
of the body sick, or altogether destroy it, it is always the
inward man who first allows himself to be overpowered by
them. As the sicknesses of the first kind are rooted in the
fact that the spirit, perverting itself to sin, perverts also the
life of the soul and body; so the sicknesses of the latter kind
are based in the fact, that the spirit having altogether, or even
only for a season, forfeited its power over itself in God, knows
not how to maintain itself against forcible impressions, but

itself exposes to their attacks, together with itself, the life of the soul and body. This powerless subjection of the spirit has its degree. If it goes down to a very low grade, the man becomes mad (מְשֻׁגָּע, Deut. xxviii. 34). Thus, also, in such cases the psychical-bodily sickness has its issue in the spirit. The essential condition of man would not be that of personal unity, if those were right who think that the human spirit would remain unaffected in such a case, and be suspended on high unapproachably, like the moon behind the clouds. But if the spirit, as we maintain, be at once interested in a primary manner, then the sicknesses of this second kind also have their mediate final source of origination in sin. For the powerlessness of the spirit, its immediate ground of origination, is the consequence of its separation and remoteness from God. United with God, it would participate in God's blessed peace, and power to subdue all disturbances of the same. We are not forgetting in this, that there is also a divine zeal which consumes the corporeity (Ps. lxix. 9); a guiltless pure love (Cant. ii. 5); a justifiable affliction over the decay of the church (Amos vi. 6); a salutary repentant sorrow, and other holy affections which draw the body into sickness in sympathy. But this proves nothing against the point that we have asserted above. For that holy affections should produce destructive effects upon the corporeity, would be impossible, if the mutual relation of man's inner and outer life had not by means of sin become an incongruity.

In the two kinds of sickness alluded to, the spirit gives the impetus to the sickness. But because the pervading reciprocally conditioning relation of the spiritual-bodily natural condition of man has become abnormal through sin, soul and spirit fall sick frequently also by the agency of the body. Morbid conditions of the body, founded in causes of an inward or outward physical nature, act upon the soul and spirit; and not merely in such a way that they beget the feeling of displeasure and of pain (חָלָה, Prov. xxiii. 35, Jer. v. 3), but also by opposing all kinds of obstacles to the psychic-spiritual activities, so far as these are instrumentally carried out and conditioned, and bringing disturbances into their action. If spirit and soul are strong enough to hold their ground against the impulse of these obstacles and disturbances, and to make an effectual resistance, they will, in the carrying on of such a contest and victory, become so much the stronger, more independent, and more rich in experience. On the other hand, the sickness of the body acts with such overmastering power, that it either loses all self-manifestation of the spirit and the soul in the passivity of the feeling of sickness, or else takes prisoner the innermost personal life by delusive ideas. In the latter case, the sickness of the soul or spirit appears in a more restricted sense. Scripture designates it as an alteration[1] of the understanding (שָׁנָה טַעְמוֹ, of which *Pi.* is, "to behave as spiritually sick"), or as a change of the heart (Dan. iv. 13). There is hardly a class of spiritually diseased persons who are not mentioned in the Scripture. The maniac is called (Prov. xxvi. 18) מִתְלַהְלֵהַ; and probably מִגְנַת לֵב (Lam. iii. 65) is a name for insanity. We have an instance of melancholy (רוּחַ רָעָה) in Saul, and an instance of metamorphosis (*insania zoanthropica*) in Nebuchadnezzar. David assumes the behaviour of a lunatic (מִשְׁגָּע) in the house of Achish, in order to preserve himself (1 Sam. xxi. 14–16). The characteristic of the frenzy, if this be apprehended as a conception of spiritual disorder, is this, that the illusion of another new personality is substituted in the place of one's own real one: wherefore, on the one hand, מְשֻׁגָּע or אֱוִיל (Hos. ix. 7) is applied as an opprobrious name to the prophet, because the word of Jehovah is derided in him as exaggerated fancy, *i.e.* sick dreams in a waking state; on the other hand, הִתְנַבֵּא (1 Sam. xviii. 10) is also used of the speech and demeanour of a really spiritually disordered person; because prophecy and mania, according to an ingenious observation of Schleiermacher, symphonize, and are associated as true speech, and deceitful speech. The former, אֱוִיל, in Hosea (properly, the loose, sluggish man), indicates rather a deranged than an insane man: the deranged or crazed man has not the compact false personality that is peculiar to the insane; the Ego of the latter is altogether decomposed by false illusions, and hurried away by desultory disconnectedness of thought. Another name of this spiritual disorder is הוֹלֵלוּת (Eccles. x. 13, comp. ii. 2), the folly enhanced to sickness (of the soul) (סִכְלוּת). Finally, the Scripture is not wanting also in an

---

[1] Not alienation; for שָׁנָה טַעְמוֹ does not mean, his understanding is gone, *alienata est*, but, it has become changed.

appropriate designation of imbecility and stupidity (*torpor*), namely תִּמְהוֹן לֵב (coupled with שִׁגָּעוֹן, Deut. xxviii. 28).

There are, moreover, bodily sicknesses which have ethical, and which have sentimental, and which have physical causes. And there are diseases of soul and spirit which proceed from ethical self-perversion, or from sentimental disturbance of equanimity, or from physical restraint and interference: the two first have bodily anomalies as their result, and the last have such as their cause. A dynamical disturbance of the cerebral life, or generally of the nervous system, is associated with every spiritual disorder, of whatever kind it may be: without an **ab**normal affection of the nerves, it can attain no substantial existence. But that, without exception, all psychical diseases have physical causes and reasons, is contrary to experience; and even if it were true that, in the *post mortem* examinations of spiritually diseased people, pathologic circumstances of the brain were found[1] for the most part to confirm this, it would still in no way follow therefrom. There are psychical diseases which have their root manifestly in the various kinds of spiritual selfishness, as pride, envy, avarice, and vices of this kind; and therefore in the personifying fundamental powers of the spirit, and which begin from thence to draw the body into special sickness. Certainly, as there are for psychical disorders of a sentimental kind physical inducements, so for psychical disorders of a purely ethical kind there are physical attractions, —to wit, for all that are associated with the sexual life. But these physical attractions still only then operate in a way of disorder, when the soul and the spirit are wanting in power of resistance, to prevent their growing powerful over themselves, to their own disturbance. The fact of the transmission of sinful dispositions embraces here, indeed, a world of mysteries which cranioscopy has undertaken to ventilate; but the hereditary

---

[1] Comp. F. W. Hagen, *Psychiatrie und Anatomie*, 1855, p. 46: "The *post mortem* results in the brains of spiritually disordered persons are not of such a kind, that we could seek in them the proximate causes of psychical disease;" and *ibid.* p. 54, "Anatomical experiments hitherto ought surely to have taught sufficiently, that as the specially inner life of the brain is not visibly material, even its aberrations cannot always be expected to be such as you can grasp with the hand." The change of substance does not usually appear till the later stages. There are abnormal conditions which predispose to disease; but most of these are not causes, but consequences.

sinful destination, in its individual blending, is just the ethical problem into which man finds himself planted; and for which, moreover, when he comes in general to full consciousness, and is not from his birth of a checked and troubled spirit, he is sufficient, so far as he draws powers from God, and collects his powers in God.

NATURAL AND DEMONIACAL SICKNESS.

Sec. XVI.

If death came into the world through Satan, who tempted the first created man, all sickness goes back to him who has the power of death (Heb. ii. 14), as its ultimate cause, but it is well to be noted, its ultimate cause within the range of created things; for the final super-creative cause of death and of sickness is God, who manifestly (Isa. xlv. 7) is as well creator of the darkness as former of the light, as well the maker of peace as the creator of evil (בּוֹרֵא רָע), *i.e.* not certainly of evil in the sense of what is done, which comes into existence from the freely-choosing created will and only from this, but of the possibility of evil, and of the self-punishment of evil, and generally of the evil that comes in the form of punishment. Satan is the first who established the possibility of evil implied in created freedom, on the ground of actuality, and thereby became the object of the divine anger, and the material of the divine vengeance of fire, which expresses itself in him, as a power to destroy his purely spiritual nature, and in the spirit-embodied man as a power of death. This power of death is God's, and it is Satan's only so far as everything which has not become absolutely free from his dominion, succumbs to this power of death set free by him: for the presence in the world of divine wrath is centralized in this spirit of wrathful fire, who was first a spirit of the light of love; and when he gave up his glorious position in the principle of love, he became a prince in the principle of wrath.

But we should greatly err, if we thought that all death and

all sickness, without exception, is only in a various manner the operation of Satan, or of other evil spiritual natures.[1] I find no such thought as this founded in Scripture. The one final cause of all evil is the divine wrath that follows as the self-punishment of sin,—a wrath which certainly Satan kindled in God's creation, and especially in humanity, but without thereby becoming also the mediator of all individual operations of the wrath of God, since God indeed makes even good angels mediators of the same; as, *e.g.*, the plague (2 Chron. xxi.) had its occasion in a satanic temptation of David (ver. 1), but in itself appears as the divine agency of the angel of Jehovah (ver. 15). Moreover, as there are sicknesses and deaths that are the divine operations of good angels (Isa. xxxvii. 36; Acts xii. 23), so there are also such as are immediately decreed by God, as *e.g.* is expressly said of the leprosy of Uzziah (2 Chron. xxvi. 20), and of the blindness of Elymas (Acts xiii. 11). Such sicknesses as do not evince any *concursus specialis* of divine interference, we call natural. As there are fleshly and satanic temptations, so also there are natural and demoniacal sicknesses. Scripture, indeed, expressly distinguishes in Matt. iv. 24, viii. 16, Mark iii. 15, and in many other passages, between these two kinds of sickness. The former have, as their immediate cause, the principle of wrath which rules over the present world together with the principle of love; the latter, on the other hand, are effected mediately by Satan and other spiritual natures. For there is beyond and beneath Satan an entire large kingdom of super-terrestrial natures, which, in self-exaltation against God, have extinguished in themselves the divine light of love, and have become wholly and absolutely vessels of divine wrath. This is the kingdom of שֵׁדִים; in Greek, of the δαίμονες or δαιμόνια.[2] That these can exercise upon men a destructive influence, not merely of an ethical, but also of a magical kind,

[1] See Hofmann, *Schriftbeweis*, i. 446, comp. 357; Hahn, *Theologie d. N. T.* i. 304, 374; Philippi, *Glaubenslehre*, iii. 322.

[2] The definition (which sounds Swedenborgian) of Josephus, *Bell.* vii. 6, 3, τὰ δαιμόνια πονηρῶν ἐστιν ἀνθρώπων πνεύματα, is false; yet there appear credibly attested experiences to affirm that the demoniacal kingdom, in its destructive influences upon men, is strengthened by the psychical spirits of those who have died in sin. Thus also judges v. Rudloff, *Lehre vom Menschen*, pp. 176, 280. But there is no Scripture testimony at hand which would be favourable to it.

SEC. XVI.] NATURAL AND DEMONIACAL SICKNESS. 347

is to be accounted for from the fact of the relation of bondage and affinity into which the human race has fallen to this invisible kingdom of darkness since the primal sin. The power of wrath of this kingdom over men, however, only reaches so far as God permits it; and this permission is measured according to His holy will of righteousness and grace, which makes all created powers, whether of wrath or of love, minister to Himself.

We first of all present to ourselves only symptomatically the demoniacal forms of sickness that Scripture places before our eyes, in order that we may then form thereupon, so far as they come within the range of our purpose, a psychological judgment.

Demoniacal sicknesses consist partly in physical, partly in physico-psychical constraint. Most of the cases of demoniacal sickness of which Scripture makes mention, are (and this is not commonly sufficiently considered) of the former kind. The elephantiasis of Job which the prologue of the book makes to proceed from Satan by God's permission, is a purely physical disease; for the high spiritual disturbances which are associated therewith, even if in the meaning of the book they are to be regarded as satanic, are still no special manifestations of psychical disease. Of a like purely physical kind, is the crooked spinal complaint of a woman for eighteen years, mentioned in Luke xiii. 11; where, moreover, πνεῦμα ἀσθενείας, without having a personal sense, indicates the hidden power of disease:[1] for the cure in this case was only the result of the laying on of hands, and was not effected by means of exorcism. Even the periodic attacks of disease, in which Paul is given to feel the buffets of the messenger of Satan, were only a bodily evil; for he calls it a thorn in the flesh, by which God would keep him in humility (2 Cor. xii. 7). A special kind of such demoniacal

[1] For Luke expressly distinguishes between πνεύματα πονηρά and ἀσθένειαι (viii. 2, comp. v. 15). On this impersonal use of רוח, see Bucher's *Magic and Magical Modes of Healing in the Talmud*, p. 177. One says, רוח צרדה, spirit of spasm; רוח חזזית, spirit of a malignant attack (see my *Commentary on the Hebrews*, p. 396, obs.), and the like; just as, on the other hand, sicknesses are certainly personified as demons, *e.g.* קרדיקום, καρδιακός (Gittin, 67b). To the impersonal pathologic use of πνεῦμα is allied the moral use of πνεῦμα, to indicate an overmastering power of a spiritual kind, as πνεῦμα ζηλώσεως, πορνείας, πλανήσεως. Vid. v. Zezschwitz, *Profangräcität u. bibl. Sprachgeist*, p. 70.

bodily diseases is the magical binding of organs that in themselves are healthy, as in the case of the dumb man (Matt. ix. 32), and the man who was at once blind and dumb (Matt. xii. 22-24). The Lord heals them both by driving out the demons. For demons have taken partial possession of their corporeity, and have insinuated themselves therein. From this possession and settlement the Lord drives them forth. The narrative gives us no right to regard the dumbness as dumbness arising from idiocy, as idiotic dulness; for on one occasion it is associated with blindness. Just so, moreover, the form of disease of the σεληνιαζόμενος, who had been dumb from childhood, whom the Lord healed on coming down from the Mount of Transfiguration, is without any special psychical feature. The symptoms consist in convulsive movements, contortions, extensions, and the like (Luke ix. 39-42); painful crying out (Luke ix. 39), foaming at the mouth, gnashing with the teeth (Mark ix. 18), wallowing on the ground (Mark ix. 20), helpless falling down at the risk of life (Matt. xvii. 15), consequent pining away (Mark ix. 18, if ξηραίνεσθαι does not here mean rather numbness or rigidity). These are all symptoms of that which, in ancient medicine, is called *morbus comitialis*, or (in Hippocrates and Celsus) *morbus sacer*,[1]—of that incurable evil [2] with which are frequently associated also mental disturbances. But those morbid phenomena of the demoniacs are still not merely epileptic. For the boy is, moreover, deaf and dumb; and the Lord cures him by driving out "the deaf and dumb spirit" (Mark ix. 25), *i.e.* the demon who stood in relation to the deafness and dumbness as cause for the effect. The question whether, according to the biblical view, the epilepsy in itself is in every case a demoniacal agency, is rather to be answered in the negative than the affirmative. The σεληνιαζόμενοι, at least (Matt. iv. 24), are expressly distinguished from the δαιμονιζόμενοι. The characteristics that are in other cases peculiar to epilepsy and lunacy, accompany, in the case of that boy, only the deafness and dumbness in which the Lord recognises the distinctive feature of the disease, and the abode of the

---

[1] *Vid.* Winer, *R.W.* ii. 163.

[2] The ancients used for it even beasts' and man's blood; *vid.* Th. Bartholinus, *De Sanguine vetito* (1673), p. 8. Even still, at the present day, there is a superstition that the blood of an executed criminal is a means of healing.

SEC. XVI.]   NATURAL AND DEMONIACAL SICKNESS.   349

demon, as is shown by the form of His exorcism ("Thou dumb and deaf spirit, I charge thee come out of him"). It is manifest from this, that even the purely physical disorders which Scripture designates as demoniacal, are of an extraordinary nature, and do not coincide with the usual diseases that are symptomatically allied with them. There are demoniacal powers by which, in these cases, the bodily life is taken hold of, as is plain from the fact that its functions are paralyzed and disordered in a way distinct from the ordinary causes of disease. The disease is a demoniacal one, but (although not without psychical reflection) it is a purely physical one.

The demoniacal sickness does not become perfect possession until it announces itself not merely in physical, but at the same time in expressed psychical phenomena. We have such an illustration of the specially possessed (δαιμονιζόμενοι, δαιμονισθέντες, δαιμόνιον ἔχοντες, in the narrower sense [1]) in the demoniacs of Gadara. We discern in them the following symptoms: they roar frightfully (Mark v. 5); they rend asunder, with unnatural strength, the bonds with which they are bound (Mark v. 3); will bear no clothes (Luke viii. 27); they rage violently against themselves (Mark v. 5); they do not stay at home, but sojourn day and night in burying-places and mountains (Matt. viii. 28; Mark v. 5), and furiously attack those who approach them (Matt. viii. 28, comp. Acts xix. 16).

---

[1] There are other designations in Luke vi. 18, Acts v. 16, viii. 7, x. 38. The later ecclesiastical designation was ἐνεργούμενοι, Guericke, K.G. i. 166 (ed. 8). The name "Possessed" is not used in the New Testament; but in Josephus, Ant. vi. 11, 2, it is said of Saul, σοῦ τοῦ πονηροῦ πνεύματος καὶ τῶν δαιμονίων ἐγκαθεζομένων. Singular, that in the Talmuds, which are crammed full of demonologic principles, there is no word for possession; and the very idea is wanting. It is said that an evil spirit abides in one, or takes hold of one, hurries one abroad, and the like; but not that it enters into one and possesses him. J. Therumoth 40b, the שׁטה (the madman) is described in a similar manner to the two Gadarenes, but there is nowhere formed an adjective from or with שׁד which corresponds to the New Testament δαιμονιζόμενος,—a proof how defectively the Talmuds reflect the position of Judaism at the time of Christ. In the language of Christendom, and also of Islam, "Possession" became the customary expression. In Arabic, the possessed is called mascûn, malbûs, m'amûr, scil. li-l-'ginn (of a genius, i.e. demon). The language of the church distinguished possessio from obsessio as a lower degree.

These symptoms correspond to that which, as a natural disease, is called intermitting insanity.[1] By the inclination to graves and desert places, this intermitting character betrays at once its demoniacal character; but the morbid type of one specially possessed is first completed in the fact that the demon, or the demons, with entire supplanting of the man's self-control, either mediately, availing themselves of the human organs, or immediately, speak out of him.[2] Thus we hear them speak out of the Gadarenes possessed (Matt. viii. 29, 31); out of the one in the synagogue at Capernaum (Luke iv. 34), from whom the demon issues, crying with a loud voice (Mark i. 26); from the one in Ephesus (Acts xix. 15). Thus they spoke out of those many whom Jesus healed, when He as the Christ constrained them to be silent (Luke iv. 41, and the parallel in Mark); thus they must also have spoken out of Mary Magdalene, as their number is specified (Luke viii. 2, comp. viii. 30). That these were spirits who spoke out of such sick people, is shown by the fact, that what was uttered betrayed a clear-sighted vision of the person and work of Jesus, which transcended the degree of knowledge of the men of that time; and that they were evil and impure spirits, is manifest from this, that they would have nothing to do with Jesus, and that His proximity enhanced the furiousness of the possessed one, so that he himself is afraid of the access of pain that approached with the accomplishment of the cure (Mark v. 7). In all these cases the Lord performed the cure by exorcism, once by means of agency from a distance (Mark vii. 30).[3] The demons of the two possessed men at Gadara pray

[1] V. Spielmann, *Diagnostik der Geisteskrankheiten*, 1855, pp. 42–45.

[2] Even the declarations of the diseased man, that he harbours the devil in him, are not yet sufficient. These declarations may, as I myself have had opportunity of observing in a sick man, depend upon delusion. The demonomaniacs, so called in the later psychiatry, are not all possessed as well; and, at all events, the possessed ones depicted in the New Testament are rather of the predominating melancholic than of the frenzied type of possession. Of the writings of the old school, compare especially, Christ. Scriver, *Das verlorene und wiedergefundene Schäflein*, 1672, etc.; and of the writings of the later school, Blumhardt's *Vertheidigungs-schrift gegen de Valenti*, 1850.

[3] How altogether different is the proceeding of the Jewish exorcists! According to Josephus, *Bell.* vii. 6, 3, there grew in Jerusalem, in the valley of Βαάρας, bounding the north, a fire-coloured plant of the same name, of which he relates fabulous things. This only needs the demoniac to be brought near, and it drives out the demons. Eleazar, whom he himself,

Jesus, in whom they recognise God's Son, their future Judge, that they may be allowed to go into a herd of swine; for, concealing themselves in bodies, and venting their rage on bodily creatures, the demons find an alleviation of the sense of wrath with which their merely spiritual nature is seized and pervaded. The Lord grants to them that which they ask for, that for the two possessed men their wonderful deliverance might be all the more convincing; but the swine, feeling themselves laid hold upon by a foreign power, plunge into the sea.[1]

Having thus stated the fact, the task is imposed upon us to make it psychologically clear to ourselves as far as it is possible. In doing so, we proceed from a treatise that introduces us into the centre of the matter by Dieringer,[2] the same Roman Catholic theologian who, in his work entitled *A System of Divine Facts* (1841), so learnedly brought together the testimonies of the ancients on the continuance of the gift of casting out of demons, and of other miraculous gifts in the first Christian centuries. Humanity ensnared in sin by the fall, as such, says he, finds itself in an inward affinity with the fallen spirits, which exposes it to their seducing and tormenting influence; but how far this power may manifest itself in the individual man, depends not only on his moral self-attestation, but generally on the kind and manner of the interest

---

in the presence of Vespasian and his son, saw make proof of his power over the demons (*Ant.* viii. 2, 5), held a ring, in which a root specified by Solomon as of healing virtue was enclosed, under the sick man's nose, and by conjuration and rehearsing of Solomon's formulas drew forth the demon. In order to convince those present of the reality of the occurrence, he placed a vessel full of water, or a foot-bath, on the ground, and bade the demon to overturn it, in order to certify the spectators of the fact that he had left the man. Thus was the art of exorcism practised also among the heathen: θυμιάμασι καὶ καταδέσμοις; see Martin's *Dial.* c. 85. In respect of such a circumstance, and of Acts xix. 13, what the Lord opposes to the Pharisees (Matt. xii. 27), is only an *argumentatio ad hominem:* if they attribute what their exorcists perform to divine power, it can certainly not be demoniacal powers by which He, Jesus, overcomes the demons in such strength and such extent as no other can.

[1] Let the Manichæans explain, says Jerome on this point, if the souls of men and of beasts are of the same nature and of the same origin, why two thousand swine are drowned for the sake of delivering one or two men.

[2] Art. "Besessenheit," in Aschbach's *Allgem. Kirchen-Lexikon.*

which the individual, according to the inscrutable decree of Providence, is to have in the common misery of the whole race: for although all sickness is a consequence and punishment of sin, still in the general, the personal guilt of a man is not to be measured according to the share which has fallen to him in the physical sufferings and privations of the race (John ix. 1-3, and book of Job). Possession is, besides, only in degree distinguished from the influence which the hostile powers strive to exercise more or less over every man; and it has its fearful aspect only in its appearances that strike the eye, while other modes of operation of fallen spirits withdraw themselves from external perception, but on that account may become all the more destructive to the souls of those who have given them admission. Judas was not a possessed man, and yet Satan entered into him, and seduced him into a blacker deed than ever demoniac could accomplish (John xiii. 27). After determining hereupon the preliminary degrees of possession,—the temptations and seductions (*tentationes*), the snares (*insidiæ*), the besieging (*circumsessio*), and the blockade (*obsessio*),—Dieringer seeks to establish the distinction of the actual possession (*possessio*) from these four degrees, and finds it in the fact, that in the possession, the juxtaposition which still finds place in the *obsessio* of the corporeally effected self-attestation of the demon on the one hand, and on the other of the human soul, has ceased, inasmuch as the demoniac force has entirely appropriated to itself the use of the bodily organs, or at least has deprived the soul of their use, in such a way that the soul appears as if in bondage; but is, in fact, only thrown back upon its own internal nature, and remains remote from the destructive influence of the evil one, so long as it does not voluntarily acquiesce in it. Seldom, moreover, is this bondage a total one in such a sense as that the soul should not still at times come forward as an active principle; so that the conditions of possession and obsession frequently alternate one with another. How such a state of things comes to pass, is one of the hardest of problems. Thus much is certain, that a demon can never substantially take up its abode in the human soul, and make this a mere instrumental agency, nor become, in place of the soul, the inner living principle of the body; for, in the former case, the freedom of the soul would be abrogated; in the latter, the living unity of the two natures of man would be rent asunder. And yet this influence of the demon is not to be thought of as merely virtual, which would on the one hand be opposed to unequivocal Scripture language, on the other, to the nature of the case itself. Probably, therefore, we shall speak most correctly, with J. von Görres, in saying, "that while the soul from within outward is sheltered under all its capacities, the demon from without inward endeavours to shelter himself under them; and when he has attained with this inward pressure to a certain point, the state of possession begins." In actual possession, therefore, there is found a sway over the capacities and domains of the soul, which is effected by external intrusion, on which account also there may be several of the demons who seize possession. The natural precedent condition may be found in a responsible or irresponsible bodily psychical and moral predisposition.

Thus the case actually stands. Nevertheless, we cannot concur in the view, that in possession culminates the same demoniac influence upon man, which begins at the lowest point with demoniacal temptations and seductions. Between such ethical influences and possession there subsists not merely a gradual but a specific difference,[1] as may be gathered from the fact that the Lord does not exercise a moral influence upon the demoniacs, as if they were corrupted, and so become preeminently evil, but regards them as only peculiarly diseased, who are to be healed first of all by loosing the ban which oppresses them.[2] In three points, however, the explanation has our entire assent. Firstly, it proceeds rightly on the supposition, that the soul is no absolutely simple monad, but a compact abstract of manifold powers. Secondly, it rightly asserts an actual irruption of the demoniac force into the region of these powers. It is not sufficient that the ancient dogmatists make the soul to be only sympathetically affected in the so-called bodily occupation.[3] Demoniac power, in the bodily occupation not less than in the so-called spiritual, takes prisoner the soul, and even the spirit; yet with the distinction, that in the spiritual occupation the will of man is slavishly forced by the evil spirit,

---

[1] Thus quite correctly, v. Rudloff, *Lehre vom Menschen*, p. 274.
[2] *Vid.* A. Zeller, art. "Irre," in Ersch u. Gruber's *Allg. Encyklopädie*.
[3] Quenstedt, *Systema*, i. 650.

without its ceasing to be actually free, and thus accountable;[1] whereas in the bodily occupation, all impulse and act of man is the involuntary result of a magical compulsion. Thirdly, it is true that the demoniacal violation takes its course from without inwards, and indeed through the corporeity. It is impossible that Satan should bind the man's freedom of action by immediate agency upon his spirit. Such a demoniacal bondage could not become possible, except by the man, as a spirit-embodied nature, coming into bodily conditions which would result in confusion, weakening, and paralyzing of his psychical and spiritual powers.

In conformity with this, the specific character of possession consists in this, that demons intrude themselves between the corporeity—more strictly, the nervous body—and the soul of man, and forcibly fetter the soul together with the spirit, but make the bodily organs a means of their own self-attestation full of torment to men. Possession—as Eschenmeyer[2] defines it on the ground of special observations—is that unnatural operation, in which one or more impure spirits through any sort of agency intrude into a human body, make themselves masters of the instruments of sensation, of movement, and of speech; attach the power of the soul to them, and in shorter or longer paroxysms make themselves manifest in strange sounds, gestures, and movements, for the most part of a mocking, licentious, and violent kind. In the same manner, also, Ebrard[3] conceives of possession as the binding and affecting of the bodily-psychical life by a foreign influence proceeding from without: " The soul finds itself no longer in possession of its body; a strange something has forced itself between it and its body, and exerts a disturbing and hindering influence upon the bodily organs of the psychical life." And in harmony with Ebrard, v. Rudloff,[4] although opposing it, explains that which is expressed in the first edition of this our system: " The soul of man is not that which is possessed, but absolutely only his

[1] Therefore Gerhard says, in his *Isagoge:* The *obsessio corporalis* is more terrible because it is manifest to the senses, but the *obsessio spiritualis* is worse and more perilous.

[2] *Geschichte Besessener neuerer Zeit*, p. 136.

[3] Art. " Dämonische," in Herzog's *Real-Encyklopädie.*

[4] *Lehre vom Menschen*, pp. 274-277.

bodily organism; for the soul, it is a mere *obsessio*, not a *possessio*. The soul of the possessed person is not even an instrument of the demon's; in his impulses it is wholly unconcerned with its self-attestation: in what the demon says or does by means of the bodily organs of the possessed person, it is not in the least degree active."

The view that the demon has established himself substantially in the soul of the possessed person, is, as I now understand, to be given up; for that a created spiritual being could transplant itself substantially into the spirit and soul of man, is at variance with the limitation drawn by the Creator round all created individual life, and with the power which belongs to the Creator alone, substantially to permeate and pervade every created thing, and even spirits,[1] without their own nature being decomposed, and ceasing to be itself thereby. The locality of possession is the human corporeity. In this—and, indeed, just where the soul exerts an influence upon it by means of the nervous system, and receives reacting influences from it—the demon establishes himself, but from here outwardly exercises a forcible influence, extending itself to soul and spirit: to the soul at once, so far as he makes the corporeity, *e.g.* the instrument of speech, a means of his self-manifestation, and thereby dislodges the soul from its relation of power to the body that it vitalizes; to the spirit, inasmuch as he degrades the will to a mere potentiality, and places it in fetters that cannot be broken. He thus affects the nature of man even to its very foundation. Even to the will, and thus even to the root of the soul, and of the spirit, his influence penetrates. He binds the will in a magical manner, and makes it subservient to himself, and thus deprives the entire man of independence, and of all further power over himself. Not as though he made himself the internally efficient principle of the human spirit, and this spirit his instrument; but from the boundary at which bodily life and psychical life are connected, he declares over the powers of the soul, especially the imaginative faculty, his urgent influence,[2]

---

[1] Augustin, *de spir. et anima*, c. 26, compared with *de eccles. dogm.* ch. 83, is right: Illabi menti illi soli possibile est qui creavit, qui naturâ subsistens incorporeus capabilis est suæ facturæ.

[2] "Diabolus," says Gisbert Voet (in Ebrard, *l.c.* p. 253), "non illabitur in mentem aut voluntatem, nec intra eas operatur, ut physica actione faciat

and thence places the spirit as in a state of siege, so that it becomes incapable of resistance in any attack. The power of freedom may in flashes of light break through the dark ban, for the freedom is restrained in its manifestation without being annihilated in its nature. But, in general, the demoniac ban, with its restraint of free agency, its darkening of the consciousness, its perversion and distraction, is established over spirit and soul and body, in all their powers, from that extreme background, the will of the spirit, outwards.

Nothing makes the condition of demoniacal possession so intelligible as the magnetic *rapport* in artificially produced magnetic states. The magnetized person there appears as the absolutely will-less instrument of the magnetizer; and the contents of the consciousness of the magnetizer are reflected in the consciousness of the person magnetized, so that the individuality of the one is, as it were, merged in that of the other. Pinch the patient, he does not feel it; pinch the operator, the patient feels it as if he had been pinched, and complains of the injury to the part affected. Put rhubarb in the patient's mouth, he has no taste of it; put rhubarb in the operator's mouth, and the patient tastes and names this drug under the impression that he has it in his own mouth. Placed on his legs, he stands as if nailed to the ground; but following the movements of the magnetizer's hands, he is put into visibly involuntary and uneasy motion. This sympathetic unity of will is raised even into sympathetic unity of consciousness. The patient understands even the unexpressed thoughts of the operator, and acquiesces in them; or he speaks as if from himself, but in such a way that it is the manner of thought and the thought of the operator transferred to him which he reproduces. That which is here exhibited to us is an intoxication, a bondage, a possession of one Psyche by the other, accompanied by an extra-natural enhancement of the powers by the intrusive co-operation of evil, or even of good, influences of the spiritual world. From this dynamical possession of one human soul by the other, we may

eas quidquam intelligere aut velle, sed in phantasiam et in reliquas facultates sensitivas aliquid potest;" and Burmann, "In animam quamquam immediate illabi eamque intime affari et quibuscunque velit formis ac ideis implere non possit, phantasiæ tamen ope ac per externos sensus valide eam quatere ac multis modis tentare potest."

form to ourselves an idea of the substantial possession of a human soul by a demon. In the former case, the possession is only dynamical, because the human soul is linked to its body; in the latter case it is substantial, although not local, because the demon, by virtue of his purely spiritual nature, can penetrate into the substantial condition of the man, without disintegrating its living unity. But, in both cases, the powers of the soul have reached even to the spiritual roots of the internal life under the unnatural pressure of a foreign power, and have become involuntary forms of a substantial existence obtruded upon them.[1]

We have been compelled to limit ourselves to the New Testament in characterizing the true possession; for the Old Testament has neither a name for, nor gives an illustration of, this demoniacal condition. It speaks of sickness and the doom of death, which come, by the agency of Satan and angels of destruction, upon men; but we nowhere meet with such demoniacally diseased persons as Jesus healed in Gadara and elsewhere. When Josephus (*Ant.* vi. 8, 2) says of Saul after the war of the Amalekites, that πάθη τινα καὶ δαιμόνια, πνιγμοὺς αὐτῷ καὶ στραγγάλας ἐπιφέροντα had attacked him, and when (*Ant.* vi. 11, 2) he makes Jonathan say to his father that τοῦ πονηροῦ πνεύματος καὶ τῶν δαιμονίων ἐγκαθιζομένων,—David has driven them out, and procured him peace of soul,—he is carrying back, here as elsewhere, a mode of view and of expression belonging to his own time, into the antiquity of the Old Testament; for the historical records of the Old Testament themselves everywhere designate the melancholy of Saul, passing from time to time into frenzy, the immediate operation of God. This opera-

---

[1] *Vid.* Fr. Fischer, *Der Somnambulismus*, 1839; Ge. Barth, *Der Lebensmagnetismus, seine Erscheinungen und seine Praxis*, 1852; and the work of Joseph W. Haddock, *Somnolism and Psychism*, 1852. Without losing sight of the fact, that involuntary dependence and phantastical delusions throw their dark shadows even into spontaneous somnambulism (*vid.* Sec. XVII.), we have purposely spoken above only of that which is actively produced. That this latter has become a trade of the most unprincipled charlatanism, Mabru has lately disclosed in his work entitled *Les Magnetiseurs jugés par eux mêmes*, 1860; who, after the example of Burdin, offers to the somnambulist who proves herself *veritablement lucide* a reward of 3000 francs. In view of this work, we must regret that we did not rather leave magnetic phenomena altogether unconsidered; but this one authority is still not of weight enough to supersede the others, which we follow.

tion of God is absolutely indicated, as well in itself as in reference to its results, just as much as that which Saul underwent in Gibeah (comp. 1 Sam. xviii. 10 with x. 10): it is in both cases God's Spirit who suddenly and forcibly overcomes him (צָלַח); and the consequence is, in both cases, a speaking and demeanour beside himself, removed beyond the region of the natural and customary (הִתְנַבֵּא). But the one time it is the Spirit of God (רוּחַ יְהוָה) which comes upon him, the other time an evil spirit from God (רוּחַ אֱלֹהִים רָעָה, 1 Sam. xvi. 15, or רוּחַ יְהוָה רָעָה, 1 Sam. xix. 9),—a designation which we would not venture to take upon our lips, if the Scripture did not so directly make use of it. The one time it is the Spirit of God which pertains to God's holy nature, and acts according to that nature of light and love; the other time it is a spiritual agency of God, which brings to bear upon Saul the dark and fiery powers of divine wrath which he has aroused by his sin. Scripture throughout makes no mention in this case of demoniacal agency; and this need not appear strange, since the assertion that all diseases of the spirit are demoniacal, is neither agreeable to Scripture nor to experience.

Are we, then, perchance to say that it is a mere chance, that the form of demoniacal disease that characterizes real possession is nowhere mentioned in the Holy Scriptures of the Old Testament? Impossible! The Thora, and the Old Testament generally, mentions, on the one hand (as we shall see in the subsequent section), all kinds of magic; on the other hand, all forms of divinely caused disease, so designedly, that such a chance as this is not to be thought of. Or are we to say, that in the Old Testament Israel, although possession might have occurred, yet it was not recognised, because the satanic background of evil and of pain was at that time still hidden from their knowledge? Even this mode of explanation is not valid, true though it is that the knowledge of the kingdom of darkness only gradually dawns in the Old Testament, and only attains to full clearness through the decisive struggle of Christ. For that there are human sufferings of which Satan is the mediate cause, is assumed by the poet of the book of Job in the time of Solomon, in such a manner that it must be regarded as a view long current among the writer's people;[1] and besides,

[1] Hofmann, *Schriftbeweis*, i. 433.

possession is a disease which exhibits its demoniacal character so palpably, that, especially from the point of view familiar to the people of Israel, it could not be mistaken. The only true explanation is found in the fact, that as there are climatic characters of disease, so also there are some special to the history of the time; and as there are diseases peculiar to the country, so also there are some peculiar to the period.[1] This is especially true of spiritual sickness or mental disorders. That insanity is distinctively developed according to the colour of the popular character, the degree of cultivation, and the relations of the period, is an acknowledged and generally familiar fact in psychiatry, from which, however, we in no way deduce the result, that even possession without objective reality rests only upon delusions which, favoured by the prevailing laxity of the spiritual life, the want of internal vigour, or the attraction towards a false passivity, may have been only the reflex of the then dominant superstition.[2] No, the kind and manner of the assertion which Satan makes of his dominion over humanity, is actually different according to times and circumstances. In the Old Testament it was idolatry, which even there, according to its true nature, is regarded as the worshipping of demons (שֵׁדִים, LXX. $\delta\alpha\iota\mu\acute{o}\nu\iota\alpha$), together with the manifold kinds of witchcraft, mania, and divination associated therewith, by which Satan held in subjection whole peoples, and even Israel before the exile, rebellious from God. In this his dominion over great masses, he did not need to manifest his power in individuals, as was the case in the special possession. But when the wholesome disciplinary sufferings of the exile had given the death-blow to idolatry in Israel for ever, the spiritual and spirit-embodied power of destruction which characterized the kingdom of darkness assumed another form; and there began among others those sporadic manifestations of bodily, or rather spirit-embodied possession, which in the time of Jesus Christ had increased with such terrible vigour in intensity and number, because the kingdom of darkness summoned all its powers to resist its vanquisher at His entry into history, and to

---

[1] It is an acknowledged fact, that not only does the geographical latitude of the situation favour different diseases, but, moreover, gives to every disease a prevailing form.

[2] Thus even Neander, *K.G.* i. 25.

contend with Him for men to be redeemed. But this was God's ordering: the kingdom of God that came in and with Christ was to announce itself unmistakeably by the visible overcoming of demons (Luke xi. 20).

Nevertheless, that prevalence of demoniacal disorders, and especially of possession, had also certainly a deep psychological reason in the superstition of that day, in virtue of which it was mingled with all kinds of magic (Acts viii. 9, xiii. 6, xix. 19). Superstition is not absolutely a mere subjective guiltless delusion; and, moreover, it is not a complication which is dissolved by truly scientific illumination into a mere nothing.[1] It opens the human soul to demoniacal influences, just as much as faith does to divine. And witchcraft is no empty guiltless legerdemain, and neither is it an empty fraud, disclosing itself to intelligent cultivation: it is, in its often sufficiently undeniable reality, the fearful opposite of the sacred miracle, which apart from God sets in movement created powers.

SUPERSTITION AND MAGIC.

Sec. XVII.

It is not the man who believes in a super-terrene spirit-world, reaching into that which is earthly, who on that account is superstitious, although he is considered so by those who think themselves enlightened. He assuredly believes what Scripture declares, what reason finds consistent with itself, and what experience confirms. But he who, in respect of supersensual things, and of the mysterious background of sensible things, regards as true, and allows impressions to be made on himself by, thoughts or occurrences, whose reality has neither the warranty of undoubtedly credible tradition, nor the warranty of internal force of conviction in their favour, is rightly called superstitious; and should he, by preference, be addicted to such a

[1] It is therefore superficial, when Richard Mead, whom we name by way of example, in his *Medica Sacra* (1749), looks on the *dæmoniaci* only as *insani et epileptici*.

pretence of mystery (περίεργα, Acts xix. 19), and act upon it
—bigoted. It is thus essential to superstition, that the object
which one believes, should either not exist at all, or at least
should not exist in the way that he believes it; whereas faith,
resting upon external and internal foundation, has for its object
and substance that which is real, though invisible. Superstition, moreover, is, in spite of the unsubstantiality of its object,
a tendency of the spirit and soul, neither subjectively indifferent nor objectively without relation. Not subjectively indifferent; for the surrender of man to that which is untrue, or
to the truth defaced, is always a self-perversion fraught with
danger, which finally makes him incapable of distinguishing
between truth and untruth, and wholly incapable of perception
of what is true. Not objectively without relation; for, inasmuch
as the superstitious man plunges with his thought and imagination into the night-side of nature, and into the invisible world,
which is the reverse side of the visible, on the one hand,—and
on the other allows himself, willingly and of set purpose, to be
affected thereby,—he comes into a condition of reciprocal relation thereto, which affords to the evil spirits sufficient points of
connection to entangle him into increasingly mischievous delusions, and to make use of him as a serviceable instrument. In
the former case, his spirit is led away further and further from
sound and wholesome perception of the truth, into errors in
which, confirmed by all kinds of illusory and marvellous experiences, he loses himself more and more deeply; in the latter
case, he involves himself actually with demoniacal powers.
This is the great wide region of magic, which by the ancients
is very rightly treated, along with the worship of idols, as a
species of superstition. On the lowest stage (φαρμακεία, Gal.
v. 20), such mysterious means are used to attain certain results
as owe their efficiency absolutely to something beyond any
natural and experimental link of causation. One is not conscious to himself of a demoniacal co-operation; indeed, one
perhaps believes himself acting altogether as an instrument of
God, because divine or other holy names are invoked therein,—
in such a way, nevertheless, as that the effect is expected, **not**
from the promise given to the prayer of faith, and from powers
obtained from God by means of prayer, but from the traditionally infallible operation of formulas and ceremonies. The form

which is apparently the most harmless of this lowest degree of magic, is the election of days; *i.e.* the superstitious opinion that certain duties, if they are performed on certain days, with observance of certain rules, infallibly have a definitely good result, and are protected against evil casualties. In this case, means and end stand in no relationship; it is a blind surrender of one's self to a causality opposed to nature, or to a mocking delusion. On a higher grade, one is conscious that there are higher spiritual beings in whose strength he is speaking or acting; but regarding them as good angelic powers, he is a dupe, to the injury of himself, and of others whom he designs to serve. To this kind belongs, for the most part, the heathen magic as pseudo-theurgy,[1] and the heathen soothsaying, which is essentially distinct from the Israelitish prophecy (Num. xxiii. 23). To this belongs the Jewish practical Cabbala (קבלה מעשׂית); the visionary heretical gnosis (Col. ii. 18), of which the pastoral epistles give warning, as of that which is falsely named; in addition to the so-called divine magic (*magia theurgica*), with its secret books, named after Adam, Abel, Enoch, Abraham, Solomon, and others. To this also belong the modern magnetic oracular speech, and the magnetic necromancy which are especially at home in Paris and in London, and which are only a new form of the old God-contemning disorder that was condemned by law (Deut. xviii. 11) and prophecy (Isa. viii. 19). On the highest grade, a man is willingly and knowingly in covenant with evil spirits, whether it be that, without intending thereby to revolt from God, he has surrendered himself to them in exchange for some deceiving assistances and glittering distinctions, or that, driven by enmity against God, he has attached himself to the side of Satan, and of the powers of the kingdom of darkness [2] enlisted under his banner. In the first two degrees, the characteristic of an evil design is not absolutely essential to magic;[3] but, in this third

---

[1] It was called in the imperial age of Rome, *ars mathematica*.

[2] "Diabolus," says the author of the *Quæstiones v. et N. Test.*, "non speciale nomen est, sed commune; operis enim nomen est, non naturæ."

[3] This in opposition to Aberle, who, in his clear-sighted article "Zauberei" in the *Wetzer-Welteschen Kirchen-Lexikon*, declares that this is an essential characteristic of all magical agency, that it proceeds from an evil will. Chr. A. Crusius has rightly avoided adopting this characteristic into the definition. He defines: Magia est genus superstitionis, ubi adhibitis formulis certis et ritibus per se ad effectum non aptis vel saltem non sufficientibus,

degree, and the highest of all, it is human and demoniac activity combined for evil purposes.

All these kinds of magic are strictly forbidden and rejected in Scripture, with an acknowledgment of their objective dark background[1] (Deut. xviii. 10–12; Jer. xxvii. 9; 2 Chron. xxxiii. 6; Mic. v. 11; Gal. v. 20). The church has from the beginning lifted up her earnestly warning voice against it.[2] Nevertheless all are still current in the present day, from the sympathetic cures, the election of days, the fortune-telling by cards, even to the conjuration of the dead; and still further, even to formal compacts with evil spirits, and formal obligation to Satan, which usually ends in despair. These kinds of superstition and of magic it is not the problem of psychology to set forth individually, but rather of the demonologic part of dogmatics; and it is the office of ethics to warn against them. But psychology, in explaining the natural condition of man,

ope potentiæ, quæ superat humanam, quæque suas operationes his conditionibus adstringit, certi effectus vel præstantur vel tentantur.

[1] Proof: The Egyptian magicians in Moses' time, whose magical works are related as such, not as jugglers' tricks (Ex. vii. 11, viii. 3); Balaam, whose incantation is regarded as a power from which Jehovah saved Israel (Josh. xxiv. 10); the witch of Endor, who actually disturbs the spirit of Samuel from his repose (1 Sam. xxviii. 15); and, according to Scripture, there are satanic miracles which, in the time of the end, will deceive many (2 Thess. ii. 9; Apoc. xiii. 13–15, xix. 20, xvi. 14). It is therefore false when Aberle maintains that the objective reality of magical agency cannot be proved from the Holy Scripture.

[2] To the teachers whose writings are full of the most terrible warnings of this kind, belongs first of all Augustine, who, prior to his conversion, glanced deeply into this abyss. Thus he says, *e.g.*, in respect of the election of fortunate days, *Sermo de temp.* 215: "Quia audivimus, quod aliquos viros aut mulieres ita diabolus circumveniat, ut quinta feria nec viri opera faciant nec mulieres lanificium, coram Deo et sanctis angelis ejus contestamur, quia, quicunque hoc observare voluerint, nisi per prolixam et duram pœnitentiam tale sacrilegium emendaverint, ubi arsurus est diabolus, ibi et ipsi damnandi sunt." And *Serm.* 241: "Ego me apud Deum absolvo, dum iterum atque iterum admoneo pariter et contestor, ut nullus ex vobis carragos vel divinos sortilegos requirat nec de qualibet eos aut causa aut infirmitate interroget." And *Tract.* xiii. *in Joan.*: "Contra mirabiliarios, ut ita dicam, istos cautum me fecit Deus meus, dicens: In novissimis temporibus exsurgent pseudo-prophetæ. . . Ergo cautos nos fecit sponsus, qui et miraculis decipi non debemus." Thus spoke the church, while at the same time the synagogue, as the Talmuds show, was becoming ever more securely entangled in the net of superstition and magic.

as we are doing in this Division, cannot avoid drawing attention to the demoniacal region, by which the natural condition of man is surrounded on all sides as the earth is by the atmosphere, or, according to a talmudic image, as the vine by the heap of mould; and from which dangers are threatening man, all the greater in proportion as he has become in addition, in consequence of the fall, the more related and the more accessible to these powers of darkness.

We revert here once again to the already more than once mentioned subject of somnambulism. That which we said of the possessed in the Gospels is true also of this state. Antiquity has nothing to produce that veils itself under this phenomenon. The waking intercourse with the outer world in some other than the customary way of the senses, the rapport, the absence of memory on the part of the person awakened, and the waking up of the memory immediately upon the re-entrance into a similar condition,—these are four characteristics which are thus found associated in no analogous phenomenon of antiquity.[1] Most of the cases of ecstasy are distinguished from the somnambulists, by the fact that the ecstasy comes on without intervening sleep as an immediate consequence of the convulsions. But Tertullian's *Exstatica*, of whom we made mention above (Sec. XIII.), even apart from the fact that she did not see in the condition of sleep, is distinct from a somnambulist, because of the remembrance of what was seen abiding with her after the ecstasy. And the maid at Philippi (Acts xvi. 16-18) runs in broad daylight after the apostles, while the state of the somnambulist is always, even when sleep-walking is

---

[1] It is in vain that Ennemoser (*Gesch. des thier. Magnetismus*), Passavant, J. A. G. Meyer (*Natur-Analogien*, 1839), Steinbeck (*Der Dichter ein Seher*, 1836), Choulant (*Vorlesung über den Animal. Magn.* 1840), Mayo[1] (*Wahrheiten im Volksaberglauben*, 1854), and others, have sought to allege similar instances of antiquity. When Aberle (art. *Verzückung* in *Wetzer-Welteschen K.L.*) says that somnambulism has been long known, and that Augustine relates several cases, it is an assertion that leads to error. The *energoumenoi* mentioned by Augustine in lib. xii. *de Genesi ad literam*, are, more closely considered, very different from somnambulists.

[1 Is this book perhaps Mayhew *On the Truths contained in Popular Superstitions?*—Tr.]

associated with it, a sleeping state. Moreover, the somnambulist himself makes a clear distinction between himself and the spirits with which he has intercourse; while that maid does not speak herself, but a πνεῦμα πύθωνος speaks out of her, making use of her organs of speech, which spirit the apostle drives out. Even in the cases in which the ancient magic produced conditions of clairvoyance, it occurred through other means than the irradiation of magnetical power; and the effect was a condition similar indeed to somnambulism, but still not identical with it.[1]

As Scripture mentions no special somnambulists, somnambulism might appear to lie altogether beyond the region of biblical psychology; but still it belongs to its region, inasmuch as, if anywhere at all, we must expect a well-founded judgment upon the subject from biblical psychology. In order to obtain this, the spontaneous somnambulism (Idiosomnambulism) and that which is induced by magnetic agency must be distinguished; wherein it may be observed, that the latter does not appear in all, but only in rare cases of magnetic agency, as the climax of the other symptomatic conditions. But it is always the boundary of the present and future, on which the somnambulist finds himself planted, at one time by the immediate direction of God, at the other by human instrumentality. The true religious-moral ground of his inward nature, withdrawn back upon itself, and thus mightily empowered, which in the waking state could not manifest itself, becomes evident. And they are actually agencies of God and of spirits which go forth upon the clairvoyant, and are reflected in his internal nature[2] laid open towards the spiritual world. So far as in this phenomenon there is an evidence to confound materialistic unbelief, and as there is always presented to the so-called reli-

[1] Thus, *e.g.*, the magical practice of the oriental *mustantikûn* (*incantatores*) places boys, in order to have clear insight, and to predict, in a benumbed state, but through enchanted potions and the like. The fact still occurs, and is attested. See thereupon Fleischer, in the Catalogue of MSS. of the Leipzig Town Library, p. 505.

[2] Both very plainly in *Selma, the Jewish Female Seer* (1838). The glimpses of light coming from above, and features of the father in the son, are here unmistakeable. But the cloud, with its phantasmagoriæ, which lies thereupon, remains unbroken. Noticeable is her confession, "I have never been able to see quite clearly" (p. 121), and "no man can see quite clearly and live" (p. 106).

gious somnambulists the separate future destiny of the pious and the godless in a manner corresponding to the divine holiness, it suggests a loud call to repentance. Moreover, it is not to be denied, that the declarations of all somnambulists coincide in certain visionary facts, which, compared with Scripture, confirm its testimony, or may avail as experimental and actual illustration of it. Apart from these fundamental facts, the value of the declaration is measured always according to the position which the somnambulist usually occupies in the deepest ground of his heart towards the word of God and the Redeemer. Even the special ecclesiastical position that he occupies has some influence in determining their value; the views and confessions have, according to the circumstances, a Catholic, a Protestant, or even an indifferent colour. In Sec. XIII. I spoke of a somnambulist, the phenomena of which case have, more than any other known to me, a power to awaken repentance, and truly sanctifying.

But the physical basis of somnambulism is always chronically morbid,—not, as in the prophetic ecstasy, only as it were a force put upon the body and its functions similar to that of morbid action, but an actual disease, which, moreover, is regarded as such by the somnambulist, although he knows at the same time that it is to serve the purpose of his cure, and of a testimony to others. This morbid basis throws its dark shadows into the clairvoyance. For the most part there are clouds ascending thence, which are formed into phantasmagoric images; and even the spiritual world, which allows itself to be seen in objective reality, suffers a more or less distorting refraction, on account of the morbid background of the revealed inward sense. Moreover, evil spirits are mingled among the good ones, and force themselves into the field of view, in order to mock the seer, and, through him, others; and in the spiritual ascendancy of which he is conscious, is only too easily aroused, and by the surrounding circumstances is frequently encouraged and fostered in an unjustifiable manner, the sin of all sins— the sin of self-reflected arrogant contemplation.[1] Thus, in the

---

[1] V. Schubert, *Die Zaubereisünden in ihrer alten und neuen Form*, p. 37; and comp. the decision of Fabri (*Die Erweckungen auf deutschen Boden*, 1861) upon the revivals associated with convulsive phenomena: "There are sudden illuminations out of the invisible world, in which angelic powers

utterances of the somnambulists, elements divine, subjective, and demoniacal occur confusedly. It would be a revolt from God's word to rely upon such utterances as upon divine revelations; but not the less would it be a closing one's eyes to the signs of the time, to refuse recognition and acknowledgment to the experimental evidence of the truth of the biblical revelation, to the call to repentance, and the trumpet sound of the coming judgment, which are suggested in this phenomenon. It is plain that it is psychologically infinitely instructive.

It cannot therefore be said that clairvoyance is a condition purely demoniacal and pernicious to the soul;[1] it is an opening of the inward perception, in which man is exposed to very various spiritual influences. But our judgment is otherwise formed upon the practice of magnetism. It is indeed a natural and no demoniacal power which the magnetizer exercises upon the patient,—namely, that power of his own Psyche, which, emanating therefrom, comprehends in itself the bodily powers as the power of the entire life; and on the first grade of its effects, where they are still of a medicinal kind, magnetism may avail as a means of cure as innocent as electricity. But when from thence its effects are enhanced, it begins in the so-called comatose state, and the symptoms associated therewith, to render the patient as it were a living corpse and a bewitched person: his eyes stare, without seeing; and the pupil, expanded and immoveable, does not shrink even at the contact of the apple of the eye with the finger, or at the approach of a blazing light. This symptom of βασκανία (Gal. iii. 1), and the rest taken together, are a state of unnatural bondage, which in Sec. XVI. we have designated as a possession of one Psyche by the other.[2]

are active; but immediately upon these there lie in wait demoniacal powers and others. The nervous convulsive casualties that not seldom appear in such cases are a result of the mighty psychical excitement, which must be first calmed and spiritually restored by the subsequent effect of the divine word and spirit, if truly a living fruit is to grow forth out of it."

[1] Read the noteworthy law-case of a somnambulist female, who in the ecstatic sleep was dishonoured by a hypocritical villain, but remained therein morally pure, in Hitzig's *Annalen*, edited by Schletter, 1855, October part.

[2] An illustration: In a moment of enthusiasm, a girl that had fallen after her first communion into the somnambulic state, cried out that she saw such beautiful and glorious things; and when the elders asked what

The impression becomes more and more terrible when the comatose state is heightened at the third stage to the somnambulic, and at the fourth to the ecstatic. The patient, if God do not for the sake of his heart-reality assist him by good spirits, here becomes an instrument of demoniacal delusion to himself and others. He finds himself hard on the limit of phrenzy and of death; for the ecstasy may become so powerful, that (according to the statement of the initiate) if one does not go cautiously to work in the matter, the soul is actually withdrawn without return; or if it return, it sinks into madness.[1] That which runs into such terrible manifestations of power over man, is suspicious even in its beginnings.[2]

Moreover, there is actually no art of dark magic which has not associated itself with this magnetic practice: not merely soothsaying professionally practised for gain,[3] and even

---

she saw, she answered, "God surrounded by the angels, the apostles, and Mary." The same girl subsequently was thrown by magnetism into the somnambulic state by a friend of the elders, who was a Voltairian; and when he asked the ecstatic patient what she saw, she replied, "God accompanied by His two apostles, Voltaire and Rousseau." Thus the soul of the magnetized person is wholly and absolutely in the power of the magnetizer. In the work of a Parisian physician, who, after long contradiction, was won over to magnetism, may be read in this matter a warning which closes with the words: Dès qu'elles sont en somnambulisme, elles se trouvent soumises comme des esclaves, plus que des esclaves, puisqu'elles sont complices à des personnes qu'elles connaissent à peine; lorsqu'elles sont reveillèes, elles ont oublié tout ce qu'on vient de leur faire. The book itself where this is to be read (J. J. Beaux, *De l'influence de la Magnetisation sur le développement de la voix et du gout en Musique*, Paris 1855) is not far from this spirit of impurity. In the Holy Scripture, unchastity and witchcraft are twin ideas. A Brazilian of the race of the Coërunas, questioned by v. Martins, comprehended the mystery of the Indian art of healing in the words: "All witchcraft comes from lust and from hatred, and thence also is healing."

[1] Cahagnet, *Der Verkehr mit den Verstorbenen auf magnetischem Wege*, i. 196–198. The translation is by an authorized magnetizer in Berlin.

[2] Aberle, *l.c.*, although acknowledging magnetism as a natural and serviceable means of healing, says, nevertheless, "Even if magnetism do not go beyond the range of that which is natural, it is still undeniable that it brings man into a condition which makes him more accessible to demoniacal intrusions than is the case in his usual state."

[3] In reference to a similar phenomenon in the Romish Church, Hermas, in the *Shepherd*, gives the criterion: "Spiritus qui desursum est nemini respondet interrogatus nec singulis respondet, neque quum vult, homini

necromancy with the table-rapping[1] and psychography, that not long ago had become almost epidemic; with those traps laid for the spiritual kingdom, in which was caught not this kingdom itself, but only a caricature of it;[2] but also the construction of all kinds of magical machinery, and magical means for healing, for defence, for disclosing and seeing forbidden things. Let one single example suffice, in which the dark magic whereunto the magnetic practice grows, is actually to be laid hold of with the hands, and is even conceded by the narrator, a magnetic physician, who stands upon the purely medicinal stage. "There are persons," says D. Ge. Barth,[3] " who possess

loquitur spiritus Dei, sed tunc loquitur, quum vult Deus." S. Hilgenfeld, *Glossolalie*, pp. 71–73.

[1] For the art of "table-turning," we have Jewish testimonies as early as the seventeenth century. Friedr. Breutz, in his *Jüdischen abgestreiften Schlangenbalg*, 1614, denounces the Jews, therefore, as practising *Kischuph* (magic). "We make the table turn in playful times with *Kischuph*, and whisper into one another's ears, *Schemoth, Schel, Schedim* (names of demons), and the table springs up then, even when laden with many hundredweight." Zalman Zebi, in his *Jüdischen Theirak*, 1615, defends this table-turning, as practised not through magic, but the power of God, *Kabbala Maasith* (practical Kabbala). "Thus, for the table-turning no *Maasch Schedim* can be employed, for we sing for it excellent *mismorim* (songs), as *Adon olam jigdal* (The Lord of the world be exalted). Thus there can be no devil's work suffered when God is remembered." See thereupon v. Harless, *Das Buch von den Ægypt. Mysterien* (1858), pp. 130–132.

[2] Examples of such deceptive intercourse with the spirits turning away from the true heavenly ladder (John i. 51) are given in Hornung's *Neue Geheimnisse des Tages, Durch Geistes-Magnetismus Vermittelte Geister-Manifestationen aus dem unenthüllten Jenseits*, 1858, 8. These manifestations of spirits reduce themselves to self-excitements of the so-called media, and only too truly reflect the cultivation and the religious standing of these personal media. Just so in Preiswerk's narrative of the superstition among the Swiss people (*Verhandlungen der Schweizerisch-reform Prediger, Gesellsch*. Schaffhausen 1856), it is decided, " that the table-rapping is only a deceiving performance, and only an echo and reflection of the persons engaged in it." It is remarkable, that even the somnambulists deny the reality of this spiritual intercourse by means of table-rapping and psychography (p. 409); nay, the pretended spirits themselves are honest enough to declare, "We can give you nothing really but what must subsist in you already;" and one says to the medium, "Thy head is my library." H. Leo and A. V. Harless deservedly lashed this spiritual disorder in the course of the year 1858 in the *Evang. K.Z.*

[3] *Magnetism of Life, its Phenomena and its Practice*, 1852, pp. 234–236.

and exercise the capacity or power of seeing in glass globes, or rock crystals, or mirrors formed in a certain manner, the past, the distant present, and the future. Some of these seers descry all this in glass bottles also, which are filled with magnetized water, or in drops of ink which are poured into their hand. I am certainly not in the position to explain the reason of this capacity, but I do not doubt its authenticity, for I have seen sufficient facts to convince me. The art of prophesying by these means is very old, and certain old formulas are known for the preparation and application of the crystals. When the crystal is formed and polished, it is dedicated to some spirit or another: this is called its consecration. Before its use, it is ' charged,' *i.e.* there is spoken an invocation of this spirit, in which a vision is prayed for of those things which are sought to be known. Usually a young person is chosen to look into the globe, and to contemplate the desired vision: after some time the crystal becomes clouded, and there appears a diminutive vision, which represents the persons, things, or scenes that are necessary for the communication of the explanation sought for, in a miniature picture to him who looks in the crystal. If the desired disclosure be received, the crystal is ' discharged,' and the spirit to which it is dedicated is thanked for the service rendered, and dismissed. I have neither time nor inclination to enter upon this matter personally. I know from facts which have come to my knowledge, that it is possible to employ supernatural agencies pertaining to the spirit-world, to produce results in this natural world. I know the fearful, shocking, and ruinous consequences which have arisen to men from the use of such agencies: although I have been summoned as a magnetizer to make good the mischief done, as a magnetizer I myself scorn this assistance."

Thus far this thoughtful physician. He makes a distinction between the magnetism which he practises and the former magic. Even v. Schubert regards magnetism as an actually tested means of cure, within the limits of a morally serious, intelligent, and conscientiously self-restrained treatment, as justifiable. It does not become, says he, the sin of witchcraft until it purposely leads the magically excited soul which is surrendered to it, beyond into the region of demoniacal enticements. But for the psychical life-breath which, proceeding from the soul of the magnetizer into the nerves, pervades his own nervous body, to be transferred by the power of the will into the bodily domain of another soul, may be in itself an altogether unexceptionable healing process.[1] Still, is not magnetism, even upon this stage, a deliberate use of suspicious doubles, or mimicries,[2] of the miracle performed by God's power? Is not this irruption of one Psyche into the sphere of another a derangement of limits contrary to nature? And are there not associated therewith, in a sequence of unregulated declivity, so many abnormal phenomena which Scripture rejects as witchcraft? Operative magnetism in itself is no magic, but it carries in itself all kinds of magic, and thus also its own decisive rejection.

We have now reached the furthest limit of the method of inquiry which in Sec. I. we proposed to ourselves to follow, for the knowledge of the natural essential condition of man as held together by the soul; and without intending it, the issues of this Division have moulded themselves for us according to the plan of Lord Bacon of Verulam.[3] This fourth Division forms, so to speak, the trunk of the entire system deduced from the Scripture. Beginning from the innermost personal life, we have advanced in a progressive method even to the visible bodily life in its reciprocal relation to the soul, and have learnt to know the manifold modes of disease to which the human natural condition is exposed in its state of nature perverted by sin. If we now compare the end of this Division (Sec. XVII.) with the end of the foregoing one (Sec. V.), we see how, since the fall of man, two principal distinct powers, a good and an evil one, have grappled in contest about his soul. On the one side there comes to aid man, the might of the divine love, which in promises, and in the gospel of their fulfilment, addresses itself to his faith; on the other side there surround him demoniacal powers which have fallen from the divine love, have their being in the divine wrath, and seek to ensnare and ruin him on the path of superstition. We shall now see how the love of the soul, situated as it is between such opposites, approves

---

[1] V. Schubert, *l.c.* pp. 11, 35.

[2] *Doppelgänger*, double-goers—an untranslateable expression.—Tr.

[3] *De augmentis scientiarum*, iv. 3: Habet etiam pars ista de facultatibus animæ appendices duas—altera harum est doctrina de divinatione naturali, altera de fascinatione.

itself, when, by the power of the redemption of the God-man, it re-attains, in the spirit and in God, once more to the position of its decayed ideal or likeness to God, and, as the Scripture expresses itself, is transplanted out of the darkness, into God's marvellous light.

APPENDIX.

I.

Passages from the Physics of Comenius.

THE post-Reformation literature has scarcely any work to point to, which in the smallest compass includes such a wealth of interesting and suggestive matter in so light a form, and so systematically put together, as the little pamphlet entitled *Physicæ ad lumen divinum reformandæ Synopsis* (1635 and 1663, in 12mo), by John Amos Comenius, the last bishop of the Bohemian-Moravian Brethren, who died in exile, at Amsterdam, in the year 1671. In addition to what had been done by precursors, such as Ludovicus Vives, Thomas Campanella, and Lord Bacon of Verulam, Comenius seeks herein to release natural science from the bondage of heathen philosophy, and especially of Aristotelian scholasticism, by vindicating, instead of this, the divine revelation in the Scripture, but besides, the perception of the senses, and reasonable investigation as its principles of knowledge; and by maintaining as certain, that the results of natural research which are attained in an empirical way, will never contradict the rightly understood testimonies of Scripture.[1]

The idea that the Holy Scripture has no reference at all to natural philosophy, is familiar to him. He refutes it in a striking manner: " Cui obsecro usui," says he among other things, " tot et tanta de mundi exordio, creationis processu, creaturarum proprietatibus possim memorantur, si nihil de natura docere nos voluit naturæ parens idemque Scripturæ dictator? Aiunt,

[1] Comp. K. v. Raumer, *Geschichte der Pädagogik*, ii. 65-68, and generally the interesting characterization there given of Comenius.

id eo spectare, ut rerum factorem agnoscere et admirari, amare et metuere discamus. Recte, sed quomodo factorem absque factura? Annon quo melius quis picturæ artem intelligit, eo magis pictoris ingenium, si excellit, miratur et laudat? Utique. Superficiaria cognitio nec amorem nec admirationem excitabit unquam. Et quæro: ea quæ de creaturis in Scriptura occurrunt (etiam per similitudines inde ductas) verant sicut necne? Si vera (quis autem absque blasphemia aliter statuat?) cur ea non conferamus cum iis, quæ Sensu et Ratione constant? ad deprehendendam scilicet eam, quæ in rebus et rerum Auctoris ore est, veritatis harmoniam!"

To quote an example: Comenius, on the ground of empirical investigation, and of the biblical narrative of creation, avows three principles of all things: matter, spirit, and light or fire. The *Thohu wa-Bohu* is matter; the Spirit of God which broods over it is the power that moulds it, and the life that vitalizes it; the light, which comes into being at God's command, is that which refines, actualizes (*inactuans*), and diversifies it. Light (Or) and Fire (Ur) are reciprocal. "Primæva lux," says he, "fuit ingens moles Ignis ardentis, in mundanæ materia massa jussu creatoris accensa." To the same purpose, Leibnitz, in his ingenious work, *Protogœa*.

Comenius comes to the conclusion, without intending it, that the created essences of the elements (*æther, aër, aqua, terra*) form a scale of seven degrees up to the pure spiritual nature. To us it is more important, that in these seven essential classes he recognises seven powers proceeding from God, of which the subsequent always includes the precedent: Esse, motus, figura seu qualitas, vita, sensus, ratio, intelligentia. He compares them to the seven pillars (Prov. ix. 1), and to the seven steps (Ezek. xl. 22); and having called attention to the significance of the number seven in all created things, he continues: Quid omnia hæc portendunt nisi ut expressa sit imago illius Dei, cujus septem oculi permeant universam terram (Zech. iv. 10) et cujus septem Spiritus sicut in conspectu throni ejus (Apoc. i. 4), imo qui ipse cum quolibet gradu creaturæ suæ mysticam constituit octavam? In ipso enim vivunt, sunt et moventur omnia quæ vivunt, sunt et moventur (Acts xvii. 28) et ipse operatur omnia in omnibus (1 Cor. xii. 6) et omnia hæc sunt quasi Ipse ille (Ecclus. xliii. 29), nec tamen quidquam eorum est Ipse ille (Job xii. 9), sed quia omnia illa aliquid de divina essentia effigiant et virtute ejus operantur quæ operantur, hinc est quod ille, super omnia, extra omnia, infra omnia existens vera sit mystica octava omnium. Others may form a different judgment; we discern herein presentiments and perceptions of the truth, and rejoice in them.

The section *de angelis* is excellent, in which Comenius distinguishes, besides other things, how far physics (in the sense of that day), and how far theology, are respectively bound to speak on this subject: we give therefrom only the second proposition, paradoxical, but thoroughly true, and its elucidation. The proposition runs thus: "Angelus est homo incorporeus;" and the explanation: " Homo dici potest angelus eo sensu, quo homo ipse Animal, Animal Planta, Planta concretum, etc., dicitur, id est, propter inclusam præcedentis formam, nova solum superaddita perfectione. Homo enim creatura est rationalis ad imaginem Dei condita, immortalis; est et angelus, sed majoris perfectionis ergo a corpore liber. Nihil igitur aliud est angelus quam Homo a corpore nudus, nihil aliud Homo, quam angelus corpore vestitus." In three points we find Comenius altogether in agreement with ourselves: (1) That the angels were created before the visible world; (2) that, not less than man, they were created after the image of God; and (3) that they are absolutely incorporeal. Each of these three points is proved by Comenius, briefly, but convincingly.

In the doctrine of man, he does homage to that trichotomy which has often been mentioned and maintained by us previously, that man consists of a body, spirit, and animal soul, which he has in common with the brutes. He calls the spirit *anima* or *mens;* that animal soul, *spiritus*. His two chief positions are these: (1) Corpus est organon et habitaculum spiritus. Spiritus vero habitaculum et organon animæ; and, (2) Ut spiritus afficitur a corpore, ita Mens a Spiritu. We have the body from the elements, as the brutes; the nature-soul (*spiritus*) from the universal spirit of nature (*spiritus mundi*), as likewise the brutes;[1] the spiritual soul, on the other hand (*anima, s. mens*), from God, but not as a part of the divine nature: Deus enim in partes divisibilis non est nec in essentiam cum creatura

[1] " Spiritus hic Comenii ex Spiritu Mundi," says Quenstedt, i. 739, " est ejusdem valoris cum Spiritu mundi h. e. æque fictitius et nullus."

coibilis. Comenius thinks so little of the doctrine of emanation, that he regards the inspiration of Gen. ii. 7 not at all as an increating of a proper spiritual soul, but as a creative deepening of the natural soul into spirit. He explains Gen. ii. 7 according to Zech. xii. 1. The natural soul, according to its innermost condition, is an immortal spirit. It propagates itself *per traducem*, but not as spirit. It only becomes spirit by virtue of a constructive divine act, associated with procreation; an act which is the continuation of that original one in Gen. ii. 7. Different as our views are from these, yet there is much in harmony with our idea, when Comenius attributes to the natural soul *attentio, judicium, memoria* (the three *sensus interni*), and makes the spiritual soul, by means of these functions of the natural soul, exercise its own functions, *intellectus, voluntas, conscientia;* and we may appropriate to ourselves the apophthegm of which Comenius makes use, as more applicable to our view than to his: Hominem dum vides, Regem te videre cogita, regie vestitum et in regio residentem solio. Rex enim mens est, vestis ejus spiritus, solium corpus.

II.

THESES ON FIRE AND LIGHT, SOUL AND SPIRIT.

BY PROF. D. JULIUS HAMBERGER.

Communicated on April 13, 1860.

BY Fire is to be understood, on the one hand, only the desire after Light and Being; but, on the other hand also (as in the thirst for the realities is announced the capability of the reality itself), the might or power for both.

In God the Father, as the absolute supporter of Fire, is contained, for that reason, the nature, *i.e.* the possibility of the Being of the divine corporeity, and again also the Light, or the idea, *i.e.* the possibility of the form of the same.

The actual supporter of the Light, or of the idea, is the Son who proceeds from the Father, begotten by Him; in whom, as the *actual* essentiality is not to be conceived without form, is given the purpose of the fulfilment of the will of His Father, through whom therefore, so far, the Father is reconciled.

The Holy Spirit, finally, is the supporter of the actual Being, in that through Him the Fire-life of the Father and the Light-life of the Son are brought together, the possibility of the Essence and the possibility of the Form are united, and thus the divine corporeity is shown forth in fact.

This forming forth ensues, according to the part in it of the one or the other divine person, in seven impulses, distinguished from one another. These impulses are effected by the divine persons : the divine persons thus stand absolutely above them.

Moreover, certainly, as this forming forth of the divine corporeity is an eternally free act of will, there must be assumed for it—ideally—one impulse or moment in which the Godhead presents to itself the mere possibility of that corporeity, which then by the power of its will it brings to realization.

As the divine corporeity has its ground in the Father as the supporter of Fire, in the Son as the supporter of Light, and in the Holy Spirit as the supporter of actual essentiality; so, moreover, the world is created from God, through God, to God, *in the sense* that by the Father first of all is established the ground of its essentiality, therefore of its distinction from God, or its independence; by the Son is established the ground of its form and figure, consequently of its analogy with God; but by the Holy Spirit both of these grounds are brought to actual existence, and consequently the world is perfected and brought back to God, from whom its being proceeded.

The individual impulses of the Mosaic history of creation correspond to the impulses of the forming forth of the everlasting corporeity of God.

The deepest ground of human being is the Fire-life bestowed upon man by God,—consequently, the longing, on the one side after Being, and on the other side after Light. This Fire-life was first of all offered to him by God, through the opening of the everlasting nature, as that which underlay all creation. But because existences were already in being, when man was to appear on the stage, and therefore man organically is linked with the whole of nature, so essentiality itself was immediately bestowed upon him, including all the powers of nature, *i.e.* in the earthly clod. Within this essentiality there already subsisted also the Light, or the divine idea, but at first still inoperative.

In the Fire-life—which, as essentiality, was given to man by the Father—was rooted his soul; in the essentiality was based his corporeity; but in the idea which had been implanted in him by the Son as the supporter of the whole ideal world, and in which the whole law of his being floated before him, is given the possibility of his elevation to spirit.

This threefold possibility became actualized by the Holy Spirit, who awakened by His breath the idea that as yet was not living, and herewith brought the corporeity of man to full manifestation, so that now man might become a living soul.

Man merely HAS the body as he has the spirit, but he himself IS the soul, and in it he has the will and the power of choice between the Fire-life (in pride) and the Nature-life (in sensual lust), and a life according to the will of God (godliness). Man is only uni-personal, and not tri-personal as God is, who bears in Himself the reason not only of His will, but also of His ideal as of His real Being.

V.
THE REGENERATION.

Τὸ γεγεννημένον ἐκ τῆς σαρκὸς σάρξ ἐστι καὶ τὸ γεγεννημένον ἐκ τοῦ πνεύματος πνεῦμά ἐστι.

By way of introduction to the following Division, I record a lay of Zion sung by a congregation no longer known in Jerusalem, whose memorable history (God willing) I shall relate elsewhere :—

> They told me that I was albumen:
> How was I then distressed!
> How did I despair,
> Because spirit and soul were gone!
>
> Then Jesus Christ found me,
> And gave me intelligence once more;
> I know surely that He is,
> And that He does not forget me:
> I know now who I am.
>
> I am the Father's child,
> And Jesus is leading me
> Whither all His people are
> Whom He has purchased with His blood. —
> I am not albumen!

THE DIVINE-HUMAN ARCHETYPE.

Sec. I.

If we were writing general instead of biblical psychology, we should require to begin phenomenally, not rationalistically; *i.e.* we should be compelled to seek to advance in an analytical manner from the psychical phenomena to their reasons, and to the nature of the soul. But biblical psychology is perfectly justified in proceeding synthetically: for its material is not now to be discovered for the first time, but it is already given; and wherever it occurs, Scripture labours not according to the manner of human science from below upwards, but sets forth the world of phenomena as an announcement of revelation, in the light of divine facts. Therefore as, when we considered the primeval and natural psychical condition of man, we proceeded from the godlike archetype, "for man was created after the image of God," so now, when we wish to consider the new spiritual life of the redeemed man, we proceed from the divine-human archetype, the person of the Redeemer: "For whom God did foreknow, He also did predestinate to be conformed to the image of His Son, that He might be the first-born among many brethren" (Rom. viii. 29).

In the original position of man, his spirit and his soul were the exact image of God; the former of His triune nature, and the latter of His sevenfold *doxa*. Both were God's likeness, not merely in their constitution, but also according to their life; for their background was the presence of God's love, by which they were maintained and pervaded. Then, when man fell from the good beginning into which he had been created, spirit and soul did not indeed cease to be God's likeness according to their constitution, for their substance remained unchanged; but they were so no longer according to their life, for their substantially undiminished powers had fallen out of the standing of peace, into that of the Turba, which is the consequence of sin, and the effect of the wrath aroused thereby. How it happened that this state of self-corruption was transferred by inheritance, and could be again made good through no moral act of man, we have already seen in Div. III. Sec. V. But even although absolutely no reasons could be discovered to make this transference intelligible, it is still a fact which confirms itself to the self-knowledge of every individual, in all times and peoples, even to this day. And how radical, how physically and ethically profound, is, at the same time, the ruin consequent upon the fall, is shown by the fact, that even the might of redemption accomplishes its reversal no otherwise than as the progressive effect of a lengthened process, which begins within the sphere of this world's life, passes through death, and is not perfected until the resurrection.

Nothing less was necessary than that, to the primitive Beginning perverted by sin and devoured with wrath, with its development into death, a new beginning of similar creative intensity should be applied; and that, by means of a progressive perfecting of this new beginning, all the mischief wherein the primitive beginning had resulted should be finally abrogated. Any ethical agency of man's on himself was incapable of accomplishing this; and still it could not be onesidedly an act of God's own, since a free nature such as man's cannot be acted upon by compulsion, like a machine. There must thus have been a spontaneous act of God, which might be at the same time a spontaneous act of humanity also. By a transaction of the internal divine nature, which would at the same time be a transaction of the history of the internal nature of man, God's wrath upon humanity must be overcome, and God's love must again be acquired,—thoughts which assuredly could not originate in us, if we did not know that God is a tri-personal being; and which would not originate in our minds, if the mystery of the everlasting counsel of grace had not become actually revealed in the fulness of times.

If God were not a tri-personal being, an Incarnation of God would be absolutely inconceivable. But being tri-personal, there can be conceived as well an event which is reciprocally accomplished within the Godhead, tending to change the divine wrath on humanity into love, as also a self-surrender of one of the three persons into humanity, without the two others renouncing on that account their supra-mundane glory. This self-surrender, indeed, would never be such, that by it the unity of the associated Trinity would be sundered, or the eternal nature of the Godhead, as it is in itself, be changed. But either result occurs in this case as little as it does generally in God's manifold relation to the world. The nature of God remains in every multiplicity of His revelation and operation, *ad extra*, always the same immutably in Himself.

This unchangeable self-identity will be found the more conceivable, if we remember that in the history of the world, and especially of humanity, nothing is realized in time which had not been from eternity in the consciousness and will of the Godhead. This is the case also with redemption. It is the eternal counsel of the Godhead. Its realization is only the temporal completion of that which had been willed from eternity. The world to be created stands eternally before God the Triune, in the mirror of His wisdom (*vid.* Div. I. Sec. II.), not without the manifestation to Him at the same time of the evil that is to usurp power over it, as something to be overcome and to be eradicated by the redemption. But it thus appears to Him, in that He regards the world, and especially humanity, in Christ (Col. i. 16), *i.e.* in the Son of God, who, having become man, will appease the future wrath, and change it into love. If the mystery of redemption had not been from all eternity hidden in God τῷ πάντα κτίσαντι (Eph. iii. 9), the world would never have come to creation at all.

Moreover, let it now be considered that, the world being created, the incarnation of the Son so little contradicts the relation of the Trinity, that rather the three persons work together for the redemption of humanity, in a manner which is the historical counterpart of their eternal reciprocal relation. That the Mediator in the Godhead becomes also the Mediator between God and man; that the Father sends the Son, and begets Him into humanity; that the Son of the Father, as Godman, is unchangeably turned to the Father, and returns back to Him; that from the Father, through the exalted Son, the Spirit proceeds and descends;—these are all images of the eternal relation of the Trinity, in the history, that is encompassed by eternity, of the realized counsel of redemption.

Moreover, this history is infinitely deep and sacred earnest! In consequence of sin, God's wrath, the wrath of the Triune against humanity, is actually enkindled. Even the Son of God, as such, cannot quench this wrath; for it is indeed His own wrath: it is the sacred wrath of the Godhead. But in that He becomes man, and opposes to this wrath a holy human life, over which the wrathful will has no power; and in that He subjects this holy life for humanity, which is His flesh and blood, to the effects of the wrath enkindled in the divine nature, and thence outwardly in the world of spirits and of man, so that this wrath is given Him to drink, even to the last dregs of the cup of death,—He suffers this wrath in a manner propitiatory and meritorious for entire humanity; and thus establishes, instead of the beginning of good that had been lost in wrath, a new beginning, which is rooted in love regained, no longer restrained by wrath. And it is the sacred loving will of the Triune Godhead itself which thus accords itself in the way discovered from eternity, with the not less holy will of wrath, and quenches the not less holy fire of wrath of the judicially aroused *doxa*. The love of God to humanity, as of the Deviser of the work of reconciliation, and the love of the God-man to humanity, as of the Mediator of the work of reconciliation, mutually moved towards one another, and broke through the wrath between them. That these two loves, the eternal love and the historical love plunged into humanity,— the atoning enduring love, and the decreed delivering love,— have joined hands by breaking through the wrath in all its forms, is the fact that has accomplished our reconciliation.

But these are truths, whose biblical and systematic establishment is not a problem of theological psychology, but of dogmatics. On the other hand, it is psychology which has to offer to dogmatics the knowledge that is required for the understanding of the human essential constitution of the God-man: and, moreover, it is incumbent upon it itself, within certain limits to bring the divine-human internal nature of the Redeemer to our comprehension. For, first of all, this divine-human internal nature of the Redeemer is in itself a phenomenon just as enigmatical as it is full of solutions of the enigmas; a phenomenon which puts the fundamental view arrived at by psychology, to a proof from whose decisive reaction it cannot withdraw itself;[1] and further, without a glimpse into the mystery of that man in whom was realized an originally new beginning of humanity, no psychological glimpse into the life of regeneration is possible.

It is confessedly one of the greatest problems of the later theology,—the most sacred and the most deserving of inquiry, in proportion to the pervading impression of true humanity and of undivided unity which the person of Christ produces, as it is presented to us in the Scripture,—to abolish the contradictory dualism beyond which the church view of the God-man has not been able to attain, in such a manner that, without a relapse into long vanquished errors, the substance of the Catholic dogma may be maintained.[2] That will be the true solution which, firstly, holds fast the divine-human double nature of Christ, without assuming, in contradiction to the eternally unchangeable self-identity of God, a changing of the divine nature into the human; which, secondly, acquiesces in the position in its scriptural truth, that in Christ, the Logos is the personifying nature, and the humanity the assumed nature; and which, thirdly, succeeds in showing how the Logos, without ceasing to be what it eternally is, could nevertheless make itself the subject of a

[1] Therefore may be mentioned the title of a book by Jac. Carpov, 1738, which otherwise is a feeble and valueless performance of Wolfianism melted down with orthodoxy: *Psychologia Sacratissima hoc est de anima Christi hominis in se spectata commentatio theologico-philosophica.* Theod. Krüger, in his *Theologia Moralis* (1747), says with reference to this work of Carpov, p. 232: Quamquam psychologia Christi principiis rationis non repugnet, transcendit tamen eandem, et non proponenda est meris sermonibus, quos docet humana sapientia, sed quos potissimum Spiritus sanctus docet, spiritualia spiritualibus comparans. The business of biblical-psychological inquiry in this region is acknowledged even by Beck, *Christliche Lehr-Wissenschaft*, i. 481.

[2] What is taught here, according to Brömel (*Kliefoth-Mejers Kirchlich. Zeitschr.* 1857, p. 144), Hengstenberg, Schenkel, Ströbel (*Luth. Zeitschr.* 1857, p. 760), Philippi (*Glaubenslehre*, iv. i. 369), by making the Redeemer actually a merely pure man, overthrows the manifestly great mystery of salvation. These all proceed upon the supposition, that the Logos, if He surrender His omnipotence, omniscience, and omnipresence, ceases to be God. But this assumption contradicts the declarations of the God-man Himself, who in the Gospels disclaims for Himself these attributes, and still does not thereby disclaim the divine nature. The historical Christ is of more importance to me than the unhistorical defenders of His divinity, and the bugbears of their bungling conclusions. The objections

being so truly human as everywhere meets us in the Christ of the Gospels. The great question is this : How could the Logos so renounce Himself as to surrender His eternal *doxa;* and still more, as to surrender His eternal mode of being, and the attributes flowing from Him to the world, of omnipotence, of omniscience, and of omnipresence, without surrendering the identity of His being? The fact in question is established. The incarnate Logos is not in possession of the eternal *doxa*, for He looks back longingly after it (John xvii. 5). He is not omniscient, for He knows not, as He himself says, the day and the hour of the end (Mark xiii. 32). He is not almighty, for the power over all things is given to Him, as He says after His resurrection (Matt: xxviii. 18). He is not omnipresent, for He ascended up, that He might fill all things (Eph. iv. 10). If these three statements be merely referred to Him as man, the unity of the person is rent by inward contradiction, and the reality of the human nature is changed into an appearance. It must therefore be shown [1] how the Logos might truly and actually surrender the eternal *doxa*, and these attributes of His divine manner of being, without nevertheless surrendering His divine

---

advanced even by Dorner against the notion subsequently set forth of the Kenosis, from the unchangeableness of God, deserve an examination which cannot here be undertaken. We observe here, in general : (1) That Dorner himself reduces the immutability to " ethical self-identity," *i.e.* the divine life of love, willing and maintaining itself ; (2) that he himself teaches that the incarnation is not merely an act of God, as others are, but that it brings with itself a new being of God Himself in the world,—a being which has come into existence through God's act, and which previously only existed potentially, or in counsel ; (3) but that his own view, according to which the *unio naturarum* in Christ did not become a full *unio personalis* till His exaltation, prejudices the truth of the incarnation, and is irreconcilable with the Incarnate One's own declarations, which everywhere express a perfect two-sided divine human self-consciousness, and thus drive him to another solution of the problem. We shall only severally reply to a few objections, especially concerning us, in what follows.

[1] There is found no inclination thereto in theosophy. "Hear dear reason," says J. Böhme, in the *Book of the Three Principles*, xxiii. 8 : " when the Word of God became man in the womb of Mary, was it not then at the same time also high above the stars? When it was at Nazareth, was it not also at Jerusalem, and everywhere in all thrones?" To a similar effect runs the magnificent passage of Melito, " Whilst He wandered on earth, He filled also the heavens," etc., in Cureton, *Spicilegium Sacrum*, pp. 52–54.

being, of which the *doxa* is the radiance, and of which these attributes are the energy.

It has been shown (Div. IV. Sec. IV. and VII.) wherein subsists the fundamental assumption of this possibility. The essence of the absolute personality consists in infinite, absolutely limitless self-determination; and the root of the essence of the Godhead chiefly, and of every one of the three persons in particular, (as, representatively, of the human spirit,) is the will which is related to the actualized self-consciousness as precedent. Thus God's Son, without foregoing Himself, might withdraw Himself to this lowest basis—this radical potentiality—this all-determining ground and origin of His nature; and thus, by renunciation of His essential development, make Himself the subject of a human personality, and become objective to Himself in a newly originating self-consciousness, which, although it has as its substance His actual twofold nature, is still no double nature, but one that arises from a compact divine human ground of life.[1] By this there neither ensued a difficulty in the immanent process of the Trinity, nor a breach in the world-maintaining and world-governing activity of the triune Godhead. There ensued no hindrance in the immanent process of the Trinity: for the act of the Father, by virtue of which He comprises His essential fulness in the Son in exact resemblance and objectively; and that of the Son, by virtue of which He comprehends Himself as God of God, and turns to His primitive source in bright love (Div. IV. Sec. IV.); and that of the Holy Ghost, by virtue of which He, proceeding from Father and Son, brings into manifestation the combined life of the two, and forms the embracing link of the Godhead;—these eternal

---

[1] The kind and manner of the apprehension of the anypostasy of human nature on the part of the ancients, suggests rather a humanity becoming God, than a God becoming man; yet it is also observed by them, that the anypostasy of human nature before its union with the personifying Logos is only an abstraction (see in Schmid, *Dogm.* p. 225). A deeper-seeing knowledge is made possible to us by the fact, that of later times the essence of personality and of life has become more transparent, and thereby the entire view of nature and of history has become organically complete. In the Incarnate One, the Logos is certainly the personifying principle; but the new self-consciousness of the Logos as the Incarnate One has both natures as coefficients, and arises out of the mutual operation of both, combining into one living centre.

acts of the internal divine nature continue in their eternally self-identical progression (to which is related the absolute present ὁ ὤν, John i. 18, iii. 13; comp. viii. 58, xvii. 24). The Son, moreover, remains—in that state of withdrawal, and, so to speak, systole of His essential development, wherein consists His privation—the other divine will, in which is reflected the prototypical will of the Father, and which has the essential fulness of the Father as its moving substance. Further, there ensued no breach in the world-supporting and the world-ruling activity of the triune Godhead: for in the self-renunciation of the Son is realized the eternal loving will of God the triune, and therefore His own eternal will; and " as its realization is one with the government of the world, so it is true not less of the human self-assertion of the Son than of the divine, not less of the mundane than of the supra-mundane, that it is a government of the world on His part. In the womb ripening towards birth,— as a youth increasing in body and spirit,—sleeping and waking, doing and suffering,—He is a sharer in the government of the world; because upon the relation of the Son to the Father herein realized, which has the eternal fellowship of both for its indwelling ground, depends the carrying into action of the eternal counsel."[1] In other words, redemption is the centre of the sustaining and ordering of the world; and when therefore God the Son, retiring to the foundation of His nature, exchanged the form of God for the form of a servant, it caused so little of a breach in the world-maintaining and world-governing activity of the triune God, that in this self-privation of the Son, this activity, without being dissolved therein, rather converged as it were centripetally upon that very self-privation, and had its centre of gravity there, so that the φέρων τὰ πάντα τῷ ῥήματι τῆς δυνάμεως αὐτοῦ (Heb. i. 3) even thus maintained its enduring truth, although under the veil of a mystery not to be penetrated even by the angels; in like manner as the human spirit continues to be the living power that pervades the body by means of the

---

[1] See Hofmann, *Schriftb.* ii. 26 (the second edition, where now also Dorner's and Gess's objections are refuted); and to the same effect, Thomasius, *Dogm.* sec. xlvii. The apparent ceasing of the world-governing activity of the Son, which was the conditioning of His world-reconciling agency, is no cessation of His interest in the government of the world; rather co-operation in it was share in the completion of it.

soul, not less in the bondage of sleep than in the full activity of waking, without any interruption of its self-identical life. The self-privation of the Son, and His divine human passion associated therewith even to death, is indeed rightly considered the most strong-willed, most energetic, most intense self-confirmation of all. In this self-privation the free self-might of the eternal Son culminates, and the eternal love which wills and accomplishes the perfection of the world is concentrated; its effects extend not alone to the whole of humanity, but to heaven and earth.

Before proceeding onwards from this point, we will examine the objections[1] first made by Dorner. To my assertion, that I had arrived in a psychological way to that apprehension of the Kenosis which coincides with that of Thomasius and Hofmann, he makes a note of interrogation; but König, Gaupp, and others also, have made a similar statement. The revision of the traditional views is actually here a necessity felt by many. My leading point of view was the perception, that the will is the essential ground of the spirit, and in archetypal manner of the Godhead also. To my assertion, that the Logos withdrew itself to this lowest basis of its nature, and thus, by privation of its essential development, made itself the subject of a human personality, he observes, " Plainly according to the connection, with privation of His hypostasis also." But no: the Hypostasis continues; only, in its retreat to its essential ground is accomplished the eternal loving counsel of the triune Godhead in a manner historical, and still not interrupted from eternity: in other words, it is perfected temporally upon an eternal foundation. To my designation of this regress from essential development on to essential being, as a systole, he observes, "Like the old Sabellianism;" but what has my ecclesiastical creed upon the triune God to do with the monad of unitarian Sabellianism enclosed in itself, and disclosing or expanding itself in the Logos? To my assertion, that the above comprehension of the Kenosis, as Thomasius shows, is the direct consequence of the ancient Catholic and Lutheran Christology, he remarks, " that the view is not new; and when it was new, and as often as it was renewed, it was rejected by the

---

[1] *Treatise on the Right Conception of the Dogmatic Idea of the Immutability of God*, in the *Jahrbb. für deutsche Theol.* 1856, p. 388: comp. 1857, p. 440; 1858, p. 579.

church." But in fact it occurs in none of the rejected heresies of the œcumenical councils from the first to the sixth, and has, moreover, never been rejected; because it grew out of perceptions which were never familiar in the old church, even to the Formula of Concord, and for that very reason also is not referred to by the more ancient judicial sentences. Finally, when I maintain that the ecclesiastical doctrine of the Trinity is not affected thereby, Dorner suggests to me to consider whether, in so saying, I may not perhaps "have forgotten the Athanasian *Non tres æterni, immensi, omnipotentes.*" Is this to signify that the Son of God cannot deprive Himself of His absoluteness and omnipotence, without this privation at the same time affecting the Father? This conclusion is of no weight. He deprives Himself indeed of His absoluteness and omnipotence, that He may accomplish in Himself, as the centre of the divine loving action, the loving will of the one Godhead, the triumph of which actually consists in this sacrifice. But He can deprive Himself, because He has the self-consciousness which pertains to the threefold self-consciousness of the Godhead. And even after the privation, He remains still the absolute, and the almighty, because, being incarnate, it is by the power of His own will that He is not actually absolute and almighty. As far as regards eternity, however, even Father and Holy Spirit, in their manner, are concerned in the historical process of the work of redemption. The unfolded nature of all the three persons, by the new relation into which the Godhead comes towards humanity, actually undergoes a change, and such a one, too, as is eternally completed, and is eternalized according to the temporal completion. But the eternal fundamental nature of the three persons, and their relation to one another, remains absolutely unchanged; and not only God's ethical, but also His metaphysical identity of Himself with Himself, reaches beyond the process which goes forth from it, and which it turns back into itself. If indeed this conception of the Kenosis led to the consequences which Gess has drawn,[1] we should hasten to reject it, as the mother of the most fatal heresies. For at once the first consequence which Gess infers—that, in order to avoid in

[1] *The Doctrine of the Person of Christ developed from the Self-consciousness of Christ and the Testimony of the Apostles*, 1856; comp. Thomasius, *Dogm.* ii. 196-199.

it that which is fruitless and illusory, the supposition of a human soul in the person of Christ, distinct from the Logos, must be abandoned—would throw us back upon a standing which the church with hard struggles has rejected. But such distortions of truth are only incurred by seeking to grasp the mystery intellectually. We are only concerned with the fact —whose right comprehension has to approve itself in this—that it allows to subsist as well the immanent Trinity of the divine nature, as the true humanity and the personal unity of the two natures constituted in the incarnation, and leaves untouched the old Catholic dogmas upon the subject.

If the Son of God became very man, we must further distinguish, according to the knowledge that we have attained from the natural condition of man, just as well a $\pi\nu\epsilon\hat{v}\mu\alpha$ beginning to be in time, as a $\psi\nu\chi\dot{\eta}$ beginning to be in time, in Him. He even attributes to Himself both: the latter when He says, "My soul is exceeding sorrowful, even unto death" (Matt. xxvi. 38); the former when at His death He exclaims, "Father, into Thy hands I commend my spirit" (Luke xxiii. 46).[1] Further, as in man his spirit, but in the God-man the Logos, is the personifying element, we must assume that, in the moment of incarnation, the eternal will of the Logos surrendered itself up to the temporal will of the human spirit; so that from thenceforward He had this His human spirit in submission to the law of human development, as the mirror of His nature and the place of His consciousness. Thirdly, as the human soul is the sevenfold *doxa* which emanates from the human spirit, so the human soul is the כָּבוֹד (Ps. xvi. 10, comp. ver. 9; Acts ii. 25–27) for which He exchanged His heavenly כָּבוֹד. And fourthly, Because it is the destination of the body by means of the soul to become as the soul itself, the *doxa* of the Spirit, or what is the same thing, a $\sigma\hat{\omega}\mu\alpha$ $\pi\nu\epsilon\upsilon\mu\alpha\tau\iota\kappa\acute{o}\nu$, so mediately also the body of the God-man belongs to the *doxa* of the Logos united to His spirit. This psychico-corporeal *doxa*, indeed, is in a position of humiliation, because the Logos appeared $\dot{\epsilon}\nu$ $\dot{o}\mu o\iota\acute{\omega}\mu\alpha\tau\iota$ $\dot{\alpha}\nu\theta\rho\acute{\omega}\pi\omega\nu$ (Phil. ii. 7), and indeed $\dot{\epsilon}\nu$

---

[1] "Immortalis veritas," says Augustine (*de Agone Christi*, c. 18), "per spiritum animam et per animam corpus suscipiens toto homine assumpto eum ab infirmitatibus suis liberavit." Thus also Hofmann; comp. the direct confession in the *Schriftb.* ii. 43.

ὁμοιώματι σαρκὸς ἁμαρτίας (Rom. viii. 3)—a *doxa* as yet veiled, and still waiting for its perfection; but even in the position of humiliation, the energy of the Logos was still so great, that the eyes of believers perceived in this man the *doxa*, as of the Only-begotten who had come into time (John i. 14); and from what they heard, saw, and tasted, received the impression of the Word of Life that had been from eternity with the Father, and was now manifested (1 John i. 1–3). But the result was, that the Logos broke through the created limits of His natural development, enhanced though they were by the consequence of sin,—a development into which He entered by the power of free agency, and swallowed up the assumed humanity into His recovered primitive *doxa*. The incarnation was a self-humiliation,[1] but now it is so no more.

This Jesus is the second Adam. The good beginning which the first Adam forfeited, found in Him a new indestructible reality, and—because He was exalted—its conclusive perfection. For the presence of God in the first Adam, which by his free agency was to have established itself into a *unio mystica*, was capable of being lost; but in the second Adam, Godhead and manhood have entered by a free agency of the Logos into the position of indissoluble *unio personalis*. This appropriation of human nature, through the Logos, and this impropriation of the Logos into the human nature, became the inviolable ground of a new humanity, which has in the God-man the creative principle and the superabundant archetype of its growth. Union of the spirit of man with God, and, what is the result thereof, perfecting of His psychico-corporeal *doxa*,—this is the twofold aim of the redemption, of which the Redeemer is the archetype for the redeemed. In that now this archetype realizes itself representatively, the psychical condition of man suffers a change, which as certainly falls within the range of biblical psychology as 1 Cor. xv. 45–49 is an apostolic instruction of psychologic character.

---

[1] A. Günther, indeed, says (*Vorschule*, ii. 447, ed. 2), " It is no humiliation of God when He takes back again into Himself that which originally proceeded from Him, by means of reunion;" but what is emptying Himself of glory (see John xvii. 5) other than humiliation? Strikingly, Thomasius had said (*Dogm.*. ii. 236), " In the humiliation, the divine fact of the beginning (the self-limitation already contained in the incarnation) became the divine-human fact of his whole life."

THE NEW LIFE OF THE SPIRIT.

Sec. II.

When, in treating of the fact of the resurrection, and especially of the constitution of the future corporeity, the apostle says, in reference to Gen. ii. 7, that the first Adam was made εἰς ψυχὴν ζῶσαν; the last, *i.e.* the Adam that concludes the history of humanity, εἰς πνεῦμα ζωοποιοῦν,—he characterizes thereby the destination for which man was originally intended, as a destination attained in Christ. For, in the first-created man, spirit and body were first of all united by means of the soul to a self-living nature (ψυχὴ ζῶσα), to whose own decision it was left whether it would allow itself to be determined according to God's mind by the spirit which immediately originates in God, or would selfishly conclude against God in its own separate life. For the soul was first of all the personal link of human nature; but the spirit was to become the personal power, *i.e.* the ruling, glorifying, and, so to speak, personifying power, of the entire personality. This object remained unattained; for the spirit—instead of proving itself ζωοποιοῦν, *i.e.* an all-pervading power of life, in ever increasing energy and with ever extending result—fell under the bondage of the flesh in such a way, that, although its God-resembling substance continues still, its God-resembling life is quenched. Man, from the good, but still in some measure undetermined, position of a self-living ψυχὴ ζῶσα (undetermined, in that it still wanted the confirmation and establishment of man's own proper self-determination), instead of becoming πνευματικὸς, *i.e.* directed on all sides by the spirit that lives and moves in the God who was its source, became ψυχικὸς and σαρκικὸς, *i.e.* altogether determined by his ψυχὴ, fallen away from the spirit, and identified in a mode adversely determined, and by the σάρξ fallen away from the spirit, and therefore, from a material nature, become a gross materialistic nature. The spirit is not what it was intended to be—the personal might of the entire life; but only still a consciousness of the individual life held together by the soul, the Psyche has usurped the right of the Pneuma; in it, and not in the Pneuma, the individual life of the person now has its compact form of existence.[1] But in Christ a new beginning is established, which bears in itself the most infallible guarantee of completion; and on account of the superabundant intensity of its power of propagation, suggests the hope of a renewal of the whole of humanity. The spirit of the first Adam had God's presence, as it were, as a productive root, from which it could be nourished and strengthened, but from which also it might be disjoined. In the second Adam, on the other hand, the Logos united Himself inseparably with the human spirit, in such a way, that in proportion as the threefold human life is developed out of its embryonic elements, the Logos also, which has made itself the personal ground of this life, proves itself more and more to be the divine personifying might of the same. Therefore the apostle says, ὁ ἔσχατος Ἀδὰμ (ἐγένετο) εἰς πνεῦμα ζωοποιοῦν. The essential condition of the Adam that brings the history of humanity to its result, was distinguished at once, à priori, from the essential condition of the Adam that begins it. The latter was a beginning to be completed; the former is the beginning of the completion itself: for His spirit, because united to the Logos, is πνεῦμα ζωοποιοῦν; and it cannot but be that it must prove itself in the region of His own personality, and thence outwardly upon humanity, an all-overpowering principle of Life, and thereby bring forward the end of the completion.

But that the history of humanity should have begun as it now ends, was an impossibility. The apostle asserts this in 1 Cor. xv. 46. The position of man as a spiritually embodied and free nature is of necessity constituted first of all psychical, i.e. subjected to the actualized dominion of the spirit by means of the Psyche. The pneumatic position is the appointed result. Pervading by the spirit, or what is the same thing, glorification of man's nature, is the end, not the beginning. Precisely because it is the end, the πνεῦμα in the New Testament is conceived as occupying a position that overtops and determines all other psychological ideas.[2]

The destination of the earthly man for a life pervaded by the spirit of free powers, which had been placed at an un-

[1] *Vid.* v. Zezschwitz, *Profangräcität u. bibl. Sprachgeist,* p. 46.
[2] *Ibid. l.c.* p. 33.

attainable distance by the fall, is realized in Christ. "The first man," adds the apostle, ver. 47, " is of the earth, formed of dust; the second man is from heaven." But is not then the spirit of the first man of heavenly origin, inasmuch as it was breathed into him from God; and, moreover, is not the corporeity of Christ also of earthly origin, inasmuch as He was born of Mary? True, in both cases: the first man had a heavenly side, and the second man has an earthly side of His nature. Even the corporeity of the Exalted One, although celestially transformed and taken up into the Godhead, is still, in consideration of its origin, no other than that which was assumed in Mary. But still the antithesis of the apostle consists in its complete sharpness; it refers to the fundamentally and essentially distinct commencements of the two founders of humanity. The one, in that God the Creator first of all formed dust of the earth into a human body, had a real earthly beginning; the other, on the other hand, had a personal heavenly beginning, in that God the Redeemer, of His own free self-power, entered into the womb of the Virgin: the one became a person, because the created spirit was united with the body which came into existence without his co-operation; the other was already a person, when He made Himself the subject of a human nature that did not come into existence without His will. While thus the task was proposed to the one, spiritually to overcome the earthly foundation of his being, which anticipated his knowledge and will,—a task which he might, and also which he might not, accomplish, and which in effect he did not accomplish; the other is immediately, *à priori*, Lord in the region of human nature, into which, descended from heaven, He entered, by the power of a consciously free will, without losing Himself; and although His spirit does not at once glorify the body, it is still in the power of the divine heavenly Ego, which is conscious in Him of itself to itself in a human manner, an *à priori* power and guarantee of an infallible glorification.[1] The

[1] I have proceeded above from the critically attested reading, ὁ δεύτερος ἄνθρωπος ἐξ οὐρανοῦ. The ὁ Κύριος which the *textus receptus* has before ἐξ οὐρανοῦ, is, however, altogether according to the meaning of the apostle; and when I consider the intentional expression ἐκ γῆς χοϊκός, it appears to me that as ἐξ οὐρανοῦ corresponds to the ἐκ γῆς, there must also be a predicative idea to correspond to the χοϊκός. The original text had, as I am

apostle is not here concerned with the path of the Lord from the power of glorification to the realization of glorification : he sees Him at once in the heavenly glory of the end attained, but with especial retrospect to the divinely-fulfilled spiritual principle, of which that life of glory must be the unfailing consequence.

When, therefore, in ver. 48 he thence concludes, that as the old humanity, according to the first Adam, must be made earthly, so the new humanity, according to the second Adam, must be made heavenly; and that as we have borne the image of the earthly (the first Adam), so also we shall bear ($\phi o \rho \acute{\epsilon} \sigma o \mu \epsilon \nu$) the image of the heavenly (the second Adam); he means thereby the consummation placed before us at the resurrection, which will bring to outward manifestation that for which the ground is prepared, by our becoming previously inwardly like to Christ, through being transplanted from the position of the $\psi v \chi \grave{\eta}$ $\zeta \hat{\omega} \sigma a$ into the position of the $\pi v \epsilon \hat{v} \mu a$ $\zeta \omega o \pi o \iota o \hat{v} v$; for without participation in the $\pi v \epsilon \hat{v} \mu a$ $\zeta \omega o \pi o \iota o \hat{v} v$ of the Incarnate One, although He was still subjected to the mortal conditions of a fleshly body, we have no part in the $\sigma \hat{\omega} \mu a$ $\pi v \epsilon v \mu a \tau \iota \kappa \grave{o} v$ of the Risen and Exalted One.

But how do we receive a part in the life-giving spirit, and in consequence thereof, also in the spiritual body of Christ, the new heavenly man? A share in the body, soul, and spirit of the first Adam, in their determination by the fall, we have by means of physical begetting, like the lower animals. A new humanity could not possibly originate from Christ in this manner. It originates by means of a new creation, which

convinced, ὁ δεύτερος Κύριος ἐξ οὐρανοῦ without the ὁ before Κύριος. For (1) Tertullian, Adv. Marc. v. 10, translates with the old Latin translation, "Primus homo de humo terrenus, secundo dominus de coelo," without here contending with Marcion. But that the latter, in ver. 45, read dominus novissimus (ὁ ἔσχατος Κύριος) pro novissimo Adam, bears an indirect witness in favour of the originality of the Κύριος in ver. 47. (2) The Greek Dial. contra Marc. writes also the reading, ὁ δεύτερος Κύριος ἐξ οὐρανοῦ, on Marcion's account, who thereby had wished to oppose the reality of the incarnation of Christ. It is plain how ὁ δεύτερος Κύριος became suspicious, as being Marcionitish : one could not reconcile one's self to the true meaning, "the second (man), the Lord from heaven ;" and so found a remedy, partly through a repetition of the ἄνθρωπος, partly by insertion of the article that was intentionally omitted before the predicative idea.

moreover is a birth, but, as a birth from above, is essentially different from the earthly birth. By the power of the eternal Word united in Him with the human constitution of nature, Christ is a person creatively powerful, which, so far generally as the distance of the creature from God permits likeness, can produce from its essence its like; in addition to which, the humanity of the God-man, after it is taken up into the circle of the absolute internal divine life, became the Pleroma and Medium of the entire triune Godhead.

But the new creation is distinguished from the first. The latter created man out of nothingness into existence; the former finds the ungodly being of man in existence, and transforms it into a godly one.[1] Its point of entrance is the conscience, that "remains of spirit in the psychical man;"[2] and it is completed by above all changing the godlessness of man— his separation from God—into fellowship with God, which is effected by the proffer of itself of the newly-acquired divine love through Christ to man, in the word that condemns sin and promises forgiveness of sins, and by man's laying hold of this word and its subject, and receiving them into himself by means of the faith which this word produces. With this most internal operation of all which addresses itself to the innermost nature of man that is unalterably referred to God, and first of all changes man's consciousness of his mutual relation to God, *i.e.* his conscience, into a good one, briefly, with justification, the work of grace begins.[3] Its first operation is a free love, that comes through on God's side to meet man; on man's side a change of consciousness effected *sola fide*. The transference of the human Ego out of the principle of wrath into the prin-

---

[1] For beyond the Sabbath of creation, into which God entered, there is no further creation, in the sense of production of new natures, but only creative confirmation of that which had been fundamentally created at the beginning. This against Schultz, *Voraussetzungen der christl. Unsterblichkeitslehre* (1861), p. 172.

[2] Thus v. Zezschwitz names the conscience (*Profang. u. bibl. Sprachg.* p. 55).

[3] In F. Weber, *Die Lehre vom Gewissen, l.c.* p. 85: "If the difference between the divine and human will came into consciousness in the conscience, there needed faith in the forgiveness of sins to do away with this difference, to receive a good conscience by means of faith, *i.e.* to change the judgment of conscience," etc.

ciple of love makes the beginning (*vid.* Div. III. Sec. V.). Thus, with the new birth or regeneration of the Ego, the work of grace began in the old covenant; and so far as it occurs in the consciousness, it remains also in the New Testament, limited within the present life to this life-giving point of origination.

But since the mystery of the incarnation has been accomplished, other divine agencies are added to this one, which make sinful man a partaker in the spirit, the soul, the body of Christ; whereby, as by his descent from Adam he was earthly, so by his derivation from Christ he may become spiritual and heavenly. These are agencies which,—just as little as in the case of the inbreathing which endued the first man with soul, and just as little as in the case of the descent of children, in respect of spirit and soul, from their parents,—are to be represented as if Christ gave up a portion of His spirit, soul, and body, which is absurd. But there proceed from Christ, according to His threefold human condition, certain agencies, which establish man, in the way of participation with Christ's spirit, soul, and body, in a fellowship which is powerful to transform his own spirit, his own soul, his own body. The work of grace is thus carried forward by the fact, that (1) we receive of the spirit of Christ, which, after it laid aside every limitation in the resurrection, was combined into one with the Holy Spirit, so that all communication of the Spirit, as is shown by the pentecostal gift, is effected since the ascension of Christ through the spirit of the Son of man. This communication of the Spirit again revives the extinguished image of God in our spirit, and keeps it living: it restores our spirit thereby to its true nature; so that man, who even naturally has not ceased to have a $\pi\nu\epsilon\hat{v}\mu\alpha$, now for the first time again begins to have a $\pi\nu\epsilon\hat{v}\mu\alpha$ rightly (Jude 19), and to be $\pi\nu\epsilon\nu\mu\alpha\tau\iota\kappa\grave{o}s$ (1 Cor. ii. 12–16; comp. $\pi\nu\epsilon\hat{v}\mu\alpha$, John iii. 6).[1] (2.) We receive of Christ's soul, for we

---

[1] The matter is clear, and yet is often lamentably confused. That Scripture distinguishes in the work of grace a human $\pi\nu\epsilon\hat{v}\mu\alpha$ from the $\pi\nu\epsilon\hat{v}\mu\alpha$ of God or of Christ, is shown by passages such as Rom. viii. 16, 2 Cor. vii. 1, comp. 1 Cor. ii. 11, v. 3, without contradiction. Looking to his substantial nature, no man is without this $\pi\nu\epsilon\hat{v}\mu\alpha$; but, looking to his destination for a divinely-associated personal power of human entire life, all who stand outside of grace are $\psi\nu\chi\iota\kappa oi$; and in so far as they have extinguished in themselves the last remains of spirit—the conscience—they

receive of Christ's blood; but the blood is the soul, *i.e.* soul and blood are involved in one another (Div. IV. Sec. XI.). It is the blood in and with which He poured out His soul for us (Isa. liii. 12), but not that blood which flowed from His dying form upon the ground, but that which remained, in identity with the former, to Him the Exalted One,—the blood which extinguished the wrath, and is now entirely pervaded in its complete perfect *doxa* by the divine love. This divine human blood of the Mediator becomes the tincture of our soul, whose *doxa* has become Turba;[1] and although, within the range of this life, it still does not abrogate this Turba, yet it removes its liability to condemnation, and therefore its curse; and by the power of love and of peace that it contains in itself, it appeases the raging wild struggle of powers; so that by virtue of this blood, and of the spirit which in Christ's spirit has again become God's, the soul recovers its godlike *doxa*, if not at once in mid-day clearness, yet still, as it were, in morning twilight and dawning. In the essential relation in which the soul stands to the body, this is also to the advantage of the body; but we receive, moreover, (3) of the flesh of Christ, which, because it came into being by means of heavenly begetting in the womb of Mary, and is pervaded by the life-giving Spirit (John vi. 63), is of the nature of spirit, and is communicable for spiritual benefit. This flesh, which He Himself called heavenly bread of life, and manna that makes immortal, enters into us without mingling with our sin-pervaded materialistic animal flesh; but in respect of this our Adamic flesh, it becomes for us a power of gracious encourage-

are absolutely without spirit, $\pi\nu\epsilon\tilde{\upsilon}\mu\alpha$ $\mu\grave{\eta}$ $\check{\epsilon}\chi o\nu\tau\epsilon\varsigma$ (Jude 19). The work of grace consists precisely in this, that it realizes again the lost godlike nature of the spirit that is called to dominion, and develops a spiritual beginning of the man thus once again restored (1 Cor. xv. 45). That in many places it is hard to say whether the human or the divine $\pi\nu\epsilon\tilde{\upsilon}\mu\alpha$ is to be understood, arises from the fact that the $\pi\nu\epsilon\tilde{\upsilon}\mu\alpha$ of the Godhead and of Christ, that has become immanent in the human $\pi\nu\epsilon\tilde{\upsilon}\mu\alpha$, or the human $\pi\nu\epsilon\tilde{\upsilon}\mu\alpha$ renewed by means of this immanence, is meant. Scripture does not in that respect keep divided in conception that which is actually involved.

[1] The seven strings of the soul, says my Elberfeld critic, are out of tune. That which has made them discordant, is the world-spirit that has got within them, and through this the spirit of darkness. If the spirit of Light do not again harmonize the seven strings, their noise and croaking will neither cease in this world nor in the world to come.

ment and of victory—an assurance and pledge of life in the midst of death—a tincture of immortality, which in spite of corruption lays hold of the essence of our flesh, in order eventually in the resurrection to assimilate to itself even its outward appearance.[1]

These three divine agencies peculiar to the New Testament, proceeding from Christ's spirit, soul, and body upon our threefold constitution (1 Thess. v. 23), may be called the regeneration of the natural life; so far as the whole circumference of the constitution innate in man, in which the merely actual Ego is established as a centre, may be comprehended under the name of nature (Div. IV. Sec. II.).

In what distinct way the means of grace, the word and sacrament, serve to this manifestation of the new man accord-

---

[1] That which Philo (who also in his fashion was a forerunner of Christianity) so often lays down as the aim of the soul, to be attained by the condescending and merciful love of God, and of His Logos, has thus first become truly attainable by the incarnation of the Logos, and the fulness of grace disclosed thereby. The ladder which Jacob saw, says Philo (*Opp.* ed. Mangey, i. 642), has a significance of a cosmologic-symbolical and of an anthropologic-symbolical kind. "If we take in view the latter, the soul corresponds to the ladder, whose basis, sensuous perception (αἴσθησις), is corporeal, and so to speak earthly; but its top, the absolutely pure spirit (νοῦς), is heavenly. In the soul, according to its entire nature, the Logoi (λόγοι) of God pass incessantly up and down, drawing it upwards when they ascend, with themselves, detaching it from this mortal state, procuring for it the glimpse of things peculiarly and alone worthy to be seen, without dragging it down when they descend. For God and the divine Logos have not injury in view, but condescend to the human race in kindness and compassion, rendering help and assistance in order to make alive again the soul that is still dwelling in the body as in a fluctuating stream, —powers of healing breathing forth upon it from them. It is true, in absolutely purified dispositions (διανοίαις) God alone dwells unheard and unseen, the director of all, as is declared to the wise man in a recorded saying of God (Lev. xxvi. 12), 'I will dwell in them, and I will be their God.' But to the souls of those who still are engaged in the process of purification, and have as yet not fully cleansed the life that has become foul and polluted by the encumbering corporeity, angels associate themselves, divine Logoi (λόγοι), refining them by the contemplation of their beauty and goodness. How heavy, however, is the evil confusion of evil indwellers, which is expelled when the One Good (εἷς ὁ ἀγαθός) makes His dwelling, is manifest. Therefore, O soul, give diligence still to become God's house—a holy temple; from a soul so absolutely weak, to become a strong; and from one so powerless, a mighty one; a prudent soul, from a foolish one; a deliberate from a frantic one."

ing to the likeness of Christ—this and other dogmatic questions are apart from the purpose of biblical psychology.[1] It would, however, be to circumscribe this science unreasonably, if it were denied the right of expanding itself, in the way in which we have undertaken to develop it, over the new spiritual life. As the naturally pneumatico-psychical constitution of man is a constitution not merely ethically, but also substantially, affected with corruption, so also is its restoration a restitution at the same time ethical and substantial; and therefore the work of grace which is the foundation of this restoration is a psychologic phenomenon. Because the theological sciences are an organism, none is so independent as not to be connected on all sides with the others, and to be articulated with them. One is incomplete without the others. How much need dogmatics have of psychology, and how rightly the latter extends its investigation, even into the soteriologic field, will be still more plainly evident, as we come to agree upon the twofold sphere of human subjectivity, in which the mysterious fact of regeneration is completed.

THE CONSCIOUS AND THE UNCONSCIOUS SIDE OF THE WORK OF GRACE.

Sec. III.

"Marvel not," says Jesus to Nicodemus (John iii. 7), "that I said unto thee, Ye must be born from above. The wind bloweth where it listeth, and thou hearest the sound thereof, but canst not tell whence it cometh, and whither it goeth: so is every one that is born of the Spirit." Nicodemus marvelled because he could not otherwise conceive of a mystery which lay out of the region of the sensible and the natural, than according to sense and nature, and therefore found it contrary to common sense. Jesus, desirous of explaining that the birth from above is not sensible and natural, in condescension to Nicodemus makes use of a parable drawn from the region of nature. The Spirit has its natural analogue in the wind, with which it

[1] *Vid.* thereupon, Thomasius, *Dogm.* iv. 112-121.

has the same name: the wind is the most essentially similar elementary phenomenon to the Spirit of God which pervades the creation, and operates through the entire life of nature. As the wind bloweth where it listeth, *i.e.* now here, now there, without being subject to limits, and without allowing its paths to be prescribed, and as its rush may be heard, although it cannot be determined where it at first began, and how far at the time it may go, or where it may cease;[1] so it is with every one that is born of the Spirit. The operation of the Spirit of regeneration is therefore, (1) a free one, withdrawn from the power of human volition, of human special agency; (2) a mysterious one, lying beyond human consciousness, and only to be recognised by its effects. The regenerated person recognises himself,—when he compares his present condition with his old one and its still uneradicated remains,—as a new man, with a fundamentally changed tendency of all his powers, released, by sprinkling with Christ's blood, from his previously evil conscience, or—what is essentially the same thing—become, by the justifying grace of redemption, instead of a child of wrath, once more a child of the God of love, and renewed in the foundations of his nature according to the image of God, even as that nature has in Christ attained a new creative energy in humanity. He hears the voice of the Spirit, like the rush of the wind, experiencing in himself the testimony of the spirit of his adoption— the groanings that cannot be uttered, mingling with his prayer —the cry of Abba—the discipline of the Holy Spirit manifesting itself in many ways, in instruction, warning, and reproof; he is enlightened once for all; he tastes the heavenly gift of forgiveness of sins, in which are comprehended all the riches of grace; he knows himself in the actual possession of the Holy Ghost; he tastes the dear comforting word of God, and the powers of the future world of perfection, which are already acting upon this present state (Heb. vi. 4 et seq.). But all these things are only the results of that which has transpired in him: the divine fact itself is, and remains for him, in an unattainable depth placed below his consciousness; and as the natural birth, which his natural conscious life has as its foundation, so the spiritual birth, the basis of his spiritual conscious life, remains hidden from him in darkness. He is conscious to himself of that which is effected,

[1] Thus rightly Paul Anton, in Hengstenberg, *in loco.*

but only as the result of a spiritual work that has transpired in the region of his unconsciousness.

It is peculiar to all God's creative agencies, that the creature which is thereby brought into existence, or in which this or that is brought into existence, has no consciousness of what is occurring. When Adam, in consequence of the divine inbreathing, came to the consciousness of himself, his creation was then already perfected; and when God would create the woman out of him, He caused a deep sleep first to fall upon him; and when he awoke, the woman stood before him. It is still just in the same way that man comes into existence. In respect of the husband and wife, who are the instruments of the propagating divine creative power, the moment of conception is associated with an actual veiling of the consciousness; and the consciousness of the spirit of the embryo is germinally restrained, and does not awake until, glimmering as a feeling of self, it finds itself born into the light of the world as a complete man. The creature, in coming into existence, is related to God the Creator as the clay to the potter, Isa. xxix. 16, xlv. 9, lxiv. 7, Jer. xviii. 6, Ecclus. xxxvi. 13, comp. Rom. ix. 20, where the apostle proceeds thereupon to prove the absoluteness of God and of His world-plan as anticipating all consciousness, and all individual agency of man. The creature which God establishes in actual existence is therein absolutely passive. Even to assume only the possibility of a conscious co-operation of the creature, would be absurd.

The like is the case also with the birth from above. Even the first operation of grace which overpowers us, while we allow ourselves to be overpowered, occurs in us as in the condition of sleep and of death (Eph. v. 14). And while the faith which the grace effects, and which lays hold upon and clings to the grace, this first stirring, and this continuous breathing of the new life, is, although in the most manifold modification, a fact of our consciousness; and the word says to our consciousness what God will further give to us by the means of grace, so that we do not take these things for granted at random; yet the events themselves, named and promised by the word, all occur in us in the depth of unconsciousness, and only now and then reflections of them fall from them upon our consciousness. We receive of the spirit, of the body and blood of Christ, and our believing

Ego is transformed into a growing new man within the husk of
the old one: we become—through the God-man, who thus communicates
to us of His essential fulness, and makes us partakers
of His nature—at the same time partakers of the divine nature
($\theta\epsilon\iota\alpha\varsigma$ $\kappa o\iota\nu\omega\nu o\grave{\iota}$ $\phi\acute{\upsilon}\sigma\epsilon\omega\varsigma$, 2 Pet. i. 4), in that the triune God is
internally present to us, and surrounds and pervades us with
His threefold love; but we are able neither to contemplate, nor
even to distinguish, these divine agencies in their beginning and
progress. We know from the word, and from the testimony of
the Spirit by means of the word, what is bestowed upon us by
grace (1 Cor. ii. 12); but we know it in faith. As we have a
natural spontaneous feeling and consciousness of our life, even
without being able physiologically to analyze the process of life
and its factors; and as this life, without our looking through its
mutually involved powers, and even without our applying to it
conscious attention, fulfils itself; so we are in faith certain of
our life from God, without being able to raise the life that is
hidden with Christ in God (Col. iii. 3) into clear and permanent
consciousness; and this life fulfils itself, without being conditioned
by our knowledge and will, sufficiently for us to maintain
that living faith, which unites our Ego with this life, and awaits
the revelation (1 John iii. 2) of the riches of the glory of this
mystery (Col. i. 27). We perceive from Scripture what
occurred to us in baptism and the Lord's Supper: we recognise
the reality of what occurred, from many kinds of consequences
and manifestations which reach into our conscious life;
but to what occurred itself we only stand in the relation of unconscious
passivity; and the fact of what occurred is purposely
withdrawn from our perception, and is, in the sense of Ex.
xxxiii. 22 (where there is permitted to Moses, not the view, but
only the back view—only an after glance of one who was withdrawing
himself), purely *à posteriori*. How could the sacramental
controversy between our Church and the Reformed
Church have arisen, if the nature of the gift and effect of the
sacraments, and especially of the Lord's Supper, were not to be
determined only according to the word of Scripture, but could
have been decided from experimental observation? And if the
fact of regeneration took place in the region of our consciousness,
how would it be possible that there could be found, even
among the most enlightened Christians, such a fluctuation of

views upon the distinction between the operations of the word and of the sacraments? How would it be possible that the question, whether there is also an extra-sacramental tasting of Christ's flesh and blood, should be answered by some in one way, by others in another? What we observed in considering the natural pneumatico-psychical life of man—viz. that as the spirit's existence commences from a condition of unconsciousness, so also all spiritual growth ripens embryonically in the dark depth of unconsciousness (Div. IV. Sec. VIII.), and that this depth conceals within, more than is manifest to man,—is true in a still higher degree, and to a larger extent, of the facts and of the substance of the spiritual life.

In all this we have not yet at all referred to infant baptism. But if, as (Div. IV. Sec. VIII.) we have shown, the embryonic beginning of human life is, at the same time, the beginning of man's threefold—*i.e.* bodily, spiritual, and psychical—life, because certainly what is not *à priori* constituted in germ cannot be developed,—and, as we have just shown, even in the adult the creation of a new beginning of this threefold life is consummated in the region of unconsciousness,—it is not to be doubted that the sacrament of holy baptism may prove, even in the newly born child, to be a bath of regeneration, and may operate in its independent natural life the beginning of a spiritual life; especially as the God-man, because He Himself was a child, became even for the age of childhood in His manner the possibility and power of regeneration.[1] But still this does not vindicate infant baptism. For all regenerate life has faith as its indispensable postulate—since above all, the Ego of the man is to be restored from perdition. Faith is just the proof to one's self of the Ego turned towards the regenerating, and first of all justifying, grace, and laying hold upon it; and baptism with respect to the man who undergoes it in right apprehension is actually a longing that appeals to God for a good conscience.[2] Rightly, therefore, has the question as to

---

[1] "Omnes enim," says Irenæus, ii. 22, 4, "venit per semet ipsum salvare, omnes inquam, qui per eum renascuntur in Deum, infantes et parvulos et pueros et juvenes et seniores. Ideo per omnem venit ætatem, et infantibus infans factus, sanctificans infantes."

[2] Thus is συνειδήσεως ἀγαθῆς ἐπερώτημα εἰς Θεόν (1 Pet. iii. 21) to be understood, with Güder (*Die Lehre vom Gewissen nach der Schrift*, in *Stud.*

the justification of infant baptism concentrated itself in the minds of our dogmatists in the question, whether infants are able to believe. They recognise the conclusion, that he who is not capable of faith (*capax fidei*), is, moreover, not capable of regeneration (*capax regenerationis*).[1] This conclusion is perfectly scriptural. The birth of the spirit cannot be a divine agency that leaves man's spirit alone; it must, before all things, be a divine agency that comprehends this. If it be supposed that a change so ethico-physical as regeneration could occur even in its elementary beginning without co-operation of the personal Ego, then the very centre of human nature is excluded from the regenerating agency of God, in a way that contradicts the personality of man; and if it be supposed that, in the child that is baptized, the necessity for redemption and the desire for redemption take the place of faith, the enigma is not solved, since this impulse for redemption, if it is not to be as a blind natural impulse, must have the Ego as its subject, no less than faith must. For although the consciousness of the Ego be not associated with all human impulses and conceptions, still they are distinguished from those of the brutes, by the fundamental notion of Ego, even although it remains in the background. Or if one supposes that by baptism—by the power of the relation of grace which the triune God introduces into it—the child is only transferred into the possibility of a regeneration to be realized subsequently (which is confessedly the prevalent view of the Reformed churches), then baptism—which nevertheless finds in the child no obstacle of opposition, as in the unbelieving adult—is emptied of the peculiar efficiency attested by the Scripture. As, after what has been above said, the view often expressed since the time of Augustine[2]—that the want of faith and intention on the part of the child may be supplied by the faith of the sponsors and of the whole church,—needs no refutation, the justification of infant baptism remains thus,

u. Kritiken, 1857, pp. 283-285), Hofmann (*Schriftb*. iii. 184), Schott, and others; for that ἐπερώτημα means not the beseeching inquiry, but the granted claim, as v. Zezschwitz (*De Descensu*, p. 45) assumes with Besser, is contrary to the logic to be presumed of the definition.

[1] See Schmid, *Dogmatik der Ev. Luth. Kirche* (edit. 4), p. 413.

[2] "In ecclesia salvatoris," says Augustine, *e.g.*, *c. duas ep. Pelag.* i. 22, "parvuli per alios credunt, sicut ex aliis quæ in baptismo remittuntur peccata traxerunt." Just so subsequently Luther also.

without evasion, conditioned by the question whether the infants can believe. If faith were a work of man's own, with a human initiative, then this question would have to be answered absolutely in the negative. But if faith is a human condition of divine operation, a work of the grace that prevents man, and takes its Ego for itself, there is left a possibility to reply to the question in the affirmative. Depending on this, our old dogmatists affirmed it when they said: Habent infantes fidem non reflexam aut discursivam, sed directam et simplicem a Spiritu sancto, cui malitiose non resistunt, per baptismum accensam.[1] For this reason, Brenz has the distinction of faith into a hidden (*abscondita*), and a manifest (*revelata*), faith. Others distinguish *fides habitualis* and *actualis*, or *actus seu operatio fidei primaria et immediata*, and *secundaria et mediata*;[2] but now that we are more closely entering upon the distinction indicated,—which, not only for the question of infant baptism, but generally for the right judgment of the spiritual life, is of the greatest importance,—it will be manifest that its most appropriate designation is *fides directa* and *reflexa*.

THE ACTUS DIRECTI AND REFLEXI OF THE LIFE OF GRACE.

Sec. IV.

In order to elucidate the meaning of this distinction, which was first applied dogmatically by Mart. Chemnitz, we proceed from a fact that belongs to the department of the revelation of creation, in which it appears accurately expressed. After Paul, in Rom. i. 20, has said how God from the beginning of the world

---

[1] Thus, for example, Hollaz in the *Cap. de gratia regenerante* of his *Examen*.

[2] See, for the history of this distinction, Dieckhoff, *Abendmahlslehre*, i. 183–186, who says here, among other things: "The precise distinctions which here become necessary, may first be found with scientific certainty on the ground of an anthropology and ethics prosecuted in conformity with the faith of the Christian revelation."

made Himself known to human knowledge by His works, so that men are without excuse, he goes on : " For although they knew God, they glorified Him not nor thanked Him as God, but became vain in their imaginations, and their foolish heart was darkened." It is surprising that the apostle here attributes to men a γνῶναι τὸν Θεὸν, whilst the heathens, who are here especially under consideration, are elsewhere called τὰ ἔθνη τὰ μὴ εἰδότα τὸν Θεὸν (1 Thess. iv. 5; Gal. iv. 8). In both cases ὁ Θεὸς is the true God; so that thus in the same subject knowledge of the true God is affirmed and denied. If γνόντες be resolved into γνῶναι δυνηθέντες, it is an unjustifiable exegetical violence. If the attempt be made to understand γνόντες as pluperfect, the 19th verse testifies, on the other hand, that the apostle considers this γνῶσις not as something past, but as something in the midst of the thanklessness and apostasy present there : for he says of men upon whom the wrath of God is revealed, because they restrain the truth in unrighteousness, that that which may be known of God, *i.e.* God Himself, so far as He has made Himself the subject of knowledge by creation, is manifest in them, and is therefore present to their consciousness.[1] Thus the question still remains, in what sense the apostle attributes to the heathens an acquaintance with or knowledge of God, which he elsewhere denies to them. The meaning of the apostle is doubtless this, that God reveals Himself to all men in His works; that they have an organ of perception corresponding to Him;[2] and that they all really acknowledge Him also

---

[1] In Ps. xix. this γνωστὸν τοῦ Θεοῦ stored up in the creature is called (ver. 3) יַבִּיעַ, "Day unto day bubbleth forth the tidings"—*i.e.* as out of a living inexhaustible opening, the knowledge of God overflows from one day to another—" and night unto night showeth forth knowledge," *i.e.* every approaching night sets forth the tidings to that which has vanished; so that thus the knowledge of the Creator which is offered to the creature, is conceived of as in incessant expression. Our forefathers call it an *objectivum vocis non articulatæ præconium.*

[2] Oetinger calls it *sensus communis;* see thereon, Fabri, *The Sensus Communis the Organ of the Revelation of God in all Men,* 1861. The *sensus communis* is the capacity—which has remained to man ever since the fall—of recognising God as Creator and Lawgiver and Lord, in the witness of the creature, and of the conscience, and of history,—the residuum left to man of his likeness to God, which may be acknowledged without thereby abating the greatness and depth of original sin and its results, and which must be acknowledged as the result of the above clear testimonies of Scripture.

actu directo;[1] but that their knowledge has never come to the inner assent to this self-revelation of God, never to the internal comprehension of Him, never to the free making-subjective (*Subjectivirung*) of the objectively revealed divine, *i.e.* it has never come to *actus reflexus.* For, as the apostle says in ver. 28, men did not regard it as worth the trouble to have God in their knowledge. He here uses ἐπίγνωσις purposely instead of γνῶσις ; for ἐπίγνωσις, as distinct from γνῶσις, is always an actually recognising apprehension of the object, whereof not the ἐπίγνωσις, although perhaps the γνῶσις, may be a false, a dead apprehension.[2] Men refused to accept God, and thus to have Him in ἐπίγνωσις, *i.e.* to make Him the reflex subject of their consciousness, although He was objectively knowable to them, and was therefore spiritually perceived by them *actu directo.* Their ungodly will permitted not that result to be produced; similarly as the Pharisees, from the works of Jesus, without being able to evade them, received the impression of the most intimate divine association of His person, but did not allow the knowledge that arises from this impression to get at them. For it is with spiritual perception as with the vision of sense. When the eye falls on an object, this object is copied in the eye, without the eye being able to evade it; but it can immediately turn away from the object perceived, or become closed to it.

We meet with the same distinction of *actus directi* and *reflexi* as in the first chapter of Romans, in the prologue of St John's Gospel. When the Evangelist says there, in ver. 4, καὶ ἡ ζωὴ ἦν τὸ φῶς τῶν ἀνθρώπων,—*i.e.* that life which was in the person of the Word, and which was the Word in person, was the light of men,—he regards in this statement[3] the operation of the Logos, inclusively of His incarnation, yet wholly apart from the relation of men to that light for which the life of the Logos

---

[1] Tholuck thinks, probably, in substance the same, when he calls this a potential latent knowledge."

[2] Comp. Huther, *On the Epistle to the Colossians,* p. 75.

[3] See Hengstenberg, *in loco:* " The thought can only be, that the Logos from the beginning was virtually the light and life of men ; so that, before He appeared in the flesh, men were excluded from light and life,"—according to my own most decided conviction contrary to the spirit of the Gospel of John,—which teaches a saving operation of the Logos even prior to His incarnation.

was disclosed to them: he expresses only the fact, that the life of the Logos disclosed itself *radio directo* for the light of entire humanity, and shone into its internal eye. For further on (ver. 5) he is constrained to complain that the light which shone in darkness was not welcomed with any desire of humanity to be enlightened by the light: the light became thus what in itself, and *actu directo*, for humanity, it was not, even in subjectively reflected operation. In the same objective sense, the Evangelist says (ver. 9) of the true light, ὃ φωτίζει πάντα ἄνθρωπον, distinguishing sharply the divine agency going forth upon man, and man's relation thereto. The true light beams without exception upon every man: it has the destination, and the power, and the desire, to enlighten every man; but here also is repeated the mournful complaint, that the world of humanity did not acknowledge Him who wished to be its light, although it was He by whom it received its existence.

The *actus directus*, in both those cases of revelation which are treated of in the introductions to the Epistle to the Romans and to the Gospel of St John, is rather divine than human. A divine power, offering and awakening acknowledgment, penetrates from what is perceived into man, who stifles the growth of the recognition at the moment when it ought to begin. Just thus it is with the means of grace, with Word and Sacrament. If no condition of external comprehension be wanting to the hearer, yet he does not receive the word without the manifestation in him of the divine energy of its power of conviction. Even although he purposely restrains all wholesome reflection of it in himself, the word, once understood and received, has attained in him, with the power proceeding *radio directo* from it, an internal objectivity: he bears it, although μὴ συγκεκραμένον τῇ πίστει (Heb. iv. 2), in his knowledge and memory; it is in him as a seed fallen upon stony ground—for the man it is as dead—but in itself it is living, and—so soon as the ground of the human heart becomes loosened—striking root and shooting forth. As long as man resists, the word in him is as a power of judgment; but in the fact that he knows the word of the grace of God in Christ, he has still great advantage over him who knows it not: for he needs only to forsake his resistance, and the word in him will be manifested as a power for the enlightenment of his spirit, and for the changing of his personal life. What is true of the word, in the event of its attaining to man's knowledge, is true also of the sacraments, in the event of man's submitting himself to them freely, with the view of receiving them. The condition of their saving reception is faith. There is no such thing as a saving effect of the sacraments that is not conditioned upon faith and that in this sense occurs *ex opere operato*.[1] Without faith, there is attained no reflex possession of the sacramental gifts, and no reflex consequences of the sacramental agencies. But even in the case where the faith of the receiver does not respond to the sacraments, and the unbelief of the receiver does not allow itself to be overcome, they remain, in their substance and power, what they are in themselves by virtue of the inviolable will of God, which is linked to no human condition. He who is baptized, even if he have not received baptism in a right mental comprehension, needs not to be baptized again : the substantial contents of the sacrament have attained in him a living presence once for all, and there needs only faith, that that may realize itself in a reflex manner in him to his salvation, which he already has inwardly present *actu directo*, and which *radio directo* ever presses to be realized in him.[2] And he who does not receive the Lord's Supper in true faith, still receives Christ's body and blood; and the sacramental gifts manifest themselves in him, in the hope that he may allow them to redound to salvation as disciplining powers (1 Cor. xi. 29–32). The substantial completeness of the sacrament is in neither case dependent on the faith of the receiver.[3] But if man in both cases receives what the sacraments by their appointment convey, their saving purpose in the case of unbelief is at least so far attained, that the saving benefits comprehended in the sacraments are brought into immediate nearness to the man. They are appropriated to him by God, for the

---

[1] This is the very kernel of the polemics of our doctrinal writings against the scholastic *opus operatum*. In remembrance of the assertion of Julius Müller (*Die Evangelische Union*, 1854, p. 290), that in the doctrine of the sacraments I find myself in contradiction to the creed of my church, I might underline the above passage three times.

[2] The passage of Schöberlein (*Jahrbb.* 1861, p. 71) goes too far : "Mere baptism without faith establishes a body of the new man without a soul: faith without baptism, a soul without a body."

[3] Thus say our creeds and dogmatists : Fides non requiritur ad substantialem sacramenti integritatem. *Vid.* Schmid, *l.c.*, p. 400.

purpose that he should appropriate them to himself by means of faith.¹

Psychologically, it is not to be wondered at. The sacramental gifts, indeed, are pneumatical. For even the God-man, in respect of the nature of His personality, is wholly πνεῦμα (2 Cor. iii. 17). But God, who is spirit, can make Himself present in man as, and by what means, He will. He can encircle man with His wrath, or in grace with His love. By the sacrament He makes Himself present to him in the whole might of His redeeming, regenerating love. That man who, nevertheless, does not believe, is as a blind man who does not see the sun which beams upon him, or as a dead man, before the door of whose grave, as before that of Lazarus, Christ the raiser of the dead is standing. Much is conferred upon him by grace—a treasure is concealed in his field—he can raise it at any time.² He needs only to open the eyes of faith, and he finds himself in a paradise, which existed without his faith, and prior to it. The true light which shines into the darkness, and enlightens every man *radio directo* (John i. 5–9), has gathered itself around the Ego of the baptized person in the narrowest circle of light. The Ego needs only to open itself in faith, and the whole man becomes a light in the Lord (φῶς ἐν Κυρίῳ, Eph. v. 8).

It is thus with the adult who, without having living faith, submits himself to baptism. It is otherwise with the child. In order to understand the difference, let the following considerations be pondered. As the direct results of the grace of God going forth upon man, and surrounding him, have faith as their first and essential reflection ; so, on the other hand, the faith itself is, according to its nature, an *actus directus* : namely, a line drawn from us up to Christ, and to God in Christ; a longing

---

¹ In my *Four Books of the Church* (1847), and my *Catechism of the House of God in the Church* (1849), I have shown what important results flow therefrom upon the doctrine of the church; and it is since more and more acknowledged, that the divine operations that are performed upon man, on his personal and natural side, by means of the word and sacrament, are the ground of the church's unity, and that the holy sacraments, according to their special agency, form the spiritual natural ground of the church, or, what is the same thing, they articulate it into the body of Christ, and establish it in the articulation.

² Thomasius makes use of this figure, *Dogm.* iv. 117.

reaching forth to the salvation offered in word and sacrament; a look turned away from the innate natural state direct to Christ; an awakened yearning for His grace; a grasp and apprehension having relation to this grace in the unity of all one's powers (Div. IV. Sec. IV.). This *actus directus* has in itself the promise of 'God. The *actus reflexi* of divine assurance, of joyous self-certainty, of experimental seeing and tasting, belong not to the essence of justifying faith; but the former *actus directus* is, as our ancients say, the *forma fidei essentialis*. "It is necessary," says one of them,[1] "to acknowledge a twofold manifestation of faith. The first is called *actio directa*, by which we lay hold of and embrace Christ; the other *actio reflexa*, by which we acknowledge our own doing, and feel or experience that we have apprehended Christ. By the former we believe, to speak accurately, on Christ; by the second, however, we become assured of the fact that we believe, and the faith which has laid hold on Christ falls back softly and sweetly into itself. But there are many who have really laid hold on Christ, although they do not feel that they have apprehended Him; and these are none the less justified. For we become incontestably righteous by the *actio directa*, and not by the *actio reflexa*: we become justified, not because we feel that we believe, but so far as we only believe." The faith is thus in its essence *fiducia supplex* (assurance of refuge), not *fiducia triumphans seu gloriosa* (assurance of experience). The faith is God's agency, as well in the former state as in the latter: in the one, it is the operation of His grace condescending towards man; in the other, it is the operation of that grace apprehended, and assuring itself, and giving itself to be apprehended by man.

But if the faith, even as *actio directa*, be God's agency, it is not to be perceived why the grace of regeneration, which is introduced into man by baptism (as also by the Lord's Supper), associated with the word, cannot effect even in the child the faith necessary to its saving reception.[2] It is said that faith

---

[1] In Pontoppidan's *Glaubensspiegel*, pp. 301-3. The divine assurance is called by him *reflexio passiva et supernaturalis:* the self-certainty that arises from self-examination according to God's word, *reflexio activa et rationalis sc. syllogistica.*

[2] See, on the older dogmatic writings belonging to this subject, the

is not possible, and not conceivable, without consciousness. But (1) the condition of the child is certainly not the absolute opposite of consciousness: the entire threefold life of the man is already existing in the child, although in the first commencement of its development; therefore even already it is the growing consciousness.[1] The unconsciousness out of which it is developed is distinct from the brute condition of impersonality, and remains indeed, even in the adult man, the reverse side of consciousness,—the ground wherein it is submerged in ceaseless variation, and whence it emerges again, as, according to God's ordinance, night and day, contrasted with one another, ceaselessly change into one another. Wherefore, then, should God not be able to effect in the remotely glimmering consciousness of the child a germinal faith, just as well as a developed faith in the daylight consciousness of the adult; especially as (2) even in the adult, not merely in sleep, but even in the midst of every strenuous labour not immediately religious, and in conditions of sickness surrounded with darkness of the most manifold kind, the *actio directa* subsides, out of the region of consciousness, into unconsciousness, without by that means losing its existence, which ever again breaks through these bonds, and

German treatment of the dissertation of J. G. Walsh, *de fide infantum*, by A. L. Müller, Jena 1729, 8.

[1] Therefore Cyprian asks, with reference to the baptism of infants, *Quid ei decet, qui semel in utero Dei manibus formatus est?* And therefore, as Dorner argues (*Jahrbb. für Deutsche Theolog.* 1856, p. 406), the union of both natures in Christ, although the divine-human self-consciousness starts from a dark ground, is from the moment of conception a *unio personalis*. The child is not *res*, which BECOMES *persona*; it is from the very beginning an entire man, growing on all sides. Not inappropriately, K. Göbel compares baptism to the so-called inoculation into the sleeping eye, which, in the hope that the eye engrafted on the wild stock will shoot in the spring, is examined in the midsummer of the second sap. The good eye remains indeed, the whole winter through, in as it were a sleeping state, and pushes forth first with stirring life and full impulse of sap in the spring; but it is already growing in the autumn, so far as it remains alive: it is then taken up into the attraction of the sap of the wild plant, although it does not till later put forth visible shoots. See Göbel's essay, *Die Kindertaufe eine Oculation aufs Schlafende Auge*, in the *Neuen Reformirten Kirchenzeitung*, 1855, Nos. 21 and 22, where nevertheless is asserted, that "the seed of life which God plants in baptism in the newly-born child must not be called faith, otherwise the idea of that faith which justifies is prejudiced."

even in powerlessness and seeming death, in phrenzy, and in the highest degrees of resistance bordering on despair, may continue to subsist, as seen by God's all-penetrating eye? Faith in its perfect matured condition certainly subsists in the perfectly conscious acts of *apprehensio cognoscitiva, approbativa,* and *appropriativa;* but every believer knows from experience, that his faith began with a secret divine agency upon his will; and that this turning of the will already included, undeveloped in itself, those acts of faith. To this point of unity faith ever and anon returns: why should it not be able to begin therewith also in the child? The glimpse of Him who has overcome curse and death for us, is compared indeed to the glimpse of the serpent lifted up in the wilderness (John iii. 14). Such an inclination to Christ, effected by God, is even possible in little children (Matt. xviii. 6, τῶν μικρῶν τούτων τῶν πιστευόντων εἰς ἐμέ), and even not impossible to newly-born children; for the consciousness begins from a remote point of growth, when it is still as none, and even indeed actually still none, thus also faith must be able to begin from a remote point of growth, when it is still as if none, and even in fact actually none, but yet is already present in seed and germ.[1] Even already in the life of the embryo the Scripture (as we saw in Div. IV. Sec. VIII.) declares secret spiritual occurrences. We are teaching in this, nothing essentially different from what is affirmed by Thomasius and Martensen also: for although Thomasius, on the one hand, indeed denies that baptism creates a conscious condition, that it creates a personal faith in the child; but, on the other hand, designates its effect as an inward laying open of the human spirit to the divine work of grace, corresponding to the natural opening of the life of the child towards the mother's love, which experimentally reaches far behind the awakening of the self-consciousness back into the earliest dawning life of the suckling,[2]—still, herewith is attributed to baptism the effect of that which determines the essential ground of faith: for what is faith, except the unclosed inner eye, which adopts into itself the form of God the Redeemer?

---

[1] It is plainly seen from St John's Gospel what kind of a progressively gradual idea πιστεύειν is: it there runs through all degrees, from the lowest to the highest.

[2] *Dogm.* iv. 141.

What we postulate is an effect of baptism comprehended in the word upon the whole man. The final aim of the new creation, says Martensen,[1] altogether in our sense, is the new man, who does not become perfectly manifest until the new heaven and the new earth become manifest,—where not only the spirit, but also the corporeity, celebrates its resurrection,—where spirit and nature dissolve into glory. The new creation, which embraces the whole man—body, soul, and spirit—must for that reason begin from an organic point, which is the point of union of spirit and nature, and in germinating fulness contains what appears disjoined in temporal development. This hidden ground of life is the mystery of baptism. Every one of these words of Martensen bears the stamp of truth. It is just this, that is wanting to our view, that baptism comprehends the natural aspect of the child not exclusively of his personality, but, in a manner exalted above the merely symbolic circumcision, places the entire personality (נפש) of the man in a living and new relation to God.

The final psychological ground of possibility of all, is found in the fact that the spiritual life, and in a typical manner also the life of the soul, have, as their lowest foundation, not the reflected self-consciousness, but the will and impulse which contain in themselves this self-consciousness unreflected; that, expressed in Hofmann's mode of viewing it, there is a natural will which precedes the personal will;[2] and that the operation of the sacraments, according to Stahl,[3] is directed not so much to our occasional determinations of will, as to the substance of our will, *i.e.* to the nature and essence of our spiritual being. To this radical unity, situated on this side of the reflected self-consciousness, corresponds a unity situated beyond the reflected self-consciousness, in which will and thought combine together to culminate in a third form of life: the region of the human πνεῦμα in the narrow sense, which we have already learnt to

[1] *Dogm.* sec. 253.
[2] See thereupon, *Schriftb.* i. 517, comp. iii. 196 : "It is the natural life of man, in which he is sold under sin; so that the effect of divine power of life upon it becomes a counter agency against the power of evil in him;" wherein, nevertheless, is to be observed, that the consequence drawn by us is not drawn by Hofmann.
[3] *The Luth. Church and the Union* (1859), p. 159.

recognise, in Div. IV. Sec. V., as distinct from the human νοῦς, according to 1 Cor. xiv., as the medium of the speaking with tongues. As there are acts of the spiritual life which precede the reflected self-consciousness, so also there are such as restrain the actual self-consciousness. These we shall now more closely consider.

THE THREE FORMS OF THE DIVINELY-WROUGHT ECSTASY, AND THE THEOPNEUSTIA.

Sec. V.

WE begin by recapitulation. The natural spirit-life of man is rooted in the still undistinguished unity of the will: it acts in the self-consciousness proceeding therefrom, which comprehends the acts of thought and will that have now become distinctive (νοῦς or λόγος); and it culminates in the mind (πνεῦμα τοῦ νοός, or πνεῦμα in the narrower sense), in which thought and will are dissolved into a third form of life—of a view or perception situated beyond their distinction.[1] Conformably to this, the supernatural spirit-life (the spiritual) is threefold. There are (1) operations of divine grace which stimulate or move our will, and precede the self-consciousness; (2) such as proceed upon our self-consciousness, and aim at becoming taken up, from conscious thought into conscious will; (3) such as give to our mind the experience of heavenly blessedness, and the view of the mysteries of the kingdom of heaven.[2] In the operations of grace of the third kind, so far as they do not transcend the mea-

---

[1] It will be remembered here that Plato distinguishes the νοῦς as seeing and as comprehending (effecting the ἐπιστήμη): the New Testament πνεῦμα τοῦ νοός corresponds in some measure to that perceiving νοῦς which Plato considers as the innermost highest pilot (κυβερνήτης) of the soul.

[2] We place first experience, as Ps. xxxiv. 8, טַעֲמוּ וּרְאוּ. "Nisi gustaveris," says Bernard, "non videbis. Manna absconditum est, nomen novum est, quod nemo scit, nisi qui accipit. Non illud eruditio, sed unctio docet, non scientia, sed conscientia comprehendit."

sure of that which is customary in the work of grace, there prevail indeed experience and perception beyond the reflecting will and discursive thought; nevertheless, these still always make themselves observable therein, as ascending and descending impulses. But there are also extraordinary operations of grace of this kind, which act on the human spirit in its disposition, in such a way that all reflection of the spirit upon itself, and upon that which happens to it, is lost in the power of the all-devouring impression. This is the state of ecstasy. We have already considered phenomena of this kind—so far as they are composed of influences natural, demoni-angelic, and divine[1]—in the final paragraphs of Div. IV. They now concern us only as pure miracles of grace.[2]

There is a threefold kind of such ecstasy pertaining to the new life from God—the mystic, the prophetic, and the charismatic. (1.) The mystic.—The more manifestly and perfectly the man loves God above everything, and the more earnestly and constantly he crucifies his flesh, with the affections and lusts, the deeper, clearer, and stronger becomes his spirit-life, the more richly his death to all earthly things is compensated by supra-terrene experiences. It happens sometimes, that the indwelling of Christ and God and His Spirit—which, besides, is the supporting and originating ground of the life of the new man (Gal. ii. 20; 1 Cor. xiv. 25; Rom. viii. 14; 1 John iii. 24) —signalizes itself with such an energy in the believer, that the human individual life is overflowed and swallowed up by the divine, as by a river of delight (Ps. xxxvi. 8), in respect of which our fathers quote the example of the holy Ephrem, who, after his conversion, experienced such wondrous consolation, that he often cried to God, "Lord, withdraw Thy hand a little,

---

[1] "L'extase n'est qu'une forme indifferente en elle même," says very truly Theophile Rivier, in his *Etude sur Balaam*, Lausanne 1856, " ce qui lui donne une valeur morale, c'est le fond bon ou mauvais qui la remplit, la puissance salutaire ou pernicieuse qui agit en elle."

[2] We call *grace* everything which proceeds from the principle of the divine love turned back again to humanity in Christ, and *nature* all that belongs to the natural constitution of man creatively established, and become through sin selfish, and subjected to the influences of the kingdom of darkness. The extraordinary phenomena of the soul-life take for granted, without distinction, so-called magic or mystic capabilities based in man; but they are distinguished according to the cause which brings these capa-

for my heart is too weak to receive such excessive joy." It is
the presence of the divine love which, in such extraordinary
cases, hurries along with it man's will and self-consciousness,
and breaks out with such force in his mind (Rom. v. 5), that it
is altogether occupied and taken possession of by it. In other
cases it is certified, that the walk of the Christian is in heaven
(Phil. iii. 20, comp. Zech. iii. 7) actually, by the fact that
the future glory is not merely revealed to his perception as a
subject of hope (1 Cor. ii. 9), but is given him for a moment
to see and to share in by way of foretaste, as *e.g.* Thomas
Aquinas, in his last illness, after a long-continued ecstasy, cried
out, *Arcana verba audivi;* and John Arndt, awaking from a
short sleep, cried, " We saw His glory;" but chiefly, as Paul
relates of himself (2 Cor. xii. 1-4), that he once was caught up
into the third heaven, and indeed into the heavenly paradise,
and there heard unspeakable things, which it is not permitted
to any man to utter. Emphatically, he repeats that he knows
not whether at that time he was ἐν σώματι or ἐκτὸς (χωρὶς)
τοῦ σώματος, God knoweth. At any rate, what is experienced
in such ecstasies is a prelude of that separation of the soul
from the body that results in death (Div. IV. Sec. XIV. towards the end), during which separation the body is usually
found in a cataleptic condition, *i.e.* a state similar to the rigidity
of a corpse : but it remains an enigma whether the soul is actually separated from the body, and whether this does not draw
death after it, only for the reason that what is experienced is
compressed, like eternity, into a momentary now ; or whether
the union of the soul with the body continues to subsist, in that
the withdrawal is an extra-local one, and therefore may be re-

bilities into action, and their moral worth is measured according thereto.
Only in the light of the religion of revelation experimentally attested, is it
possible to see one's way in this region. The works of Bastian (*Der Mensch
in der Geschichte. Zur Begrundung einer psychologischen Weltanschauung,*
3 vols. 1860) and of Perty (*Die mystischen Erscheinungen der menschlichen
Natur*, 1861) show in what a labyrinth one is lost who despises the
criteria offered to Christians in God's word. The former refers everything
to nature and deception ; the latter to the magical power of man, to which
he most credulously entrusts the incredible, and to the participation in
the knowledge and power of the Geo-dæmon (earth-spirit), which his
fancy (like Fechner's, in his *Zendavesta*) interpolates between the universal
Spirit (God) and man.

garded just as much as a condescension of that which is heavenly, as an exaltation to the same.[1]

We distinguish this kind of ecstasy which has as its aim the strengthening and recompensing of personal faith, from the prophetic. For (2) the prophetic has, as its characteristic attribute, the purpose, according to its vocation, of announcing that which is given to be experienced and to be seen. If we consider prophecy in general, there cannot be perceived a qualitative distinction between that of the Old and New Testament. They are distinguished neither in regard of manifold spiritual operations, which are removed sometimes more and sometimes less remotely from the limits of natural life; nor in respect of the manifold vocation, which is by no means exhausted in special foreseeing and foretelling. That which is common to all prophecy of both Testaments, subsists in the fact, that it is the receiver and the bearer of direct revelations of God, significant in respect of salvation.[2] The prophet speaks always on divine impulse, with divine power, from divine communication or information, which has to justify its authenticity as well by its substance as by the circumstances that accompany it (1 Cor. xiv.; Eph. iii. 5). Among the many Hebrew synonyms of vision, חָזָה is the standing general expression for prophetic perception, whether vision or word be the form in which the divine is announced to the prophet.[3] In both cases he sees it, in that he distinguishes, by means of the spiritual eye of the inward sense—which is designated after the noblest of the five external senses—this divine thing in its supernatural objectivity

---

[1] Tertullian considers this question, *de anima*, c. 44. Lactantius expresses the view, *abit animus, manet anima;* but Tertullian, *omnia magis conjectes, quam istam licentiam animæ sine morte fugitivæ et quidem ex forma continuam* (read *continuæ*); but he does not venture to deny the possibility of a rapid anticipatory loosing of the soul from the body. V. Rudloff believes that in such cases the soul remains united to the body by the nerve-spirit. But in the supposition that the soul, remaining within this neighbouring medium of bodily animation, is removed out of the body, the riddle becomes still more insoluble.

[2] The name נָבִיא, نبي, signifies the announcer. See Fleischer, in my *Commentary on Genesis*, pp. 634–636.

[3] The Indian name of the prophet, *rishi*, is explained, "seer of the divine word." See Nève, *Etudes sur les Hymnes du Rig-Veda*, p. 21.

from his own imagination and thinking. For the manner of revelation is not always the specifically visionary. Prophecy, even in respect of the mode of revelation, has a progressive history. In the range of the later prophecy, the dream almost wholly disappears: it is the lowest stage of revelation. And the ecstasy or vision in the waking state, in the maturity of prophecy that came in with Joel and Obadiah, serves only for extraordinary purposes. The forms of revelation named in Num. xxiv. 3 continue, but only as extraordinary occurrences, within the range of a more constant intercourse with God, which approximates to God's revelation by Moses,[1]—an intercourse which is effected without vision only by means of the word, and therefore after the manner of inspiration; while the willing, thinking, feeling spiritual life of the prophet, in the condition of perfect waking power over himself, is elevated and supported by a gentle divine influence, which he (as is indispensable) is able clearly to distinguish from his own personal agency (2 Pet. i. 21). This is the condition of inward penetration by which is explained the change of persons so frequent in the Old Testament books of prophecy. The prophet himself sometimes speaks from God, sometimes God Himself speaks from the prophet; sometimes the divine Ego asserts itself with a supreme power that absorbs all other, sometimes the human in the entire fulness of sanctified humanity; but in both cases it is the personality of the prophet, in the totality of its pneumatico-psychical powers, which becomes the more active or passive organ of God. Ecstasy, on the other hand, consists in this, that the human spirit is seized and compassed by the divine, which searcheth all things, even the deep things of God, with such force, that being averted from its life in itself and in the soul and in the body, and fixed in the third of its forms of life, it is altogether a seeing eye, a hearing ear, a perceiving sense for the world and the things of eternity, or of the future, whither the mighty agency of God has withdrawn it from its customary sphere of life. Thus Isaiah in ch. vi. is withdrawn into the temple-palace of the heavenly King, where he is consecrated as a prophet; thus he exists and lives in ch. xl. to lxvi., as if cut off from his actual presence in the exile; and

[1] More cannot be said, for the standing of Moses is not attained to; comp. Kurtz in the *Dorpater Zeitschr. für Theologie in Kirche*, 1861, p. 127.

from this his ideal presence, held fast through twenty-seven chapters, looks forth with an excellent spirit ($\pi\nu\epsilon\acute{u}\mu\alpha\tau\iota$ $\mu\epsilon\gamma\acute{a}\lambda\wp$, as Ecclus. xlviii. 24 says) upon the last things; and from the clear vision which in the exile has become in form his natural condition, he announces as with angel tongues the coming redemption. The withdrawal is in both cases a purely spiritual event, and to be distinguished from such occurrences as that at the baptism of Jordan, and on the mount of transfiguration, where there are external facts of sacred history, which are not merely represented in a spiritually perceptible manner for those for whom they are intended, but are actually transacted. That which is to be perceived has in these cases a subsistence independent of perception—of external, although not of grossly external historical reality: it happens not merely in the domain of the inward nature, as in the case of the prophetic withdrawal. The objectivity of the latter consists in the fact, that it is not a state into which the spirit of the prophet transposes itself out of itself, but into which he is transplanted by the spirit of prophecy. The future, indeed, has besides, at the time in which the prophet is enabled to see it and to experience it, only an ideal reality. But, moreover, the other world does not take up the prophet into itself, as if he were one blissfully separated thereto; but from the spiritual agency which operates on the prophet's spirit there is developed the supersensual, which he is to be permitted to behold, in that it becomes visible and audible to him by the mediation of his psychico-corporeal nature,[1] and according to the measure of his temporal limitations; but so that by virtue of the divine agency which rules future and present, heaven and earth, these are objective realities, into whose contemplation the prophet is transported,—objective

---

[1] An irritation of the nerves of seeing and hearing proceeding from within (see Luthardt, in Tholuck, *Die Proph.* p. 56) is herein not to be supposed; only the affected ganglionic parts of the brain, as in all conceptions, so also in these, are projected outwardly, but in fact are engaged with internal forms. For the ecstasy is indeed, as Augustine rightly defines it, *alienatio mentis a sensibus corporis;* and even hallucinations do not always originate through irritation of the nerves of sense, but through irritations which may proceed from the most distinct points of the body furnished with nerves, and thence lay hold of the brain-ganglia,—in other words, through any influence upon the brain, and indeed upon those parts of it which are the media of the impressions of sense for the subject, and

occurrences, which bring their nature to manifestation in his mind, in a clothing which is borrowed from the individual nature of the prophet.

Scripture calls this ecstatical state γενέσθαι ἐν ἐκστάσει (Acts xxii. 17), or else γενέσθαι ἐν πνεύματι (Apoc. i. 10); for although εἶναι ἐν πνεύματι (Rom. viii. 9) is the fundamental state of the regenerate person generally, so far as his personal life has broken with the fleshly life, and is the life of the spirit in God's Spirit, yet in those passing acts of ecstasy, as in the mystic ecstasy, this habitual reciprocal immanence of the human and the divine spirit is so greatly enhanced, that the essential connection of the human spirit with all that lies on this side, and below this immanence, is, as it were, severed. Thus upon the prophets of the schools of Samuel came the "hand of Jehovah," not without abeyance of the external man. Saul is violently taken hold of by the spirit of prophecy in Gibeah, and goes thence with another heart (לֵב אַחֵר, 1 Sam. x. 5). In Naioth of Ramah, overcome by the Spirit, he strips off his clothes, in order to make (so it appears, comp. Jer. xx. 9) the inward burning more supportable, begins to prophesy, and lies naked the whole day and the whole night on the ground (1 Sam. xix. 20-24). It may be easily explained why precisely the prophetic endowment of the time of the judges has this violent form. We are reminded of Balaam (Num. xxiv. 4): "That falling down," observes Baumgarten,[1] "from which Balaam calls himself נֹפֵל, is the perfect prostration, the sinking away of the directly natural standing and condition. The less the natural life is glorified into the spirit, the more forcibly is expressed the might of the divine Spirit that comes over the man." And, in fact, where the Spirit of revelation has to make use of

which are able to represent the places of actual impressions of sense. Since, for the rest, through pathologic irritation, or moreover internal spiritual causation, lively perceptions may come into our circle of vision without external agency, it will have to be conceded from the scientific standing, that such like subjective seeing and hearing in certain cases may be produced by God; and there may be due to what is perceived at the same time a higher truth and reality, a divine objectivity. I miss the acknowledgment of this possib:lity in Hecker's *Vorlesung über Visionen*, 1848, according to which Th. Sickel, in his treatise on Jeanne d'Arc, 1861, estimates the visions of the heroine.

[1] *Theologischer Comm. zum Pentateuch*, ii. 370.

instruments such as Balaam and the Samson natures of the time of the judges, it does not occur without such violence, and constraint, and rending asunder of the strong links that still unite spirit and flesh. But even still later, when the prophetic endowment has already, so to speak, a nobler form, although the prophetic state is not in itself associated with *abalienatio mentis* and *deliquium sensuum*,[1] yet probably the ecstasy is so, which generally is not to be conceived without cessation of the external agency of the senses, and without a temporary death to the external world. The true prophets, however, are distinguished from the false, by the fact that there are no special pathologic phenomena under which the visionary state comes on; further, by the fact that they do not, by any influence upon themselves, throw themselves into this state, and that generally in order to be able to behold divine visions, they are not first thrown into this state by way of preparation; but the continuity of their spirit's life is suddenly broken through by the extraordinary operation of God, as when Ezekiel, sitting before the elders of the exiles, is seized by the hand of Jehovah, and snatched away to Jerusalem, and not till after long vision is placed back by the Spirit of God which has taken him away, into the external and conscious reality of his situation (Ezek. viii. 1–3, comp. xi. 24); and it is the awe-inspiring, overpowering impression of the vision itself which throws them upon their face (Ezek. i. 28, iii. 23, xliii. 3),—that they are, as it were, sunken in deep sleep (Dan. viii. 18, x. 9, comp. Zech. iv. 1), and lie upon the ground, as if, as far as the outer man was concerned, they were dead (Dan. x. 8; Apoc. i. 17). Their ecstatic state, moreover, is distinguished from the forced false one ($παρέκστασις$), by the fact that they remember what has been given them to see, hear, and speak in the ecstasy: their consciousness therefore suffers no dislocation in the withdrawal; it does not happen to them as to the Cumæan Sibyl,[2] who, when the inspiration left her, had no memory of what had been spoken.[3] But, in all cases, the

---

[1] Thus Philippi, *Kirchliche Glaubenslehre*, i. 169. This is the Montanist view, which Ritschl (*Die Entstehung der altkatholischen Kirche*, pp. 465–477, ed. 2) rightly refers to the heathen-Christian confusion of prophecy with soothsaying.

[2] Justin, *Cohort. ad Græcos*, c. xxxvi.

[3] Comp Kurtz' *Darstellung der Unterschiede der prophetischen und*

ecstatic vision never comes on without the life of the prophet withdrawing itself from without, inwardly to the innermost ground of the spirit. And, moreover, Balaam and Caiaphas are not the only examples of the prophet prophesying what he would not, and prophesying without knowing the prophetic character of what was said. As Balaam blesses where he would curse, so Jehovah's prophets at times are compelled to curse where they would bless; and as Caiaphas prophesied on account of his high-priestly office, so David also prophesies frequently in the Psalms without knowing it, on account of his typical character. The prophecy in all these cases is of like character. The hand of God is laid on the prophet; the Spirit of God effects the capacity, and the substance of the prophecy; and it ranges from perfectly conscious free service, to unconscious or unwilling instrumentality, down through a number of mingled relations.

Whilst, however, the mystic ecstasy is not able to grasp that which is seen, for the most part, in words, although it has been seen in clear and not restrained but exalted consciousness—and thus the remembrance of it remains present—it is involved in the purpose of the ecstasy of the prophet who is so by his calling, that he should bring the visions, seen $\dot{\epsilon}\nu$ $\pi\nu\epsilon\acute{\upsilon}\mu\alpha\tau\iota$, and, becoming gradually conscious to him under the influence of the $\nu o\hat{\upsilon}\varsigma$ and of the psychical agencies, to adequate and intelligible expression. For that which the prophet, as such, receives to see and to apprehend, he sees and apprehends, not for himself alone, but, as being the appointed mediator of the divine thoughts respecting the order of salvation and divine decrees, for his people and for humanity. Thus the prophetic ecstasy is distinguished, as from the mystic, so also (3) from the charismatic, for instance, the glossolalic ecstasy, *i.e.* from that whence proceeded the speaking with tongues, or speaking in strange languages (whether they be languages actually existing, as at Pentecost, or languages newly created[1])—an exalted speech in an ecstatic state,

---

mantischen Ekstase, l.c. p. 129. Meanwhile, also, a striking treatise by Oehler, on the relation of the Old Testament prophecy to the heathen soothsaying, appeared in 1861 (*Programm zur Beglückwünschung der Univ. Breslau bei ihrem Jubiläum*).

[1] In this accidental double form subsists the essential unity of the Glossolalia in the First Epistle to the Corinthians, and in the Acts of the

which did not bring to the congregation any conscious advantage, until either some other (1 Cor. xii. 10, xiv. 27) or the speaker himself (*ibid.* v. 13) interpreted it (διερμήνευε), and so translated it out of the eternal sphere of the πνεῦμα into the region of the νοῦς. Hilgenfeld, indeed, is mistaken in explaining the unintelligibility of the γλῶσσαι, only by the transcendent nature of what they expressed to the merely human consciousness;[1] but he observes with great truth, that that which is common to prophecy and to glossolalia consisted in the exaltation of the consciousness above the merely human sphere, but that which is distinct consisted in this: that he who was prophetically inspired was in the full possession of his reflecting spiritual powers; whilst the other inspiration expressed itself only by the agency of the intuitive God-directed side of the human spirit, with suppression of the discursive thought (νοῦς). We have already spoken on this subject, Div. IV. Sec. V., where we showed that there is a human πνεῦμα in a narrower sense, a capacity of immediate perception and insight. As all ecstasy, so also glossolalia was perfected in this πνεῦμα:[2] it was a miraculous agency of the Spirit of God (Acts ii. 4, x. 45,

Apostles. For that the ecstatic sayings of the apostles had first been, by additional interpretation, transferred into the special popular languages, as Wieseler (*Studien u. Krit.* 1860, p. 117) supposes, is contrary to the verbal tenor of the narrative; and that the proclamation was made in a spiritual language, distinct from all popular tongues, is contrary to the historical import of the fact (see v. Hofmann, *Schriftb.* iii. 22). Whether glossolalia repeated itself in this prominent pentecostal form, we know not; it cannot be gathered from Acts x. 46. In 1 Cor. xii.-xiv. it appears throughout as a speaking in unknown, new spirit-created tongues, which, instead of ἕτεραι γλῶσσαι or καιναὶ γλῶσσαι, are called absolutely γλῶσσαι, because γλῶσσαι in itself has also the meaning of a foreign obscure language; wherefore Wieseler refers to Plutarch, *de Pyth. orac.* c. xxiv., where the expressions of the Pythia are called γλῶσσαι, and Pollux, *Onom.* ii. 4, according to which even poetical expressions were so named (καὶ τὰς ποιητικὰς φωνὰς γλώττας ἐκάλουν). Irenæus (v. 6, 1) says, παντοδαπαῖς γλώσσαις; comp. ξενοφωνεῖν by Montanus in *Euseb. h. e.* v. 16.

[1] *Glossolalia in the Ancient Church*, 1850; comp. the work of Rossteuscher, that appeared about the same time, *The Gift of Tongues in the Apostolic Age*, 1850. The charisma in itself is in the latter work more justly apprehended.

[2] See Burger on 1 Cor. xiv. 2, 31, where, moreover, the ecstatic character of the speaking with tongues, which von Rudloff (p. 241) will not allow, is acknowledged.

comp. Mark xvi. 17, 1 Cor. xiv. 22) in the human πνεῦμα τοῦ νοός, *i.e.* in the depth that lies below the customary daylight consciousness. He who spoke with tongues was in the condition of προσευχή, *i.e.* of adoring, praising prayer,[1] and indeed, as the activity of his νοῦς ceased, of supernatural prayer, as our fathers call it,[2] and whereof *e.g.* Joh. Arndt[3] says, "Our spirit dissolves therein, and is absorbed into the uncreated Spirit of God: the heart therefore becomes, by true faith, filled with God's love, in such a way that it can remember nothing but God. What the soul then perceives is inexpressible; and if in such high devotion it should be asked, What perceivest thou? it would answer, A good above all good. What seest thou? A beauty which transcends all beauty. What feelest thou? A joy above all joy. What tastest thou? A graciousness above all graciousness." In such a state of mystical ecstasy surrendered to God (1 Cor. xiv. 2, 28, comp. 2 Cor. v. 13), in which the influence of the Holy Ghost, which moreover otherwise flows forth to the prayers of the faithful (Rom. viii. 26), is enhanced to the highest degree,[4] he who speaks with tongues finds himself speaking to his own edification (1 Cor. xiv. 4); and this mystic ecstasy becomes a charismatic ecstasy, intended for a miraculous sign (1 Cor. xiv. 22), in that this prayerful disposition, triumphant and absorbed in God, creates to itself a form of speech in which it incessantly breaks forth from the heart as in sacred dithyrambics.[5]

[1] Confessedly, this is the idea of προσευχή, in distinction from δέησις, ἔντευξις, and εὐχαριστία (1 Tim. ii. 1). Εὐχαριστία, thus distinguished, is giving thanks, not for the ordinary human, but for the special experiences of grace. But the apostle (1 Cor. xiv.) uses for προσεύχεσθαι, of the speaker with tongues, εὐχαριστεῖν also; and εὐλογεῖν, so far as it is thanks and praise (בְּרָכָה), is also the general nature of προσευχή.

[2] In Tertullian, *adv. Marc.* v. 8, *oratio spiritalis.*

[3] *True Christianity*, ii. 20, comp. the division on charismatic prayer in R. Lobers's *Lehre vom Gebet* (2d edit. 1860), p. 100, especially the beautiful and genuine Paulinian expression: "In the charismatic prayer, a man maintains a testimony of the living Christ, and a breathing of His power, but not in order to build tabernacles on the mount of transfiguration, but in order to carry the heavenly life into the valley of death, where resounds the cry for help."

[4] Hilgenfeld, *l.c.* p. 57.

[5] That, as Wieseler supposes (*l.c.* pp. 113-116), the unintelligibility of the speaking with tongues (1 Cor. xiv. 7-11, where it is compared with the

A phenomenon very similar to glossolalia has often been observed in clairvoyance. Not only that the soul, in all conditions of more solemn excitement, or of enhancement of its powers, associated with a gradual detachment from the body, is accustomed to speak a purer, more select, more picturesque, and more rhythmic language: in the state of clairvoyance, moreover, it begins—as if feeling the insufficiency of customary language, and the need of one fuller of meaning and expression—to speak in tongues that are unintelligible to the hearers, but produce an effect upon them as if of spiritual voices from a distant world.[1] The degree of the soul's flight in the case of the female seer of Prevorst, was in this respect, as generally, only a very low one. Instead of other instances, I recur again here also to the case of the somnambulist, already more than once mentioned, who, although not without obscure intervals, still beyond all doubt, during his somnambulic state, continued under the protection of the Lord, to whom he was devoted in his waking state with simple, childlike faith. "The songs, prayers, and the like, which were made by our somnambulist in foreign languages," says the narrator of the account, "contain sounds akin to the oriental and classic, but not to the northern languages; yet he in no way confuses these languages together. But if, for example, he begins a song with Hebrew intonations, he continues to use them to the end. Many known words occur from the language chosen; but nevertheless, according to the judgment of one who knows the language, the whole is not to be understood. Often, moreover, he sings very softly, with trembling voice, a sorrowful oriental melody. Sometimes he begins in a whisper, sometimes he concludes thus, and speaks at length only in pantomime. Although in unintelligible language, he speaks with the most delicate voice. In the beginning of his somnambulism, he only at first spoke such words and sentences isolated, but now in connected discourses. It is

---

effects of sounding instruments) is maintained in respect of the delivery, and equally in vers. 10-12 (where the languages of intercourse are opposed) in respect of the language, I cannot find; but certainly there was associated with the foreign language of the ecstatic speaker with tongues (as Wiesinger acknowledges), doubtless also a foreign delivery or address.

[1] Steinbeck, *Der Dichter ein Seher*, p. 547.

as though at first he had learned by degrees to imitate these heavenly tones, these angelic voices." When the narrator once asked him, What sort of strange languages are they that thou so often speakest; and wherefore dost thou speak and sing in these languages, although none of the hearers understand them? he answered, It is the Spirit's language, which only somnambulists understand, and can weakly imitate. Further, who has taught thee these languages? He replied, Elias speaks to me, and I hear his voice, and give heed to his words. Thou often breakest off when thou wishest to disclose to us the future, and then speakest in strange language: wherefore doest thou this? He said, My angel of peace, Elias, then enjoins me silence: he checks my speech, so that I can only speak to him.

This comparison of the somnambulic glossolalia with the charismatic is justified; for nothing is more true than (to adopt J. H. Pabst's view [1]) that the supernatural and the natural ecstasy produce in many ways altogether similar phenomena. What the apostle says (1 Cor. xiv. 21) of glossolalia, that it is a sign of a judicial kind for the unbelieving, is also true in some measure even of the somnambulist. But our point of view in the comparison is not the similarity, but the great distinction in all this similarity. The charisma was conditioned by no kind of bodily constitution. There was no cataleptic state associated with it, such as is inseparable from the somnambulic clairvoyance, and such as occurs even in the mystic and prophetic ecstasy. He who possessed this charisma had himself so far in his own power, that he could come forth with it in the congregation or not (1 Cor. xiv. 18, 28). He was bound to, and was able to, enjoin silence on himself, if no interpreter were there; for God had ordained for the gift of languages, as its complement, also the gift of interpretation, which, even in somnambulic cases as relatively pure as the one just mentioned, has never appeared. And whilst idio-somnambulism, especially on this grade of clairvoyance, is always an exceedingly rare occurrence, the early church gift of speaking with tongues was possessed at the same time by several. It was one of the many fruits of the pentecostal Spirit shed forth upon the primitive congregation. It was a purely spiritual phenomenon. For whilst the somnambulist converses with the outer world in

[1] *Ein Wort über die Ekstase*, 1834, p. 29; comp. above, p. 355.

the full activity of his psychico-pneumatical powers, although not by means of the external senses, the speaker with tongues was altogether turned towards God with his heart, and an incomparably purer mirror of the divine mysteries.

Nevertheless, we should be convinced, if a glossolalic discourse could be preserved to us in a faithful translation, that there is no lifting away of the man out of the bonds of the body,—no withdrawal of the spirit from the flesh-enslaved Psyche,—no ravishing of the spirit into the directness, proportionally freed from self, of his feeling and perceiving mind, wherein nevertheless, in spite of all the brightness, a shadow of the limited human individuality, and its temporal necessities, allows itself to be perceived. Between the future intuition of the blessed, and the visions of the most favoured seer of this world,—between the being at home with the Lord, and every kind of spiritual ecstasy,—there is, and will be, a large interval. In all prophetic visions, the power is given to contemplate the Godhead, and the spirit-world, and the decreed future, in a manner accommodated to the individuality of the prophet and the circumstances of the time. He therefore beholds that which is seen, not as it is in itself, but as it becomes visible to him in a symbol that yet is formed for the purpose, chiefly from materials that are found in his subjectivity. And even if the prophet apprehends the divine word in itself, in a condition distinct from ecstasy, it does not come to him without having first of all entered into the form of his individuality. The divine thoughts take their way to the Ego of the prophet through his nature. They clothe themselves in popular human language, according to the prophet's individual manner of thinking and speaking; and they present themselves in a form manifoldly limited, according to the existing circumstances, and the horizon of contemporary history. They maintain themselves in the objectivity and transcendency of their nature (1 Pet. i. 10), but in a human, finite, accidental expression, which often makes that which is in itself mysterious still more enigmatical Even the glimpse into the future which is granted to the prophet, is conditioned, so to speak, according to the optical laws of his internal perception.[1] Things which are widely removed

[1] Comp. on this subject the interesting remarks in the work of v. Baader, *Ueber die Ekstase oder das Verzucktsein der magnetischen Schlafredner*, 1818,

from one another, approach in the perspective: the prophet sees the conclusive future on the brink of the present, without the long ascending and descending road that lies between. By the side of the remote perspective that is rendered possible by the spirit of prophecy, there is always also a close view that is not cancelled by the former; and hope, moreover, does its work of drawing near the remote future into the closest neighbourhood of the gloomy present. Prophecy is, indeed, not merely a $\theta\epsilon\hat{\iota}ov$: it is, moreover, an $\dot{a}v\theta\rho\dot{\omega}\pi\iota vov$, and both aspects of its nature subserve the divine plan of salvation. God could do away with the limits that are incident to the prophetic view of the remote future; that He does not do so, is of His disciplinary wisdom. The like, moreover, is obvious with the THEOPNEUSTIA, the divine factor in the origination of the canonical Scripture (2 Tim. iii. 16). It is inadmissible to distinguish between *inspiratio realis* and *verbalis*. Substance and form are both the effect of the one divine act. As the soul came into existence when God breathed the spirit into man, so come into existence words of divine nature and human form, when God breathes thoughts into man. This is a fact of experience, which is not so altogether exclusively pertinent to the future life, that every Christian has not occasionally been able to experience it in himself. Moreover, Theopneustia is a conception of a species which comprehends within itself variously diversified spiritual operations,—even according to the special charisma, the special professional position, and special literary occupation, *i.e.* even according as the writer is related productively and continuously, or reproductively and applicatively, to the revelation and the history of redemption. But in both cases the divine appears under the affections of the human. In the latter case, even errors are possible in the reproduction of the historical and transacted: failures of memory, failures of combination, generally failures above which the most spiritual human activity of all is not absolutely exalted. Our ancient dogmatists evade this avowal, but their idea of inspiration neither approves itself psychologically nor historically. It makes the influence of God, who takes the writer into the service of the revealed history, into a too stiff, uniform, forceful one-sidedness, without duly appreciating the co-opera-

p. 15; and, in addition, Hamberger, *Cardinal Points of the Philosophy of Baader* (1855), pp. 43-45.

tive individual manifold free agency of the writer. The act of inspiration should, and must, be represented as an organic vital interworking of the divine and human factor, without thereby jeopardizing the infallibility of the revealed truth written in the Scripture, and the faithfulness of the fundamental history of redemption contained therein for all times. Or are we, in order to open no breach to unbelief, to declare even the punctuation of the Old Testament to be inspired, and the New Testament Greek to be free from all offences against classicality of form?[1] The time when such assertions were possible is irrevocably past. Scripture is no book fallen from heaven: its origination is just as much human as divine—$\pi\acute{\alpha}\nu\tau\alpha\ \theta\epsilon\hat{\imath}\alpha\ \kappa\alpha\grave{\imath}\ \grave{\alpha}\nu\theta\rho\acute{\omega}\pi\iota\nu\alpha\ \pi\acute{\alpha}\nu\tau\alpha$.[2] He who is offended at this, sins against the Holy Spirit, whose condescension into humanity, by no means docetic, and full of love, he ought rather to admire and praise.

Man, indeed, is no angel, no pure spiritual nature perfected by trial. However mightily God may remove man above the limits of finite existence, of embodied spirituality, of nationality, of the ideal range, of his language, of the individuality of his endowment and his education, of the standing and the circumstances of his time, and commune with him, as it were, isolated from his natural self in the $\pi\nu\epsilon\hat{\upsilon}\mu\alpha\ \tau o\hat{\upsilon}\ \nu oo\grave{\varsigma}\ \alpha\mathring{\upsilon}\tau o\hat{\upsilon}$,—the limits continue to subsist still within the present state, because only an immediate sudden magical power could annihilate them; and their shadows reach even into that sanctuary of communion with God, and tinge the light that thence breaks forth on man. Therefore even the New Testament apostle, who possessed the gifts of prophecy and of speech with tongues in the highest measure (1 Cor. xiv. 18), and was favoured with lofty ecstasies, declares that prophecy is a fragment, and that we (including him) look upon the divine only through a mirror in an enigmatic form (1 Cor. xiii.). It is the same apostle who in Rom. vii. 24 sighs, "O wretched man that I am! who shall deliver me from the body of this death?" The divine does not give itself to us to inspect, without its beams being refracted in our

---

[1] See Schmid, *Dogmatik der Ev. Luth. Kirche*, p. 25.

[2] This expression, first of all transferred by Hamann to the spiritual province, is from Hippocrates, who says it, with reference to the ἱερὴ νοῦσος (epilepsy), of the diseases (*Opp.* ed. Littré, vi. 394).

manifoldly limited nature; and our life in God is not maintained, without being under the necessity of constantly resisting the pressure of our sinful nature.

THE UNABOLISHED ANTINOMY.

Sec. VI.

THERE is no portion of Scripture which affords us a more profound psychological insight into the internal condition of the regenerate than Rom. vii. in association with ch. viii. But in order to avoid misapprehension in the psychologic application of this portion, we must first of all transport ourselves vitally and fundamentally into the current of thought involved in the apostolic argument.[1]

In v. 12, etc., Paul has instituted a parallel between Adam and Christ. There is in the world a dominion of death, as there is of sin, which is caused by the one man in whom humanity originates. All men die, because (ἐφ' ᾧ) in the sin of one all have sinned. The death of individuals is, even apart from their special sins, the infallible consequence of the sin of the one. This may be seen from the fact, that death reigned even in the period before the law, when sin had not yet, as in the case of Adam, the form of a transgression of law. But with Adam, the One, stands contrasted Christ, the One, who has earned for humanity that which in the first instance the individual does not require to earn, as Adam incurred for it that which in the first instance the individual does not require to incur. As the sin of Adam had the doom of death as its result, which is completed on all men by reason of sin, so the obedience of the one man Jesus Christ, on the other hand, brought about righteous-

---

[1] Among the most solid things that have been produced on this subject, is Hofmann's treatise on the Epistle to the Romans, in the course of his treament of the history of the origination of the Scriptures, *Zeitschrift für Protest. u. Kirche*, 1860, p. 65. This treatise is subsequent to vol. i. of the 2d ed. of the *Schriftbeweis* (1857), and to Schott's work, *Der Römerbrief seinem Endzweck und Gedankengang nach ausgelegt* (1858).

ness and life, which are offered to all men as a gift of grace, and are manifested as a contrary power far transcending the consequences of the disobedience of the one. What position is attributed to the law in this opposition, is declared in ch. v. 20, 21: it was brought in to make sin all the more evident in its manifestation, and so to reveal in its fulness the superabundance of grace. It was to be shown, that the dominion of sin which effectually declares itself in death, is far exceeded by the dominion of the New Testament grace, which is fulfilled by righteousness in everlasting life. The apostle then anticipates the immoral result which might perchance be gathered from this, as though, in declaring the triumph of grace to be greater in proportion as the sin is greater, he were giving to the sinner a ground of palliation. He obviates this, by showing that the Christian, by virtue of baptism into the death of Christ, has died to the old life conditioned by sin, and by virtue of the resurrection of Christ is empowered and engaged to lead a new divine life in the service of God (ch. vi. 1-14). That mischievous consequence of the relation of grace to sin is thus void. The apostle from this also obviates another false deduction from the Christian's freedom from the law, as though a licence were thus set up for the sinner. This deduction also is futile; for the standing of grace, as the position of a servant under righteousness, is the absolute opposite of the standing of a servant under sin. To be under grace is not only to be freed from the bondage of sin, and its wages of death, but to have entered into the service of righteousness,—into the service of God, whose gift of grace is eternal life in Christ Jesus τῷ Κυρίῳ ἡμῶν (ch. vi. 14 et seq.). That Christ is our master, and no longer the law, is proved by the apostle, with especial reference to the members of the Jewish community (ch. vii. 1-6). He appeals to a fundamental principle of the positive law. Man is subject to the law so long as he lives, but no longer: only death abrogates the obligatory relation of man to the law; but this abrogates it effectually. He illustrates this by an example. So long as the husband lives, the wife, as under the husband, is thus bound to the law, which is represented with its weight of obligation in the husband; only death looses the legal bond, which otherwise is indissoluble. Hereupon he concludes in ver. 4a, from ver. 1: We have died in and with the crucified

One; over a dead man the law has no further power, therefore we are free from the law. And from vers. 2 and 3 he infers in ver. 4*b* (εἰς τὸ γενέσθαι, κ.τ.λ.) that the church of God is first the church of the law; but in Christ, who in the body of His flesh represents the law, the law is dead for the church of God, that the church might belong to Christ the risen, to whom the law with its claims and its curse has no more right, and espoused to whom the church is a church of grace and of life. In ver. 5 he specifies the reason why man, in order to bring forth fruit unto God, must be made to belong to another than the law: "for when we were in the flesh" (the condition of moral weakness and corruption, which the law only enhances, and does not abrogate), "the sinful passions that were called forth by the law were operative in our members to bring forth fruit unto death; but now we are delivered from the law, having died to that wherein we were held" (the power of the law which enhances sin), "so that now we serve in newness of the spirit, and not in the oldness of the letter" (*i.e.* not in the old form of life, which the letter of the law acquiesces in, but in the new, which is the operation of the Spirit).

Only misunderstanding can thus, from the principle that the law enhancing sin treats the power of grace as folly, infer such consequences as imperil sanctification. The freedom from the law is no licence to sin; rather it is the condition of enfranchisement from sin. But thence it might appear as though the law itself were sin. The apostle cannot carry on the argument begun ver. 12 to the end, without first having demolished this false appearance also. He accomplishes this ch. vii. 7-12, by experimentally showing that the law brings to man the consciousness of what sin is, and by its prohibition occasions the transition from lust after that which is forbidden, into the death-causing act of sin; and that, far from being itself sin, it actually thereby proves its holiness, in opposition to the sinfulness of man; or, as Hofmann[1] combines these thoughts of the apostle, created by experience, "that the law is only abused by sin, to make the beginning of personal self-determination the beginning of personal forfeiture to death. By nature every individual man stands in an attitude of will opposed to God and of being out of God, in sin and death, even before he

[1] *Schriftbeweis*, i. 459, 1st ed.; comp. 544 of 2d ed.

becomes personally conscious of himself in his relation to God. But thence, moreover, he enters upon such a consciousness, only in virtue of his own decision as Ego to make that ungodly will his own; and herewith as the Ego, which he has now become, to fall into that being out of God, within which he was when he became Ego." Manifestly ἐγὼ ἔζων and ἐγὼ ἀπέθανον stand in contrast to one another. When Augustine explains the former, *vivere mihi videbar quia ante mandatum latebat peccatum*, it is insufficient. There is an existence meant, which, in comparison with the condition of death subsequently self-produced by personal sin, deserved the name of life,—an existence in some measure like the paradisaic *status integritatis* (only in some measure similar, because sin, although as in a kind of death-sleep, was already in being), namely, the condition of the child not yet entered into the so-called *status discretionis* (Div. IV. Sec. III.), in which sin and death have not yet grown from slumbering potentialities into personally realized facts. In the divine law, the ripening man attains to the consciousness of that which is good and evil: there begins now a self-conscious conduct, and self-determining moral agency is perfected; but this beginning of personal moral self-attestation is also the beginning of personal involvement in sin and death. The law, therefore, is not itself sin; but that it makes sin and death personal facts of experience for us, is the effect—which is established in our natural, *i.e.* inborn, condition inherited by birth— of the revelation in itself, holy and just and good, of that which God claims from us.

To this setting aside of the one counter-question, whether the law is ἁμαρτία, is linked another counter-question: Is therefore τὸ ἀγαθὸν, *i.e.* the law which proceeds from God, originating in goodness, having good as its aim, and promising good— is this become my death? To this the apostle replies, Not the law, but sin. This was to be evident precisely from the fact, that by means of that which is good it wrought death in me, and thus perverted the God-ordained means of life into a means of death: it was thus to become manifest, in the abundance of its ungodly nature, by the commandment which it thus misused. "For we know," continues the apostle, associating himself with all the faithful, who understand how to appreciate the significance of the law in the whole of the divine institution,—" we know that the law is spiritual; but I am carnal, sold under sin." It is the knowledge of a continual state of things that the apostle here expresses. The declaration that the law is spiritual, while he himself is flesh, and in bondage under sin, is related to the present. For that very reason it is said, not σαρκικός, but σάρκινος: for σάρκινος is one who has in himself the bodily nature and the sinful tendency inherited with it; but σαρκικός is one whose personal fundamental tendency is this sinful impulse of the flesh.[1] Flesh, born of the flesh, are we all, and so remain until the regeneration is completed in the resurrection; and, because with this inborn nature sin also is inborn in us, we are and remain also inalienably burdened with sin, or, as may moreover be said, since we cannot release ourselves from it, imprisoned under it. Every Christian, as a child of Adam, must acquiesce in what the apostle confesses. Thus, and no otherwise, we appear to ourselves universally in the mirror of the law. It is precisely this knowledge of our natural constitution that contradicts the law, that we owe to the law. It is this acknowledgment which the law has it in view to produce in man as he is descended from Adam. How this acknowledgment, and with it the feeling of the necessity of redemption, originates, the apostle explains further in the 15th and following verses, from his own experience of life.

The law is spiritual in kind and nature, and therefore claims a conduct which has the mastery over that which is material and over itself; but I am of flesh, and disposed accordingly. "For"—thus the apostle makes good this 15th and 16th verse—"that which I do I know not," *i.e.* it is foreign to my most special self-determination; "for not what I wish to do I accomplish; but what I hate, that do I. If then I do that which I would not, I consent unto the law, that it is justly ordered." It is precisely this contest between my will and my conduct that gives to the law this testimony, in that that proportion of the law which I do not accomplish is that which is properly willed by me, while that which is sinful which I do is what I hate. The law requires of me spiritual conduct, powerful over myself, conformed to the sanctity of God, to the Spirit, and to the

---

[1] Thus in this way are distinguished εἶναι ἐν σαρκί and εἶναι κατὰ σάρκα. See Hofmann, *Schriftb.* i. 562. In Meyer and Schott I do not find this distinction properly regarded.

divine likeness of my spirit. That in spite of my will I never accomplish this, is not the fault of the law, but of my own fleshliness.

The apostle deduces from this, with reference back to the preceding πεπραμένος ὑπὸ τὴν ἁμαρτίαν, ver. 17, that in such a state of things it is no longer he that does such things, but the sin that dwelleth in him; and proves (vers. 18–20) that sin, and nothing else, is this power, distinct from his Ego, opposed to his true nature. What the apostle here declares, can only be repeated after him by one in whom a knowledge and will of what is willed by God, opposed to the inborn nature, is present,—one in whom Ego and sin are in such a manner isolated, that the sin, instead of passing as the action of his Ego, may rather be regarded as the act of the sin that enslaves it contrary to his will; for the Ego is no longer one with sin— it is free from it; sin resides in such a man still, only as a foreign power: there has come to pass in him, consequently, a process of separation which is still foreign to the natural man, and is thus effected by grace. But the apostle cannot by possibility mean, that in any such an one a sinful act could be accomplished without his Ego being concerned therein. This would be just as contrary to the idea of sin, which as an act is always a personal fact, as it is contrary to all experience. For instance, no sin of unchastity is possible, so long as the man is able to hold his Ego at a distance absolutely from the urging fleshly enticements: it is possible only when the might of temptation succeeds either in overmastering, or even in interesting, the Ego of the man. At times there are mingled in the range of man's thoughts impure thoughts, which he acknowledges as not less thought by his Ego than the pure ones which it opposes to them in order to dislodge them. Sometimes temptation succeeds in drawing in the man's Ego into itself; but in the midst of the sinful act, the man draws it back from it, full of loathing for it. Sometimes, moreover, the Ego, in order to complete the sinful act unrestrainedly, is voluntarily absorbed into unconsciousness, and does not until after its completion return with horror to recollection of itself; and the spirit with shame becomes conscious of its having been veiled by its own responsibility. When, therefore, in the 18th verse, the apostle says, "I know that in me (that is, in my flesh) dwelleth no good thing," he cannot thereby intend to say that the flesh, and not the Ego, is the subject of sin. The meaning is rather this, that in him—to wit, as he explains by way of restriction, in him so far as he is σάρκινος, *i.e.* consists of flesh, and is thus easily overpowered by flesh—no good thing dwells. It is false if it is said that σάρξ in such an ethical connection does not mean the sensible flesh; but it is not less false if it be said that it signifies this in respect of itself alone. It is the entire nature of man, sinful, and subject to death, which is called σάρξ. But Hengstenberg[1] rightly suggests the question, how it happens that it should be called exactly σάρξ. He replies, that it is because the impulses that proceed from the spirit make an impression upon the flesh, the material nature, because sins are accompanied with bodily excitements, and as it were encamp in the body; because sinful impulses are, moreover, already in the material nature in consequence of inherited sin: for how else could there be family sins? This is all true; but the true final answer is that which we gave in Div. III. Sec. I. towards the end. The entire natural man is called σάρξ, because he has fallen absolutely into the power of the evil potentialities of his fundamental nature, which the original sin has set free. This setting free is the work of an ungodly will; but having once taken place, it is a fact that can only be remedied by regeneration. The breadth of the idea of σάρξ, in an ethical sense, is only thus to be explained. In this sense σάρξ is the palpable material flesh, inclusive of its human existence from the beginning, the psychico-pneumatical internal nature homogeneous with it, and standing in mutual relation with it, and even inclusive of the Ego that suffers itself to be limited by the inborn fleshly nature (Div. IV. Sec. II.), which, in complying with the sinful dispositions, restraints, and allurements of his nature, enhances its own inborn corruption.

It is not at all possible that the New Testament conception σάρξ (comp. Gen. vi. 3, בָּשָׂר) should be otherwise intended. For (1) the material flesh in itself can neither experience, nor imagine, nor desire. All these things, although effected by means of the body, are yet impossible acts without a psychical

[1] See his *Explanation of the Gospel of St John*, vol. i. (1861), pp. 189-192 (on John iii. 6)

background. Thus, when the New Testament, and especially Paul, speaks of ἐπιθυμίαι τῆς σαρκὸς (Gal. v. 16; Eph. ii. 3), θελήματα τῆς σαρκὸς (Eph. ii. 3, comp. John i. 13), and even πράξεις τοῦ σώματος (Rom. viii. 13), the idea of σάρξ cannot be satisfied with the meaning of the tangible flesh. It is necessary, in order to avoid attaching absurdity to these biblical expressions, to suppose that the flesh is conceived of together with a fleshly soul pertaining to it. This view was widely diffused among the most ancient fathers. Man was almost generally defined as a nature consisting of a rational immortal soul, and a body with a vegetative-sensitive soul. But, in opposition to the Manichæism which supposed a good and an evil soul in man, and to the Apollinarianism which explained the incarnation as a union of the Logos with a corporeity consisting of flesh and fleshly soul, it was decided, after careful consideration, for the most part, that there is no inferior soul distinct from the reasonable soul, but that the one spirit-soul (μία ψυχὴ λογική τε καὶ νοερὰ, as the eleventh canon of the eighth œcumenical council expresses it) is that which animates the body without the intervention of a fleshly soul.[1] This opposition to the view of two souls, although in this conception very insufficient, was still justified. For (2) there is not actually any fleshly soul distinct from the spiritual soul, capable of experience, of imagination, and of desire. The school of Günther, which maintains this view with great acuteness, and not without many respectable predecessors,[2] proceeds therein

[1] In favour of the identity of the reasonable and the vegetative-sensitive soul, there are, among others who specially treat on this question, Tertullian and John of Damascus. Origen is rather in favour of the distinction. Lactantius calls the question *inextricabilis*. Augustine is in favour of the identity, but not without hesitation. Among the scholastics, Thomas Aquinas and Duns Scotus are in favour of the identity: the former teaching that the *anima rationalis virtualiter* is at the same time the *vegetativa et sensitiva*; the former, that the *anima rationalis* imparts to the body its vegetative and sensitive life (*dans esse corpori*). Thus also the Councils of Vienna (1311), and of Lateran (1513), explain themselves, *anima rationalis est forma corporis per se et essentialiter*. In favour of the difference, there are among the more celebrated scholastics only Alanus *ab insulis* and Occam.

[2] See Zukrigl's *Critical Inquiry into the Nature of the Reasonable Spirit-soul and of the Psychic Corporeity of Man, with reference to the Conflict of the present time, and to the Councils, Ecclesiastical Fathers, and Scholastics*, 1854.

on the supposition that the brute-soul is only the highest intensification of matter, and is therefore no substance essentially distinct from matter; and on the not less unscriptural supposition, that the body with which in man the spirit-soul is united, contains in itself a soul similar in qualification to the brute-soul, which only becomes awakened or actualized by the super-addition of the spirit-soul. From these two unscriptural assumptions, it is then further asserted, that when Scripture speaks of a contrast of the flesh and the spirit, the flesh, with the experiencing, imagining, and desiring internal character peculiar to it as such, is meant, whose impure disorderly affections are urgent against the spirit-soul, and by its consent become sin. If we remember that by scholasticism there are distinguished in the *locus de concupiscentia*, firstly, *motus primo-primi*, i.e. such as for a moment, benumbing the free-will, anticipate its exercise; then *motus secundi*, i.e. such as proceed directly from the free-will; and thirdly, *motus secundo-primi*, i.e. such as the free-will suffers itself to be hurried away in; then, according to the Güntherish theory, the *motus primo-primi* proceed from the fleshly soul. As this, although conscious, is yet impersonal and not free, those *motus primo-primi* are in themselves guiltless and irresponsible. Confessedly this is a symbolically accepted proposition of Roman Catholic morality. That the Güntherish theory finds so much contradiction in the Romish Church, is a fact which proves that that position (which our church decidedly rejects) may be held without accepting the Güntherish *anima carnis*. But the true refutation of this latter is, at the same time, also the refutation of the former position, which is perilous to the acknowledgment of sins and reality of sanctification. We have already sufficiently proved above, that Scripture only knows of one soul of man, which is at once spiritual and fleshly soul.[1] That, even in reference to the moral dualism in man, this essential unity

[1] The third of the views given by Origen, *de princ.* iii. 4, that the essentially one soul consists of a reasonable and an unreasonable part, and that the latter again consists of the θυμικὸν and the ἐπιθυμικὸν, comes the nearest to the truth, but still is some distance from it. It is brought to an issue in Nemesios' book, περὶ φύσεως ἀνθρώπου, against which the author of the Δόξαι maintains the view, that man has three souls (φυσική, ἄλογος, and λογική), but that they are one—διὰ τὴν συμφωνίαν αὐτῶν καὶ τὴν συμπάθειαν.

of spirit and soul is held by Scripture, is proved 1 Pet. ii. 11. Scripture nowhere speaks of an opposition of the soul and the spirit, but only of the flesh and of the νοῦς; of the καρδία, Rom. ii. 28; of the πνεῦμα; or even, as in 1 Pet. ii. 11, of the ψυχή. For not soul and flesh, but soul and spirit, are essentially one; and even experience confirms this unity. When an enticement to sin, *e.g.* to sensuality, proceeds from the body to the inner man, this enticement is certainly as yet no sin, although it belongs to the consequences of the sinfulness which has distorted the true relation of the body to the spirit-soul, or, as we say, to spirit and soul; and therefore, even in itself, is to be bewailed with penitence. But this blind, unconscious natural impulse never becomes concupiscence, or lustfulness, until it is reflected in the psychico-spiritual internal nature of man. That such an enticement can originate in us against our will has its reason in the fact, that in our present natural condition we are no longer lords of the material and power of our body. But the enticement to sensuality never becomes the form of sensuality; or, as the scholastics formulate it, the *concupiscentia informis* never becomes the *concupiscentia formata* without the spiritual soul according to its nature, and this form of sensuality is not, moreover, held by us for one minute without the will of the spirit which is immanent in, and which personifies the soul; and the changes in the body which minister to sensuality do not originate without the impulse of the will upon the nerves of motion, and the intentional agitations of the flesh that are linked with this impulse. It is our Ego which is carnalized in every act of sensual lust: the personifying spirit which, by means of the Psyche belonging to it, ought to rule the corporeity, sinks down into it, and darkening itself, succumbs to its impressions. For the very reason that the Ego of man, as he is from birth, has fallen under the superior authority of the flesh, the natural man is called σαρκικός, or even, as his soul is fallen away from its destination, and the soul conformed to its corporeally turned aspect has the dominion, ψυχικός. Of the flesh in this ethical sense, which embraces the whole natural man, Paul says (Gal. v. 17), ἡ σὰρξ ἐπιθυμεῖ κατὰ τοῦ πνεύματος. But he says it of the man in the position of μετάνοια: he says it, speaking out of the New Testament present, of the regenerate, in whom the Ego itself is divided, that is, has separated itself into a spiritual Ego turned to God, and a fleshly Ego turned away from God. In the one Ego is a double will,—a will which is founded in that which it is by nature, and a will which is founded in that which it is through grace,—a will conformed to the fleshly determination inherited by the inborn nature, and a will conformed to the spiritual determination received with the new beginning established by the grace of regeneration. This twofold will is as an impelling power and tendency simultaneous in man; but its actual movements always follow one another in time, as is shown by close self-observation; and the one spirit-soul is, as our consciousness tells us, the subject of both, even although it may be in a different relationship to the corporeity. The former may be called, as Hofmann calls it,[1] the nature-will; the latter, the personal-will; but this distinction cannot be properly applied to the man who is matured to moral self-responsibility. Certainly an Adamitically determined nature-will precedes the personal-will of the perfectly conscious man,—an inherited individualized participation in the ungodly human will of the race, which may be called a will, for the very reason that the growing man even from the outermost point of his growth is a growing person; but the personal will of the perfectly conscious man, who is not yet effectually laid hold of by grace, is actually itself the nature-will, which has now become personal-will. And in the man effectually laid hold on by grace, the Adamitic nature-will may indeed be distinguished from the new person-will; but not in such a way that the one Ego should not be the subject of both. Immediately the man is awakened to self-consciousness, it is always he as Ego who himself determines himself, either in conformity to the inborn sinful constitution of nature, or, by the power of grace, in conformity to the divine will.[2]

[1] See *Schriftb.* i. 517, as a corrective explanation to *Weiss. u. Erfüllung* ii. 16: "The materiality of our $\sigma\tilde{\omega}\mu\alpha$, in consequence of Adam's transgression, has a will directed to the world in its death, which may be distinguished from the $\theta\acute{\epsilon}\lambda\epsilon\iota\nu$ of the $\nu o\tilde{\upsilon}\varsigma$, of the self-conscious and the self-determining Ego;" and, "If the personal will of man surrenders itself to the will of his flesh, he has no other object for which he lives than the world."

[2] See Thomasius, *Dogm.* i. 280; comp. my *Biblisch-prophetische Theologie*, 207. Since even Hofmann understands by $\sigma\acute{\alpha}\rho\xi$ = nature, not only the palpable bodily, but the entire sensuous-spiritual nature of man, the inborn natural-will must from this premiss be received by him as a growing

The apostle considers his personality from the two several points of view, of grace and of nature, when he says (ver. 18*b*), "To will is present with me; but how to perform that which is good, I find not." The will to do that which is good—which, as the tendency of his true Ego, is most internally present to him—is established by grace; but the flesh does not permit it to come to the performance of that which is willed,—either altogether frustrating it, or so defiling it, that that which is performed is no more purely καλόν. The apostle cannot here by possibility mean such cases as if, *e.g.*, I wish to write a letter that is intended to rescue an erring man, and it becomes wholly impossible to me, through any sort of indisposition of body. In such a case, the will to do good is of equal value with the carrying out of the same. But if I have purposed to allow my power of labour or prayer to be weakened and abridged by no darkening pleasure, and yet such a pleasure exercises over me a power of attraction that I am not able to withstand, what the apostle says is confirmed. It is not the flesh in itself which frustrates my good determination, but the flesh with the nature-will that is stimulated by it, *i.e.* the will of natural or inherited sin, whereby the energy of the will most specially conformed to God is scattered.

The apostle has now explained, that between his will and his deed subsists a contradiction which gives a testimony to the goodness of the law to which the will is directed, and the opposed constitution of his own nature (vers. 15, 16). In that case, it is the sin which dwells in him, that is, in his flesh (or, what is the same thing, his nature), which performs that which is thus opposed to the will of his Ego (ὁ οὐ θέλω ἐγώ, vers. 17–20); and in returning to the thought (ver. 14) from which he proceeded, and which he now experimentally establishes, he concludes thence (vers. 21–24), that the spiritual law of God reveals to him in his nature a fleshly law, and thus (which is just the redeeming purpose of that law of God) awakens and sustains in him the longing after deliverance from this nature which has fallen into the power of sin and death. This result-

person-will; for nature-will, as the designation of his idea, proves the inborn impulse of will of the personally interested human nature, growing to conscious self-determination immediately the man begins to act self-consciously. The flesh, as such, has indeed no will, and (even according to Hofmann) there is not a natural soul distinct from the spirit.

ing statement he begins in ver. 21, with the inference, "I find then a law, that when I would do good, evil is present with me." To change this juxtaposition of his Ego that wills what is good, and of the evil that thwarts its performance, or that mingles itself with it, is beyond his ability: it is a νόμος, *i.e.* it is for him an inscrutably present fact, and a fact that inevitably limits him.[1] "For"—thus he continues establishing and explaining his position (vers. 22, 23)—"I delight in the law of God after the inward man; but I see another law in my members warring against the law of my mind, and bringing me into captivity to the law of sin which is in my members." There are two correlative pairs of laws which the apostle distinguishes: (1) an objective pair, ὁ νόμος τοῦ Θεοῦ, the law of God which is exalted over man by coming before him in the way of a revelation, and ὁ νόμος τῆς ἁμαρτίας, which subsists independently of the Ego of man, inasmuch as he finds himself subjected to it; and then (2) a subjective pair, ὁ νόμος τοῦ νοός, the law of his capacity of will and knowledge determining itself, and indeed determining itself according to God's law; and ὁ νόμος ἐν τοῖς μέλεσι, the law of the corporeity, which serves his Ego as an outward means of manifestation, which likewise ought to be constituted in conformity to the law of God, but in reality is determined by the law of sin that dwells in it. The genitives in "law of God" and "law of sin" indicate, as *genitivi auctoris*, the law-giving powers: the genitive in "law of the mind," on the other hand, and the attributive "in my members," designate the two laws of his own which are personal and natural to man, which are the reflex of the two other ones, in respect of the place and means of their determining opera-

[1] Hofmann reads otherwise, *Schriftb.* i. 549: "I thus find the law to me who wills to do it, as the *good*, because evil dwelleth in me." But the obvious connection of ποιεῖν τὸ καλόν contradicts this; and Meyer (edit. 2 and 3): "I find then in me, while my will is directed to the law in order to do good, that evil is foremost to me." But this is inconsistent, because of the hard inversion of the τὸν νόμον τῷ θέλοντι ἐμοί, which would only be supposable if ποιεῖν τὸ καλόν were in any way indicated as the point in view. The supposition of Meyer, that τὸν νόμον must be the positive law, is erroneous. The law is meant which the apostle in ver. 22 distinguishes from νόμος τοῦ Θεοῦ as ἕτερος νόμος. The objection against our explanation, that the idea νόμος does not agree with the relation intimated by ἐμοὶ τὸ κακὸν παράκειται, is met above.

tion.[1] The law in the members is the law of sin imprinted on the members, which Job xxiii. 12 calls חֻקִּי, " my own statute or law," as opposed to God's commandments; and the law of the *nous* or mind is the delight of the inward man in the law of God—his wish and will to allow himself to be determined by this law, and to put this law into practice. That ὁ ἔσω ἄνθρωπος is not without some modification identical with ὁ καινὸς ἄνθρωπος, is at once understood. Every man is, in psychical association, an inner and an outer nature: he has a dynamically manifold and characteristically formed internal self, and a dynamically manifold peculiarly and physiognomically formed outer self. The apostle might have written κατὰ τὸν νοῦν also, instead of κατὰ τὸν ἔσω ἄνθρωπον.[2] On the other hand, it cannot be said that the apostle might also have written κατὰ τὸν καινὸν ἄνθρωπον. For elsewhere, ὁ ἔσω (ἔσωθεν) ἄνθρωπος certainly[3] designates the regenerate internal nature of man (2 Cor. iv. 16, Eph. iii. 16; comp. ὁ κρυπτὸς τῆς καρδίας ἄνθρωπος, 1 Pet. iii. 4), although even there also, not in itself, but only in respect of the connection;[4] but here the inward man comes into consideration, not yet as a new, *i.e.* a regenerate man, but first of all only in his separation from the outward man effected by the revelation of the law. Nevertheless, even here ὁ ἔσω ἄνθρωπος does not signify the reasonable moral nature of man as such, as Meyer declares,[5] just as in Plato and Porphyry ὁ ἐντὸς ἄνθρωπος is the denomination of the human innermost nature partaking

[1] Thus Hofmann, i. 551, and similarly also Ewald, against whom Meyer, as Calov., says: "Lex membrorum et lex peccati idem sunt." They are, moreover, truly essentially one, but they are distinguished as affected and affecting; comp. for the rest, Besser on Rom. vii. (*Bibelst.* vii. 1), where the double pair of laws is acknowledged, and the law of sin is comprehended as the "power of sin" (1 Cor. xv.).

[2] As, for example, Philo says, i. 301, ἄνθρωπος ὁ ἐν ἑκάστῳ ἡμῶν τίς ἂν εἴη πλὴν ὁ νοῦς, κ.τ.λ., and i. 533, ὁ νοῦς, κυρίως εἰπεῖν, ἄνθρωπός ἐστιν ἐν ἀνθρώπῳ, κρείττων ἐν χείρονι; or Gregory of Nazianzum, ii. 88, ed. Bened., τοῦ νοῦ ὅ καὶ μᾶλλον ἄνθρωπος; comp. Cicero, *Somn.* ch. viii., "Mens cujusque is est quisque, non ea figura, quæ digito demonstrare potest;" and Lactantius, *de opificio Dei*, ch. xx., "Ipse homo neque tangi neque adspici neque comprehendi potest, quia latet intra hoc quod videtur."

[3] *Vid.* Lechler, *Die neutest. Lehre vom heiligen Amte* (1857), p. 24.

[4] *Vid.* Schott on 1 Pet. iii. 4, p. 180.

[5] Thus also Stirm, in his *Anthropologico-exegetic Inquiries*, in the *Tubinger Zeitschr. für Theologie*, 1844, 3; and not otherwise Osiander on

in the idea. The apostle does not mean a higher and better self that is left to man after the fall, but a self that is effected by grace; or, as may also be said, released by grace,—to wit, the training of the law according to the order of salvation.[1] For, in the natural state, inner and outer man are both equally under sin. It is therefore a work of grace when a man has attained to the position of having an inward delight in God's law according to his inward man, and according to his own absolute prevailing personal life desires that which is good—that which is conformed to the spiritual law of God; whilst in his outward man, *i.e.* in his members, and generally in his natural life, the law of sin still prevails, but in such a way as that he hates sin, and as far as concerns his own prevailing Ego, does not so much do it as suffer it. It is not merely un-Lutheran, but it is also un-Pauline, when Meyer[2] says, "Here the entire connection determines that the ὁ ἔσω ἄνθρωπος of the unregenerate man is meant. Moreover, to him belongs (which Philippi altogether arbitrarily denies) the συνήδομαι τῷ νόμῳ τοῦ Θεοῦ, and must belong to him, since the sinful nature is in the σάρξ. This does not, indeed, agree with the hypothesis that just the higher powers of the natural man are *e diametro* in contest with God and His law (*Form. Conc.* p. 640); but it is nevertheless exegetically established." We agree with the view in some measure, that Paul means the inward man of the unregenerate man. He speaks, indeed, of himself the regenerate, *i.e.* of experiences still continuing, and not absolutely passed away; but he does not speak of himself *quà* regenerate, *i.e.* not of experiences which he has received by the specifically New Testament grace of regeneration, but of experiences which the divine law calls forth in every man who does not harden himself against the grace that corresponds to the purpose of his salvation, and prepares and continually disciplines him for it. That even in the heathen world similar experiences may be associated with

2 Cor. iv. 16. That which is capable of regeneration (and therefore is also in need of regeneration) is the true kernel of human nature.

[1] *Vid.* Preger, Flacius, ii. 411. Man has in himself a divine ground of life, which would not at all come into his consciousness apart from prevenient grace. But through the influence of that grace it certifies itself in man since the fall, and becomes to him a law in his heart, which resists the law of sin in the members in the flesh.

[2] *Commentary on the Epistle to the Romans* (3d edit.), p. 265.

the knowledge of the divine law imprinted, according to Rom. ii. 15, upon every man, we do not deny; but the apostle is here speaking of the positive historical law of salvation, and in any case, of such a moral separation of the outer and inner man as does not subsist in man as such, but is effected by the Holy Spirit, who also is effectual by the law, although otherwise man may allow himself to be brought to self-consideration, *i.e.* to the knowledge of his duty to make God's will the substance of his own will. For transmitted sin resides not merely in the flesh. The proof that Paul does not derive sin from the sensuous nature, *i.e.* the material nature of man, has been lately again deduced by Ernesti with fundamental completeness.[1] The state which Paul (vii. 5) indicates by εἶναι ἐν τῇ σαρκὶ is a condition of the whole man, who is in the bonds of fleshly destination: it is, considered in the relation to God, a state of death (ch. vi. 13). The man who desires the good and hates the evil, and yet must experience the power of the flesh that neutralizes the God-willed good, but always with pain and shame, has already felt in himself the wholesome separation of a divinely-produced inner man, and an innate outward man. For that which is born of the flesh is flesh. The entire man is by nature formed fleshly. He may, indeed, in his conscience know what God claims from him, but the knowledge of that which is good is not of itself the decided will to do good. He does not fear God, does not love Him, does not trust Him, as he ought: the alienation from God, which is the reverse side of fleshliness, lords it over him within and without. The view of Philippi, and the hypothesis of the *Concordien-formel,* that the natural man is, " according to his highest powers and the light of reason," in an ungodly state, is thoroughly scriptural, and especially Pauline: for man's νοῦς is naturally νοῦς τῆς σαρκὸς (Col. ii. 18), and therefore μάταιος (Eph. iv. 17) and ἀδόκιμος (Rom. i. 28); his affections and tendencies of will are θελήματα

[1] H. Fr. Th. C. Ernesti, *Die Theorie vom Ursprunge der Sünde aus der Sinnlichkeit im Lichte des Paulinischen Lehrgehalts betrachtet,* 1855. Moreover, Hahn's *Theology of the New Testament* teaches very distinctly, that sin is rooted not in the flesh, but in man's supersensual inward nature; and it is gratifying that Tholuck has again borne a decided witness for the more comprehensive and deeper significance of σάρξ, defended by him in the *Commentary on the Epistle to the Romans.* See his renewed inquiry about σάρξ as the source of sin, in *Stud. u. Krit.* 1855, iii.

τῆς σαρκὸς καὶ τῶν διανοιῶν (Eph. ii. 3), *i.e.* originating in his innate sinful nature, and his selfish God-estranged mental capacities which are organized in accordance therewith. This view of the profound inwardness of human corruption is so little arbitrary, that if inherited sin were anything of less importance, the Pauline doctrine, as well of reconciliation as of the justification by grace by faith alone, would give way.

It is God's grace that divides man thus dualistically, as we read vers. 14–23. He who is carnally secure, feels nothing of it. But the more earnest is a man's moral contest, the more painfully he feels this twofold division. And probably there passes no one day in the life of any Christian, in which this twofold division does not extort from him a similar complaint to that of the apostle, ver. 24, "O wretched man that I am! who shall deliver me from the body of this death?" Even the form of this complaint shows that it comes from the breast of a converted man. An unconverted man would, before all, have longingly to aspire after the deliverance of his Ego from the will to do that which is ungodly, and from having pleasure therein, and after power earnestly to will that which is good; but the converted man knows that in his own personal life he is free from sin, and turned to God and to good. He sighs now for final deliverance from this body of death, through which his personal life is so burdened and disordered; free from that natural element that is spread around that *punctum saliens* of a will conformed to the will of God, and in which sin, with its wages of death, is ruling.[1] It is a yearning, not generally after redemption, but after perfect redemption, which is expressed in the question, Who shall deliver me, etc.? The apostle himself immediately answers this question to himself in ver. 25a: "I thank God through Jesus Christ our Lord." It is the work of Jesus Christ, that his yearning sigh can be transformed into triumphal thanks. In Jesus Christ he has that after which he sighs. Being in this body of death, he is still, because he is in Jesus Christ, free from sin and death. That it is such thoughts

---

[1] It is therefore no specifically Platonic, it is a truly Christian thought, when the book of Wisdom (ix. 15) says, "The corruptible body presseth down the soul, and the earthy tabernacle weigheth down the mind that museth upon many things." The body, as the actual σῶμα τοῦ θανάτου, is actually for the spirit a prison and a burden.

as these that are contained in this short word of thankfulness, may be known even from ch. v. 12 and ch. vi.

The apostle now sums up what he has said in vers. 14–25a about his condition, by first of all drawing, in ver. 25b, a consequence from vers. 14–24, and then in ch. viii. 1, a consequence from ch. vii. 25a. The first, the result of vers. 14–24, runs, "So then with the mind I myself (*ipse ego*) serve the law of God, but with the flesh the law of sin." As the verbal proposition appropriate to this "I myself" (not I, the same) is a united one, and is antithetically divided by μὲν-δέ, I give up the view that "I myself" means as an equivalent I, according to my true Ego.[1] The apostle means himself, for his own person; he means himself, as he is in himself, as contrasted with him as he is in Christ. Not only the thanksgiving just uttered brings with it this contrast, according to which he, who in himself must lament his miserable condition, knows, on the other hand, that he is delivered from it through Jesus Christ; it comes, moreover, to expression in the two resulting propositions by means of ἄρα (consequently), where the self-finding of the Christian in Christ Jesus (τοῖς ἐν Χριστῷ Ἰησοῦ) is opposed to his self-finding in himself in the face of the Sinaitic law (αὐτὸς ἐγώ). What the apostle says in ver. 25 by means of ἄρα οὖν, is the statement of the condition in which he finds himself since he has learnt to know God's law, and has become fond of this holy spiritual law. Since, then, he serves, with his free self-determining *noûs*, God's law, but with the flesh, in consequence of a calamitous necessity of nature, the law of sin, the law has attained in him its purpose of salvation. Sin appears to him in the light of this law all the more sinful; but he feels himself also all the more unfortunate, as his natural constitution, resisting the law, does not allow him to get free from sin. The law has not been able to bring him further than to the yearning cry of complaint after redemption from this body, which bears in itself death with sin. But he must not sigh only, he can also thank. For he is not merely himself; he is also in Christ. After what he is in himself, he finds himself still always subjected to that disunion that is called forth in him by the law. But this disunion, although in the present

[1] Combated by Hofmann, i. 556, and Meyer, p. 270 of the 3d edit. of his Comm.

it still continues, is yet not his whole, not his true present.[1] The νῦν, ch. viii. 1, is only meant of time.

How the two consequent propositions are included in one another by ἄρα, is understood when we analyze the meaning and substance of the cry of joy, "I thank God through Jesus Christ our Lord." The apostle thanks God through the Lord Jesus Christ, that he, continuing in life, has become free and released from this body of death, *i.e.* from this nature that imposes upon him a sinful death, and which brings coercion. If, on the one hand, he is thus, so far as he is out of Christ, a servant of the law of God with his own real will, but one hurried away sometimes by his sinful nature into the service of sin; still, on the other hand, for him, and for all who are in Christ Jesus, and are able through Him to thank God as being delivered and enfranchised from their body of death, all and every condemnation has now an end. "There is therefore now (actually at this time) no condemnation to them which are in Christ Jesus;" "for the law of the spirit of life in Christ Jesus hath made me free from the law of sin and death." Through the law there has arisen in him, not without the operation of the Holy Spirit, a will to do good, but a will that is powerless on account of the flesh; a will which, precisely as being without result, does not relieve him from condemnation. But if, at the same time, he is in Christ, no more condemnation of any kind touches him now; for he is no longer under that law which could not bring him further than to that powerless unblessed state of disunion: he has in himself a law removing him away above the law of sin and death,—namely, the spirit of the life of Christ, which now just as much determines his Ego to prevail and to participate in the capacity for good, as, when he regards himself as out of Christ, his Ego is determined by the overmastering sinful nature that makes all will to do good impossible. The incapacity of our Ego to accomplish the good that is willed, and the constraint of the flesh, which hurries us away against our better knowledge and will to the commission of sin, and thereby—since will without acting of good cannot avail before God as the fulfilment of law—binds us under the curse of the law,[2] subsists no more,

[1] *Vid.* v. Hofmann, in the *Erlanger Zeitschr.* 1860, p. 82.

[2] See Schott, *Römerbrief*, p. 284, with reference to v. Hofmann, *Schriftb.* i. 556.

since the spirit of life acts upon us in Christ; and in this is bestowed the power that capacitates us for the doing of good, and therewith takes us away from the state of death incurred by sin.[1] The law, far from being itself sin, and in itself the cause of death, serves therefore, as being in itself holy and spiritual, a purpose of salvation, in revealing to us sin, as a death-bringing transgression of the divine will, in its full sinfulness; but it is incapable of procuring salvation of itself: it effects only, and continually sharpens, the urgent longing after the divine fact of redemption, which has made possible that which was impossible to the law. "For what the law could not do, in that it was weak through the flesh," *i.e.* through the guilt of our flesh, which being in contradiction to its spirituality opposes it, God has accomplished for our salvation, sending His Son in the flesh, and indeed in likeness of our sinful flesh, and for an atonement for sin ($\pi\epsilon\rho\grave{\iota}$ $\dot{\alpha}\mu\alpha\rho\tau\acute{\iota}\alpha\varsigma$, *i.e.* as חַטָּאת). He has, for instance, in the flesh, *i.e.* in the flesh of Jesus for the flesh of all of us, once for all fulfilled the judgment of condemnation; so that in no way the $\kappa\alpha\tau\acute{\alpha}\kappa\rho\iota\mu\alpha$ of the law cleaves to us, but the $\delta\iota\kappa\alpha\acute{\iota}\omega\mu\alpha$ (the justification and emancipation, comp. vers. 16, 18, and therefore the promise of life) of the law becomes fulfilled in us, who walk not after the flesh, but after the spirit.[2] The sin that dwells in the flesh is condemned for us all in the flesh of Jesus in a substitutionary atoning manner. Thus in us there is no more anything to be condemned in us, who, as the apostle (ch. vii. 14–24) has shown, hate it, fight against it, and bemoan it,—in us who, indeed, as he further

---

[1] Comp. Frank, *Lehre der Concordienformel*, ii. 301: "The reception of the Holy Spirit by the preaching of the gospel proves something altogether different from this, that it is not without the Spirit's operation when the law punishes man's sin. A reception of the Holy Spirit is not yet established where only the operation of the Spirit is established in the view of its object."

[2] See my *Commentary on the Epistle to the Hebrews*, pp. 716–718. That $\delta\iota\kappa\alpha\acute{\iota}\omega\mu\alpha$ may mean the same as the law has rightly established (Meyer), and therefore may imply the moral claim of the law (Hofm., Schott, and others), I regard as possible; but in the New Testament *usus loquendi* in question, it means the sentence (Rom. i. 32), the judgment (Rom. ii. 26, etc.), the doom (Apoc. xv. 4), righteousness (Rom. v. 18; Apoc. xix. 8), and justification (Rom. v. 16); and of these meanings, the last is the fitting one here.

says, walk not κατὰ σάρκα, but κατὰ πνεῦμα; which is possible to us, as, through the judgment of God accomplished in the flesh of Jesus, not only the curse, but also the power of sin, has been broken, and a new νόμος established, which is not a death-bringing γράμμα, but a life-giving πνεῦμα, founding in us a new spiritual beginning of life, by which the body of sin and death, as we have been already withdrawn from it in its condemnation and bondage, will finally be fully overcome.

If we now look back from ch. viii. 1–4 to ch. vii. 15–23, it is first of all as clear as sunlight, that the apostle is not speaking of himself as regenerate. But just as certain is it, that he does not describe himself as he is by nature without God's influence. By nature he is "carnal, sold under sin;" and still more than that, by nature he is fleshlike, *i.e.* not merely suffering the constraint of his sinful nature, but even under its influence and direction in respect of his thoughts and will. The will to do good, the counter will against evil, is not inborn in him. That he desires the good and hates the evil, and does not succumb to sin, although in his inmost nature he is no stranger to it,—for this he has to thank God's law, which he has learned to like, because it has won his love. This is not the effect of the spirit of regeneration.[1] For the will to do good, which we have described, is a powerless one. Moreover, the powerless will to do good is not, as such, the operation of the law. The powerlessness is the result of the overmastery of the flesh, which continually diverts from this purpose the will to which the divine law has given the tendency to good. It is true, therefore, when it is said that in ch. vii. 15–23 are depicted the moral experiences of the man under the law, of whom grace has laid hold. The man is thus desirous of doing what the law puts before him as God's will; but the sin that dwells in his nature makes it impossible to him. But does the apostle describe this state as one which for the regenerate person has absolutely passed away?

This is the main and fundamental question, to which we

---

[1] Philippi in the Comm., comp. *Dogm.* iii. 229, maintaining this, asserts at the same time, that in ch. vii. 14 the regenerate person, as such, is speaking; but to this view is decidedly opposed ch. viii. 22. To this effect also what is said in my *Biblisch-prophet. Theologie*, p. 260, must be rightly added.

reply in the negative. We maintain now, as ever, that even in Rom. vii. 14-24 Paul is speaking "out of the consciousness of the regenerate person,"[1] without thereby meaning to say that he is giving utterance to experiences which are permitted to the regenerate as such; rather experiences which even the regenerate person is not spared. It certainly appears an irreconcilable contradiction, to say that one and the same man is fleshly, sold under sin (ch. vii. 14), and yet, on the other hand, is freed from the law of sin and death by the spirit of life that is in Christ Jesus (ch. viii. 2). But the apostle actually places the two states in juxtaposition, as belonging to his present condition. He does not say in ch. vii. 14, that he was previously consisting of fleshly material, and was sold under sin, but that this is his natural constitution, and that this contrariety subsists between him and God's spiritual law. He speaks in the present; and when he sets forth, in continuation, that his acknowledgment of the law does not help him to do the prescribed good, but that sin, in spite of his own will, makes him do that which is against God's will, he speaks throughout in the present. This established present claims to be all the more considered, that the apostle (ch. vii. 7-13) also actually speaks in historical form of a fact of experience which at that time belongs to the past. He looks back there into his childhood, and shows how, in the degree that the claim of law entered into his consciousness, the sin which was present in him, but not present as his personal conduct, became his personal sin, and the cause of his self-incurred death. It was the saving purpose of the law declared in ver. 13 which he thus painfully experienced. From ver. 14 onwards, the apostle then depicts how he, the self-consciously willing one, finds himself and his doing disposed in the light of the law. Every Christian is compelled to confirm what the apostle here says, from his own personal experience. And well for him if he can also confirm the fact that God's law, and therefore God's will, is his delight,—that he desires the good and hates the evil; and, indeed, in such a way that the sin to which, against his will, he is hurried away, is foreign to his inmost nature. But woe to him, if from his own personal experience he could only confirm this, and not also the

---

[1] Thus, for example, also v. Harless, *Ethik*, p. 45. Meyer does not justly appreciate this view, and therefore wrongly classifies it.

fact that the spirit of the new life that has its source in Christ Jesus, has freed him from the urgency of sin, and the condition of death, which were not abrogated through the law, but only brought to light; so that his will, which by the law was inclined towards what is good, although powerless, now actually capable of good, is opposed, as a predominating overmastering power of life which will finally triumph in glory, to the death that continues to work in him.

We agree with Hofmann[1] in Philippi, that the two passages, ch. vii. 14–24 and viii. 1–11, must be taken together, if the form of the regenerate life is not to be left one-sided. Meanwhile, ch. vii. 14 is not the one side of the form of life of the regenerate, as such: it is only the dim foundation of this form of life, that has not yet disappeared even in the condition of regeneration. For what Hofmann says is no less true, that the apostle in ch. vii. 14 represents himself in respect of his own moral relation to God, apart from the moral capacity which accrues to him from his community of life with Christ,—a capacity which does not come into expression till ch. viii. Philippi,[2] on the other hand, has objected, "If I am in Christ, and am depicting that which I am out of Christ, I depict *in concreto* not what I actually am, but what I once was out of Christ." It is only necessary to look into one's own heart to feel what a sophism this is. The man who is in Christ, just this very man, is divided indeed into a man actually living in Christ, and a man who, although surrounded by the new life, is not yet pervaded by it, and therefore is in effect out of Christ; as Flacius[3] remarks on Rom. vii., "That two men are found in the skin of the one man, *i.e.* that two kinds of power exist in the regenerate person." In other words, there is, as our every-day experience teaches us, in our life referred to God, a region pervaded by grace, and a region only, so to speak, shone upon (illuminated) by grace. Certainly, in the regenerate person, an all-powerful might of good shows itself effectual; but, opposed to it, there is also a power of evil, which, although overcome, is still constantly needing to be restrained; and in this contest, which ought to be a

---

[1] *Vid. Schriftb.* i. 556, and, as an explanation, *Erlanger Zeitschr.* 1860, pp. 82–84.

[2] *Römerbrief*, p. 250, Anm.; comp. *Dogm.* iii. 228.

[3] *Vid.* Preger's work on Flacius, ii. 218.

constant victory, a mournful powerlessness of good purposes remaining unaccomplished throws its long dark shadows, as we are compelled to avow in daily contrition, on every evening self-examination. The separate representation of this light and this twilight aspect in ch. vii. and viii., depends certainly upon an abstraction; but this abstraction, far removed from being, according to Schott's[1] expression, *a casus non dabilis*, is perfectly justified in the history of redemption, inasmuch as the description in ch. vii. corresponds to the Old Testament condition under the law; and is experimentally justified, inasmuch as this Old Testament condition is overcome in us, but not so annulled that it does not constantly from time to time, in conformity with its general ethical nature, intrude into our actual present state, *i.e.* the being and walking in Christ. The abstraction, therefore, only subsists in separate consideration of that which *in concreto*, unfortunately, is only too manifoldly involved together."[2]

The unhappy disunion which the apostle depicts is, moreover, not foreign to the regenerate. Even he is still σάρκινος, for his body is not yet spiritual. Even he is πεπραμένος ὑπὸ τὴν ἁμαρτίαν; for, so long as we are compelled to implore the forgiveness of our sins daily, yea hourly, we are still, as it were, fettered to sin. But this disunion is not the Christian's entire, not the Christian's proper and true present condition, but only its twilight background, which is still waiting for its perfect enlightenment. He bears in himself also a fundamentally new life, which, peaceful in itself, floats over that disunion. This new life is inwoven in his νοῦς, which desires the good: it has its place in the πνεῦμα τοῦ νοὸς αὐτοῦ (Eph. iv. 23, comp. 1 Pet. iii. 4), and subsists in the God-resembling nature which there is once more enlivened and realized by actual communication of the πνεῦμα of Christ. Here there has broken forth to him a light eminent above the sorrowful disunion, that is not to be done away in this mortal state; a light, moreover, which shall become a glorification even for his corporeity. His Ego that desires God's will, knows already that it is redeemed, in that it is removed away from the body of sin and death, into the divine, God-resembling life-principle of the spirit which is exalted above

[1] *Römerbrief*, p. 276.
[2] *Vid.* Thomasius, *Dogm.* i. 276, and Harless, *Ethik*, p. 45.

the φθορὰ, i.e. sin and death (ἐν τῷ ἀφθάρτῳ τοῦ πνεύματος, 1 Pet. iii. 4). It has received Christ's Spirit as the principle in which it dwells and takes root,—as the sphere in which it feels itself living, enfranchised, satisfied, and thus even here below blessed,—as the power by which it is impelled, and empowered to rule over sin, and to act in a way that shall be pleasing to God.[1]

This is the twofold condition of the Christian, the unabolished dualism, or, as we may say, following Scripture testimony still more closely, the unabolished antinomy. The state described in ch. vii. 14-24, and that described ch. viii. 5-17, are involved in one another, as the apostle says in a way that is altogether unmistakeable, in ch. vii. 25b and viii. 1. The Christian is not privileged to experience the latter state, without at times also being compelled to experience the former; and he does not experience the former, without being able to patiently wait for the latter, (but of pure and unqualified grace.) If he withdraws himself into the πνεῦμα of his νοῦς, where, by communication of Christ's Spirit, is laid the foundation of a new man, there subsists a wall of separation between him and the unblessed disunion: he enjoys righteousness, life, and peace; and he performs holy deeds from

---

[1] As a sketch of what is stated in the section of the Epistle to the Romans just explained, occurs Gal. v. 16-18. In ver. 17, the disunion depicted in Rom. vii. 14-24 is declared; in vers. 16 and 18, the spiritual elevation above that disunion, which the New Testament standing of grace makes possible. Πνεῦμα, in ver. 17, inclusively of the νοῦς, is generally the internal nature of the man, so far as it is defined by the divinely originated beginning of a new personal life. In a similar connection, Peter says even (1 Pet. ii. 11) ψυχή. By the latter as by the former denomination, is meant the pneumatico-psychical internal nature of the man, not as it is by nature, but through grace by the power of the indwelling of the Spirit of Christ. "The power of sin," strikingly says H. W. Rinck, agreeing with us in the interpretation of Rom. vii., " which before had its citadel in the spirit and in the soul, is broken and forced back into the flesh. It certainly has still an existence in the soul: it is busy in the lower life of the soul, and reaches even into the spirit, and pollutes body, soul, and spirit; but the new Ego, the new man, ever overcomes it anew, and—what we especially insist on here, in conformity with Rom. vii.—it remains uninvolved with sin, even although sin exercises a power that is still often victorious. The innermost Ego, when it is renewed by the Holy Spirit, remains separated from sin, and subsists in constant struggle with it, until, after many defeats and victories, it finally has possession of the field."

this centre,—deeds which indeed are not without any blot, but still are accepted before God as holy, because they have their origin and nature from the Spirit of His Son, the beloved one. The corporeity with its members ($\sigma\hat{\omega}\mu\alpha$ and $\mu\acute{\epsilon}\lambda\eta$) is not yet spiritual, but fleshly, darkened by sin and death: the *nous* is involved in a struggle for the light, in favour of which it has decided against the darkness, and is imprisoned in the never-resting struggle; but the spirit of the *nous* is redeemed from darkness and contest in Christ the Redeemer. Here the Christian has his life-ground, and therefore he is no longer $\dot{\epsilon}\nu\ \tau\hat{\eta}\ \sigma\alpha\rho\kappa\acute{\iota}$ (ch. viii. 9). In the forecourt is the darkness of death ($\tau\grave{o}\ \sigma\hat{\omega}\mu\alpha\ \nu\epsilon\kappa\rho\grave{o}\nu\ \delta\iota'\ \dot{\alpha}\mu\alpha\rho\tau\acute{\iota}\alpha\nu$, ch. viii. 10); in the holy place the light glimmers through the darkness with which it struggles (ch. vii. 23; Gal v. 17); in the holiest of all are enthroned righteousness, life, peace (ch. viii. 6, 10): there is the gentle stillness, which in 1 Pet. iii. 4 is said to be the essence of true womanhood: there is light, and thence come the fruits of light, or, which is the same thing, of the Spirit; for in the scriptural language, and even in the Pauline, $\pi\nu\epsilon\hat{\upsilon}\mu\alpha$ and $\phi\hat{\omega}\varsigma$ are one and the same thing[1] (comp. $\kappa\alpha\rho\pi\grave{o}\varsigma\ \tau o\hat{\upsilon}\ \phi\omega\tau\grave{o}\varsigma$, Eph. v. 9, with $\kappa\alpha\rho\pi\grave{o}\varsigma\ \tau o\hat{\upsilon}\ \pi\nu\epsilon\acute{\upsilon}\mu\alpha\tau o\varsigma$, Gal. v. 22).

We have now examined the substance of the fact of the life of regeneration. If we were to consider the fact of justification, and all the agencies and experiences of grace which are linked with this fundamental fact, we should overstep the limits of our science. Mindful, however, of the risk which we suggested to ourselves in the Prolegomena, we have only examined the fundamental facts and relations which proceed from the grace of God in Christ. Even these would not indeed fall into the

[1] The object of the spiritual affection, says J. H. Ursinus in his *Theologia Mystica*, is rest in God, that sleep of grace (*somnus gratiæ*) contrasted with the sleep of nature, by means of which the spirit enters as into a sacred gloom, so that in the closed eyes of the understanding (*intellectus*) it understands nothing else than God above all understanding: the will reposes from all desires, and the heart from all affections; and the peace of God embraces and encircles the whole new man, the peace which is higher than all reason, which passes all understanding. This repose is experienced more or less by all those whom the Spirit of God impels in the spirit of their mind (*in spiritu mentis suæ*); but the struggle continues none the less, because sin continues to subsist in and around us: we taste the peace, but its full enjoyment awaits us in that home where God shall be all in all.

domain of psychology, if grace only made an ethical alteration in the inner man; but they become the subject of psychology, by the fact that grace penetrates and changes fundamentally, newly creating and newly moulding, the natural pneumatico-psychical condition. The constitution of our pneumatico-psychical internal nature, in the condition of its integrity, in the state of the ruin that followed the fall, and in the state of the begun process of its restoration, is indeed not merely distinct superficially, but to its profoundest core. The human soul has a changeful history, within which its God-created substance continues to subsist indeed, undestroyed, although it passes through the most diverse kinds of phases and forms of being. Pursuing the history further, we now accompany the soul into the future state. Were it here only speculation that leads us where our own immediate experience ceases, it would be a daring and ineffectual attempt. But our guide is the divine revelation that is put before us in Scripture. To exhibit the psychological intimations presented by Scripture, and which are not limited to this present temporal state of things, but reach backwards and forwards into the everlasting spiritual world—this is our problem.

APPENDICES.

I.

LUTHER'S TRICHOTOMY.

From his Exposition of the Magnificat of the Year 1521.

VOL. VII. OF THE EDITION OF WALCH, VOL. XLV. OF THE ERLANGEN EDITION.

SCRIPTURE divides man into three parts, as says St Paul (1 Thess. v. 23): "God, who is a God of peace, sanctify you through and through; that thus your whole SPIRIT, SOUL, and BODY, may be preserved blameless unto the coming of our Lord Jesus Christ." And every one of these three, together with the entire man, is also divided in another way into two portions, which are there called SPIRIT and FLESH. Which division is not natural, but attributive; *i.e.* nature has three portions—spirit, soul, and body—and they may be altogether good or evil. And this is called being spirit or flesh, of which at present we are not to speak.[1]

THE FIRST DIVISION.—The spirit is the highest, noblest part of man, wherewith he is fitted to apprehend intangible, invisible, eternal things; and it is briefly the house within which the faith and word of God dwells. Of this David (Ps. li. 10)

---

[1] "Man," says Luther elsewhere, "with reason and will, internal and external, with body and soul, is called flesh, for the reason that he, with all his powers, internally and externally, only seeks that which is flesh, and is advantageous to the flesh. The soul is thus deeply immersed into the flesh, so that it wishes to preserve and protect it from suffering prejudice; and therefore that it is more flesh than the flesh itself." In the preface to the *Epistle to the Romans*, "Thou art not to understand flesh and spirit here in such a way as that flesh alone should be that which has to do with impurity, and spirit that which concerns what is internal in the heart; but St

says, "Lord, make in my most inward part a right spirit," *i.e.* an upright strong faith. Again, of those who were unbelieving he says (Ps. lxxviii. 37), "For their heart was not right towards God, and their spirit was not in faith towards God." (If the spirit be no longer holy, nothing besides is holy. But the spirit's holiness subsists in the simple, sincere faith, because the spirit does not concern itself with tangible things. Only the faith of the spirit is important.)

THE SECOND—the soul—is just the same spirit conformed to nature, but still in another agency; namely, in that in which it vitalizes the body and operates through it, and is often taken in Scripture for the life. For probably the spirit might live without the body, but the body does not live without the spirit. We see this division as it lives and acts even in sleep also, and without intermission; and its manner is not to apprehend intangible things, but such as the reason can recognise and estimate. And thus the reason is here the light in this house; and when the spirit does not enlighten, as with a higher light, this light of reason rules; and therefore it can never be without error. For it is too feeble to act in respect of divine things. To these two divisions Scripture appropriates many things as *sapientiam* and *scientiam*—the wisdom to the spirit, the knowledge to the soul; and accordingly, also, hatred, love, desire, horror, and the like.

THE THIRD is the body with its members, the agencies of which are only bringing into exercise and use what the soul knows and the spirit believes. And to adduce a parallel to this from Scripture, Moses made a tabernacle with three distinct compartments (Ex. xxvi. 33, 34, xxvii. 9). The first was called *sanctum sanctorum*, within which dwelt God, and there was no light therein. The second *sanctum*, within which stood a candlestick with seven pipes and lamps. The third was called

Paul, as Christ (John iii. 6), calls flesh, all that which is born of flesh, the whole man with body and soul, with reason and all senses; for the reason that everything in him is stirring towards the flesh. Therefore thou mayest know to call him fleshly who without grace thinks, teaches, talks of high spiritual matters, as thou probably mayest learn it from the works of the flesh (Gal. v. 19), since he also calls heresy and hatred works of the flesh; and Rom. viii. 3 says, that through the flesh the law is weakened, which is said not of uncleanness, but of all sins, and most of all of unbelief, which is the most spiritual sin of all."

atrium, the court; and it was under the open heaven, in the light of the sun. In the same figure a Christian man is depicted. His spirit is *sanctum sanctorum*, God's dwelling-place in dim faith without light. For he believes what he does not see, nor feel, nor apprehend. His soul is *sanctum:* there are seven lights; that is, all kinds of understanding, discrimination, knowledge, and perception of bodily visible things. His body is *atrium*, which is manifest to every man, that it may be seen what he does and how he lives. [If to a Christian his spirit be maintained entire and complete ($\pi\nu\epsilon\hat{v}\mu\alpha$ $\delta\lambda\delta\kappa\lambda\eta\rho o\nu$), the soul and the body may also continue accordingly without error and evil works. Otherwise it is not possible, where the spirit is faithless, that in such a case the soul and the whole life should not go wrong and ill; although probably they avail themselves of good intentions and imaginations, and use special devotion, and have pleasure therein. Let this for the present be sufficient for the illustration of the two words SOUL and SPIRIT, for the reason that they are almost used in common in the Scripture.]

II.

UPON THE "SPIRIT OF THE MIND."

A. *From the " Scriptural Thoughts of the Powers of the Human Soul," of Heinrich Wilh. Clemmens (Prof. and Preacher at Bebenhausen).*[1]

HEILBRONN, 1760, 8.

THE powers of grace that operate in the soul, and new beget the man, determine the spirit of the man, which afterwards penetrates the entire soul; and in so far as the spirit's abode is in the innermost recesses of the soul, it is called the spirit of the mind, $\pi\nu\epsilon\nu\mu\alpha$ $\tau o\nu$ $\nu o o \varsigma$. As such a spirit it is again afterwards specially subjected, in a gratefully passive manner, to the Holy Spirit, and to His gracious influences, which are always carried

[1] Communicated as the only endeavour known to me to establish the idea of $\pi\nu\epsilon\nu\mu\alpha$ $\tau o\nu$ $\nu o o \varsigma$, *spiritus mentis.* See above, p. 185; *vid.* Observation 2.

forward and exalted in the hearts of the faithful, and is related to these operations of the Holy Spirit, as human feeling considered in itself is related to the general assistance of grace, or to that grace which is common to the first man as to all men. "Spiritus est facultas animæ," says in this sense Bengel, "quum ea spiritus divini operationem suaviter patitur; at $νοῦς$ est facultas animæ foras progredientis et cum proximo agentis, 1 Cor. xiv. 14."

In respect of the Reason, so far as it alone rules, the word $πνεῦμα$, which points to a foreign power, not for one time only, stands as a manifest proof, that in the Reason man has a definite ground of his doings—peculiar, it is true, but altogether corrupted by sin. If, on the other hand, the Reason is used in good understanding, and by those who are brought under grace, it occurs that now and then such an epithet as $πνευμα$ is applied thereto; while the faithful, for the very reason that they are under grace, allow their reason and all their senses to be animated by the operations of grace, and receive a spirit in themselves which afterwards may receive and retain in the innermost ground of the soul the impressions of the Holy Spirit, that does not until then rightly carry on and complete the condition of grace. Thus at least speaks the Holy Scripture; for otherwise it could not be known why, in 1 Cor. xiv. 14, $πνευμα$ and $νους$, spirit and understanding, should be distinguished, and why, according to Eph. iv. 23, the believer is daily to allow himself to be renewed in the spirit of the understanding, $πνευμα \, του \, νοος$.

If the Reason works under grace, it becomes ever more qualified to comprehend with all saints what is the breadth and length, and the depth and height, of the knowledge of God which is in Christ Jesus. At the beginning, it abides by the first omnipresent grace which is near to all men; and if it here proves faithful, it will become from time to time invested with new grace, and so pervaded, that a spirit of understanding enlivens its doing and pleases God; and that these powers daily become renewed, awakened, and set in movement to the praise of the wisdom and glory of the great God and the Saviour Jesus Christ; and by the help of the good Spirit, and the gracious work of the perfecting Spirit, and His constant influx,

> Even in the innermost ground of the soul,
> Mingle themselves with the most childlike sighs.

Thus, then, in this innermost ground of the soul, the πνευμα του νοος, the spirit of the mind and of all the powers of the soul, has its dwelling.

B. *From a mediæval pamphlet, entitled "The Life of the Thinking Soul."*

(MS. OF THE YEAR 1486, IN THE POSSESSION OF THE AUTHOR.)

HERE it is to be observed, that the soul is divided into three parts in the Scripture, and each part has its specific name. The lowest part is referred to the lowest powers; therefore it is named a soul when it is united with the part that is with the body, and gives to the body a life. The middle part of the soul is called a spirit, and is that which is conformed to the three highest powers. The highest part of the soul is that in which these three powers are originally in union; and when effluent, like the ray from the sun, it is called a mind or thought, and is the apex sharp and pointed of the soul, wherein (*scil.* the apex) the image of the Holy Trinity is impressed. And it is so noble, that no appropriate name can be given to it; but it is described in many words as best it can be. And this is the highest point in the soul, and the elevation of the spirit. These are the highest powers, which must precede a separation of the soul, that is, between the soul and the spirit. When this elevation transpires with the spirit, all is free. The division which, according to St Paul's words, is operative in us, is the living and powerful word of God, which is penetrating more than a sword that cuts on both sides, by which the spirit, free from all things, may prosecute its subtle work of inspection; and, as St Augustine says, nothing is more wonderful than this dividing between the soul and the spirit, since they are essentially one thing. But this division takes place for this reason, that in man might not be left that which is brutal and sensual, and that that which is spiritual in man might soar aloft in freedom; so that he may thus become fitted for the dignity of beholding the divine glory, and so be united to God, and transformed into God's own image. If he thus depends on God, he becomes a spirit with God.

VI.
DEATH AND THE INTERMEDIATE STATE.

———◆———

Ἄγκυραν ἔχομεν τῆς ψυχῆς ἀσφαλῆ τε καὶ βεβαίαν, καὶ εἰσερχομένην εἰς τὸ ἐσώτερον τοῦ καταπετάσματος.—Heb. vi. 19.

SOUL AND SPIRIT IN THE MIDST OF DEATH.

Sec. I.

SLEEP, as we have shown in Div. IV. Sec. XIV., is the periodical sinking down of the seventh, sixth, fifth psychico-somatical form of life retrogressively into the fourth, towards the first. The activity of the fourth, third, second, first, continues in sleep, and is partly even more intense and perceptible than in waking. If the activity of these lower forms of life ceases also, and is changed into its opposite, death supervenes. The heart stiffens (1 Sam. xxv. 37), or is broken (Jer. xxiii. 9); the blood stands still, or flows forth (in the case of a violent death); the last breath is drawn, to which no further one succeeds; the body, thrown back into the first form of life (that of the נְּוִיָה), sinks, after complete extinction of all animal and vegetative functions, into the purely elementary (psychico-chemical) decomposing process of corruption ($\delta\iota\alpha\phi\theta o\rho\acute{a}$) in the womb of the earth (Job i. 21 ; Ecclus. xl. 1),—the absolute reverse of the embryonic process of formation in the womb of the woman (Ps. cxxxix. 15).

Death therefore is, as it is very generally named in Scripture, a falling asleep, but such an one as overpasses the natural limit which is set to mere sleep. For sleep is only the relative, while death is the absolute, opposite of waking; falling asleep, therefore, is a euphemism for dying (John xi. 11, etc.). He who has fallen into the sleep of death (יָשֵׁן הַמָּוֶת, Ps. xiii. 3), sleeps שְׁנַת עוֹלָם (Jer. li. 39, 57). In the sleeper, the soul has withdrawn itself to the four lowest forms of life; in the dead person, it has wholly retired in the direction of these lower forms out of the body. The spontaneous power of reawakening is no longer there (Job xiv. 12).

It is the נֶפֶשׁ which, in scriptural language, is poured out in violent death (Isa. liii. 12; Ps. cxli. 8), and is breathed forth in every kind of death (Job xi. 20, xxxi. 39, Jer. xv. 9; comp. Lam. ii. 12, 1 Kings xvii. 17). Scripture says directly, even that the soul dies (תָּמוּת). That in this mode of expression (Num. xxiii. 10, Judg. xvi. 30, Job xxxvi. 14; comp. Wisd. i. 11, Mark iii. 4) נֶפֶשׁ does not synecdochically denote the person who possesses the soul, but the soul itself, is proved by the frequent form of speech הִכָּהוּ נֶפֶשׁ, Gen. xxxvii. 21 (comp. רְצָחוֹ נֶפֶשׁ, Deut. xxii. 26), according to which it is the soul of the man which in killing by violence is fatally stricken. This sounds wholly materialistic; and, indeed, what is true in materialism is seen without qualification in Scripture.

But not as though the soul in itself, as distinct from the spirit, were mortal. This view, which attributes to man a brute and perishable soul as the link of his spirit and body, we must, after having often postponed its discussion, here finally get rid of. In Scripture, that which passes over from man when he dies, into the unseen world, Ps. xlix. 19, comp. ver. 16, xvi. 10 (Acts ii. 25), xxx. 3, is called, indeed, not only רוּחַ, but also נֶפֶשׁ, as well as that which returns to the body when man again comes to life (1 Kings xvii. 22); and the departed are called as well ψυχαί (Apoc. vi. 9, xx. 4, comp. Wisd. iii. 1) as πνεύματα (1 Pet. iii. 19, Heb. xii. 23).[1] Of the dying person is said just as much, his soul goeth forth (Gen. xxxv. 18), as his spirit goeth

---

[1] From the ἐκκλησία πρωτοτόκων ἀπογεγραμμένων ἐν οὐρανοῖς, i.e. the church which is still struggling here below, with certain expectancy of the heavenly inheritance,—the church, whose new birth in relation to the still unglorified remaining creation is called a first birth,—are here distinguished the πνεύματα δικαίων τετελειωμένων, i.e. the spirits of the righteous, of the old covenant, and of those added to them of the new covenant, which exist as spirits withdrawn from all inward and outward disturbances of the fleshly life, already in the position of completion, and are only still waiting for the exaltation of their bodies also into the position of completion; comp. the song of the three children, v. 63, where πνεύματα καὶ ψυχαὶ δικαίων are called upon to praise the Lord. The Sohar calls the blessed in heaven רוּחִין דְּצַדִּיקַיָּא. Moreover, we remember the remarkable saying of Cicero: O præclarum diem, cum ad illud divinum animorum concilium cœtumque proficiscar cumque ex hac turba et colluvione discedam. In Homer, the departed are usually called ψυχαί; but he also says, Il. vii. 129, θυμὸν ἀπὸ μελέων δῦναι δόμον Ἄϊδος εἴσω.

forth (Ps. cxlvi. 4; Ecclus. xxxviii. 23; Wisd. xvi. 14): of the person who dies voluntarily, just as much that he surrenders his spirit (John xix. 30), or yields it up (Matt. xxvii. 50), as that he surrenders or yields up his soul (Acts xv. 26). This going out, this surrender of the spirit, attends the last drawing of breath (Eccles. viii. 8): the breath is the sensible manifestation of life, which, in the widest extent, has its causal subject in the spirit, רוּחַ or נְשָׁמָה (*vid.* Sec. II.). Therefore, in the New Testament, the designation of dying is as well ἐκπνέειν as ἐκψύχειν; in respect of which it is to be observed that the former is used thrice, for an obvious reason, of the death of Jesus: the latter is used thrice (in the Acts of the Apostles) of the punishment of death of sinners.

How could this interchange of רוּחַ, πνεῦμα, and נֶפֶשׁ, ψυχή, be possible when death is spoken of, if the soul perished in death, and if it were not attested, even in the midst of death, that spirit and soul, as *principium principians* and *principium principiatum* of human individual life, are inseparably united in unity of essence and causal connection?[1]

Plainly, therefore, according to Scripture, soul and spirit outlast the corruption of the body. And, nevertheless, it is true of the soul, in a certain sense, that it dies! It dies, so far as it was wont to centralize in itself the natural powers of the body, and to pervade the organs of the body with its own spirit-like life. It does not die, so far as it is of the spirit (Matt. x.

[1] As once in earlier times was expressed by Heyder in his work, *Ecclesiastæ de Immortalitate animi qualis fuerit sententia* (1838), that, according to Old Testament representation, the spirit returns to God, the soul, on the other hand, enters into Hades, so lately, Ströbel (*Zur Eschatologie, Luth. Zeitschrift*, 1855, iii.) has sought to prove that Scripture teaches that the departed soul enters into the kingdom of death (Hades); the separated spirit, on the other hand, into a condition of bliss, or perdition. Upon the anthropological fundamental text, Gen. ii. 7, he says (*l.c.* p. 494), "He who doubts of the possibility of the separation in question, should consider that Gen. ii. 7 does not stand thus: God made the body out of the earth, and breathed into it soul and spirit, and thus man was made. Having first already created body *and soul* (man), the Lord breathed into him the life-giving spirit, by which his soul, as distinguished from that of the brute, became a *living* one. Spirit and soul are not contemporaneous in Adam, were not even given in one kind of manner: he received the latter, like all other psychic creatures, by his creation from the earth; the former subsequently out of God's mouth." But I find it now, as ever, just as much

28); but it dies, so far as it has become of the body. Its life that has emanated from the spirit, endures; but its life that is immanent in the body, perishes with the body itself.[1]

The matter of fact is not, however, this, that the soul withdraws itself gradually from the body, in the degree in which the body dies. If the case were thus, we could only speak figuratively, only *per zeugma*, of a death of the soul. But the fact, as both Scripture and experience attest, is otherwise. The soul goes forth from the body (יֵצֵא, Gen. xxxv. 18) not without resistance: it seeks to maintain itself in the body as long as possible (1 Kings xvii. 17), until at length it succumbs powerlessly, when its connection with the body is forcibly severed (Job xxvii. 8, vi. 9; Isa. xxxviii. 12). It is the light of the bodily life; and when this light burns clearly no longer, it still flickers and glimmers on, until it finally goes out (Isa. xliii. 17). It would lead to no result if we were to consider at length the biblical figures of that power which comes more especially over the body and the soul in dying (*vid.* Div. IV. Sec. X.). It is indeed intelligible of itself, that man would experience no pain at all if he had not a soul in which the pain-exciting bodily affections are reflected. Therefore the soul, because it is the subject of the bodily life, of sensation, and all its shadowings, is moreover the peculiar subject of the suffering of death; and being this, it is impossible that the suffering of death should

---

contradictory of this scriptural statement as generally of the scriptural representation, that the human soul was already in existence before the divine inbreathing, and did not come into existence by means of this inbreathing. It is true, Ströbel reminds me (*Luth. Zeitschr.* 1857, p. 764) that I teach what is substantially the same, when I say that "in the body formed by God there were living powers, but they were not yet combined into unity of life." But in vain: in my view, the soul is not, even in the brute, to say nothing of man, a resultant of natural forces; for in all creatures, whether they be unendowed with soul, or endowed with soul, or deprived of soul, natural powers are actually operative.

[1] Materialism only acknowledges the latter life. Of old it said, ὁ λόγος σπινθὴρ ἐν κινήσει καρδίας ἡμῶν (Wisd. ii. 2); in the present day, "thought is a phosphorescence of the brain;" in opposition to which, J. von Liebig has observed that the brain does not contain phosphorus, but only phosphoric acid, which does not shine at all; and that our bones, which contain four hundred times more phosphorus, ought in such a case to possess the wisest thoughts. More cautiously, and not assailable in this manner, runs the saying, "Without phosphorus, no thought."

result in death, unless the soul itself were stricken with death. The soul dies, and yet it subsists on. The body, moreover, continues to exist, but decomposing and decomposed in its fundamental elements. The soul continues to exist as the emanating *doxa* of the spirit. In what else, therefore, can its death consist, than in the fact of its being driven forcibly back to that from which it originated? The body continues to exist, even in corruption, *i.e.* while its elements, passing forth from the bond of the living organism, arrange themselves in new and more simple partially gaseous and putrid associations. But the soul—that monad which united the body into a compact life—cannot corrupt as the body corrupts. Its life subsists in emanation; and its death, or, if it be preferred thus to speak, its corruption, consists in remanation. It can no longer hold its ground against the Turba, which has possessed itself of the body with its natural powers, and its own powers. Constrained to recoil to the lowest forms of its bodily self-manifestation, it must at length vacate the body, the place of its dominion. Dethroned and driven to flight, it returns to the spirit from which it went forth royally and masterfully to conquer and to rule.

But, inasmuch as the soul forsakes the body, the spirit also which pervaded the body by means of the soul is isolated therefrom. This isolation, if we regard death in itself as the punishment of sin, is nothing at all of an enfranchisement. For, to dwell in the body, to endow it with soul, and to live itself forth therein, is the innate nature and destination of the human spirit. It is therefore an unnatural condition into which the spirit is thrown back by means of death. The downfall of the soul is also the downfall of the spirit. Deprived of the body of which it ought to be the life culminating in self-consciousness, and in which it has the proximate material and the proximate means of this life, even the spirit becomes surrounded with darkness. For death is νύξ (John ix. 4). But such a surrounding with night is possible. For the essence of death consists in the man's becoming again the same as he was. And the existence of the spirit which began with unconsciousness, may also be thrown back into unconsciousness. The spirit which proceeded from God, when He created man (Gen. ii. 7), when it was to become a human spirit, did not attain to self-consciousness until its association with the body; and since humanity has propagated itself, by the mode of begetting, forth from that creative beginning, that is also the way of its development. Therefore, when the association of the spirit with the body ceases, that which is agreeable to nature, in that which is contrary to nature, is this: that the spirit is transplanted back into that restraint of its self-consciousness with which its existence began. That actually, through the darkening of death, the most intense effulgurations of its nature springing from God thrill throughout it,—as Cicero says, "appropinquante morte anima multo est divinior,"—does not prove the contrary. This is usually explained by the fact, that the spirit, in proportion as its union with the body becomes more loose, becomes the more capable of purely and freely attesting its own self;[1] but this view of death as a process of enfranchisement according to natural law, is unscriptural. Only this is true, that with the final sinking into sleep are associated intense dreaming phenomena,[2] in that the spirit does not suffer the violence wherein death consists without collecting together its whole power, in order to defend itself therefrom, and to lift itself above it. But it does suffer it, as every injury of the body that brings it near to death proves. This is the fact to which materialism points with contemptuous look of triumph. It may not be denied. Death as such, does not, it is true, force man back into absolute nothing, but back within the limit of that nothingness which preceded his coming into being. That man continues self-conscious throughout death, and that it is possible for him to live although he dies,—this is the operation of redeeming grace, which, for all who lay hold on it, changes death into life, and permits us sometimes to behold in the countenance of dying persons the bright gleam of the heaven opened to them.[3] This redeeming grace has, even for those who reject it, placed a limit to the power of death.

[1] See, for example, Petöcz, *Ansicht der Welt* (1838), p. 403.
[2] Göschel, *Der Mensch diesseits und jenseits*, p. 43. In death, sleep is perfected, as καταφορά, sinking; and again, the dream is perfected as ἀναφορά, raising.
[3] An illustration, confirmed to me by an eye-witness, is the death of a lad of five years old, related in the *Kleinen Barmer Missionsfreund*, 1858, No. 9. About half-past one o'clock he bowed his dear head: the eye appeared broken. Then at once he folded his hands, raised his head, opened his eyes wide, and looked in silent amazement for about two minutes

THE TRUE AND THE FALSE IMMORTALITY.[1]

Sec. II.

It is contrary to experience as well as to Scripture, to say that man is immortal; for man, in fact, dies. He is spoken of as the frail and perishable אֱנוֹשׁ; he resembles, in respect of mutability, a fading flower and a fleeing shadow (Job xiv. 2, and *passim*). The son of Adam is not immortal—οὐκ ἀθάνατος (Ecclus. xvii. 30). Moreover, it is just as little scriptural to say that the soul is immortal, and that the spirit is immortal: for Scripture does not hesitate to say of the soul, that it dies; and of the spirit, although it does not indeed say that it dies, yet it says nowhere that it is immortal. Man was created by God in the position of *posse non mori*, that he might thence attain to the position of *non posse mori*, or of everlasting life (ἐπ' ἀφθαρσία, Wisd. ii. 23): he was, according to the design, and so far certainly by nature, immortal.[2] But after he had fallen from this his destination, immortality (ἀθανασία or ἀφθαρσία) only exists for him

upwards. An inexpressible loftiness sate upon his countenance, his eyes lightened, and his face was overflowed with a bright gleam. Full of amazement, and with the cry of astonishment, we stood around his bed. None of us, although some had already stood by many hundred deathbeds, had ever seen such an one: it was a lightning flash of eternity, granted bodily for a few moments, according to God's gracious pleasure, to mortal sinful eyes.

[1] As, from this paragraph forward, spirit and soul come into consideration almost entirely in respect of the similarity of their future destiny, founded in their indissolubility and unity of nature, therefore henceforth "soul" will be used more frequently than elsewhere, in such a way as that the spirit is included in the idea—in like manner as God, in respect of His *doxa*, is named, inclusively of His essence, שָׁמַיִם, οὐρανός, or even directly the *Doxa*.

[2] Hahn, *Theologie der N. T.* i. 389. I so far also agree with Hermann Schultz, *Die Voraussetzungen der christl. Lehre von der Unsterblichkeit*, 1861, that the personal continuance of being, and especially the everlasting life of man, has no physical necessity actually founded in creation. But the moral conditioning is not such as that therefrom would follow a conclusive annihilation of evil, to which the chain of this theologian's argument amounts. Scripture teaches an eternal personal continuance of being of all personal natures.

as a future spiritual gift to those who are reunited with God the Immortal (1 Tim. vi. 16), and a grace that recompenses faithfulness towards Him (Wisd. iii. 4, Rom. ii. 7, and elsewhere). It is this which the oldest teachers of the church opposed to philosophical heathenism. "The soul," cries Tatian, "is not in itself immortal, O ye Greeks." And Justin Martyr says, "It participates in life, so far as God wills it to live." "For God alone," says Athanasius, "has immortality, and is Himself immortality."[1]

Where Scripture speaks of death as of a κρίμα common to men (Ecclus. xli. 4), it is everywhere the whole man who suffers it. Death is a breaking up of the divinely ordained substance of a living being.[2] In this disruption—the issue of the Turba, which has laid hold of body, soul, and spirit, each according to its manner (Div. III. Sec. II.)—body, soul, and spirit also share, each in its own way. Body and spirit fall away from one another; and the spirit, to which the soul has retreated, finds itself, so far as it is disembodied, in the condition of death. Even of the spirits of the just made perfect this is the case, although it is said only *per zeugma*.[3] Scripture calls the deceased altogether, not merely their bodies, νεκροί; and teaches that the dead, not merely that their bodies, rise again, for the resurrection is a restoration of the personal condition that is dissolved by death.

Death is consequently the final destiny of the whole man. How then is it possible, apart from redemption, to speak of the immortality of man, or even only of the immortality of his soul? If we understand, by immortality of the soul, its indissolubility as the result of its simple nature, the expression does not affirm what we have in view. For that that which is not compounded cannot be dissolved, is self-evident; but is everything which cannot perish in the way of dissolution, therefore of necessity eternal?

[1] See the passages in v. Harless, *Das Buch von der ägyptischen Mysterien* (1858), pp. 14, 111.

[2] Λύσις or Διάλυσις, as Zacharias, bishop of Mitylene, loves to say in his Διάλογος *of the Beginning of the World and of Humanity.*

[3] This distinction is to be observed. In the Old Testament it might be said the dead in Hades, but in the New Testament it cannot be said the dead in heaven, although they are included when we acknowledge a resurrection of the dead, and Christ as the judge of the living and the dead.

Even if we understand, by the immortality of the soul and the spirit, their incapability of annihilation, the expression is, to say the least, unscriptural. For death and annihilation in Scripture are not by any means coincident ideas. In general, Scripture nowhere says that anything whatever of what has been created is annihilated; and, so far as our inquiry reaches, we see no atom perish. But, from the nature of things, it by no means follows, that God's word of might cannot again transplant into nonentity that which it has called into existence. And if such a conclusion followed from the nature of the soul, still actual continuance of being and self-conscious continuance of being are far from being necessarily associated. Whence can it be concluded that human souls continue to subsist individually, since the souls of the brutes are confessedly taken back into the entire spirit of nature, of which they are individuations? That which is constituted by way of emanation may also be taken back by way of remanation (Ps. civ. 29; Job xxxiv. 14).

But in view of the personality which distinguishes the human soul from the brute soul, annihilation, or remanation of the former, is assuredly an idea of extreme improbability. For personal freedom is the inexhaustible ground of possibility of an endless development; and it is extremely improbable that this development, in its origin, or broken off from its middle, and the fulness of substance which the human soul has attained by means of free life, should be forcibly extinguished. With equal conviction, the doubt is met by another consideration. To the doubting question of Eccles. iii. 21, the Preacher's own declaration of ch. iii. 11 may be used as a reply, in case this is to be translated, " God has given eternity in the heart of men."[1] In the nature, *i.e.* in the inborn constitution of man, there is the capability of conceiving of eternity, the struggle to apprehend

---

[1] Just in the same way Oehler translates in his able work, *Die Grundzüge der alttest. Weisheit* (1855). " The satisfaction," thus he explains it, " which man attains from his action and work is wasted, as has been shown chap. ii. 12, as soon as he reflects that he thereby attains no result which lasts beyond his passing existence. That man cannot help striving after that which is imperishable, is the first meaning of the words,—God has put eternity in man's heart." In post-biblical Hebraism עוֹלָם signifies not only eternity backwards and forwards as incalculable duration, but also

the everlasting, the longing after eternal life. Although we may not thence conclude that man is derived from eternity, it is yet certain that he is designed for eternity. The conclusion is irrefragable, as also the Cartesian conclusion from the idea of a God to the being of a God is irrefragable. This is the, so called by the ancients, *argumentum ab appetitu æternitatis*.[1]

Pantheism, indeed, which makes a divinity of an absolute nature that individualizes itself in a blind necessity, and takes itself back out of the individualization, escapes both arguments for personal continuance of existence, by being satisfied with an impersonal expansion in that absolute nature,—an issue of life which may please an eccentric or thoughtless person, but which surely sheds no smile upon a dying man. The existence of man, if it has its end in such a hopeless drowning death as this, becomes the most desperate enigma. Only in view of personal continuance of being, is it such an enigma as can hope for solution : and personal continuance of existence has as its fundamental postulate the existence of a personal God; for its final ground, the free determination of will of this God. But immortality and personal continuance of being are, in Holy Scripture, not at all co-extensive ideas. Only the man who is united with God the immortal, through Christ who is risen again, is immortal. For such an one temporal death has lost the nature of death; for all other men, a limit is only placed to temporal death. Personal continuance of existence, moreover, has its final reason in the counsel of redemption, whose self-realization demands the continuance of personal being of entire humanity. Without, therefore, dwelling long upon the probable reasons for that future continued existence that are based in the nature of the human soul, biblical psychology has to seek for the solution of its eschatological enigma in the revealed mystery of the counsel of redemption.

the world as that which endures incalculably ($\alpha i\acute{\omega}\nu$, *seculum*). Biblical language as yet knows not the word in the latter signification; and therefore the words of the Preacher must not be understood of the impulse of man to reflect upon the universe.

[1] *e.g.* in Dannhauer, *Collegium Psychologicum* (1627), p. 128, and Christ. Aug. Crusius, *Metaph.* sec. 483. Comp. Oetinger in Barth's *Süddeutschen Originalien*, i. 42. The *sensus communis* is the hidden thing of man, a *sensus tacitus æternitatis;* or as Solomon says, " God has placed עוֹלָם, *i.e.* the hidden eternity, in the heart of man."

THE FUTURE STATE AND THE REDEMPTION.

Sec. III.

DEATH in its sensible aspect is a return to the dust (Gen. iii. 19). This is the destiny of the body. On the particular destiny of the spirit and the soul, the word of divine wrath was silent. Therefore there was thought to be no special revelation; but on the ground of that word of wrath, the destiny of the spirit was conceived to be analogous to that of the body. As the body is inherited by the grave, thus the inner part of the earth[1] receives, as into a retreat, the bodiless spirit,—a representation not contradictory of the nature of the spirit. For although the spirit is no *extensum*, it may still be locally restrained; it is indeed so restrained so long as man lives in the

---

[1] That Scheôl was conceived of as sub-terrene, is manifest not only from the collective expressions referring thereto, *e.g.* Ps. lxiii. 10, Ezek. xxvi. 20, xxxii. 18, Job xxvi. 5, but also from the history of the company of Korah (Num. xvi. 30, 33), and the appearance of Samuel (1 Sam. xxviii. 13). Certainly we are not to conceive of any localization, after the fashion of the present state; and perhaps it is this which Hofmann means to say, *Schriftbeweis*, i. 492, " When the Scheôl is called deep, it is not meant to be so understood as if it were anywhere deep down under us, but it goes down subterraneously, just as immeasurably deep as it goes up on high towards heaven;" for the last " it " is not to be referred to Scheôl. Ströbel goes further when, *l.c.*, he teaches that "the separated souls partially sojourn also in the regions of the invisible world, which in the Apocalypse are called heaven, *i.e.* not in the home of the blessed, but in that part of the invisible world which bodiless creatures of good and evil kind have in common with one another." He asserts of the souls under the altar, Apoc. vi., " For them Hades is in heaven," with the remark, " A super-terrene, supramundane Hades of souls is far more consistent with Scripture teaching than a sub-terrene and sub-mundane one." I am compelled to declare the limitation of Hades in this form, even in spite of Ströbel's reply (*Luth. Zeitschr.* 1857, pp. 769–771), to be unscriptural; because he proceeds from the assumption that soul and spirit separate themselves in death, and that the former always is allotted to Hades: he is compelled to make the heavenly state of the martyr-souls (Apoc. vi. 9) one which, although it is found in heaven, is yet in Hades. Hades is, indeed, the kingdom of death; but where God's eternal altar stands, there is heaven in the highest sense— αὐτὸς ὁ οὐρανός, into which Christ has entered (Heb. ix. 24). This one text

present state. Although itself unallied to space, it is limited in the local body, and within and not outside of it.¹

The state of the spirit, or of the soul, in Scheôl,² was not conceived of as an enfranchised and more perfect state, but—since all the life of man is naturally carried on by means of the body—as a state deprived of actuality—bound ; and, as death is a doom of God's wrath,—as a state cut off from God's grace, and from communion with Him,—as a half-life in the darkness of the abyss, not without consciousness and remembrance and fellowship, but all only in feeble passing remnants, and the like in respect of good and evil, without any view of a return to the upper world, or, which is the same thing, without any prospect of redemption.

This is the most ancient notion of Scheôl. It was, especially in that want of distinction and want of hope that it assumed, the pure reflex of the word of divine wrath, not without admixture of the hyperbolic fear of death found in the Old

---

overthrows that false assumption. All souls do not come into Hades ; and that the soul of a man may be found there while his spirit is in the heaven of the blessed, is a notion just as contrary to reason as to Scripture ; opposed to which, the view of Jung Stilling (in his *Knowledge of Saints, and its Apology*), who places the peculiar hell in the centre of the earth, and regards Hades as the mid-region between hell and heaven, is indeed not contrary to reason, but at least finds no support in Scripture. For the rest, we acknowledge with v. Rudloff, p. 331, "If even Holy Scripture points very definitely to earthly localities of the kingdom of death, still that kingdom cannot, as a region of immaterial, and therefore of spiritual being, be subjected to the laws of locality of material beings, in the degree in which the things of the visible world are so. There are spiritual localities, of which we can have no idea, very probably extending themselves throughout the whole dimension of visibility, and beyond it." Still, we here commend to inquiring comparison the chapter upon the localities of the intermediate state, in C. W. Rinck's work upon the state after death (1861).

¹ In the local body, as say the ancients, the spirit is *non localiter seu dimensive, sed definitive.* The scholastics (Bonaventura, Occam, and others) say instead *diffinitive* as the opposite of *circumscriptive.*

² For what of man could be in Scheôl unless it were his soul? When in Baruch ii. 17 it is said of the dead in Hades, ὧν ἐλήφθη τὸ πνεῦμα ἀπὸ τῶν σπλάγχνων αὐτῶν, from whose inward parts the spirit was taken, "spirit" is not the *spiritus vitalis* withdrawn from them (as Schott in his *Licentiatenschrift* at Göttingen, *Veteris testamenti de hominis Immortalitate Sententia illustrata*, 1860, declares), but the spirit itself disembodied, and leading a shadowy life in Hades.

Testament, and, in its fantastic picturing, not without mythologic elements.¹ But in itself it was no mythus.² Death is, indeed, the punishment of the entire man. To the state of punishment of the body corrupting in the grave, there must correspond an analogous state of the incorruptible soul. Death, grave, Scheôl, therefore, are in the Old Testament most closely associated ideas, interchanging with one another, and passing over into one another.

New Testament Scripture puts to the existence of Hades its seal in the history of redemption. In doing this, it at the same time denies objectivity to the ideas of indiscrimination and hopelessness associated with Scheôl in the Old Testament: to the former by the parable of the rich man, and by the word of the crucified Lord, "This day shalt thou be with me in paradise;" to the latter by the whole work of redemption, as a reward of which the keys of death and of Hades (Apoc. i. 18) are in the hand of the God-man.

But, at the same time with God's wrath, God's love had after the fall of man announced itself. The Old Testament declarations of the future state are not merely reflections of the former, but also of the latter. Even in the Old Testament, those confused mythologic representations are in many ways broken through. The facts of the rapture of Enoch and Elijah throw on to them their beams of light: Faith, the Chokma, and Prophecy lay hold of them together, and overthrow them. Faith takes refuge in Jehovah, the ever-living, the redeemer (see especially Ps. xvi. xvii. xlix. lxxiii.³). The Chokma points the lover of wisdom with a promise upwards (Prov. xv. 24, xii. 28, Wisd. vi. 13–20, comp. Eccles. iii. 21⁴),

---

¹ The name of the dweller in Hades, רְפָאִים, the loosed (from רָפָא, weak, languid), agrees with the Homeric designations οἱ καμόντες, the relaxed, ἀμενηνὰ κάρηνα, the heads without power (μένος), σκιαί, εἴδωλα, and occurs also in the inscription of the Sidonian king Sargon.

² That Scheôl is only the shadow which the temporal horror of death projects upon the spiritual world (Fr. Beck in the *Theol. Jahrb.* 1851, p. 473), is an unhistorical view.

³ Jul. Müller, *Unsterblichkeitsglaube und Auferstehungshoffnung* (1855), pp. 21–23.

⁴ Heyder, *l.c.*, translates this passage, " Quis est qui cognoscat spiritum hominum? hic est qui ascendit sursum; et spiritum pecoris? hic est qui," etc.; and certainly the vowel arrangement seems to require this translation,

and declares already the mighty word, "In the midst of death the righteous is comforted" (Prov. xiv. 32, comp. Job xxvii. 8-10). The thought of a redemption out of Scheôl already appears, at least in the form of a wish (Job xiv. 14); and the thought of a future vision of the God who reveals Himself as a redeemer, appears in the form of a postulate of faith, to which the righteous man, misapprehended and persecuted even to the death in this world, is urged (Job xix. 25-27[1]). The truth of such glimpses of light into the future state does not annul the truth of the existence of Scheôl. The truth of Scheôl subsists in the fact, that by the power of the word of wrath (Gen. iii. 19) every man who dies comes under the principle of wrath with body and soul; and the truth of those better views consists in the fact, that he who in this state has loved Jehovah, even in the future state, although encompassed by the principle of wrath, nevertheless, as waiting for a certain redemption, is in the principle of love. He is with his soul in Scheôl, as certainly

for הֲ before עַ in a questioning significance is certainly elsewhere without example. Yet the interrogative הַאֲתֶּם (Judg. vi. 31) may be compared to הַעֲלֹה, and the interrogative הַיֵיטַב (Lev. x. 19) to הַיֹּרֶדֶת; and as well the collocation as connection permit no other comprehension than that which is repeated, moreover, by LXX., Targ., Syr., Jer., Luther: "Who knows of the spirit of the children of men, whether this goeth upwards; and of the spirit of the brute, whether this goeth down below towards the earth?" As also elsewhere in this book (ch. ii. 19, vi. 12), מִי יוֹדֵעַ lays open a doubtful question; and there subsists between it and ch. xii. 7 no contradiction which could determine us to lean towards its exegetic removal. For in ch. xii. 7 is declared the fact, in itself comfortless, that the elements of man return to their original; and in ch. iii. 21, the uncertainty whether the spirit bestowed upon man goes back in any other way to its original source than does that of the brute. None the less, I have with careful deliberation quoted above Eccles. iii. 21. In the doubt there is a longing, and even the acknowledgment of the dilemma is an important step in advance.

[1] Everywhere in such passages of the books belonging to the literature of the Chokma, there is anticipated a meaning which transcends the degree of knowledge of redemption of the time then present; so that observations such as Hitzig's on Prov. xiv. 32, "The proverb touches upon an earlier time than that in which resurrection or immortality was believed in," depend upon ignorance of the peculiar nature of the spiritual tendency of that time, which was hurrying on a tendency which brought forth in the midst of Israelite people, books bearing the stamp of common humanity, such as the book of Proverbs and the book of Job.

as the body is in the grave; but resting in the depth of love from which, in the fulness of time, the Overcomer of death and of Hades will go forth. Looking beforehand to Him, Isaiah prophesies the future swallowing up of death; the waking up of the bodies of the righteous, and the redemption of their souls from Hades (Isa. xxiv.–xxvii.); and Ezekiel beholds the restoration of Israel, as the animating of a large field strewed with corpses, by the resurrection word of power of Jehovah. In the book of Daniel (xii. 2), moreover, the general rising of the dead is declared without a figure, and plainly as the final fact of time. The apocryphal literature shows us this new light still in conflict with the ancient gloom. For the horizon of the books of Baruch and Sirach is still bounded by the old Hades view. The book of Wisdom teaches a blessed future of the souls that have been united to God here below; and a finally determining judgment, which raises the righteous to eternally blessed dominion, and rejects the godless into everlasting shame, but without giving expression to the statement so closely suggested of a twofold resurrection. And the second book of Maccabees, arming its martyrs with the hope of resurrection, confesses a resurrection of the godless as of the righteous,—without, however, expressly extending it (*vid*. vii. 14) to the whole of humanity, or even beyond the limits of Israel. Near to the Christian times, however, the hope of resurrection was already part of the inalienable substance of the believing consciousness of Israel.[1] And it need not surprise us, since the eternal counsel of redemption presides over temporal history; and the historical future of salvation is withal a coming one, which, as it approaches nearer to the end, leaves behind it clearer traces as well in history as in consciousness.

The more nearly the manifestation of Jesus Christ drew nigh, the more preparatory became, as in the Christologic questions the perception of His person, so in the eschatologic questions the perception of His work.[2] This His work consists

---

[1] Only the Sadducees denied it. When in Acts xxiii. 8 it is said that they generally denied the existence of a πνεῦμα, it is explained from Josephus, *Ant*. xviii. 1, 4, according to whom they taught τὰς ψυχὰς συναφανίσαι τοῖς σώμασιν. They were materialists.

[2] Böttcher, in his learned and careful work, *de inferis* (1846), represents this process of development; but without considering it from the point of

in reconciliation, redemption, and perfection: reconciliation through an atonement, which in love does away with the wrath of God upon humanity; redemption, by the breaking up of all powers and circumstances which bind humanity under the wrath of God; perfection, in the exaltation of humanity to the height of its destination. In Him arose the Sun which in eternally decisive manner enlightened the gloom of futurity, and maintained the hope of the faithful by facts of redemption that were rich in results, and proved itself the essential unity of those beams which had announced its coming.

In order to redeem humanity from death, the Redeemer must, as the Sinless One, suffer the wrathful destiny of death. He must die and be buried without seeing corruption, and go down into Hades without being holden of Hades (Acts ii. 27).[1] The descent εἰς τὰ κατώτερα μέρη τῆς γῆς, i.e. into Hades, which with the burial is comprised in the sojourn ἐν τῇ καρδίᾳ τῆς γῆς (Matt. xii. 40), is the extreme lowest point contrasted with the ascension above all the heavens (Eph. iv. 9); for heaven and Hades (Matt. xi. 23), or heaven and the under world (Phil. ii. 10; Apoc. v. 3), or heaven and the abyss (Rom. x. 6), or heaven and the prison (1 Pet. iii. 19, 22), are opposite poles.

This lowest point of His humiliation was also the turning-point and commencement of His exaltation. He did not appear in Hades as the dead one, without immediately approving Himself ἐν πνεύματι to the spirits in prison as the living one; for He went thither ἐν πνεύματι, which could not, like His flesh, be slain, but which, in the midst of the condition of death awaiting the reunion with the body through the creative might of the Father, asserted itself as an undestroyed power of life. It is thus that we must understand ἐν ᾧ (1 Pet. iii. 18).[2] He

view of its object, without which, according to our conviction, neither insight into the unity of the several Old Testament views of the future state, nor their just criticism, is possible.

[1] See my *Psalm-Commentary*, on Ps. lxiii. 10 (i. 470), where the LXX. translates τὰ κατώτατα τῆς γῆς; and Hölemann's argument on behalf of the reference of the passage, Eph. iv. 9, to the *descensus ad inferos* in his *Bibelstudien*, Div. ii. p. 89.

[2] Not only H. W. Rinck, *Vom Zustande nach dem Tode* (1861), p. 87, where the degree of consistency of the mention of the descent into Hades in that passage is very well authenticated, but Wold. Schmidt, *De Statu animarum medio inter mortem et resurrectionem* (1861), agrees with us in

appeared in the world of the dead as a spirit,[1] while His incorruptible but not yet glorified and risen body was at rest in the grave; but He appeared none the less in the undissolved unity of His divine-human person as the Prince of Life breaking through the bands of Hades and the grave.

Thus manifesting Himself to the dead in Hades, He preached to them (ἐκήρυξεν) the victory that had now come to pass. He preached to the Old Testament dead the New Testament gospel (νεκροῖς εὐηγγελίσθη) of the now completed redemption (1 Pet. iii. 19, iv. 6). There the fallen angelic powers beheld Him as the conqueror; the Old Testament saints, as the Redeemer; those who had died in the attitude of hardening themselves, as the Judge; and for many who, as in the judgment of the deluge, had been swallowed up by Hades in very unequal measure of sin, there were glimpses of deliverance still

this, that the Lord went bodilessly into Hades, according to His spiritual nature, and there manifested Himself not only as a Judge, but chiefly as a Redeemer; but both, after the example of Bengel, allow the ζωοποιηθείς to coincide with the death in which His spirit indeed is for a moment enwrapped, but is at once forced through the night of death to life; wherefore the latter is to be regarded as the correlation of the μὲν-δὲ, which infers contemporaneousness, and the former corresponds to the prophecy according to which the Christ of God should assuredly not be left in Hades. All this is untenable. The words ζωοποιηθεὶς δὲ πνεύματι, according to the New Testament use of language (John v. 21; Rom. iv. 17; 1 Cor. xv. 22), can only be understood of the awakening of which the resurrection was the consequence. The assertion of the fact of the intermediate state begins for the first time with ἐν ᾧ, and precisely by this ἐν ᾧ (not merely ᾧ) it is characterized as a fact that occurred apart from the body. The spirit, since it was the might of indissoluble life (δύναμις ζωῆς ἀκαταλύτου, Heb. vii. 16), needed no making alive. For the same reason, however, we are not compelled to the supposition (last suggested by Schott) of a double *descensus*; such an one as perfected the reality of death, and such an one as had for its subject the bodily aroused but yet not risen one. We subscribe to the words of Bengel, "Christus vitam in semet ipso habens et Ipse vita spiritu vivere neque desiit neque iterum cœpit, sed simul atque per mortificationem involucro infirmitatis in carne solutus erat, statim vitæ solvi nesciæ virtus modis novis et multo expeditissimis sese exserere cœpit," referring the *vivificatio* not to this unfettering, but to the awakening, and comprehending the descent into hell as the dividing limit and turning-point of the two *status*.

[1] This is the view which has become symbolical in the Romish Church, and moreover is defended in our church by ancient teachers, as Urbanus Rhegius, Lucas Osiander, and others, which, as I believe, is more conformed

possible. There also the soul of the penitent thief beheld Him in the bliss of Paradise.

Then ascending out of Hades, arising out of the grave, and rising towards heaven, the Lord led captivity captive ($\mathring{\eta}\chi\mu\alpha\lambda\acute{\omega}$-$\tau\epsilon\upsilon\sigma\epsilon\nu$ $\alpha\mathring{\iota}\chi\mu\alpha\lambda\omega\sigma\acute{\iota}\alpha\nu$) : the gifts which the Exalted One sends down, are the fruits of His victory; and, as it were, benefactions out of the spoils of a triumphant victor (Eph. iv. 8). For He has triumphed over the angelic powers (Col. ii. 15); and when He had subjected to Himself the spirits that rule in the kingdom of death and of darkness, He led the men who in Hades honoured Him as a Redeemer with Himself toward heaven,[1] for the Paradise is from that time forth above the earth (2 Cor. xii. 1–4). And the souls of the blessed dead are, according to the constant testimony of New Testament Scripture, henceforth in heaven—in the Jerusalem which is above, under God's altar; or, according to the synonymous expression of the old synagogue, under the throne of glory. The enigma of the prophetic word, which far transcended the prophet's own

to the Petrine assertion than the view that has become symbolical in the Greek church, and even in our own (although in a less stringent manner). Yet $\zeta\omega o\pi o\iota\eta\theta\epsilon\grave{\iota}\varsigma$ $\delta\grave{\epsilon}$ $\pi\nu\epsilon\acute{\upsilon}\mu\alpha\tau\iota$ is meant, as it is said, of the awakening of the corpse coincident with the resurrection, with which awakening the spirit-life of glorification took its beginning, as the dying put an end to the fleshly life of humiliation; and only $\grave{\epsilon}\nu$ $\tilde{\dot{\omega}}$ will be so understood, as that He went in the spirit, according to which (so that the now commencing life had its determinate character in the spirit) He, in awakening up, was again living. Little as I, with Besser (*Zeitschr. für Protest.* 1856, p. 294), can approve of Hofmann's interpretation of this passage—of Christ—of the not yet incarnate testimony to the race of men during the deluge—during the 120 years of grace (Gen. vi. 3),—yet I regard as just what he remarks, ii. 1, 474. By $\grave{\epsilon}\nu$ $\tilde{\dot{\omega}}$ $\pi o\rho\epsilon\upsilon\theta\epsilon\grave{\iota}\varsigma$ $\grave{\epsilon}\kappa\acute{\eta}\rho\upsilon\xi\epsilon\nu$ is designated a going and preaching of Christ, for which the spirit served Him as an agent, in opposition to the flesh; and it is not said in the state characterized as $\zeta\omega o\pi o\iota\eta\theta\epsilon\grave{\iota}\varsigma$ $\pi\nu\epsilon\acute{\upsilon}\mu\alpha\tau\iota$, that He went and preached. Thus also judges Martensen, *Dogm.* sec. 171.

[1] Even Hofmann finds in that which is related by Matthew (xxvii. 51-53), that this is at least hinted at; but observes, nevertheless, "Although the intelligence of the church of the earliest times has given this perhaps not unjustifiable expansion to the event testified, still the silence of Scripture is for us a consenting testimony, that the scientific declaration of Christendom has nothing to announce respecting it." We go further; for what we teach above, proceeds on the assertions of Scripture of necessity beyond the distinction of the spiritual condition of the Old Testament and New Testament believers, and is supported by the direct evidence of Scripture.

understanding (Hos. vi. 2), is solved: Hades has now, according to the prophecy of Isaiah (xxvi. 19), yielded up the dead that belong to the Israel of God;[1] it now only remains.as the fore-hell (Apoc. xx. 14),[2] although only in such a way as there

---

[1] It is there predicted, that while the oppressors of Israel are pressed down into the shadowy kingdom, without the possibility of thinking of a raising of themselves again, or a lifting of them up again (xxvi. 14), the power of God's grace prepares for His people the restoration which they long desired while under punishment, and in vain strove to attain by their own efforts. "We have not wrought deliverance to the land—the dwellers on the land have not come to light (בַּל־יִפְּלוּ)," *i.e.* a new race which shall people the desert land (ver. 18). But now it has happened, instead of celebrating the event in song, the prophecy transplants itself into the midst of it: the people, in consequence of their long sufferings and chastisements, is melted away to a small remnant; and many of them that might in truth be numbered among them, lie in the dust of death. Then it cries to itself, as if present to itself, pervaded with a hope which will not be ashamed, THY DEAD MEN SHALL LIVE AGAIN—consoles itself with the operation of God's power and grace, even now exhibiting themselves in completion—THE CORPSES OF MEN SHALL ARISE; and cries, as certain of the purpose of God, the mighty word of faith over the field of dead bodies, AWAKE, AND SING, YE THAT DWELL IN THE DUST; and justifies this believing word of power in its own sight, by acknowledging, with a glance upwards to God: FOR THE DEW OF THE LIGHTS,[1] *i.e.* the powers of life, IS THY DEW; AND THE EARTH WILL BRING FORTH SHADOWS, *i.e.* will again bear forth the dead who are sunk down into it. Hofmann does not find prophesied here any peculiar arising of the dead, but only that under the form of raising, which is presupposed as an element of the Israelitish consciousness of faith, is predicted the restoration of Israel: "The people of redemption does not awake by any effort of Israel's own to new-create itself; but when it is all over with it, God wondrously transforms it as out of death into life, although of its own impulse there had been no hope for it for ever" (*Schriftb.* ii. 2, 511). My conviction is different. Even (Ezek. xxxvii. 1-14) the rising of the dead, which the prophet sees, is to me more as an image of the restoration of the people buried in exile. The two prophets here prophesy what the apocalyptic seer calls "the first resurrection;" the latter certainly in more special and continuous connection, and in less enigmatical fashion. Isaiah and Ezekiel unfold what is announced in Ps. xlix. 15. They unfold it by the power of divine revelation, which has previously set forth the hope of the rising of those that have died in the Lord, as the expectation of the resurrection of the dead in general.

[2] The idea of שְׁאוֹל is already on the way to this change in the Old Testament, especially in the Proverbs; *vid.* Oehler, *Veteris testamenti Sen-*

---

[1] *Ros lucis*, Vulg., the dew of the morning.—TR.

can be a fore-hell prior to the absolutely final decision. The hope that the souls of the righteous are in God's hand, and in the enjoyment of rest and peace (Wisd. iii. 1, 4, iv. 2), has now its heavenly seal: the curtain is rent,[1] and the new and living way is opened, on which henceforth all the faithful follow their Redeemer, without being compelled to pass further through any veil, to the place where God's loving presence is revealed in glory (Heb. x. 19). Thither look the eyes of the dying; thither, when their eyes fail them, their hands still point; there they are in the presence of their risen and glorified Saviour, who guarantees to them their own resurrection and glorification, even in their disembodied state, blessed and waiting in peace the dawning which will make even their bodies alive again. They are in the enjoyment of the peace of blessed inward contemplation, and blessed exaltation.[2] They are in the heaven of glory, but this glory is still awaiting an increase. The history upon earth must first have passed away before the completion in heaven comes on (Heb. xi. 40). This completion is their sweet longing, their blessed hope. "Interim ergo," says the holy Bernhard, in profound and beautiful figures, " sub Christi humanitate feliciter sancti quiescunt, in quam nimirum desiderant etiam angeli ipsi prospicere, donec veniat tempus, quando jam non sub altari collocentur, sed exaltentur super altare." [3]

tentia de rebus post mortem futuris. Our limitation above, "although only," etc., has not been strictly rendered by v. Rudloff, p. 329 : it indicates the extreme limit of what biblical psychology is authorized to say.

[1] Such an occurrence, says Göschel, *Letzte Dinge*, p. 78, with reference to Matt. xxvi. 51, stands alone, as the death itself, of which it was the result; but something similar, a shadow of that solitary fact, accompanies every hour of death, where one soul passes away in the Lord, and another looks after it. It is as if the veil were not closed until a little later. Gradually therefore, even the sharpest anguish is lightened at the beginning: the deepest affliction comes after.

[2] Göschel, *Der Mensch diesseits und jenseits*, p. 91, thus distinguishes $κατάπαυσις$ and $ἀνάπαυσις$. To this belongs also the thoughtful expression in his work upon old age. The exit of the soul from the body first completes its entrance into itself.

[3] In the first of the sermons on the Festival of All Saints. In agreement with us, H. W. Rincke remarks (*Vom Zustande nach dem Tode*, p. 61): "The purification which is completed by becoming enlightened and pervaded with light by the glorious light, and the heavenly glance of God's fire, is something very distinct from an intermediate state of purgatory."

This is, in outline, the doctrine of the Old and New Testament of the intermediate state between death and resurrection. Of a purgatory we can say nothing, for Scripture teaches none. The scriptural passages on which it is founded, impartially looked at, and intelligently explained, prove quite other things. The chief argument for purgatory is found in the assertion of its psychologic-ethical necessity. "It is the most complete contradiction," it is said,[1] "to enter into heaven polluted with sin, whether it be covered by atonement, or uncovered. Therefore the question obtrudes itself, How is man finally delivered from sin, and holiness established in him as a fundamentally living principle? Or, if we leave the earthly world still stained with any sort of sinful character, how are we to become purified from the same?" This question assuredly presses upon us. Released from the body, we are not on that account released from sin. And justification through the grace of God in Christ, releases us from the guilt of our sin in the way of responsibility, without therefore uprooting sin itself in us. This continues to be weakened in us here below; and the most earnest endeavour after holiness gains the mastery over it indeed—rules it, banishes it within narrower and narrower limits, but without being able entirely to separate and eradicate it from us. How then is the soul which has found grace in God, freed from sin at its translation into the future state? Let it be done as it may, it is by no means effected by a fire which is needed to help forward the effect of the holy baptism, and the blood of the Son of God, which have both in themselves the virtue of fire: it is by no means effected through an expiating suffering, which would have to assist the saving purpose of the reconciling passion of Christ, for the first time to attain the effectuation of its final object. How then? It has been said that death itself is our purgatory; and the final shock of death also the final dividing (Heb. iv. 12), which pierces through and through, even to the finally decisive purification.[2] And, in fact, who could deny that every well-resisted death-struggle is, moreover, a finally determining crucible, which absolutely detaches the gold of the divinely wrought spiritual life that will stand the fire, from the dross which

[1] Thus *e.g.* Möhler in his *Symbolik.*
[2] Thus Göschel, in his work, *Der Mensch diesseits und jenseits.*

burdened and disintegrated it here below? But not every soul is led through by God, by means of such a confirming and refining fire of a long sickness and a victorious dying bed. It must therefore be assumed that the spiritual life, begotten and nourished in us by word and sacrament, is in itself actually sufficiently powerful,—when it has rid itself of the world lying in the wicked one, or is suddenly withdrawn from it,—to break forth in the view of the manifest reality of that which has been believed here below with such intensity, that it drives out the sin which is still dwelling in human nature, even to the last trace of its consequences. Whether this may happen to one suddenly, to another by degrees, we know not. Scripture on this matter says nothing. And as far as concerns those who, in the present state, are unconverted and unbelieving, certainly the hope is at hand, that on this side of the final destiny, the breaking through God's wrath to God's love is still, under certain circumstances, possible; but Scripture says of it nothing, either direct or indirect, but contains expressions which rather leave the opposite to be dreaded. And we therefore decline taking our flight into inferences and presumptions, or following other lights than the one whose clearness, measured by the divine wisdom, ought to be sufficient for us here.

But we hold all the more strenuously to the doctrine of the intermediate state which we have sketched above. In all its details it depends upon irrefragable exegetic foundations, and can appeal to the believing consciousness of the church brought by Scripture and tradition from those times in which it had not yet, in order to oppose superstitious disfigurements, exchanged the primitive Christian views for a heartless dialectic rigidity foreign to Scripture. That such passages of Scripture as 1 Pet. iii. 18, iv. 6, speak of a subterraneous self-manifestation and declaration of power on the part of Christ, seems to me as clear as the sun; although, because they appeared to militate against the *analogia fidei*, they were banished[1] out of the range of the

---

[1] Thus, for instance, David Chyträus' book, *de morte ac vita æterna*. Polemics against the Romish purgatory have here operated mischievously. The able John Heinr. Ursinus, in his work, *On the State of Faithful Souls after Death* (1663), makes a glorious exception as well in the doctrine of the descent into hell as of the intermediate state. "The descent of the Lord into hell," says he, p. 285, "belongs partly to His true death; be-

SEC. III.]   THE FUTURE STATE AND THE REDEMPTION.   489

illustria verbi divini testimonia; and, as if blinding by their intense brightness, they were sought to be dimmed and obscured by other scriptural passages, especially Heb. ix. 27, where is signified not a judgment immediately following death, but the conclusive general judgment. In the meantime, it is not a problem of biblical psychology to bring scriptural proof for the above positions. These are *lemmata* from dogmatics, against which one must be on one's guard, not to wish to know either less than Scripture or more than Scripture.[1] To this is essential quotation and scriptural proof ; wherefore we, in order not to trench upon a foreign region of science, have been thus aphoristically brief. But those disclosures of Scripture upon the intermediate state are the indispensable postulates of certain questions, to the discussion of which dogmatics are

cause He, as all men as far as their souls are concerned, was gathered to His fathers, and of His free-will for us was given up to the dominion of death, in order to abrogate it for ever. But partly also it belongs to His triumph; because He as a victorious Prince, and a hero of two parent stems, overcame death thereby, and bound the devil. When the holy body of Christ was borne to the grave, the soul of the Lord was gathered to the fathers, and continued under the law of death till soul and body were united. Thus He also triumphed over death, and awakened the dead fathers to be the trophies of victory, and led them with Himself out of the condition of death." "From which it plainly shines forth," adds Ursinus to this, "that our Lord maintained this triumph, not only in respect of the making alive of His soul, but of the making alive of Himself in the grave with body and soul; for how could He have triumphed over death if He had been subjected in respect of the body to its laws?" For this same reason, in later times, a twofold *descensus* is distinguished by Wiesinger, v. Zezschwitz (*De Christi ad inferos descensu*, 1857), Engelhardt (*Zeitschr. für Protest.* 1856, p. 285), Schott, and others : one at death, involved in the death itself; and one at the awakening (which would therefore have preceded the rising), subsequently in reassumed and glorified corporeity. "It was an exegetical error," says Schott, *On the First Epistle of Peter*, p. 240, "when the fathers regarded the *descendit ad inferos* of the Apostles' Creed, and the πορευθείς ἐκήρυξεν of 1 Pet. iii. 19, as referring to one and the same event." We are not of this opinion ; and similarly, then as now, are we certain that ἐκήρυξεν cannot be understood of a preaching which had no saving object in view : He who preaches κηρύσσει, provided that his preaching always has in view whatever saving determination of themselves may be possible in the case of those to whom He preaches. The absolute κηρύσσειν cannot signify a partial *concio damnatoria*.

[1] Schleiermacher, *Dogm.* sec. 161, 2, may serve as a representative of the former error ; Jung Stilling of the latter.

not directed; but upon which psychology, at least this especially, is called to enter.

THE FALSE DOCTRINE OF THE SOUL'S SLEEP.

Sec. IV.

PROCEEDING from the sound premises, that the combination and unity of spirit and body is the peculiar nature of man as a created whole; that therefore the rending of this link puts the soul-spirit not less than the body into a state of death, but that the soul-spirit cannot die in the same way that the body does, which latter is dispersed into its elementary constituents; that in general, on account of its divinely-formed nature, it cannot perish, and by the might of the revealed will of God continues to exist independently (which Origen maintained in opposition to the Θνητοψυχῖται of Arabia),—in primitive times some have here and there chanced upon the thought, that the separated soul is in a state of sleep without consciousness, and without sensibility, until God wakens it up at the last day, together with the body. Even Tertullian (*de anima,* ch. lviii.) is aware of this opinion, and controverts it. Vigilantius, whom Jerome attacked, appeared inclined to it. The schismatic Armenians entertained it. Even Luther expressed it here and there, although only conjecturally and vaguely.[1] The sup-

---

[1] He writes to Nic. Amsdorf about the 13th Jan. 1522 (see De Wette's edition of the *Letters of Luther,* part ii. p. 122): "De animabus tuis non satis habeo quod tibi respondeam. Proclive mihi est concedere tecum in eam sententiam, justorum animas dormire ac usque ad judicii diem nescire ubi sunt. In quam sententiam me trahit verbum Scripturæ *dormiunt cum patribus suis.* Et mortui resuscitati per Christum et apostolos idem testantur cum velut a somno evigilarunt, ignari ubi fuerint." In what follows, he concedes that there must be exceptions to this sleep of the soul as well in the sphere of the blessed (Elias, Moses, Abraham, and Lazarus) as of the lost (the spirits in prison, 1 Pet. iii. 19, who at least to the time of Christ's preaching did not sleep; and the people of Sodom, of whom Jude 7 says, in the present tense, "ignis æterni pœnam sustinentes"). But his conclusion remains: "Verisimile autem, exceptis paucis omnes dormire insensi-

porters of the special doctrine of the soul's sleep in the time of the Reformation were the Anabaptists. Against these Calvin wrote in 1534 his *Psychopannychia*.[1] It is only the coarsest form of the doctrine which is here combated by Calvin, and is touched by his counter-argument. The later advocates, especially among Socinians and Arminians,[2] limited themselves to denying all external activity to the soul in its separate state. Subsequently, with the increasing insight into the corporeal mediation of the soul's activities, the adoption of an absolutely unconscious sleep of the soul recurred all the more frequently.[3]

biles." The letter is of an earlier date, but the view here expressed occurs still even in the *Enarrationes in Genesin*. It is true he says here, on Gen. xv. (Erl. edit. pt. vi. p. 120), distinguishing the sleep of the future state from natural slumber: " Anima non sic dormit, sed vigilat et patitur visiones, loquelas Angelorum et Dei;" but on ch. xlix. (Erl. edit. pt. xi. pp. 301-306), he compares the intermediate state with the condition of the fœtus in the womb, and seems to regard it as unconscious. " We pass on and come again to the last day before we perceive it; moreover, we know not how long we have been in that state." We do not wish to deny that this is the doctrine of the sleep of the soul, which, together with its scriptural reasons, we shall proceed to confute; but Luther does not teach thus: he expresses himself in this way in all modesty being hypothetically, being very willing to be corrected, and at length declares that the manner and the place of that rest of the future state are things that are placed beyond our knowledge.

[1] The completion of the *Psychopannychia* belongs to the year 1534. In the year 1536, Calvin added a second preface, moderating the polemical bitterness; and in the year 1545, the book appeared at the same time in two Strasburg editions, with somewhat differing titles. At the close, Calvin put the seal to his refutation, saying: " Istud rursum lectores omnes (si qui tamen erunt) memoria tenere volo, Catabaptistas (purposely, instead of *Anabaptistas*) quos ad omne genus flagitiorum designandum nominasse satis est, esse præclari hujus dogmatis authores." Comp. for the rest on the history of the doctrine of the sleep of the soul, *Sylloge Scriptorum de Spiritibus puris et animabus humanis, etc.* (Ratisb. 1790), pp. 87-92 (a classified catalogue, whereas Grässe's *Bibliotheca Psychologica*, 1845, is alphabetical); and especially V. E. Löscher, *Select Collection of the Best Writings on the State of the Soul after Death*, 1735, excerpted and enriched in Herbert Becker's communications from Dr Valentine Ernst Löscher's *auserlesener Sammlung, etc.*, two parts, Augsburg 1835-36.

[2] But also among those who were theosophically disposed, as Ph. Matth. Hahn, and his associates, Goltz, Thomas Wizenmann, the friend of Fr. Heinr. Jacobi, vol. i. (1859) p. 88.

[3] Even about the middle of the previous century this was the solution of the "Soul-sleepers (Hypnopsychites)," that as soon as the ORGANS of

There are certainly scriptural passages which may apparently be made available in favour of the sleep of the soul, especially in a period which, without distinguishing as to the history of redemption between the Old and New Testament, argues from isolated scriptural texts, no matter out of what kind of books and connections. The many scriptural texts were appealed to in which dying is called a falling asleep, and death a sleep; for instance, 1 Cor. xv. 20, 1 Thess. iv. 13. Complaints and questions were depended upon, such as those of Ps. lxxxviii. 10-12 (comp. Ps. vi. 5, xxx. 9, cxv. 17; the whole of the book of Job, nearly akin to Ps. lxxxviii., Isa. xxxviii. 18, Ecclus. xvii. 27):

> Wilt Thou show wonders to the dead,
> Or do shadows rise up to praise Thee?
> Shall Thy grace be declared in the grave,
> Thy faithfulness in the under-world?
> Shall Thy wondrous might be known in the darkness,
> And Thy righteousness in the land of forgetfulness?

but especially upon Eccles. ix. 4, "A living dog is better than a dead lion. For the living know at least that they shall die: but the dead know nothing, and have no reward to hope for; for the memory of them is forgotten;" and ix. 10, "All that thy

---

the body were destroyed, the soul must sink into its original *assoupissement*, its previous powerlessness. Thus, for example, Thom. Burnet (*mort.* 1715), in his work *de statu mortuorum et resurgentium* (in French, by Bion, 1731): L'ame ne peut avoir aucune sensation ou perception du monde extèrieur, de quelque phenomêne que ce soit, ni d'aucun mouvement de la matière, à moins qu'elle ne soit unie a quelque corps, ou à quelque portion de la matière. Thus in Germany, Heyne, in *Werder*, the chief advocate for the soul's sleep. The best counter arguments are those of Simonetti and Timoth. Seidel. Many of the productions on both sides are anonymous, as *A Treatise of the Sleep of Souls after Death* (1754), and a letter to the anonymous author of the *Treatise on the Sleep of Souls after Death* (in the same year 1754). Both treatises proceed on the ground that every finite actual spirit must have a body; but says the latter, "It is true that after man's death the soul passes out of association with this body, but not generally out of association with matter." In the frankest way, Fries (*Jahrbb. für deutsche Theol.* 1856) has lately expressed himself in Heyne's view. That the personal Ego of man, says he, should be without the body, is altogether not conceivable, and the soul can therefore only lead a dream-life in the intermediate state. We cherish for this dear friend, who in the meantime has gone to his home, a better hope than this.

hand is able to do, do it with thy whole might; for there is no work, nor device, nor knowledge, nor wisdom, in Scheôl, whither thou art going;" with which John ix. 4, "A night cometh in which no man can work," appears to agree. Finally, also appeal was made to those who were wondrously recalled from death into this present life—to Lazarus, Jairus' daughter, the widow's son of Nain, and Tabitha. None of them that were thus aroused from the dead gave any information upon the condition of the spiritual world. For what other reason than because not only their bodies, but also their souls, had slept in unconsciousness? The foil to this mode of argument is furnished in such statements of Scripture as characterize the state of separate souls before the resurrection, certainly as a state that still waits for its decided completion. At the head of these scriptural assertions was placed Heb. xi. 39. But the final ground of the assumption that the disembodied souls sleep, was the presumption that the soul without the body cannot be active; because, as the author of the *Quæstiones ad Antiochum* expresses it, soul and body are related as musician and lyre; or because, as it is formulated by Lactantius, there is wanting to the soul separated from its body the capacity of perception, no less than to an eye torn out of the body is wanting the faculty of vision.

The futility of all this reasoning may be easily shown. Scripture calls death a sleep, so far as the disappearance of the soul of a dying person out of the body resembles the retreat of the soul of a person falling asleep out of the corporeally evidenced external life; but it nowhere says that souls departing out of their bodies sleep. And although it compares the entire state of the deceased person to sleep, yet from this comparison is not to be deduced a continuance of the soul in a state without consciousness, and without sensation; since, although the soul of the sleeper has retreated from the full activity of waking life, as carried on by the body, still it is not sunk into a state of passivity without consciousness and perception. Now there certainly, in places such as Eccles. ix. 10, appears to be attributed to the separate existences in Scheôl such a numb, dull, self-contained passivity; but by the side of such passages there are others which show that the separate souls are neither without consciousness, nor without memory, of what passed in this world, nor without fellowship with one another, although, on account of their bodilessness and of their state of death, in a shadowy manner. Read the scene represented by Isa. xiv. 9 in Scheôl, at the entrance of the king of Babel: "The kingdom of the dead is moved from beneath, to rise up and meet thee: it stirreth up the shadows for thee; even all the lewd ones of the earth; it raiseth up from their thrones all the kings of the nations. All rise up and say, Art thou also become weak as we? art thou become like unto us?" In Ezek. xxxi. 16 all the trees of Eden and Lebanon (princes) were comforted in the under-world at the similar fate of the cedar (Pharaoh); and in the description, Pharaoh, on his entrance into Scheôl (Ezek. xxxii. 17), is accosted by the mighty ones of the people, as in Isaiah is the king of Babylon. The objection that these are poetic fictions, does not set aside their demonstrative power. For the history of the citation of the spirit of Samuel (1 Sam. xxviii.[1]) proves in a similar way that the separated souls in Scheôl were not conceived of as without consciousness and without perception: those prophetic pictures, therefore, proceed from prevailing ideas, as moreover is confirmed by the Hades-doctrine of other peoples, especially the Egyptians, according to which the separate souls in *Amentes* do not sleep, but find themselves, according to their position and character in this world, unhappy or happy. The fact that in the Old Testament we read nothing of the Egyptian distinction of the under-world into hell and Paradise,[2] and on the other hand, that we find such absolutely mournful lamentations as in Ps. lxxxviii. 11–13, arises from this, that the sense of death as a wrathful punishment was deeper in Israel than elsewhere, and that, in default of a word of revelation, men did not dare to picture to themselves more endurable representations of Scheôl.

That souls in a separate state, because they are bodiless, are incapable of perceiving what is external to themselves, and of giving external evidence of themselves, is, as is manifest from the representations of the events of the under-world above quoted, an assumption foreign to the Holy Scripture. Cer-

---

[1] The evasion that this was a juggling or a diabolical deception (*e.g.* Turretin, Tertullian, and Jerome), is a self-delusion. See, on the other hand, 1 Chron. x. 13, LXX., and Ecclus. xlvi. 20.

[2] See Duncker, *Geschichte des Alterthums.* i. 70–76 (ed. 2).

tainly the putting off of the body cuts through the intercourse of man with this present world, as it has been corporeally and especially sensibly effected; but instead of the present world, another surrounds him, and his life, far from being an unconscious and absolutely inactive one, is still, although with a predominating inward direction, a life manifoldly related externally to that world of the future.[1] The Old Testament shows to us the inhabitants of Hades in communion with one another; the parable of the rich man gives us the same representation; and the visions of the spirit-world in the Apocalypse present to our eyes anything rather than quietistic assemblies, or even silent sleeping chambers.[2] Certainly it cannot be physiologically proved at all, that the soul associated with the body into a combined life, can moreover, without the body, continue to lead a self-conscious active life; and moreover, it can only be approximately proved psychologically from the double life which the spirit-soul leads already in this present state. But biblical psychology, in the presence of the doctrine of the soul's sleep, may be content with this, that the Holy Scripture assumes as actual that which is not capable of proof by natural means.

That people raised from the dead—such as Lazarus—had nothing to relate of the other world (as it is taken for granted that it must be concluded from the silence of Scripture on the subject), is absolutely no proof of the sleep of the soul, as little (as we have shown in Div. I. Sec. I.) as our knowing nothing of a life that preceded our present life is a proof against the doctrine of our pre-existence. The spirit of Samuel (1 Sam. xxviii.) knows of the other world, and speaks forth from it, for he remains in his sphere. But when a sphere of life is exchanged for one wholly different, as *e.g.* also in the magnetic sleep, in that case the consciousness of the one is merged in that of the other, and does not return till it reverts into the condition that has been left.

But the chief mistake of those fruitless efforts of the

[1] Thus also judges v. Hofmann, ii. 2, 482, where the idea is rejected, that the incorporeity of the soul implies that it only regards itself, and is deprived of the outward expression of its life.

[2] Or even, to speak in human language, "a monastic world," as Martensen (*Dogm.* sec. 276) thinks.

Psychopannychia to establish itself, lies in the denial of the difference of the two Testaments in their degree of development of the plan of salvation.[1] There is a considerable difference between the condition of the souls of the departed prior and subsequent to the advent of Jesus Christ. If he who believeth on Christ shall live, though he die—if he shall not see death for ever—if he have eternal life now present, and be passed from death unto life,—in the light of these declarations of the Lord, it is every way objectionable to conceive of the spiritual existence of those whose spirit even here below was life ($\zeta\omega\grave{\eta}$ $\delta\iota\grave{\alpha}$ $\delta\iota\kappa\alpha\iota o\sigma\acute{\upsilon}\nu\eta\nu$, Rom. viii. 10), as an existence still subjected to the supremacy of death, whether it be by the expression of this

---

[1] Even the work of the able Capadose, directed against the sleep of the soul, suffers from this deficiency, *Gedanken über den Zustand der Seelen in der Abgeschiedenheit zwischen Tod und Auferstehung* (Dutch 1845; German by Dammann, Düsselthal 1846). As Capadose interprets the Old Testament declarations of the future world in a New Testament way, so Maywahlen, in his book, *Der Tod das Todtenreich und der Zustand der von hier abgeschiedenen Seelen* (1854), transplants the Old Testament kingdom of the dead as such into the New Testament period, thinking that not until the *parousia* of Christ do those who believe on Him break through the bonds of Hades, and are taken up into heaven as those who are raised again. We cite these two works only by way of illustration. Both errors against the truth are old and widely diffused. Even König and Güder, although acknowledging a history as belonging to Hades, teach, that even the souls of the faithful come into Hades; and the latter even refers the word of the Lord to Hades, which says, "In my Father's house are many mansions." Nevertheless, in the art. "Hades," in Herzog's *R.A.*, he declares it to be only probable that Hades is the middle place for the totality of the dead, especially pointing to Apoc. xx. 13 as an apparent counter evidence. But this passage (if there were no other important reasons to be found) would prove nothing against it, since by $\theta\acute{\alpha}\lambda\alpha\sigma\sigma\alpha$ on the one hand, and $\theta\acute{\alpha}\nu\alpha\tau o\varsigma$ and $\mathring{q}\delta\eta\varsigma$ on the other, are only indicated *per merismum* collective spaces which conceal the dead (see v. Hofmann, *Schriftb.* iii. 725). An inside of the earth concealing the dead will not be proved from that. On the other hand, H. W. Rinck, in his work on the condition after death, of the view that is declared in the Old Testament of Scheôl as the place of assembly of all the dead, even of the faithful, denies the objective actuality, and maintains, concerning the assumption that the pious of the Old Testament were in Hades, that it is without any scriptural foundation; and yet nothing is more certain than that the Old Testament knows as yet nothing of blessed men who are in heaven. It was not until the ascension of Christ that heaven became open for men, and became the place of assembly for a human *ecclesia triumphans*.

supremacy in them as suffering, or only as bondage. The souls of the righteous are only still awaiting the overcoming of death in their bodies (Rom. viii. 11), and the overcoming of death generally. They are νεκροί, so far as the totality of their essential state is not yet restored; but in respect of the souls, they are living in the land of the living: they are at home with the Lord, after whom they longed: they are in that Paradise where Paul heard unspeakable words: they are before God's throne, and serve Him day and night in His temple, as John sees in Apoc. vii. 15, when that which is to happen on this side of the judgment of the world and the glorification of the world is revealed to him;—for that these apocalyptic visions are anticipations of that which first awaits the blessed on the other side of the resurrection, or that those blessed are already risen from the dead,[1] as if the first resurrection were to be considered as extending throughout the whole of secular history—these are idle and arbitrary subterfuges. No; they even now as blessed spirits behold God who is a Spirit, and the God-man who is the Lord of the Spirit, through which He has already in this life changed them by degrees into His image (2 Cor. iii. 18). At least the degree of blessing of vision (*visio beatifica*) is even now a manifest one, and many are partakers of it, although certainly, beyond that closing act of the world's history, the bliss even of the most favoured will experience a manifest enhancement.

In respect of those who have died in Christ, therefore, the thought of a sleep of the soul ought never to have arisen. The death of those who die in the Lord has only the mask, but not the nature of death.[2] Considered in itself, it is the opera-

[1] Thus v. Rudloff, *Die Lehre vom Menschen*, p. 395. Rightly on the other hand, Karsten, *Die Letzten Dinge* (ed. iii. 1861). John sees especially at five several periods of the history of the end, the souls of the faithful standing before God; and from this fivefold image we can not only see what sort of a condition the intermediate state is, but also how far and in what direction we can speak of a process of development therein.

[2] Thus it must be; and yet it would not be thus, if, as Ströbel thinks, even the soul of the believing Christian passed into Hades, and found itself there, not indeed in sleeping, but perchance in waking death, with more or less dull pain or longing to retrace its steps. Such a notion is rejected by Schleiermacher himself, when he, on the other hand, says of the idea of a sleep of the soul, "that our Christian self-consciousness can put in no definite protest to the contrary" (*Dogm.* sec. 161, 2). But to him who rests on God's word, both representations are

tion of divine wrath; but this operation of wrath, regarded with respect to them, the dying, is penetrated through and through by divine love. In the might of this love they break through, and are found in the place where they already were in this life in respect of their true nature; in the principle of love, of light, of life, of liberty.[1] They are only dead κατὰ σάρκα, but alive κατὰ πνεῦμα; they sleep not, but they enjoy a sabbatical rest from their temporal trouble (Apoc. xiv. 13); they wait in peace, as already perfected, for the conclusive perfection even of their bodies, by their being made alive again and glorified. But it was not till the completion of the work of redemption that the destiny of the pious had this heavenly issue. The souls of the Old Testament dead, and indeed of those who died in faith in God the Redeemer, not less than of the godless, went to Hades. The souls of the former were, it is true, in the midst of Hades in God's hand, but still in a state of subjection to wrath and need of redemption. Perhaps the parable of Lazarus and the rich man (Luke xvi. 19), and the word of the Lord (Luke xxiii. 43), "To-day shalt thou be with me in Paradise," might be regarded as a confirmation of the faith that was at that time general among the Jewish people, —that Hades was divided into one place for the pious, and into another place for the godless—into Geenna (*Gehinnom*) and Paradise (*Gan Eden*), which, moreover, was called the bosom of Abraham (חיקו של אברהם),[2] and is designated there in the parable as the consolation which indemnifies for the affliction

equally opposed to the Christian self-consciousness realized by him. It is true Ströbel replies (*Luth. Zeitschr.* 1857, p. 772), "It is rhetoric—nothing further—troublesome philosophizing rhetoric — melting away before the divine word of the Holy Scripture like butter in the sun;" but we refer then, as now, to the Epistle to the Hebrews, and the Apocalypse, which afford us the deepest glimpse into the spiritual archetypal world, and to the condition of those who are separated there in faith; and we will rejoice, living and dying, that in front of the light that beams towards us from thence, those thoughts of Hades concerning the intermediate state must melt away like ice.

[1] The kingdom of God is in us, says Ph. Nicolai, in Rocholl, *Luth. Zeitschr.* 1860, p. 216; the young infant comes from the body of its mother into the world, *tanquam ab intra ad extra;* but the regenerate soul of a dying Christian passes out of the world into the kingdom of God's glory, *velut ab extra ad intra.*

[2] See thereupon v. Rudloff, *Die Lehre vom Menschen,* p. 310.

of this present time. The expressions of the Old Testament Scripture itself give us no clear image, because for the most part they are coloured subjectively, and we might almost say mythologically. Nevertheless they all agree in this, that the state of Hades is a state of death still unabolished,—a life not void of consciousness and perception, but certainly dreamlike, and only darkly conscious in the shadows of the previous bodies; and that the special horror of the destiny of Hades consists in the being cut off from the revelation of God's love in the land of the living.

THE PHENOMENAL CORPOREITY AND INVESTITURE.

Sec. V.

WHEN, by God's permission, Samuel appeared to king Saul, the latter asked the witch, "What seest thou?" "I see," said she, "Elohim (a lofty being) ascending out of the earth." What form is he of?" asked he further. She answered, "An old man cometh up, and he is covered in a robe" (1 Sam. xxviii. 13). Samuel, who came up out of Hades, had therefore form and clothing as he had had in this world; and when on the mount two men approached Jesus the glorified, appearing likewise $\dot{\epsilon}\nu$ $\delta\dot{o}\xi\eta$, and spoke with Him, the disciples immediately recognised in them Moses and Elias (Matt. xvii. 3; Luke ix. 30). These also appeared therefore in an external form, corresponding to their temporal history, and are therefore unmistakeable. But this external form is a spiritual one. For Samuel is invisible to Saul, and only visible to the witch. Moses and Elias are visible to the three disciples, but then these latter are in a state of ecstasy.

Putting Elias out of the question, it was not their material bodies in which Samuel and Moses appeared, for both of them after their death had been committed to the earth. But that material bodies were assumed for the occasion is contrary to all analogy; for, to say nothing of the Theophanies, even the angels, when they appear in the form of men, assume no material bodies; but, by virtue of an internal power, they give themselves human form when they make themselves visible to whom they will, and whose inner sense is opened to see them. We thence conclude, that even the external appearance conformed to the form that they had previously worn in this state, wherein Moses and Samuel were manifested, was the immaterial product of their pneumato-psychical nature; and this conclusion is confirmed by the fact, that as well in its pictures of Hades, as in its pictures of heaven, Scripture shows us the spirits or souls that are transferred thither, although actually incorporeal, yet with a corporeal form.[1] But if we compare Isa. xiv., Ezek. xxxi., with Apoc. vii. and other passages, the bodily form of the spirits that are in Hades is the copy of that which they had worn in this world;[2] and the bodily form of those that are in heaven is the pattern of their future glorified body. And this is confirmed by the expressions of all to whom, since the apostolic times, a glimpse into the spiritual kingdom has been vouchsafed.

We are far from desiring to raise a dispute on what has been said by the Smalcaldian Articles (ii. 2) of our ecclesiastical confession, "that evil spirits have made a great deal of mischief by appearing as human souls, with unspeakable lies and deceptions." But still we do not decide, on that account, that we can regard all appearances of the dead as a mocking game of lying demons. For the reasons which Ströbel[3] opposes to us will not stand the test. He maintains (1) that a reappearance of the departed is not possible without resurrection; that no soul can come forth from Hades, without at the same time breaking the bars of death; but that Scripture knows only one key to Hades, the key of death in the hands of the Risen One (i. 18). We no less distinctly acknowledge, that no soul can be

[1] There remains to souls, says Umbreit in his work *On Sin*, 1853, p. 128, after the flesh has passed from them, a certain corporeity, not further described. In the same way, Heyder, *l.c.* p. 48, *animæ in Hade versanti umbra corporis vindicatur.*

[2] In Ps. xlix. 14, this form, corresponding to that of the present state, in which the ungodly appear, is called צוּר = צוּרָה, image, form, pattern: "their image is given up to the hell for consumption, without any place remaining for it (in the upper world)."

[3] In his notice of this book of ours, *Luth. Zeitschr.* 1857, pp. 777–783.

free from the bands of Hades and of death unless this key opens the way for it; but we reject the inference, that all appearances of the dead must therefore be appearances of those who have risen again. The saints which manifestly appeared, according to Matt. xxvii. 52, after the resurrection of Jesus in Jerusalem, were raised from the dead; but Samuel, who appeared to king Saul, was no raised person; and Moses, who spake with Jesus on the mount of transfiguration, had not risen from the dead. It is true Ströbel refers to both appearances in the chapter *de bis mortuis;* but that Samuel and Moses were raised up from the dead for the purpose of a passing appearance, to die again afterwards, is a romantic invention. Both of them were manifested, not as redeemed out of Hades either for ever or for a period: they appeared within the unabrogated limits of their spiritual state as bodiless,—and yet in conformity with their previous corporeity—visible spirits. But (2) how then, asks Ströbel, is a soul to make itself perceptible to the inhabitants of the earth, if it have no body? With as much reason it might be asked, How then can angels make themselves perceivable if they have no body? They do not appear in assumed human bodies, which they afterwards lay aside like a mask; and yet they appear in human form, which they give to themselves from within, and in which they operate upon material nature. But with respect to the souls ($\psi v \chi a i$, Apoc. vi. 9), or, as Scripture expresses itself (without, like Ströbel, wrenching asunder soul and spirit), to the spirits ($\pi \nu \epsilon \acute{v} \mu a \tau a$, 1 Pet. iii. 19, Heb. xii. 23) of departed men, they, as creatively intended for bodily manifestation, are even in themselves not, according to the biblical view, without form. Wherefore should they not be able to make themselves perceptible, on the assumption that God wills it, and opens man's eyes for the purpose of discerning them? But (3) God will not do so, says Ströbel, referring to the parable of the rich man and Lazarus. From this parable we perceive, that the information upon God's will which we have in God's word needed no filling up by means of the preaching of those who for this purpose should be raised from the dead, and sent to the living. But are we thence to conclude, that the dead do not under any circumstances return to life, in order still to tarry among the living for awhile as testimonies of the divine power of miracle, and thus of the truth of divine revelation? The dead who were raised by the Lord Jesus prove exactly the contrary. And are we at all to conclude thence, that the dead even before their resurrection, and without awakening of their bodies, are not able to appear again? The appearances of Moses and of Samuel prove the contrary. We stand upon the testimonies of Scripture, without interpreting therein in favour of any dogmatic prejudices; and we still even now say with Erich Pontoppidan,[1] "What is acknowledged to be possible in the Holy Scripture, must even outside of it still be possible."

Even the ancients objected that the Samuel who appeared in 1 Sam. xxviii. could not have been the true one; because it was not written that he had re-assumed his body, without which he could not have been seen. One of our old theologians[2] answers thereto, "Non opus fuit redassumptione corporis sui; spiritus Samuelis enim potuit vel alio quodam corpore aëreo, uti angeli, apparere in eoque figuram prioris humani corporis repræsentare, vel etiam sine illo cerni, facta solum elevatione sensus oculorum mulieris et Saulis ad lumen e spiritu prodiens recipiendum." We believe, on the other hand, that the spirits of the departed are even in themselves not without a phenomenal bodily form. It is true it may not be assumed that the soul, when separating from the body, continues to exist within its nerve-spirit as its immaterial body:[3] for this nerve-spirit is of very doubtful authenticity; and even if it were not so, would belong to the region of power and matter without being of a pneumatico-psychical nature. We find it therefore inadmissible that the soul retains the same nature which, in Div. IV. Sec. XIII., we called its nerve-body, or rather which is called by others[4] its nerve-spirit-body: it is contrary to the nature of

---

[1] In his scriptural and intelligent treatise, *On the Immortality of Human Souls, etc.*, ed. 2, 1766.

[2] Dachselt, in his *Biblia Accentuata* (1729), p. 434.

[3] V. Rudloff, *Lehre vom Menschen*, p. 62, and elsewhere.

[4] This view is widely circulated. "Perhaps," says Kästner himself, in his *Considerations on the Influence of Natural Study on Metaphysics*, "there is a certain portion of matter constantly associated with our soul, and the rest no further than to form the clothing for the body which we call ours." More definitely, v. Rudloff teaches an intermediate condition of immaterial corporeity of the soul, which consists of its *nephesch, i.e.* (as he understands this word) the nerve-spirit, or is formed through it.

death, which consists in total separation of the soul from the body, as well in its most subtle, as in its grossest, materiality. Yet it is true—as maintained by Tertullian and Irenæus, appealing to the parable of the rich man and Lazarus—that the soul in the future state has *ejus corporis quod circumtulit effigiem* (*de anima*, c. ix.), or preserves *characterem corporis, in quo etiam adaptantur, eundem* (*c. hær.* ii. 34, 1). "The soul of the spirit," we say with Göschel,[1] "after the separation from its body, is not wholly without a body—the inward body follows it." We think that we must form for ourselves the conceptions that follow therefrom, in which, moreover, we may do justice to the truth contained in the confused heathenish representations of the shadowy corporeity of the other world.[2]

As the soul is a principle of bodily life derived from the spirit, it is even in itself probable, that although immaterial, it is still a manifestation of the spirit, formed conformably to the organism which it enlivens by its universal presence. This is an old view. To the question whether it is possible to see the soul, Macarius answers (*Hom.* vii. 6 s.), "Like as these eyes behold the sun, thus the enlightened, but only a few, behold the form of their souls;" and to the question whether the soul is in any manner formed, "As the angels have a form and likeness, and as the outward man has a definite external appearance, thus also the inner man has an angel-like form, and on the other hand, a form like to the outer man." And Tertullian relates, in ch. ix. of his book *de anima*, a story of a Christian woman well known to him, who often fell into a state of ecstasy (similar to a so-called religious somnambulist, but unlike in this particular, that after the ecstasy she was able to remember what she saw), and who once declared, "Among other things, the soul was shown to me corporeally; and I saw it as spirit, but not of an inane and void (shadowy and spectral) character: no, as capable of being grasped by hand, tender and light, and of an aerial colour, and in altogether human form." In agree-

---

[1] *Letzte Dinge*, p. 150.
[2] See Nägelsbach, *Homerische Theologie*, vii. 27 (of the Autenrieth ed.), together with the discussions of Cæsar upon the life of the Psyches as εἴδωλα of the living, according to Homeric ideas, in the *Zeitschr. für A. W.* 1842, c. 991; Thiersch's *Pindar*, pt. ii. p. 233, on the words ζῶον δὲ λείπεται αἰῶνος εἴδωλον; and Böttcher's *Ideas on Art-Mythology*, ii. 477.

ment with this vision—which certainly becomes suspicious as a vision, from the fact that it only confirmed what Tertullian himself taught—is what J. B. von Helmont, in his treatise upon the image of the spirit (*imago mentis*), relates of himself.[1] Three-and-twenty long years having been occupied with large aspirations after knowledge of the soul, he finally in the year 1633, when he in the midst of outwardly troubled circumstances was in a sabbatical mood, saw in a vision his spirit in a human form. "It was a light, absolutely pure, active Vision, a spiritual substance, crystalline, enlightening in its own brightness, but enveloped in another cloudy portion as in its husk (*siliqua*), in which I could not distinguish whether it had a brightness from itself, on account of the predominating flashing of the crystalline brightness therein contained." Moreover, J. Böhme answers to the question, how the soul is specially formed and shaped: "The soul is formed according to the entire body, with all the limbs; the spirit portions it into the whole body; all the limbs are its boughs: its whole form looks like a tree with many twigs and branches." We leave it to the reader to confront these testimonies of the ancients with our representation of the nature of the soul, and its relation to the spirit, and are satisfied ourselves with the hint. It is the *doxa* of the spirit, immaterial, but similarly formed to the body, which the spirit through it ensouls; it is, as the outside of the spirit, so the inside of the body, which in every change of its material condition maintains it in identity with itself.

When the soul has thus been linked with a body thus or thus articulated, has acted upon it, and has been subjected to its influences, it has become a natural necessity for it to exhibit itself conformed to the constitution of that body formed under its physical and ethical co-operation, and the temporal relations associated therewith. It continues, moreover, in the other world in that form which, as the living principle of the body, it had assumed. Its appearance remains a corporeal one, although

---

[1] *Opp.* ed. Francofurt, i. 256 (not exactly communicated in Barth, *Lebensmagnetismus*, p. 8). The "cloudy portion" is, in Helmont's mind, the *anima sensitiva*, by him regarded as mental, which has its place *circa os stomachi*, and pervades the whole body *per ministrum organum archei;* this *archeus*, according to our ideas, being the nervous power. S. Spiess, J. B. von Helmont's *System der Medicin*, p. 46.

immaterial. We are constrained thus to express ourselves. For although we hesitate to speak of an immaterial corporeity of God and of the angels, because certainly materiality (even although spiritualized) is an essential characteristic of corporeity; still it is precisely in this case that the idea of immaterial corporeity is no self-contradiction, because it is only in this case that the form of corporeity will be conceived of abstracted from its matter. For this intermediate state of corporeity, as compared with the material corporeity, is on the one hand only a shadow of the latter, but on the other hand is, so to speak, its essence or extract, so far as it is a far more immediate and more transparent image of the actual nature of man, and is related to the corruptible body as the cast is to the broken mould.[1] As, generally, what the man has been and how he has been in this life is not extinguished in the future state, but becomes essentially manifest; so there is reflected in this material, or (as, to guard ourselves against misconstruction, we prefer saying) this phenomenal psychical corporeity, all that man has become through his own self-destination among divinely-appointed relations. In this life, the soul has only a limited power over the corporeity. In noble bodily forms dwells often a hateful soul; in hateful forms, a noble soul. In the other world it is otherwise. The phenomenal corporeity, laying aside all that is inadequate, will be the adequate bodily copy in human form of the ethical self-formation of the soul. All that is good and divinely wrought in man, and all that is evil, with the exception of that which is blotted out in the blood of Christ Jesus, comes then to manifestation; for as well good as evil deeds leave behind lasting traces in the soul, and give to it a permanent character.[2] Happy then is the soul, which, purified by Christ's word, is pervaded by the cleansing fire of death as a light in the Lord![3]

[1] Just in this way Gregory of Nyssa. See Möller, *l.c.* p. 93, *forma quædam* (εἶδος) *semper manens.*

[2] Therefore it is prayed at the close of the Σχολαστικός of Zacharias (ed. Boissonade, p. 151): τοὺς κακοὺς χαρακτῆρας καὶ τύπους τῆς ψυχῆς ἐξελάσαι, δεῖξαί τε τὴν εἰκόνα τὴν πρώτην ἀθόλωτον. By these are meant *stigmata et vibices, quibus vitia animas maculant et deformant, quæque eis etiam a corporibus separatis insident.*

[3] See Göschel, *Der Mensch diesseits und jenseits,* p. 71: "Death is the final washing of the feet, for purification through the blood."

I cannot refrain from citing here some expressions of the two clairvoyants already often mentioned, which, on account of their manifest piety, and on account of visible indications of grace, of which they were thought worthy in their state, deserve special consideration. No psychologist will deny that the circumstances which I communicate are deep glimpses into the mystery of the life of the soul, although the actual fact of that which was seen only allowed itself to be beheld by them in symbolical refraction. "In every human soul," says one, "is formed first of all a tree of life. This has its roots in the heart, its several kinds of branches expand themselves in the breast, and the tenderest twigs in the brain. The most various kind of flowers—as roses, lilies, tulips, and the like—and its just as various kinds of fruits, show forth from it outside the head in the crown of the rays of righteousness. Thus, as by the tree of life, the kingdom of plants is represented in the soul: thus there are formed in it also, by strong spiritual operation, lifeless forms, more strongly or more weakly stamped as animal, which encamp around our heart; and there, even although they have no life of their own, are stirred at the heaving of the passions. There appears the serpent, as a symbol of malicious cunning; the peacock, as that of vain pride; the goat, as that of sensuality; the toad, as that of covetousness, and the like. And where these dark brute-forms are encamped in more vivid character, there the stream of life which pours from the heart to the brain and again returns to the heart suffers, and there also the tree of life suffers, an absolute darkening and change." "Even the evil men," says the other clairvoyante, a little girl of ten years old, "have flowers around their head; but I cannot in any wise tell you how terrible, how disgusting they are. In the same way that a darkness surrounds their whole body, which terrifies me, and causes me cramps, so also are their flowers darkened. They hang down all withered and heavy; many appear absolutely dark, many as if mouldered. Ah, no corrupted, rotting earthly rose appears so loathsome as the black rose on the darkened head of an evil man: its leaves are wildly torn to pieces, and ragged in many withered rags; and its darkness is so frightful, that I cannot look upon it."[1]

If these pictures must be regarded as visionary or poetical,

[1] See M. Beesel, *Letzte Aussagen* (1851), p. 47.

at any rate they are pictures of what is actual. "The will of the soul-spirit"—thus J. Böhme[1] expresses this matter of fact—"is eternal; that which is comprehended in the will of the soul-spirit is taken along with the soul, when body and soul are severed. Therefore it is necessary for us to aspire after something good, in which the soul can find its eternal occupation, and within which it may have its enjoyment; for the works of our soul follow us, and the works of the hands and of the external spirit remain in this world, for the soul is in eternity. What it makes and imagines its own in this state, this stands ever before it, unless it shatters it again, and then it is as a shattered work, on which it spends no more effort; for it is delivered from it. For eternity carves an eternal model, and that which is fragile and incipient carves a perishable model; for all things of this state shall stand every one in its own model. For what the eternal will grasps, lays hold of an imperishable form; therefore it does not itself break that in pieces."[2]

There is a spiritual form of the soul which is the sum of its present ethical conduct and condition.[3] This, even in the future

[1] *Of the Threefold Life of Man*, xii. 2 (works published by Schiebler, iv. 183).

[2] If the testimony of the theosophist be rejected, let that of a late philosopher be heard: "Every individuality," says J. H. Fichte, in his work on the idea of personality, and of individual continuance (ed. ii. p. 168), "takes over along with it, in itself, its judgment, to the rest of blessedness, or to ever unblessed rending opposition. The sum of its inner and outer works, which it has lived in its passions and endeavours, its capacities as its incapacities, it continues to take with it, as spiritually formed habit and fundamental tendency. The self-conviction of this sum of life establishes thereby at once the soul's condition after death. It is the conditioning and the basis of the future corporeity."

[3] Dante has this in mind when he sings (*Purg.* x. 121-126):

"Christians, and proud! O poor and wretched ones!
That, feeble in the mind's eye, lean your trust
Upon unstayed perverseness: know ye not
That we are worms, yet made at last to form
The winged insect,[1] imp'd with angel plumes,
That to heaven's justice unobstructed soars?"[2]

He who wishes to read another commentary upon these profound poetic

[1] "*Nati a formar l'angelica farfalla.*"
[2] Carey's translation.

intermediate state, will come to a more transparent manifestation, in that the soul by the power of the spirit makes itself visible, in conformity with its present corporeity and its present *habitus*, allowing for all the inadequacy of its spiritual form. The godless person will then not be able to conceal his internal condition, and will so far go γυμνὸς, as that his shame appears (Apoc. xvi. 15). But he who already here below has lived in God, and has put on righteousness in the faith of Christ, and has been nourished by Christ's flesh and blood, his self-manifestation is the serene prelude of that perfection for which he waits in peace; and there shall appear upon him nothing of sin, or standing in closer or remoter connection with sin: for that is all swallowed up by justifying grace.

The phenomenal body, in which such an one manifests himself, is as the embodied blissful hope of his coming glorification; and as a pledge of this, he receives a white raiment, in which the garment of salvation, wherewith even here below he was invested inwardly, makes itself visible; and the faithfulness with which he watched over the purity of his robe of salvation finds its recompense.[1] The Apocalypse makes mention of these ἱμάτια λευκὰ, or στολαὶ λευκαί, so frequently and continually (iii. 4, 5, vi. 11, vii. 9, 13, xix. 14, comp. iii. 18, iv. 4), that it is exegetically impossible to regard this white raiment as a mere figure of speech.[2] Moreover, none who at any time have been thought worthy to catch a glimpse of the eternal state, have known how sufficiently to extol this heavenly whiteness in which the spirits of those who have died in the Lord are clothed. It is the white raiment which Dante so ingeniously distinguishes,

---

words than the one above given by us, may read what Schöberlein says in the *Jahrbb. für Deutsche Theol.* 1861, p. 74, upon the corporeity of the intermediate state; among other things, "The soul which is separated in the Lord will after death be supported and surrounded by the internal spiritual corporeity, which it has worked out here below in the silent hidden way of faith through the power of the Holy Spirit."

[1] Comp. H. W. Rinck, *Vom Zustand nach dem Tode*, p. 133; against whom Woldemar Schmidt, *De statu animarum medio inter mortem et resurrectionem*, p. 31, will only allow the one passage 2 Cor. v. 1–4 to be of effect, and will not receive the στολαὶ λευκαί as a testimony on behalf of the corporeity of the intermediate state.

[2] Thus v. Hofmann, ii. 2, 483–486. The garment white as light is the glory of the saints; the palm, the adornment of their joy.

as the first raiment, from the second raiment—the resurrection body.[1] But he mistakes (if in other respects I here penetrate the meaning of the Scripture) in identifying this first garment of the soul-spirit with the self-likeness of its body in the intermediate state,[2] and regards the air as the material of this self-likeness, when he, who even in this matter is otherwise an incomparable theologian, sings of the soul causing its first clothing (*Purgatorio*, xxv. 88–108):

> " Soon as the place
> Receives her, round the plastic virtue beams,
> Distinct as in the living limbs before :
> And as the air, when saturate with showers,
> The casual beam refracting, decks itself
> With many a hue ; so here the ambient air
> Weareth that form, which influence of the soul
> Imprints on it ; and like the flame, that where
> The fire moves, thither follows ; so henceforth,
> The new form on the spirit follows still ;
> Hence hath it semblance and is shadow called,
> With each sense,[3] even to the sight, endued :
> Hence speech is ours, hence laughter, tears, and sighs,
> Which thou may'st oft have witnessed on the mount.
> The obedient shadow fails not to present
> Whatever varying passion moves within us,
> And this the cause of what thou marvell'st at." [4]

---

[1] This distinction of a *stola prima* and *secunda* (*binæ stolæ*) is ancient ; it occurs in Augustine (*Serm.* iv. *in solennitate sanctorum*), Gregory the Great (*Dial.* i. iv. ch. 25), Beda, Haymo, Anselm, Bernhard, etc.

[2] Göschel, *Dante Alighieri's Osterfeier*, pp. 73, 77, 98, comp. *Letzte Dinge*, p. 13 ; Althaus, *Letzte Dinge* (1858), p. 33 ; Hebart, *Die zweite sichtbare Zukunft Christi*, p. 234, where it is cautiously said, " The white garments POINT to corporeity ;" Osiander, *Commentary on the Corinthians*, ii. 181, " The position and the clothing of the soul between death and resurrection is to be thought of as a mediation between the new life and the old."

[3] In the original, *e quindi organa poi ciascun sentire.*

[4] Cary's *Dante*. [The translator ventures to transcribe the marvellously accurate and beautiful German version of the passage by Kopisch :

> " Sobald der Stätten eine die umfähet,
>   Erstrahlt die bildnerische Kraft nun ringshin,
>   So und so weit, wie in lebendgen Gliedern.
> Und wie die Luft, wenn sie des Regens voll ist
>   Vom fremden Strahl, den sie in sich abspiegelt,
>   Geschmücket wird mit mannigfachen Farben :

My purpose in this discussion on the soul's clothing in the intermediate state, is to leave aside the passage 2 Cor. v. 1, which even to this day is so variously explained. The heavenly habitation which the apostle refers to, is here in no respect the intermediate body, but the body of the resurrection or glorification, which he, as in 1 Cor. xv. 48, calls a heavenly one, because it originates through a heavenly agency of power, is of a heavenly nature, and has heaven as its place of residence. "We know," says he in ver. 1, "that when our earthly house of this tabernacle is dissolved, we have a building of God, an house not made with hands, an eternal dwelling-place in heaven." It pertains to the substance of the Christian's believing consciousness, that when our earthly pilgrimage is at an end, we receive as our own, a body of heavenly nature and abode. The apostle transfers himself, in saying ἔχομεν, into the period of the parousia; or this ἔχομεν is an expression of the possession which, after death has resulted, is future, but certain, and therefore already as good as present. In the expectation of the parousia that fills the apostle, as of something that is immediately at hand, it cannot be surprising that the intermediate state is passed over by him, or has almost wholly disappeared from his view. In ver. 2, this certainty of ours of such a heavenly body present to us after death is founded upon the fact, or is explained by it, that with our present groaning is associated the longing

> So ordnet sich die nachbarliche Luft dort.
>   Zu der Gestalt, die ihr die Kraft der Seele
>   Aufpräget an dem Orte, wo sie weilet.
> Und dann vergleichbar einer Flamme, welche
>   Dem Feuer immer folgt, wo man es hinträgt,
>   Folgt nun dem Geiste seine neue Bildung.
> Dorther empfähet er dann sein Erscheinen
>   Und heisst ein Schatten, rüstet auch ein jedes
>   Empfinden völlig aus,[1] bis dass es sichtbar.
> Deswegen reden wir dahier und lächeln,
>   Deswegen bilden Seufzer wir und Thränen,
>   Die der am Berg kannst wahrgenommen haben.
> Nachdem uns Neigungen und andre Triebe
>   Festhalten, bildet sich der Schatten, siehe:
>   Dies ist der Grund des Vorgangs, dem du staunest."
>   KOPISCH.]—TR.

---

[1] In the original, *e quindi organa poi ciascun sentire*.

after a clothing upon with the heavenly investiture, *i.e.* after a clothing with the same, which ensues immediately, and does not wait until beyond death. "For in such a case[1] we groan moreover, earnestly desiring to be clothed upon with our house which is from heaven" (the immortal heavenly body). We long for immediate clothing upon, "although it is true," adds the apostle in ver. 3, "that being clothed" (and not clothed upon), "we shall not be found naked;" for even those who have already fallen asleep, are at the parousia clothed with a heavenly body, and at the same time with those who are alive and are clothed *upon* with the same, are brought to meet Christ (1 Thess. iv. 15–17, comp. 1 Cor. xv. 48). The future εὑρεθησόμεθα refers to this meeting of Christ of the returned spirit, and of His people who are taken up by Him now bodily from death, and the aorist participle ἐνδυσάμενοι confirms what will have happened there in the case of the latter: even having attained the heavenly body by means of clothing (not clothing upon), they become such, that they are not found naked.[2] Nevertheless we long after clothing upon; "for"—thus ver. 4 founds or explains the fact of longing—"we that are in this tabernacle" (the present body of dissolution through death) "do also groan, feeling ourselves burdened, for the reason that we may not be unclothed" (in order that we might be clothed on the other side of death for the first time), "but clothed upon"

[1] I refer ἐν τούτῳ no longer to τοῦ σκήνους (ver. 1), but I take it in the meaning "according to this" (in such a state of things), as John xvi. 30, Acts xxiv. 16; although, moreover, the meaning "presently," "in the meanwhile," "now," is suitable. Both meanings of the ἐν τούτῳ (ἐν τούτοις) are frequent in classical Greek. See the new edition of Passow on Οὗτος, p. 599*b*.

[2] That εἰ καί, moreover, in the New Testament *usus loquendi*, means "if also = although," and that καί in this connection may belong to the chief verb of the hypothetical sentence just as well as to a special member of the sentence, needs no proof. In the only New Testament passage where εἴ γε καί occurs, it is in another meaning. The apostle says in Gal. iii. 4, "Have ye submitted to so immense an injury, as that which ye had received, εἰκῇ, for nothing, at random, without having anything substantial therefrom?" and adds, εἴ γε καὶ εἰκῇ, *i.e.* if indeed it be so, that ye have suffered it for nothing, and something has not assuredly rather grown up to you therefrom, — to wit, corruption. In conformity with this use of εἴ γε καί, 2 Cor. v. 3 would be explicable, "if indeed we also, in putting it on (the heavenly habitation), be found to be not naked," *i.e.* so far as we, when

(at the parousia without previous death), "so that thereby mortality may be swallowed up" (at once transformed) "of life." The Christian does not fear death, but he sighs for redemption from this body of death (Rom. vii. 24), by which he feels himself burdened; and the dearest thing that could happen to him, and which therefore he thus longs for, is that immediate clothing upon with the body of glorification which awaits the faithful who live to see the day of the Lord,—a spiritual disposition which lies remote from our present life of experience, because the day of the Lord is more or less pushed out of its just place in our believing consciousness, and therefore the longing after it no longer fills our hearts as it did those of the first Christians.

Our interpretation of ver. 3 essentially agrees with that of Reiche.[1] Nevertheless the latter decides for the reading ἐκδυσάμενοι : "although moreover, we, being unclothed from our present body by death, shall not be found naked." In this reading, the thought lies proportionally nearer to a corporeity of the intermediate state; and accordingly the whole passage has been recently interpreted by Ernesti.[2] But if the apostle looks upon death as ἐκδύσασθαι, and the change at the day of the coming of Christ as ἐπενδύσασθαι, there is left for ἐνδύσασθαι only the idea presented by 1 Thess. iv. 16; and the rather, as οἰκοδομή, οἰκία, οἰκητήριον of ver. 1 can in no

the Lord comes, shall not already be among those who have fallen asleep. But this view, in itself forced, and loosening the strict connection between vers. 2 and 4, is wrecked on the *part. aor.* ἐνδυσάμενοι. Bengel and others explain *siquidem etiam indutos nos, non nudos* (*h. e. si vivos nos*) *inveniat dies novissimus;* but this must (in spite of J. Müller's defence, ii. 413), require ἐνδεδυμένοι. De Wette and Meyer translate εἴγε καί,—for the rest explaining differently,—in the certain presumption to wit, (εἴγε) that actually (καί), and so on. But this apprehension of the particles corresponds rather to the rationalistic theory of their use, than to their use itself. One thing of the two, either the sentence with εἴγε καί is restrictive (if indeed also), or it is concessive (although indeed also). Only in the latter view is a perfectly satisfactory meaning obtained.

[1] See his *Comm. crit.* i. 353-365, and also Kling, *St. u. Kr.* 1839, 511.

[2] In his *Theorie vom Ursprunge der Sünde aus der Sinnlichkeit*, pp. 117-121. Moreover, Roos, Flatt, Schnekkenburger, Schott, J. P. Lange, Kern, Nitzsch, Martensen, Göschel, v. Rudloff, and in the latest times H. W. Rinck and Wold. Schmidt, understand the passage of an intermediate corporeity.

case designate the corporeity of the intermediate state which is referred to in ver. 3. An intermediate corporeity to which these designations were appropriate, is known neither by Paul nor by the Holy Scripture in general. Rightly, Reiche rejects this reference of ver. 3 to a *mortui organum quasi provisorium*. There is no intermediate corporeity which can be named a habitation, and of which an ἐνδύσασθαι can be predicated. That self-embodiment of the soul represented by Dante, and here and there by later writers,[1] by means of an investiture of any kind of substance external to itself, and still material, however delicate and subtle it might be, is a wholly untenable fantasy. The intermediate state is actually, as referred to the resurrection and glorification, a γυμνὸν εἶναι. Not till the day of the appearance of Christ will the essential condition of man be restored as a synthesis of the soul with a body. The immaterial corporeity, which we assume on the ground of other scriptural testimonies beside 2 Cor. v. 1, is nothing else than the corporiform appearance of the soul itself, nothing else than the shadow of that which is put off, held fast, and conformed to the true internal condition of the soul. It is as little in contradiction to the assumed nakedness referred to by the apostle, *i.e.* bodilessness, as is the white clothing with which God's grace clothes the spirits in heaven.

THE RELATION OF THE SOULS OF THE RIGHTEOUS TO THE CORPOREITY OF CHRIST.

SEC. VI.

" THE οἰκία ἀχειροποίητος," says v. Hofmann, adopting another course in the interpretation of 2 Cor. v. 1,[2] " is neither a provisional dwelling appropriate to the dead nor their own for ever glorious body. The former would give a romantic conception absolutely foreign to Scripture [an assertion by which our

[1] See Güder, *Lehre von der Erscheinung Jesu Christi unter den Todten*, 1853, p. 336.
[2] *Weissagung und Erfüllung*, ii. 190.

idea discussed in Sec. V. is not affected]; the latter would contradict either the doctrine elsewhere maintained by the apostle, if the clothing with this body were to happen immediately after death, or could not be reconciled with the present ἔχομεν if it were not to take place until the resurrection of the righteous [but ἔχομεν with transposition into the time of the death following, or of the *parousia*, is not at all a surprising expression of that which is certain to happen afterwards, or then]. Of the glorified corporeity of Christ, it may, on the other hand, be said that we have in it, even now, an οἰκία αἰώνιος for our souls, even when our ἐπίγειος οἰκία is dissolved. Of it we might, while living in this our mortal body, receive, and thereby be changed into, the fellowship of its glory without death. Εἴγε καὶ ἐνδυσάμενοι οὐ γυμνοὶ εὑρεθησόμεθα, adds Paul by way of reminder; which words, as it appears to me, have therefore been so manifoldly and so terribly misunderstood, because οὐ γυμνοὶ has not been regarded as in apposition with ἐνδυσάμενοι, and the latter not as a characterization of a conduct, and indeed of such a conduct as must have been pursued by us before the appearance of Christ, if this manifestation be to tend to our glorification. Only upon the supposition that we are already clothed with Christ, and are not found naked, have we to expect that if we are alive at the day of the manifestation of Christ, and are in the flesh, we shall also see our σῶμα τῆς σαρκὸς clothed upon with the σῶμα τῆς δόξης of Christ, and thus shall see τὸ θνητὸν swallowed up ὑπὸ τῆς ζωῆς." Elsewhere,[1] v. Hofmann recapitulates the declaration of the apostle in the following manner: "The Christian, when dying he puts off his earthly body, will exchange the earthly dwelling-place which he possessed therein for a heavenly one: he will be taken up bodilessly in Christ the glorified, or, which is the same thing, he will be taken up into the heavenly house of God. Even without a body he will be included in Christ, in whose glorified nature the entire fulness of the divine essence has its bodily dwelling-place."

We willingly concede that against this view of the third

[1] *Schriftbeweis*, 2, ii. 477. I have again tested my view of 1 Cor. v. 1-4 by the criticism to which it is there—466-474—subjected; but I find myself corrected only in one essential point—the reference of the ἐν τούτῳ to the τοῦ σκήνους.

verse[1] nothing is to be objected in terms: the reading εἴγε accommodates itself to it as well as εἴπερ; moreover, it gives to the ἐνδυσάμενοι a meaning which elsewhere (comp. Gal. iii. 27; Eph. iv. 24; Col. iii. 10) in Paul it actually has, although never without a corresponding definition of the object. But we must not set aside the consideration, that it estranges the ἐνδυσάμενοι (with which 1 Cor. xv. 53 is rather to be compared) from the eschatological connection of the range of conception, ἐκδύσασθαι (death), ἐπενδύσασθαι (a change in the bodily life), and ἐνδύσασθαι (resurrection). Let it be as it will with the meaning of the third verse, in any case we insist upon this, that the apostle, by the heavenly habitation, understands the resurrection body,[2] not an intermediate corporeity, and still less the glorified corporeity of Christ; for this yields a view neither declared by any appendix, nor otherwise to be authenticated in the apostolic form of doctrine. The apostle teaches that the word and sacrament make us members of the church, which is the body of Christ. He teaches that our mortal bodies are one day, whether by changing or by raising again, to become conformed to the glorified body of Christ (see 2 Cor. iv.); but he nowhere teaches, that in the intermediate state Christ's glorified body will be to the hope of the resurrection our habitation, and so to speak, the universal body, which embraces the souls of all believers.

The case would indeed be somewhat otherwise, if in the

[1] It has precursors in Jerome, Anselm, Luther, Calvin, Calixtus, Calovius, Baldwin, Vitringa, Olshausen, Usteri; moreover, it occurs in the Greek fathers, and in other teachers of the time of the Reformation. Macarius, for instance, is worthy of consideration (*Hom.* v. 6-8), who understands by the heavenly habitation of ver. 1 the house of the spirit which remains to the soul that is at home there at the breaking up of the body, and by the power of the spirit maintains its final development in the spiritual corporeity (Rom. viii. 11). This house of the spirit is to him the immaterial corporeity of the intermediate state: for the soul appears to him in itself as bodily (iv. 9, vii. 7), and God Himself has embodied Himself (ἐσωματοποίησεν ἑαυτόν, iv. 9) in order to be able to become soul like to soul. "Let us strive," says he (ver. 8), "to attain to this clothing by faith and by a divinely blessed walk, whereby we shall not be found naked when we must put off the body, and have nothing which may make our flesh predominant in that day."

[2] Thus also the latest interpreters of the Epistle to the Corinthians, Osiander and Burger, although (the former reading ἐκδυσάμενοι, the latter

Epistle to the Hebrews, which in any case is in some sort Pauline, viii. 2, ix. 11, and elsewhere, were to be understood by the heavenly archetypal and antitypal σκηνή, as Hofmann explains it, the glorified body of Christ.[1] This view, which is maintained also by J. Gerhard, Eg. Hunnius, Bengel, is certainly suggested, when John ii. 21, where the body of Christ is called a temple, is placed side by side with Eph. ii. 19-22, according to which Christ and the church together form a holy temple. Moreover, the Epistle to the Hebrews itself appears in x. 20 to suggest this view; for if the flesh of the crucified One is the veil which must be rent, the glorification of the corporeity of Christ is the uncovering of that which was hidden by this veil. But I consider that, in the decisive passage (Heb. ix. 11), where Hofmann associates ἀρχιερεὺς τῶν μελλόντων ἀγαθῶν διὰ τῆς μείζονος καὶ τελειοτέρας σκηνῆς (an high priest of good things to come by means of His glorified human nature as the tabernacle where now God dwells in humanity), the association of διὰ τῆς μείζονος καὶ τελειοτέρας σκηνῆς with εἰσῆλθεν εἰς τὰ ἅγια is the most obvious;[2] that, according to viii. 3-6, the original Mosaic tabernacle was the copy of a heavenly model, and accordingly the image and adumbration of heavenly archetypes (τῶν ἐπουρανίων);[3] that, according to the universal testimony of Old Testament Scripture, there is a heavenly temple-palace, where God is enthroned in the midst of blessed spirits; that even the consciousness of the faith of the synagogue is aware of a parallel heavenly sanctuary antitypical of the earthly sanctuary, which is neither the Shechina

ἐνδυσάμενοι) they understand ver. 3 of the necessity of a precedent covering of our nakedness with the righteousness of Christ.

[1] Hofmann, *Weissagung und Erfüllung*, ii. 190; *Schriftbeweis*, 2, i. 411. "The name σκηνή designates the house of God's dwelling in humanity as the copy in the history of redemption of the habitation of God established by Moses; whereby alone every other interpretation appears excluded but that which harmonizes with Col. ii. 9,—that the divine fellowship of the glorified Son of man must be thought of, whose bodily nature is the dwelling-place of all the fulness of the Divine Being.

[2] Bengel indeed thinks, even in this obvious association, that he must understand σκηνή of the body of Christ: *Tabernaculo opponitur corpus, ut sanguis sanguini.* But as the σκηνή is designated as belonging to the future world, this is impossible. Christ may be said to have passed through His σάρξ, but not through His σῶμα τῆς δόξης.

[3] See my *Commentary on the Epistle to the Hebrews*, p. 337.

(*i.e.* the manifestation of the Godhead dwelling among men) nor the church, but the everlasting place of worship of the latter;[1] that even the seer of the Apocalypse gains a sight of this ναὸς τῆς σκηνῆς τοῦ μαρτυρίου (xv. 5), and thoroughly describes it in his book, even to the detail, without there being given to us in xxi. 22 (where the new Jerusalem, as that which is absolutely filled with the presence of God and of the Lamb, is contrasted with the lower Jerusalem, in which city and temple are distinct) a right to a spiritualistic interpretation of these manifold and certainly pneumatistic realities. Therefore I cannot appropriate to myself the view of Hofmann, that the author of the Epistle to the Hebrews means by the σκηνὴ ἀληθινὴ the glorified human nature of Christ. But where, then, would be that archetypal and antitypal place of worship? It is said in Heb. ix. 11, that "Christ being come as a high priest of good things to come, by the greater and more perfect tabernacle, one not made with hands, that is, not belonging to this creation; moreover, not by blood of goats and calves, but by His own blood, He entered in once for ever into the Holy of holies, effecting an eternal redemption." It is through the tabernacle—a tabernacle of the other world, belonging to the world of glorification—that entrance is made into the holy place, *i.e.* as everywhere where ἡ σκηνή and τὰ ἅγια are distinguished,—the holiest of all. The two, moreover, are distinguished in the future world, although separated by no dividing wall. The holiest of all—τὰ ἅγια—is the place of God absolutely elevated above place and time. This place of God is not anywhere in the region of the *created*. It is heaven beyond all heaven, filling everything, without being limited by anything whatever; it is the uncreated heaven of God, His eternal *doxa*. But God the Eternal is He who constitutes space and time. He reveals Himself to His creatures in a manner that is appreciable according to laws of space and time. He reveals Himself thus also to them who have entered into the repose of eternity. Their life is rooted in eternity; but it is lived there, not outside of those forms which are inseparable from all created existence. Accordingly there is a heaven of glory which does not belong to the portions of the world-system which were created once for all, and yet is somewhere,—to wit, continually

[1] Schöttgen, *Horæ Hebraicæ et Talmudicæ*, p. 1212.

produced and brought forth by God's will there, and throughout there, and only there, where God will reveal Himself in His bodily glory to angels and men. There also is that σκηνή, or rather, this heaven of glory is that σκηνή, through which Christ entered into the doxa (John xvii. 5), or the essence of the Godhead self-revealed to Himself. "Against this distinction," observes Hofmann,[1] "the remembrance appears to me to be sufficient, that thereby both designations are applied concerning its condition to the Old Testament sanctuary." But this condition is there indeed fully justified. The tabernacle is, in the form of expression adopted by Isaiah, the place of the heavenly altar of incense (Isa. vi. 6), and the holiest of all is the throne of the Lord: these two are not separated, for the borders of His robe fill the temple; but in order to attain to the throne, which is its infinite background, the place of the altar of incense must be passed through. On this throne Christ is seated at the right hand of the Majesty, having passed through the outer tabernacle, or, as it is called in Isaiah, the Hêchal. Subsequently this is the place of the angels; now, moreover, a place of blessed men. And the *sanctum sanctorum*, where now the God-man is enthroned with God, by the power of Christ's atonement once for all accomplished, is not now, as it was here below, veiled, obstructed, and unapproachable, but manifest and open to the blissful inhabitants of the σκηνή by the power of our High Priest enthroned there, and ruling in the σκηνή.

Psychology is not called upon to say more upon these things; but to the inquiry, whether souls transplanted into the invisible world have from that time an existence bearing no relation to the world, to space, and to time, it may perhaps propose this question in order to answer it in the negative on scriptural ground. That which we call, in a metaphysical sense, eternity, Scripture calls the absolute life of God.[2] He who has God, through Christ, dwelling in him, has God's absolute life for

---

[1] *Schriftbeweis*, 2, i. 412.
[2] Boethius, *de consolatione philosophiæ*, v. 6, defines thoroughly, according to Scripture, æternitas est interminabilis vitæ tota simul et perfecta possessio, remarking by way of explanation: Quod interminabilis vitæ plenitudinem totam pariter comprehendit ac possidet, cui neque futuri quidquam absit, nec præteriti fluxerit, id æternum esse jure perhibetur.

his own living foundation, and is therefore rooted in eternity. It is thus even here below, and in the other world it becomes manifest. That which the God-blessed man only perceives here below, when he is withdrawn to the innermost ground of his spiritual life, becomes in the other state manifest even in his outer life. When the eternal life that is latent in us shall be emancipated from the conditionality of time and space, which has become by sin a painful restraint, then we shall become, as internally, so also externally, exalted above time and space. Just as for God a thousand years are as one day (Ps. xc. 4), and one day as a thousand years (2 Pet. iii. 8),—*i.e.* as a thousand years are for Him, who pervades them all, like a vanishing point—and, moreover, the most minute time is not so minute that He could not in it perfect the greatest matter, the work of a millennium,—so then will no time seem to us too long or too short, no space too wide or too narrow. We shall still be living in time and space, but in such a way that in the midst of the course of æons, and in the midst of our movement from one divine dwelling-place to another, nevertheless our existence floats in the limitless freedom of eternity, and is founded in the still sabbath of eternity. It is the principle of everlasting love which in heaven pervades the forms of time and of space, and makes them the most appropriate conditions of the free and blissful personal self-power of the creatures that dwell there; whereas in Hades or in hell the principle of eternal wrath pervades the forms of time and space, and changes them into those which in this world have emptied their being of all their eternal and divine substance, in endlessly afflicting and tormenting fetters.

As, therefore, eternity and infinity are in such a way immanent in time and space, that these forms of existence continue to subsist for the creature, unabrogated even in the future world, therefore the blessed souls—which are within the range of eternity and infinity, so far as on the one hand the foundation of their life is there, but on the other hand, are within the range of time and space wherein they manifest themselves and their life—find themselves absolutely penetrated by eternity and infinity, and therefore these are no limits prejudicial to their blessedness. Their ground of life is the Godhead, into which the Redeemer has gone back as the God-man. They are with

Christ (Phil. i. 23). Even in this life they were, in respect of their inmost personal life, in Him; but now they have departed out of the body of sin and death, and they are at home with Him (2 Cor. v. 6–8). They are naked (2 Cor. v. 3), for they have put off the mortal body, and have not yet received it back glorified. Yet, moreover, they are not naked: for because they have put on Christ here below, and have been nourished with His flesh and blood, their true nature, now released from the body of sin and death, comes to a manifestation all the more serene and undisturbed; and already this manifestation is a clothing for their nakedness. But not only this: the grace of God in Christ, which even here below had put on them the garments of salvation, adorns them also in that future world with garments of glory. The white robes promised by Christ to those that overcome, temporarily supply the place to them of the glorification of their bodies; and the assurance that they may await this glorification, and all that they will have in it with certainty, is given to them and pledged to them by the contemplation of their Saviour risen again and glorified, and by the close unchecked intercourse with Him from which Mary Magdalene was repelled when He cried to her, "Touch me not, for I am not yet ascended unto my Father." Now He is ascended; and nothing further separates Him and the loving souls who have ascended after Him, whom even here below He has fed with His body, and has given to drink of His blood.

THE RELATION OF SOULS TO THEIR SOULLESS CORPOREITY.

Sec. VII.

"THE souls of the righteous are in God's hand, and there shall no torment touch them" (Wisd. iii. 1). This assertion of an apocryphal book is conformed to the sense of canonical Scripture, in proportion as it is certain that there is a justifying grace which delivers from wrath and its effects. When, therefore, Job (xiv. 21) says of the dead,

> "Should his sons come to honour, he knoweth it not;
> Or into affliction, he perceiveth it not:
> Only his own flesh suffereth pain,
> And his own soul mourneth,"—

it might thence be concluded, with the addition of Isa. lxvi. 24, Judith xvi. 17, that the process of bodily corruption casts its painful reflection on the separated souls; but the souls of the righteous are in peace, and, to use the words of Mayfart,[1] wait for the resurrection of their bodies with longing, but still not with pain, but with joy.

Yet an assumption underlies that representation of Job, darkened as it is by spiritual opposition,—an assumption which meets us everywhere in the Holy Scripture,—that the union of the soul and its body, namely, is indeed severed by death, but is not annihilated. "The soul," says Göschel,[2] "proves itself even in death the middle term; it performs even after death the function of mediating between body and spirit; it maintains during the external separation deep within the threads of the connection of all the three powers. The continuous life of the spirit preserves the connection with the forsaken body and the bodily life in its memory; and there continues also between the soul of the spirit and the dead body, during the intermediate period, a secret relation, somewhat akin to a relation of polarity, a mutual attraction, a *rapport*." There needs, after what was said in the fifth section, no further proof of the scriptural character of this assertion. But there are still at our disposal other proofs.

When the son of the woman of Sarepta died, Elijah stretched himself three times upon the corpse, and prayed that the soul of the child might come back to it (1 Kings xvii. 21). In a

[1] *Himmlisches Jerusalem* (1664), book ii. ch. i.
[2] *Letzte Dinge*, pp. 172, 150, comp. also Heyder, *l.c.*, p. 47 : " Quæritur, num distracta ea, quæ in homine vivo sunt conjuncta, nullo jam cohæreant modo ? Vix credibile id quidem videbitur, si ad illam respexeris rationem quæ inter corpus, animam, spiritum e sacrorum autorum sententia intercedit;" and Beck, *Seelenlehre*, p. 40 : "The individual living constitution appears rent and loosened asunder, but still not unconditionally abolished; but as, in a chemical analysis, the agents obtain a new union, so, while there remains to the soul its capacity of perception as akin to the body, to the spirit the capacity of soul, they must still be held together by the united effort after a new living formation of the dissolved individuality."

similar manner, Elisha in prayer lays himself upon the corpse of the child of the Shunammite woman, mouth to mouth, eyes to eyes, hands to hands, pressing himself closely to it, and thus warms the chilled flesh, and brings it to that point at which the boy sneezes and opens his eyes (2 Kings iv. 34). In both these cases death is not only apparent, but it has actually ensued. But that the soul in both cases can be, and must have been, brought back, entitles us to conclude that its relation to the body is still one that is closer, in proportion to the shortness of the time that it has left it. Precisely in the same way is explained the wondrous miracle that is recorded in 2 Kings xiii. 21). Moreover, the New Testament raisings of the dead (Jairus' daughter, the widow's son of Nain, Tabitha) occur shortly after death has taken place. Only the raising of Lazarus that had been dead four days, as an isolated act of the kind by the future Raiser of the dead, makes an exception. Otherwise all the miracles of resurrection are recalls of the soul, as it were, on the way from this world to the other. We say "as it were;" for in fact the soul, from the moment at which the thread of life is severed, is in the other world, but still in such a lively relation of itself to its forsaken body, that a miraculous reunion with the latter is permissible.[1]

It is, moreover, consistent with this, that in the Old Testament, according to a mode of speech which occurs for the first time wholly unartificially in Lev. xix. 28, the corpse is called נֶפֶשׁ.[2] It is a task for biblical psychology to solve the enigma of this *usus loquendi*. J. D. Michaelis asks whether נֶפֶשׁ, in the sense of dead body, does not probably refer to the verb נָפַשׁ in

---

[1] *Vid.* Schubert, *Gesch. der Seele*, ii. 446. The Talmud says, with reference to 1 Sam. xxviii. 3, "Twelve months, as long as the body is still uncorrupted, the soul hovers up and down," etc. (*b. Sabbath* 152*b*). That the soul continues still in a certain association with the corpse, and through it with the earthly life, is a view very widely diffused in antiquity.

[2] That נֶפֶשׁ has this meaning is shown by Num. xix. 13, comp. 11, where it is an explanatory permutative of מֵת: comp. נֶפֶשׁ מֵת, in association with the genitive, Lev. xxi. 11, Num. vi. 6; טְמֵא־נֶפֶשׁ, Lev. xxii. 4, Hag. ii. 13; comp. לְנֶפֶשׁ, Lev. xxi. 1, Num. v. 2, ix. 6, vii. 10; חָטָא עַל־נֶפֶשׁ, Num. vi. 11; שָׂרַט לְנֶפֶשׁ, Lev. xix. 28. Therewith accords the talmudic and Syriac use of נֶפֶשׁ, *nafscho*, in the meaning—a monument, *e.g.* in the beautiful expression of Simon b. Gamaliel, "No נְפָשׁוֹת are raised to the pious,

the sense of *exspirare*? Impossible, because the verb only means to breathe, *respirare*, not to breathe out, to expire, ἐκπνέειν. Gesenius thinks that נֶפֶשׁ מֵת is used as of *mortuus quis*; but, on the other hand, that נֶפֶשׁ means nothing but *aliquis*, implies that נֶפֶשׁ, even in respect to itself alone, is already the name of the corpse. Böttcher explains in a similar way, that נֶפֶשׁ implies the person, and only (first of all in the association נֶפֶשׁ מֵת) the corpse, for the reason that even the unsouled body was regarded by the Hebrews still as a person;[1] but he proceeds upon the false assumption that נֶפֶשׁ cannot by itself alone signify the corpse (which is contradicted by the previously occurring mode of speech), and substantially the explanation is as good as none: for as נֶפֶשׁ, even in the sense of person, maintains, for the consciousness of the Hebrew speech—its fundamental significance—the question recurs, how the corpse can be called נֶפֶשׁ, *i.e.* soul = person. Rather might it be said—since, according to biblical and especially Old Testament representation, the death of man is a death of his soul—that the corpse is called נֶפֶשׁ as a dead soul; but even this is not likely to be possible, as the soul, according to biblical ideas, dies indeed, but is not, in the sense of materialism, mortal, but, separated from the decaying corpse (פֶּגֶר, גְּוִיָּה, πτῶμα, σῶμα), continues to subsist without annihilation or remanation. How then? Is the corpse perhaps called נֶפֶשׁ as being divested of soul? Such a nomenclature *per antiphrasin* is in Hebrew without example. Even in Greek it is true the butterfly is called ψυχή, but not the chrysalis or the caterpillar.[2] Or is the corpse called נֶפֶשׁ, soul,

their works are their honourable remembrance" (*Schekalim* ii. 7); and in the Syriac translation of 1 Macc. xiii. 28, of the monument with seven pyramids which Simon Maccabeus erected to his fathers and their sons. This נֶפֶשׁ does not signify the tombstone, but a stone edifice built over the grave with exalted walls. See thereupon *Zunz zur Gesch. u. Literatur*, p. 390; comp. Perles, in Frankel's *Monatsschrift*, 1861, p. 392.

[1] See *de inferis*, sec. 127. Knobel also says, נֶפֶשׁ of the corpse signifies the person as dead.

[2] J. Grimm, *Mythologie*, ii. 789 (ed. iii.), and especially Böttcher's *Ideas on Art-Mythology*, vol. ii. (1836), Cursus 4; the fable of Amor and Psyche. On sarcophagi, Eros and Psyche mean the soul, as it were, having burst the cocoon, escaped from the dungeon, reunited with the heavenly body, the object of its longing; comp. Ottfried Müller, *Handbuch der Archäologie*, p. 591 (ed. ii.).

per euphemismum? This explanation would be relatively the best, but only in default of another which should be better.

The true reason of the designation is found in the impression which a corpse makes. The body of a person just dead gives a far more direct impression of soul than the body of a living person. The lively and plain bodily effected activity has ceased; its psychical background appears in the solemn stillness that has now supervened as an open secret. The whole internal nature of the man lies in the corpse, as if turned out before us; we look there into the depth of the soul's struggle and of the soul's peace under which the separation of the soul and the body ensued; and the soul still hovers, to brighten or to disfigure, over its structure so lately forsaken. Therefore every corpse makes an impression so gloomy, spiritual, and phantom-like; and therefore it is called נֶפֶשׁ. The corpse of the person just dead still bears the recent traces of its soul, which, separating itself, has, as it were, impressed itself upon it: it is the dwelling of the soul that is left behind; it is, as it were, itself that which was soul. Therefore the Romans also call it *manes* (*e.g.* Lucan: *inhumatos condere manes*); therefore in Homer occurs the notion, that the Psyches in Hades have the appearance of the dead person at the moment of his death (*Od.* λ. 38–43); therefore, also, an old funeral urn itself has the inscription, Ἐν μύροις, ὦ τέκνον, ἡ ψυχή.[1]

In thus designating the corpse, therefore, is affirmed the principle that, although death abrogates the living association of the soul and body, it still does not neutralize the relation of the former to the latter. Soon after the occurrence of death, this relation is still so near a one, that the corpse may be called נֶפֶשׁ. As corruption gradually advances, it then becomes more and more vague, but still continues to subsist undestroyed; so that although, on the one hand, the resurrection is indeed a new creative work of divine omnipotence, yet, on the other, to use the words of Gregory of Nyssa,[2] it is a concurrence of things that belong to one another, and of elements combining again by virtue of a mysterious natural attraction (τῷ

---

[1] Gaetano Marini, *Iscrizioni antiche*, p. 184.

[2] *Vid. de hominis opificio*, p. 116, and especially the detailed elucidation of the matter in the *Dialogue with Makrina*, pp. 213–219, in vol. iii. of the Paris edition.

οἰκείων συνδρομὴ, ἀρρήτῳ τινὶ τῇ τῆς φύσεως ὁλκῇ πρὸς τὸ ἴδιον ἐπειγομένων). Still even a later and well-known physiologist says that, in the relation which still continues to subsist between the soul and the earth to which its body is committed, are based the conditions of the restoration of the organic individuality dissolved by death, or the re-creation of a new bodily life for it.[1]

[1] Purkinje, in R. Wagner, *H. W.* iii. ii. 470.

APPENDIX.

UPON THE INTERMEDIATE STATE OF SOULS.

By JOHANN HEINRICH URSINUS.

It is certain and undeniable, if it be only rightly understood, that even the souls of the righteous—although, according to their nature, so far as it alone is concerned, they live immortally, and by God's grace are blessed through Christ, and in heaven—are nevertheless subjected to the condition of death, or, as the fathers say, to its laws, sway, and dominion, so long as they are severed from their bodies. The Holy Scripture describes such a state by the word *Scheôl*, as a common place whither all men descend, good and evil (Gen. xxxvii. 35, xlii. 38; Ps. lv. 15). No one can deliver a soul from the hand of hell, *i.e.* from the might and power of death (Ps. lxxxix. 48); and thus death and hell are usually associated, when not only the godless, as Ps. xlix. 15, but also the elect are spoken of (Hos. xiii. 14), until the Lord by His glorious appearing shall destroy death, the last enemy (1 Cor. xv. 26), and the land of the dead shall perish (Isa. xxvi. 19);[1] which passage nobody interprets better than St John in his Revelation (xx. 14), that the Lord shall cast death and hell into the lake of fire. Thus hell is distinguished from the lake of fire, and therefore signifies nothing else than the kingdom and dominion of death, which Isaiah calls the land of the dead, indicating that after the resurrection none of His elect shall either die

---

[1] Ursinus follows the translation of Luther (which, according to the Masoretic vocalization, is impossible to be justified); but Luther himself had previously translated—as the passage is generally rendered now—*and the land shall cast out its dead.*

or be under the mastery of death as heretofore; but death and all his might, dominion, and kingdom, shall only take effect upon the condemned—which is the second and eternal death. Even as St Paul says of Christ our Head, Henceforth He shall die no more, death shall have no more dominion over Him (Rom. vi. 9). And as now such a state of death as that to which all men are subjected is named in Holy Scripture a land of the dead, and *Scheôl*, the grave; not as if it were a natural positive place in the world, but according to its custom *per condescensum* of speaking thereof after human fashion;— therefore the fathers of the church cannot be blamed who retain such a manner of speaking; thus they elsewhere do not reject the divine doctrine of the blissful condition of souls, but believe that all souls, because they are in the like state of death, by reason of the severance of their bodies in a similar manner, await the last day in a common keeping, in an invisible place, but that they nevertheless, as immortal spirits, have also for themselves their appointed dwellings; and especially the faithful souls, when they must go the way of all flesh, in the midst of death, immediately press through the dark valley into heaven, to eternal bliss. And this is the common dwelling, and, as it were, the grave of souls, of which *Dr. Lutherus* at various times makes mention, of which those who see the truth and yet wilfully abuse it make so much complaint. For he certainly expressly establishes both positions: that the souls *ratione compositi* in respect of their natural condition into which they are created by God,—that body and soul should be one man,—are subjected to the common dominion of death and its laws; and yet, moreover, *ratione sui* in respect of their own spiritual immortal nature, retain their life outside of all the power of death, and are either blessed in heaven or cursed in hell.[1] Hence follows of itself,

Secondly, That the souls of the righteous are confessedly still

---

[1] Thus Hades is no place, but a state; so that the separated souls of the righteous are at the same time in heaven and in Hades. Scripture nowhere thus expresses itself, and certainly does not wish thus to be understood. If Hades were actually only the name of a state, it could not then be said that the souls of the righteous are in Hades: they are in eternal life, which they had even here below, free from the troubles that in this world accompany their possession.

until the last day, in a position constrained, unnatural, and incomplete, contrary to their nature and the final cause for which they were created by God; and thus they have not yet attained their *consummatam beatitudinem*, as Bernhard rightly says. This is the common doctrine of all the fathers of the church, thoroughly based in God's word and Christian teaching, whence we know that the soul was not for itself before and external to the body, independently with God, but was first given after the formation of the body to man by God in the creation; that accordingly the soul by the intention and plan of its Creator an *ens incompletum*, was indeed thus constituted and endowed with immortality, that even after death it may and should remain, subsist, and live apart from the body, although contrary to its nature and final cause. Thence, moreover, is gathered incontrovertibly the resurrection of bodies, because it is impossible that the soul should continue in an unnatural state for ever, into which it has fallen *per accidens* by means of sin, and for which God did not create it. For although after death souls live and praise the Highest, yet they are not the entire man (Ecclus. xvii. 27), as the Platonic wisdom was apt to fancy, but only an essential piece of man. On this account, that God might not have created man in vain,—which is contrary to His wisdom,—man must, although by death perchance he have ceased to be a man,[1] nevertheless, by resurrection from the dead, again become a man, and remain one to eternity; that God's honour, either in respect of His mercy to the elect, or His justice to the condemned, but to all in respect of His power and divine wisdom, might be manifested and praised to eternity.

Accordingly, (3) the soul of the righteous remains from death to resurrection in a mediate condition; blessed indeed in heaven, so far as in its own nature it is an immortal soul, and still not yet perfect, so far as it is a human soul. And in this understanding, the Romish theologians rightly said at

---

[1] Not so: the body without the soul is, indeed, only a thing; but the spiritual soul, as that which personifies man, is, even without the body, still a person. Death robs the human personality of the body belonging to it, as its immediate means and object of attesting itself; but the soul, which in its double-sidedness is the peculiar essential form of man, continues to exist, and is therefore the man in respect of the essence of his spiritual corporeity.

Ferrara,[1] that the souls of the blessed, according to their nature, considered specially for itself, so far as they are souls, had already their perfect blessedness. On the other hand, the fathers were also right in saying that such souls, so far as they were human souls, and are so constituted that they inhabit bodies, and are meant to be an essential part of man, had not yet their perfect blessedness. If there were some among the ancients (which cannot be denied) who left such a distinction out of consideration, and attributed to the souls of the righteous only a *privativam beatitudinem*, or such a blessedness as that of being in their own nature freed from all evil, they have given too little attention to the matter. On the other hand, Popish teachers of the present day make too much of it, in assigning to such souls entire perfect blessedness in such a way, that they had nothing more to expect or to receive beyond the glorification of their bodies. We adopt the middle course, with all the fathers. And in this concurs also the saying of the ancients, that the souls of the righteous had already received *primam stolam*, the first white robe, but still had to expect *duplicia vel binas stolas*.

But that (4) the perfect contemplation of the holy threefold nature belongs to this separate blessedness of the righteous souls, —as the decree of the Florentine *Concilii* declares,—remains a matter of dispute. Bellarmine, who takes great pains to maintain this, has not strictly proved it by any single clear testimony of Holy Scripture—by any single express affirmation of the old church teachers—by any reasonable argument. The condemned, says Bellarmine, are already in torment (Luke xvi.); therefore the righteous are already in bliss. Answer: But as the former are not yet in perfect torment (even the devils are not, as Bellarmine himself teaches); therefore the latter also are not in perfect bliss. Further, the day of death of the saints is their day of birth; therefore it is a beginning of their blessedness, for when they die on earth they are born in heaven. Answer: Amen! A beginning in the same way as a new-born infant looks upon the light, lives upon earth, is his father's heir, is nourished, cared for, beloved by his parents, is honoured by the whole household as an heir, learns to know his father day

[1] At the Council of Ferrara-Florence (1438–39), where the above specified view of the Latins obtained the victory over the Greeks.

by day, until a perfect man is formed therefrom; so also it is in this case. Further, the hope which is deferred, pains the souls: therefore the souls have at once what they hope for without delay; for it is not fit that they should be pained which have no sins. Answer: If the conclusion were true, the souls in heaven would have to hope for no resurrection of their bodies, no avenging judgment of God upon their enemies, no new world and heavenly new Jerusalem. But such a hope, because it is wholly certain, and unfailing, and depends upon the time which God has appointed, causes neither fear nor pain, but yet certifies that the souls have not yet attained the perfect good.

But if the souls of the righteous regard their own blissful condition, no time is long to them; no time is, in fact, long: they have already what alone, according to God's counsel and promise, is proper for their satisfaction, and can desire for themselves in such a state nothing beyond; because they know that, according to God's will, they ought for themselves to desire nothing further. The blessed souls live in no human time that is reckoned by days, months, and years, but in an angelic time, where a thousand years are as a watch in the night; even as God's eternity is only a little point—so little, that nothing there is past or future, and so infinitely great, that it comprehends and circumscribes in itself all times. Seven years Jacob served Laban for Rachel with extreme labour; yet they appeared to him as it were but a single day, for the love that he bore her (Gen. xxix. 20). How, then, could the time be long to elected souls in the home of their Father, more beloved than all, and with their Bridegroom, the fairest of all? But because they know that God has prepared for them a still greater blessedness; know that their brethren on earth are still engaged in contest; know that their adversary the devil still has dominion upon the earth, as if there were no God in heaven, and His vengeance were to sleep for ever; know that, separated from their bodies through the power of death, they must live out of their constituted position; know that everything of such a kind comes from sin (for death came into the world by sin, so that it has dominion over all men till Christ shall put an end to its dominion by His glorious appearing);—therefore they long thereafter with heartfelt longing, but still in moderation, without fear, anguish, fretfulness, impatience, wholly acquiescing in God's will and ordinance, and well satisfied. That there is still something wanting to infinite perfection, disturbs them as little, as it does a youth that he is not yet a man. But they long that body and soul should be crowned together on the great coronation day of the Lord. Their longing especially is indulged after the redemption of their bodies and reunion with them, as Bernard writes. This natural craving is so strong in them, that even their whole love and desire does not yet freely go forth towards God; but, as it were, it is indented and wrinkled, etc. [The bold passage occurs in *Sermo* iii. *in festo omnium Sanctorum:* Unde hoc tibi, O misera caro, O fœtida, unde tibi hoc? Animæ sanctæ, quas propria Deus insignivit imagine, te desiderant, quas redemit proprio sanguine te exspectant, et ipsarum sine te compleri lætitia, perfici gloria, consummari beatitudo non potest. Adeo viget in eis desiderium hoc naturale, ut necdum tota earum affectio libere pergat in Deum sed contrahatur quodammodo et rugam faciat, cum inclinantur desiderio tui.] Bernard regards the longing question of the souls (Apoc. vi. 9) as proceeding not so much from desire after judgment, as rather from longing after the resurrection and glorification of their bodies, which will follow the day of judgment. The holy souls are *sine macula* (Apoc. xiv. 5), but to this well-justified longing they have aspired, yet not *sine ruga*. The end of the history of redemption, however, is a glorified church, which has neither spot nor wrinkle.

VII.
THE RESURRECTION AND CONSUMMATION.

Erimus idem qui nunc, nec alii post, Dei quidem cultores apud Deum semper, superinduti substantia propria æternitatis; profani vero et qui non integri ad Deum in pœna æque jugis ignis, habentes ex ipsa natura ejus divinam scilicet subministrationem incorruptibilitatis.

TERTULLIANUS (*Apologeticus*).

SPIRIT AND SOUL IN THE ACT OF RESURRECTION.

Sec. I.

THE creation of man began with the formation of his body: for the design of the creative wisdom contemplated a twofold being, which should unite in itself spirit and nature in combination, and should in itself peaceably harmonize the spirit-world with the material-world. Sin frustrated the effectuation of this exalted destination of man, but redemption made it once again possible: it is now completed by death, in the way of a new-creative miracle. If death were not an actual disembodiment of man, but a loosening, as of the spiritual nature of his soul, so also of the true nature of his corporeity concealed here below,—of an inner body, which is further organized out of the atoms of the higher world of light, in a manner conformable to his progressive development,[1]—it could not be comprehended for what purpose the miracle of the resurrection was still needed; for the death itself of those who die in the Lord would then be their resurrection. But Scripture looks upon the death as an unclothing of man from that element of his personality which makes him the point of union of both worlds.

---

[1] Thus Schelling, in the beautiful discourse now first published, *On the Connection of Nature with the Spirit-World*, Works, Div. i. vol. ix.; and thus also Fichte, in his work upon the *Idea of Personality*, and elsewhere. "Death is a necessary event in the development of life,—the complete separation of the internal body from its copy woven out of the elements, and even in this world constantly changing and transforming itself;" comp. Böhner, *Naturforschung und Kulturleben* (1858), p. 222: "Bodily death is an accelerated process of life, in which absolutely nothing is lost; but spirit and body only unfold themselves according to their further destination." In his *philosophia secunda*, however, Schelling teaches in the future life an intermediate state of mere being and of extinguished capability requiring a resurrection, and thus teaches a state of restraint like a sleep of the soul. See *Works*, Div. ii. vol. iv. 210.

The corporeity of souls that have passed over into the other world is only a phenomenal one, not a material, and therefore no actual one That which is effected in man by Christ's word and sacrament, comes also in this phenomenal corporeity to provisional manifestation; but their actual bodies lie in the dust of the grave in hope: for they have received here below the tincture of immortality, by virtue of which they cannot abide in death; and this tincture of their immortality is at the same time the power of the glorification of the world.

Therefore the separated souls long for reunion with their bodies; nevertheless, they are unable to complete the reanimation of these latter. It is a creative act of God the Father, completed through the Son, and brought about by the Holy Ghost, whereby they receive back their bodies. This act of new creation is different in manifold ways from the creative act of the primeval beginning. There, when the body was formed, the personifying spirit who was to endow it with soul was not yet present: here the self-conscious spirit is already at hand; and the creative restoration of the body—with which it has already lived through a history conscious to its memory, —is an act of God, which does not come to it unforeseen, but is longed for by it, is guaranteed to it, and, as in this state, so in the world to come also, is prepared for it. This is the psychological point of view under which the transaction of the resurrection falls. It is asked, How is the self-conscious spirit related to this act of restoration? Does the beginning of a new bodily life resemble the embryonic commencement of the old one, so far as the self-conscious spirit is pressed back into unconsciousness; and attaining from this once more into full and waking consciousness, does it find itself within the created and restored body?

No express answer to this question is given us in the Holy Scripture. On the contrary, it says, without reconciling the two passages, just as definitely that the separated souls are partly in heaven and partly in Hades, as that all the dead shall arise from their graves. It is confessed what mistakes have been made by the adoption of one of these two facts, and shutting one's eyes to the other. Either it was thought that the souls were even to the resurrection day in a state of sleep with their corrupting bodies, or " resurrection" was explained as a designation used only figuratively and by way of accommodation.

We let both facts stand, even although we should be unable to reconcile them. Nevertheless, the informations of the Scripture upon the resurrection of the dead are so copious, that even psychologic consideration finds a point of junction in order to sketch for itself a picture of the mysterious procedure conformed to revelation.[1]

The restoration of the human body results when God the triune "supplies to the soul from the then glorified world of nature materials for the new formation of its body, similar to those of which its earthly body was formed, and with which, when the soul impresses upon them the form of its inner spiritual body, its spiritual nature may attain to full manifestation even in the external body."[2] The assertion *anima corpus suum creat* (thus formulated by Erigena), which we have already rejected in respect of the primitive beginning and the propagation of man, we must here also reject. The soul is neither the creative principle of the body, nor the plastic and organizing principle of its materiality. None the less on that account is it true, that the formation of our bodies in the womb is not completed without the co-operation of the soul; and when it is added thereto, that death, although it severs the living union of the soul and the body, yet, as we have shown in the concluding paragraph of

---

[1] Even J. P. Lange (*Biblisch-theologische Erörterungen in Studien und Krit.* 1836) and Kling (the same, 1839, p. 512) attempt this; but the former in a manner that reminds one of Origen—too boldly picturing; the latter in a way which touches the truth of the resurrection as a going forth from the grave, and otherwise wholly incapable of being carried into effect even ideally. On the other hand, among the fathers of the church is hardly found a disposition thereto, not even in Tertullian's work, *de resurrectione carnis*, although this outweighs all which had previously been written upon resurrection.

[2] Thus Schöberlein, *Jahrbb.* 1861, p. 77. Our own previous idea did not sufficiently observe the sameness of the future body with the present. The question, whether the glorification of the earth will precede or follow the resurrection, we leave unanswered; but in any case, the materiality of the resurrection body is essentially of a similar nature with the materiality of the glorified earth (as also v. Rudloff, p. 421, supposes), and essentially identical with the materiality of the body that has become subject to corruption (as we maintain with Schöberlein, *Stud. u. Krit.* 1860, p. 164, against v. Rudloff).

the foregoing division, does not destroy the real relation of the soul to its corrupting and perishing body, it becomes more than probable that this real relation, enhanced to attractive power, is drawn into the creative restoration of the body. Thus Thomas Aquinas and Dante conceive. And, in fact, assumption and glorification in pure passivity of the soul are not perhaps conceivable.[1] Nevertheless, the transaction is a mystery, and moreover an uncompleted mystery, and the completion is, even although many creative potencies interact within it still an absolutely creative mystery, not successive, but momentary.[2]

The creative act of restoration, and the yearning, joyous eagerness of the soul for its body to be again received from death—these are two acts that meet one another, and coincide in one lightning-like now (comp. 1 Cor. xv. 52 with 1 Thess. iv. 16). The reunion results in waking consciousness of the soul, but in a condition of pleasurable awe, in which all reflecting will and thought are merged; and the formation of the body which the soul finds in the moment of reunion as already prepared, is a mystery withdrawn from its testimony and its knowledge. Even the transformation of the bodies of the living occurs so rapidly, that it withdraws itself from all observation, and no subsequent reflection is able to fathom the secret.

The resurrection body is not, as was the body of the first created man, psychical, with the destination that it should become pneumatical; but it is immediately pneumatical, because the spirit which, by means of the soul, seizes possession of it, finds itself in the position of perfection (Heb. xii. 23). The soul, besides, gives to that which in design is formed upon it, in the measure of the immaterial shadow which is left to it, its perfected individual stamp; for everything which it has here

---

[1] See Göschel, *Der Mensch diesseits und jenseits*, p. 46.

[2] Gregory of Nyssa, in his *Dialogue with Macrina* (*Opp.* ed. Paris, iii. 212-216), goes too far when he compares the soul, in respect of the dissolved elements of its body, to an artist who knows how to unmix the colours of a picture blended together and dispersed, and to combine them into the same picture, or to a potter who can easily find the broken pieces of several vessels from the rude mass of clay among which they are mixed; or when he says that all the elements of the body run together, like many strings in the soul, and therefore $\mu\iota\tilde{\alpha}\ \tau\tilde{\eta}\ \tau\tilde{\eta}s\ \psi\upsilon\chi\tilde{\eta}s\ \delta\upsilon\nu\acute{\alpha}\mu\epsilon\iota$ can be again drawn together and combined. What is so said of the soul, is only true of God, and of it as co-operating.

below collected to itself as a treasure, as Macarius (*Hom.* v. 8) says, will then become manifest and openly plain outwardly in the body. That shadow of the spirits of perfected righteous men was already a type of the glorification which is now bodily perfected in them when they have again attained their bodies,[1] which cannot abide in death after the Holy Ghost has made them His habitation (1 Cor. vi. 19; Rom. viii. 11[2]); and Christ's body and blood have become for them the tincture of everlasting life (φάρμακον ἀθανασίας). It is obvious that the sacramental gifts do not remain with the corpses. They become absorbed by the full possession and full enjoyment of Christ, into which the separated soul enters. That the Lord gives to these, in their state of intermediate corporeity, to enjoy the vision and the embrace of His gracious glorified humanity, is a fact related to the sacramental gifts, in the same way that the perfect actual performance is to the earnest that guarantees it. It is, however, the effect of the sacramental gifts, that bodies do not corrupt without an expectation of the restoration of their nature.

The human body formed by the hand of God, since it has become materialistic, is as an overcrusted mystery. It is wholly inconceivable that this mystery is not one day to become revealed to the joy of all beings. The resurrection will place it

---

[1] "The adjustment of the identity of the rising body with the body of this state," says Nitzsch, *System*, sec. 217, obs. 2, "will have to be sought for in the same corporeity in which the soul that is being severed remains ; and which, according to the constitution of the cosmical sphere to which it now first of all in every case pertains, and according to the impulses of its own internal formation, is changed for it even to that point at which it attains the final condition." Martensen (sec. 276, obs.) even calls this preparatory process a "concealed natural development" (*i.e.* development of the soul's nature that is not to be thought of as purely out of nature). On Kling, who describes this oddly, we have already spoken. The view of these inquirers (including also Julius Müller, *Sünde*, ii. 416) of the intermediate corporeity is a different one from ours. To us this is an absolutely immaterial—purely psychical—phenomenon. A substantial (not merely typical) preparation of the resurrection body on behalf of the soul is to us inconceivable.

[2] Not only internal but external reasons (see Reiche, *Comm. criticus*, i. 54, 67) declare here for the reading διὰ τὸ ἐνοικοῦν πνεῦμα ἐν ὑμῖν,—διὰ of the objective moving cause, according to 2 Cor. v. 5 and other places. The reading διὰ τοῦ, κ.τ.λ., is contrary to the doctrinal scheme of the apostle.

in the clearest light. But as yet we are not in a position to make to ourselves a clear conception of the pneumatic bodies of those who are risen again. If we attempt it,—as, for example, Origen did, who attributed to the risen, σῶμα αἰθέριόν τε καὶ σφαιροειδὲς τῷ σχήματι, — our powerlessness and limitation prove themselves here, if anywhere at all. They will become of like form with the glorified body of the second Adam (Phil. iii. 21). They will be as the body of the first Adam prior to the establishment of the sexual distinction (Div. II. Sec. V. VI.); but more glorious than this, because they will have attained the glory which the psychical body of the first Adam ought to have attained, but forfeited by the fall.[1] They will also be actual human bodies, essentially even in respect of form identical with those of this present state, and yet in quality infinitely different from them. The perfected realization of the human

[1] Tertullian (*de resurr.* c. 60-62) maintains the continuance of all human members, notwithstanding the cessation of the sexual and other functions, *et hodie*, says he, with respect to fasting and chastity, *vacare intestinis et pudendis licebit*. In order to weaken the proof from Luke xx. 36, he says, that as angels appearing in human form (*e.g.* Gen. xviii.) maintained their angelic nature, so also men in the angelic form of the future life may maintain their bodily nature: Non magis solemnibus carnis obnoxii sub angelico indumento quam angeli tunc solemnibus spiritus sub humano. Just so Jerome, allying himself to Tertullian, makes use of Luke xx. 35 for the purpose: Ubi dicitur; non nubent neque nubentur, sexuum diversitas demonstratur (in the *Epitaphium Paulæ*). In an altogether similar way, Hahn, *Neutest. Theol.* i. 268, and Kurtz, *Bibel und Astronomie*, iv. sec. 18 (ed. 4), express themselves; and just so decides Besser, who on 1 Cor. vi. 13 (*Bibelst.* viii.) remarks, " Stomach and intestines, in their special character of belly, serve the maintenance of this natural life. Although, therefore, the spiritual resurrection body shall have ALL ESSENTIAL PARTS of the natural body in a new manner (xv. 44), it will still be without the necessity of the belly. For the belly changes the nourishing part of the food into blood, and prepares that which is not nourishing to be again rejected. In the kingdom of glory, on the other hand, we shall so eat and drink (Matt. xxvi. 29), that the flesh and blood, glorified into spiritual life, shall be pervaded with living food, as the atmosphere is impregnated with sunbeams for the purpose of becoming transparent and warm." The direction of κοιλία is here limited, as it is by Keil (see above, p. 102, obs. 1), to the organs that serve for digestion. And certainly thus say we also: an absolute abolition of the sexual distinctions would not be different from an abolition of personal identity. But its continuance does not necessarily imply a continuance of that bodily external manifestation of it which was its characteristic in this life.

body as such, the mystery of its organism, become manifest—the heavenly antitype of its earthly type. Their identity with the bodies of this present state is not founded in similarity of material; for even now in this state this identity is contained in an unceasing origination and passing away.[1] But, moreover, it is not merely in likeness of form (εἶδος), with entire distinction of substance;[2] for such a merely formal identity as of a mould gives no satisfaction to the idea of the resurrection, and militates against the character of the grain of wheat which befits the corrupting corpse (1 Cor. xv. 42-44). The true identity lies in the mean, between the former grossly material, and the latter merely formal, identity. Within the world once created, no single atom is ever annihilated. The elementary materials whereof the now corrupted body was composed, are therefore still in existence; and the Omniscient knows where they are, and the Omnipotent can collect them together again. But, in the meanwhile, together with the world of nature in which they are laid up, they have undergone the process of fire, out of which heaven and earth issue in brighter glorification. From this glorified world, He who at first formed the body of man of the earth of Eden, brings together again the elementary materials of our bodies, in similar destination of the powers per-

[1] See Julius Müller in *Studien und Kritiken*, 1835, p. 777. "Resurrection of the flesh" is nevertheless a justifiable expression, and one that has become necessary in the face of the Origenistic doctrine of resurrection. It cannot indeed be justified from Job xix. 26, where is only expressed the hope of a future fleshless, therefore spiritual, vision of God, but perhaps from John vi. It is certainly not Pauline: see, upon the Pauline distinction between σάρξ and σῶμα, Tijssen, *Pauli Anthropologia* (Groningen, 1847), and especially Holsten, the meaning of the word ΣΑΡΞ (1855), pp. 1-6. The idea of *flesh* has, in the view of Paul, the essential characteristic of earthly material nature. The resurrection body is σῶμα, not σῶμα τῆς σαρκός. The substance, of which it is a living articulation, is not σάρξ; but that the essential characteristic of that which is earthly material in "flesh and blood" is no absolutely inalienable one, is shown by the holy communion, to which Irenæus expressly points.

[2] The Origenistic view, λόγος τις (σπερματικός) ἔγκειται τῷ σώματι, ἀφ᾽ οὗ μὴ φθειρομένου ἐγείρεται τὸ σῶμα ἐν ἀφθαρσίᾳ (c. Cels. v. 23). See Thomasius, *Origen*, p. 255. Æneas of Gaza (ed. Boissonade, pp. 65-67) cites the parable: If a statue of Achilles, made of brass, and grown old, were shattered, and an artist were to make a golden one of a like form, that would be the same Achilles (ὀφθείη ἂν χρυσοῦς ὁ πάλαι χαλκοῦς Ἀχιλλεύς, Ἀχιλλεὺς μέντοι).

vading them, and similar mingling of their essential elements, so far as this purpose and this mingling are the conditions of the individuality of each person remaining to him after sin, with its precedents and results, has been deducted; and the soul, with that form of body brought together again, takes possession of it, as a queen takes possession of her throne, and pervades it with its heavenly light, and makes it a transparent manifestation of the soul's spiritual nature, uniting itself therewith as the object of the soul's longing into a compact self-completion of its personality. The natural constitution of man had from the beginning this design, that corporeity might be elevated into the sphere of the spirit, and become a manifestation of the spirit. This purpose was withal its problem, and this problem is now solved. When the discord of the spirit and the soul shall have already ceased with the victorious irruption through death into life, the discord of the spirit and flesh which at death resulted in absolute ruin of both shall be abrogated also. Man is now, in the unity of his three constituent elements, spiritual. The synthesis which distinguishes man from the pure spirit is again established, but the dualism is compensated and balanced. In the spirit is reflected the Godhead, and in the soul the spirit, and in the body the spiritual soul. Man is now a microcosm in the position of glorification. For as God the triune fills the new world with the sevenfold *doxa*, so the human spirits created after the image of the Godhead fill with their souls which portray the divine *doxa*, their bodies that have become σώματα τῆς δόξης.[1]

Of the bodies of the ungodly this indeed cannot be said. The bodies of these also shall arise. But this cannot possibly be as spiritual. For they have not sought to attain the redemption as a renewing of the godlike actuality of their spirit. Their spirit is powerlessly imprisoned in the *turba* which has laid hold of the powers of the soul. They are psychical and fleshly, and therefore their bodies will be so also. Scripture

---

[1] The divinely-formative process which herewith is completed, is otherwise apprehended by Böhme and Baader: Soul (∾ Father), Idea (∾ Son), Spirit (∾ Holy Spirit), spiritual body (∾ eternal divine corporeity). Thus also my Elberfeld-critic: "Soul does not correspond to *doxa*; *doxa* is corporeity." Just so also v. Rudloff and Schöberlein. Let the reader test these views and ours by the Scripture!

does not expressly assert this, as it nowhere designedly declares itself in general upon the resurrection to judgment,—that night-side of the general resurrection; but that without a spiritual internal nature there cannot be a spiritual external nature, is self-evident.

It is the call to judgment penetrating through heaven and Hades, in consequence of which even the souls of the ungodly hasten to their bodies, which arise by God's creative mighty operation contemporary with the call. It occurs with that awful fear (Heb. x. 27), which even in this world shook their carnally secure peace; perhaps also not without that vain hope that is comparable to the wish of the demons (Matt. viii. 31), that they might find in their bodies a covering for the disgraceful nakedness of their souls, and a shield from God's anger. The assumption of a participation of souls in the restoration of their bodies is here, moreover, in the resurrection of the ungodly, even more inevitable. For the human body is established again, in order that man may come to stand before God's judgment in the totality, and indeed in the true physico-ethical nature of his spirit-embodied personality. The resurrection is not yet the judgment itself, but only the preparation for it. Therefore also the reconstitution of the bodies of the ungodly is no purely judicial act of God. But if it be not this, it must be supposed that the souls of the ungodly partake in the reconstitution of their bodies, so far as they express in those bodies, rising by God's might and power, the alienation from God of their individuality. In the bodies of the righteous, God sets aside everything which is the consequence of sin; and in the bodies of the ungodly, He sets aside everything which could delusively conceal their internal sinfulness; but that which is sinful itself, as well in its internal nature as in its external manifestation, is the operation of souls concurring in the act of reconstitution.

To this operation of souls, the finally decisive judgment adds the judicial operation of God. As well *turba* as *doxa* of those who have risen, there attain their final climax, their eternally valid seal.[1] For not until the blissful spiritually

---

[1] Julius Müller places the ascension of Christ in a similar relation to His resurrection, when he assumes a process from within outwards between both facts,—a process in which the Spirit of Christ progressively pervaded

embodied vision of God, is perfected the *doxa* of the righteous, when the *doxa* of the Triune is stamped upon them who behold it (1 John iii. 2, comp. John xvii. 24); and only in hell—where wrath and love are not mingled as in the present world, but wrath, or what is the same thing, darkness and fire, reign exclusively—is perfected the *turba* of the ungodly, in that the wrathful fire of hell (whereof elementary fire is only a remote created type) sets on fire its natural wheel of life (Jas. iii. 6).[1] Beyond the acts of God which close the history of salvation which are recorded in Apoc. xx. 11-xxi. 1, the present world, mingled of wrath and love—this world of *Paidagogia* to Christ —is for ever put aside. There subsist only still the kingdom of exclusive love infinitely exalted above the present world, and the region of exclusive wrath lying at an infinite depth below the present world, and therefore strikingly designated by Baader as sub-material, sub-local, and sub-temporal. A state such as the present—into which the soul can return, in order, after many changes, to attain finally again into the blissful, bright region of love—exists no more. The metempsychosis is a lie.

His corporeity, and imparted itself thereto (*Christian Doctrine of Sin*, transl.; Clark, *For. Theol. Libr.* vol. ii. p. 328); a not improbable view, in which, however, this is not acceptable, that the body of the Risen One was still σῶμα χοϊκόν, and did not become σῶμα πνευματικόν, except as a result of this development. Better is Keerl, *Schopfungsgeschichte*, p. 785. His body, which originally was paradisaical, is glorified with His entrance into the heavenly sanctuary, into the heavenly nature.

[1] Karsten, in his work upon the last things, teaches that the ungodly only arise in order to be unclothed, in the judgment of the world, of their body that has been raised by the power of redemption, and then to continue to exist as disembodied spirits; but Scripture says nothing to favour this view.

THE METEMPSYCHOSIS.

Sec. II.

The metempsychosis[1] is the doctrine commonly, although not always, associated closely with that of pre-existence, which we have already passingly referred to in Div. I. Sec. I. We should not here recur to it, if it had a history only external to Judaism and Christianity. But it has found advocates of a decided character as well in the synagogue as in the church. The Pharisees, according to the testimony of Josephus, taught that the souls of the wicked continue in everlasting punishment; but the souls of the good, on the contrary, pass into other bodies.[2] This sounds as if the Pharisees had taught the transmigration of souls; but, in fact, it is only the biblical doctrine of resurrection maintained by the Pharisees in opposition to the Sadducees, on which Josephus, that it might not be used to put him to shame before the Romans, puts this Pythagorean-Platonic garment.[3] How frequently we hear in the Talmuds the Pharisees contending with the Sadducees about the resurrection (תְּחִיַּת הַמֵּתִים); but about transmigration of souls nothing is whispered, beyond that here and there appears to be supposed that one and the same man may emerge at several times under different names in the current history of this world,[4]—an idea which, at the time of Jesus, appears to have been a popular superstition: for Herod the tetrarch thinks that Jesus is only another incarnation of the soul of John, who was beheaded (Matt. xiv. 1, comp. Mark vi. 16, Luke ix. 9); and as well John

---

[1] Instead of μετεμψύχωσις, it is called also μετενσωμάτωσις, μετένδεσις, *i.e.* reuniting of the soul from one body to the other; μεταγγισμός, *i.e.* transfusing from one vessel into the other; in the Latin fathers, *animarum transmigratio, translatio, revolutio, reciprocatio,* etc.

[2] *Bell. jud.* ii. viii. 14 (comp. iii. viii. 5), *Ant.* xviii. 1, 3. The chief passage runs, ψυχὴν πᾶσαν ἄφθαρτον, μεταβαίνειν δὲ εἰς ἕτερον σῶμα τὴν τῶν ἀγαθῶν μόνην τὴν δὲ φαύλων ἀϊδίῳ τιμωρίᾳ κολάζεσθαι.

[3] See Böttcher, *de inferis,* sec. 518, p. 552; Winer, *R.W.* ii. 247.

[4] *e.g. b. Sanhedrin* 105*b*, according to which Beor (the father of Balaam, not Balaam himself, as Bottcher supposes, sec. 552), Cushan Rishathaim, and Laban the Aramæan, are one person.

the Baptist (John i. 21) as Jesus (Matt. xvi. 14; Luke ix. 19), are taken by the people for great personages of the past days, appearing again. It has been thought also, that the question of the disciples (John ix. 2) must be explained of a presumed transmigration of souls, or at least, as De Wette, with Brückner's concurrence, supposes, of a presumed pre-existence ; but it is not at all necessary to suppose that the disciples regard the one of the two cases suggested as possible, as being just as conceivable as the other. The question is the expression of the embarrassment into which they were thrown by the false premiss, that bodily suffering of the individual is always the punishment of sin. The Zohar first of all teaches not only, as the Talmud, the pre-existence of souls, but also the transmigration of souls from one form of temporal life into the other, till they finally become worthy to return into the palace of the heavenly King.[1] In the ancient church, Origen awakened the suspicion of a similar view, by declaring himself often expressly against the transmigration of souls; and a continued embodiment of the soul in this world is, moreover, actually foreign to his system,[2] which teaches for it a continual new creation of material worlds, destined for places of purification of spirits, and thus prides itself on establishing, in the place of the doctrine of the transmigration of souls, a far more exalted theory. None the less Jerome accuses him of unmistakeably defending the transmigration of souls,[3] in the sense of Plato and Pythagoras; and laments that the serpent's poison, so nearly allied to this of the doctrine of pre-existence held by Origen, still always was secretly entailed upon the church from Egypt and the East.[4]

[1] See Franck. *Cabbala*, p. 177. The transmigration of souls is called גִּלְגּוּלָא דְנִשְׁמָתָא (*revolutio animarum*), probably to distinguish it from גִּלְגּוּל in another eschatological meaning. See Buxtorf, *Lex. Chald.* c. 438, 440.

[2] Observe; a metensomatosis OF THIS WORLD. See his disputing this at the beginning of vol. xiii. *in Matthæum*.

[3] In the Epistle 59, *ad Avitum* (*Opp.* ed. Vallarsi, i. c. 923); and equally the Emperor Justinian, in his writings in respect of the fifth Council of Constantinople (550), in vol. ix. of the *Collectio* of Mansi. In Photios we read also that Origen was responsible for the view, that the soul of the Redeemer was the soul of Adam.

[4] In the *Ep. ad Demetriadem* (*Opp.* i. c. 992); comp. *Epitaphium Paulæ* (*ib.* c. 715–719).

The Gnosticism as well of the Jewish as of the Gentile Christians, adopted the erroneous doctrine thus favoured by philosophy and the Cabbala, and nurtured it up.

And how is it proved from Holy Scripture? How Basilides attempted it, we are informed by Origen on Rom. vii. 9 : " I died, says the apostle, for sin began to be attributed to me. But Basilides, without considering that this is to be understood of the natural law, refers the apostolic word to absurd and ungodly fables, to the Pythagorean dogma, seeking to prove from this assertion of the apostle, that souls are continually transfused into other bodies. When the apostle says, I lived once without law, he means, according to Basilides: Before I came into this my present body, I lived in the bodily form of a being that was not under the law,—namely, of a four-footed beast or of a bird. Basilides therein shuts his eyes to what follows: but when the commandment came, sin revived again (*revixit*)."[1] Carpocrates taught that the world is a work of world-spirits, whose place is far beneath the true and highest God; and that the soul, passing through the region of the world-spirits, and emancipated from their trammels, has to take its way upwards to the eternal uncreated Father. In this manner he interpreted the parabolic saying of Jesus, " When thou art in the way with thine adversary, give diligence that thou mayest be delivered from him, that he may not hale thee perchance to the judge, and the judge deliver thee to the officer, and the officer cast thee into prison. Verily I say unto thee, Thou shalt not depart thence till thou hast paid the very last mite" (Luke xii. 58; Matt. v. 25). The adversary, he said, is the devil, one of the world-spirits who brings the departed souls before the judge the chief of the world-spirits, who delivers them to the officer another of the world-spirits, in order to enclose them in other bodies; for the body, say they, is a dungeon from which the soul does not depart until it has lived through and experienced all that belongs to this world, and has therein approved its freedom, in order to soar upwards to the God who is exalted above the world-forming angels.[2]

Such a mode of scriptural argument needs no refutation.

---

[1] Stier's *Ausg. des Irenäos*, i. 903.

[2] Irenæus, *c. hær.* i. 25; Tertullian, *de anima*, c. 35; Epiphanius, *hær.* xxvii. (*Opp.* ed. Petav. i. 106).

It is still more absurd than if any one, as Augustine observes, were to quote Ps. xlix. 12, 20, lxxiv. 19, on behalf of the transmigration of souls, or than when Juda b. Aser, Abarbanel and other Jewish religious philosophers, find in it the reason of the Levirate law (טעם היבום), and appeal to Job xxxiii. 29 as a proof text.[1] Scripture contains no intimation which even remotely favours it. For even Matt. xi. 14 (comp. xvii. 12) is not such an intimation. John himself denies that he is Elias (John i. 21); he is therefore not Elias in the sense of the Jews, but he is so nevertheless in a certain sense: for he is the second Elias, who, according to scriptural prophecy, precedes the Lord; and it was of great importance that he should be so regarded, that the day of redemption which was then breaking, the heavenly kingdom of the second David that was appearing, should not be mistaken. For the rest, Elias was already, according to Scripture, bodily taken into heaven. That his soul should be clothed upon with a new temporal body in the womb of Elisabeth, would be a contradiction of Scripture by itself.

The metempsychosis has therefore no biblical testimony to adduce for itself; it only abases the word of God, as all false wisdom does, to paint itself up withal. It is, on the contrary, thoroughly contradictory to Scripture. For (1) it deranges, contrary to reason and experience, the limits established by creation, as the Holy Scripture testifies, between natural class and class (מין), according to which it is impossible that one nature should pass over into the other, which is substantially the same as that the soul of one being should become the soul of another. That the souls of those men whose god is their belly, and whom their own greediness has stricken with stupidity and sluggishness, pass into swine, asses, and similar brutes; the souls of those who loved unrighteousness, exercised tyranny, and were given to robbery, into wolves, hawks, and other creatures of prey; that the souls of those, on the other hand, who lived morally and peaceably should pass, not essentially but habitually, into bees or ants; and that these degraded souls should ever, according to their conduct, be changed from brute souls back into human souls, as we read in Plato, whether it be regarded physically or ethically, is alike an absurdity. It is

[1] See the two Hebrew treatises on the transmigration of souls in the collection טעם זקנים, Frankfort-on-Maine 1854.

absurd in a physical view; for "every body," says Aristotle with absolute truth,[1] "has its peculiar internal form and external formation; and that every soul can without distinction enter into every body, is therefore a fiction just as romantic as if it were said that an architect can accomplish his work by playing on the flute. In the same way that every art must have its appropriate tools, the soul also needs a body corresponding to it." It is absurd in an ethical view; for a state of punishment, without consciousness of the foregone sins to be expiated, cannot possibly serve for man's moral purification; and a human soul that has become the soul of a brute, is absolutely no longer a being capable of moral accountableness and improvement. The proof of this twofold (physical and ethical) absurdity of the Pythagorean-Platonic dogma, is found as early as the writings of Justin Martyr.[2]

Now it cannot indeed be said of the metempsychosis, if it abandons that change of men into brutes, any more than of the doctrine of pre-existence (Div. I. Sec. I.), that it is contrary to reason. But it is contrary to revelation and contrary to Scripture in all forms. For, (2) according to Scripture, death

---

[1] In the three books, περὶ ψυχῆς, i. 3.

[2] At the beginning of the dialogue, *c. Tryphon:* comp. Irenæus, *c. hær.* ii. 33, which takes its counter proof from the want of all recollection of the earlier condition; Theodoret, *Græcarum affectionum curatio,* c. xi. (p. 431, s. ed. Gaisford), which, in connection with the migration into wasps, bees, and ants, wittily remarks, that, according to Plato, the reward of those who in their life have done wrong to no one, is to wound and injure others; Augustine (*civ.* x. 30), who with satisfaction appeals to the fact, that even Porphyry limited the doctrine of Plato and Plotinus his own master, to a migration into human bodies: Puduit scilicet illud credere ne mater fortasse filium in mulum revoluta vectaret, et non puduit hoc credere, ubi revoluta mater in puellam filio forsitans nuberet. Unsurpassed in this kind of contest is Tertullian, who, in his *apologeticus,* c. 48, and especially *de anima,* c. 32–35, heaps upon the philosophico-gnostic *metempsychosis s. metensomatosis,* in the mocking designation of which he is inexhaustibly inventive, the most biting sarcasm of the coarsest wit. Æneas of Gaza is the only one besides the above-named that embarks in a searching refutation, in his dialogue *Theophrastos;* Hermias scoffs not without wit; Lactantius and Chrysostom lose themselves in empty tirades. What elsewhere is found in the fathers, consists partly of insignificant historical notices (among the apologists, Clemens Alexandrinus, Epiphanius, Eusebius), partly of insufficient attempts at refutation (Cyril of Alexandria, Isidorus Peleusianus, l. iv. ep. 163). Besides Porphyry, Jamblichus and

is the absolute end of the temporal history of every individual man, and the *parousia* of Christ is the absolute end of the temporal history of the whole of humanity. A general judgment decides finally upon the destiny of all men, and of all the beings that have been involved in the history of humanity; and when the present world shall have passed away, whose characteristic is the mingling of wrath and love, there is no further world beyond the new one which proceeds from the destruction of the old world. The essence of eternity that has been immanent in temporality has come to its breaking forth: the two principles are for ever unmingled, and there remains still only a kingdom of love or of light—heaven; and a kingdom of wrath or of darkness and fire—hell.

In the scriptural doctrine of the last things, therefore, there is absolutely no place for a gradually progressive embodiment of the separate souls, whether it be in the present world or in another future one. Even Origen is compelled to allow this, although his exegetical method permitted him to twist the Scripture like a kaleidoscope. But if, among the great thinkers of modern days, Lessing[1] so lightly spoke in behalf of the

---

Hierocles (according to the information in Photius) limited the human metempsychosis to a transition into human bodies. Proclus and Syrianus made another wonderful attempt to vindicate the Platonic dogma. They said that the brute kept its own soul, but that the human soul, which passed into the brute body, was bound in sympathy to the brute soul. Ὁ δὲ ἀληθὴς λόγος, says Proclus in the sixth book to Timæus, εἰσκρίνεσθαι μὲν εἰς θηρία φησὶ τὴν ἀνθρωπίνην ψυχὴν, ἔχουτα δὲ τὴν οἰκείαν ζωὴν, καὶ ἐπὶ ταυτῇ τὴν εἰσκριθεῖσαν ψυχὴν οἷον ἐποχουμένην καὶ τῇ πρὸς αὐτὴν συμπαθείᾳ δεδεμένην. We recall therein the cabbalistic doctrine of עִבּוּר, *i.e.* of the impregnation of a soul by another married in union with it. Æneas banters the new device of his contemporary Proclus in a very successful manner.

[1] In *The Education of the Human Race* (1780), where, in sec. 95, it runs: "Is this hypothesis so ridiculous for the reason that it is the oldest—because the human understanding chanced upon it before the sophistry of the schools had dissipated and weakened it?" That the oldest view of futurity is that of metempsychosis, is false. It was first developed among the Egyptians as well as the Indians, from the notion of Hades and its two-fold state. In Israel no step was made beyond the revealed fundamental view, either in the mythologic or in the speculative direction. Zschokke has represented the faith of the transmigration of souls in a sentimental novel entitled *Harmonius:* "I knew three beings," says *Harmonius* there, " with which I was associated in a wondrous involuntary manner, as I was

transmigration of souls, it is explained from the fact that he wholly lost the idea of a positive although progressive revelation, and was only groping in the dark according to a position that was spiritually just as free, as it was restrained to the divine-human canon of Scripture. Both these things are true in a more limited degree of Herder also, who closes his confutation of Lessing with the words: " Purification of heart, improvement of the soul, with all its impulses and desires: this, it seems to me, is the true *palingenesia* of this life; after which assuredly a more joyous, a loftier metempsychosis, but which is unknown to us, awaits us."[1]

This "unknown" metempsychosis — the only one that Scripture teaches—is the resurrection. As there their God-resembling nature comes to manifestation in the bodies of the righteous—the nature in which Christ's blood has effaced every stain—so, through the not less humanly formed bodies of the ungodly, will break through their nature, on the one hand devilish, on the other brutal, and make them a dreadful and loathsome reverse of glorification. This, but nothing further than this, is the truth of the metempsychosis. The scriptural revelation leaves unabolished the dualism of hell and heaven, which the metempsychosis has it in view to cancel.

THE DOCTRINE OF RESTORATION.

Sec. III.

WHEN the existing form of the world—which is absolutely a bridge thrown to man, whereby he may attain from wrath to love, from curse to blessing, from death to life—shall be destroyed, man will be for ever established in the principle into which in this world he has sought to enter in habit and life by virtue of his own free determination. The fiery side, as the

with no other being during my life of seventy years' duration. In all these three was the same tenderness, the same faithfulness." The first of these beings was a bird, the second a dog, the third his wife.

[1] *Postscenien zur Geschichte der Menschheit*, Werke (1807), vii. 277.

light side of the divine *doxa*, will have in hell, as in heaven, an eternal objectivity apart from God. There needs no final abolition of hell in heaven, that the whole creation may be a copy or expression of the everlasting triumph of light over darkness, which is set forth by the divine *doxa*, considered with respect to the internal nature of God (Div. IV. Sec. VI.). This triumph is completed. If the whole of creation were one being, it would indeed have to be perfected in such a manner as that the darkness should be in this one nature abolished in light. But as the entire creation is an infinite number of beings, that triumph is then already perfected, when those beings which have taken their stand in the principle of wrath are capable of nothing further in opposition to the holy one whose hereditary portion is in light, and which have become the footstool of God and of his Christ, *i.e.* the dark ground on which is enhanced the glory of the divine dominion. God is thus, moreover, πάντα ἐν πᾶσιν. He who, in respect of His triune nature, is love, embraces all who have laid themselves open to this love with the light of His *doxa;* and all who have shut their hearts to this love, He encircles with the darkness and the fire of His *doxa*. Love has conquered. Evil is placed under bonds. There needs not its absolute annihilation that the hexaëmeron of the world's history may close, as did that of the world's creation, with והנה טוב מאד (Gen. i. 31).

There is no doctrine that contradicts the Holy Scripture in a more unwarrantable manner than that of the so-called *Apokatastasis*. There is only needed one glance into the life of Joh. Wilh. Petersen († 1727), in order to be convinced how even the noblest soul may be absolutely perverted in all its relations by this doctrine. It is no postulate of reason for which it is passed off. For as it has of late been observed with perfect justice, the anthropologic, psychologic, and ethic view of the case claims, on the contrary, the possibility of an eternal condemnation. " Since man is not to be blessed by means of a natural process, must it not be possible to his will to establish his own induration, to continue rejecting grace for ever, and thus himself to choose his own condemnation? Will it be said that this possibility of a continuous induration must include also a constant possibility of conversion? This will be found to be a precipitate conclusion. For this earthly life has already proved to us the fearful law of necessity, according to which evil progressively assumes an unchangeable natural impress in the individual. It is true that psychological experience also shows us, that in the human soul may be introduced a mighty turning-point, whereby the old is broken away from, and the development of the character takes a new direction. But there arises here the old question, whether, for the conversion of man, there is not a *terminus peremptorius*—an extremest limit, beyond which atonement and conversion are no longer possible. Although we dare not place this limit arbitrarily at any point whatever within the range of time (*e.g.* at the end of this life), still we must unconditionally place it at the end of time and of history itself, which is exactly the idea of the final advent of the Lord. So long as there is Time, conversion must be possible, for it is actually the Christian idea of the significance of time, that it is a period of trial and of grace; and as long as the sinner finds himself within the range of time, he exists under the patience of God. But when not merely this or that defined section of time, but Time itself, has passed by, then it cannot be understood how conversion is still possible, because conversion cannot be conceived of without a history of conversion. The possibility of conversion depends, for instance, not merely on the fact that there is good essentially present in man, and can never be extinguished, which is just as much the possibility of condemnation; but on the fact that internal and external conditions of effectiveness for the development of this possibility are present, that the sinner is still in that order of things which bears in itself the stamp of that which is undecided,—a state of the world where trial and temptation may still be talked of." [1]

What Martensen thus says of the natural character which evil assumes, agrees with what, from Div. III. 2 onwards, we have already frequently represented with respect to the consequences not merely ethical, but also physical, of sin. What he says of time is true in general of the present world, which, in its temporally limited constitution—its constitution calculated not less to conceal than to reveal the Godhead—its constitution mingled of self-evidences of divine love and divine wrath—is purposed to make man aware of his conditionary state, to render sin distasteful to him by means of its own necessary conse-

[1] Martensen, *Dogmatik*, sec. 286.

quences, to check the enhancement of his sin to a demoniacal character, and to train him to the salvation which is to be attained by means of faith. If this pædagogic form of world be destroyed, man is, and remains, that which he has become within himself. He is, and remains; he is not annihilated: for Scripture no more teaches the final annihilation of the wicked, than it does their apokatastasis or restoration. Human reason would like in one way or another to abolish the dualism with which the history of the world closes. Let her do it upon her own responsibility, but let her not falsify the Scripture. This teaches an eternal personal continuance of all personal beings, and a continuance fundamentally conditioned by what they have become in time.

Here in this life, says Jac. Böhme,[1] the soul is on the balance, on the hinge; and if it is evil, it can be born again in love; but when the hinge is shattered, then it is in its own territory, in its principle of being.

But within the two principles there is movement, and that not only in a circle. The history of this world has ceased, yet experience does not also cease; and therefore it is not the close of all history.

[1] See Hamberger, *Lehre Jac. Böhme's*, p. 302. Jac. Böhme is decided against the apokatastasis. His doctrine of the last things is therefore found unsatisfactory by Hamberger (*ibid.* p. 331); as, moreover, Franz v. Baader in this point became unfaithful to the master. We bow, as does also v. Rudloff with J. Böhme, to the word of Scripture, and reply to the apokatastasis with Augustine (*civ.* xxi. 23): Ita plane hoc erit, si non quod Deus dixit, sed quod suspicantur homines plus valebit. Also the sound decision of H. W. Rinck (*Vom Zustand nach dem Tode*, p. 291) deserves here distinguishing mention: "It seems to us to be very precipitate to decide, with Jung Stilling, that the supposition of an eternal condemnation prejudices God's honour, and is unbecoming to God. Do we, then, so thoroughly understand the proprieties of God? Do we fundamentally understand the nature of Him before whom the seraphim with veiled faces sing, Holy, holy, holy is the Lord of Sabaoth?"

fection in the intermediate state does not exclude enhancement (comp. Heb. xii. 23 with xi. 40; Apoc. vi. 9-11; 1 Cor. xv. 23-28); so it will not exclude it, moreover, after the new creation of heaven and earth. If there be, as undeniably there is, a multiplicity of degrees in the glory of the future state, there is no reason why there should not, moreover, be exaltation from the one degree to the other, since the highest good which is the possession of all the blessed—fellowship with God—allows of continually deeper and deeper sounding, a continually richer giving and receiving, a continually and increasingly glorious disclosure of itself. Therefore it is observed by von Gerlach upon that passage of the Apocalypse referred to, with a full apprehension of its meaning, "There shall also be there one more unceasing creation—a reception of God's gifts of grace—as of the tree of life in Eden, and no unbending sameness, but an eternal becoming and growing."

The seer can even say, "every month," for the blissful world of spirits indeed is not compounded of an irrecoverable past, a passing present, and a dim future; but, on the other hand, it is anything but a numb quietude and a uniform absence of events: it is a lapse of αἰῶνες τῶν αἰώνων filled and pervaded by eternity. Time is therefore, after its manner, glorified, as are the bodies of the blessed. The eternal source whence it proceeded is broken through by it, and overflows it. The blessed strike the root of their life in the eternal life of God. In the lapse of æons this is a present which is always alike to them. There is no past which they should wish back, and no future which should make the present painful to them. Their present is God. To be deprived of this present, and still to subsist without end—this in itself alone is a torment of hell for the condemned.

· · · · · ·

Our plan, as we sketched it in the *Prolegomena*, is now accomplished. We have traced the history of the soul from its eternal antecedents up to its eternal ultimate destiny. It is a system that now stands before us, not a system built up of scientific categories, but constructed in conformity with the ways of God with the soul of man—ways which proceed from eternity, and return to eternity,—a completed circle, whose living centre is the Name which is above every name.

That which from eternity was in the presence of God as an ideal in the mirror of His wisdom, we now behold in self-living eternal fulfilment and completion. The idea of humanity, in its process of realization, disturbed by sin but renovated anew and guided to victory by redemption, is now perfected eternal reality. Enfranchised in God through Christ, man is henceforth absolutely exalted above evil; and his body is not merely, as it was in its primitive origin, immortal in design, but immortal in nature. The spirits of the redeemed are now, in conformity with their destination, in blessed actuality the image of God the Triune; and their souls the image of the divine *doxa;* and their bodies the image of the body of the glory of the God-man. The spirit of man lives and moves in God's triune love; the soul of man reflects in incessant delightful vision the loving triumph of the divine *doxa;* and the body of man, whose spiritual and microcosmic typical meaning is now no longer a concealed mystery but a revealed marvel, shines, as pervaded with the loving light of the spirit and the soul, in the loveliest beauty. But everything that redeeming love repelled to self-induration is for ever absorbed into the wrathful aspects of the *doxa*, and there leads a life self-consuming, and, as it were, non-existent.

APPENDIX.

From a Sermon of the Author's on the Fourth Sunday after Trinity, 1854.

ON ROM. VIII. 18-23.

WHENCE comes it, then, that our joy in nature, and the joy of nature herself, is changed from time to time into mourning? The answer to this question stands in the closest connection with the state of our own soul and of our own body. It is therefore sufficiently within our reach; but by our own reason we do not discover it, and in the wisdom of this world we shall seek for it in vain. Whence comes it, then, that the body of man, made in God's image, becomes at last a corrupting carcase, as do the bodies of unreasoning brutes? Whence comes it that heat and cold, moisture and drought, wind and weather, continually shake and wear it, as if it were a ruinous house? Whence comes it that, even before it is deprived of soul, it is a habitation for worms? Whence the sicknesses numberless, and deformities and imperfections? whence that life, which, even in the case of people in health, is more or less unsound, with its seeds of death developing themselves more tardily or rapidly? Ask the wisdom of this world. It will give you the absolutely comfortless disclosure: The constitution of man, and his relation to the whole of nature, is the cause of these results. And truly it is so; but was it so originally, and is it therefore to continue so for ever? To these questions natural wisdom either answers not at all, and lets the enigma stand; or it answers yes, and so makes the enigma more enigmatical still. But the Holy Scripture teaches us to understand the present in the light of the past and of the future; and perhaps no passage is so specially instructive in this respect as Rom. viii. 18-24.

I.

When a creature wishes to be emancipated from that which God has imprinted upon it, there must, in respect of that which is thus imprinted, have preceded a terrible change; and when even those who, according to their inner man, know and feel themselves redeemed, nevertheless, as the apostle says, wait with sighing and longing for the redemption of their body, the human body must have come into a condition which is the most lamentable disfigurement and perversion of the primitive one. Thus it must be; and when we look back to man's creation, thus also we actually find it. You have perchance seen statues hewn out of stone—human forms wrought by human skill—which, by the perfect symmetry and by the majestic beauty of their outlines, filled you with amazement. If even human skill can produce that which is thus glorious, how glorious must that have been which God's omnipotence produced, when, according to His eternal counsel, He went about to lay the foundation of humanity; when He, as the Scripture narrates, formed man out of the dust of the ground! (Gen. ii. 7.) In the creation of the beasts He had said, "Let the earth bring forth living creatures;" but in the creation of man He did not say, "Let the earth bring forth man." Men did not come into existence by such a creative command; but God Himself laid hands to the work (to speak humanly), and formed the body of the one first man out of the earth, moistened by the primal dew of the delightsome land of Eden. LORD! how this was done we know not: for Thou art not a man, to have done it with hands, and God the Son had not yet become man. Thine invisible omnipotence it was, which in a manner inconceivable to us formed the dust of the garden of Eden into the body of Adam; Thine omnipotence,—which also will form the dust of the graves one day into bodies for those who shall rise again. It was an act of Thine own love, according to the plan of Thine eternal wisdom, and in the power of Thine omnipotence. And when the human body was formed, then the Lord God breathed into it the created, but God-like and God-related, breath of life; and proceeding from it, the soul pervaded the frame of the body, and subjected to itself the powers that move therein. Thus originated man. His God-like spirit lived and moved in the God of its original source, and thence by the soul ruled over the divine image of the earthly body. He ruled therein as a king on his throne, and was appointed from this throne to govern the creatures around him. The whole condition of his being was peace, and all creatures around him were with him in peace; and their progress to glory depended on the fact that their king continued in the holiness imprinted on him. For bodily he belonged to them, and spiritually, to the heavenly spirits. Thus he stood there as the link of two worlds,—for heaven and earth might claim him for their own,—an object of wonder to heavenly angels, and a delight to heavenly wisdom, but moreover envied by Satan, who succeeded in ruining him.

II.

What became of man when he broke up his fellowship with God by disobedience, our text does not actually say; but it suggests what was the result to the unreasoning creature. It became subject, it says, to vanity, to the service of perishing nature, on account of Him who hath subjected it. It is God who, on account of man, has inflicted a curse on the ground. The field is primarily meant, where now to man's careful sowing are opposed weeds which threaten it with suffocation, and wildness, and all kinds of risks, which often, even at the end, bring to nothing the hope of the harvest. The apostle says to us, moreover, that that curse extended over all creation for the sake of man; and that vanity and corruption, to which it is now subjected, are the result of man's fall. What consequences the fall had for man himself, may be gathered from this. The light of the spirit is quenched; and in the place of the glorification of the body by the spirit, has now appeared the reverse of glorification: the body of man has become a body of death, and nakedness is thenceforward a shame. Man, who was summoned to dominion over the earth, is now no longer endowed with power over himself. The peace of the spirit, the soul, and the body, has been changed into confused discord. The soul has choked the image of God in the spirit, and disordered the body by its lust; and the body also entices the soul against its will. In one word, man has fallen away from the love of God. He has aroused the anger of God by sin, and that has now taken entire possession of him and of nature. For the comprehension of the whole of nature with man for the glorification of both had fallen out to the corruption of both. God's plan was hindered, God's good-will was made of no effect; therefore God's wrath kindled in the entire circumference whose centre was man. But the apostle says—in hope. If that has reference to the creation, it is also true of man; for the creation is just on that account not without hope, because man is not without hope. With the wrath of God arose, at the same time, the grace of God, and opposed itself to the wrath. That humanity still subsists—that the creation which pertains to it still subsists—that they still subsist, not without an evening glow of their original beauty,—this is God's grace. God promised to humanity to overcome the wicked one. The overcomer of the evil one is Jesus. Therefore I rejoice always when I find the cross, which stands on our altars, also planted upon the hills, or anywhere else under the open heaven. For the cross is not only the standard of redemption for us men, but also for all creatures that surround us. The blood which flowed down therefrom, not only extinguished the anger upon us sinners, but has also broken the power of the curse upon the earth. When thou, then, standing on the mountain top, kindled with the view which is presented around, criest out, How marvellous is God's earth !—do not forget how infinitely more marvellous it will be, when it has wholly become the reflection of God's love, which the crucified One has won back again for us.

III.

Our body, and with it the creation, are to become spiritual, free, and glorious. For the painful expectation of creation, says the apostle, waiteth for the revelation of the children of God. Revelation is a turning out of that which is within, that the external may be like to the internal. Revelation of the children of God is an unveiling of their sonship, which now is veiled by our fleshly body; an unveiling of this, so that it appears in the body—which itself has become spiritual—visibly to all creatures. And further, the apostle says that the creature shall be delivered from the bondage of the perishing being, into the glorious liberty of the children of God. In what this glorious liberty consists, is indicated in the closing words of our text; it consists in the redemption of our body from sin and death.

For sinlessness, that is liberty; and immortality, that is glory! Our worthless bodies, says the apostle in another place, shall be like to the glorious body of Christ. For, for that purpose did the Son of God become man, that He might descend into the abyss of misery, into which our spirit and soul and body have come by sin, and that He might wrest them free from the dominion of darkness, and that He might lead them up with Himself, by His reconciling suffering and death, to a glorious liberty. The body in which He arose from the dead, is the same in which He had been crucified; but it is, nevertheless, another. For, of the Lord in the days of His flesh, the contrite Israel confesses, He had no form nor comeliness; He was the most despised and the most rejected of all men, full of pains and sickness; He was so despised, that men hid their faces from Him; therefore we esteemed Him of no account (Isa. liii. 2, 3). But when He appeared to Saul the persecutor, on the way to Damascus, light from heaven shone around him (Acts ix. 3). And when John received his revelation, he saw His eyes as flames of fire, His feet as brass that glows in the furnace, His countenance lightening like the sun. In this glorified body of the God-man, we have the type of that of which our bodies shall be representations. For the righteous, says He Himself, shall shine as the sun in the kingdom of their Father (Matt. xiii. 43). It is sown, says our apostle (1 Cor. xv. 42–44), corruptible, and shall arise incorruptible; it is sown in dishonour, and shall arise in glory; it is sown in weakness, and shall arise in power; it is sown a natural body, and shall arise a spiritual body. And this great Easter of humanity, wherewith its redemption is completed, is also the Easter of all creation. But before the Easter comes, the Good Friday and the Sabbath of the tomb must be undergone.

IV.

The redemption has already begun. But it has begun from within, not from without. For, as a tree does not begin to grow from its crown, but from the seed that lies in the concealment of the earth; so also is the new life in Christ. It began with the fact that, as our text expresses it, the first-fruits of the Spirit are given to us. For as the creation of the world began with the Spirit of God brooding upon the waters of the yet unformed mass, so also the new creation of man. We are flesh, born of flesh. Our whole natural being, the invisible as well as the visible, is a mass of corruption. But God hath taken pity upon us. We are all washed. There has passed over us the gracious water of life, the bath of regeneration, and of the renewing of the Holy Spirit, which He hath shed upon us abundantly through Jesus Christ our Saviour. Whether ye allow this Spirit to work in you or not, ye have all received Him, and He is near to you all by the power of the holy baptism. But those who allow it to produce an effect on them, experience it in themselves as the spirit of adoption, which cries in us, Abba, dear Father; and as the spirit of life in Christ Jesus, which makes us free from the law of sin and death. And yet we still groan, longing after the adoption, and waiting for the redemption of our body. Even we, says the apostle, who have the first-fruits of the Spirit, even we ourselves groan. For we are God's children—are delivered by the Holy Spirit from the law of sin and death; but it is not yet abolished in us—we still bear it about with us in our sinful dying body : we are endued with power to gain the victory over sin, but yet we conquer not without daily bitter and hard struggle. When we would labour in the Lord's service, we feel the leaden weight of this body, and the shadow that it casts upon our devotion; and when we strongly purpose in God to tread it under foot, and to crucify it with its affections and lusts, it has nevertheless again enticed us before we are aware of it, with its sensual fantasies: we strive, and strive, and become weary even unto death, and weary of life. We hate sin—we desire to be rid of this bondage—we lift ourselves up with ever newly collected power, and soar upwards with wings as eagles; but we soon sink, as if drawn back again to the earth with the power of its fascination. We cannot otherwise rejoice in our adoption, than when we hide ourselves in faith in God's free undeserved grace, and retreat into the innermost sanctuary of our heart, where God's Spirit has restored again the image of God in us: for in our soul and our body burns an unblessed fire; and if thou, O Christian, thou child of God, dost not daily extinguish this fire with tears of repentance, and with the blood of the Lord Jesus, it becomes a larger burning that consumes thee, and at length it becomes a fire of hell. And to these experiences of sorrows that we ourselves undergo in ourselves, and besides, the sufferings of this time which come from without,—the sorrow at the want of faith—the lukewarmness, the lovelessness which surround us—the conditions of life often so perilous and yet so unchangeable, within which we are imprisoned—the wounds which the death of our beloved ones rends in our heart—the isolation into which we are thrown by the loss or the want of faithful friends—the frequent frustration of our purest designs, and the disappointment of our most well-founded hopes; and—shall I go on? It would be a long catalogue. The apostle is thinking chiefly of ignominy and persecution for Christ's sake. Of these we suffer now little or nothing. But these sufferings also will, as in the first centuries, break out again over the church of Christ; and if our Christianity were less conformed to the world, we should even now experience sufficient preludes of them. This is the state of things in us; this is the state of things around us: therefore we groan, even we who have the first-fruits of the Spirit; and we groan, as our text says, within ourselves; that is, we groan in the very depth of our inward nature—we groan from our deepest heart. For I ask all of you who have found the one pearl of great price, Where, then, have ye this pearl of great price? Must ye not say with the apostle (2 Cor. iv. 7), We have such a treasure in earthen vessels? The pearl is enclosed in a coarse hard shell, and this shell has grown on to a ledge of rocks, and the waves of the sea wash over it. Therefore we groan within ourselves, desiring that the Lord would bring up this pearl from the sea of this world, and that He would break it off from the rock of the bondage of sin and death, and that He would shatter the coarse hard shell of our body, and set this pearl free.

V.

And we do not groan alone. Since God laid the earth under the curse in consequence of the fall of man, the whole creation longs with us, and is in pain, as the apostle says, continually still,—that is to say, from that time even to this present day. It groans with us, and, as the apostle in the original text suggestively allegorizes it, it is in pangs as a travailing woman; and as one who longingly expects a messenger from a distance, lifts up his head with outstretched neck, as though he could draw the person waited for towards him, so is the creation around us in the state of strained expectation. And what is the message that it awaits? It is the revelation of the sons of God. To many of you this will sound altogether strange. But the apostle does not think that he is saying an unfamiliar thing to the Roman Christians; "for we know," says he, associating himself with them, "that the whole creation longs with us, and is in pain still continually." Let me render the matter plain by a simile. When the sun shines, it is the delight of creation—it is the condition of its growth and increase. Now, conceive for a moment that the sun in heaven should be extinguished: it would not only become night for ever; all creature life, moreover, would pine away, and finally perish. In a similar relation to creation to that of the sun, but an incomparably richer one in attraction and influence, man was placed; his spirit, the lamp of God in him, was destined to become the light of glorification for all the creatures that surrounded him. But this light is quenched by sin. A profound change resulted then in all creatures: the sun of heaven still shines on them, but the sun of the Spirit has passed away from them. Now indeed, God, who bade the light to shine forth out of the darkness, has given again a bright light to shine into our hearts (2 Cor. iv. 6); but this bright shining is still invisible to creation, for it is concealed by our flesh, as the sun behind thick clouds. When one day this clear effulgence shall also be revealed in our bodies, and the glorious liberty of the children of God shall be discernible therein as in a crystal mirror, then will the whole creation rejoice in the light of its king,—Man; and it is just that after which it longs. It is no longing with consciousness, but it is yet a longing; and the object of its ardent craving is that which is named by the apostle. All the tortures which men inflict upon brutes—all the tortures under which brutes mutually tear and rend one another —all the sufferings of their ceasing to be—express themselves in cries of pain, which, rightly understood, are at the same time cries of longing; and all the forcible destruction of the vegetable world that was intended to be serviceable to man by its fruit, gives the impression of this craving; and all the discord, all the disturbance of the elements, is, as it were, the birth-pangs of this craving. And it is not therefore to continue.

Throughout the whole of Scripture is promulgated the Evangel of redemption and glorification even to the unintelligent creation. When God redeems His people, then, as Isaiah prophesies (xxxv. 1), the wilderness and the solitary place shall be glad for them, and the plain shall rejoice and shall blossom as the lilies : then nature, as all the prophets foretell, shall put on her blissful festal attire ; and as it has been compelled to share in the sorrows of men, it shall also be a participator in their glory.

VI.

The apostle intimates to us how glorious it will be when this groaning and longing is stilled, when he says that the sufferings of this present time are not worthy to be compared with the glory that shall be revealed in us. When grief and necessity are gnawing thee in body and soul here below—when sickness and disease weigh down thy spirit—when all kinds of affliction assail thee,—consider, if in one scale were placed this present temporal sorrow and suffering, and in the other, the future eternal glory, how infinitely more important thou wouldest find the latter than the former ! When the Lord shall deliver the captives of Zion, then shall we be like unto them that dream. As a dream of the night which we can hardly remember, as a little cloud that vanishes before the sun, so all that we have endured in this world will be cast behind us. How soon thou forgettest the sickness that has been overcome, when thou once once more feelest thyself sound in body; and how frequently sayest thou in such a case, that until now thou hast not known rightly how to value the blessing of health ! How completely, then, will all temporal pain shrink together in thy remembrance, and how well shalt thou then feel thyself, when this thy body shall have become an external manifestation, a glorious vessel, and a free instrument (freed from sin and all its consequences) of thy inward spiritual life; and when even all possibility of disease, and of disaster, and of pain, all possibility of temptation to sin, and of abuse to sin, and of disfigurement by sin, is taken from it ! As those who are set free from a dungeon, we shall then rejoice with the Psalmist (Ps. cxxiv. 7): Our soul is escaped as a bird out of the snare of the fowler; the snare is broken, and we are delivered. If we look, then, above us and around us, we see ourselves surrounded by a new heaven and a new earth. It is the same heaven and the same earth, but they are nevertheless different, as it is the same body which enclothes us, and yet another. The whole world appears to us now as a new creation of divine love. Hitherto wrath and grace reigned in the world; now the wrath is extinguished—the blood of Jesus Christ has quenched it: the wrath is extinct, the grace has completed its work, and love reigns. The groaning of creation has vanished in delight, and its throes in exultation, and its expectation in satisfaction, and its corruption in glory, and its bondage in triumph. Humanity, believing in Christ, is now glorified into the image of the glorified God-man, and all the visible creation is glorified into the image of the glorified humanity. There is peace between God and man, peace between man's body and spirit, peace between humanity and creation, peace between all creatures. The blood of Jesus Christ has made peace; through Him, God hath reconciled all to Himself, whether it be on earth or in heaven.

VII.

But this is not true without exception of all men. Only that which in this temporal world groaneth and longeth shall rejoice; only those who weep shall laugh; only they who mourn in Zion, as Isaiah predicts (lxi. 3), shall receive beauty for ashes, and the oil of joy for mourning, and beautiful garments for a spirit of heaviness; and only those who in this world of time possess the first-fruits of the Spirit, shall experience the glorification of their body, and the joy at the glorification of nature,— only such as even now have the Spirit which gives them witness that they are God's children, which cries in them, Abba, dear Father! The apostle, indeed, calls the fulfilment after which all creation longs with us, the revelation of the children of God, the perfect realization of their divine and glorious freedom. How can he who is no child of God be revealed as a child of God; and how can he who so loves the bondage of this perishing worldly life, that he would gladly enjoy it for ever, have the glorious freedom of the children of God obtruded upon him? To you whose god is your belly, how is the body of glorification fitted for you? What advantage is it to you, who have yielded your members as instruments of unrighteousness? Ye also shall not remain without bodies—ye also shall arise; but in your body shall be manifest what is in you,—not God's image, which was quenched in you, and has remained quenched because ye have resisted the restoring grace of God, but the form of the brutes, after whose manner ye have been enslaved to vice, and the form of the devil, whose serpent-seed ye have cherished and fostered within you. For when the mighty call of God's Son, the first-born from the dead, goes forth to those who thus lie in the graves, then, as in the Old Testament God's angel said to Daniel (xii. 2), shall the many who sleep under the earth awake, some to everlasting life, some to everlasting disgrace and shame.

INDEXES.

I.

PASSAGES OF SCRIPTURE REFERRED TO OR ILLUSTRATED.

Gen. i. ii. p. 45.
  i.-ii. 3, p. 63.
  i. p. 18, 87, 88, 89.
  i. 1, p. 75; 2, p. 75, 76, 96, 140; 20, p. 87; 21, p. 96; 24, p. 29, 87; 26, 27, p. 28, 30, 48, 80; 27, p. 84; 30, p. 29, 97; 31, p. 552.
  ii. p. 88, 105.
  ii. 1, p. 75; 4, p. 87; 7, p. 14, 15, 26, 88, 90, 91, 92, 94, 99, 100, 107, 113, 114, 115, 140, 213, 231, 233, 234, 249, 250, 251, 253, 257, 268, 273, 318, 376, 393, 469, 472; 15, p. 74; 17, p. 151; 19, p. 87; 96, 215; 21, p. 132, 325.
  iii. 2, p. 96; 3, p. 151; 8-10, p. 97, 157; 13, p. 150; 17-19, p. 74; 19, p. 151, 338, 477, 480; 22, p. 194.
  iv. 1, p. 139; 10, p. 286.
  v. 3, p. 137.
  vi.-ix. p. 29.
  vi. p. 149.
  vi. 1-4, p. 140; 2, p. 78, 261; 3, p. 104, 109, 125, 170, 268, 439, 484; 5, p. 294; 7, p. 29; 17, p. 34; 19, p. 30.
  vii. 15, p. 288; 22, p. 29, 94, 100, 253, 273, 288.
  viii. 21, p. 293, 294.
  ix. 4-6, p. 282; 4, p. 274; 6, p. 85, 285; 16, p. 96; 22, p. 157.
  xv. 4, p. 314; 12, p. 325; 17, p. 61, 223.
  xvii. 17, p. 293.
  xviii. p. 81.
  xviii. 5, p. 292.
  xx. p. 333.
  xxii. 2, p. 126.
  xxiv. 45, p. 293.
  xxv. 22, p. 255; 23, p. 314.

Gen. xxvii. 35, p. 526.
  xxviii. 10, p. 214; 12, p. 334.
  xxix. 6, p. 338; 20, p. 530.
  xxxi. 10-13, p. 334; 20, p. 293; 24, p. 333.
  xxxii. 21, p. 283; 33, p. 275.
  xxxv. 18, p. 468, 470.
  xxxvii. 5, p. 330; 21, p. 468.
  xxxvii. 35, p. 526.
  xl. p. 331.
  xl. 8, p. 331.
  xli. p. 335.
  xli. 16, p. 331; 40, p. 239.
  xlii. 9, p. 331; 38, p. 526.
  xliii. 30, p. 315.
  xlvi. 26, p. 132, 138, 240.
  xlviii. 14, p. 301.
  xlix. 6, p. 119, 268, 316; 26, p. 301.

Ex. iii. 2, p. 225; 14, p. 195, 203.
  iv. 15, p. 213.
  vii. 11, p. 363.
  viii. 3, p. 363.
  xiii. 21, p. 223.
  xiv. 24, p. 223.
  xv. 7, p. 225; 8, p. 102, 274; 10, p. 102.
  xvi. 16, p. 301.
  xix. 16, p. 223.
  xx. 7, p. 118.
  xxiii. 9, p. 239, 241.
  xxiv. 15, 16, p. 223.
  xxvi. 33, 34, p. 461.
  xxvii. 9, p. 461.
  xxviii. 3, p. 294; 42, p. 157.
  xxxiii. 14, p. 301; 22, p. 404; 19, p. 60, 196; 25, p. 285.
  xxxiv. 29, p. 301.
  xxxv. 21, 26, p. 195, 293; 29, p. 293.
  xxxvi. 2, p. 195.

INDEX OF TEXTS.

Ex. xxxviii. 26, p. 301.
  xl. 38, p. 223.

Lev. i. 3, p. 300; 5, p. 290.
  iii. 17, p. 285.
  vii. 7, p. 283; 25, p. 285; 26, p. 285.
  viii. 10, p. 301; 12, p. 301; 20, p. 300.
  ix. 7, p. 282; 24, p. 226.
  x. 2, p. 225, 226; 19, p. 480.
  xii. 2, p. 140.
  xv. 2, p. 157; 16, p. 332.
  xvii. 10-14, p. 282, 285; 11-14, p. 274; 17, p. 290.
  xix. 17, p. 293; 26, p. 285; 28, p. 28, 522; 29, p. 126.
  xxi. 1, 11, p. 522.
  xxii. 4, p. 522.
  xxvi. 11, 30, p. 258; 12, p. 400; 36, p. 294.

Num. v. 2, p. 522; 8, p. 283.
  vi. 6, p. 522; 11, p. 522.
  vii. 10, p. 522.
  ix. 6, 7, 10, p. 522.
  xi. 31, p. 102.
  xii. 6-8, p. 336; 8, p. 61.
  xiv. 32, p. 270.
  xv. 28, p. 235.
  xvi. 22, p. 97, 137, 258; 30, p. 477.
  xvii. 11, p. 225.
  xix. 11-13, p. 522.
  xxiii. 10, p. 468; 23, p. 362.
  xxiv. 3, p. 338, 421; 3, 15, p. 311; 4, p. 423.
  xxvii. 3, p. 338; 16, p. 97, 137, 258.
  xxxi. 17, p. 139.

Deut. i. 33, p. 223, 278; 34, p. 278; 39, p. 186, 192.
  ii. 30, p. 108.
  iv. 9, p. 241; 11, p. 274; 12, p. 223; 24, p. 225; 29, p. 297; 33, p. 278; 37, p. 301.
  v. 25, p. 278.
  vi. 5, p. 297.
  viii. 5, p. 293.
  ix. 3, p. 225.
  xi. 18, p. 293.
  xii. 15, p. 241; 16, p. 285; 23, p. 285.
  xiii. 2, p. 336; 7, p. 239.
  xv. 23, p. 285.
  xviii. 10-12, p. 362, 363.
  xix. 6, p. 294.
  xx. 8, p. 294; 16, p. 181.
  xxi. 14, p. 191.
  xxii. 26, p. 468.
  xxiii. 10, p. 285, 332.
  xxiv. 5, p. 191, 285; 6, p. 242.
  xxvii. 25, p. 286.
  xxviii. 12, p. 62; 28, p. 294, 344; 34, p. 342; 58, p. 59.

Deut. xxix. 3, p. 293.
  xxx. 17, p. 293.
  xxxi. 21, p. 295.
  xxxii. 18, p. 137; 40, p. 59; 46, p. 293.
  xxxiii. 3, p. 149.

Josh. v. 1, p. 294; 8, p. 339.
  x. 40, p. 181.
  xi. 11-14, p. 181.
  xiv. 7, 160.
  xxii. 5, p. 297.
  xxiii. 14, p. 293, 297.
  xxiv. 10, p. 363; 23, p. 293.

Judg. v. 9, p. 293; 15, p. 294; 30, p. 301.
  vi. 31, p. 480.
  vii. 13, p. 331.
  viii. 3, p. 235; 18, p. 279.
  xi. 34, p. 126; 39, p. 139.
  xvi. 30, p. 468.
  xix. 5, p. 292.

1 Sam. i. 13, p. 293; 15, p. 241; 26, p. 107.
  x. 5, p. 423; 10, p. 358.
  xiv. 32, p. 285.
  xvi. 15, p. 358.
  xviii. 1, p. 239; 10, p. 343, 358.
  xix. 9, p. 358; 20, p. 423.
  xx. 4, p. 241.
  xxi. 14-16, p. 343.
  xxii. 8, p. 341.
  xxiv. 6, p. 160.
  xxv. 31, p. 160; 37, p. 313, 467.
  xxvi. 12, p. 325.
  xxviii. p. 494.
  xxviii. 6, p. 335; 13, p. 477, 499; 14, p. 279, 363.

2 Sam. xiii. 2, p. 341.
  xvii. 11, p. 301.
  xviii. 14, p. 274.
  xix. 36, p. 186.
  xxi. 3, p. 283.
  xxii. 16, p. 273.
  xxiv. 10, p. 160.

1 Kings ii. 4, p. 297; 44, p. 160.
  iii. 5, p. 334; 26, p. 314; 28, p. 313.
  viii. 17, p. 293.
  x. 2, p. 293.
  xii. 33, p. 294.
  xv. 29, p. 181.
  xvii. 17, p. 468, 470; 21, p. 313, 521; 21-23, p. 468.
  xviii. 12, p. 102.
  xix. 11, p. 125.
  xxi. 7, p. 292.

2 Kings i. 2, 7, p. 339.

INDEX OF TEXTS. 573

2 Kings ii. 16, p. 102.
  iv. 34, p. 522.
  v. 26, p. 293.
  viii. 1, p. 196; 12, p. 248.
  x. 27, p. 49.
  xiii. 21, p. 522.
  xv. 5, p. 191; 16, p. 248.
  xx. 7, p. 339.
  xxiii. 3, p. 297.

1 Chron. x. 13, p. 494.
  xii. 23, p. 301; 33, p. 295, 301; 38, 295.
  xvi. 27, p. 60.
  xxii. 12, p. 246.
  xxviii. 9, p. 195, 297; 12, p. 234.
  xxix. 11, p. 230.

2 Chron. ii. 11, p. 246.
  vi. 38, p. 297.
  vii. 11, p. 293.
  xxi. p. 346.
  xxvi. 20, p. 346.
  xxxiii. 6, p. 363.

Neh. v. 7, p. 180, 293.
  vi. 8, p. 294.
  ix. 6, p. 30, 75.

Esther iv. 13, p. 241.
  vii. 5, p. 293.

Job i. 2, p. 78; 21, p. 249, 467.
  ii. 6, p. 239.
  iii. 3, p. 247; 20, p. 107, 274.
  iv. 12-21, p. 333; 13, p. 214; 15, p. 273; 19, p. 268; 21, p. 268.
  vi. 9, p. 269, 470.
  vii. 13, p. 333.
  viii. 10, p. 294.
  ix. 18, p. 273.
  x. 1, p. 107; 8, p. 88; 9, p. 27; 8-12, p. 134, 248; 11, p. 268, 275.
  xi. 20, p. 273, 468.
  xii. 3, p. 294; 9, p. 375; 10, p. 30, 258.
  xiv. 2, p. 473; 8, p. 232; 12, p. 467; 14, p. 480; 21, p. 520.
  xv. 13, p. 235; 35, p. 313.
  xvi. 13, p. 317.
  xvii. 4, p. 294; 11, p. 294.
  xix. 17, p. 313; 25-27, p. 430, 541; 27, p. 317.
  xx. 2, p. 214; 8, p. 328; 23, p. 313.
  xxi. 24, p. 275.
  xxiii. 12, p. 446.
  xxiv. 12, p. 286.
  xxvi. 5, p. 477.
  xxvii. 3, p. 98, 100, 273; 6, p. 160; 8, p. 268, 269, 470; 8-10, p. 480.
  xxviii. 28, p. 223; end, p. 53.
  xxix. 3, p. 269.

Job xxx. 16, p. 180; 18, p. 268; 27, p. 314.
  xxxi. 15, p. 134; 39, p. 273, 468.
  xxxii. 8, p. 101, 109, 246; 19, p. 313.
  xxxiii. 4, p. 95, 109, 134; 6, p. 134, 249, 268; 8, p. 278; 15, p. 333; 19, p. 338; 29, p. 548; 30, p. 274.
  xxxiv. 10, p. 294; 14, p. 113, 152, 475; 34, p. 294.
  xxxvi. 14, p. 468.
  xxxvii. 1, p. 297.
  xxxviii. 4-7, p. 75, 76; 7, p. 78; 28, p. 137; 36, p. 317.
  xli. 13, p. 273, 288.

Ps. iii. 6, p. 333.
  iv. 9, p. 333.
  v. 10, p. 244, 292, 313.
  vi. 5, p. 492.
  vii. 6, p. 119; 10, p. 317.
  viii. p. 78.
  viii. 2, p. 83, 257; 5, p. 79, 81.
  x. 18, p. 92.
  xi. 1, p. 126; 5, p. 258.
  xii. 3, p. 293.
  xiii. 3, p. 241, 295, 467.
  xv. 2, p. 294.
  xvi. p. 479.
  xvi. 2, p. 126; 7, p. 317; 9, p. 119, 297; 10, p. 391, 468.
  xvii. p. 479.
  xvii. 15, p. 61.
  xviii. 15, p. 158.
  xix. p. 78.
  xix. 3, p. 408; 5, p. 277; 15, p. 294.
  xxi. 3, p. 293.
  xxii. 10, p. 134, 255; 20, p. 126.
  xxiv. 4, p. 117, 258.
  xxv. 16, p. 126.
  xxvii. 8, p. 294; 12, p. 239.
  xxix. 1, p. 78, 238.
  xxx. 3, p. 468; 6, p. 273; 9, p. 492; 13, p. 119.
  xxxi. 9, p. 277, 314.
  xxxiii. 6, p. 90, 278; 7, p. 133; 15, p. 98, 138.
  xxxiv. 5, p. 156; 9, p. 218, 417; 19, p. 235.
  xxxv. 4, p. 156; 9, p. 228, 315; 17, p. 126; 25, p. 239, 241.
  xxxvi. 9, p. 228, 418.
  xxxvii. 31, p. 314.
  xxxviii. 10, p. 292, 297.
  xxxix. 4, p. 292, 294.
  xl. 8, p. 314; 13, p. 292.
  xli. 7, p. 294.
  xlii. 5, 6, 7, 12, p. 180.
  xliii. p. 126.
  xliii. 5, p. 180.
  xliv. p. 126.
  xliv. 16, p. 156; 22, p. 296; 24, p. 328.

Ps. xlviii. 14, p. 293.
  xlix. p. 479.
  xlix. 4, p. 294; 12, p. 292, 313, 548; 15, p. 485, 526; 19, 468.
  l. 2, p. 60.
  li. 7, p. 247; 8, p. 315, 317; 10, p. 117, 460; 12, p. 125, 173, 313; 14, p. 195; 19, p. 235, 295.
  lv. 15, p. 526.
  lvi. 5, p. 181; 14, p. 274.
  lvii. 5, p. 214; 9, p. 119, 126.
  lviii. 4, p. 255; 9, p. 232.
  lxiii. 10, p. 477, 482.
  lxiv. 7, p. 292.
  lxvi. 9, p. 107, 342.
  lxix. 9, p. 342; 21, p. 271.
  lxxi. 6, p. 255.
  lxxiii. p. 479.
  lxxiii. 7, p. 294; 20, p. 328; 21, p. 294, 317; 26, p. 174, 295.
  lxxiv. 19, p. 548.
  lxxvi. 13, p. 235.
  lxxvii. 7, p. 234.
  lxviii. 8, p. 173; 14, p. 223, 328; 38, p. 225, 461; 47, p. 232.
  lxxxiv. 3, p. 294, 297; 11, p. 78; 7, p. 556.
  lxxxvi. 11, p. 240.
  lxxxviii. p. 492.
  lxxxviii. 5, p. 191; 10, p. 492; 11-13, p. 494.
  lxxxix. 6, p. 78; 49, p. 276, 526.
  xc. 2, p. 137; 4, p. 41, 519; 7, p. 337.
  xcii. 5, p. 78.
  xciv. 9, p. 261; 19, p. 214; 21, p. 286.
  xcv. 10, p. 235.
  c. p. 134.
  ci. 5, p. 242.
  cii. 5, p. 274, 294.
  ciii. p. 126.
  ciii. 1, p. 314; 5, p. 268.
  civ. p. 126.
  civ. 29, p. 30, 152, 475; 30, p. 113, 288; 31, p. 261.
  cv. 2, p. 239.
  cvii. 5, p. 180.
  cviii. 2, p. 119.
  cix. 22, p. 294.
  cx. 3, p. 195.
  cxi. 10, p. 222.
  cxii. 4, p. 226, 268.
  cxv. 7, p. 271; 17, p. 492.
  cxvi. 7, p. 126, 173.
  cxix. 73, p. 134.
  cxxi. 4, p. 324, 328.
  cxxiv. 7, p. 567.
  cxxvii. 2, p. 329.
  cxxix. 5, p. 156.
  cxxxi. 2, p. 126, 173, 340.
  cxxxiii. 2, p. 301.
  cxxxv. 17, p. 273, 278.

Ps. cxxxix. 1, 17, p. 212; 5, p. 186; 8, p. 226; 13-16, p. 134, 226, 248; 14, p. 234, 241; 15, p. 134, 272, 467; 16, p. 48, 247; 17, p. 214; 18, p. 333; 23, p. 214.
  cxli. 8, p. 274, 468.
  cxlii. 4, p. 180.
  cxliii. 4, p. 180, 294; 7, p. 173.
  cxliv. 6, p. 158.
  cxlvi. 4, p. 467.
  cxlvii. 3, p. 295; 18, p. 101.
  cxlix. 6, p. 271.

Prov. i. 7, p. 223.
  ii. 10, p. 297.
  iii. 3, p. 293; 8, p. 275; 19, p. 78; 22, p. 107.
  iv. 23, p. 274.
  vi. 6-8, p. 34; 18, p. 294; 21, p. 293; 30, p. 242.
  vii. 23, p. 316.
  viii. p. 232.
  viii. 5, p. 293; 23-31, p. 53, 229; 24, p. 137; 30, p. 229.
  ix. 1, p. 229, 374.
  x. 6, p. 301; 11, p. 271; 13, p. 294; 31, p. 214.
  xii. 10, p. 315; 14, p. 214; 25, p. 294; 28, p. 479.
  xiii. 2, p. 214; 12, p. 341; 25, p. 313.
  xiv. 10, p. 293, 296; 30, p. 296; 32, p. 480; 33, p. 294.
  xv. 11, p. 296; 24, p. 479; 28, p. 294; 32, p. 294.
  xvi. 1, p. 294; 9, p. 293.
  xvii. 22, p. 296.
  xviii. 4, p. 271; 15, p. 246; 20, p. 214, 313.
  xix. 2, p. 234; 25, p. 246.
  xx. 27, p. 34, 98, 118, 182, 234, 239, 313; 30, p. 313.
  xxi. 11, p. 246.
  xxii. 11, p. 295; 18, p. 313.
  xxiii. 2, p. 239, 241; 7, p. 293; 15, p. 179; 16, p. 317; 17, p. 294; 26, p. 293; 33, p. 294; 35, p. 342.
  xxiv. 2, p. 294.
  xxv. 20, p. 294.
  xxvi. 18, p. 343.
  xxvii. 17, p. 286; 25, p. 242.
  xxx. 19, p. 139; 25, p. 34.
  xxxi. 2, p. 313; 3, p. 219.

Eccles. i. 13, p. 293; 16, p. 293.
  ii. 2, p. 343; 14, p. 300; 19, p. 480; 20, p. 294.
  iii. 11, p. 42, 475; 21, p. 152, 288, 475, 479.
  v. 3, p. 331; 6, p. 328.
  vi. 3, p. 255; 9, p. 241; 12, p. 480.
  vii. 4, p. 235; 25, p. 179; 29, p. 194.
  viii. 1, p. 301; 8, p. 469; 11, p. 293.

INDEX OF TEXTS.

Eccles. ix. 3, p. 293; 4, p. 492 ; 9, p. 276; 10, p. 492, 493.
  x. 13, p. 343; 20, p. 160.
  xi. 5, p. 139, 248.
  xii. 6, p. 269; 7, p. 44, 152, 270, 480; 14, p. 152.

Cant. ii. 5, p. 342.
  iv. 1-5, p. 271; 3, p. 278.
  v. 2, p. 327; 4, p. 314; 10, p. 92.
  vii. 10, p. 328.
  viii. 6, p. 293.

Isa. i. 14, p. 231, 258.
  ii. 22, p. 98, 100, 253, 273.
  iii. 9, p. 280, 301; 20, p. 97.
  iv. 3, p. 49.
  v. 14, p. 239, 242, 288; 27, p. 324.
  vi. p. 79, 421.
  vi. 3, p. 63, 264 ; 6, p. 518 ; 10, p. 295.
  vii. 15, p. 186, 192; 16, p. 254.
  viii. 9, p. 190 ; 19, p. 362.
  x. 7, p. 293; 17, p. 226.
  xi. 2, p. 61, 222, 240; 4, p. 273.
  xiv. 9, p. 494 ; 12, p. 75 ; 12-15, p. 148.
  xvi. 11, p. 313, 314, 321.
  xvii. 11, p. 341.
  xviii. p. 277.
  xx. 14, p. 526.
  xxii. 11, p. 46, 48.
  xxiv.-xxvii. p. 481.
  xxiv. 5, p. 163 ; 10, p. 76 ; 23, p. 156.
  xxv. 1, p. 46; 4, p. 235.
  xxvi. 9, p. 116, 179, 239, 313, 333 ; 14-19, p. 485, 526; 21, p. 60.
  xxix. 7, p. 328 ; 8, p. 242 ; 16, p. 403; 22, p. 156; 24, p. 235.
  xxx. 27, p. 59; 33, p. 273.
  xxxi. 3, p. 103, 104, 219.
  xxxii. 4, p. 293; 6, p. 242.
  xxxiii. 11, p. 235, 276 ; 14, p. 225, 226; 18, p. 294.
  xxxiv. 9-11, p. 76.
  xxxv. 1, p. 567.
  xxxvii. 26, p. 46, 48, n.; 36, p. 346.
  xxxviii. 12, p. 268, 269, 470; 18, p. 492.
  xl.-lxvi. p. 46, 421.
  xl. 4, p. 340; 13, p. 214; 28, p. 133.
  xlii. 1, p. 258; 5, p. 98, 133.
  xliii. 17, p. 470.
  xliv. 2, p. 134; 16, p. 276.
  xlv. 7, p. 225, 345; 9, p. 403.
  xlviii. 8, p. 255.
  xlix. 1, 5, p. 255.
  li. 7, p. 295, 314; 13, p.134.
  liii. 2, 3, p. 563 ; 12, p. 274, 286, 399, 468.
  lvi. 10, p. 328.

Isa. lvii. 15, p. 235; 16, p. 98, 134; 19, p. 214; 20, p. 189, 190.
  lviii. 1, p. 271; 10, p. 242.
  lix. 13, p. 294.
  lxi. 3, p. 568.
  lxiii. 9, p. 301 ; 15, p. 314 ; 17, p. 295.
  lxiv. 7, p. 403.
  lxv. 12, p. 192 ; 14, p. 294 ; 17, p. 293.
  lxvi. 2, p. 235 ; 3, p. 192, 285 ; 24, p. 521.

Jer. i. 5, p. 45, 255.
  ii. 13, p. 228; 24, p. 271; 34, p. 286.
  iii. 16, p. 293.
  iv. 19, p. 126, 241, 276, 294, 314, 315; 23-26, p. 76.
  v. 3, p. 342; 9, p. 258; 21, p. 294.
  vi. 7, p. 189.
  viii. 18, p. 180.
  xii. 2, p. 317.
  xiv. 6, p. 271 ; 14, p. 294 ; 19, p 258; 30, p. 232.
  xv. 9, p. 273, 468.
  xvi. 12, p. 295.
  xvii. 4, p. 225 ; 9, p. 296, 340 ; 13, p. 229.
  xviii. 2, p. 27; 6, p. 403; 16, p. 49; 19, p. 27.
  xx. 9, p. 295, 311, 423.
  xxiii. 9, p. 271, 295, 467; 16, p. 294; 20, p. 294; 24, p. 260; 26, p. 327; 32, p. 336.
  xxv. 4, p. 235.
  xxvii. 9, p. 363.
  xxix. 8, p. 336.
  xxx. 15, p. 341.
  xxxi. 20, p. 314; 33, p. 295, 323, 314; 39, p. 277.
  xxxii. 39, p. 295; 40, p. 294.
  xxxiii. 24, p. 276.
  xxxviii. 16, p. 98, 134, 240.
  xlviii. 36, p. 321.
  li. 14, p. 118; 39-57, p. 467.

Lam. i. 20, p. 180, 314.
  ii. 11, p. 314, 316.; 12, p. 286, 468; 15, p. 60; 18, p. 296; 19, p. 271.
  iii. 13, p. 317; 20, p. 180; 24, p. 241; 33, p. 293 ; 41, p. 296 ; 48-51, p. 277; 65, p. 295, 343.
  iv. 7, p. 92; 20, p. 273.

Ezek. i. 4, p. 224, 228; 20, p. 96; 28, p. 61, 424; 27, p. 224; 28, p. 224.
  iii. 12, p. 60; 23, p. 424.
  viii. 1, p. 335, 424; 2, p. 224.
  x. 17, p. 96.
  xi. 5, p. 235; 19, p. 295; 24, p. 424.
  xiii. 2, p. 311.
  xvi. 4, p. 274; 30, p. 295.

INDEX OF TEXTS.

Ezek. xviii. 4, p. 30, 134, 258.
  xix. 10, p. 83.
  xx. 32, p. 235.
  xxii. 20-22, p. 225.
  xxvi. 20, p. 477.
  xxviii. 2-5, p. 295; 13-15, p. 83.
  xxxi. 16, p. 494.
  xxxii. 18, p. 477; 17, p. 494.
  xxxiii. 25, p. 285.
  xxxvii. 1-14, p. 101, 485; 5, p. 273; 6, 8, p. 275.
  xl. 22, p. 374.
  xliii. 2, p. 228, 264; 3, p. 424.
  xlvii. 12, p. 556.

Dan. i. 8, p. 293; 17, p. 331, 336.
  ii. 19, p. 336; 22, p. 60, 228; 28, p. 298; 30, p. 294, 298.
  iv. 2, 7, 10, p. 298; 13, p. 297, 343; 23, p. 59.
  vii. 1, p. 298, 336; 10, p. 224; 15, p. 268, 298.
  viii. 18, p. 335.
  x. 7, p. 311, 335; 8, p. 424; 9, p. 335.
  xii. 2, p. 481, 569.

Hos. iv. 11, p. 294.
  v. 15, p. 60.
  vi. 2, p. 485.
  vii. 11, p. 294; 14, p. 296.
  ix. 7, p. 343.
  xi. 8, p. 295.
  xii. 4, p. 255.
  xiii. 14, p. 526.
  xiv. 1, p. 248.

Joel iii. 1, p. 336.

Amos i. 13, p. 248.
  vi. 6, p. 342; 8, p. 231.

Jonah ii. 4, p. 274.

Mic. i. 3, p. 60.
  iii. 6, p. 78.
  v. 11, p. 363.
  vii. 3, p. 244.

Hab. iii. 16. p. 313.

Hag. ii. 13, p. 522.

Zech. iii. 7, p. 419.
  iv. p. 223, 269.
  iv. 1, p. 424; 1-4, p. 61; 5, p. 61; 10, p. 374.
  v. 6, p. 61.
  xii. 1, p. 98, 108, 134, 138, 313, 376.

Mal. iii. 1, p. 45; 20, p. 78.

Judith xvi. 17, p. 521.

Ecclus. xv. 14, p. 193.
  xvii. 27, p. 492, 528; 30, p. 473.
  xix. 12, p. 313.
  xxxi. 1, p. 328; 3, p. 331; 5, p. 327.
  xxxiii. 5, p. 314.
  xxxiv. 2, p. 325, 328.
  xxxv. 13, p. 166.
  xxxvi. 13, p. 403.
  xxxvii. 13, p. 166.
  xxxviii. 23, p. 469
  xl. 1, p. 467.
  xli. 4, p. 474.
  xliii. 26, p. 260; 27, p. 260; 29, p. 374.
  xlvi. 20, p. 494.
  xlviii. 24, p. 422.
  li. 21, p. 313.

Wisd. i. 6, p. 317; 7, p. 260; 11, p. 468.
  ii. 2, p. 470; 23, p. 473.
  iii. 1-4, p. 468, 474, 486, 520.
  iv. 2, p. 486.
  vi. 13-20, p. 479.
  vii. 3, p. 271; 22, p. 126; 26, p. 227; 27, p. 295.
  viii. 17-19, p. 331; 20, p. 44.
  ix. 15, p. 268, 450.
  x. 5, p. 315.
  xii. 1, p. 260.
  xv. 11, p. 91, 101.
  xvi. 14, p. 469.

Baruch ii. 17, p. 478.

Song of Three Children 63, p. 468.

1 Macc. ii. 24, p. 317; xiii. 28, p. 523.

2 Macc. vii. 14, p. 481; 22, p. 248; 28, p. 47.

Matt. i. 2, p. 334.
  iv. 24, p. 346, 348; 8, p. 148.
  v. 9, p. 229; 25, p. 547.
  vi. 23, p. 118, 183, 277; 18, p. 349; 25, p. 103; 30, p. 134.
  viii. 17, p. 338, 346; 22, p. 152; 28-31, p. 349, 350; 31, p. 543.
  ix. 4, p. 294; 18, p. 301; 32, p. 347.
  x. 28, p. 115, 469; 39, p. 190.
  xi. 14, p. 548; 23, p. 482; 25, p. 257.
  xii. 18, p. 258; 22-24, p. 347; 27, p. 351; 34, p. 294, 295; 40, p. 274, 482; 41, p. 165; 43, p. 82.
  xiii. 19, p. 295; 43, p. 563.
  xiv. 1, p. 545; 12, p. 270.
  xv. 19, p. 294.
  xvi. 14, p. 546; 28, p. 276.
  xvii. 2, p. 301; 3, p. 499; 12, p. 548; 15, p. 348.
  xviii. 6, p. 415.

INDEX OF TEXTS.

Matt. xxi. 25, p. 59.
xxii. 30, p. 82.
xxiii. 35, p. 286; 37, p. 192.
xxiv. 48, p. 293.
xxv. 5, p. 324.
xxvi. 29, p. 500; 38, p. 391.
xxvii. 19, p. 333; 50, p. 469; 51, p. 484, 486; 52, p. 502.
xxviii. 3, p. 81, 280; 18, p. 386.

Mark i. 26, p. 350.
iii. 4, p. 468; 15, p. 346; 21, p. 144.
iv. 15, 19, p. 295.
v. 3-5, p. 349; 7, p. 350; 38, p. 276.
vi. 16, p. 545.
vii. 21, p. 295; 30, p. 350.
viii. 12, p. 220.
ix. 18, p. 348; 20, p. 348; 24, p. 191; 25, p. 348.
xiii. 32, p. 386.
xvi. 17, p. 427.

Luke i. 25, p. 255; 35, p. 136, 140; 36, p. 247; 41, p. 45, 255; 47, p. 220; 51, p. 210; 66, p. 293; 80, p. 257.
ii. 9, p. 82; 19, p. 293; 26, p. 276; 40-52, p. 257; 47, p. 144; 51, p. 293, 295; 52, p. 247.
iv. 34, 41, p. 350.
v. 15, p. 348; 22, p. 294.
vi. 18, p. 349; 19, p. 301; 45, p. 295.
viii. 2, p. 348, 350; 15, p. 296; 27, 29, 30, p. 349, 350.
ix. 9, p. 545; 19, p. 546; 29, p. 280; 30, p. 499; 32, p. 324; 39, p. 348; 42, p. 348; 47, p. 294.
x. 18, p. 75, 154.
xi. 20, p. 360.
xii. 19, p. 126; 58, p. 547.
xiii. 11, p. 347.
xv. 18, p. 59; 24, p. 152.
xvi. 19, p. 498; 25, p. 529.
xx. 35, p. 82, 123, 540; 36, p. 84, 540.
xxi. 14, p. 293; 34, p. 292.
xxiii. 38, p. 294; 43, p. 498; 46, p. 391.
xxiv. 25, p. 210; 32, p. 295; 38, p. 294.

John i. 1, p. 210, 211; 1-4, p. 63, 227; 3, p. 90; 4, p. 409; 5-9, p. 410, 412; 13, p. 290, 440; 14, p. 392; 18, p. 388; 21, p. 546, 548; 51, p. 369.
ii. 21, p. 516; 22, p. 210.
iii. 6, p. 398, 461; 7, p. 401; 8, p. 244; 13, p. 59, 388; 14, p. 415; 17, p. 192; 36, p. 172, 276.
iv. 24, p. 62, 103, 119, 196; 37, p. 210.

John v. 17, p. 133; 21, p. 483; 37, p. 61.
vi. p. 541.
vi. 63, p. 97, 104, 399; 68, p. 211.
vii. 38, p. 314.
viii. 9, p. 161; 12, p. 227; 31, p. 210; 44, p. 76; 51, p. 276; 58, p. 388.
ix. 1-3, p. 352; 2, p. 546; 4, p. 471; 493; 39, p. 192.
x. 11, p. 239; 35, p. 210.
xi. 11, p. 467; 12, p. 325; 33, p. 220.
xii. 38, p. 210; 41, p. 80; 47, p. 192.
xiii. 2, p. 296; 21, p. 220; 27, p. 352.
xiv. 2, p. 556; 23, p. 42, 210.
xv. 25, p. 210.
xvi. 6, p. 294; 13-15, p. 228; 30, p. 511.
xvii. 5, p. 386, 392, 518; 17, p. 210; 24, p. 388, 544.
xix. 30, p. 469.
xx. 22, p. 94.

Acts ii. 3, p. 301; 4, p. 426; 25, p. 468; 25-27, p. 391; 27, p. 276, 482; 46, p. 294.
iv. 32, p. 295.
v. 3, p. 296; 15, p. 349.
vii. 23, p. 293; 54, p. 294; 55, p. 335.
viii. 7, p. 349; 9, p. 360; 22, p. 295; 23, p. 316.
ix. 3, p. 336; 7, p. 311, 336.
x. 9-16, p. 324, 335; 10, p. 335; 38, p. 349; 45, p. 426; 46, p. 426.
xi. 5, p. 335; 23, p. 293.
xii. 11, p. 335; 23, p. 346.
xiii. 6, p. 360; 11, p. 346; 48, p. 49.
xiv. 17, p. 292.
xv. 18, p. 48; 20, 29, p. 286; 26, p. 469.
xvi. 9, p. 334, 335; 14, p. 293; 16-18, p. 364.
xvii. 25, p. 28; 26, p. 132, 139, 290; 28, p. 95, 170, 181, 186, 260, 374; 29, p. 245.
xviii. 9, p. 334, 335; 25, p. 219.
xix. 13, p. 351; 15, p. 349, 350; 19, p. 360, 361.
xx. 9, p. 324; 28, p. 288.
xxi. 13, p. 294; 25, p. 286.
xxii. 9, p. 336; 17, p. 335, 423.
xxiii. 1, p. 165; 8, p. 481; 11, p. 334.
xxiv. 16, p. 160, 165, 511.
xxvi. 13, p. 225; 18, p. 154.
xxvii. 23, p. 334.

Rom. i. 19-28, p. 408, 409; 20, p. 55, 62, 78, 212, 407; 21, p. 295; 24, p. 295; 26, p. 185; 28, p. 449; 32, p. 452.

INDEX OF TEXTS.

Rom. ii. 7, p. 474; 9, p. 182; 12, 13, p. 163; 14, p. 165; 15, p. 160, 161, 162, 295; 26, p. 452; 28, p. 442.
iv. 17, p. 46, 483.
v. 5, p. 296, 419; 12, p. 36, 151; 18, p. 452.
v. 12-vii. 6, p. 433.
vi. 7, p. 331; 9, p. 527; 13, p. 448; 17, p. 293; 20, p. 195.
vii. p. 212, 433.
vii. 5, p. 448; 9, p. 547; 14, p. 193; 19, p. 193; 20, p. 194; 22, p. 220; 24, p. 512.
vii. 6-viii. p. 433.
viii. 3, p. 392, 461; 7, p. 153; 9, p. 423; 10, p. 496; 11, p. 497, 515, 534; 13, p. 440; 14, p. 418; 16, p. 107, 108, 161, 183, 235; 18, p. 559; 20, p. 74; 24, p. 432, 556; 26, p. 427; 27, p. 296; 28-30, p. 49; 29, p. 381.
ix. 1, p. 161, 167; 11-13, p. 45; 20, p. 403; 22, p. 50.
x. 1, p. 293; 6, p. 482; 10, p. 174, 295.
xi. 33, p. 54, 64, 240, 246; 34, p. 214.
xii. 2, p. 235; 11, p. 219.
xiii. 1, p. 182; 5, p. 161.
xiv. 5, p. 212; 23, p. 166.
xvi. 25, p. 50; 27, p. 53.

1 Cor. i. 27, p. 257.
ii. 9, p. 293, 419; 11, p. 98, 107, 108, 118, 183, 197, 199, 234, 398; 12, p. 232, 404; 12-16, p. 398; 16, p. 214.
iv. 4, p. 160, 168; 5, p. 294.
v. 3, p. 218.
vi. 12, p. 540; 13, p. 123, 540; 16, p. 133; 19, p. 539; 20, p. 103.
vii. 34, p. 218; 37, p. 193, 293.
viii. 6, p. 104; 7, 12, p. 166; 9, p. 166.
x. 29, p. 164, 166.
xi. 3, p. 128, 301; 7, p. 60, 86, 128; 8, p. 132; 29-32, p. 411.
xii.-xiv. p. 426.
xii. 6, p. 374; 23, p. 123.
xiii. 11, p. 205; 12, p. 175, 432; 13, p. 556.
xiv. p. 218, 220, 417, 420.
xiv. 2, p. 335, 426; 14, 15, 19, p. 217, 220, 463; 20, p. 315; 22, p. 427; 25, p. 418; 33, p. 153.
xv. 20, p. 492; 22, p. 483; 23, p. 557; 26, p. 526; 36-38, p. 134; 40, p. 81; 42-44, p. 540, 541, 563; 45, p. 15, 28, 97, 112, 119, 399; 46, p. 394, 395; 48, p. 396, 510; 49, p. 84; 52, p. 538; 53, p. 515; 54, p. 96.

2 Cor. i. 11, p. 180; 12, p. 161; 22, **p.** 296.
iii. 2, p. 298; 13, p. 301; 14, p. 295; 17, p. 412; 18, p. 149, 497.
iv. p. 515.
iv. 2, p. 164; 4, p. 148; 6, p. 210, 296, 566; 7, p. 269, 565; 16, p. 220, 446; 17, p. 60.
v. 1, p. 88, 268, 510, 513; 3, p. 511, 520; 5, p. 539; 6-8, p. 520, 556; 11, p. 164; 13, p. 335, 427.
vii. 1, p. 108, 218, 396; 3, p. 293.
viii. 16, p. 296.
ix. 7, p. 293.
xi. 3, p. 150.
xii. 1-4, p. 336, 419, 484; 7. p. 347.
xiii. 5, p. 176.

Gal. i. 8, p. 48, 336; 15, p. 255.
ii. 20, p. 418.
iii. 1, p. 367; 4, p. 511; 13, p. 172; 27, p. 515.
iv. 3, p. 266; 8, p. 408.
v. 16, p. 440, 457; 17, p. 189, 442, 458; 19, p. 461; 20, p. 361, 363; 22, p. 458.

Eph. i. 4, p. 48, 51; 10, p. 51; 18, p. 210.
ii. 1, 5, p. 152; 2, p. 231; 3, p. 172, 189, 219, 440, 449; 19-22, p. 516.
iii. 5, p. 420; 9, p. 240, 247, 383; 10, p. 54, 229; 16, p. 220, 446; 17, p. 296.
iv. 8, p. 484; 9, p. 482; 10, p. 386; 17, p. 448; 18, p. 33; 20-24, p. 219; 21, p. 317; 23, p. 183, 210, 217, 219, 235, 456, 463; 24, p. 84, 515.
v. 8, p. 412; 9, p. 458; 13, p. 279; 14, p. 152, 403; 19, p. 296; 22, p. 133; 23, p. 128, 301.
vi. 6, p. 113, 239; 12, p. 77, 231.

Phil. i. 7, p. 293; 23, p. 520; 27, p. 113.
ii. 6, p. 61; 7, p. 391; 10, p. 482.
iii. 20, p. 419; 21, p. 540.
iv. 7, p. 210, 220.

Col. i. 9, p. 247; 15-17, p. 211; 16, p. 86, 383; 17, p. 261; 26, p. 50; 27, p. 404.
ii. 8, 20, p. 266; 9, p. 516; 15, p. 484; 18, p. 217, 218, 362, 448; 19, p. 301.
iii. 3, p. 404; 10, p. 84, 515; 15, p. 296; 23, p. 113, 239, 241.

1 Thess. iv. 5, p. 408; 13, p. 492; 15-17, p. 511, 536.
v. 19, p. 219; 23, p. 103, 109, 110, 119, 400, 460.

INDEX OF TEXTS. 579

2 Thess. i. 8, p. 225.
 ii. 9, p. 363.

1 Tim. i. 5, p. 165, 293 ; 17, p. 229 ; 19, p. 165.
 ii. 1, p. 427; 14, p. 150.
 iii. 9, p. 165.
 iv. 2, p. 166.
 vi. 4, p. 340 ; 16, p. 60, 474.

2 Tim. i. 3, p. 165; 9, p. 49, 50, 51.
 iii. 8, p. 340; 16, p. 431.

Tit. i. 2, p. 51; 15, p. 166.
 iii. 5, p. 117.

Philem. 12, p. 315; 14, p. 195.

Heb. i. 2, p. 90; 3, p. 32, 61, 180, 211, 227, 388; 14, p. 103.
 ii. 14, p. 31, 345.
 iii. 12, p. 295.
 iv. 2, p. 410; 12, p. 24, 31, 103, 109, 110, 112, 275, 294, 487.
 v. 14, p. 192, 276.
 vi. 4, p. 402.
 vii. 5, p. 138; 10, p. 138; 16, p. 483.
 viii. 2, p. 516; 3-6, p. 516.
 ix. 1, p. 266; 8, p. 32; 9, p. 168; 11, p. 516 ; 14, p. 168, 273, 288 ; 24, p. 477; 27, p. 489.
 x. 2, p. 164, 168; 19, p. 486; 22, p. 160, 166, 295; 27, p. 225, 543.
 xi. 1, p. 32, 180 ; 3, p. 47, 90, 212 ; 11, p. 140 ; 40, p. 486, 493, 557.
 xii. 9, p. 137, 138; 19, p. 237, 278; 23, p. 468, 501, 536, 557 ; 24, p. 286; 29, p. 225.
 xiii. 18, p. 165.

Jas. i. 17, p. 61, 224, 225; 18, p. 137; 23, p. 279.
 ii. 26, p. 103, 114, 233.
 iii. 6, p. 227, 274, 544 ; 7, p. 185, 187; 9, p. 85, 87; 14, p. 294; 15, p. 247; 17, p. 229.
 v. 5, p. 109, 292.

1 Pet. i. 1, p. 48; 3, p. 137; 10, p. 430; 20, p. 52; 23, p. 137; 24, p. 60.
 ii. 11, p. 239, 442, 457 ; 16, p. 195 ; 19, p. 161, 501.

1 Pet. iii. 4, p. 220, 295, 446, 456; 16, p. 165; 18, p. 468, 482, 488; 19, p. 482, 489 ; 20, p. 181; 21, p. 165 ; 22, p. 482.
 iv. 6, p. 483, 488.

2 Pet. i. 4, p. 172, 185, 188, 404 ; 13, p. 268; 19, p. 296; 21, p. 421.
 ii. 12, p. 185, 187.
 iii. 5, p. 32, 90; 8, p. 41, 519.

1 John i. 1, p. 210; 1-3, p. 392 ; 5, p. 148, 204, 225; 7, p. 149.
 ii. 10, p. 149.
 iii. 2, p. 404, 544; 8, p. 75; 9, p. 137; 14, p. 152; 19, p. 160 ; 19-21, p. 295; 24, p. 418.
 iv. 8, p. 203; 16, p. 148; 18, p. 158.

Jude 5, p. 332; 6, p. 140; 7, p. 490; 10, p. 185, 209; 12, p. 232; 19, p. 398; 25, p. 60.

Apoc. i. 2, 9, p. 211; 4, p. 61, 374; 10, p. 336, 423; 17, p. 424; 18, p. 479.
 ii. 11, p. 152.
 iii. 1, p. 152, 222 ; 4, p. 508 ; 18, p. 158, 508.
 iv. 3, 5, 8, p. 61.
 iv. 3, p. 61, 224, 229 ; 4, p. 508 ; 5, p. 61, 224; 8, p. 61.
 v. 3, p. 482; 6, p. 61.
 vi. 4, p. 273 ; 9, p. 286, 468, 501, 531; 11, p. 508, 557.
 vii. 9, 13, p. 477, 508; 15, p. 497.
 viii. 9, p. 232.
 xi. 11, p. 96.
 xiii. 8, p. 49, 50; 13-15, p. 363; 18, p. 212.
 xiv. 5, p. 531; 13, p. 497.
 xv. 2, p. 224; 4, p. 452; 5, p. 517.
 xvi. 3, p. 96; 14, p. 363; 15, p. 508.
 xvii. 8, p. 49; 9, p. 212.
 xviii. 7, p. 293; 14, p. 241.
 xix. 8, p. 452; 13, p. 210; 14, p. 508; 15, p. 158; 20, p. 363.
 xx. 4, p. 468; 6, p. 152; 13, p. 496; 14, p. 152, 485.
 xx. 11-xxi. 1, p. 544.
 xxi. 6, p. 228; 8, p. 152; 11, p. 224; 19, p. 224; 22, p. 517.
 xxii. 1, p. 224; 2, p. 556.

II.

INDEX OF SUBJECTS.

	PAGE
Absolute pre-existence of humanity,	50, 51
Absorption of spirit into matter in man,	262
Adam and Christ,	433
Adam not created glorified,	119
Advantage of man over Satan,	157
Analogy between the natures of God and the creature,	58
Analogies of the spirit with its archetype,	206
Angelic source of man's ruin, scriptural hints on,	74
Angels in the image of God,	79
Anima vegetativa,	232
Annihilation of the wicked denied,	554
Anthropomorphism,	79
Apostolic expectation,	510
Apostle Paul's statement of his own condition,	450
Appearances of angels in Scripture,	81
Appearance of Samuel to Saul,	499
As for sinners,	568
Baptism to the unbeliever,	412
Beginning of a human life,	140
Bellarmine's argument on the intermediate state,	529
Bengel's treatment of biblical psychology,	8
Biblical psychology and physiology,	267
Birth a type of primeval creation,	249
Birth from above,	401
Blessedness of the intermediate state,	529
Blood the basis of the physical life,	289
Blood the life,	283
Blood the means of atonement,	284
Blood of man not forbidden,	291
Blood the source of the physical life,	290
Böhme's doctrine of the Trinity,	67
Bodily condition of spiritual appearances,	500
Body not the spontaneous formation of the soul,	320
Body of man prior to his soul,	91
Bodies of the ungodly in a future state,	542
Brain the organ of conscious vital activity,	303
Bread of life,	399
Breathing into man's nostrils,	94
Breathing of Christ on the disciples,	94
Characteristics of false and true prophecy,	311
Characteristics of man as created,	88
Characters of masculine and feminine beauty,	125
Charismatic ecstasy,	425
Christianity and Hellenic philosophy,	211
Christ's first coming, in respect of demoniacal power,	360
Christ the second Adam,	392
Christ preaching to the spirits in prison,	482
Christ leading captivity captive,	484
Christ's work in the grave,	488
Church without spot or wrinkle,	531
Clothing upon of the body,	511
Commenius on the angels,	375
Communication between spirit and body,	259
Communication of spirit and body solved in Scripture,	260
Commencement of human life,	247
Communication of Christ,	399
Communion between God and man, fallen and unfallen,	169
Conception, problems of,	141
Conclusion,	558
Condemnation of sin in the flesh,	452
Condition of waking,	328
Conscience, a good,	165
Conscience in fallen men,	167
Conscience in unfallen men,	166
Conscience of the heathen,	165
Conscience, precedent and subsequent,	166
Conscience, vitality of man's,	159
Conscience, nature of man's,	159
Conscience, definitions of,	160
Conscience and heart,	160
Conscience God's witness,	161
Conscience the knowledge of divine law,	163
Consciousness of a foregone state,	43
Consciousness of man progressive,	121

INDEX OF SUBJECTS. 581

	PAGE
Consciousness of God's Spirit,	198
Consciousness of the soul after death in Scripture,	494
Continuance of humanity,	531
Continual progress in God,	554
Conversion, its limits,	553
Co-operation in the threefold life of the spirit,	221
Corporeity of God, scriptural meaning of,	80
Corpse called Nephesch,	523
Created natures variously created,	90
Creation and God,	63
Creation, scriptural account of,	26-28
Creation of angels,	75
Creation by the Logos after the image of the Elohim,	86
Creation of man not mechanical,	88
Creationism possibly defensible from Scripture,	137
Creative word peculiar to man,	89
Creative process, comprehensive view of,	102
Dante's view of the intermediate state of souls,	509
Death,	36, 474
Death existing before the fall,	74
Death referred to the spirit,	152
Death and Scheôl,	527
Decisive reasons for this second edition,	252
Degradation by sin,	156
Demoniacal possession,	348
Demoniacal sickness,	347
Demoniacal temptation,	353
Demoniacs not read of in the Old Testament,	359
Departure from God, spiritual disease,	340
Desire a faculty of the soul,	245
Designations of the heart,	297
Destruction of death,	526
Development of the Mosaic account,	77, 78
Development theory condemned,	73
Development of Old Testament teaching,	481
Dichotomic and trichotomic view of man,	103
Distinction of spirit and soul,	99
Distinction between sin of Satan and sin of man,	148
Distinction between "Pneuma" and "Noûs,"	218
Distinct soul and spirit in Christ,	391
Distinction between charismatic and somnambulic tongues,	429
Divine Doxa,	60
Divine Doxa, its nature,	62
Divine nature not a development,	65

	PAGE
Divine likeness in the creature direct or inverted?	68
Doctrines of psychology found in Scripture,	16
Dorner's view of the equality of the Son,	388
Doxa of man, woman the glory of,	128
Doxa of human spirit,	288
Dreams, their nature,	327
Dreams in relation to the heart,	328
Dreams, their illusiveness,	328
Dreams, their reality,	328
Dreams, the background of life,	329
Dreams, sacred and secular,	329
Dreams, their forebodings,	330
Dreams, their ethical aspect,	331
Dreams, their possible guilt,	332
Dreams, their spiritual aspect,	333
Dreams from God,	334
Dualism of Psyche and Pneuma caused by sin,	114
Dualism of spirit and matter,	103
Dualism of the Christian,	457
Early treatment of biblical psychology,	4
Effect of death,	535
Effect of the fall on man,	561
Effect of mental affections on the heart,	302
Essential distinction between soul and body,	104
Essential distinction between spirit and matter,	105
Eternity of the procession of the Trinity,	58
Eternity the life of God,	518
Excess of the brain life,	312
Explanation of scriptural figures,	226
Explanation of scriptural raisings of the dead,	523
Faculties of the soul,	241
Faith, character of,	174
Female seer of Prevorst,	428
Fides directa and reflexa,	176
Figurative expression of the sevenfold divine nature,	224
Fire and light in the soul,	236
Fire and light, soul and spirit,	376
First and second Adam,	395
Fleshly heart,	376
Fleshly and spiritual soul,	440
Form of souls,	504
Foundation of soul's existence,	236
Free agency in man,	171
Freedom in God,	196
"Geist" and "Seele," derivation of,	142
Gess on the infinity of the Son,	390

INDEX OF SUBJECTS.

	PAGE
Glorification possible, to glorification actual,	122
Glorified body of Christ,	514
God, fire and light,	225
God's likeness in man,	381
Groans of creation,	559, 565
Healing of the nations,	556
Heart and feeling,	304
Heart the centre of bodily life,	292
Heathen ideas of the heart,	298
Hidden man of the heart,	220
Hints from somnambulism,	307
History of man a history of the world,	266
Hofmann's trichotomic teaching,	107
Holy of holies,	517
Hope of creation,	567
House not made with hands,	513
Human soul after death,	37
Human development,	254
Human constitution of the divine Son,	384
Human history progressive,	394
Ideal and historical world,	52
Ideal world of Scripture,	46
Identity of soul and spirit,	115
Image of God in man,	31, 78
Immortality, its nature,	475
Inbreathing, is it the source of the soul?	97
Inbreathing, scriptural doctrine of,	98
Incarnation an argument for traducianism,	136
Inclination and determination of will,	207
Infant regeneration,	405
Infants, capacity of regeneration in,	406
Infants, conditions of regeneration in,	406
Influence of demons on humanity,	346
Inherited sin an argument for traducianism,	134
Inner man,	446
Inspiration, its nature,	433
Institution of the Sabbath an argument for traducianism,	133
Intermediate state of souls,	490
Intermediate state of corporeity,	505
Interpretation of Luke xii. 58,	547
Intrusion of angels into human history,	76
Kenôsis,	203, 387
Knowledge of God,	409
Knowing and having in knowledge,	409
Lapse of time in the intermediate state,	530
Language a shadow of the Logos,	216
Law of God and law of sin,	445
Life of man twofold,	34
Life under penalty of death,	152
Life begins before consciousness,	416
Life of regeneration,	458
Light which lighteth every man,	410
Limitations of the Logos,	386
Limit to the body of death,	472
Liver,	316
Living soul, its distinctive meaning,	96
Locale of feeling, according to Scripture,	313
Logos not the ideal-world,	53
Logos and Sophia,	54
Logos the archetype of humanity,	209
Logos the product of the Noûs,	213
Loss of God's image in man,	84
Love is will,	244
Luther's view of spirit, soul, and body,	472
Magic entirely forbidden in Scripture,	363
Man not constrained by God,	193
Man never absolutely indifferent,	194
Man free to sin,	195
Man a microcosm,	265
Man not immortal,	473
Man a threefold spiritual nature,	542
Man the link of two worlds,	561
Man, his existence and origin,	29
Man, why called Adam,	82
Man God's offspring, in what sense,	95
Man, his spiritual characteristics,	126
Manifestation of spirit,	122
Man's judgment,	192
Man's freedom of choice since the fall,	193
Man's will free in form, not in substance,	194
Man's freedom to righteousness,	195
Man's freedom and God's freedom,	196
Man's choice,	192
Materials of the body, whether in the blood,	290
Meaning of sickness,	337
Meaning of being in the flesh,	448
Meaning of 1 Thess. iii. 23,	110
Meaning and effect of shame,	156
Means of human salvation,	173
Mediæval treatment of biblical psychology,	5
Metempsychosis, no biblical testimony for,	548
Metempsychosis not unreasonable,	549
Metempsychosis,	43

INDEX OF SUBJECTS.

Method of divine work in redemption, . . . 172
Mode of scriptural treatment of psychology, . . . 19
Modern psychological manifestations, . . . 25
Mode of man's appearance and existence, . . . 89
Motives, their operation, . 441
Mystery of the body, . . 539
Mystery of the Ego, . . 191
Mystic ecstasy, . . . 418

Naming of the creatures, . 215
Narratives of the creation of man, ... 87
Natural life and Ego life, . 186
Natural life not free, . . 186
Nature in two senses, . . 187
Nature of the soul's Sophia, . 246
Nature of human endowment with soul, . . . 253
Nature of sleep, . . . 324
Nature will and personal will, . 443
Necessity of doctrine of traducianism, . . . 139
Necessity for the embodiment of the creature, . . . 231
Nerve-spirit, . . . 318
Nervous atmosphere . . 319
Nervous system generally, . 318
New Testament use of the Logos, 209
New creation distinct from the first, ... 397
New Testament teaching on Hades, ... 479
New Testament teaching on future state, . . . 480
No condemnation in Christ Jesus, ... 451
Noûs, ... 212

Objections of Harless to scientific biblical psychology, . . 13
Objective reality of tongues, . 430
Office of the Spirit in man, . 120
Opposition of will and deed, . 444
Order of creative works, . 71
Origen's view of the soul, . 43
Origen's view of a previous consciousness, . . . 45
O wretched man that I am! . 444

Palæontology confirming Scripture, ... 72
Partaking of humanity in the spiritual body of Christ, . 396
Pauline view of man's essential constitution, . . . 110
Paul speaks of himself as regenerate, . . . 453

Paul refers also to his unregenerate state, . . . 454
Peace of the righteous, . . 486
Peculiar forms in magic, . 362
Penalty of death, its meaning, . 151
Personal existence, its continuance, ... 476
Personality of the soul, . . 233
Personality of man, . . 179
Personality distinct from individuality, . . . 180
Phenomenal body of souls, . 453
Philosophy of the phenomenal appearance of souls, . 503
Philosophy of possession, . 351
Philosophy of the incarnation, . 383
Physical and divine nature, . 185
Physical degradation of man, . 157
Pneuma, ... 217
Possession defined and illustrated, . . . 354-356
Possibility of annihilation, . 475
Post-mortem investigations in brain and heart, . . 305
Potential constitution of mankind, ... 139
Power of the soul, . . 34
Pre-existence, mistaken notions of, ... 43
Present state a perversion of the natural, . . . 560
Priority of soul's creation, . 254
Process of divine development, 202
Process of sleep, . . . 325
Process of redemption, . . 384
Process of glorification, . . 120
Procession of the Trinity, . 56
Procreation, spiritual and psychical elements in, . . 140
Progression in the future state, 555
Progressive character of redemption, ... 382
Progressive embodiment of spirits denied, . . 550
Prohibition of beast's blood for man's food, . . 282, 285
Promise of a Messiah, . . 173
Propagation of the soul, . 129
Prophetic ecstasy, . . . 420
Prophetic vision, . . . 420
Prophetic teaching of the future state, ... 485
Psyche, its scriptural meaning, 113
Purgation of souls, . . 488
Purgatory not a scriptural doctrine, ... 487
Purpose of the diaphragm, . 315
Purpose of the restoration of the body, ... 543
Purposes and foreknowledge of God, ... 49

INDEX OF SUBJECTS.

	PAGE
Quickening spirit,	393
Reality of magic,	361
Reappearance of departed souls,	500
Reason of sickness,	338
Reason and its acts in man,	33
Reason of creative breathing into man's nostrils,	100
Reason of the divine procedure in redemption,	171
Reception of the first edition of this work,	11
Redemption and death,	482
Redemption from within,	563
Reformation treatment of biblical psychology,	6
Refraction of divine truth through humanity,	433
Regeneration an unconscious process,	404
Reins,	317
Relation of the blood indirectly to the spirit,	288
Relation of the body to the soul,	286, 321
Relation of the Ego to nature,	189
Relation of psychology to dogmatics,	18
Relation of psychology to physical science,	23
Relation of soul to spirit, as divine Doxa to Trinity,	118
Relation of Christ to humanity,	175
Relation of spirit and nature,	201
Relation of soul to the blood,	281
Relation of the various forms of life,	278
Relation of sacraments to faith,	411
Relation of the Christian to the law,	437
Relation of the Ego to temptation,	442
Relation of the reason to the spirit,	463
Relations in the Trinity,	57
Relations between men and angels,	83
Relations of soul, spirit, and body in death,	521
Remoteness of man from God,	170
Renewal of the spirit,	219
Restoration of the body,	536
Results of man's sin,	150
Resurrection body, its nature,	515
Return for the soul not possible,	544
Reunion of body and soul a mystery,	538
Rewards and punishments for souls,	498
Risen body, its relation to existing materials,	541
Romans vii. and viii., its exposition,	433
Sacramental gifts in respect of the corpse,	539
Sacraments, their operation,	416
Sacraments, their effect on the infant,	413
Σαρξ, its meaning,	439
Satanic agency peculiar to time and circumstances,	359
Satan's relation to sickness,	345
Scientific treatment of biblical psychology possible,	12
Scriptural teaching of biblical psychology,	16
Scriptural dichotomy,	109
Scriptural passages bearing on creationism,	138
Scriptural figures of the body,	263
Scriptural views of the heart,	301
Scriptural teaching of relation of head and heart,	311
Scriptural narratives of raising of the dead,	522
Scripture consistent with itself,	17
Scripture teaching on pre-existence,	47
Scripture statements on the mystery of divine nature,	61
Scripture teaching on succession of facts in creation,	91
Self-consciousness of man as Ego,	180
Self-consciousness of the soul,	184
Self-consciousness, why needed at the first,	255
Senses, of the,	29
Seven, significance of the number,	71
Seven-flamed lamp of Zechariah,	223
Sevenfold nature of the soul,	222
Sevenfold wisdom,	229
Seven powers in the divine nature,	228
Seven powers of the soul,	232
Seven powers of life,	272, etc.
Sexual distinctions, man subject to,	123
Shame of man,	154
Sickness a gradual dying,	339
Sickness of the soul,	340
Sickness caused by excessive affection,	342
Sickness, natural and demoniacal,	346
Silver cord and golden bowl,	269
Sinner's fear of God,	158
Sin of Adam and sin of Satan,	153
Sin a disturbance,	189
Sin the cause of sickness,	341
Sleep of our soul,	336
Somnambulism, its uses,	364
Somnambulism a morbid state,	366

INDEX OF SUBJECTS

	PAGE
Somnambulism, its terrible results,	368
Son of man, the purpose of creation,	77
Son partaking in the infinity of the Father,	388
Soul and Ego,	181
Soul the object of redemption,	183
Soul the counterpart of spirit,	235
Soul, its substance,	237
Soul the candlestick of the sanctuary,	238
Soul the type of the divine Doxa,	239
Soul at birth,	250
Soul and spirit present from begetting,	255
Soul the link between spirit and matter,	265
Soul sevenfold in its relation to the body,	271
Soul of possessed person,	355
Soul between divine and demoniacal agency,	371
Source of man's individuality,	93
Speech, nature of human,	278
Speech inseparable from thought,	213
Spirit of man a created thing,	95
Spirit and soul,	96
Spirit capable of sin,	105
Spirit of God dwelling in man,	108
Spirit and soul not absolutely distinct natures,	112
Spirit of child,	257
Spiritual significance of the heart,	366
Spiritual form of the soul,	507
Spiritual body,	563
Stasis and upostasis,	32
Synthetical consideration of biblical psychology,	381
Table-turning,	369
Teaching of temptation and fall,	162
Temptation addressed to woman, and why,	127, 147
Temptation, its manner and nature,	147
Temper and disposition,	280
Testimony of a physician,	369
Testimony of clairvoyance on the state of souls,	506
Theopneustia,	431
Thought of Ego,	121
Threefold personality of God,	64
Threefold life of the human spirit,	205
Time and eternity,	41
Time and space still existing in eternity,	519
Time glorified,	557
Traducianism (*per traducem*),	131
Transmigration of souls,	545
Trinity, doctrine of,	55
Trinity consistent with historical revelation,	56
Trinity of human nature,	197
Trinity shadowed forth in human spirit,	200
Trinity a manifestation of love,	204
Trinity of the divine acts,	201
Trinity of power,	227
Triplicity of man's spirit,	196
Triplicity of the soul,	464
True and false prophecy,	424
Turba, the condition of sickness,	328
Twofold nature of Christ,	385
Two natures in regenerate persons,	455
Types of the glorified body,	516
Ultimate issue of the world,	551
Unclothing of the body,	512
Unconsciousness at birth,	403
Value of somnambulism,	310
Varieties of possession,	352
Vegetable creation not animated,	28
Victory of love,	552
Viscera the seat of the affections,	314
Visibility of departed souls,	501
Vision by crystals,	370
Waiting of righteous souls,	497
Waking and sleeping, health and disease,	323
Waking vision an ecstasy,	335
White raiment of souls,	508
White robes,	520
Will of the flesh,	190
Will, man's characteristic,	242
Witchcraft, when it begins,	370
Woman the psychical element in humanity,	126
Woman dependent on man,	127
Woman's creation an argument for traducianism,	132
Word to express spirit and wind the same,	101
Word and sacraments,	400
Word and hearer,	410
Wrath and love mingled in the world's constitution,	77
Wrath of God for sin,	158

THE END.

www.ingramcontent.com/pod-product-compliance
Lightning Source LLC
Chambersburg PA
CBHW052042290426
44111CB00011B/1588